LARGE
PRINT
EDITION

RANDOM
HOUSE

MY AMERICAN JOURNEY

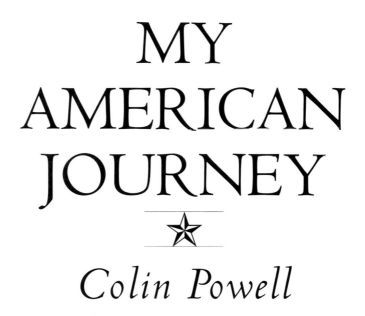

Colin Powell
with Joseph E. Persico

Published by Random House Large Print
in association with Random House, Inc.
New York   1995

LIBRARY OF CONGRESS CATALOGING-IN-PUBLICATION DATA
Powell, Colin L.
My American journey : an autobiography / Colin L. Powell,
with Joseph E. Persico.   p.   cm.
Includes index.   ISBN 0-679-76511-5
1. Powell, Colin L. 2. Generals—United States—Biography.
3. Afro-American generals—Biography.
4. United States. Army—Biography.
5. Large Type Books.
I. Persico, Joseph E. II. Title.
E840.5.P68A3   1995   355'.0092—dc20
[B]   95-17119   CIP

Manufactured in the United States of America
FIRST LARGE PRINT EDITION

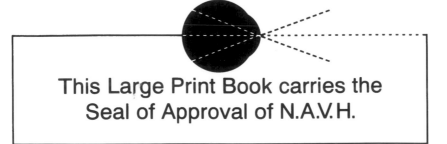

This Large Print Book carries the
Seal of Approval of N.A.V.H.

To my family . . . past, present, and future

COLIN POWELL:
SCENES FROM MY EARLY YEARS

Perhaps this is the beginning of my fascination with automobiles. We are on a summer Sunday outing to Uncle Joe and Aunt See's house in Jamaica, Queens, around 1942. The family dream was to move "up" from renting an apartment in the city to owning a house in the suburbs.

Maud Ariel Powell   **Luther Theophilus Powell**

MY PARENTS

These are the earliest pictures I have of my parents, which I found after their deaths. These are their original British passport photos. Pop's is from 1920, when he was twenty-two, and Mom's is from 1924, when she was twenty-two. It was with these documents that they came to the United States, met each other, and began new lives.

"THE LION KING"

I was too young to protest the indignity of this photo. It was not even our trophy skin! In those pre-animal rights days—this was 1937—proud parents eager to show off their pride and joy asked for such photographic-studio props to suggest an affluence and level of importance the family did not yet enjoy.

A SUNDAY OUTING WITH MY FATHER

**Luther Powell, a snappy dresser, with his well-togged,
big-footed son, Colin, around 1943 on a Sunday morning on
167th Street, just down from Prospect Avenue. We were
on the way home from paying our ritual after-church visit
to my Aunt Beryl, Luther's sister.**

Above: The cottage at Top Hill in St. Elizabeth parish, where my father was born, photographed when Alma and I visited in 1992. The cottage is referred to as "the old house" and is still being used. My grandparents are buried in the front yard just to the right of this homecoming scene.

Right: Kelly Street, where I was brought up, is being readied for a block party to celebrate V-J day in 1945. Our apartment is at 952 Kelly Street, the first building in the row of lower housing on the right. The picture was taken at the corner of 163rd Street, looking toward Westchester Avenue, with the elevated section of the IRT subway in midpicture.

Below: Hanging out with my sister, Marilyn, in front of our first apartment house in the Bronx, 980 Fox Street.

A YOUNG MAN IN THE BRONX

I am in my Sunday best near Hunts Point in the Bronx
in 1953. The following year I entered the City College of
New York to study engineering. I dropped engineering
after one semester and switched to geology to
stay in college.

My "gang" in the early 1950s, two blacks, two Lithuanians, and a Puerto Rican: typical of the ethnic mix of Banana Kelly then. From left to right: Victor Ramirez; Eddie Grant; me; Tony Grant, Eddie's brother, on leave from the Navy; and Robley McIntosh.

Left: Gene Norman, my best friend on Kelly Street, lived just across the street from us. He served in the Marine Corps and then went into architecture, rising to become Landmarks Commissioner for the City of New York.

Right: I entered ROTC in the fall of 1954. Here I am in my first uniform. I had found something that I loved and that I did well.

Below: **The summer of my junior year in college was spent at ROTC summer camp at Fort Bragg, North Carolina. Complete with .45 caliber pistol, safely without ammo, I am getting ready to start my tour as the Company D duty officer.**

THE PERSHING RIFLES, A TURNING POINT IN MY LIFE

The CCNY Pershing Rifles in 1957. I am seated in the front row. On my right is my friend and role model, Ronnie Brooks. Seated next to Ronnie is our faculty advisor, Major Jones, who kept us off probation. Directly behind me (second row, fourth from right) is Antonio Mavroudis, who saw me as his role model. Tony was killed in Vietnam. John Young, behind Tony (third row, third from right), was also killed in Vietnam, as was another Pershing Rifleman, Alan Pasco (not pictured). Ronnie died of a heart attack in 1989. The rest of us are still in touch as a group and have frequent reunions.

**I BECOME A RANGER, AND
GET MY FIRST FOREIGN POST**

Inset: **Coleman Barracks, Gelnhausen, Germany, in 1960.
As a first lieutenant, at right, swagger stick in hand, I watch
with some anxiety as Lieutenant Colonel Jim Carter,
commander of the 2d Armored Rifle Battalion, 48th
Infantry, makes a final inspection of the honor guard I**

have trained and am about to take to the 7th Army
Noncommissioned Officers Academy at Bad Tölz.

Above: Smiles of relief from young second lieutenants who
have just finished the final field exercise at the Ranger
school mountain training camp in Dahlonega, Georgia. I'm
in the back row just about under the helicopter mast.

MY LUCKIEST DAY

I met Alma Vivian Johnson on a blind date in the fall of 1961. She was twenty-four. This is her at age fourteen.

Alma and I were married on August 25, 1962, at the First Congregational Church in Birmingham, Alabama, where Alma grew up. My parents are to the left. Alma's parents, Mildred and Robert "R. C." Johnson, are to the right. R. C. has a resigned expression on his face: he's not quite sure what his daughter has gotten into. He'd only met me thirty-six hours before the wedding.

A GROWING FAMILY, AN ABSENT FATHER

Our marriage was blessed with three children. Alma is with Mike, age five, and Linda, age three, in 1968, in Birmingham, Alabama. Alma sent this picture to me in Vietnam for Christmas. I stared at it for hours.

The growing Powell family in 1975, after Vietnam and another year I had spent away from them in Korea. From left to right, Annemarie, five, Linda, ten, and Mike, twelve.

Top: **We take a break in the tropical jungle. I'm the big one with a bulging pack at left center. Directly in front of me is Captain Hieu, and in the immediate foreground is Lieutenant So. I lost track of them both for over thirty years, but they came back into my life.**

ON PATROL IN VIETNAM

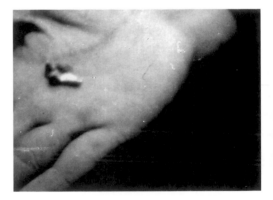

Center: **A smashed Viet Cong bullet I've just pried out of an armored vest of our point man. It took persuasion to get the point squad to wear vests, but after this incident, I could do no wrong.**

Bottom: **Treating a wounded Viet Cong cadre member we ambushed in the A Shau Valley. He and his team were armed, carrying documents and heading to a meeting in one of the villages along the coastal plain.**

**Standing outside my hootch at A Shau in 1963. This is
my showoff uniform. On patrol, the white name tag
disappeared, as did the silver insignia. The hand
grenade was carried much more carefully and not just
tucked in my belt by its handle.**

Minutes after General Gettys's helicopter crashed in Vietnam in 1968. The injured have been removed and the GIs are bending wreckage out of the way to allow rescue helicopters to get closer and lower evacuation winches. I am the character with the bruised face in the right-hand corner, keeping an eye on the circling helos.

IN THE JUNGLE

U.S. ARMY PHOTO

U.S. ARMY PHOTO

The general we pulled from the wreckage, my commander in the Americal Division, Major General Charles M. Gettys.

ON MY WAY TO A WHITE HOUSE FELLOWSHIP

After finishing graduate school at The George Washington University in 1971, I served on the Army staff for a year before being selected for a White House Fellowship. On my last day on the Army staff, I was presented a Legion of Merit by my boss, Major General Herbert McChrystal. Alma is holding Annemarie, while Mike and Linda look on with reasonable interest.

I met President Nixon for the first time in the fall of 1972, after my selection to be a White House Fellow.

Above: This was about as close to the White House as I got when I was a White House Fellow in 1972 and 1973. The Fellowship was a unique program, which gave me invaluable insight into the workings of Washington.

Below: My White House Fellows class on the South Lawn of the White House in 1972. I am at the right, rear. The director of the program, Lieutenant Colonel Bernard Loeffke, is kneeling at the left. Kneeling second from the right is Jim Bostic, who became the younger brother I always wanted. All my classmates went on from this program to distinguished careers.

I WAS PROUD OF MY BATTALION IN KOREA

Above: "My God, will you look at these winners!" says my division commander in Korea, the legendary Major General Henry E. Emerson, as we move down the line presenting Expert Infantryman Badges to men in my battalion in 1974.

Below: With several of my company commanders in Korea. Left to right: Captains Baird and Behrens, and First Lieutenant Garnett.

"GUNFIGHTER" EMERSON

Hank Emerson as a lieutenant general in 1977 while commanding XVIII Airborne Corps. He was known affectionately as "The Gunfighter," as reflected in his preference for a six-shooter rather than a regulation .45 caliber pistol.

In the field in Korea as commander of the 1st Battalion, 32d Infantry, "The Queen's Own Buccaneers," in 1974.

COMMANDING THE 2D BRIGADE, 101ST AIRBORNE

Visiting soldiers of my brigade in field training at Fort Campbell, Kentucky.

Greeting Secretary of Defense Donald Rumsfeld when he visited Fort Campbell in 1976. I could never quite get my beret to look stylish.

Right: My official file photo as a colonel in the 101st Airborne. I looked like this and was no doubt an odd sight when I went to Washington in February 1977 to be interviewed by Zbigniew Brzezinski for a job on the National Security Council staff of the new Carter administration.

U.S. ARMY PHOTO

Below: In the field at Fort Chaffee, Arkansas, in the summer of 1976, training the 39th Infantry Brigade of the Arkansas National Guard. The brigade commander, Brigadier General Harold Gwatney, is on the left. General Bernard Rogers, the commander of Forces Command, is on the right. Rogers went on to become the Army Chief of Staff.

U.S. ARMY PHOTO

ON THE RUN AT FORT CARSON, COLORADO

At Fort Carson, Colorado, 1982. The command group of the 4th Infantry Division (mechanized) leads the division in an annual organization day run. As a brigadier general, I am running behind the division commander, Major General John W. Hudachek. Hudachek found my performance wanting and said so in an efficiency report that could have ended my career. Behind me is Colonel William Flynn, division chief of staff. To my left is Brigadier General Rock Negris, my fellow assistant division commander. Behind Negris is Colonel Bob Dupont, the deputy post commander.

FROM THE FIELD TO
THE WASHINGTON BELTWAY

DEPARTMENT OF DEFENSE PHOTO

Secretary of Defense Caspar Weinberger, in 1984, presents President Reagan with a mounted AK-47 rifle that was captured during the 1983 Grenada invasion. From left: Vice President George Bush; me, military assistant to Secretary Weinberger; Secretary Weinberger; General Jack Vessey, Chairman of the Joint Chiefs of Staff; William Howard Taft IV, deputy secretary of defense; and President Reagan. Within five years I would become National Security Advisor for President Reagan and then Chairman of the Joint Chiefs of Staff for President Bush.

Preface

I have had a great life, and this is the story so far.

I was not planning to write an autobiography and had even helped other authors write biographies about me. In my final months as Chairman of the Joint Chiefs of Staff, however, I began to change my mind. The commercial prospects could not be ignored. Friends encouraged me to do it, but still I hesitated until one particularly close friend said, "Oh, stop being afraid, Colin. You owe it to your grandchildren, and you have a story to tell. Do it!" And so I have.

This is a personal memoir. It is not a definitive history of the major events in which I was privileged to take part. An autobiography is much too self-serving for that purpose. I hope the book will prove useful to historians of our times; but I wrote it principally to share my story with my fellow Americans.

I faced the problem all authors have to contend with, that of selection. There is neither time nor space to tell everything. I was determined to produce a single volume of reasonable length, and avoid a "doorstopper" of the kind I was warned about by one of my media friends: "For heaven's sake, don't write another of those long, bloody 'And then I had lunch with . . .' books."

Mine is the story of a black kid of no early promise from an immigrant family of limited means who was raised in the South Bronx and somehow rose to become the National Security Advisor to the President of the United States and then Chairman of the Joint Chiefs of Staff. It is a story of hard work and good luck, of occasional rough times, but mostly good times. It is a story of service and soldiering. It is a story about the people who helped make me what I am. It is a story of my benefiting from opportunities created by the sacrifice of those who went before me and maybe my benefiting those who will follow. It is a story of faith—faith in myself, and faith in America. Above all, it's a love story: love of family, of friends, of the Army, and of my country. It is a story that could only have happened in America.

Contents

Preface vii

Part One: The Early Years

1. Luther and Arie's Son 3
2. A Soldier's Life for Me 59
3. Courting Alma 96

Part Two: Soldiering

4. "It'll Take Half a Million Men to Succeed" 119
5. Coming Home 158
6. Back to Vietnam 196
7. White House Fellow 227
8. "Go, Gunfighter, Go!" 270
9. The Graduate School of War 309

Part Three: The Washington Years

10. In the Carter Defense Department 351
11. The Reaganites—and a Close Call 384
12. The Phone Never Stops Ringing 424
13. "Frank, You're Gonna Ruin My Career" 477
14. National Security Advisor to the President 531

Part Four: The Chairmanship

15. One Last Command 605
16. "Mr. Chairman, We've Got a Problem" 626

17. When You've Lost Your Best Enemy   658
18. A Line in the Sand   696
19. Every War Must End   770
20. Change of Command   826
21. Mustering Out   867
22. A Farewell to Arms   900

Colin Powell's Rules   933

Acknowledgments   935
Index   941

Part One

THE EARLY YEARS

1 ☆ *Luther and Arie's Son*

I USUALLY TRUST my instincts. This time I did not, which almost proved fatal. The day was pure Jamaica in February, the sun brilliant overhead, the air soft with only the hint of an afternoon thundershower. Perfect flying weather, as we boarded the UH-1 helicopter. My wife, Alma, and I were visiting the island of my parents' birth at the invitation of Prime Minister Michael Manley. Manley had been after me for a year, ever since the Gulf War. "Get some rest, dear boy," he had said in that compelling lilt the last time he had called. "Come home, if only for a few days. Stay at our government guesthouse." This time I accepted with pleasure.

Even with Desert Storm behind us, the pressure on me as Chairman of the Joint Chiefs of Staff had been relentless over the past year. With the Cold War fast fading, we were trying to rethink and reshape America's defenses. The world had altered so radically that we were presently organizing a relief airlift to help feed the Russians. We had a festering situation at our base at Guantanamo in Cuba, with Haitian migrants piling up under conditions starting to resemble a concentration camp. And a defeated but incorrigible Saddam Hussein was trying to thwart UN inspectors' efforts to put him out of the nuclear, biological, and chemical weapons business. I welcomed a chance to get out of cold, gray Washington and into the island sun for a few days. And, on the way down, I could stop and check out conditions at Guantanamo.

We arrived in Jamaica the afternoon of February 13, 1992, and were swept up in a whirlwind of West Indian hospitality. The next morning, Alma and I were whisked off to the Ward Theatre, where the mayor of Kingston, Marie Atkins, presented me with the keys to the city. "I'm American-born, Madame Mayor," I said in my response, "but you've handed me the keys to my second home." I recalled boyhood memories, listening to calypso melodies like "Fan Me, Saga Boy," hearing the pidgin-English poetry of Louise Bennett, and feasting on plantain, roast goat, and rice and peas. After my speech, Councillor Ezra Cole observed: "Only in Jamaica do we call it rice and peas. Everywhere else in the Caribbean, they have it backward, peas and rice. General Powell is a true Jamaican."

We next visited the Jamaica Defence Force headquarters at nearby Up Park Camp, where the chief of the JDF, Commodore Peter Brady, took me on a tour and had his troops go through their paces. The drill was carried off with great skill and flair. Much foot stomping, smart saluting, slapping of sides, and shouting of "Suh!" this and "Suh!" that. All very British and very professional.

After lunch, we boarded a Jamaica Defence Force helicopter for a quick hop across the bay to Manley International Airport. There we were to transfer to an American Blackhawk helo to visit U.S.

units on temporary duty in Jamaica. The original plan had been for us to fly the Blackhawk all the way, but our hosts wanted us to use the U.S.-built Jamaican helo to leave their headquarters, and I could not easily reject their gesture of pride, though my antennae quivered. Kingston faded behind us as the helicopter rose, leveling off at about fifteen hundred feet. Alma smiled at me; it had been a lovely day. I was gazing out at the soothing aquamarine of the Caribbean when I heard a sudden sharp *crrraack.* Alma looked at me, puzzled.

I knew instantly that we were in trouble. The helicopter's transmission had seized. The aircraft began to sway wildly. We were dropping into the bay. I had already experienced one helo crash in Vietnam. I knew that if the UH-1 struck water, it would probably flip, and the blades would snap off and cut the air like shrapnel. And with the doors open, the aircraft would sink like a stone. What flashed through my brain was, we have three children and their mother and father were about to die.

"Hunch over! Grab your legs!" I shouted to Alma.

"Why?" she asked.

"Dammit! Just do it!" I yelled, as we continued to plummet. I saw the two pilots snatching at the controls, racing through emergency procedures. They shut off the engines, and the only sound now was the whopping of the blades as we continued to drop toward the bay. At the last moment, the pilots managed to nurse the helo over the shoreline for a hard landing, scarcely twenty feet from the water's edge. I unhooked my seat belt, grabbed Alma, and dragged her away. This thing might still burst into flames.

"What happened?" she asked, when we were at a safe distance.

"We crashed," I told her. I went over to the Jamaican pilots and congratulated them on an impressive piece of emergency flying.

Later, Michael Manley phoned me. "My dear Colin, do you know what is causing the rustling of the trees you hear? It is my immense sigh of relief." Prose poetry, the language of my forebears. And the irony of the moment did not escape me. What had been the land of my folks' birth had nearly become the site of their son's death.

We boarded the Blackhawk and resumed the tour. We visited an Ohio National Guard unit that was helping the Jamaicans with a roadbuilding project and a U.S. Air Force drug-tracking radar site poised on a breathtaking bluff called Lover's Leap. With these stops completed, the official visit was over. Now the sentimental journey began.

We piled into jeeps provided by the Jamaican government and headed north into the interior. We turned onto a dirt road that cut through the red earth like a gash. Handsome homes gave way to humble cottages. The road dwindled to a path, and we finally had to get out and walk. We had been on foot for about fifteen minutes when, out of nowhere, the "custus"—the local government head—and the police chief and several other officials appeared and greeted our party. We walked behind them across gently rising fields to a crest, then started down a rut-ted trail into a small valley where something quite magical happened. People seemed to emerge out of nowhere. Soon, about two hundred people surrounded us, young and old, some colorfully dressed, some in tatters, some with shoes, some barefoot. All at once, the air was filled with music. A band appeared, youngsters in black uniforms playing "The Star-Spangled Banner."

"The children are from the school your father attended," the custus informed me. The musicians then shifted to calypso tunes as familiar to me as our national anthem. The crowd began clapping, reaching out to Alma and me, taking our hands, smiling and greeting us. From a distance, a smaller group started toward us. The crowd parted to let them pass. I was choked with emotion. This was my family. No one needed to tell me. Some I had met before. As for the others, it was in their faces, in their resemblance to each other, in their resemblance to me. We had arrived at Top Hill, land of my father's birth. They embraced me and started introducing themselves, Aunt Ivie Ritchie, Cousin Muriel, Uncle Claude, Cousin Pat, in a blur of faces and family connections.

Alma and I were led to folding chairs and asked to sit in the place of honor while Joan Bent, a schoolteacher and the wife of one of my cousins, delivered a speech of welcome full of colorful flourishes. We started walking again past several comfortable houses, with porches painted a rich red earth color, to a tiny cottage. Its walls were made of rough stucco, the roof of rusted sheet metal, the eaves of hand-hewn boards. Brown shutters flanked six-over-six windows, giving this tropical dwelling an unlikely New England touch.

The cottage contained four cubicles, no running water, no electricity, no kitchen, no indoor plumbing. The entire house was smaller than an average American living room. My relatives had shooed the chickens out of the place, scrubbed it, and swept it, but that was all. I was standing in the house where my father had been born in 1898.

We went out back to the family burial plot, freshly weeded and tended. Once again the crowd surged around, waiting for me to say something. I thanked them for their welcome, and hoped to be left alone for a while. I wanted time to retrace my father's footsteps through the fields, to roam among trees he must have known. I wanted to imagine what it was like to live here, scratching out a subsistence living from these austere patches of earth. But people kept pressing in on us. Alma and I said a prayer over the graves of my grandmother and grandfather. We exchanged a few simple gifts with members of the family; the women gave Alma lovely hand-embroidered linens. And then the visit was over.

We made our way back to the Blackhawk and flew over Westmoreland, the birthplace of Maud Ariel McKoy Powell, my mother. As we traveled along, I wondered what dreams or fears had prompted two young Jamaicans to cut the roots to their native soil, leave the people they loved, and emigrate to a land so foreign to what they knew. And I wondered if they could have imagined how much this act of courage and hope would shape the destiny of their son.

.   .   .

I was born on April 5, 1937, at a time when my family was living on Morningside Avenue in Harlem. My parents' first child, my sister, Marilyn, had been born five and a half years before. I have no recollection of the Harlem years. They say our earliest memories usually involve a trauma, and mine does. I was four, and we had moved to the South Bronx. Gram Alice McKoy, my maternal grandmother, was taking care of me, since both my parents worked. I was playing on the floor and stuck a hairpin into an electrical outlet. I remember the blinding flash and the shock almost lifting me off the floor. And I still remember Gram scolding and hugging me at the same time. When my mother and father came home from work, much intense discussion occurred, followed by more scolding and fussing. My keenest memory of that day is not of the shock and pain, but of feeling important, being the center of attention, seeing how much they loved and cared about me.

The dominant figure of my youth was a small man, five feet two inches tall. In my mind's eye, I am leaning out the window of our apartment, and I spot him coming down the street from the Intervale Avenue subway station. He wears a coat and tie, and a small fedora is perched on his head. He has a newspaper tucked under his arm. His overcoat is unbuttoned, and it flaps at his sides as he approaches with a brisk, toes-out stride. He is whistling and stops to greet the druggist, the baker, our building super, almost everybody he passes. To some kids on the block he is a faintly comical figure. Not to me.

This jaunty, confident little man is Luther Powell, my father.

He emigrated from Jamaica in his early twenties, seventeen years before I was born. He left his family and some sort of menial job in a store to emigrate. He never discussed his life in Jamaica, and I regret that I never asked him about those years. I do know that he was the second of nine children born to poor folk in Top Hill. No doubt he came to this country for the reason that propelled millions before him, to become something more than he had been and to give his children a better start than he had known. He literally came to America on a banana boat, a United Fruit Company steamer that docked in Philadelphia.

Pop worked as a gardener on estates in Connecticut and then as a building superintendent in Manhattan. Finally, he found the job that was to provide the base of our family's security and make him the patriarch of our clan. He went to work for Ginsburg's (later elevated to the Gaines Company), manufacturers of women's suits and coats at 500 Seventh Avenue in Manhattan's garment district. He started out working in the stockroom, moved up to become a shipping clerk, and eventually became foreman of the shipping department.

My mother was the eldest of her generation—of nine children—and came from a slightly more elevated social station in Jamaica. She had a high school education, which my father lacked. ("Him who never finished high school," she would mutter, when Pop pulled rank on family matters.) Before emigrating, Mom had worked as a stenographer in a lawyer's office. Her mother, Gram McKoy, was a small, lovely woman whose English wedded African cadence to British inflection, the sound of which is still music to my soul. The McKoys and the Powells both had bloodlines common among Jamaicans, including African, English, Irish, Scotch, and probably Arawak Indian. My father's side even added a Jewish strain from a Broomfield ancestor.

Some of Gram's nine children were grown, but most were still dependent on her alone when she separated from Edwin McKoy, a sugar plantation overseer who lent the Scottish line to our ethnic mix. To support her family, Gram left Jamaica in search of work, first in Panama, then in Cuba, finally in the United States. She sent for her eldest child, my mother, to help her. She labored as a maid and as a garment-district pieceworker and sent back to the children still in Jamaica every penny she could spare. She eventually sent for her youngest child, my Aunt Laurice, whom she had not seen for twelve years. To those of us spared dire poverty, such sacrifices and family separations are all but unimaginable.

Gram had named my mother Maud Ariel, but she was known all her life as Arie. She was small, five feet one, plump, with a beautiful face, soft brown eyes, and brown hair done in the forties style, and she had a melting smile. When I picture Mom, she is wearing an apron, bustling around our apartment, always in motion, cooking, washing, ironing, sewing, after working all day downtown in the garment district as a seamstress, sewing buttons and trim on clothing.

Mom was a staunch union supporter, a member of the International Ladies Garment Workers Union. My father, the shipping room foreman, considered himself part of management. Initially, they were both New Deal Democrats. We had that famous wartime photograph of President Franklin D. Roosevelt, with the Capitol and the flag in the background, hanging in the foyer of our apartment for as long as I can remember. My mother remained a diehard Democrat. But Pop, by 1952, was supporting Dwight Eisenhower.

He was the eternal optimist, my mother the perennial worrier. That never changed, no matter how much our fortunes did. After my father died, I would come home on leave to visit Mom and she would say, "Colin, take the book to the bank so they can show my interest."

And I would explain, "Mom, you don't have to do that. The bank will post the interest on the statement they mail you. The interest isn't going anywhere."

"How do you know they won't 'tief' me?" she would say, using an old Jamaican expression for stealing. She would go to her bedroom, fish out an old lace-covered pink candy box from under the bed, and hand me the bank book.

I would dutifully trot down to the bank, stand in line, and say, "Will you please post the interest on this account?"

"Of course, Colonel Powell. But we also show it on the statement. That can save you a trip down here."

"No," I would say. "My mother has to see those red numbers you print sideways to show her interest." And, I wanted to add, to prove you didn't "tief" her.

According to my Aunt Beryl, Pop's sister, in her nineties as of this writing, my parents met at Gram McKoy's apartment in Harlem. Besides raising her own children, Gram took in relatives and Jamaican immigrants as boarders to earn a few extra dollars. One such boarder was Luther Powell. Thus, my parents courted while living under the same roof.

After early years in Harlem and at a couple of other addresses, I grew up largely at 952 Kelly Street in the Hunts Point section of the South Bronx, where my family had moved in 1943, when I was six. The 1981 movie *Fort Apache, The Bronx,* starring Paul Newman, takes place in the police precinct where I lived. In the movie, the neighborhood is depicted as an urban sinkhole, block after block of burned-out tenements, garbage-strewn streets, and weed-choked lots, populated by gangs, junkies, pimps, hookers, maniacs, cop killers, and third-generation welfare families—America's inner-city nightmare come true. That is not quite the Hunts Point I was raised in, although it was hardly elm trees and picket fences. We kept our doors and windows locked. I remember a steel rod running from the back of our front door to a brace on the floor, so that no one could push in the door. Burglaries were common. Drug use was on the rise. Street fights and knifings occurred. Gangs armed with clubs, bottles, bricks, and homemade .22 caliber zip guns waged turf wars. Yet, crime and violence in those days did not begin to suggest the social breakdown depicted in *Fort Apache, The Bronx.* That was yet to come. When I was growing up in Hunts Point, a certain rough-edged racial tolerance prevailed. And, critically, most families were intact and secure.

We lived in a four-bedroom apartment on the third floor of a four-story brick tenement, two families on each floor, eight families in all. When I stepped out the door onto Kelly Street, I saw my whole world. You went left three blocks to my grade school, one more block to my junior high school; between the two was a sliver of land where stood St. Margaret's Episcopal Church, our church. A few blocks in the opposite direction was the high school I would later attend. Across the street from us, at number 957, lived my Aunt Gytha and Uncle Alfred Coote. On my way to school, I passed 935 Kelly, where Aunt Laurice and Uncle Vic and their children lived. Farther down, at 932, my godmother, Mabel Evadne Brash, called Aunt Vads, and her family lived. And at 867 were Amy and Norman Brash, friends so close they were considered relatives. "Mammale and Pappale" we called them. Don't ask me why the Jewish diminutives, since they were also Jamaicans. Most of the black families I knew had their roots in Jamaica, Trinidad, or Barbados, or other islands of the West Indies.

The Brashes' nicknames may have reflected the fact that in those days Hunts Point was heavily Jewish, mixed with Irish, Polish, Italian, black, and Hispanic families. The block of Kelly Street next to ours was slightly curved, and the neighborhood had been known for years as "Banana Kelly." We never used the word "ghetto." Ghettos were somewhere in Europe. We lived in the tenements. Outsiders often have a sense of New York as big, overwhelming, impersonal, anonymous. Actually, even now it's a collection of neighborhoods where everybody knows everybody's business, the same as in a small town. Banana Kelly was like that.

There was a repeating pattern to the avenues that connected our streets. On almost every block you would find a candy store, usually owned by European Jews, selling the *Daily News* and the *Post* and the *Mirror.* No one in my neighborhood read the *New York Times.* These little stores also carried school supplies, penny candy, ice cream, and soft drinks. As every New Yorker knows, the specialty of the house was the egg cream, consisting of chocolate syrup, milk, and seltzer. If you did not have a dime for the egg cream, you could just get the seltzer— "two cents, plain." Every few blocks you found a Jewish bakery and a Puerto Rican grocery store. Italians ran the shoe repair shops. Every ten blocks were big chain stores, clothing and appliance merchants, and movie houses. I do not recall any black-owned businesses. An exciting event of my boyhood was the arrival of laundromats after World War II. My mother no longer had to scrub our clothes on a washboard and hang them out the window on a clothesline. Pop, however, insisted on having his shirts done at the Chinese laundry.

The South Bronx was an exciting place when I was growing up, and I have never longed for those elms and picket fences.

My father adored my sister, Marilyn. Thanks to his job in the garment district, she was always well dressed, and she led a sheltered life by Kelly Street standards. She ran with the good girls. The Teitel-baum sisters, whose father owned the pharmacy on the corner, were Marilyn's closest friends. I played the role of pesky little brother. Marilyn's first serious boyfriend was John Stevens, whose family was also active in St. Margaret's Church. John was an only child, and was being groomed to become a doctor (he made it). He and Marilyn were matched up by their parents. My idea of fun was to sneak up on them in amorous embrace and make a nuisance of myself. John would buy me off with a quarter. Marilyn would rage at her little brat brother. I thought of her in those days as a fink who turned me in for playing hooky, and I'm sure she found me a pain in the neck. On the whole, it was a normal sibling relationship.

One summer, when I was eight, my folks and some relatives rented cabins at Sag Harbor on Long Island. I was outside by myself playing mumblety-peg, trying to make the knife stick into the ground, when a piece of dirt flew up and lodged under my eyelid. I ran crying into the cabin, where my Aunt Laurice managed to get the irritant out, while I continued bawling. When I went back outside, I over-heard her say to Aunt Gytha, "I don't know about that boy. He's such a crybaby." It stung me then, and the fact that I vividly remember the incident almost fifty years later suggests my youthful devastation. I remember thinking, nobody's ever going to see me cry again. I did not always make it.

When I was nine, catastrophe struck the Powell family. As a student at P.S. 39, I passed from the third to the fourth grade, but into the bottom form, called "Four Up," a euphemism meaning the kid is a little slow. This was the sort of secret to be whispered with shaking heads in our family circle. Education was the escape hatch, the way up and out for West Indians. My sister was already an excellent student, destined for college. And here I was, having difficulty in the fourth grade. I lacked drive, not ability. I was a happy-go-lucky kid, amenable, amiable, and aimless.

I was not much of an athlete either, though I enjoyed street games. One of my boyhood friends, Tony Grant, once counted thirty-six of them, stickball, stoopball, punchball, sluggo, and hot beans and butter among them. One day, I was playing baseball in an empty lot and saw my father coming down the street. I prayed he would keep on going, because I was having a bad day. But he stopped and watched. All the while Pop was there, I never connected. A swing and a miss, again and again, every time I was at bat. I can still feel the burning humiliation. It was always painful for me to disappoint my father. I imagined a pressure that probably was not there, since he rarely uttered a word of reproach to me.

I did enjoy kite fighting. We would smash up soda bottles in a big juice can and lay the can on the trolley tracks until the passing cars pulverized the glass. We then glued the powdered glass onto a kite string. We fixed double-edged razor blades at intervals on the kite's tail. Then we flew our kites from the roofs of the tenements. By maneuvering the glass-coated string and razored tail, we tried to cut down the kites of kids on other roofs, sometimes a block away, and watch the kites flutter to earth—our version of World War II dogfights.

I have no recollection of the Depression. My parents were lucky enough to stay employed throughout the thirties, and we were never really in want. And I was only four when America entered World War II, almost ending hard times overnight. Young as I was, I have vivid memories of the war years. I remember assembling ten-cent model airplane kits of balsa wood and colored tissue paper. I deployed legions of lead soldiers and directed battles on the living-room rug. My pals and I scanned the skies from the rooftops looking for Messerschmitts or Heinkels that might get through to bomb Hunts Point. We sprayed imaginary enemies with imaginary weapons. "Bang! Bang! You're dead!" "I am not!" One thrill of my childhood occurred when Uncle Vic, who had served in the 4th Armored Division, came home after the war and gave me a yellow German Afrika Korps helmet. I carried that helmet around for forty years until it finally disappeared on a move between Germany and Washington, liberated, I am sure, by the German movers. In 1950, when I entered high school, the country was at war again, in Korea this time. Warfare held a certain fascination for me, as it often does for boys who have not yet seen it up close.

World War II changed my name. Before, I was *Cah*-lin, the British pronunciation that Jamaicans used. One of the first American heroes of the war was Colin P. Kelly, Jr. (pronounced *Coh*-lin), an Air Corps flier who attacked the Japanese battleship *Haruna* two days after Pearl Harbor and won the Distinguished Service Cross posthumously. Colin Kelly's name was on every boy's lips, and so, to my friends, I became Coh-lin of Kelly Street. To my family, I remain Cah-lin to this day. I once asked my father why he had chosen the name, which I never liked. Was it for some illustrious ancestor? Pop said no, he had read it off a shipping ticket the day I was born.

As a boy, I took piano lessons; but the lessons did not take with me, and they soon ended. I later studied the flute. Marilyn thought the noises coming out of it were hilarious. I gave up the flute too. Apparently, I would not be a jock or a musician. Still, I was a contented kid, growing up in the warmth and security of the concentric circles my family formed. At the center stood my parents. In the next circle were my mother's sisters and their families. My father's only sibling in America, Aunt Beryl, formed the next circle by herself. These circles rippled out in diminishing degrees of kinship, but maintained considerable closeness. Family members looked out for, prodded, and propped up each other.

I sometimes felt as if I were half spectator and half participant in a play populated by character actors. We usually went to my Aunt Dot's house in Queens on New Year's Day for curried goat. Dinner was followed by much drinking of Appleton Estate rum, dancing of the chotisse and singing of calypso songs.

A note on the etiquette of Jamaican rum. Appleton Estate is the most famous. It comes in different colors, proofs, and ages. In my family, to serve anything else was considered an affront; to serve Puerto

Rican rum, such as Bacardi, was an insult. Appleton Estate ninety proof golden was the most popular. A white version of 150 proof was used for punch. Real men drank the 150 proof neat. The smell stayed with them for a week, which is also about how long it took a drinker to recover. Rum to Jamaicans is like tea to an Oriental or coffee to an Arab, a sign of hospitality and graciousness, usually served over ice with ginger ale or Coke. The Coke version later became too Americanized for us because of the Andrews Sisters' hit song "Rum and Coca-Cola." Ladies, especially my mother, when offered a snort would respond with a demure "Just a touch." My mother would then complain that I had made her "touch" too strong and had put it in too big a glass, just before she downed it.

As a kid, I did not understand the lyrics of the calypso songs I heard at family gatherings. But as I grew older I started to decode the sly double entendres. My favorite calypso singer was Slinger Francisco, a Trinidadian known as "the Mighty Sparrow," a master of the naughty phrase. I played calypso tapes in my office even after I became Chairman of the Joint Chiefs of Staff. My aides did not get the pidgin lyrics and missed most of the innuendo in such tunes as "The Big Bamboo" and "Come Water Me Garden." But then, you do not hear much calypso music in the Pentagon's E-Ring.

At family gatherings, talk would invariably turn to "goin' home." No matter how many years my aunts and uncles had been in America, when they said home, they meant Jamaica. "Hey, Osmond, you goin' home this year?" "No, don't have the money.

Next year, for sure." "Hey, Laurice, you goin' home?" "No, but I'm packin' a barrel to send to the folks." They would slip into nostalgia, all but my godfather, Uncle Shirley, Aunt Dot's husband, a dining-car waiter on the Pennsylvania Railroad. Uncle Shirley was Jamaican too, but in their eyes, he had gone "American," even shedding much of his West Indian accent after riding the rails for so many years with native-born blacks. "Goin' home?" Uncle Shirley would say. "You damn fools sit around talking about 'home.' You forget why we left? Ain't been home in twenty years, and I ain't never going home." At which point the kids would laugh uproariously, delighted to see Uncle Shirley provoked to heresy.

We liked to get Aunt Dot and Uncle Shirley into an argument, because their spats had the reliability of a Punch and Judy show. "Shirley, you come over here with the folks, instead of sitting in front of that TV all day," Aunt Dot would begin. Shirley do this, and Shirley do that. It was like watching a fuse burn. Finally, Shirley would explode: "Woman! Mind your own damn business!" I later understood that the only way those two could fight like that for over forty years had to be out of deep love.

During summer vacations, I sometimes stayed with Aunt Dot and Uncle Shirley. I especially enjoyed my godfather's idea of breakfast on his day off, steak, eggs, and ice cream. Dottie and Shirley are gone now; yet every time I spend an evening with their sons, my cousins, Vernon, Roger, and Sonny, we amuse ourselves by reenacting one of their parents' long-ago tiffs. Sometimes these memories will strike me suddenly out of nowhere, and I start laughing all by myself.

Our family was a matriarchy. I loved my uncles—they were the sauce, the fun, and they provided the occasional rascal. But most were weaker personalities than their wives. The women set the standards, whipped the kids into shape, and pushed them ahead. The exception was my father. Luther Powell, maybe small, maybe unimposing in appearance, maybe somewhat comical, was nevertheless the ringmaster of this family circle.

In 1950, my sister transferred to an upstate New York college, and Marilyn's send-off was pure Pop. We all went down to Grand Central Station to put Marilyn on the Empire State Express bound for Buffalo State Teachers College. My father strode into the station, overcoat flapping, smiling through his tears, tipping everybody in sight, the porter, the conductor, the trainman, telling them, "Take care of my little girl, make sure she gets there safe and sound." I was embarrassed to see him doling out the money, but that was his way. Around the holidays, he would tip the mailman, the fuel man, the garbageman. When he was young, living in Harlem, Pop would dress up every Saturday in a vested suit, a checkbook with a zero balance stuffed into his pocket. He would start off the weekend at a shoeshine stand, where he also had a reputation as a heavy tipper. Afterward, as he strode down Morningside Avenue, the world was his oyster.

During football season, his son had to have the best helmet on the block, though I was far from the best player. My first two-wheeler bike had to be a Columbia Racer, with twenty-six-inch whitewall balloon tires. When I needed a suit, it was "Son, here's the charge card—go to Macy's and take care of yourself." All this from a shipping room foreman who never earned more than $60 a week. One Christmas, my mother objected to my father's inviting so many people over, which he did every year. The work was getting too much for her, she said. He went out and invited about fifty people and told Mom that if she could not handle it, he would hire a caterer.

His take-charge manner was reassuring. Luther Powell became the Godfather, the one people came to for advice, for domestic arbitration, for help in getting a job. He would bring home clothes, seconds and irregulars, end bolts of fabric, from the Gaines Company, and sell them at wholesale or give them to anybody in need. Downtown, Pop was not always able to play this lordly role. Maybe that was why it meant so much to him on Kelly Street. When Gaines changed hands, he tried to buy a piece of the company, but he was turned down. He had given the firm twenty-three years of his life, and, in his view, had been unfairly frozen out. Whether or not Pop was a serious bidder, I never knew. But after this disappointment, he left Gaines and went to work in a similar position for Scheule and Company, dealers in wholesale cloth. And that is where he spent the rest of his working days until the firm folded, and he was too old to get another job.

Luther Powell never let his race or station affect his sense of self. West Indians like him had come to this country with nothing. Every morning they got on that subway, worked like dogs all day, got home at 8:00 at night, supported their families, and educated their children. If they could do that, how dare anyone think they were less than anybody's equal? That was Pop's attitude.

Of course, there was always the dream that it might not have to be earned by the sweat of your brow, that one day Dame Fortune might step in. I remember the morning ritual, my father on the phone talking confidentially to his sister: "Beryl, what you doing today? Four-three-one? Hmmm. Straight or combination? Okay. Let's make it fifty cents." Later, the numbers runner would come by to pick up the bet. Someday, they knew, they were going to strike it rich.

In 1950, I entered Morris High School. Instead of turning left when I went out of the house I turned right for a few blocks. Marilyn had gone to the elite Walton High School. And, at my parents' prompting, I tried to get into Stuyvesant High, another prestigious school. I still have the report card with the guidance counselor's decision: "We advise against it." Morris High, on the other hand, was like Robert Frost's definition of home, the place where, when you show up, they have to let you in.

I was still directionless. I was not fired by anything. My pleasures were hanging out with the guys, "making the walk" from Kelly Street, up 163rd Street around Southern Boulevard to Westchester Avenue, and back home. Our Saturday-morning rite was to go the the Tiffany Theater and watch the serial and then a double feature of cowboy movies.

Sundays meant attending St. Margaret's Church, where we had our own family pew. Pop was senior warden, Mom headed the altar guild, and Marilyn played the piano at children's services. I was an acolyte. My folks always worked on the bazaar, the bake sale, and the annual dance, where you could let your Episcopalian hair down, do the calypso, get a little tipsy, and even share a nip with the priest.

In our neighborhood, we also had Catholic churches, synagogues, and storefront churches. On Friday nights I earned a quarter by turning the lights on and off at the Orthodox synagogue, so that the worshipers could observe the sabbath ban on activity. I had definite ideas of what a church was supposed to be, like the high Anglican church in which my family was raised in Jamaica, with spires, altars, priests, vestments, incense, and the flock genuflecting and crossing itself all over the place. The higher the church, the closer to God; that was how I saw it. At Christmas, our priest, Father Weeden, turned St. Margaret's into a magical place of candles, lights, ribbons, wreaths, and holly. The incense burning during the holidays almost asphyxiated Marilyn. I loved all of it.

I can still remember confirmation, watching those sweet, scrubbed children as the bishop seized them one by one by the head: "Defend, O Lord, this thy Child with thy heavenly grace; that he may continue thine forever; and daily increase in thy Holy Spirit more and more, until he come unto thy everlasting kingdom." I would swing the incense burner, lustily chanting "Amen," convinced that I was witnessing the spirit of God entering that child's head like a bolt of lightning. St. Margaret's was imagery, pageantry, drama, and poetry. Times change, and the liturgy has changed with the times. I suppose I have to yield to the wisdom of the bishops who believed the 1928 *Book of Common Prayer* needed updating, just as it replaced its predecessor. But in the change, something was lost for me. Long years afterward, I buried my mother from St. Margaret's Church at a time when the old liturgy had been displaced by the new. God now seemed earthbound and unisexed, not quite the magisterial, heavenly father figure of my youth. It saddened me. I miss the enchantment of the church in which I was raised.

I was a believer, but no saint. One summer, in the early fifties, Father Weeden selected me, the son of two pillars of St. Margaret's, to go to a church camp near Peekskill. Once there, I promptly fell into bad company. One night, my newfound friends and I snuck out to buy beer. We hid it in the toilet tank to cool, but our cache was quickly discovered. The priest in charge summoned all campers to the meeting hall. He did not threaten or berate us. Instead, he asked who was ready to accept responsibility. Who would own up like a man? We could probably have gotten away with our transgression by saying nothing. But his words struck me. I stood up. "Father, I did it," I said. When they heard me, two more budding hoodlums rose up and also confessed.

We were put on the next train back to New York. Word of our sinning preceded us. I dragged myself up Westchester Avenue and turned right onto Kelly

Street like a felon mounting the gallows. As I reached number 952, there was Mom, her usually placid face twisted into a menacing scowl. When she finished laying into me, Pop began. Just about when I thought I was eternally damned, Father Weeden telephoned. Yes, the boys had behaved badly, he said. "But your Colin stood up and took responsibility. And his example spurred the other boys to admit their guilt." My parents beamed. From juvenile delinquent, I had been catapulted to hero. Something from that boyhood experience, the rewards of honesty, hit home and stayed.

As for the neighborhood gang I traveled with, getting thrown out of church camp, plus having my father catch me playing poker in Sam Fiorino's shoe repair shop—with off-duty cops, no less—boosted my image. Usually, the other guys looked on me, not quite as a sissy, but as a "nice" kid, even a bit of a mama's boy.

One day when I was fourteen, my mother sent me to the post office to mail letters. I was passing Sickser's, on the corner of Westchester and Fox, a baby furnishings and toy store, when a white-haired man crooked a finger at me. Did I want to earn a few bucks? he asked in a thick Yiddish accent. He led me to a truck backed up to the warehouse behind the store, where I proceeded to unload merchandise for the Christmas season. The man was Jay Sickser, the store owner. Later, when he came by to check on me, he seemed surprised that I had almost finished the job. "So you're a worker," he said. "You want to come back tomorrow?" That day began an association with Sickser's that was to last throughout my youth.

Many of the store's customers were Jewish, and after a while I started picking up Yiddish. Relatives of Jay's would come in looking for a deal. Jay would call me over and say, "Collie, so take my cousins upstairs and show them the good carriages." I would escort them to the second floor, where they would talk confidentially in Yiddish—which model they liked, how much they were ready to spend. This *schwarz knabe,* what could he understand? I'd excuse myself and go down and report to Mr. S., who would come up, armed with my intelligence, and close the deal.

After I had worked at Sickser's for a few years, Jay took me aside one day. "Collie," he said, "you got to understand, I got two daughters. I got a son-in-law. Get yourself an education someday. Don't count too much on the store." He evidently thought that I had worked out well enough to deserve being brought into the firm, which I had never considered. I took it as a compliment.

I have been asked when I first felt a sense of racial identity, when I first understood that I belonged to a minority. In those early years, I had no such sense, because on Banana Kelly there was no majority. Everybody was either a Jew, an Italian, a Pole, a Greek, a Puerto Rican, or, as we said in those days, a Negro. Among my boyhood friends were Victor Ramirez, Walter Schwartz, Manny Garcia, Melvin Klein. The Kleins were the first family in our building to have a television set. Every Tuesday night, we crowded into Mel's living room to watch Milton Berle. On Thursdays we watched *Amos 'n' Andy.* We thought the show was marvelous, the best thing on television. It was another age, and we did not know that we were not supposed to like *Amos 'n' Andy.*

Racial epithets were hurled around Kelly Street. Sometimes they led to fistfights. But it was not "You're inferior—I'm better." The fighting was more like avenging an insult to your team. I was eventually to taste the poison of bigotry, but much later, and far from Banana Kelly.

The inseparable companion of my youth was Gene Alfred Warren Norman, also West Indian, a year or two older, a better athlete, and a more restless soul. A close white friend was Tony Grant. I remember their haste to get out of the neighborhood, to peer over the horizon, Gene via the Marine Corps and Tony via the Navy. Tony remembers two groups on Banana Kelly in our youth, "the drugged and the undrugged." Among the latter were the three of us. Gene went on to become landmarks commissioner of New York City, and Tony corporation counsel for White Plains.

In February of 1954, thanks to an accelerated school program rather than any brilliance on my part, I graduated from Morris High School two months short of my seventeenth birthday. My picture in the *Tower,* the yearbook, shows a kid with an easygoing smile and few screen credits beside his name. My page in the yearbook also reflects the Hunts Point mix of that era, three blacks, one Hispanic, four Jewish kids, and two other whites.

Except for a certain facility in unloading prams at Sickser's, I had not yet excelled at anything. I was the "good kid," the "good worker," no more. I did well enough at Morris to win a letter for track, but after a while I found slogging cross-country through Van Cortlandt Park boring, and so I quit. I switched to the 440-yard dash, because I could get it over with faster, but I dropped out after one season. We had a church basketball team at St. Margaret's. I was tall, fairly fast, and the senior warden's son, and the coach was inclined to give me a chance. I spent most of the time riding the bench, so I quit the team, to the relief of the coach. In later years, I frequently found myself asked to play or coach basketball, apparently out of a racial preconception that I must be good at it. As soon as I was old enough to be convincing, I feigned a chronic "back problem" to stay off the court.

My inability to stick to anything became a source of concern to my parents, unspoken, but I knew it was there. I did, however, stand out in one arena. I was an excellent acolyte and subdeacon, and enjoyed my ecclesiastical duties. Here was organization, tradition, hierarchy, pageantry, purpose—a world, now that I think about it, not all that unlike the Army. Maybe my 1928 prayer book was destined to be Field Manual 22-5, the Army's troop drilling bible. Had I gone into the ministry in those days, it would have pleased my mother. I did not hear the call.

I remained unprecocious and unaccomplished in another department. I never received a word of sex education at home. The street was my teacher, and a crude one. All the guys carried condoms in their wallets, mine yellow and brittle with age. I had a puppy-love romance with a girl who lived a few blocks away that lasted throughout high school. I invited her to a family party once, where Marilyn spent the whole evening giggling at her. Later, my sister said, "What's so special about that girl?" Not special? I had thought my girl was beautiful. For all our squabbling, Marilyn's opinion mattered to me. If my girlfriend was not pretty in Marilyn's eyes, she began to look less attractive in mine, and the romance faded.

In later years, I would turn out to be a good student, but no one would have predicted it then. Marilyn continued to set the Powell standard in education. She had been an honor student at Walton High, and she excelled at Buffalo State. And so, in spite of my final high school average of 78.3, I started looking at colleges because of my sister's example and because my parents expected it of me. Education meant the difference between wrapping packages or sewing buttons all day and having a real profession. Education had led to an extraordinary record of accomplishment in my family. Among my blood relatives and extended family of lesser kinship, my cousin, Arthur Lewis, served as U.S. ambassador to Sierra Leone, after a career as a Navy enlisted man. His brother, Roger, became a successful architect. Cousin Victor Roque became a prominent lawyer. James Watson became a judge on the U.S. Customs Court of International Trade. His sister, Barbara, was U.S. ambassador to Malaysia and the first woman assistant secretary of state; another sister, Grace, served as an official in the Department of Education.

Another cousin, Dorothy Cropper, became a New York State Court of Claims judge. My cousin Claret Forbes, one of the last to migrate from Jamaica, is a nurse, with two children in Ivy League colleges. My sister's daughter, Leslie, is an artist with an M.A. from Yale. Yet another cousin, Bruce Llewellyn, Aunt Nessa's son, is a businessman, philanthropist, former senior political appointee in the Carter administration, and one of this country's wealthiest African-Americans.

Not every cousin became a professional. Some worked as motormen on the New York subway, some had small businesses, some clerical jobs. But all of them have been good providers and parents, keeping their families together and educating offspring who continue to turn out well. I look at my aunts and uncles, their children and their children's children, and I see three generations of constructive, productive, self-reliant members of society. And all my relatives, whatever their professional status, enjoy equal standing in the family. No cousin stands above another in respect or affection. Some have experienced disappointment. Some did not achieve the success they desired. But they have all been successful in what counts in the end; they are useful human beings, useful to themselves, to their families, and to their communities.

Most of my parents' brothers and sisters stayed in Jamaica, and their children have turned out well there too. My Meikle cousins, Vernon and Roy, went to the University of Toronto and the University of London respectively. In the 1970s, when the Jamaican government took a socialist turn and practically wrecked the economy, more relatives left the island, this latest immigrant wave settling in Miami. And the pattern of success began repeating itself.

American blacks sometimes regard Americans of West Indian origin as uppity and arrogant. The feeling, I imagine, grows out of an impressive record of accomplishment by West Indians. What explains that success? For one thing, the British ended slavery in the Caribbean in 1833, well over a generation before America did. And after abolition, the lingering weight of servitude did not persist as long. The British were mostly absentee landlords, and West Indians were left more or less on their own. Their lives were hard, but they did not experience the crippling paternalism of the American plantation system, with white masters controlling every waking moment of a slave's life. After the British ended slavery, they told my ancestors that they were now British citizens with all the rights of any subject of the crown. That was an exaggeration; still, the British did establish good schools and made attendance mandatory. They filled the lower ranks of the civil service with blacks. Consequently, West Indians had an opportunity to develop attitudes of independence, self-responsibility, and self-worth. They did not have their individual dignity beaten down for three hundred years, the fate of so many black American slaves and their descendants.

Of course, my ancestors had also been ripped ruthlessly out of Africa, the ties to their past severed by slave traders. In Jamaica, some blacks replaced this hole in their culture with British culture, its church, its traditions, its governmental institutions, its values. Others remained attached to their African roots through the Rastafarian movement with its religious linkage to the late Emperor Haile Selassie of Ethiopia. I appreciate and admire the impulses that have led many African-Americans as well to reclaim the culture that was stolen from them and to draw spiritual sustenance from it.

American blacks and West Indians also wound up on American soil under different conditions. My black ancestors may have been dragged to Jamaica in chains, but they were not dragged to the United States. Mom and Pop chose to emigrate to this country for the same reason that Italians, Irish, and Hungarians did, to seek better lives for themselves and their children. That is a far different emotional and psychological beginning than that of American blacks, whose ancestors were brought here in chains.

There is, undeniably, a degree of clannishness among West Indians, Jamaicans included. My family socialized and found friends almost entirely within the Jamaican community. Consequently, my sister Marilyn's behavior came as a real jolt. Ever since she had gone off to college, Marilyn had been bringing home girlfriends, some of whom were white. The South Bronx was a bit different from what they were used to, but Marilyn was not concerned. She was proud of her family, and my parents welcomed all her friends. In 1952, she announced that she was bringing home a boyfriend. She was in love. They wanted to get married. His name was Norman Berns, and Norman was white.

This bit of proposed integration was occurring two years before *Brown* v. *Topeka Board of Education,* a time when few people, black or white, could have identified Martin Luther King, Jr., when Americans would not have known a sit-in from a sofa. Marilyn's choice was the source of much tut-tutting in the family. Our girl from Banana Kelly going with some white boy from Buffalo? What's going on? Why do they want to get married?

The time came for Norm to meet the family and answer the question. He turned out to be a prince and obviously in love with my sister. An interracial marriage, nevertheless, troubled Pop, and he understood the shelf life of youthful passions: "You two want to marry. Fine. Wait a year," he said. "See if you still do."

In the meantime, we went to meet Norm's folks. An adventure for me. Buffalo, New York, *460 miles* from New York City. Out West! The Berns, it turned out, were a little more tolerant than the Powells. They took the attitude that if the kids were in love and wanted to get married, let's wish them godspeed.

In the end, love triumphed, and the wedding was planned for August 1953. Luther Powell's only daughter was getting married, and only the best would do: best caterer, biggest cake, finest band, and poshest site, the Concourse Plaza Hotel on the Grand Concourse, the biggest hotel in the Bronx. A decade of skimping, saving, and sacrifice must have vanished that day. But the light dancing in my father's eyes said, what's money for?

I might add that Marilyn and Norm, with their two daughters and one granddaughter, recently celebrated their fortieth wedding anniversary.

. . .

Following Marilyn's example and Mom and Pop's wishes, I applied to two colleges, the City College of New York and New York University. I must have been better than I thought, since I was accepted at both. Choosing between the two was a matter of simple arithmetic; tuition at NYU, a private school, was $750 a year; at CCNY, a public school, it was $10. I chose CCNY. My mother turned out to be my guidance counselor. She had consulted with the family. My two Jamaican cousins, Vernon and Roy, were studying engineering. "That's where the money is," Mom advised. And she was not far wrong. In the boom years of the fifties, demand for consumer goods and for engineers to design the refrigerators, automobiles, and hi-fi sets was strong. And so I was to be an engineering major, despite my allergy to science and math.

The Bronx can be a cold, harsh place in February, and it was frigid the day I set out for college. After two bus rides, I was finally deposited, shivering, at the corner of 156th Street and Convent Avenue in Harlem. I got out and craned my neck like a bumpkin in from the sticks, gazing at handsome brownstones and apartment houses. This was the best of Harlem, where blacks with educations and good jobs lived, the Gold Coast.

I stopped at the corner of Convent and 141st and looked into the campus of the City College of New York. I was about to enter a college established in the previous century "to provide higher education for the children of the working class." Ever since then, New York's poorest and brightest have seized that opportunity. Those who preceded me at CCNY include the polio vaccine discoverer, Dr. Jonas Salk, Supreme Court Justice Felix Frankfurter, the muckraker novelist Upton Sinclair, the actor Edward G. Robinson, the playwright Paddy Chayefsky, the *New York Times* editor Abe Rosenthal, the novelist Bernard Malamud, the labor leader A. Philip Randolph, New York City mayors Robert Wagner, Jr., Abraham Beame, and Edward Koch, and eight Nobel Prize winners. As I took in the grand Gothic structures, a C-average student out of middling Morris High School, I felt overwhelmed. And then I heard a friendly voice: "Hey, kid, you new?"

He was a short, red-faced, weather-beaten man with gnarled hands, and he stood behind a steaming cart of those giant pretzels that New Yorkers are addicted to. I had met a CCNY fixture called, for some unaccountable reason, "Raymond the Bagel Man," though he sold pretzels. I bought a warm, salty pretzel from Raymond, and we shot the breeze for a few minutes. That broke the ice for me. CCNY was somehow less intimidating. I was to become a regular of Raymond's over the next four and a half years. And it either speaks well of his character or poorly of my scholarship that while my memory of most of my professors has faded, the memory of Raymond the Bagel Man remains undimmed.

As I headed toward the main building, Sheppard Hall, towering like a prop out of a horror movie, I passed by an undistinguished old building. I do not remember paying any attention to it at the time. It was, however, to become the focus of my life for the next four years, the ROTC drill hall.

My first semester as an engineering major went surprisingly well, mainly because I had not yet taken any engineering courses. I decided to prepare myself that summer with a course in mechanical drawing. One hot afternoon, the instructor asked us to draw "a cone intersecting a plane in space." The other students went at it; I just sat there. After a while, the instructor came to my desk and looked over my shoulder at a blank page. For the life of me, I could not visualize a cone intersecting a plane in space. If this was engineering, the game was over.

My parents were disappointed when I told them that I was changing my major. There goes Colin again, nice boy, but no direction. When I announced my new major, a hurried family council was held. Phone calls flew between aunts and uncles. Had anybody ever heard of anyone studying geology? What did you do with geology? Where did you go with it? Prospecting for oil? A novel pursuit for a black kid from the South Bronx. And, most critical to these security-haunted people, could geology lead to a pension? That was the magic word in our world. I remember coming home after I had been in the Army for five years and visiting my well-meaning, occasionally meddling Aunt Laurice. What kind of career was this Army? she asked, like a cross-examiner. What was I doing with my life? Snatching at the nearest defense, I mentioned that after twenty years I would get a half-pay pension. And I would only be forty-one. Her eyes widened. A pension? At forty-one? The discussion was over. I had it made.

During my first semester at CCNY, something had caught my eye—young guys on campus in uniform. CCNY was a hotbed of liberalism, radicalism, even some leftover communism from the thirties; it was not a place where you would expect much of a military presence. When I returned to school in the fall of 1954, I inquired about the Reserve Officers Training Corps, and I enrolled in ROTC. I am not sure why. Maybe it was growing up in World War II and coming of age during the Korean conflict: the little banners in windows with a blue star, meaning someone from the family was in the service, or a gold star, meaning someone was not coming back. *Back to Bataan, Thirty Seconds over Tokyo, Guadalcanal Diary,* Colin Kelly, Audie Murphy, the five Sullivan brothers who went down with the cruiser U.S.S. *Juneau, Pork Chop Hill,* and *The Bridges at Toko-Ri.* All these images were burned into my consciousness during my most impressionable years. Or maybe it was the common refrain of that era—you are going to be drafted anyway, you might as well go in as an officer. I was not alone. CCNY might not have been West Point, but during the fifties it had the largest voluntary ROTC contingent in America, fifteen hundred cadets at the height of the Korean War.

There came a day when I stood in line in the drill hall to be issued olive-drab pants and jacket, brown shirt, brown tie, brown shoes, a belt with a brass buckle, and an overseas cap. As soon as I got home, I put the uniform on and looked in the mirror.

I liked what I saw. At this point, not a single Kelly Street friend of mine was going to college. I was seventeen. I felt cut off and lonely. The uniform gave me a sense of belonging, and something I had never experienced all the while I was growing up; I felt distinctive.

In class, I stumbled through math, fumbled through physics, and did reasonably well in, and even enjoyed, geology. All I ever looked forward to was ROTC. Colonel Harold C. Brookhart, Professor of Military Science and Tactics, was our commanding officer. The colonel was a West Pointer and regular Army to his fingertips. He was about fifty years old, with thinning hair, of only medium height, yet he seemed imposing because of his bearing, impeccable dress, and no-nonsense manner. His assignment could not have been a coveted one for a career officer. I am sure he would have preferred commanding a regiment to teaching ROTC to a bunch of smart-aleck city kids on a liberal New York campus. But the Korean War had ended the year before. The Army was overloaded with officers, and Brookhart was probably grateful to land anywhere. Whatever he felt, he never let us sense that what we were doing was anything less than deadly serious.

That fall, I experienced the novel pleasure of being courted by the three military societies on campus, the Webb Patrol, Scabbard and Blade, and the Pershing Rifles, ROTC counterparts of fraternities. Rushing consisted mostly of inviting potential pledges to smokers where we drank beer and watched pornographic movies. The movies, in the sexually repressed fifties, were supposed to be a draw. I hooted and hollered with the rest of the college boys through these grainy 8-millimeter films, in which the male star usually wore socks. But they were not what drew me to the Pershing Rifles. I pledged the PRs because they were the elite of the three groups.

The pledge period involved typical ritualistic bowing and scraping before upperclassmen, and some hazing that aped West Point traditions. A junior would stand you at attention and demand the definition of certain words. To this day I can parrot the response for milk: "She walks, she talks, she's made of chalk, the lactile fluid extracted from the female of the bovine species . . ." and on and on. I can spout half a dozen similar daffy definitions. When we finished the pledge period, we were allowed to wear distinctive blue-and-white shoulder cords and enamel crests on our uniforms. I found that I was much attracted by forms and symbols.

One Pershing Rifles member impressed me from the start. Ronald Brooks was a young black man, tall, trim, handsome, the son of a Harlem Baptist preacher and possessed of a maturity beyond most college students. Ronnie was only two years older than I, but something in him commanded deference. And unlike me, Ronnie, a chemistry major, was a brilliant student. He was a cadet leader in the ROTC and an officer in the Pershing Rifles. He could drill men so that they moved like parts of a watch. Ronnie was sharp, quick, disciplined, organized, qualities then invisible in Colin Powell. I had found a model and a mentor. I set out to remake myself in the Ronnie Brooks mold.

My experience in high school, on basketball and track teams, and briefly in Boy Scouting had never produced a sense of belonging or many permanent friendships. The Pershing Rifles did. For the first time in my life I was a member of a brotherhood. The PRs were in the CCNY tradition only in that we were ethnically diverse and so many of us were the sons of immigrants. Otherwise, we were out of sync with both the student radicals and the conservative engineering majors, the latter easy to spot by the slide rules hanging from their belts. PRs drilled together. We partied together. We cut classes together. We chased girls together. We had a fraternity office on campus from which we occasionally sortied out to class or, just as often, to the student lounge, where we tried to master the mambo. I served as an unlikely academic advisor, steering other Pershing Rifles into geology as an easy yet respectable route to a degree.

The discipline, the structure, the camaraderie, the sense of belonging were what I craved. I became a leader almost immediately. I found a selflessness within our ranks that reminded me of the caring atmosphere within my family. Race, color, background, income meant nothing. The PRs would go the limit for each other and for the group. If this was what soldiering was all about, then maybe I wanted to be a soldier.

I still worked occasional weekends and the Christmas season at Sickser's. But as the school year ended, I wanted a summer job that paid more. And that is how I became a member of the International Brotherhood of Teamsters, Local 812. I had started out the summer in a Harlem furniture plant, screwing hinges on cabinets. My father was delighted to see me get up every morning and head for a paying job. But within three weeks, I told him that I had decided to leave. Pop was not happy. "You work three weeks and just up and quit? What are you gonna tell the boss?" I explained to Pop that I could make more money shaping up every morning with the Teamsters. I could read the message in Pop's eyes. Shape up? When is this kid going to shape up? I made up some excuse for quitting and, to avoid embarrassment, sent a friend to pick up my last paycheck at the furniture plant.

I did earn more shaping up every day at the Teamsters Hall, usually working as a helper on soft drink delivery trucks. One day the Teamsters agent announced a steady summer job that did not require shaping up, porter at a Pepsi-Cola bottling plant in Long Island City. None of the white kids raised a hand. The job was mine, though I was not quite sure what a porter did in a bottling plant. When I reported in, I was handed a mop, an experience that black workers have had for generations. I noticed that all the other porters were black and all the workers on the bottling machines were white. I took the mop. If that was what I had to do to earn $65 a week, I'd do it. I'd mop the place until it glowed in the dark. Whatever skill the job required, I soon mastered. You mop from side to side, not back and forth, unless you want to break your back. It could be godawful work, as it was the day fifty cases of Pepsi-Cola bottles came crashing down from a forklift and flooded the floor with sticky soda pop.

At the end of the summer, the foreman said, "Kid, you mop pretty good."

"You gave me plenty of opportunity to learn," I told him.

"Come back next summer," he said. "I'll have a job for you." Not behind a mop, I said. I wanted to work on the bottling machine. And the next year, that is where he put me. By the end of summer, I was deputy shift leader, and had learned a valuable lesson. All work is honorable. Always do your best, because someone is watching.

I returned to college in the fall of 1955, commuting from Kelly Street. I did not have to be an urbanologist to see that the old neighborhood was deteriorating. The decline was just the latest chapter in the oldest story in New York, people moving up and out as their fortunes improved, and poorer people moving in to take their places. The Jewish families who had escaped Lower East Side tenements for the South Bronx were now moving to the suburbs. Poor Puerto Ricans were moving into their old apartments. Hunts Point had never been verandas and wisteria. And now it was getting worse, from gang fights to gang wars, from jackknives to switchblades, from zip guns to real guns, from marijuana to heroin. One day, I came home from CCNY to find that a kid I knew had been found in a hallway, dead of a heroin overdose. He would not be the last. I had managed to

steer clear of the drug scene. I never smoked marijuana, never got high, in fact never experimented
with any drugs. And for a simple reason; my folks
would have killed me.

As better-off families continued to flee, proper-
ties began to decay, even to be abandoned. Landlords
cut their losses short and walked away from their
buildings. In years to come, my own 952 Kelly Street
would be abandoned, then burned out and finally
demolished. But that was all in the future. For now,
conversation among my relatives typically began,
"When you getting out?" Aunt Laurice moved to the
northern edge of the Bronx. So did Godmother
Brash. Aunt Dot was already in Queens. When were
Luther and Arie going to leave?

The secret dream of these tenement dwellers
had always been to own their own home. And so the
Powell family began heading for the upper Bronx or
Queens, Sunday after Sunday, house hunting in
desirable black neighborhoods. But the prices were
outrageous—$15,000, $20,000, with my parents'
combined income totaling about $100 a week. Week-
ends often ended with the real estate agent sick to
death of us and my sister embarrassed to tears.

My father also dreamed about numbers. He
bought numbers books at the newsstands to work out
winning combinations. And he still went in every day
with Aunt Beryl. They usually played quarters. Then,
one Saturday night, my father dreamed a number,
and the next morning at St. Margaret's the *same*
number appeared on the hymn board. This, surely,
was God taking Luther Powell by the hand and lead-

ing him to the Promised Land. Somehow, Pop and Aunt Beryl managed to scrape up $25 to put on the number. And they hit it, straight.

I still remember the atmosphere of joy, disbelief, and anxiety when the numbers runner delivered the brown paper bags to our house. Pop took them to his room and dumped the money on his bed, $10,000 in tens and twenties, more than three years' pay. He let me help him count it. The money was not going into any bank. This strike was nobody's business. The bills were stashed all over the house, with my mother terrified that the tax man or thieves would be coming through the door any minute.

And that was how the Powells managed to buy 183-68 Elmira Avenue, in the community of Hollis in the borough of Queens—for $17,500. The house was a three-bedroom bungalow in a neighborhood in transition; the whites were moving out and the blacks moving in. My folks bought from a Jewish family named Wiener, one of the few white families left. The neighborhood looked beautiful to us, and the Hollis address carried a certain cachet, a cut above Jamaica, Queens, and just below St. Albans, then another gold coast for middle-class blacks. Our new home was ivy-covered, well kept, and comfortable, and had a family room and a bar in the finished basement. Pop was now a property holder, eager to mow his postage-stamp lawn and prune his fruit trees. Luther Powell had joined the gentry.

But owning a home frightened Mom. She worried constantly about making the mortgage payments. She talked incessantly about her old friends left at Banana Kelly. After a few months, my father came to me almost in tears. "I don't think we can stay," he said. "Your mother can't take the loneliness. I'm not sure she'll make it through the winter." Two years passed before Mom overcame her fears, realized they could carry the mortgage, and stopped running back to the South Bronx.

I now began commuting from Queens to CCNY via the subway, which led to my first serious romance, with a CCNY student. We began riding the A train from the campus downtown, where we would transfer, I out to Queens and the girl out to Brooklyn. I took her to meet my parents. They were perfectly polite to her, but reserved.

My main college interest remained ROTC and the Pershing Rifles. Geology continued to be secondary, though I did enjoy the field trips. We went upstate and clambered over formations of synclines and anticlines. We had to diagram them and figure out their mirror images. If you had an anticline here, you should be able to predict a complementing syncline bulging out somewhere else. Very satisfying when I got it right. Geology allowed me to display my brilliance to my noncollege friends. "You know, the Hudson really isn't a river." "What are you talking about? College kid. Schmuck. Everybody knows the Hudson River's a river." I would then explain that the Hudson was a "drowned" river, up to about Poughkeepsie. The Ice Age had depressed the riverbed to a depth that allowed the Atlantic Ocean to flood inland. Consequently, the lower Hudson was really a saltwater estuary. I proudly pinpointed the farthest advance of the Ice Age. It stopped at Hillside Avenue running through Queens. You can see the ground sloping down along that line into St. Albans and Jamaica. I was startled to earn an A in one of my geology courses and wound up with three A's in my major by graduation.

In my junior year, I enrolled in advanced ROTC, which paid a princely $27.90 a month. My idol was still Ronnie Brooks. In his first two years at CCNY, Ronnie had become a cadet sergeant. I became a cadet sergeant. In advanced ROTC, Ronnie became a battalion commander. I became a battalion commander. Ronnie was a drillmaster. I became a drillmaster. Ronnie had been the PRs' pledge officer, and in my junior year I became pledge officer, which allowed me to do something about the way we went after pledges. I told the brothers there was something wrong if the only way we could attract members was with dirty movies. Besides, I said, all the fraternities are doing the same thing. So what's our edge? Let's use a little imagination. Let's show movies of what we do, like drill competitions. Let's show them what we're all about.

The Pershing Rifles had a basement room in one of the houses along Amsterdam Avenue, provided by the CCNY administration to give this largely commuter campus a touch of college social life. I told the brothers to go out on the street, corral kids after they had gotten their jollies from porn movies at other houses, and bring them over to our place to see movies about what the PRs did. I was taking a risk. Success as a pledge officer was easy to measure. Pledges were either up or down from previous years. I anxiously awaited the day the rushees made their choice. When it was over, the Pershing Rifles had attracted the largest pledge class in years. This was a defining moment for me, the first small indication that I might be able to influence the outcome of events.

One of the student pledges during this period was a rough diamond whose destiny was set the day he joined ROTC and the Pershing Rifles. His name was Antonio "Tony" Mavroudis, a Greek-American, also from Queens, who worked part-time as an auto mechanic. Tony was coarse, profane, street-smart, full of life. I loved him. Just as I had found my model in Ronnie Brooks, Tony found his model in me. We became as close as brothers, commuted together, dated together, raised hell together. And our lives were to be indelibly marked together, Tony's more fatefully than mine, by a place neither of us had probably heard of at the time, Vietnam.

During my last three college years, the drill hall became the center of my universe. A Major Nelson was in charge under the more remote Colonel Brookhart. The major ran interference for us with the college administration as we courted probation for mediocre grades, cutting classes, and pledge-week pranks. ROTC was also my introduction to the backbone of the Army, the NCOs who drilled us and taught the nuts-and-bolts courses. I remember most vividly a rough master sergeant named Lou Mohica: "Gentlemens, this is the Browning Automatic Rifle. I am going to teach youse how to disassemble and assemble the BAR. Listen to me, cuz if youse don't youse could die in combat. Any questions so far?"

I spent almost every Saturday at the drill hall, up to seven hours at a stretch, drawing an M-1 rifle with the rest of the PR drill team, practicing the Queen Mary salute, rifle spins, and diagonal marching with fixed bayonets, a perilous business if you were careless. The Pershing Rifles took part in two competitions, regular drill, which Ronnie led, and trick drill, the fancy stuff, which he entrusted to me. In the spring of 1957, my junior year, we participated in a competition at the 71st Regiment Armory in New York against ROTC units from Fordham, New York University, Hofstra, and other institutions in the metropolitan region. We arrived with our mascots, Coke and Blackjack, two squirrels.

Ronnie took his team out on the floor and scored 460 out of a possible 500 points to win the regular drill competition. Then it was my turn to lead the eighteen-man trick drill team. We had polished our brass with blitz cloths until we'd almost worn out the metal. Our faces were reflected in our shined shoes. And I had a few surprises in store that we had secretly rehearsed. Ordinarily, the drill team captain would just mark time as the team moved into its next maneuver. Instead, I launched into a dance solo, a step popular at the time, the camel walk. The audience went wild. We scored 492 out of a possible 500 points and took first place. My ambition for the next year was to succeed Ronnie as cadet colonel of the entire CCNY regiment, become company commander of the Pershing Rifles, as Ronnie had been, and sweep both ends of the drill competition.

Needless to say, none of the Pershing Rifles' successes cut much ice with the general CCNY student body, which at best tolerated us as chauvinist nuts. At worst, the campus newspaper called for dissolving ROTC.

I have a desk set that I have carried with me for over thirty-five years, two Scheaffer pens and pen holders mounted on a marble base. I kept the set on my desk in the White House when I was National Security Advisor and at the Pentagon when I was Chairman of the Joint Chiefs of Staff. I cherish it for what it says on a small attached plaque, a story that begins on a day in the summer of 1957.

It was an anxious moment for my father. Pop had taken me to lunch with two ROTC pals, Tony DePace and George Urcioli, and then to the Greyhound bus terminal in Manhattan. He was fidgeting, full of dire warnings, convinced he was never going to see his son again. My friends and I were off to Fort Bragg, North Carolina, for ROTC summer training, my first venture into the South. Pop told me that he had asked our priest, Father Weeden, to find some black Episcopalians in Fayetteville, near Fort Bragg, to look after me. I was embarrassed and told him to stop fussing.

As it turned out, we were picked up by the Army at the bus depot immediately and whisked off to Fort Bragg, where I spent the next six weeks isolated from Southern life. If Fort Bragg was an ethnic awakening for me, it was in meeting whites who were not Poles, Jews, or Greeks. Here I met virtually my first WASPs. We spent our days training on the rifle range, firing 81mm mortars, learning how to camouflage and how to set up roadblocks, and I loved every minute of it. I also got off to a running start. My reputation for drilling troops had preceded me, and I was named acting company commander.

At the end of our six weeks, we fell out on the parade ground for presentation of honors. We were judged on course grades, rifle range scores, physical fitness, and demonstrated leadership. I was named "Best Cadet, Company D." These are the words engraved on the desk set that was presented to me that day and that I still treasure. A student from Cornell, Adin B. Capron, was selected Best Cadet for the entire encampment. I came in second in that category.

I was feeling marvelous about my honor. And then, the night before we left, as we were turning in our gear, a white supply sergeant took me aside. "You want to know why you didn't get best cadet in camp?" he said. I had not given it a thought. "You think these Southern ROTC instructors are going to go back to their colleges and say the best kid here was a Negro?" I was stunned more than angered by what he said. I came from a melting-pot community. I did not want to believe that my worth could be diminished by the color of my skin. Wasn't it possible that Cadet Capron was simply better than Cadet Powell?

I got a more elemental taste of racism while driving home. I left Fort Bragg with two white noncommissioned officers from the CCNY ROTC unit. We drove straight through the night, occasionally stopping at gas stations that had three rest rooms, men, women, and colored, the one I had to use. Blacks were apparently ahead of their time, already unisex. I did not start to relax until we reached Washington, didn't feel safe until we were north of Baltimore. I was reminded of that old routine from the Apollo Theater: "Hey, brother, where you from?" "Alabama." "I'd like to welcome you to the United States and hope you had a pleasant crossing."

These brief episodes apart, the summer of '57 was a triumph for me. I was returning home to my girl. I was bringing my parents something they had never had from me—proof, with my desk set, that I had at last excelled. And I had found something that I did well. I could lead. The discovery was no small gift for a young man at age twenty.

Back in college, I continued doing just enough to get by, my other mediocre grades pulled up by straight A's in ROTC. The previous spring, Colonel Brookhart had informed me that I was going to succeed Ronnie Brooks. I was to be cadet colonel, running the entire CCNY regiment, then one thousand strong. I was also elected company commander of the Pershing Rifles. I was intent on winning both the regular and trick drill competitions for the PRs at that year's regional meet, as Ronnie had done before me. I led the regular drill team and delegated the trick drill team to an imposing fellow named John Pardo, a fine leader.

I sensed early on, however, that the drill team was losing its edge. John was distracted by girlfriend problems. Other members came to me complaining that his mind was not on the upcoming competition.

I wanted to take the team away from John and give it to somebody else. The best solution was probably to take it over myself, since I had led the winning team the year before. But John kept saying, "I can do it." We competed that year, as I recall, at the 369th Regiment Armory. We won the regular competition, which I led, but lost the trick competition. Overall, we came in second. I was angry, mostly at myself. I had failed the trick drill team, and I had failed John Pardo too, by letting him go on that floor unprepared, when I knew better.

That day, I started absorbing a lesson as valid for a cadet in a musty college drill hall as for a four-star general in the Pentagon. I learned that being in charge means making decisions, no matter how unpleasant. If it's broke, fix it. When you do, you win the gratitude of the people who have been suffering under the bad situation. I learned in a college drill competition that you cannot let the mission suffer, or make the majority pay to spare the feelings of an individual. Long years afterward, I kept a saying under the glass on my desk at the Pentagon that made the point succinctly if inelegantly: "Being responsible sometimes means pissing people off."

That brief lapse was not fatal to John Pardo. Nearly thirty years later, soldiers at Fort Myer were treated to a rare sight: the deputy national security advisor to the President and a prominent New York graphics designer (Powell and Pardo, respectively) and other paunchy, middle-aged men carrying out a rusty version of their old trick drill fireworks in front of my residence at a reunion of the Pershing Rifles.

We all still remain in touch—Tony DePace, Mark Gatanas, Rich Goldfarb, Bill Scott, John Theologos, and others who made Army careers, retiring as full colonels, and Sam Ebbesen, a black, who rose to lieutenant general. Some who stayed in were killed in Vietnam. Most of those who did not remain in the military have been successful, like Pardo, in civilian careers. Vietnam also killed the ROTC program and the Pershing Rifles at CCNY in the early seventies, which I deeply regret. Not only did our citizen Army lose a special kind of officer, one coming out of the inner city, but we have denied to these young people an opportunity to maintain structure in their lives and to make a useful contribution to their country. Too bad.

On June 9, 1958, at 8:00 P.M., I entered CCNY's Aronowitz Auditorium. A few weeks before, my father had come into my room, sat on the edge of the bed, and, with a twinkling eye, handed me an envelope. He had cleaned out a savings account that he and my mother had been keeping for me since I was a child. Six hundred dollars. I was rich! The first thing I did was to head downtown to Morry Luxenberg's, regarded as the best military haberdasher in New York, to be outfitted.

The First Army band was playing and I was wearing Morry's uniform when I strode past my parents onto the Aronowitz Auditorium stage. "I, Colin Luther Powell, do solemnly swear that I will support and defend the Constitution of the United States against all enemies foreign and domestic," I repeated with my classmates, "and that I will well and faith- fully discharge the duties of the office upon which I am about to enter, so help me God." We live in a more cynical age today. We are embarrassed by expressions of patriotism. But when I said those words almost four decades ago, they sent a shiver down my spine. They still do.

Because I was a "Distinguished Military Grad- uate," I was offered a regular rather than a reserve commission, which meant that I would have to serve three rather than two years on active duty. I eagerly accepted.

For me, graduation from college the next day was anticlimactic. The night before, after our com- missioning, I had gone out celebrating with the boys. We had resumed the revelry the following noon at a college hangout called the Emerald Bar. My mother, knowing where to find me, had to send a cousin to haul me over to my graduation, which in her mind had been the whole point of the previous four and a half years. I tended to look on my B.S. in geology as an incidental dividend.

For much of our growing up, Marilyn and I had been "latchkey kids," left by ourselves or with neigh- bors and relatives after school. This situation is sup- posed to be a prescription for trouble. But that day, Luther and Arie Powell, Jamaican immigrants, garment-district workers, were the parents of two college graduates, with their son now an Army offi- cer as well. Small achievements as the world mea- sures success, but mountaintops in their lives. Thirty-five years later, I was asked by *Parade* magazine to talk about those two people. "My parents," I said, "did not recognize their own strengths." It was nothing they ever said that taught us, I recalled. "It was the way they lived their lives," I said. "If the values seem correct or relevant, the children will follow the values." I had been shaped not by preaching, but by example, by moral osmosis. Banana Kelly, the embracing warmth of an extended family, St. Margaret's Church, and let's weave in the Jamaican roots and a little calypso—all provided an enviable send-off on life's journey.

I also owe an unpayable debt to the New York City public education system. I typified the students that CCNY was created to serve, the sons and daughters of the inner city, the poor, the immigrant. Many of my college classmates had the brainpower to attend Harvard, Yale, or Princeton. What they lacked was money and influential connections. Yet they have gone on to compete with and often surpass alumni of the most prestigious private campuses in this country.

I have made clear that I was no great shakes as a scholar. I have joked over the years that the CCNY faculty handed me a diploma, uttering a sigh of relief, and were happy to pass me along to the military. Yet, even this C-average student emerged from CCNY prepared to write, think, and communicate effectively and equipped to compete against students from colleges that I could never have dreamed of attending. If the Statue of Liberty opened the gateway to this country, public education opened the door to attainment here. Schools like my sister's Buffalo State Teachers College and CCNY have served as the Harvards and Princetons of the poor. And they served us well. I am, consequently, a champion of public secondary and higher education. I will speak out for them and support them for as long as I have the good sense to remember where I came from.

Shortly before the commissioning ceremony in Aronowitz Auditorium, Colonel Brookhart called me into his office in the drill hall. "Sit down, Mr. Powell," he said. I did, sitting at attention. "You've done well here. You'll do well in the Army. You're going to Fort Benning soon."

He warned me that I needed to be careful. Georgia was not New York. The South was another world. I had to learn to compromise, to accept a world I had not made and that was beyond my changing. He mentioned the black general Benjamin O. Davis, who had been with him at West Point, where Davis was shunned the whole four years by his classmates, including, I assumed, Brookhart. Davis had gotten himself into trouble in the South, Brookhart said, because he had tried to buck the system. The colonel was telling me, in effect, not to rock the boat, to be a "good Negro."

I do not remember being upset by what he said. He meant well. Like all of us, Brookhart was a product of his times and his environment. Beneath the West Point armor, he was a caring human being. I thanked him and left.

I took my girl out to Coney Island for a final fling, and a few days after graduation, I headed for Georgia. My parents expected that I would serve the three years, and after that, come back to New York and begin to make something of my life.

2 ★ A Soldier's Life for Me

I CAN REMEMBER the moment I had my first doubt about the career I had chosen. It happened in the mountains of northern Georgia as I hurtled along a cable at a height of one hundred feet, seconds from being smashed against a large tree. This exercise was called the Slide for Life, and the Army was making me perform it to see if I was scared. I was.

The slide also tested our willingness to obey what seemed like suicidal orders. The cable had been strung across a river, attached to trees at either end, starting high, then sloping steeply. At my turn, I climbed the tree and looked down at the troops on the other side, who from this height looked small. I grabbed a hook attached to a pulley that ran along the cable. The challenge was to ride the cable and not let go until the instructor on the other bank yelled, "Drop!" Before I had time to think, another instructor pushed me off. Suddenly I was careening down the wire at terrifying speed, the tree on the other side, looking bigger and bigger, rushing up to meet me. Would that bastard ever say the word? At what seemed the last possible second, he yelled, and I plunged into the water a dozen feet from the tree. It was one of the most frightening experiences of my life.

The Slide for Life was one of the joys cooked up for us during the two months at Ranger school that followed eight weeks of basic infantry training at Fort

Benning, Georgia. The first two weeks of Ranger school had involved physical challenges, designed to make the basic course seem like a stroll down Westchester Avenue. The idea was to weed out the weak before we moved on to Ranger training in the Florida swamplands. A couple of weeks of wading in swamp water and living off alligator and rattlesnake cured me forever of any desire to invest in Florida real estate.

We then went to northern Georgia for mountain training. Our Ranger instructors led us to wild terrain near Dahlonega, where the nights were cold and the mornings damp. We were supposed to bunk in wooden cabins, though we rarely saw the inside of them. We lived outdoors, scaling cliffs, crossing gorges on three-rope bridges, patrolling in the dark of night in hip-deep water, and sleeping on the ground, never for very long. We learned the Australian rappel. With a rope slung behind, you stepped off the edge of a cliff so that you were facedown, horizontal to Mother Earth. You then proceeded to "run" down the cliff by letting out slack on the rope, a little like Fred Astaire tap-dancing on a wall. It was quite thrilling, once you accepted that you were not going to land face first on the rocks 150 feet below.

My Army career had begun a few months before on a gloriously sunny morning in June 1958. That day, I found myself standing in front of the bachelor officers' quarters at Fort Benning, Georgia, which would be my home, on and off, for the next five months. Across the road from the BOQ was the airborne training ground, and rising above it, like a thrill ride at an amusement park, stood three 250-

foot practice jump towers. I studied them with considerable personal interest. If you were regular Army, if you were infantry, then you wanted to be the best, and that meant becoming a Ranger *and* a paratrooper. Those jump towers, however, looked terribly high.

Newly commissioned lieutenants from ROTC killed time waiting for the latest class of West Pointers to finish their graduation leaves and join us for the basic course. This marked the first time any of us would be competing head to head with academy graduates, and the ROTC guys seemed to think West Pointers had a median height of ten feet. When they arrived, they turned out to be like colts happily out of the corral after four years of regimentation, and we all got along fine.

That first day, we mustered in front of the Infantry School by the legendary Follow Me statue, a bronze infantryman, rifle held high, leading men into battle. It was only forged metal to me at the time, but in the weeks to follow I was to learn that this statue captured perfectly the infantry officer's code. We were about to be taught a deadly serious calling, and its creed was "Follow Me."

I found the class work and weapons training easy enough. But the field course turned out to be tough. One feat especially tested a lad from the gridlike streets of the South Bronx—a five-mile, nighttime compass hike to locate a stake planted somewhere in the Georgia wilds.

By the time the basic course ended, the meaning of "Follow Me" had been hammered home. The infantry's mission was "to close with and destroy the enemy." No questions asked. No ambiguity. No gray areas. The infantry officer was to go into battle up front, demonstrating courage, determination, strength, proficiency, and selfless sacrifice. We were to march into hell, if necessary, to accomplish the mission. At the same time, we were taught to fulfill this responsibility while trying to keep ourselves and our men from being killed. For years, I have told young officers that most of what I know about military life I learned in my first eight weeks at Fort Benning. I can sum up those lessons in a few maxims:

—"Take charge of this post and all government property in view"—the Army's first general order.
—The mission is primary, followed by taking care of your soldiers.
—Don't stand there. Do something!
—Lead by example.
—"No excuse, sir."
—Officers always eat last.
—Never forget, you are an American infantryman, the best.
—And never be without a watch, a pencil, and a notepad.

The soul of the Army, particularly the infantryman's Army, was captured for me in an old poem by Colonel C. T. Lanham that I first read at Fort Benning. It tells the plight of the lowly foot soldier, going all the way back to the Roman legions, and describes the fear, the death he has to face with blind obedience. It ends:

I see these things,
Yet am I slave,
When banners flaunt and bugles blow,
Content to fill a soldier's grave,
For reasons I will never know.

We were taught at Fort Benning, however, that American soldiers must know the reason for their sacrifices. Our GIs are not vassals or mercenaries. They are the nation's sons and daughters. We put their lives at risk only for worthy objectives. If the duty of the soldier is to risk his life, the responsibility of his leaders is not to spend that life in vain. In the post-Vietnam era, when I rose to a position where I had to recommend where to risk American lives, I never forgot that principle.

I finished the basic course in the top ten of the class, validating my ROTC and Pershing Rifles preparation. I was now a certified professional. The Ranger school that followed, with its tests like the Slide for Life and the Australian rappel, occupied us for the next two months. One of our most memorable Ranger instructors was a black first lieutenant, Vernon Coffey, who seemed to be made of flexible steel. Coffey drove us mercilessly, push-ups, sit-ups, and running until we were ready to drop. Lack of motion offended Ranger Coffey. We stood in awe of the man. I could not imagine myself ever matching his strength and endurance. Coffey was the first black officer I knew who was at the top of his game, the first so good that respect for him transcended race.

The Army was becoming more democratic, but I was plunged back into the Old South every time I

left the post. I could go into Woolworth's in Columbus, Georgia, and buy anything I wanted, as long as
I did not try to eat there. I could go into a department store and they would take my money, as long
as I did not try to use the men's room. I could walk
along the street, as long as I did not look at a white
woman.

While we were training in the north Georgia
mountains, the only black church was some distance
away in Gainesville. I wanted to go to services on
Sundays, and the Army thoughtfully provided me
with a half-ton truck and a driver, a white corporal, to
take me to Gainesville. There I sang and swayed with
the rest of the Baptist congregation. The next Sunday, the corporal pointed out that because he had to
drive me to church, he could not attend services himself. Would it be all right, he wanted to know, if he
joined me? The minister was a kindly man and said it
would ordinarily give him great pleasure to have the
corporal among his flock. But his presence in a black
church might not sit well with the local white folks.
It might be wiser if the corporal waited in the truck.

What my father had feared, what Colonel
Brookhart had warned me of, the reality I wanted to
ignore, was forcing its way into my life, the lunatic
code that made it wrong for two men to sit together
in a house of God, or share a meal in a restaurant, or
use the same bathroom.

Racism was still relatively new to me, and I had
to find a way to cope psychologically. I began by
identifying my priorities. I wanted, above all, to succeed at my Army career. I did not intend to give way

to self-destructive rage, no matter how provoked. If people in the South insisted on living by crazy rules, then I would play the hand dealt me for now. If I was to be confined to one end of the playing field, then I was going to be a star on that part of the field. Nothing that happened off-post, none of the indignities, none of the injustices, was going to inhibit my performance. I was not going to let myself become emotionally crippled because I could not play on the whole field. I did not feel inferior, and I was not going to let anybody make me believe I was. I was not going to allow someone else's feelings about me to become my feelings about myself. Racism was not just a black problem. It was America's problem. And until the country solved it, I was not going to let bigotry make me a victim instead of a full human being. I occasionally felt hurt; I felt anger; but most of all I felt challenged. I'll show you!

After Ranger school, I reported for airborne training, physically exhausted, underweight, and fighting a leg infection that I had picked up sliding down a mountain. I said nothing about the leg and just kept slathering the wound with antibiotic ointment. I was determined not to fall behind. First week: dropped from parachute trainers a few feet off the ground. Second week: dropped from the top of those 250-foot towers, astonished that the parachute actually saved me from being pulped. Third week: into the air aboard a twin-engine C-123 transport. I felt a cold anxiety as I stood in the door of the plane, battered by the wind, waiting for the jumpmaster's signal. Jumping into nothingness goes against our deepest human instincts. Nevertheless, I made five jumps in two days.

Rappelling off cliffs, sliding for life, and jumping out of airplanes answered a question that I think everyone secretly asks: Do I have physical courage? I dreaded doing these things. If I never have to parachute again, that will be fine with me, yet there was never any doubt in my mind that I would do what had to be done. I usually volunteered to go first to get the chore out of the way, which may reveal more practicality than courage. These experiences are rites of passage. Physical danger that people face and master together bonds them in some mystical way. And conquering one's deepest fears is exhilarating.

The day came when we mustered on the parade ground under the jump towers, standing stiff as pikes in our Corcoran commercial jump boots (paid for out of pocket, since no self-respecting paratrooper would be caught dead wearing Army-issue boots), and received paratrooper wings to complement our black-and-gold Ranger tabs. We were not just infantrymen, we were airborne Rangers; and the way we said it was "airborneranger," all one word. In all the American infantry, there is no cockier soldier.

I went home on leave like someone returning from another planet, from the Deep South to Queens, from rigid military discipline to casual civilian life, from the rugged companionship of young men to mothers, fathers, aunts, and uncles. One of my first stops was at CCNY to visit the Pershing Rifles and let them see this extraordinary five-month transformation in one of the brothers. "Colin! Airborneranger." I could see the wonder in their eyes, and I reveled in it. I was twenty-one and on the launchpad of life. I had a girlfriend. My parents were proud of me, though horrified when I told them I had jumped out of a plane. And I was about to see the world. My first orders sent me to the 3d Armored Division in West Germany. In that Cold War era, when the globe seemed divided between white and red, I was excited to be going to the front line, with our godless communist adversary deployed just across the Iron Curtain.

While home, I met a new member of the Powell household. Ever frugal, ever eager to earn an extra buck, Mom and Pop had taken in a boarder named Ida Bell. Miss Bell turned out to be a kindly soul, prompt with the rent and always ready to pitch into household chores. She even trimmed my father's fingernails from time to time. But when Mom came into the living room one night to find Ida Bell cutting Pop's toenails, she drew the line. My sister and I remain forever in Ida Bell's debt. In difficult times to come, when both of us would be far from Elmira Avenue, Ida Bell would serve as our parents' angel of mercy.

I was sent to Gelnhausen (which the GIs had Americanized to "Glenhaven"), a picturesque town nestled in the valley of the Kinzig River, about twenty-five miles east of Frankfurt. The Soviet zone was forty-three miles to the east. My unit, Combat Command B of the 3d Armored Division, occupied Coleman Kaserne, a former German army post near the Vogelsberg mountains, where most of the troops lived in modern concrete barracks clinging to the hillsides. I was assigned as a platoon leader to Company B, 2d Armored Rifle Battalion, 48th Infantry, my first field command—forty men. The first morning I faced them, shivering in the cold at reveille, my reaction was mixed. On the one hand, these soldiers, all shapes, sizes, colors, and backgrounds, were much like the guys I had grown up with at home. On the other hand, the Benning ethic had taken over. These men were not my buddies; they were my responsibility. I was to take care of them. I felt instantly paternal toward men close to my own age, and some even older.

I was also about to discover an Army far different from the romping, stomping, gung ho airborne-rangers of Fort Benning. Captain Tom Miller, B Company Commander, my new superior, typified the breed. Miller was one of the battalion's five company commanders, mostly World War II and Korean-era reserve officers, barely hanging on. If lucky, they would stay on for twenty years and retire as majors, maybe lieutenant colonels. If less lucky, they would be reduced back to the enlisted ranks. If really unlucky, they would be mustered out and thrown onto the civilian job market in middle age.

These men may not have been shooting stars, yet there was something appealing about them, something to be learned from them, something not taught on the plain at West Point or in the texts on military science and tactics, as my experience with Captain Miller and a pistol was about to illustrate.

In those days, the Air Force and the Navy had nuclear weapons, and so the Army had to have its nukes. Our prize was a 280mm atomic cannon carried on twin truck-tractors, looking like a World War I Big Bertha. The Russians obviously wanted to know where our 280s were so that they could knock them out if and when they attacked. Consequently, the guns were always guarded by an infantry platoon as the trucks hauled them around the German forests to keep the Soviets guessing. One day Captain Miller summoned me. He was assigning my platoon to a secret mission. We had been selected to guard a 280. I eagerly alerted my men. I loaded my .45 caliber pistol, jumped into my jeep, and headed for battalion headquarters to be briefed. I was excited; I was going to guard a weapon that fired a nuclear warhead!

I had not gone far when I reached down for the reassuring feel of the .45. It was gone. I was petrified. In the Army, losing a weapon is serious business. I was torn between taking time to look for the pistol and getting on with the mission. Finally, I realized that I had to radio Captain Miller and tell him what had happened.

"Powell, are you on your way yet?" he asked right off the bat.

"Yes, sir. But, you see . . . I lost my pistol."

"You what?" he said in disbelief, then, after a few seconds, added, "All right, continue the mission."

After being briefed at battalion headquarters, I returned to pick up my unit, uneasily contemplating my fate. I had just passed through a little German village when I spotted Captain Miller waiting for me in his jeep at the wood line. He called me over. "I've got something for you," he said. He handed me the pistol. "Some kids in the village found it where it fell out of your holster." Kids found it? I felt a cold chill. "Yeah," he said. "Luckily they only got off one round before we heard the shot and came and took the gun away from them." The disastrous possibilities left me limp. "For God's sake, son," Miller said, "don't let that happen again."

He drove off. I checked the magazine; it was full. The gun had not been fired. I learned later that I had dropped it in my tent before I ever got started. Miller had fabricated the whole scene about the kids to scare me into being more responsible. He never mentioned the incident again.

Today, the Army would have held an investigation, called in lawyers, and likely have entered a fatal black mark on my record. Instead, Miller concocted his imaginative story. He evidently thought, I've got this ordinarily able second lieutenant. Sometimes he gets a little ahead of his skis and takes a tumble. I'll teach him a lesson, scare the bejeezus out of him; but let's not ruin his career before it gets started.

Miller's example of humane leadership that does not always go by the book was not lost on me. When they fall down, pick 'em up, dust 'em off, pat 'em on the back, and move 'em on.

I gave Miller and my other superior officers plenty of opportunities to pick me up—for example, when I lost the train tickets for my platoon en route to Munich and found myself and my men stranded in the Frankfurt Bahnhof. I have never spoken of these embarrassments until now. Maybe they will help young officers learn a lesson: nobody ever made it to the top by never getting into trouble.

. . .

The Army's mission in Germany was to man the GDP, the General Defense Plan line. The line cut north-south across the Fulda Gap, a break in the Vogelsberg mountains through which the Iron Curtain ran. Every piece of artillery, every machine gun, rifle, mortar, tank, and antitank weapon in our division was intended to hit the Russians the moment they came pouring through the gap. My platoon guarded a little stretch of the Iron Curtain. Why would the Russians be coming? I did not know; the answer was above my pay grade. But we assumed the assault could come at any time. The Cold War was frigid then. The Russians had leaped ahead in space the year before with Sputnik. They were blocking our traffic to Berlin on the autobahn. The Eisenhower administration had adopted a policy of massive retaliation, which meant keeping conventional forces on short rations while beefing up our nuclear punch. Our strategists assumed that we were inferior to the Russians in conventional weaponry, so we had to rely on our nuclear superiority. All Lieutenant Powell understood of this was that we were thinly deployed along the GDP, and that once the Russians started coming, we were to fight like the devil, fall back, and watch the nuclear cataclysm begin.

I went home on leave during the summer of 1959 for the wedding of good CCNY friends, Chris and Donna Chisholm, and to see my new niece, Marilyn's baby, Leslie, and her older sister, Lisa. Mostly I went to see my girl. We talked about getting married before I went back. If we did, she intended to stay in

New York until she finished nursing school. I would have to return to Germany alone for another sixteen months, not a promising start for newlyweds. I needed Pop's advice. And so, late one night, in the basement family room, I gingerly raised the subject. His reaction stunned me. Pop thought I wasn't ready. He did not elaborate. But he made no bones about it; he was dead set against this marriage. He had never rejected an idea of mine so flatly. Family approval was all-important to me, and I was not ready to go up against Luther Powell, the Godfather. My leave ended and I returned, still a bachelor, to Gelnhausen.

By the end of that year, I got my first promotion, to first lieutenant, an automatic advancement that had only required my staying out of trouble for eighteen months.

I had my first experience with military law in Germany. Three Army truck drivers had decided to turn a German road into a racetrack, speeding and passing each other on the way back to their post. One of these five-tonners skidded out of control and slammed into a Volkswagen in the oncoming lane. Three German civilians were killed. I was tapped to prosecute these drivers for manslaughter in a special court-martial. The GIs had engaged a civilian lawyer to defend them.

Starting from ground zero, I immersed myself in the facts and law of the case. Still, I was not Mr. District Attorney. On the appointed day, I entered the tent where the trial was to be held, a young infantry lieutenant up against professional lawyers engaged by the defense. I nevertheless managed to win convictions against two of the defendants, including the sergeant in charge.

As I walked out of the court, I felt that I had learned as much about myself as about military law. I had first filled leadership roles with the ROTC and Pershing Rifles. Since going on active duty, I had assumed more serious responsibility. These situations, however, largely involved passing along canned orders. The trial marked almost the first time that I had had to do much original thinking, and a lot of it on my feet. That day marked an awareness of an ability I apparently had. I seemed to be able to assimilate a mass of raw information, pound it into coherent shape, and communicate it intelligibly, even persuasively.

The trial assignment continued another pattern that emerged early in my career. I was often pulled off my regular assignment for unusual duties. Once I was directed to run the division pistol team. We took the championship. Another time I was sent to command an honor guard for two months. I was detailed to brigade headquarters as assistant adjutant. I was moving around so much that I was afraid I might slip off the career track. Still, my efficiency reports were encouraging. One, dated July 20, 1959, by Captain Wilfred C. Morse, ended, "[Powell] is tenacious, firm, yet polished in manner and can deal with individuals of any rank. His potential for a career in the military is unlimited and should be developed on an accelerated basis." I was twenty-two years old, and I was being taken *seriously*. But just six months after that report had me floating on air, the next one brought me back to earth.

Among the easygoing reserve officers in the battalion, we were about to meet an exception. I had recently been reassigned as executive officer, Delta Company, 2d Battalion, 48th Infantry, and we were due for a new company commander. When he was named, near panic set in. Captain William C. Louisell, Jr., was a West Pointer and a former tactics instructor at the military academy. Some of our junior officers had been cadets under Captain Louisell, whom they judged one of the all-time hardnoses. Louisell turned out exactly as advertised—tough, by-the-book, brilliant, sometimes unreasonable.

I got an early taste of Louisell in the matter of the armored personnel carriers. One of my responsibilities was to see that our APCs were always parked headed downhill, with the left front corner of one vehicle aligned with the right front corner of the next, ready to pounce against the Red Army. Louisell measured the placement of these vehicles practically with a surveyor's transit, and God help us if any corner was out of alignment.

One day, I was in the orderly room on the phone, shouting at a fellow lieutenant at the top of my lungs, when Louisell walked in. He took me aside and chewed me out for my behavior. Shortly afterward, I received my efficiency report. To the layman, it might not seem disastrous. Louisell had said of me, "He has a quick temper which he makes a mature effort to control." But in the code of efficiency report writing, I had taken a hit. These words marked the only negative comment on my performance since the first day I had put on a uniform in

ROTC. Louisell called me in, sat me down, and raised the matter of the blowup on the phone. "Don't ever show your temper like that to me or anyone else," he warned. It was demeaning to everybody. I still have a hot temper. I still explode occasionally. And whenever I do, I hear Bill Louisell's warning voice.

While working as Louisell's exec, I got a foretaste of what hot war could be like if the Cold War ever ignited. It was a morning after payday in the summer of 1960. Our brigade had gone to Grafenwöhr for field training. The troops were to be billeted in over six hundred general-purpose tents. Our company had not yet arrived in force, but a sister unit, the 12th Cavalry, had come in the night before. Its tents were full of troops, still asleep at this early hour.

I was returning from a bartering mission with another company's exec, bringing rations I had traded for back to our mess hall. My ears pricked up at an odd, whistling sound overhead. In about a nanosecond, I realized it was an artillery shell that had strayed wildly out of the impact area. I stopped, frozen, and actually saw the 8-inch round come in. It struck a tent pole in the 12th Cavalry's sector, detonating in an airburst. The roar was deafening, followed by a terrifying silence. I dropped the food and rushed toward the blast as dismembered legs, hands, and arms thumped to the ground around me. Money from payday came fluttering to earth. Some other soldiers joined me, wading through the acrid smoke and fumes. Inside the tent, I zipped open a sleeping bag, and what was left looked like an illustration of viscera in a medical textbook. In an instant, a dozen lives had been snuffed out and more men wounded. The tragedy was later found to have been caused by human error in aligning the gun, and the battalion commander and other officers were relieved of their duties. I had seen a hundred war movies, but nothing had prepared me for the sights I saw that day.

ROTC and Fort Benning had been about officers. Gelnhausen was my indoctrination into what the Army is really about—soldiers. Here in the 48th Infantry, life revolved around the care of our men. In those days, the Army was composed mostly of draftees. They tended to be better educated than the volunteers, some even college-trained, and we chose our clerks and technical staff from them. The draftees wanted to put in their two years and get back to school, jobs, wives and kids, or girlfriends. We called them the "Christmas help," the people who came in, fought the nation's wars, and went home. They were not looking for trouble.

The volunteers were a different lot. Most were well motivated, and many would eventually work their way up to sergeant, becoming part of the Army's backbone. Others had enlisted aimlessly, and some out of desperation, since in those days judges often gave troublemakers the choice of jail or the Army. I had one eighteen-year-old volunteer come to me for permission to marry a German girl whom he had gotten pregnant. At the time, the Army deliberately made it difficult for young GIs to marry foreigners. Many of these couples were immature, and we tried to slow down their passion. Later, in the 1970s, we were instructed not to interfere with love—an eighteen-year-old private had a constitutional right to make a fool of himself as much as any eighteen-year-old civilian. In the case of the private who came to me, since he and his girlfriend had obviously held their honeymoon in advance, I told him I would try to expedite the paperwork. That was not the whole problem, he said. He also needed permission to get his prospective mother-in-law into the United States because he had gotten her pregnant too. This situation had not been covered in the basic course at Fort Benning.

Getting rid of troublemakers and misfits in the fifties consumed months and required piles of paperwork. We tried to persuade ourselves that all we needed was better leadership to bring the delinquents around. Meanwhile, the good troops saw the bad ones getting away with murder, a situation destructive of morale overall. It would take another twenty years before the all-volunteer Army gave us the luxury of turning down people whom judges did not want to jail and to "fire" GIs who could not meet our standards.

Sergeants were a tough breed in those days. The wise lieutenant learned from them and otherwise stayed out of their way. My first platoon sergeant was Robert D. Edwards, from deepest Alabama, which was initially a cause of concern to me. I need not have worried. My color made no difference to Edwards; I could have been black, white, or candy-striped for all he cared. I was his lieutenant, and his job was to break in new lieutenants and take care of them. He always addressed me in the old Army third-person style: "Does the lieutenant want a cup of coffee?"

The troops feared Edwards, and with reason. Once, I had to explain to him why he could not keep a soldier who had gone AWOL chained to the barracks radiator. Edwards found my reasons puzzling and went off muttering about the decline of discipline. While he was feared, he was, at the same time, respected and revered by the men. They understood Edwards. He was in their corner. No matter how primitive his methods, he had one concern—the welfare of the platoon and the men in it. If they soldiered right, he looked out for them.

I came to understand GIs during my tour at Gelnhausen. I learned what made them tick, lessons that stuck for thirty-five years. American soldiers love to win. They want to be part of a successful team. They respect a leader who holds them to a high standard and pushes them to the limit, as long as they see a worthwhile objective. American soldiers will gripe constantly about being driven to high performance. They will swear they would rather serve somewhere easier. But at the end of the day they always ask: "How'd we do?"

And I learned what it meant when soldiers brought you problems, even problems as perplexing as that of the eighteen-year-old dual lover. Leadership is solving problems. The day soldiers stop bringing you their problems is the day you have stopped leading them. They have either lost confidence that you can help them or concluded you do not care. Either case is a failure of leadership.

Another of my memorable mentors was Major Raymond "Red Man" Barrett, our battalion executive officer. His wife, Madge, was a den mother to young officers. We adored her. One late night at the officers' club bar, the Red Man explained the essence of Army leadership to us: "You go to bed at night. Everything is hunky-dory. The unit is humming. Everyone's accounted for. You think you're doing a helluva job. You wake up the next morning and discover that in the middle of the night, when no one was looking, things got screwed up bad. Stuff happens. You guys understand? Stuff happens. And a leader's just got to start all over again." Many a morning I entered the Pentagon, as Chairman of the Joint Chiefs of Staff, with the Red Man's wisdom ringing in my ear.

I have a warm spot in my heart for those long-ago officers. Men like Major Barrett and Captains Miller, Blackstock, Watson, and even Louisell taught us to love soldiering and to care about and look after our troops. And they passed on to us the fun of the Army. Do the job right, but don't take yourself too seriously. And we certainly did have fun. Our social life revolved around the O-club, which was perched on a hill overlooking the Kinzig River Valley. Every evening the lieutenants adjourned to the bar to drink Löwenbräu beer served by Friedl, the bartender, while the old captains held court, regaling us with war stories and passing on legends. Dinner was followed by more drinking, after which we staggered into our Volkswagens and careened rashly downhill to our quarters.

In those socially incorrect days, we played several drinking games, at which I excelled until I encountered "7-14-21." In this game, we took turns rolling a cup of five dice, counting only aces. Whoever rolled the seventh ace ordered a twelve-ounce drink that Friedl concocted of straight bourbon, scotch, gin, brandy, and crème de menthe. As Friedl whipped this green concoction in a blender, the game continued. Whoever rolled the fourteenth ace paid for the drink. The game ended when the person who rolled the twenty-first ace was obliged to chugalug Friedl's vile brew. One night, I hit twenty-one three times in a row. I, who am today a social sipper, fulfilled my obligation, downed the stuff, and on the third glass passed out. I was poured into bed only to be hauled out again at 2:00 A.M. for a surprise alert. I had to be strapped to the backseat of my jeep to hold me up. Fortunately for this near-brain-dead lieutenant, that was not a night the Russians chose to come roaring through the Fulda Gap.

For black GIs, especially those out of the South, Germany was a breath of freedom—they could go where they wanted, eat where they wanted, and date whom they wanted, just like other people. The dollar was strong, the beer good, and the German people friendly, since we were all that stood between them and the Red hordes. War, at least the Cold War in West Germany, was not hell.

You can serve thirty-five years in the Army and rise to the top, yet your first assignment always stands out as the most unforgettable, the one against which all future posts are measured. That is what

Gelnhausen meant to me. It marked the beginning of lifelong friendships among my class of lieutenants. We needed each other to survive. We shielded each other from occasional assaults by senior officers. We covered each other's mistakes and posteriors. And we competed against each other. Steve Stevens, Keith Bissell, Ike Smith, Hal Jordan, Tiger Johns, Walter Pritchard, Bill Stofft, Jim Lee, Joe Schwar, and others remain vivid in my memory. Joe and his wife, Pat, were to save the Powells four years later when my pregnant wife and I were practically left out in the street in a less than hospitable Southern city. Some decided the Army was not for them and left. A handful made general. We were a new officer generation, post–World War II, post-Korea. We would serve our apprenticeship in places like Gelnhausen, but we would undergo our baptism of fire halfway around the world in Southeast Asia, where some, like Pritchard and Lee, would die.

However memorable and valuable it was, I discovered a downside to the German experience. An unhealthy attitude had infected these garrison soldiers, a willingness to cut corners and make things look right rather than be right. Here is a small but telling illustration. The Army had installed a new equipment maintenance system for ordering parts. Nobody could figure it out. Rather than blowing the whistle, rather than saying this system stinks, it was easier to go to military junkyards and salvage the parts we needed. Then we would fudge the paperwork to make it look as if the cockamamie system had worked, thus perpetuating poor management practices. Senior officers went along with the game, and junior officers concluded that this was how it was played. This self-deception would be expanded, institutionalized, and exported, with tragic results, a few years later to Vietnam.

In November 1960, while I was overseas, a presidential election took place, the first in which I was old enough to vote. Not much of the campaign penetrated Gelnhausen; I didn't see the famous televised Nixon-Kennedy debates. I did vote, however, and cast my absentee ballot for JFK. Not much searching analysis went into my choice. In those days, he and his party seemed to hold out a little more hope for a young man of my roots.

I completed my two-year tour in Germany at the end of 1960. By then, I had succeeded Bill Louisell as Delta Company's CO. I was the only lieutenant in the battalion commanding a company, a job usually held by a captain. My battalion commander, Lieutenant Colonel Jim Bartholomees, asked me to extend. But I was homesick. I had a girl whom I had not seen for sixteen months. And I was ready for a change. Infantry Branch had assigned me to Fort Devens, Massachusetts, where I expected to have an opportunity to command another company. And Devens was just a few hours' drive from New York City, which appealed to me. I bid a sentimental goodbye to the 48th Infantry. I had joined as a rookie, and I was leaving as a fairly seasoned pro.

Long afterward, I was telling my children about this period, and they perked up at only one story. One morning, during maneuvers, we had come upon a scout jeep from another unit parked on a narrow road near Giessen.

"Hey, Lieutenant," one of my men shouted. "Come on over. Look who's here."

I walked over to the jeep, where a grimy, weary-looking sergeant saluted me and put out his hand. It was Elvis Presley. That their father had shaken the King's hand astonished my kids. What impressed me at the time was that instead of seeking celebrity treatment, Elvis had done his two-year hitch, uncomplainingly, as an ordinary GI, even rising to the responsibility of an NCO.

Fort Devens is located near Ayer, Massachusetts, about thirty miles west of Boston, a post then maintained mostly through the tenacity of the Massachusetts congressional delegation. I reported to Devens in January 1961 in three feet of snow. The obsessive topic among the troops was the bitter cold. Puerto Rican GIs were especially vulnerable. We had one whom we called "Private TA-21," in reference to the Army's Table of Allowance at that time for clothing. Whenever Private TA-21 had to leave the barracks, he put on *everything* issued, and he was still miserable. Alas, he went AWOL, and the MPs found him weeks later sensibly basking in Santurce, Puerto Rico. Interestingly, on Saturday afternoon, after inspection, the same troops who had been shivering and griping all week could be seen in their lightest, sharpest civvies, hitchhiking to the fleshpots of Boston and New York.

I was assigned to the 1st Battle Group, 4th Infantry, 2d Infantry Brigade. The brigade commander was Brigadier General Joseph Stilwell, Jr., son of the legendary World War II general "Vinegar Joe" Stilwell. Our Joe was known as "Cider Joe" or "Apple Juice Joe." He took up parachuting in his fifties. Not content to risk his own neck, Stilwell cajoled the brigade chaplain into jumping, after a ten-minute lesson. The chaplain hit the ground and shattered like Waterford crystal, content never to jump again. Years later, long after Devens, Stilwell taught himself to fly a DC-3, or maybe did not learn all that well, since he disappeared on a flight from California to Hawaii. Those of us who knew him expect Cider Joe to show up someday, still in the pink, on the beach at Waikiki.

My first assignment at Devens was as liaison officer in the battle group headquarters, essentially a "gofer" for Major Richard D. Ellison, the group's S-3 officer, in charge of operations and training. Ellison was a genial Irishman, a World War II and Korean War veteran several cuts above most of my recent superiors in Germany. Commanding the battle group was a straitlaced colonel, Robert Utley, and our deputy commander, Colonel Tom Gendron, added the desired spice. Gendron, a veteran of the legendary 1st Infantry Division, "the Big Red One," lived, breathed, and slept his old outfit. He named his sons after 1st Infantry Division generals. Only at his wife's insistence were his daughters spared that honor. "You ain't got one," Gendron liked to say, "unless you got a *big red one.*"

Between Cider Joe, Utley, and Gendron, ideas, good, bad, and ridiculous, bubbled up constantly. I learned from the adroit Dick Ellison how to push the smart proposals, derail the dumb ones, and strangle the most embarrassing in the cradle, all the while keeping our superiors happy. Dick and his wife, Joy, were a gregarious, fun-loving couple, and they practically adopted this lonely bachelor. Dick's death in Vietnam a few years later robbed me of a beloved friend much too soon.

I eventually managed to escape the liaison job and became executive officer of Company A, making me second in command. Shortly afterward, the company commander was reassigned and I found myself in command of my second company since I had entered the Army, and while still a first lieutenant. My fellow company commanders and I were simultaneously competitors and partners. We passed along to each other tricks of the trade. If, for example, you found yourself short on sheets, you tried the hospital trash dump or the mortuary. They always had plenty, somewhat used but recoverable.

I learned a valuable lesson about competition at Devens: it does not have to be cutthroat. I came up with competitions for my company—not just in sports, but for best barracks, best day room, best weapons inspection, any performance that could be rated and rewarded. The more competitions, the more each individual GI or platoon had a chance to stand out. I was keenly aware of this need. I had discovered my own self-worth in uniform, and I intended to help my troops find theirs. I saw far less value in "Super Bowl" competitions requiring Olympic-class performers who spent all their time training. The event was secondary. The point was to build confidence and self-esteem among a lot of soldiers. The healthiest competition occurs when average people win by putting in above-average effort.

The 2d Infantry Brigade was part of STRAC, the Strategic Army Corps, composed of elite units prepared to fight on any front on short notice. We used the acronym interchangeably as a noun and an adjective. STRAC was a state of being, a sharpness, a readiness, an esprit de corps. ("Sergeant, is the platoon STRAC?" "Yes, sir. We're STRAC.") And, as often happens in the Army, we overdid it. Style overran substance. Being STRAC came to mean looking sharp more than being combat-ready. We had our field uniforms starched stiff as boards to achieve knife-edge creases. "Breaking starch" meant using a broom handle to open up the pants so that we could get our legs into our fatigues without ripping off our skin. We dressed for inspection at the last possible minute; we left the pants unbuttoned and the fly unzipped; we put on our boots last—all in the interest of dressing without wrinkling the uniform. The effort was pointless, since within an hour everybody's uniform was a mass of wrinkles. But being STRAC meant breaking starch, and I broke starch with the best of them. It was tradition.

Breaking starch is an example of foolish tradition. Since Vietnam, the Army has tried to eliminate pointless practices. We have sought to make military life a little more like civilian life, with five-day work weeks and weekends free. Barracks today resemble junior college campuses rather than minimum-security prisons. We still hold inspections, but they are designed to assess the preparedness of a unit rather than to gig a soldier for having his canteen a quarter of an inch out of line.

I accept and support most of the sensible changes we have made, and the abandonment of the senseless, like breaking starch. At the same time, traditions and rituals remain essential to the military mystique. They instill a sense of belonging and importance in the lives of young soldiers. I have to confess my nostalgia for some of the lost practices of the past. Company commanders, for example, used to handle minor infractions and record them in a green-covered company punishment book: "Private Russo, AWOL, fined $50." Today the company punishment book is gone. To carry out routine punishment, you have to read a Miranda-like statement, provide witnesses, make a lawyer available, and submit to review by higher authority. All that may have a nice civil rights ring. But it damages something vital in small army units, the sense of a family responsible for itself, of officers and noncoms, like wise parents, looking after the young people and yanking them back into line when they stray. Undeniably, occasional abuses occurred under the old system. But the benefits far outweighed the risks. Today's situation is like dragging the family into domestic court every time there is a kitchen spat. The Army lost something valuable as the power to discipline drifted upward to higher headquarters and the lawyers.

Personnel and payroll used to be managed at the battalion level. But today, computers allow the Army to consolidate these tasks higher up. It is more cost-effective, but we pay a price in an impersonalized service. Officers are not as involved in the lives of their soldiers; they have a lesser role in advising and straightening out their problems. In some measure, we have depersonalized the human links that bind soldiers and their leaders together and make for high morale, that family feeling. I am sure that every ex-GI of a certain age remembers his company mess hall, a wooden building perched on cinder blocks, the kitchen at one end, picnic-style tables and benches on wooden floors, a rail in one corner separating the officers' eating area, another corner reserved for sergeants, the garbage cans at the exit, and the mop rack outside. I know that today's big, consolidated "dining facilities" make more economic sense than the old company mess halls. But the hum and clatter of a company mess hall is nostalgic music to me, and I miss the feeling of comradeship. Of course, I am mixing nostalgia with reality; and, intellectually, I know that today's GI and today's Army are superior. But I cannot help recalling those days through mists of fond memory, as all old soldiers do.

My tour as commander of A Company was short. I was sent off to become adjutant of a new unit, the 1st Battalion, 2d Infantry. Once again, I was a first lieutenant in a captain's job. A battalion adjutant handles personnel, promotions, assignments, discipline, mail, and "morale and welfare." My new commander was Lieutenant Colonel William C. Abernathy, a teetotaling Baptist from Arkansas and a graduate of Ouachita Baptist University who never uttered an expletive stronger than "golly." I was going to have to clean up my act.

Lieutenant Colonel Abernathy was no swashbuckler, but he was a solid performer who gave troop morale top priority. He expected a promotion to private first class to be handled with the same importance as a promotion to colonel. The men were to be paid on time. Soldiers freezing their butts off in the field were to have hot coffee and soup available. Any sign that a GI was not being properly looked after meant trouble right up the chain of command. Abernathy did not pamper the troops; he worked them hard and disciplined them, which was another way of caring.

One day, the colonel informed me that I was to set up a system of "Welcome Baby" letters. My mystification must have shown in my face. Every soldier whose wife had a baby, Abernathy explained, was to receive a personal letter from the battalion commander congratulating the parents. A second letter would go to the baby, welcoming the tot into the battalion. Abernathy demanded that I get these letters out the very day the child was born.

How was I supposed to know which men were about to become fathers? I could picture the battalion, massed on the parade ground: "Every man whose wife is pregnant, take one step forward! All right.

When's she due?" I suspect my bachelor status also had something to do with my lack of enthusiasm. In any case, I dragged my feet in setting up this stork-alert system. Abernathy called me on the carpet. "Gee whiz, Colin," he said. "I'm disappointed you haven't done this yet." I would rather have had Red Barrett blister me with four-letter words than hear Abernathy's pained reprimand. I returned to my office and immediately added population reporting to my duties.

To my surprise, once we had the system in place, we started getting positive feedback. The soldiers were impressed by Abernathy's thoughtfulness. Mothers wrote us that they appreciated being considered part of their husband's Army life. The babies were not talking yet, but I imagine, somewhere out there, a thirty-five-year-old woman is wondering how a letter making her a member of the 1st Battalion, 2d Infantry, got into her baby book.

Another lesson learned and filed. Find ways to reach down and touch everyone in a unit. Make individuals feel important and part of something larger than themselves. Abernathy had found a way to demonstrate caring in a fundamentally rough business. And this he achieved at a time when the Army's attitude was, if we had wanted you to have a wife, we would have issued you one.

I still chafed at the adjutant's job and wanted to be commanding troops. I kept nagging Abernathy for another company until, one day, he said something curious. "You've already commanded two companies, even if only for short periods. You're working now in a captain's slot for the third time in less than three years in the Army. At this rate, it's not likely anyone is going to assign you back to company level." He seemed to be saying I had already cleared the bar at that height. I still hoped for another company, but he was right.

In the summer of 1961, in the words of my relatives, I was "goin' home" for the first time. For all the professional challenge, Devens was not as exciting as manning the Cold War ramparts in West Germany. I was looking for an adventure; and so I scraped together $182 round-trip air fare (I was earning $290 a month at the time) for my first trip to Jamaica. Before leaving, I spent time with the family, poring over genealogical data explaining who was related to whom so that I'd be spared any social blunders.

Could two parts of the same planet differ more than Fort Devens and Jamaica? I was suddenly drenched in sunlight, surrounded by lush flowers, and enveloped by aunts, uncles, and cousins who took me in as if they had known me all my life. In applying for my Army commission, I had had to list relatives living abroad; my answer totaled twenty-eight Jamaicans within the first degree of kindred. I did, however, commit one gaffe on this visit. I failed to bring the presents expected from a "rich" relative arriving from the bountiful U.S.A. Nevertheless, I found myself shuttled from town to town, house to house, aunt to uncle, like a prize catch.

I soon recognized the reason for the matriarchy I had observed among West Indians back home. The women here were harder-working, more disciplined. They set the standards, raised the kids, and drove them ahead. And some of the menfolk were not considered quite presentable. I had met all my aunts but fewer uncles. One day, I was driving through Kingston with my cousin Vernon Meikle, on the way to visit Aunt Ethlyn and Uncle Witte. Vernon slowed at a light and pointed to a man standing on a corner. "That's your Uncle Rupee," Vernon said.

"I want to meet him," I answered.

"Can't," Vernon said.

"Why not?" I wanted to know. Rupee, it seemed, was the black sheep of the McKoys. Too many girlfriends and no visible means of support. I insisted that we bring Uncle Rupee along. After all, he was my mother's brother.

Vernon proved right. Aunt Ethlyn was not happy. But I was fascinated. In this clan of characters, Uncle Rupee turned out to be a particularly lovable rogue, willing to keep up his stories as long as I was willing to underwrite his rum consumption, my money and his stories lasting three days. I spent the last two days of my leave back in Queens getting rid of a headache, and then returned to Fort Devens.

By the summer of 1961, I could have left the Army, since my obligated three years of service were over. The thought never entered my head. I was a young black. I did not know anything but soldiering. What was I going to do, work with my father in the garment district? As a geology major, go drilling for oil in Oklahoma? The country was in a recession; if I stayed in the Army, I would soon be earning $360 a month, a magnificent $4,320 a year. I was in a profession that would allow me to go as far as my talents would take me. And for a black, no other avenue in American society offered so much opportunity. But nothing counted so much as the fact that I loved what I was doing. And so, much to my family's bewilderment, I told them that I was not coming home.

A certain ambivalence has always existed among African-Americans about military service. Why should we fight for a country that, for so long, did not fight for us, that in fact denied us our fundamental rights? How could we serve a country where we could not even be served in a restaurant and enjoy the ordinary amenities available to white Americans? Still, whether valued or scorned, welcomed or tolerated, hundreds of thousands of African-Americans *have* served this country from its beginning. In Massachusetts, where I was now serving, blacks, free and slave, were inducted into the militia as far back as 1652. During the Revolution, over 5,000 blacks served under General Washington, helping the country gain an independence that they themselves did not enjoy. Nearly 220,000 blacks served in the Union ranks during the Civil War; 37,500 of them died. Blacks were emancipated, but they still returned home to suffer bigotry, the rise of the Ku Klux Klan, and lynchings.

After the Civil War, Congress authorized four colored regiments, the 24th and 25th Infantry and the 9th and 10th Cavalry. They became known as the "Buffalo Soldiers," so called by the Indians, according to legend, because of their dark skin, kinky hair, buffalo-pelt coats, and courage in battle. The creation of these regiments, however, was no act of racial enlightenment. Washington merely wanted white settlers protected from the Indians as the West was settled. The Buffalo Soldiers were to help white folks acquire and defend land that blacks, for the most part, were not allowed to own.

You can search the paintings of Teddy Roosevelt and the Rough Riders charging up San Juan Hill in the Spanish-American War and you will not find a single black face portrayed. A camera, however, would have recorded them, because *they were there.* Seven of them were awarded the Medal of Honor in Cuba. In World War II, nearly a million blacks wore the uniform. Some, like the Tuskegee Airmen, the first black fighter pilots, proved that no mission was beyond the skills or courage of black men. Still, these black GIs came home in 1945 to Jim Crow in the South, to separate but unequal schools and colleges, to poor job prospects, and to demeaning restrictions like separate toilets and water fountains for the "colored." Racism in much of the rest of the country was less blatant only in degree.

Why have blacks, nevertheless, always answered the nation's call? They have done so to exercise their rights as citizens in the one area where it was permitted. They did it because they believed that if they demonstrated equal courage and equal sacrifice in fighting and dying for their country, then equality of opportunity surely must follow. General Andrew

Jackson, for example, promised to give land to blacks who fought with him, particularly at the Battle of New Orleans. They fought and some died. But when the shooting stopped and the danger had passed, they got nothing.

Not until July 26, 1948, did President Harry S Truman sign the executive order ending segregation in the armed forces. If black American soldiers were to be allowed to die equally for their country, they would finally be permitted to serve equally in the military. I entered the Army only ten years after that historic turning point. I still remember two of my closest friends in the Infantry Officers Basic Course at Fort Benning, Don Phillips and Herman Price, the three of us standing next to each other at muster, in alphabetical order, looking as if the Army were still segregated. Phillips eventually made full colonel and became the first black to command the Army's Honor Guard Regiment in Washington. Price went into medicine and became the Army's chief cardiologist. Their careers, and that of other black officers, like Ranger Coffey, who became military aide to President Richard M. Nixon, benefited from a fact that gets too little recognition. The Army was living the democratic ideal ahead of the rest of America. Beginning in the fifties, less discrimination, a truer merit system, and leveler playing fields existed inside the gates of our military posts than in any Southern city hall or Northern corporation. The Army, therefore, made it easier for me to love my country, with all its flaws, and to serve her with all my heart.

3 ★ Courting Alma

ONE NOVEMBER DAY in 1961 I was stretched out in my room at the bachelor officers' quarters at Fort Devens when a friend, Michael Heningburg, popped in to ask me for a buddy-in-a-pinch favor. Mike was also from Queens and had a background about as mixed as my own. The Heningburgs were a black family with a German strain; Mike's father was named Alfonse and his brother was Gustav. Mike had met a girl in Boston, Jackie Fields, and had flipped over her. "I'm asking you to go into town with me to pick off her roommate," he pleaded.

"A blind date?" I asked warily. Mike nodded. I had never been on a blind date. The odds of success seemed better in the numbers racket. Yet, my relationship with my girlfriend in New York had not survived the sixteen-month separation, and I was at loose ends. I had plenty of friends at Devens, Tony DePace and his wife, Sandy, from my Pershing Rifles days, Herman and Madeline Price from Fort Benning, and new friends, Costelle "Coz" Walker and Ezra "Chopper" Cummings among them. But as far as romance, I was on the inactive list. "Okay, Mike," I said. "I'll run interference for you."

We drove to the Back Bay section of Boston to pick up the girls at 372 Marlborough Street. We were buzzed into a one-bedroom apartment on the ground floor in the rear of a brownstone. Jackie Fields greeted us, and a few minutes later, the other girl emerged. "This is my roommate, Alma Johnson," Jackie said.

She was fair-skinned, with light brown hair and a lovely figure. I was mesmerized by a pair of luminous eyes, an unusual shade of green. Miss Johnson moved gracefully and spoke graciously, with a soft Southern accent. This blind date might just work out.

Long afterward, Alma gave me her version of that first meeting. "I had had an argument with my roommate for getting me involved," she told me. "I do not go on blind dates," Alma had told Jackie. "And I definitely don't go on blind dates with soldiers. How do I know who's going to walk through that door?" Alma had worked off her annoyance by dressing up weirdly and piling on makeup to put off the unknown suitor when he arrived. But when she peeked into the room, she was surprised, she said, to see a shy, almost baby-faced guy, his cheeks rosy from the cold. She was used to dating men four or five years older. "You looked like a little lost twelve-year-old," she later told me. She had then disappeared into the bathroom to change her clothes, redo her face, and unvamp herself.

We took the girls out to a club in the Dorchester section. We had a few drinks, listened to music, and talked. After almost exclusive exposure to girls with New Yawky voices, I was much taken by this soft-spoken Southerner. And Alma did talk, most of the evening, while I listened entranced. At one point, she put a question to me natural enough in that era of compulsory military service: How much time did I have left in the Army? Young men she knew went into the service and got out as soon as possible; they could practically tell you how many minutes they still had to serve. I was not getting out, I told her; I was career military. She looked at me as if I were an exotic specimen.

Finally, the most enjoyable night I had had in ages came to an end, and Mike and I drove back to Fort Devens. I called Alma the next day and asked her out again.

We began to see each other regularly, and the more I saw, the more I liked. Alma Johnson had been born and raised in Birmingham, Alabama. Her father, Robert C. "R.C." Johnson, was principal of Parker High School, one of the city's two black high schools. Her uncle, George Bell, was principal of Ulman, the other black high school. Mildred Johnson, Alma's mother, was a pioneer in black Girl Scouting and a national leader in the Congregational Church. Alma had skipped grades in school and graduated from Fisk University in Nashville, Tennessee, at the age of nineteen. She went back home after graduation and had her own radio program for a while, *Luncheon with Alma,* on which she dispensed household hints and played music, mostly the rhythm and blues that the station management wanted. But when Alma substituted for a nighttime disc jockey, she got to play her kind of music, progressive jazz.

Alma had never liked her hometown. It was not so much the institutionalized racism of Birmingham. Actually, as R. C. Johnson's daughter, she led something of a privileged life. But Alma had an adventurous spirit; she found Birmingham stifling and wanted to see more of the world. And so she had moved to Boston to do graduate work in audiology at Emerson College. When I met her, Alma was an audiologist for the Boston Guild for the Hard of Hearing, driving a mobile van all over the area giving people hearing tests. Her greatest coup was getting inside a monastery in Cambridge to test the Jesuits' hearing.

About a month after we met, Alma went home to Birmingham for Christmas. We worked it out so that she would return via New York to meet my folks at a New Year's Eve party on Elmira Avenue. I was sure Alma would love my relatives—but maybe not immediately. A well-bred girl from a proper Southern family needed to be exposed gradually to nosy, noisy, fun-loving West Indians.

The party was going to be held in our basement family room. Vinyl tiles hid the concrete floor. The walls and ceiling were covered in hideous brown cork panels. A tiny bar stood in one corner, barely big enough to hold the glasses, bottles, and bartender. Coconuts carved in the form of pirates' heads hung over the bar. President Roosevelt's picture had been transported from the Bronx and now occupied a place of honor behind the bar. Benches lined the walls, and in one corner were two tourist-class seats that my Pershing Rifles friends and I had rescued from an abandoned El Al plane at Idlewild (now Kennedy) Airport.

By the time Alma and I arrived, the place was jammed with my relatives, dancing, laughing, drinking, eating, singing, and still talking about "goin' home." Food kept pouring down from the kitchen and a stack of 78-rpm calypso records ran nonstop on a record player that Pop had bought my sister, Marilyn, for her sweet sixteen party.

I escorted Alma into this joyous chaos, where Pop was presiding as sublimely as Don Corleone at his daughter's wedding in *The Godfather.* He and Mom warmly embraced Alma and then started introducing her around the room, from aunt to uncle to cousin, giving everybody a close look.

Alma managed to survive the first round. The acid test came when she sat down in one of the El Al seats to catch her breath. Aunt Beryl, my father's sister, circled in for the kill. Aunt Beryl had no children of her own and compensated by doting on her nephews and nieces, of which I was the chosen, her "Col-Col." In Aunt Beryl's eyes, Alma started out with serious handicaps. She was not Jamaican, not even West Indian, and not from New York. Beryl planted herself next to Alma and eyed her up and down, wordlessly. The guests pretended to keep partying but watched Aunt Beryl out of the corners of their eyes. Alma finally got up. Aunt Beryl got up. Alma moved two steps. Beryl moved two steps. Every time Alma turned around, there was my aunt at her shoulder, her face scrunched in skepticism. Still, she never said a word.

At long last, Aunt Beryl drifted away and began talking to the other relatives. Alma could breathe again. Col-Col, Aunt Beryl told the folks, was going to be twenty-five soon, marrying age. The family could not wait forever. The courtship could proceed, even if the poor child was not Jamaican. I did not know it was a courtship. I just thought I had a new girlfriend and we were dating. What an idiot.

Back in Massachusetts, Alma began coming by bus to Fort Devens on weekends to visit me. We hung out with my bachelor pals in the Club Rathskeller eating cheeseburgers, and spent the rest of the time visiting my married friends. Alma met the Prices, the Abernathys, the Ellisons, and the DePaces, and she began to get a picture of Army life beyond that of draftees aching to get out. And, as a black Southerner, she was struck by the social integration among Army couples. She fitted in from the start, getting along with the wives of my seniors through her appealing combination of deference and independence, as if she were born to the game.

Alma and I soon became inseparable. I could not wait for Saturday inspections to end so that we could be together. I was oblivious to what was happening. I was in love, but I thought it would clear up.

Chubby Checker and the twist were all the rage in those days, but dancing had never been my strong suit. I was good enough at calypsos if sufficiently lubricated, and I could stumble through the lindy, merengue, and cha-cha. Jamaican miscegenation, however, had blocked passage of both the basketball and the dance genes in me. Nevertheless, when you are not white and have kinky hair, certain things are expected of you. Alma did a mean twist and tutored me until I became an acceptable twister.

By the summer of 1962, I had been at Fort Devens for eighteen months and was due for orders. They arrived in August; I was going to South Vietnam. I knew little about the country, except that President Kennedy had sent a few thousand men there as advisors. Scattered reports had filtered back from the first batch. We were involved in something called "nation-building," trying to help South Vietnam save itself from the Red Menace that stretched from the Berlin Wall (thrown up the year before) to the rice paddies of Southeast Asia. I was excited; I was going to war.

Of course, I felt some anxiety. A test pilot is anxious before a flight. So is a soloist before a concert or a quarterback before the kickoff. But we are eager to do the thing we have spent our lives preparing for, and I was a soldier. I became the envy of my fellow career officers, since those picked to go as advisors to South Vietnam were regarded as comers, walk-on-water types being groomed for bright futures. I was to report to Fort Bragg, North Carolina, in the fall for a five-week course as a military advisor. And I could expect to be promoted to captain before being shipped out.

I eagerly called my parents and friends. And then I called Alma. I sensed that she did not share my enthusiasm. I drove to Boston to explain to her why this was good news. I was going off to practice my profession in earnest. When that failed to register, I mentioned the upcoming promotion. All Alma wanted to know was what my orders meant for us. I told her that the Vietnam assignment was for one year, and that I had no idea where I would be sent afterward. I told her that I cared deeply for her, and I hoped she would write me often. Her reply floored me: "I'm not going to write to you." If she was going to be only a pen pal, she said, "we might as well end it now." She was almost twenty-five, Alma went on, and she had no intention of sitting around waiting to see if I was still in the picture a year from now.

I drove back to Devens dejected. Her reaction forced me to ask myself something I had not faced so far. How much did this woman mean to me?

That night, I lay in my bunk taking emotional inventory of the relationship. Alma Johnson was beautiful, intelligent, refined, and fun to be with, and, all too rare in a romance, she was my friend. She came from a fine family, got along with my circle of friends, and was even a great cook. I knew that she loved me, and I loved her. My folks loved her too. What was I waiting for? Alma had everything I would ever want in a wife. I was a jerk for not acting before she got away. This nonsense that if the Army wanted you to have a wife it would have issued you one had to go.

I could barely wait to drive back to Boston the next day and ask her to marry me. Thank God, she said yes.

Alma must have loved me, because I was not a romantic suitor. I did not even buy her an engagement ring. I told her that we would be better off spending the money on household items. Alma had already gone through one engagement with a ring and the works, and it had not turned out well. She was wise enough to know that the trappings tell little about success in marriage. "Don't worry about the ring," she told me. "You can make it up to me later." Which I eventually did, with a fairly nice rock.

When we called my parents to tell them we were getting married, they sounded relieved. Alma called her folks too. I had met her mother, Mildred, who seemed to approve of me. But I had yet to meet R.C., who sounded formidable. Alma told me that her father had never found any of her beaus good enough. When they came to the Johnson home, R.C. would give them the silent treatment.

We had to move quickly if Alma was to come with me to Fort Bragg for my training. We decided on a wedding just two weeks off, Saturday, August 25, 1962, in Birmingham, to be performed at the Congregational Church, with a reception at the Johnson home.

I alerted Ronnie Brooks, who was in Providence, Rhode Island, completing doctoral work in chemistry at Brown University. Ronnie, my role model, the perfect soldier, had served the minimum six months of obligated service on active duty and then had chosen civilian life. "Whoa," Ronnie said, when I told him about my imminent marriage. "Hold everything." I was to wait until he came up to Boston to see what kind of jam I had gotten into. When Ronnie arrived a few nights later, Alma had a delicious Southern dinner waiting for him. That settled it for Ronnie Brooks. He got up, walked around the table, kissed Alma, and nominated himself best man.

And then we hit a snag. "I'm not going to the wedding," Pop informed me. "You wouldn't catch me dead in Birmingham." Luther Powell was not about to go anywhere where he would have to assume second-class citizenship. "I'll send you a telegram with my best wishes," he said. Mom, bless her, said that she did not care what Luther did; she was going to see her son get married. Marilyn and Norm reported in from Buffalo that they were coming to the wedding. Pop had to rethink his position. As an interracial couple in the South, his daughter and son-in-law were bound to get into trouble. "If they're gonna lynch Norm," Pop said, "we might as well all be there. I may have to buy off the lynchers."

I went to see my boss, Lieutenant Colonel Abernathy, and asked for a weekend pass to get married. I promised that I would be back on the job Monday morning. Abernathy shook my hand warmly and said, "I think the battalion might survive three days without you, Lieutenant."

The next ten days were a blur as Alma and her mother went about the preparations with the zeal of the Allies planning D-Day. Mildred found spare rooms in her friends' homes where my family could stay. She produced a relative who volunteered to host the wedding-eve dinner. Alma's sister, Barbara, was to be the maid of honor. Ronnie and I were instructed to wear our summer tan dress uniforms, assuming Ronnie still fit in his, after a couple of years on civilian rations. In Boston, Alma and I bought simple gold wedding bands to exchange, and then she went on ahead to Birmingham. I arrived in time for the dinner and reception the night before.

R. C. Johnson turned out to be a big, deadly serious man and not one to mince words. In later years, I would occasionally run into black soldiers from Birmingham who had gone to Parker High,

R.C.'s school. When I mentioned that their old principal was my father-in-law, I got a fairly standard reaction: "You married R.C.'s daughter? You're one brave dude." Actually, R.C. was glad that Alma was getting married, though he was not crazy about my occupation or the fact that I was about to go off for a year. And he definitely was not overjoyed at having a West Indian son-in-law. After we had phoned to tell the Johnsons that we were getting married, R.C. had muttered to his wife, "All my life I've tried to stay away from those damn West Indians and now my daughter's going to marry one!" Between Luther, who resisted the South, and R.C., who resisted Luther's kind, this should be some weekend!

My folks arrived in Birmingham, and Pop, having survived so far unlynched, began having a grand old time. He loved parties, baptisms, weddings, wakes, and funerals, anything that brought people together. The Johnsons and their circle were now his lifelong friends, even if he had never laid eyes on them until a few hours before.

August is Alabama at its hottest. On the wedding day, in the packed church, you could hear the rustling as women tried to cool themselves with fans provided by a local funeral home. As the Reverend J. Clyde Perry began the ceremony, Ronnie and I marched in smartly from a side entrance, came to a halt as we hit our mark, did a right-face, clicked our heels, and stood at attention as if we were in drill competition. The funeral-home fans created a veritable wind as the congregation oohed and aahed. Alma, attended by her sister Barbara, came down the aisle on the arm of a solemn-faced R.C. I was struck by how radiant she looked and by her serene self-possession. In a few minutes, this beautiful woman was going to be my wife.

Afterward, we retired to the Johnsons' home for the reception. Here my folks discovered that they do it differently down South. No booze. No music. Few refreshments. You entered the front door, dropped off your gift, signed the guest book, went through the receiving line in the parlor, continued on to the dining room, where you were handed a glass of punch and a piece of cake, and kept moving toward the kitchen, where you deposited your empty glass and plate before being ushered out the back door. The reception lasted a little over an hour. On the spot, Luther and Arie started planning a different kind of wedding party for New York.

We spent our honeymoon night at the A. G. Gaston Motel, the only decent place in town for a black couple. A. G. Gaston was a millionaire black entrepreneur who had made a fortune selling life insurance to blacks, business white insurance companies ignored. The next day, Alma and I flew back to Boston. Jackie had conveniently moved out of the apartment on Marlborough Street, and I moved in. After its having played a fateful part in our lives, nothing more came of the budding romance of Jackie Fields and Mike Heningburg. Monday morning, as promised, I reported in to Lieutenant Colonel Abernathy, and Alma returned to work at the Boston Guild for the Hard of Hearing.

A few days later, I answered the phone in our apartment. The caller was obviously puzzled to hear a male voice on the line. "Who are you?" he asked.

"Colin Powell," I answered. "And who are you?"

"I'm Alma's fiancé," he informed me.

"How do you do," I said. "I'm her husband."

The conversation stumbled to an awkward close. We evidently had not had enough time to put my earlier rivals on notice that Alma was now spoken for.

A week later, on a Saturday morning, I answered a knock at the door barefooted, wearing only a T-shirt and chino pants. There stood a nice-looking guy with a box of candy under his arm and a smile on his face, which vanished at the sight of me. "What are you doing here?" he asked indignantly.

I explained my status in the household. Alma came into the room, and I thought it politic for me to fade. From the bedroom, I could hear parts of a brief, tense conversation. And then our visitor was gone. When I came back, I noticed that he had taken his candy with him. He was just an old friend, Alma told me, with an exaggerated notion of the degree of their friendship. She has stuck to this story for over thirty years.

The Powell wedding reception took place not long afterward at Elmira Avenue. Our guests showed up early in the afternoon, jamming the basement family room, carrying on until the last drop of rum gave out, which was at 4:00 A.M. Alma survived this second test of Jamaican hospitality, charming everybody in sight. What delighted me most was to see Luther and Arie beaming over their new daughter-in-law. After the staid, clockwork Johnson reception, the Powell party was a cultural one-eighty.

My cousin Vernon Lewis, whose interests included cake-baking, poker, the track, and his job as a cop, in that order, had been commissioned by Mom to bake a cake for this event. As the cake and Vernon failed to materialize, Arie became increasingly distraught, fearing that Vernon's number two and three interests had overtaken number one, not an unheard-of development. At long last, Cousin Vernon appeared with the Versailles of wedding cakes and disarmed my mother with his usual charm: "Auntie Arie, how, even for a minute, could you have ever doubted that I would come through with a glorious creation?" And when, Alma wondered, would this parade of in-law characters ever end?

I enjoyed being married. I liked shopping with Alma on weekends. I liked having my wife meet my friends. I would race from Devens to our little nest in my car, a blue 1959 Volkswagen I had bought in Germany for $1,312. On one of these mad dashes, I was zipping along Route 2 when I noticed a convertible coming up fast behind me. Obviously, some New England Yankee intended to show me his dust. I pushed the Beetle to the limit. Then, to my astonishment, a siren sounded. I pulled over. The driver got out, identified himself as a state trooper, and informed me that I was doing ninety in a fifty-five-mile-an-hour zone. "Officer," I said, "you know and I know this car can't go that fast." My defense fell on unsympathetic ears. In those days, and occasionally today, I tend to want to see what my automobiles can do.

. . .

The carefree life that Alma and I were living was about to end. On September 24, a month after the wedding, the battalion threw a farewell party for us. Bill Abernathy read from a beautifully hand-lettered scroll emblazoned with the insignia of the 1st Battalion, 2d Infantry. "Hear ye, hear ye," Abernathy began. "The chief paper shuffler of the battalion, being sent to the exotic land of poisoned darts and sharp bamboo sticks . . ." He went on to cite some of the memorable features of my service at Devens: "Battalion headquarters will miss the slam of the telephone, the bang of the clenched fist on the desk, the violent movements of your swivel chair." Bill Louisell would have nodded.

Soon afterward, Alma and I packed everything we owned (which one Volkswagen could accommodate), made a brief visit to Elmira Avenue, and headed for Fort Bragg, North Carolina, where I was to take the Military Assistance Training Advisor course. Driving through Dixie with a new wife was more unnerving for me than the trip a few years before with a couple of Army buddies. I remember passing Woodbridge, Virginia, and not finding even a gas station bathroom that we were allowed to use. I had to pull off the road so that we could relieve ourselves in the woods.

At Fort Bragg, we tracked down a black rental agent and started looking for a furnished place in nearby Fayetteville where we could stay while I completed the MATA course. The kind of black middle-class neighborhood we hoped to find scarcely existed.

I remember our first stop, a dilapidated house on a lot overgrown with weeds and strewn with rusty tin cans, plastic bags, and other rubbish. Inside the house, the floors were covered with cracked linoleum and the furniture looked as if it belonged outside with the trash. We shook our heads and went on to the next. Nothing else was much better. Finally, the agent told us that he had a solution. He was going to put us up in his own home. Our hopes rose. He stopped in front of a grim-looking place. The inside was even grimmer, with old people sitting around a dark room staring ahead vacantly. The agent showed us a bedroom in the back. We would have to provide our own bedding, and we would share the kitchen and bathroom with the rest of his boarders. We said thanks anyway and left.

We faced the bitter truth. I would have to send Alma back to Birmingham to stay with her parents while I spent my time at Bragg alone. The prospect was all the gloomier because this separation would be on top of the year I would be away. And Alma by now was pregnant.

On my first day at Bragg, I ran into an old Gelnhausen buddy, Joe Schwar, who was assigned there with the Special Forces, the Green Berets. Joe and his wife, Pat, invited us to dinner on what looked like the Powells' last night together for a while. I was eager to have the Schwars meet Alma, though I wished we were in better spirits.

The Schwar household was a happy bedlam. Joe and Pat were living in a small government-issue three-bedroom duplex on the post with their three boys, Joey, Kevin, and Steve, all under age four. During dinner, I enjoyed swapping stories with Joe about Tom Miller, Red Man Barrett, and other characters we had known in Germany and watching Alma and Pat get acquainted. In the meantime, Joey and Kevin used the living room for the Indianapolis Speedway while baby Steve squealed enviously from his high chair.

Inevitably, the conversation got around to our housing plans. I explained that Alma would have to go back to Birmingham. Oh no, Pat said. She wouldn't let that happen. We could stay with them. Joe chimed in, saying, "Sure you can." The house was barely big enough for the five Schwars, and Alma said, "That's nice of you, but we can't impose." Pat insisted. She had it all figured out. The two older boys could leave the bunk beds in their room and sleep on cots in baby Steve's room. Alma and I would take over the boys' room and sleep in their kid-size bunks. Not exactly the honeymoon suite; but their offer was so genuine and Alma and I hated so much to part that we said yes, and moved in the next day.

The Schwars' kindness was not cost-free for them. Pat took heat from some of her neighbors, who were repelled by the idea of blacks moving in with a white family, even sharing the same bathroom. Pat Schwar is from South Philadelphia and as tough as she is kind. She told these people what they could do with their prejudices. What the Schwars did for two desperate newlyweds long years ago is one of the greatest kindnesses that Alma and I have ever experienced.

. . .

For five weeks at Fort Bragg's Unconventional Warfare Center, I sat in classes studying French colonial
history, learning the methods of communist take-
overs, and trying to master a few Vietnamese
phrases. We reviewed the history of U.S. involvement—how President Eisenhower had refused to
intervene in the fifties when France was losing its
eight-year war against Vietnamese nationalists and
communists under Ho Chi Minh; how the country
had then been divided between Ho in the North and a
Western-oriented government in the South pending
elections in 1956; how Ngo Dinh Diem, president of
South Vietnam, had canceled the election in his half
of the country and, facing communist attacks, had
appealed to President Kennedy to save Vietnam from
"the forces of international communism." Kennedy
had committed the United States to support the Diem
regime by sending in more counterinsurgency advisors, all the rage then. By the end of 1961, 3,205
advisors were in Vietnam. The group I was part of
would bring the total to well over 11,000. We felt we
were in the thick of things, especially in October
1962 when the Cuban missile crisis erupted. Rumors
swept the school that we were to be pulled out of
class to fight the communists much closer than in
Vietnam. I came home one night to find that Joe
Schwar was gone and that his Special Forces detachment had been alerted for movement to a staging area
in Florida. After days of heart-stopping tension, the
superpowers backed away from the brink, and we
completed our advisor course on schedule.

We had cause for celebration in the Schwar-Powell household that fall. Both Joe and I were promoted to captain several months early.

I was still excited over the Vietnam assignment as the course wrapped up in early December and I prepared to leave my wife of four months and the child she was carrying. By God, a worldwide communist conspiracy was out there, and we had to stop it wherever it raised its ugly head. I had helped man the frontiers of freedom in West Germany. Now it was time for me to man another frontier in the same fight on the other side of the world. It all had a compelling neatness and simplicity in 1962.

Shortly before Christmas, we said goodbye to Joe, Pat, and the little Schwars and headed for Birmingham, where Alma would stay while I was gone. The city lay in the heart of the Old South, incorporating all the menace that phrase conjured up for blacks. Alabama Governor George C. Wallace's policy of "segregation forever" had become the white rallying cry. Birmingham was turning into a racial war zone, the rising civil rights movement, with its sit-ins and demonstrations, pitted against Eugene T. "Bull" Connor, the city's brutal police chief, determined to hold Negroes down and keep agitators out, white or black. Not a happy time; not a happy place. Still, I felt reasonably relaxed about leaving Alma there. Her folks and her aunt and uncle had just built a new home for the four of them just outside Birmingham in what was regarded as a safe neighborhood. The house had a spare room for Alma and the baby, and nearby was the Holy Family Catholic Hospital for Alma's confinement. Should the racial time bomb in Birmingham go off, Alma's dad, tough old R.C., had a house full of guns that he had taken away from students over the years at Parker High.

I remember the mixed emotions of those last days at the Johnsons'. Alma and her mom went out and cut a Christmas tree, and we decorated it. We celebrated early, since my orders called for me to leave by December 23. If the Army sent me to Vietnam *after* Christmas, I cannot imagine it would have upset the Cold War balance; but mine was not to reason why. We exchanged presents early, and I felt harsh reality intrude when we opened my mother-in-law's gift to us, a pair of tape recorders so that Alma and I could communicate while I was gone. We said our goodbyes that morning, two days before Christmas, and I went to the airport by myself, since I am not comfortable with public displays of emotion.

I had learned something about Alma in those final weeks. Here was a young woman, soon to become a mother, whose husband was leaving for a long time for a far-off, dangerous place. She accepted our separation with stoic calm. Before meeting me, Alma had never imagined herself as an Army wife. But I knew that she was going to make the perfect life partner for this soldier.

I left Birmingham for Travis Air Force Base in California and arrived in Saigon on Christmas morning, 1962.

Part Two

SOLDIERING

4 ★ "It'll Take Half a Million Men to Succeed"

MY IMAGES of going to war were formed by forties newsreels, fifties movies, and early-sixties TV documentaries, and war was always in black and white. My arrival in Vietnam shattered all the preconceptions. I did not cross the Pacific in a crowded troop transport; I came on World Airways, a chartered commercial flight. I did not storm down the ramp of an LCI and hit the beach in waist-high water. I checked into the Rex, a hotel in Saigon turned into bachelor officers' quarters. And I entered a world, not black and white, but painted in the colorful palette of a semitropical capital.

They say Irving Berlin was inspired to write "White Christmas" after spending the holidays amid palm trees during a Los Angeles heat wave. I had the same out-of-sync sensation checking into the Rex that muggy Christmas. That night, after a dinner in the hotel's rooftop restaurant with other lonely new arrivals, I looked down on Tu Do Street, a handsome boulevard with a touch of Paris. White-uniformed traffic cops directed a flow of cars and "cyclos," Vietnamese pedicabs, while fashionable women in silk ao dais moved in and out of elegant shops. The night air was soft, and, in the background, a jukebox played "Moon River," a song whose lyrics did not ease my loneliness.

The next morning, Major General Charles M. Timmes gathered us in a conference room at the U.S. Military Assistance Advisory Group headquarters and delivered a rousing pep talk. Why had we left our loved ones behind? Why had we come here to fight halfway around the world? To stop the spread of Marxism; to help the South Vietnamese save their country from a communist takeover. That was the finest thing we could do for our families, our country, and freedom-loving people everywhere. I was fired up all over again. That afternoon we were driven out to the American military side of Tan Son Nhut Airport to be issued field gear, jungle fatigues, jungle boots, helmets—reminders of where we were headed.

After a few more days of indoctrination in Saigon I was to head north to join up with the Army of the Republic of Vietnam (ARVN). I was to serve as advisor to the four-hundred-man 2d Battalion, 3d Infantry Regiment, of the 1st Division, posted in the tropical forest along the Laotian border at a place called A Shau. I had arrived in Vietnam in the rainy season, and getting to A Shau was not easy. You could either fly there in thirty hair-raising minutes or take weeks to walk in. The bad weather grounded flights for days, while I grew increasingly itchy to get moving. Finally, on January 17, at Quang Tri, I boarded a Marine H-34 helicopter loaded with ARVN replacements, bags of rice, and live chickens and pigs. We darted and bounced through thunderheads and showers over dense jungle terrain and plopped down onto a crude perforated-metal airstrip stamped out of the jungle. The pilot shouted for soldiers to unload the helo before the Viet Cong started taking potshots at us.

I jumped to the ground, looked around, and felt as if I had been propelled backward in time. Shimmering in the heat of the sun was an earth-and-wood fortress ringed by pillboxes. But for the greenness, A Shau had a French Foreign Legion quality, *Beau Geste* without the sand. I stood there asking myself the question I am sure Roman legionnaires must have asked in Gaul—what the hell am I doing here? The A Shau Valley ran down the narrow northern neck of South Vietnam near the Laotian border and contained a crucial stretch of the Ho Chi Minh Trail, the main supply artery of our enemy, the Viet Cong. A Shau was one of four fortified bases running up to Laos, from which we were to interdict the flow of goods and men to the south. Rugged mountains rose up on the western side of the valley, and a wooded jungle bordered the east. Somewhere under that triple canopy of growth was the enemy.

ARVN troops trotted out to the helicopter and began unloading. An American soldier came up, saluted, and introduced himself as Sergeant First Class Willard Sink. Sink led me through a barbed-wire gate into the compound, where a Vietnamese officer saluted and put out his hand. "Captain Vo Cong Hieu, commanding 2d Battalion," he said in passable English. Hieu was my ARVN counterpart, the man I would be advising. He was short, in his early thirties, with a broad face and an engaging smile. But for the uniform, I would have taken him for a genial schoolteacher, not a professional soldier.

The three of us headed toward a thatched hut of bamboo and grass, my new quarters. Inside was a frame cot, also of bamboo, set on a dirt floor, and not much else. A huge rat scampered from under the bed. "The A Shau Hilton," Sink said. I threw my pack onto the cot and told Hieu I would like to go outside and have a look around the compound.

Directly behind A Shau, a mountain loomed over us. I pointed toward it, and Hieu said with a grin, "Laos." From that mountainside, the enemy could almost roll rocks down onto us. I wondered why the base had been established in such a vulnerable spot.

"Very important outpost," Hieu assured me.

"What's its mission?" I asked.

"Very important outpost," Hieu repeated.

"But why is it here?"

"Outpost is here to protect airfield," he said, pointing in the direction of our departing Marine helo.

"What's the airfield here for?" I asked.

"Airfield here to resupply outpost."

From my training at Fort Bragg, I knew our formal role here. We were to establish a "presence," a word with a nice sophisticated ring. More specifically, we were supposed to engage the Viet Cong to keep them from moving through the A Shau Valley and fomenting their insurgency in the populated coastal provinces. But Hieu's words were the immediate reality. The base camp at A Shau was there to protect an airstrip that was there to supply the outpost.

I would spend nearly twenty years, one way or another, grappling with our experience in this country. And over all that time, Vietnam rarely made much more sense than Captain Hieu's circular reasoning on that January day in 1963. We're here because we're here, because we're . . .

My first sensation at being among Vietnamese troops was one of towering over them and presenting a choice target. They were short and slight, and with their smooth faces they looked like kids, though most were in their twenties. They seemed barely trained but willing and obedient. What went on in their heads I had no idea, since they were mostly conscripts who hid their feelings behind a mask of polite submission. At our A Shau base camp, I was surprised to find families of Montagnards, nomadic people who populated this part of the country. Almost no Vietnamese lived here, only these mountain tribesmen and a few other indigenous minorities. I had expected to find the reputedly independent Montagnards living in the hills rather than on a military post, and I wondered what they were doing here. I would find out soon enough. After a couple of weeks, Captain Hieu came to my hut with the news I had been waiting for. We had our orders—we were going out on Operation Grasshopper, an extended patrol down the A Shau Valley. I had become restless at the base camp, working with Sergeant Sink, training the Vietnamese in marksmanship on the rifle range, teaching patrol tactics, helping with disciplinary problems, trying to be useful without taking over. The high point of my day, much of it spent in my hooch devouring paperback novels and smoking too much, was anticipating dinner, as the livestock that had flown in with me began appearing on the menu. The Americans ate what the Vietnamese ate. Breakfast: rice stuck together with some glutinous substance and shaped into what looked like an edible softball. Lunch: rice with vegetables. Dinner: more rice, with chunks of pork or goat and, as an occasional treat, a two-inch-square omelet, actually quite tasty. I was introduced to the ubiquitous Vietnamese fish-based sauce, nuoc mam. Nuoc mam was used so commonly that it entered the GI vocabulary as a good-natured gibe at anything Vietnamese. The national airline became "Air Nuoc Mam." An older Vietnamese woman was a "nuoc mam mama."

At 3:00 A.M. on February 7, I threw my pack over my back, slung my M-2 carbine over my shoulder, and joined Hieu for a last inspection of the battalion before we moved out. Soon the long green line of troops was swallowed up by the dark jungle. I felt a tingling anticipation. A force of armed men moving into the unknown has a certain power, even a touch of majesty, although the squealing pigs and cackling chickens accompanying us in wicker baskets detracted somewhat from the martial aura.

On this march, I discovered the reality of a triple-canopy tropical forest. The lowest stratum consisted of saw grass, bushes, vines, and small trees struggling for air. Adolescent trees formed the second canopy, densely packed, rising thirty or forty feet. The third canopy consisted of mature hardwoods, some over one hundred feet high. Unless we broke out into a clearing, we could go all day long without seeing the sun. Even in the shade, sweat bathed our faces and our uniforms turned soggy. The salt from our perspiration formed gray-white semicircles under our armpits and blotches on the backs of our fatigues. We constantly popped tablets to replenish our bodies' salt supply. A distinctive smell clung to us, a pungent mixture of mud, dirty bodies, and rotting vegetation. Every day was an endless obstacle course, as we tried to make contact with the Viet Cong. We were constantly going "cross compartment," following trails down one steep side of a valley and up the other, clambering over craggy rocks and fording streams. The physical demands validated every test the Army had put me through in Florida swamps and Georgia mountains.

We moved in clouds of insects. Worse were the leeches. I never understood how they managed to get through our clothing, under our web belts and onto our chests, through our bloused pants and onto our legs, biting the flesh and bloating themselves on our blood. We stopped as often as ten times a day to get rid of them. It did no good to pull the leeches off. Their bodies simply broke and the head remained biting into the skin. We had to stun them with bursts of insect repellent or the lit end of a cigarette, which made a hissing sound on contact.

The trails we followed had been sown by the VC with snares and punji spikes, bamboo stakes concealed in a hole, the tip poisoned with buffalo dung. The first casualty I witnessed was a soldier who stepped onto a punji spike. For all the hardship, I was still excited to be on the trail, testing my endurance, feeling especially alive as strength and fatigue flowed alternately through my limbs.

Our column stretched for nearly a mile, four hundred men trying to be quiet, the noncoms constantly shushing the troops, everyone taking care not to rustle a dry twig or step on a branch, eyes darting left and right, grinding out our meager advance in eerie silence, except for the calls of exotic birds and the chatter of monkeys. Then, at nightfall, when we made camp, all hell broke loose. The Vietnamese lit campfires, the flames rising and smoke billowing high into the air. The animals screeched as they were slaughtered for our evening meal. The men sat around the fires, mess kits clattering, talking freely as they ate. It was futile to try to keep them quiet. The noise, fire, and smoke must have announced our presence for miles. In the morning, after making tea, dousing the fires, cleaning out the rice pots, and dumping the hot water down the hillside, we would resume the trails, shushing each other again and making our silent way.

It happened on the sixth day out as we were coming down a steep hillside. I was a quarter of the way back in the column, the customary place for advisors. It had been raining earlier, and the men ahead of me had churned the trail into a quagmire. As usual, we were moving in single file, which meant that the VC could halt the entire column by picking off the first man. I had repeatedly urged Hieu to break the battalion into three or four parallel columns, but the forest was so dense and the passes so narrow in places that Hieu let this bit of American wisdom go politely unheeded.

I had just arrived at the bottom of a narrow creek bed when I heard several sharp cracks. Incoming fire, the first I had ever experienced, rifles and submachine guns, I guessed. I heard a scream up ahead. The men began shouting and running around in utter confusion. I repressed my own terror and started to make my way forward to find out what had happened. When I got to the head of the column, I saw a knot of Vietnamese huddled around a groaning soldier, a medic kneeling at his side. An ARVN non-com gestured toward the creek. Another small figure lay there in a fetal crouch. His head was turned sideways, and the creek flowed across his face. This man was dead. We had been ambushed. We had taken casualties from attackers who had vanished before we had ever seen them. The whole cycle—silence, shots, confusion, death, and silence again—was over in a couple of minutes.

I wondered what you did with a dead man in the middle of the jungle. The Vietnamese rolled the body into a poncho and trussed it to a bamboo pole. The terrain, Hieu told me, was too wild and rocky to bury the soldier. Besides, it was Vietnamese custom to try to return a dead man to his native village. The troops put the wounded soldier in a litter, and we resumed the march. The Vietnamese took turns lugging our twin burdens through the entangling underbrush until we reached high ground, where our radioman used a hand-cranked AN/GRC-9 portable radio to call a helicopter to evacuate the casualties. The radio was primitive; the operator had to tap out the message in Morse code, the same way news was telegraphed a hundred years before, during the Civil War.

Within a surprisingly short time, I heard the throb of an H-34's rotors and watched the aircraft approach a clearing. The Vietnamese pilot skillfully corkscrewed the helo earthward in a tight circle to minimize flying over the jungle at low altitude. The Vietnamese loaded the wounded man and the body aboard. The helo quickly disappeared, and we were alone again.

As night fell, we camped on high ground where we would be less vulnerable to attack than down in the valley. The usual tumult of rattling pots, squealing animals, shouting men, and billowing fires began. I threw down my pack, my carbine, my helmet damp with cold sweat, and slumped to the ground. I felt drained. The lark was over. The exhilaration of a cocky twenty-five-year-old American had evaporated in a single burst of gunfire. Somebody got killed today. Somebody was liable to get killed tomorrow, and the day after. This was not war movies on a Saturday afternoon; it was real, and it was ugly.

It turned cold at night in the mountains, sometimes dropping to forty degrees. I inflated my air mattress, set it on the ground, stretched my down sleeping bag over it, and crawled in, shivering. I needed to steel myself to get through tomorrow and all the other tomorrows until they added up to a year. I was gripped by a terrible loneliness made all the more acute because I could not share my fears. I was the senior American advisor, the one the others looked to for strength and guidance. Those lines from Fort Benning came back to me: "Content to fill a soldier's grave, for reasons I will never know." Yet, I wanted to know why. And then I fell into a fitful sleep.

I woke up with the sun splashing across my face, feeling oddly invigorated. Someone else was dead, but not me, a sense of elation, I was to learn, common to men in the wake of battle, even as they mourn dead comrades. Somehow, the world did not look so frightening in the light of day. This awareness—that things will look better in the morning—was to get me through many a dark night. We packed up and started making our way along the valley, and within an hour, we were ambushed again, but, this time, suffered no casualties.

I tried to blend in with the ARVN. I wore the same uniform and carried the same pack. I pinned my captain's bars onto the front of my blouse, concealed by my gear. And, for once, my color provided an advantage. I was color-coordinated with the Vietnamese and by slouching became virtually indistinguishable from Hieu's men. I kidded Sink. What the VC really were after, I told him, was a white hide.

As they had taught us at Fort Benning, I always carried a pencil and notebook, the latter green, government-issue, stamped "Memorandum" across the front. It fit neatly into my shirt pocket. By now it was discolored by sweat and coffee stains. Typical entries read:

> 10 Feb.: Rain. Located evacuated village; destroyed houses and 100 K [kilos] rice, 20 K corn. Harassing fire on 3rd Co.
>
> 11 Feb.: Rain. Killed 3 buffalo, pigs, chickens. Harassing fire from VC.
>
> 13 Feb.: 2nd Co. made contact with VC. Blood-stains indicate cas [a possible casualty, since we still had not seen the enemy]. Crossbows, quiver of possible poison located vicinity of river.
>
> 18 Feb.: Sprayed 2 hec [hectares] sweet potatoes, manioc destroyed.
>
> 21 Feb.: 0910. Ambushed. 1 KIA [killed in action]. 1 WIA [wounded in action]. 1610, 1 KIA. 1 unconfirmed VC cas. 2 houses destroyed.

On February 18, we came upon a deserted Montagnard village. The people had fled at our approach, except for an old woman too feeble to move. We burned down the thatched huts, starting the blaze with Ronson and Zippo cigarette lighters. The ARVN troops slashed away with their bayonets at fields of corn, onions, and manioc, a Montagnard starch staple. Part of the crop we kept for ourselves. On later occasions, the destruction became more sophisticated. Helicopters delivered fifty-five-gallon drums of a chemical herbicide to us, a forerunner of Agent

Orange. From the drums, we filled two-and-a-half-gallon hand-pumped Hudson sprayers, which looked like fire extinguishers. Within minutes after we sprayed, the plants began to turn brown and wither.

Why were we torching houses and destroying crops? Ho Chi Minh had said the people were like the sea in which his guerrillas swam. Our problem was to distinguish friendly or at least neutral fish from the VC swimming alongside. We tried to solve the problem by making the whole sea uninhabitable. In the hard logic of war, what difference did it make if you shot your enemy or starved him to death? As for the poor Montagnards, caught in the middle, with their crops and huts ruined, they were forced to rely on the South Vietnamese for food. That explained why these nomadic people were living on the dole at base camps like A Shau. The strategy was to win their hearts and minds by making them dependent on the government. I am sure these mountain people wished they had never heard of the ARVN, the Viet Cong, or the Americans.

However chilling this destruction of homes and crops reads in cold print today, as a young officer, I had been conditioned to believe in the wisdom of my superiors, and to obey. I had no qualms about what we were doing. This was counterinsurgency at the cutting edge. Hack down the peasants' crops, thus denying food to the Viet Cong, who were supported by the North Vietnamese, who, in turn, were backed by Moscow and Beijing, who were our mortal enemies in the global struggle between freedom and communism. It all made sense in those days.

. . .

My notebook for Saturday, February 23, read: "Rain/Fair. Marine H-34 evac. 2 KIA; 1 WIA; about 1235 VC delivered harassing fire." This terse entry covered a bad patch. The day before, we had taken casualties, and the following day, we radioed the base camp to evacuate our dead and wounded. We climbed up to high, level ground to give the helicopter a quick approach in and out and to set up a perimeter to protect the aircraft while it was on the ground. Two U.S. Marine helos appeared, one circling while the other descended into the perimeter. We loaded the casualties aboard and signaled the pilot to take off. A young Marine wearing an armored vest, no shirt, his bare arms covered with tattoos, crouched in the doorway behind an M-60 machine gun.

As the helo lifted off, the VC, unseen in the jungle, started firing at it. The pilot threw on full power and tried to pull the aircraft straight up. The ARVN soldiers on the defensive perimeter began shooting into the jungle. I watched in horror as I realized what was happening. The young Marine gunner, seeing muzzle flashes from the perimeter, assumed he had spotted the VC and started blazing away. As the drone of the helos faded over the ridge, I heard shouts and screaming. I headed toward the commotion. A soldier was hunched on the ground holding his right hand, which hung from a scrap of flesh where a bullet had torn away his wrist. Two other men lay dead. The Vietnamese looked at me, hurt, shocked. "Why you do this?" a noncom asked. "Why shoot us?" I had no answer. War is hell? Terrible things happen? Slowly but steadily, I had been gaining the confidence of these men, becoming something more than a tourist shadowing their daily encounters with death. And now this bloody blunder had undermined their belief in me. During a long, lonely night, my worst since we had taken that first casualty, I had trouble erasing the look of betrayal on the Vietnamese soldiers' faces.

We were ambushed almost daily, usually in the morning, soon after we got under way. The point squad took the brunt of the casualties. We switched companies around, giving everybody an equal chance at being blown away. I tried repeatedly to get Captain Hieu to have at least the men on the point wear armored vests. "Armored" was something of a misnomer. The vests were crisscrossed layers of densely woven nylon. Still, they offered good protection. The Vietnamese were small, Hieu pointed out, and the vests were heavy and uncomfortable in the sweltering jungle. Still, I kept badgering him. The next time we were standing over one of his men writhing in agony, I finally persuaded Hieu to have the point squad use the vests.

We had been out for nearly two months. I had seen men hurt. I had seen men die. But I had yet to see the enemy. After a firefight, we would pursue the VC in the direction of the incoming fire, blasting away at an invisible foe. Sometimes we spotted bloodstains, and I would dutifully enter into my notebook, "VC cas unconfirmed." One day after we had been attacked again, I became annoyed because the ARVN troops just stood around. My Benning syndrome kicked in. Don't just stand there, do something. "Follow Me!" I picked up a trail of blood and headed into the jungle, glancing over my shoulder. Suddenly, I realized I was alone. No one had followed me.

"Captain, come back!" the men shouted. The greatest shame that could befall Hieu was to lose his American. I might be following a trail of pig blood, a VC trick, the men warned me. I turned back. Still, I found it maddening to be ambushed, to lose men day after day to this phantom enemy who hit and ran and hit again, with seeming impunity, never taking a stand, never giving us anything to shoot at. I often wondered if we were achieving anything. How did we fight foes who blended in with local peasants who were sympathetic or too frightened to betray them? How did we measure progress? There was no front, no ground gained or lost, just endless, bloody slogging along a trail leading nowhere.

On March 18, the rain momentarily ceased and the day turned fair. We had been under way for less than an hour when enemy fire erupted, and, from the head of the column, I heard our return fire. The shooting ended in the usual sudden incongruous silence, but this time without the screams and groans of our casualties. Instead, I heard laughter. A couple of ARVN came to me, gesturing me forward. At the head of the column stood a private giggling nervously. He was wearing an armored vest with a dent punched in the back, a flattened bullet still embedded in the thick nylon layering. From his few words of English, I pieced together what had happened. He had been point man, breaking the trail for the column. When the firing started, he rose and turned around to signal to the rest of the squad where the enemy was. At that moment, he took a slug in the back which, but for the vest, would almost certainly have killed him. I pried out the spent bullet and passed it around to the Vietnamese, who fingered it with exclamations of awe. My stock was back on the rise. I was a leader of wisdom and foresight. The only problem now was that during the next supply delivery, I could not get enough vests for all the men who wanted them.

Toward the end of March, our mission changed. We were to build a new base camp at a place called Be Luong on a hill in the southeast corner of the A Shau Valley overlooking a confluence of streams. I had a chain saw airlifted in, which dazzled the Vietnamese, who had never seen one before. Until now, they had used axes or dynamite to cut down trees. One day, as the camp went up, I kept hearing an oddly regular bang, bang, bang of rifle fire. I tracked it down and found two ARVN troops methodically loading and firing clip after clip of ammunition from their M-1s into a tree. What were they doing? I wanted to know. Dynamite was too valuable, they explained. They were shooting down the tree. These moments tested an advisor's diplomatic skills. A straight U.S. Army chewing-out would be counterproductive. At an appropriate point, I mentioned to Captain Hieu that cartridges cost eight cents apiece. Hieu thought for a moment, then his eyes brightened and he expressed an opinion with which I instantly concurred. The men must not commit such waste. Trees should be cut down, not shot down. I have always liked the maxim that there is no end to what you can accomplish if you don't care who gets the credit.

One day the resupply helo delivered, along with our rations, a blond-haired, sturdily built artillery officer, First Lieutenant Alton J. Sheek. Sheek was a welcome sight, since he was to be my assistant battalion advisor and was another American to talk to in this lonely world. He was a quiet man with a reserved manner and proved to be all soldier, solid and reliable.

Along with fortifications at Be Luong, the ARVN constructed a cozy bunker of coconut logs for Captain Hieu, Sheek, Staff Sergeant Wesley Atwood, who had replaced Sergeant Sink, and me. By now, Hieu and I got along extremely well. As soon as he concluded that I was not an American know-it-all, Hieu warmed to me. My Vietnamese was limited, but his English was good enough to sustain a conversation. We never talked about the politics of the war. We talked about our families. Hieu showed me pictures of his wife and five children. After a while, I knew his plans for each child. Hieu was especially curious about America, and as I explained the wonders of the Interstate system and fast food, he would exclaim, "True? True?" I came to consider him a good friend, and was sure he felt the same way. I had crossed a cultural divide. I was no longer excess baggage to be pampered and protected. I was accepted by him and his troops. He told me that the men knew I was a new husband and about to become a father, and they were touched that at such a time in my life I was far from home, sharing their lot.

Unfortunately, soon after the Be Luong base camp was finished, Hieu got orders. His replacement was Captain Kheim, uncharacteristically big and blustery for a Vietnamese. I felt the loss of Hieu deeply. Besides being a friend, he was an able leader, respected by his men. And something told me that Kheim was going to be neither of these. Hieu left, and thirty years would pass. But I would see him again.

It was pleasant to be out of the line of fire for a while. I carried a little AM radio, and at night I could pick up a distant English-language broadcast. On Saturday night, the station played country-and-western music. Marty Robbins's "El Paso" was a big hit at the time, and something about the melody appealed to the Vietnamese. They asked me to translate the lyrics. I told them the sad tale of the west Texas cowboy who falls in love with a Mexican girl. He goes into a bar where one of the patrons mocks his love for a Mexican, and the cowpoke shoots his tormentor. As a posse tracks down and kills our hero, we hear the tragic refrain, "I feel the bullet go deep in my side. From out of nowhere, Felina is calling. One little kiss and Felina goodbye." Every verse ended with an aye-aye-aye that the Vietnamese loved. Soon I was leading them in choruses of "El Paso."

A Marine captain, his name lost to memory, became my closest link to the world I had left. Every two weeks, when his helo was due in, my anticipation was almost sexual. This flier brought my latest batch of paperbacks, my carton of Salems, and my mail—and I was anticipating a letter from Alma telling me that I had become a father. I never had a real conversation with the Marine, since he stayed in the cockpit high over the troop compartment, engine running at full power, ready for a hasty exit. I would stand up on the tire, he would lean out, and we would shout to each other over the engine's roar. He was a big, bluff man with a reassuring smile that said, you boys get into trouble, you know I'll get you out. For a few lonely Americans wandering around in an alien wilderness, this Marine represented home. My attachment to him and his helo took on the desperation of a man clinging to a life raft.

However rough the routine, I never felt physically better in my life. I looked gaunt, but was in superb condition. I had lost twenty-five pounds of German beer blubber and Fort Devens cheeseburger fat in the steambaths of the A Shau Valley. And rice starts to agree with you when you eat it three times a day, twenty-one times a week. At first, the glutinous blobs had repelled me. In time, I became quite fond of rice dishes of every kind. Our dining followed a pattern. The menu was hearty the first days after a resupply, when we had fresh vegetables, meat on the hoof, and poultry on the run. The animals were slaughtered and the meat cut into small pieces, cooked in pots, and stored in ammunition cans still greasy from the Cosmoline coating on the inside. The cans had a warning printed on them: "Do not use as food container." After a while, pork *au Cosmoline* tasted fine. Either this diet explains my present good health or something is lurking somewhere in my system waiting to destroy me. After a few days, the meat would run out, then the vegetables, and the last few days before resupply we lived on rice alone. If the rice ran out, the war was over. The Vietnamese would endure almost any hardship except rice deprivation. They would not move without it. Rice nourished the Oriental body and spirit, and when the rice sacks began to empty, I started scanning the terrain nervously for a landing zone where our Marine savior could deliver the next shipment.

My only diversions were writing letters and reading. I recorded in my notebook everything that I read, Fitzgerald's *Tender Is the Night,* McCullers's *The Heart Is a Lonely Hunter,* Hersey's *The Child Buyer,* Stegner's *Shooting Star,* Ryan's *The Longest Day,* and enough pulp whodunits to stack the bookshelves of a half-dozen motel offices.

During March, I had a temporary respite from the camp and patrolling. I was called to Quang Tri, our regimental headquarters. I was to report the 2d Battalion's progress and to learn the latest strategic fashions concocted by Secretary of Defense Robert McNamara's whiz kids back at the Pentagon. Quang Tri was not quite going home, it was not even Saigon, but it meant the familiarity of American faces and voices and not being shot at for a while. My American superior at Quang Tri, the advisor to the entire ARVN 3d Regiment, was Major George B. Price, a bold, brassy guy with a booming voice and near-lethal self-confidence. Price was tall, powerful, athletic, and articulate—he never stopped talking. In Army parlance, he was a "burner," a guy going places. He evidently came by his theatricality and voice genetically. George's sister was the opera star Leontyne Price. He became another mentor in my career, a black officer, one career generation ahead of me, who was making it himself (he retired as a brigadier general) and was generous in helping younger blacks along the way.

On this visit, I became acquainted with the latest Pentagon theory, the "oil slick." By securing one hamlet, we would generate security in neighboring hamlets, a benign slick spreading stability to areas threatened by the VC. What I remember most about those few days in Quang Tri, however, was not fashionable strategies, but George Price taking me to the officers' mess for a real American breakfast—eggs, bacon, pancakes, cereal. By now, however, my stomach had taken out Vietnamese citizenship, and this rich American diet made me sick.

I was counting the days on two timetables, when I would become a father and when I would go home. The tape recorders Alma and I had gotten for Christmas had proved inconvenient and inadequate for expressing our feelings. We had fallen back on timeless letter writing. What Alma did not tell me in her letters, thinking that I had enough trouble, was the race situation back home. The *Pittsburgh Courier,* a black weekly, had designated Birmingham the "worst big city in the U.S.A." The honor was not bestowed lightly. While I was in Vietnam, there occurred the eighteenth bombing of black neighborhoods in Birmingham ("Bombingham," as blacks then called it). While I was fighting the VC, a young Baptist minister, Dr. Martin Luther King, Jr., had been arrested for leading a protest march on Birmingham's city hall, after which he issued a document arousing America's conscience, his famous "Letter from a Birmingham Jail." While I was patrolling the A Shau Valley for communists, R.C., my father-in-law, sat up nights, a shotgun across his lap, ready to defend his home against fellow Americans of a different color. I never knew that my folks had called Alma and pleaded with her to get out of Birmingham. I knew almost nothing of all this. Little news penetrated the A Shau Valley, and Alma wanted her letters to support me with her love, not alarm me with her concerns.

As for my impending fatherhood, Alma and I had worked out a signal. When the baby arrived, she was to write me and print on the envelope "Baby Letter." I had already asked regimental headquarters at Quang Tri to be on the lookout for this letter and to open it and radio the contents to me the minute it arrived. Something about the imminent arrival of a new, innocent life in the midst of this small hell made my own life seem more valuable, my own survival more critical.

I had lost confidence in Hieu's replacement. Captain Kheim failed to connect with his men and did not know how to use advisors. I discussed the problem with Alton Sheek. Kheim was a kind of officer we both knew, an insecure man who expressed his authority by barking foolish orders rather than exercising sound judgment.

On April 3, I was in my Be Luong bunker stretched out on a bamboo shelf bed, trying to read a paperback by candlelight. Sheek was out with the men, and Kheim was asleep. In the distance I heard the crump of mortar fire and went outside to see where it was coming from. The VC were trying to drop a calling card on the new camp, but did not have the address right yet. The rounds were exploding in the jungle, missing us widely.

Captain Kheim came bounding out of the bunker and gave the order to return fire. I told him that this response might not be wise. We were on a hilltop. We had cleared the surrounding trees, and our fire would reveal our exposed position. They were not hitting us, I said, because they could not see any better in the dark than we could. No, Kheim said, doctrine called for returning fire.

Out went a few rounds. Within a minute, a huge white flash exploded about twenty feet above my head. Instinctively, I hit the dirt and scrambled back into the bunker before the next mortar round could find us. I checked myself. I was all right, but outside, I could hear shouts and moaning, and I went back to help.

The next morning, I saw exactly what had happened. The VC round had struck a branch of a tree that I had been standing under. Shrapnel had scattered to the left and right of me, wounding a half-dozen men on either side, but leaving me unscathed. If the round had not hit the branch, it would have hit me, and I almost certainly would have been killed. The men wounded in this attack included Kheim, who, by his rashness, had acted as the VC's spotter. His leg wound was just serious enough that he had to be evacuated and replaced, no great loss to the profession of arms. Kheim was succeeded by Captain Quang, a capable officer, though he was a bit reserved toward his advisors. I admired Quang, but we never struck friendly sparks the way Vo Cong Hieu and I had.

The day after the mortar attack a resupply helicopter hovered into view over the camp. In the mail was a letter from my mother. I planted myself under a tree and read the usual family chitchat. "Oh, by the way," Mom had written, "we are absolutely delighted about the baby."

What baby? What had happened to the baby letter? Was Alma all right? Was it a boy or a girl? I had the radio operator raise the base camp on the ancient AN/GRC-9, and we managed to get patched through to Quang Tri. The letter had suffered from something not unheard of in military operations, a failure of communication. The envelope, clearly marked, was sitting in a stack of undelivered mail. "Tell them I want it read *now*," I told the radio operator, and that was how I learned of the early arrival of Michael Kevin Powell, born March 23, 1963, in the Holy Family Catholic Hospital in Birmingham. He was reverse-named after Kevin Michael Schwar, one of the sons of our Fort Bragg samaritans, Joe and Pat Schwar.

My emotions at this time were an odd mixture—elation that I had a healthy son and a strong wife; bewilderment as I looked around at the alien world in which this had happened to me; and a nagging anxiety. I had come so close to being killed, to never knowing I had become a father. A family back home was depending on me, including a small new person. I wanted desperately to see this child. I had to make it through the year.

Quang was technically the battalion commander, and he was a good soldier. But since I was senior in terms of service with the unit and had the confidence of the men, something curious began to happen. The sergeant major was a lean, leathery veteran of the French colonial army, the ARVN equivalent of tough old Sergeant Edwards back in Gelnhausen. He trusted me, and we began playing a little game, with me pretending I was not in charge, the sergeant major pretending he was not taking orders directly from me. I was supposed to be an advisor, not the leader. Nevertheless, the two of us were in quiet collusion. Leadership, like nature, abhors a vacuum. And I had been drawn in to fill a void.

The ARVN soldiers were courageous and willing but not always easy to train. I instructed. They smiled, nodded, and often ignored what I said. I drilled them for hours on how to unload a helicopter. The key was speed. The helicopter was vulnerable. It drew fire. We needed to unload it as fast as possible. The quickest way was for two men to jump inside the aircraft as soon as it landed and start throwing out the cargo. The rest of the squad should form a line from the helo into the jungle, passing the supplies from man to man, bucket-brigade style, and stockpiling them under cover of the trees. I scratched an outline of a helicopter into the dirt, and we drilled again and again. Aircraft lands. Two men inside. Others form line. Pass supplies. Over and over.

The next day, a resupply helicopter put down inside our perimeter. I gave the unloading crew the signal, and the whole squad raced for the doorway, all trying to climb inside the aircraft at once. They were uncomplaining as I began drilling them all over again, and finally, they got it.

It was a hot afternoon in May. We were on patrol wading through the saw grass, sweating and slapping at insects, when the puttering of an L-19 "Bird Dog" observation plane sounded overhead. The pilot radioed that he had special-delivery airmail for me, which soon came swaying to earth at the end of a big yellow handkerchief. I ran to the drop zone and found a box full of Reese's peanut butter cups. At the bottom of the box was an envelope marked "Baby Letter." I tore it open, and a photograph fell out. A puffy red face peered out at me with all the wonder of someone who has spent one day on earth. Who did he look like? What did he look like? I could not tell much, but he was real, and he was mine. Welcome, Michael Powell. The Vietnamese crowded around, clucking and smiling. I let them see the photo. Then it went into my breast pocket and stayed there.

Later that May, I had another brief respite from combat. I was called back to Hue, where the advisory group to the 1st ARVN Division was headquartered. I was to meet with an Infantry Branch assignments officer, since, assuming I came through the A Shau Valley in one piece, the Army had to assign me somewhere else after my tour. I helicoptered in directly from the field, and as we approached the ancient Vietnamese capital I was struck by the beauty of the city, with its shimmering Perfume River, the landmark Citadel, and the charming French colonial aura. Once on the ground, I experienced what every combat veteran feels when he is suddenly yanked to the rear— the unnatural cleanliness, the illusion of order, the abnormally normal sounds, the incongruity between where I was compared to where I had been. I had my M-2 slung over my shoulder and a hand grenade and knife dangling from my belt, and my boots still carried the mud of the A Shau Valley. I had not bathed for a month, except for a quick splash in a stream. My underwear was a shade of yellow-gray and almost eaten through by sweat. I headed first for the officers' mess for an American meal. There the neatly dressed staff types looked at me as if to say, what do you think you're doing here? And I returned a look that said, I know why I'm here. But maybe you've forgotten. I waded into a steak and french fries, drank a milk shake, and again felt sick. I left the mess hall feeling lethargic, queasy, longing for my rice balls.

I checked in with a Lieutenant Colonel Spears, the assignments officer, at division headquarters. By now I had been in the Army almost five years. I had about seven more months to pull in Vietnam. I was eager to know what the infantry had in mind next. In those days, the Army had an ingenious system for

ranking officers in merit order. The key was a number arrived at by assigning points to factors in our
efficiency reports. The colonel thumbed through my
personnel file, looked up, and said, "Infantry Officers Advanced Course, Fort Benning, Powell."

I was surprised. "I'm barely out of the basic
course," I said.

"Doesn't matter," he answered. He had that
magic number in front of him, which he was not
about to divulge. But he did say, "Don't be surprised
if you get an early promotion to major."

I had been a captain for only seven months, and
this guy was already talking about an oak leaf. In
spite of the cannonball rolling around in my stomach, I walked out of that office on air. All the hardship and horror of the past months and the months to
come seemed somehow more bearable.

Back in the A Shau Valley, my notebook entries
resumed their monotony:

> **16 May, Thurs. Contact 0810. 3 WIA by VC
> grenade. 2 houses destroyed, 3 hec manioc, 1
> hec rice, by hand.**
> **17 May, Fri. 1st Co. contact 1615 1 KIA.**

The entry for May 18 is significant. "Contact
0805. 1 VC KIA. . . ." We had been patrolling a gorge
fed by a rushing stream that covered up our noise.
For once, our point squad spotted the VC before they
spotted us. For once, we did the ambushing. We
nailed them. A hail of fire dropped several VC, and

the rest fled. We approached gingerly. One man lay motionless on the ground, the first dead Viet Cong that I could definitely confirm we had killed. He lay on his back, gazing up at us with sightless eyes. The man was slightly built, had coarse, nut-brown features, and wore the flimsy black short-legged outfit we called pajamas. My gaze fixed on his feet. He was wearing sandals cut from an old tire, a strip of the sidewall serving as the thong. This was our fearsome unseen enemy. I felt nothing, certainly not sympathy. I had seen too much death and suffering on our side to care anything about what happened on theirs. We took the wounded VCs prisoner and left.

The first confirmed kill produced a boost in morale among the ARVN. The numbers game, later termed the "body count," had not yet come into use. But the Vietnamese had already figured out what the Americans wanted to hear. They were forever "proving" kills to me by a patch of blood leading from an abandoned weapon or other circumstantial evidence. Not good enough, I told them. I became the referee in a grisly game, and a VC KIA required a VC body. No body, no credit.

Soon after the first sure kill, a Vietnamese lieutenant came to me excitedly reporting another sure KIA. "Show me," I said. "Too far, too dangerous," he replied. I repeated the rule. He shook his finger as if to say, I'll show you. Half an hour later, he returned and handed me a handkerchief. I opened it and gaped at a pair of freshly cut ears.

That night around the campfire, I summoned the company commanders and senior noncoms. The rules needed refinement. A kill meant a whole body, not component parts. No ears. And no more mutilation of the enemy.

July 23. Six months in the boonies and, at last, the battalion was getting a break. We had orders to leave the Be Luong base camp and proceed east out of the A Shau Valley to a Special Forces camp for a rest. We resumed the trail and were marching late one morning along a creek bed. The sun was shining directly over us, and I had moved up toward the head of the column. Suddenly my right leg went out from under me and I felt a sharp sting. I yanked my foot out of a small hole about a foot deep. I had stepped into a punji trap, and the spike had pierced through my boot into my foot. I cursed my stupidity and continued limping toward the camp, still a couple of hours away. If anything, I felt more embarrassment than pain and did not want to let the Vietnamese know what had happened.

I had not gone for twenty minutes, however, when the pain became excruciating. I found a branch to use as a crutch and kept moving. I staggered the last mile, barely making it. In the camp, the American medic did not bother trying to unlace my boot but cut it off. He took one look at the wound and called for a helicopter. The spike had passed from the sole clear through the top of my instep. My foot was hugely swollen and had turned purple as the poison from the dung spread. He bandaged the wound, and I was soon airborne, headed for Hue.

On my arrival, an L-19 Bird Dog pilot, Jack Dunlap, took charge of me. I had never laid eyes on the man, though Dunlap immediately treated me like an old friend. He was the one, he told me, who had delivered the baby letter. Dunlap made sure that I got to a dispensary set up in the bachelor officers' quarters, where a doctor cleaned the wound by a memorable procedure. He shoved a treated fabric called iodoform gauze into the bottom of the wound, pulled it through the top, and ran it back and forth through my foot like a shoeshine rag. I was sure I was going to faint with the pain, as I squeezed Dunlap's hand. Afterward the doctor pumped me full of antibiotics and put me in a room in the BOQ.

I recovered quickly, but my days as a field advisor were over. I had too few months left to rejoin the battalion. In the seven months I served, I was the unit's thirty-fourth casualty—seven killed and twenty-seven wounded. It would be dishonest to say I hated to leave combat. Hardship and death are easily abandoned companions. But by the time I was injured, I had become the battalion commander in all but name. I had taken the same risks, slept on the same ground, and eaten from the same pots as these men and had spilled my blood with them. Challenges shared on Georgia cliffsides had bonded me to my own kind. Shared death, terror, and small triumphs in the A Shau Valley linked me just as closely to men with whom I could barely converse. I left my comrades of the 2d Battalion with more than a tinge of regret.

I tried to stop the Army from pushing the buttons that automatically advise the next of kin when a soldier is killed or wounded. I had stepped on a sharp stick, not a land mine, and I did not want my family unnecessarily alarmed. But the wheels of bureaucracy grind relentlessly. Notification that I had suffered a minor wound went by telegram to both Alma, who took it calmly, and Pop, who was sure the Army was holding back the worst. Matters were not helped by a practice of the South Vietnamese ruling family. Madame Nhu, sister-in-law of the bachelor President Diem—she was the wife of his brother Ngo Dinh Nhu, who was head of the secret police—acted as South Vietnam's "first lady." Whenever a GI was killed or wounded, Madame Nhu sent a letter to the man's family. Her message had a curious tone. It seemed to say, sorry, but you should know the sacrifices *our* people are making. American GIs referred to Madame Nhu as the Dragon Lady, a title richly deserved.

Since I was out of action, I was reassigned to 1st ARVN Division headquarters as an assistant advisor on the operations staff. One day in the officers' mess, I heard a familiar booming voice. I turned to see George Price, now promoted to a key job, G-3 (operations and planning) advisor to the 1st ARVN Division and my new boss. I felt reassured working with George. He still talked nonstop, but I listened closely, since what he said usually made sense.

And much of what I observed at headquarters badly needed explaining. When I left the A Shau Valley, I shifted from a worm's-eye to a bird's-eye view of the war, and the new vantage point was not comforting. One of my assignments was to feed data to a division intelligence officer who was trying to predict when mortar attacks were most likely to occur.

He worked behind a green door marked "No Entry" doing something called "regression analysis." My data got through the door, but not me. I was not cleared to enter. One day, the officer finally emerged. There were, he reported, periods when we could predict increased levels of mortar fire with considerable certainty. When was that? By the dark of the moon. Well, knock me over with a rice ball. Weeks of statistical analysis had taught this guy what any ARVN private could have told him in five seconds. It is more dangerous out there when it is dark.

The infantryman in the boondocks, slogging back and forth over the same terrain, ambushed daily, taking casualties from an enemy who melts away, wonders, understandably, what good he is accomplishing. He seeks comfort in assuming that while he might not know, up there somewhere, wiser heads have the answer. My service on the headquarters staff exploded that assumption. We were the most sophisticated nation on earth. We were putting our superior technology in the service of the ARVN. Deep thinkers, like my intelligence officer behind the green door, were producing printouts, filling spreadsheets, crunching numbers, and coming out with blinding flashes of the obvious, while an enemy in black pajamas and Firestone flip-flops could put an officer out of the war with a piece of bamboo dipped in manure.

In the jungle we carried only what proved useful or life-saving. Yet at Hue, every helicopter crew chief sported a big knife with a carved handle and a gleaming blade, ideal for reflecting the sun and giving away one's position. Eighteen-year-old truck drivers hauling trash to the division dump wore tooled shoulder holsters custom-made by leatherworkers in Hue, who must have been getting rich on this sucker trade. I saw guys carrying six-guns into mess halls with the bullets arrayed, cowboy-style, on the back of their belts. How did they expect to load in a sudden firefight? That didn't matter. The ammo looked sharper in the back. It was STRAC all over again.

This kind of behavior was just silly. What seriously disturbed me was my first exposure to the upper ranks of the Vietnamese military command. Most officers and noncoms in my battalion had been dedicated, able professionals. The foot soldiers were brave and uncomplaining. But incompetence, corruption, and flashy uniforms seemed to increase in direct ratio to rank. One such rising rocket was Nguyen Cao Ky, on his way to becoming chief of the South Vietnamese air force at age thirty-two. The flamboyant Ky, with his pencil mustache and dark sunglasses, his pearl-handled, chrome-plated revolver, his scarf trailing from his black flying suit, fought the war with equal panache in the air and in Saigon nightclubs. Were these the people, I wondered, for whom ARVN grunts were dying in the A Shau Valley?

I must admit that having paid my combat dues, I found service in the rear pleasant. As a wounded combat veteran, I enjoyed a certain status. And Hue, with its delicate beauty, good restaurants, and diversions for the troops, was no hardship post. Even a trip to the barbershop was a treat. The barber not only trimmed my hair but massaged the tension from my scalp, neck, and shoulders with skilled hands. I started to regain some of the weight sweated off in the A Shau Valley by retooling my digestive tract for steaks and Ba Muoi Ba, "Number 33," a popular Vietnamese beer. And I tried to keep the weight down by playing softball.

Soon after I joined the headquarters staff, I flew to Hong Kong for rest and recreation. For some GIs, R and R in this indulgent city meant wall-to-wall sex. For others, Hong Kong meant a shopping spree. I picked up the mandatory custom-made shoes ($10 a pair) and tailored suits ($30) and the lowest-priced stereo in the world. I bought Alma Mikimoto pearls, a silk dress, and a bolt of silk cloth. Within four days I was broke and back in Hue.

There I received another of the offbeat assignments that had marked my career. As an additional duty, I was assigned as commander of the Hue Citadel airfield, which handled C-7 Caribou transports, L-19s, and other small aircraft. One cocky pilot clearly resented that a nonaviator was running *his* airfield. He challenged me one day to go up for a spin in his Bird Dog. My ego was on the line, so I accepted. It immediately became clear that this hotshot was trying to dump me or my stomach out of the L-19 as he performed barrel rolls, vertical dives, and other nauseating aerial capers. I thought that I was going to die, but refused to out of sheer spite. Finally, as he leveled off, I looked down and was shocked to see an unfamiliar landmark, a railroad track running on top of an embankment. I did not remember any such feature in our area.

"You know where we are?" I shouted.

"A little north of Quang Tri," my pilot announced confidently.

"You damn fool," I hollered through the howling wind, "turn this thing south and get us out of here. We're over North Vietnam!"

It turned out I was right. After dealing with intelligence wizards and puffed-up pilots, I began developing another rule: don't be buffaloed by experts and elites. Experts often possess more data than judgment. Elites can become so inbred that they produce hemophiliacs who bleed to death as soon as they are nicked by the real world.

On November 1, I was back in Saigon, my tour over. I had to be processed out and would soon be headed home. South Vietnam, at the time, was in turmoil. President Diem, a Catholic, was trying to suppress Buddhist ceremonies and Buddhist demonstrations against his regime. A stark photograph had shocked the world: a Buddhist priest sitting cross-legged in a Saigon intersection had poured gasoline over himself, lit a match, and burned to death without moving a muscle, to protest the Diem regime. In August, while I was still in Hue, the city had been placed under martial law, and American forces were confined to quarters. About a week later, President Diem had put the whole country under martial law.

As I rode out to Tan Son Nhut Airport this day to ship my gear home, something more serious was evidently under way. The Presidential Palace was shot up, and the streets were empty, except for troops in personnel carriers. I had arrived in Saigon in the middle of a coup. A cabal of South Vietnamese generals had just overthrown the government and had executed President Diem and his brother, Ngo Dinh Nhu, the secret police chief. At age twenty-six, I had no penetrating political insights into what was happening. I thought like a soldier who knew his perimeter, and not much more. To me, the coup was just another baffling facet of this strange land.

In spite of the most recent upheaval, I was being sent home a month early, because we were supposedly doing so well in Vietnam. The number of American advisors had actually dropped slightly from a high of 16,600 to 16,300. The McNamara-era analytic measurements that were to dominate American thinking about Vietnam were just coming into vogue. We rated a hamlet as "secure" when it had a certain number of feet of fence around it, a militia to guard it, and a village chief who had not been killed by the Viet Cong in the last three weeks. While I was in the Be Luong base camp, Secretary McNamara had made a visit to South Vietnam. ". . . every quantitative measure," he concluded after forty-eight hours there, "shows that we are winning the war." Measure it and it has meaning. Measure it and it is real. Yet, nothing I had witnessed in the A Shau Valley indicated we were beating the Viet Cong. Beating them? Most of the time we could not even find them. McNamara's slide-rule commandos had devised precise indices to measure the unmeasurable.

The Army's attitude seemed to be, don't question those who know better, including these slide-rule prodigies. If it ain't working, pretend it is, and maybe it will fix itself. The flabby thinking that I had first witnessed in West Germany had been shipped to Vietnam. This conspiracy of illusion would reach full flower in the years ahead, as we added to the secure-hamlet nonsense, the search-and-sweep nonsense, the body-count nonsense, all of which we knew was nonsense, even as we did it.

And, slowly at first, American casualties began to mount. Familiar names began showing up among the dead—Jim Lee, with whom I had served in Gelnhausen; Alan Pasco, the first of my Pershing Rifles buddies to die in Vietnam, but not the last.

Still, few people in America knew or cared what was happening in that faraway country. Vietnam was strictly a back-burner issue. At the time, the United States had 252,000 Army troops in Europe and 49,000 in Korea, compared to the 16,300 in Vietnam. And there was no antiwar movement to speak of in 1963.

In spite of my misgivings, I was leaving the country still a true believer. I had experienced disappointment, not disillusionment. I remained convinced that it was right to help South Vietnam remain independent, and right to draw the line against communism anywhere in the world. The ends were justified, even if the means were flawed. In spite of what Secretary McNamara had found, the mission was simply bigger and tougher than we had anticipated. While I was at Hue working with the intelligence staff, an analyst had asked me, as a guy who had been in the field, what the job was going to take. I pulled a number out of thin air. "It'll take," I said, "half a million men to succeed."

I was sitting in the airport in Nashville, Tennessee, thumbing through a magazine while waiting for an afternoon flight to Birmingham, when I noticed people clustering around a TV set in the lounge, staring in a strange silence. The date was November 22. Three weeks before, I had been in Vietnam on the day that that country's president had been assassinated and the government overturned. This afternoon, the President of my country had been murdered. And while I had been off fighting for the freedom of foreigners, four little black girls had been killed by a bomb planted in Birmingham's 16th Street Baptist Church. I had returned home, it seemed, to a world turned upside down.

5 ✯ *Coming Home*

ONE OF NORMAN ROCKWELL'S classic paintings is called *Homecoming GI,* a *Saturday Evening Post* cover that appeared just after World War II. The young soldier, duffel bag in hand, has just arrived back at the old neighborhood; his family runs out to greet him, including the dog; a pretty girl waits demurely around the corner; grinning neighbors lean out of doorways and windows; kids wave at him from up in a tree, welcoming home the conquering hero. That is not the way it was coming back from Vietnam in 1963.

As I stepped out of the Birmingham airport, one person was waiting for me. She looked beautiful and vaguely familiar. When two people have known each other for only a year, and are separated for another year, they are, even if man and wife, something of strangers. As I took Alma in my arms, the strangeness began to dissolve, though I am sure she was thinking, who is this guy? Do I really know him? We got into my old blue Beetle, another familiar sensation, and headed for her parents' new home in a north Birmingham area called Tarrant City. It was dusk when we pulled up and parked behind the house. Alma urged me to go on ahead toward a large sliding glass door. My in-laws, for the moment, were keeping out of sight.

I had been preparing myself for this encounter for months. Behind the glass door I saw, in the soft light of a lamp, a playpen. I slid the door open, and a little eight-month-old person, clinging to the bars, stared up at me, wide-eyed, tousled curls piled on top of his head and dressed to kill in a red suit. I picked him up. "Hi, Mike," I said. "I'm your pop!" He looked bewildered and kept gazing around for Alma. It happens in almost every man's life. The eternal triangle. Now it was happening to Michael Powell.

I had a homecoming feast with Alma and her folks, R.C. and Mildred, while the baby continued to gape at me from his high chair. When it came time to put Mike to bed, the little tot was in for another shock. He had been sleeping with Mom. Now he was dispatched to a crib. The next morning, I came down to breakfast. Mike was happily cooing in the high chair, until he saw me. This guy is still here? When is he going? Maybe he's never going? A disturbing thought. Over the next few days, he started to thaw. This big person fusses over me. He plays with me. Maybe he's not so bad, though I certainly prefer Mom. And that is how it would remain for a time, until stranger and boy became father and son.

Next stop, Elmira Avenue in Queens for Christmas with Mom and Pop. While we were there, Mike came down with a hoarse, racking cough. We rushed him to the nearest military facility, the St. Albans Naval Hospital, near my parents' home. The young Navy doctor who saw us seemed to have had about as much experience with babies as I did. He elevated what we thought was a cough to a crisis. Mike had an acute case of the croup, the doctor said, and he put Mike in a crib under an oxygen tent. He placed an emergency tracheotomy kit at Mike's bedside and asked permission to use it if the baby stopped breathing normally. What did that mean? I wanted to know. He would have to incise the child's throat and insert a tube, the doctor explained. They were going to cut open my little boy? The jungle warrior turned to jelly. Alma was distressed too, but managed to stay calm and ask intelligent questions. She explained to the doctor that the baby was still nursing; he had never seen a bottle. How would he be fed? The doctor suggested we go home and relax. We did the former, and I failed miserably at the latter. I could not sleep. We raced back to the hospital at the crack of dawn, and there, sitting up in the crib, guzzling milk from a bottle, sat little Mike, weaned, apparently free of the croup, and smiling.

I was standing on the open ramp of a cargo plane, at twelve hundred feet, eyes shut, wind buffeting me, a T-10 parachute on my back, the old terror gripping me once more. I had already jumped five times before during airborne training and had no desire to toy with gravity again. Yet off I went, into the wild blue yonder.

I had been assigned from Vietnam to Fort Benning, Georgia, to attend the Infantry Officers Advanced Course. However, the "career course," as it was known, would not begin until August 1964, still almost eight months off. To fill part of the time, the Army had dispatched me to a one-month-long Pathfinder course, advanced airborne Ranger training.

On my arrival, I immediately set out to find a place for my family to live. I was entitled to government housing when the career course began in the summer. But until then, I needed to find something off-post, if Alma and the baby were to join me. Fort Bragg all over again. Plenty of housing available for white officers in the Columbus area. But I was limited to black neighborhoods, and nothing remotely comparable to the Johnsons' home in Birmingham was available. After a discouraging start, I met a black real estate agent who offered me a house belonging to a Baptist minister in Phenix City, across the border in Alabama. I was wary. Phenix City was rough, a sin town that the National Guard had been sent in to clean out a few years before. The minister's house was located on a back road, among a bunch of shacks. Still, the house itself was a solid brick rambler with a yard for the baby. I grabbed it for $85 a month, grateful to find anything suitable.

In the meantime, I roomed at the Fort Benning BOQ while I got the new place in shape for Alma and Mike. One night, exhausted and hungry, I locked up the house and headed back toward the post. As I approached a drive-in hamburger joint on Victory Drive, I thought, okay, I know they won't serve me inside, so I'll just park outside. I pulled in, and after a small eternity, a waitress came to my car window. "A hamburger, please," I said.

She looked at me uneasily. "Are you Puerto Rican?" she asked.

"No," I said.

"Are you an African student?" She seemed genuinely trying to be helpful.

"No," I answered. "I'm a Negro. I'm an American. And I'm an Army officer."

"Look, I'm from New Jersey," the waitress said, "and I don't understand any of this. But they won't let me serve you. Why don't you go behind the restaurant, and I'll pass you a hamburger out the back window."

Something snapped. "I'm not *that* hungry," I said, burning rubber as I backed out. As I drove away, I could see the faces of the owner and his customers in the restaurant windows enjoying this little exercise in humiliation. My emotional reaction, or at least revealing my emotions this way, was not my style. Ordinarily, I was not looking for trouble. I was not marching, demonstrating, or taking part in sit-ins. My eye was on an Army career for myself and a good life for my family. For me, the real world began on the post. I regarded military installations in the South as healthy cells in an otherwise sick body. If I hurried, I could get to the snack bar or the officers' club before closing and be served, just like everyone else.

Pathfinders form an elite within an elite, paratroopers who jump in ahead of airborne and heliborne assault units to mark landing and drop zones. The Pathfinder course turned out to be incredibly demanding. My classmates were senior and master parachutists attached to airborne units, while I was a reluctant novice who had not jumped in five years. We started off with the daily dozen calisthenics, each exercise performed until the last man collapsed. We recovered with a five-mile run. And then the day began—classes in navigation, marking drop zones, using radio beacons, guiding in aircraft. And more jumping.

Pathfinder teams needed to hit the ground close together. Consequently, rather than our going out of a doorway, one at a time, the pilot lowered the rear ramp of a twin-engine Caribou, and we were all supposed to jump rapidly off the back end. Jumps were usually made at night, adding another dollop of excitement. What body of water, rock outcropping, or cliff lurked below? In my case, night operations made little difference; I always jumped with my eyes shut anyway. And instead of making a macho leap into the unknown, I tended to shuffle to the rear and baby-step off the ramp. As a result, while others soared like eagles, I managed to bang my butt on the ramp and bounce out of the plane. Once free, however, I experienced the thrill that hooks people on parachuting, that magical sensation of floating to earth while the wind sighs in the chute above you. If only you did not have to jump first.

Near the end of the course, we were to parachute from a helicopter. First we marched cross-country all day long, until sufficiently exhausted. By the time we got to the helo, it had grown dark, the wind had come up, and it was pouring. We clambered aboard, the cold January rain pelting our faces, and jammed ourselves onto the cramped floor. I was the senior officer on board, but the jumpmaster was a hard-faced, highly experienced NCO. As the helo took off, I hollered over the roar of the engine for all the men to make sure their static lines, which automatically opened the chutes when we jumped, were hooked to the floor cable. In the dark, I could hear hands rummaging along the cable on the floor. The helo leveled off. The wind had whipped up to a point where the jump could be hazardous. I yelled for the men to recheck their hookups one last time. Then, like a fussy old woman, I started checking each line myself, pushing my way through the crowded bodies, running my hand along the cable and up to each man's chute. To my alarm, one hook belonging to a sergeant was loose. I shoved the dangling line in his face, and he gasped. It was a triple failure. He was supposed to check his line. His buddy was supposed to check it. The jumpmaster was supposed to check it. This man would have stepped out the door of the helo and dropped like a rock. And he would have had only four seconds to pop his reserve parachute.

The weather worsened, and the jump had to be canceled. As we piled out at Lawson Army Airfield, the sergeant with the unhooked static line hugged me, practically blubbering his gratitude. The lesson about experts had been reaffirmed. Don't be afraid to challenge the pros, even in their own backyard. Just as important, never neglect details, even to the point of being a pest. Moments of stress, confusion, and fatigue are exactly when mistakes happen. And when everyone else's mind is dulled or distracted the leader must be doubly vigilant. "Always check small things" was becoming another of my rules.

On graduation day, I added the Pathfinder insignia to my Combat Infantryman's Badge, airborne wings, and Ranger tab, the equivalents, in my world, of degrees strung out after an academic's name. And to my surprise, this ground-loving soldier graduated number one in the class. I was proud of the honor, but I do not regret that I never again found myself in a situation where I had to jump.

I am a marginal swimmer at best, and here I was on a hunk of Canadian hardware sinking in the middle of a Georgia lake. With six months still to go before the Infantry Officers Advanced Course began, the Army again had to stash me somewhere. The answer was a deadly-sounding assignment, "test officer" with the

Infantry Board, also located at Fort Benning. Our job was to test new weapons and equipment and decide if they were acceptable to the infantry, anything from a redesigned bayonet to a new machine gun. Each item was to be judged by three criteria—did the thing work, how available was it, and how much cost and effort were required to keep it working. The Army had acronymed these standards as RAM—Reliability, Availability, and Maintainability. My job was to design RAM standards and put an item through these paces.

I was entrusted with testing the Canadian-made XM571 Articulated Carrier, an awkward-looking vehicle, supposedly ideal for carrying troops over sand, snow, or water. Accompanying this iron horse was a Canadian liaison officer, Major Colin G. Forrest, a big, ruddy-faced Irishman who wore a regimental kilt. As descendants of ex-colonials with the same first name, Forrest and I hit it off immediately. With him was the manufacturer's representative, a fellow I remember only as Bill. Both were eager to have the XM571 make a good showing. Canadian pride and profits were riding on the U.S. Army's decision.

We had put this ugly duckling through her land trials, and except for a couple of unplanned rollovers she had done well. The last remaining hurdle was a swim test. I set it up for 11:00 A.M. on Victory Pond. The entire Infantry Board was invited to observe, including my boss, Lieutenant Colonel James Sudderth. To be on the safe side, I planned a rehearsal for 7:30 that morning. Bill, the manufacturer's rep, and

I, both wearing life jackets, boarded the vehicle and gave the driver the order to shove off. I was a little concerned that the XM571 rode so low in the water. We had about six inches of freeboard between us and the lake. And as we got a third of the way across, I realized we were losing even that margin. My feet felt wet, and I looked down to see water filling the bottom. I pointed this out to Bill, who waved aside my concern. No problem; the bilge pump would kick in any second now. And it did, with one slight glitch. The pump discharged twenty gallons a minute, but the water was coming in at about forty gallons a minute.

"Bill," I pointed out, "we're sinking."

"Son of a bitch," he concurred, "we are."

We jumped out, paddling furiously, and watched the XM571 disappear from sight as a rescue boat came out to pick us up. Approaching the embankment, I looked up to see the thick, red-freckled legs of Major Forrest. The man was in a state of understandable agitation. This was not the sort of news he wanted to send back to Canada.

Fortunately, the lake was only about ten feet deep, and I soon had a wrecker and winch hauling this sinkable *Molly Brown* out of the drink. I checked my watch. Still two hours to go before the board would arrive. We waited impatiently for the water to drain, watching it spurt from every aperture in the carrier. We soon figured out the problem. The XM571's earlier rollovers had cracked the chassis. We tried to start her. No luck. We kept trying. Coughing and sputtering, but no gratifying roar. I had the carrier towed to the demonstration site anyway, while I ran off to get myself into a set of dry fatigues.

What should I tell the Infantry Board? When the members arrived and we had all of them seated, I stood beside this product of Canadian enterprise and matter-of-factly described the tests it had gone through, including this morning's failure. Just tell what happened. Don't crawl. People want to share your confidence, however thin, not your turmoil, however real. Never let 'em see you sweat. We completed the demonstration, and, I should add, the XM571 never became part of the U.S. arsenal.

I stayed for almost five months with the Infantry Board. As the time neared for me to begin the career course, Lieutenant Colonel Sudderth asked if I would like to come back to the board afterward. In an Army of Rangers, Green Berets, and airborne elites, reassignment as an Infantry Board testing officer somehow did not sing. Still, the board possessed one clear advantage: it meant that I could stay on at Benning after I finished the Infantry Officers Advanced Course. And I was becoming happily adapted to a stable home life. Yes, I told the colonel, I would be pleased to come back.

The Army has its own rites of passage. The career course at Benning was intended to prepare infantry captains to take over command of a company and to serve on a battalion staff. For all practical purposes, I had already completed this course, as a first lieutenant in a captain's slot commanding companies in Germany and Fort Devens. And I had been a battalion commander in all but name in classrooms in the A Shau Valley where they fired live ammunition, not over your head as on the practice range, but at you. And I had also logged staff-level duty in Germany, Devens, and Vietnam. Still, the course was a required part of my professional development; and in beginning it, I could now bring my family into government housing on the post.

I was curious to meet my classmates. In a sense, this was the first career cut. Many infantry officers served their obligated two or three years, then were mustered out. At the advanced course, I was among four hundred captains, buddies and competitors likely to make the Army a career. We were divided into two classes of two hundred men each. In the other class was a true walk-on-water phenomenon, Pete Dawkins, West Point All-American running back, 1958 Heisman Trophy winner, and a Rhodes scholar to boot. And we had other burners, like Thomas Griffin, who would rise to three stars and become chief of staff of the NATO Southern Command. The competition inspired and intimidated in about equal doses.

During the course, the "prefix 5" designator was added to my military occupational specialty. In Army lingo, that meant I was now certified in the use of tactical nuclear weapons. I presumably knew when to employ them (though approval still had to come from well above my pay grade), how many enemy troops, civilians, and trees a particular atomic round would likely vaporize, how to shield our men during a nuclear exchange, the amount of radioactive fallout we could expect, and when it would be safe for our troops to pass through an affected area. We were not thinking in terms of Armageddon. A nuclear shell fired from a 203mm artillery piece, for example, yielded between .1 and 10 kilotons, compared to 15 kilotons for the bomb dropped on Hiroshima. Ours was not to question the wisdom of using these nuclear weapons on the battlefield. Nor did the likelihood of the enemy's escalation figure into our calculations. The Navy and Air Force had gone nuclear. Was the Army supposed to use muskets and minié balls? Besides, the Red Army had tactical nukes. Long afterward, when I rose to the policy-making level, I would cast a far more skeptical eye at the battlefield use of nuclear weapons. But at this stage, I was just another unquestioning captain, learning my trade.

In the summer of 1964, I went to the same drive-in on Victory Drive and ordered a hamburger without being told to go around to the back. Since my previous stop, President Lyndon Baines Johnson had signed the Civil Rights Act, outlawing discrimination in places of public accommodation. That fall, LBJ was running against the conservative Republican candidate, Senator Barry Goldwater. I was no political partisan, but Goldwater had disappointed me by casting the lone vote in the Senate against the civil rights bill. Goldwater was not a racist—he had opposed the bill on constitutional grounds—but his opposition nevertheless gave unintended encouragement to segregationists. I went out and slapped a red-white-and-blue sticker on the bumper of my Volkswagen reading "All the Way with LBJ," probably violating post regulations on political activity in the process.

One evening that fall, while I was driving from Birmingham to Fort Benning, an Alabama state trooper flagged me down near the town of Sylacauga. Speeding? Not outside the realm of possibility. To my surprise, the trooper was not concerned about my driving. He was handing out bumper stickers for Goldwater! He looked over the Volks, an alien vehicle in sixties Alabama. Strike one. He checked my license plate—New York State. Strike two. He spotted the LBJ sticker. Strike three. And a black at the wheel. I had somehow managed to accumulate four strikes. He shook his head, "Boy," he said, "you ain't smart enough to be around here. You better get going." Which I did, quickly.

Soldiers like Price, Mavroudis, DePace, and me had a future in the Army. Still, the officer corps had a dominant culture in those days, and it was white, Protestant, and heavily Southern with a dash of Midwest. Far more officers came out of Wake Forest, Clemson, the Citadel, Furman, and VMI than out of Princeton, or certainly CCNY.

Our career course classes often met in small, windowless rooms, and it was a relief to get out in the hallways to stretch a leg and have a smoke. I came out one day to find a cluster of white classmates discussing the presidential election, all praising Goldwater. "Hey, Colin," one of them called out to me, "come on over." I joined them, a little wary.

"Are we prejudiced?" he asked. "Hell, if we were, would we all be sitting in the same classes together?" It was not a question of liking or disliking "colored people," the guy continued. He and his friends just did not care for this pushy stuff, the government telling people how to live their lives. "It's a question of property rights," another classmate chimed in. "A man sets up a business, he ought to be able to do what he wants with it."

I could have put my back up and lashed out, or I could have pulled away in hopeless resignation. Instead, I tried to open their eyes. "Let me tell you what property rights mean," I said. "If you're a soldier and you're black, you'd better have a strong bladder, because you won't be stopping much between Washington, D.C., and Fort Benning." I told them how it was trying to find a decent place to eat on the road in the South, or a motel where you, your wife, and your kid could stay, as darkness began to fall. Medgar Evers of the NAACP had been murdered the year before in Mississippi. Sheriff Bull Connor had set police dogs against people. Murderers had blown up four children in a Birmingham church. And these people were arguing about "property rights"! "You can't reduce this issue to whether or not a white hotel owner should have to rent a room to a black. You can't put property in the same league with human beings," I told them.

I don't know that I made any converts. But it was good to get these feelings off my chest, and to let these men know that tolerance meant more than just sitting next to a black man in a classroom.

The soldiers whose stock shot up in my esteem during this period were black officers from the South. After a lifetime of second-class treatment, segregation, and isolation in black colleges, they had found themselves competing alongside whites whom they had not been allowed to live, study, or eat with, people before whom they had been expected to bow and scrape. During my growing-up years, I had never felt uncomfortable around whites; I never considered myself less valuable. Different, yes; inferior, never. These Southern blacks had never been told anything else. Through the years that followed, as I watched them rise in the Army, my admiration grew. Most of them simply refused to carry the baggage that racists tried to pile on their backs. The day they put on the same uniform as everybody else, they began to consider themselves as good as anyone else. And, fortunately, they had joined the most democratic institution in America, where they could rise or fall on merit. These Southern black soldiers stand tall in my hall of heroes.

Shortly before election day, November 3, 1964, I mailed in my absentee ballot to my New York voting address. LBJ, all the way. And I treated myself to another burger on Victory Drive.

This period was turning out to be one of the happiest in my life. For an infantryman, Fort Benning, home of the infantry, holds a sentimental place. The bachelor lieutenant sows his wild oats, gets married, makes captain, gets orders to the career course, and brings his wife to Fort Benning, often her first post. We bought our first furniture on credit from the same Columbus department stores, delivered in one load, living room, dining room, bedroom, and kitchen. We visited each other in our look-alike houses, small two- and three-bedroom ranches set on concrete slabs. Except for the rare couple with inherited wealth, there was scant room for snobbery, since most of us were bringing home the same paycheck and living the same standard.

On weekends, Alma and I often packed little Mike into the Volks for a visit to her folks in Birmingham. On the way out, we passed through the senior officers' quarters, grand, gracious white stucco homes built by the WPA during the Depression. Most impressive of all was Riverside, an earlier antebellum mansion dripping with wisteria and ringed with magnolias, the residence of Fort Benning's commanding general. Every year, the CG hosted a reception for career course students. The men wore dark civilian suits. The women went out and bought the best dress a captain's pay allowed. And we walked up that clipped lawn toward Riverside as if we were bit players in a scene from *Gone with the Wind.*

After the reception for our class, Alma asked me if I could guess her dream. An upgrade from the Volkswagen to a station wagon? No, she said, to live at Riverside one day as the general's lady. I kidded her over what her father liked to say about her mother, that Mildred Johnson still had a slave mentality; she wanted to live in the big white house with the columns. Alma's dream seemed harmless enough and about as remote in 1964 as men going to the moon.

Benning is also where Linda Powell arrived on April 16, 1965. I had missed out on Mike's earliest infancy. By the time I saw him, he was a little person. But that day, at Martin Army Hospital, as I studied that tiny, helpless creature, I was overcome with the feeling a father has for a little girl. I was going to catch up on what I had missed in my first round as a parent. The career course involved little heavy lifting, and I took advantage of the situation to spend as much time as I could with Linda, becoming an accomplished nanny. Alma was tied up in Red Cross volunteer work at the time of Linda's six-week checkup, so I tucked the baby under one arm, held her diaper bag under the other, and took her to the hospital myself. I happily joined the young mothers in the waiting room, dispensing advice on treating croup and colic and other lore in which I was now parent-qualified.

Anybody entering my class that day would have found a U.S. Army major flinging a rubber chicken at a roomful of officer candidates. I had entered the teaching profession. And I was engaged in that *sine qua non* of all learning, motivation.

I had completed the Infantry Officers Advanced Course in May 1965, ranking first among infantry-men in my two-hundred-man class. But I came in third in the whole class, topped by a tanker and an artilleryman, which I found humbling.

As planned, I returned to the Infantry Board after the career course. My reasons were mostly personal—to keep the family in one place awhile longer. I spent several relatively uneventful months again evaluating new infantry equipment. Then one day, in the spring of 1966, I got word to report to Infantry Hall. I was being assigned to the faculty of the school where I had recently been a student.

It was now about eighteen months since President Johnson had used an "unprovoked" attack by North Vietnamese gunboats in the Tonkin Gulf to push through a Senate resolution amounting to a virtual American declaration of war against the Viet Cong and North Vietnam. When I left Southeast Asia, it had still been a Vietnamese conflict involving some 16,000 American advisors. By the time I was asked to join the Infantry School faculty, the American involvement had begun to approach 300,000 troops, and the Army needed to produce more officers. Infantry Hall, a spanking-new building, had just been completed to accommodate the expansion. Duty as an instructor was a coveted assignment, much sought after and an impressive career credential. Instructors taught the officers who would be leading the troops in battle, not a mission the Army entrusted lightly.

Before I could go near a classroom, I had to complete an instructors course. For three intense weeks, we learned how to move before a class, use our hands, adopt an authoritative tone, hold center stage, project ourselves, and transmit what was inside our heads into someone else's. We were peer-evaluated, merit-boarded, scored, graded, and critiqued to death. If I had to put my finger on *the* pivotal learning experience of my life, it could well be the instructors course, where I graduated first in the class. Years later, when I appeared before millions of Americans on television to describe our actions in the Gulf War, I was doing nothing more than using communicating techniques I had learned a quarter of a century before in the instructors course at Infantry Hall.

I entered my own classroom with something new, an oak leaf. I had received the accelerated promotion to major that the assignments officer had predicted back in Hue. I had been in the Army less than eight years, and I had attained a rank usually reached after ten or eleven years. And I had just entered another league. Army officers are divided into three broad categories: company grade, field grade, and general officers. I had just made field grade.

As an instructor, I taught students from officer candidates to reserve generals. I teamed up with a feisty Marine lieutenant colonel, P. X. Kelley, who later became the Marine Corps Commandant, to teach amphibious operations. But my most important classes involved officer candidates, young men in their early twenties who would be shipping out to Vietnam as new infantry second lieutenants, where they would suffer the highest casualties among officers. A fair percentage of those eager faces in my classes were not coming back, I knew, no matter what I taught them.

A healthy competition existed among the instructors. My chief rival was Major Steve Pawlik, a Polish-American live wire, a superb instructor, and my patient coach in handball. Steve and I were always trying to upstage each other, devising ways to grab and hold the students' attention. One approach was humor. In those less correct days, with no woman within a mile of Infantry Hall, part of the macho culture was to open the class with a joke, usually of the raunchiest kind. These stories were not my forte. But I had one surefire joke I told to every new class. It involved a missionary about to be pounced on by a tiger. The missionary starts to pray. The tiger starts to pray. The missionary says, "What a Christian thing, to pray along with me." "Pray with you?" the tiger says, "I'm saying grace." It always got a laugh.

One day my story was greeted with thunderous silence. I tried a backup joke. Grim, stone faces. What was going on? Had I possibly exceeded even the Benning bounds of corny jokes? Afterward, a deadpan Pawlik asked me how the class had gone. "Awful," I said, puzzled. Later I learned what had happened. Pawlik had gotten to my class ahead of me and persuaded the students to stiff me. He had then slipped behind the one-way glass on one wall of the classroom and thoroughly enjoyed my agony. Steve carried his fierce competitiveness to our off-duty games of hearts with another instructor and friend, Major Bill Duncan. To us hearts was a game, to Steve a vendetta.

Our ultimate challenge was teaching OCS candidates to prepare a Unit Readiness Report. The conditions were diabolical. The class was held at 4:00 P.M., at the last hour of the last day before graduation—and after a three-day field exercise of forced marches and mock battle, ending with a sleepless all-night operation. Nevertheless, the readiness report had to be mastered before a student was allowed to graduate.

This report would have been a crashing bore even for the most dedicated nerd. It involved a two-page form in which the officer recorded the percentage of equipment in state Green, ready to go, Yellow, not quite ready, and Red, out of commission. The officer had to report the unit's training status, squad by squad, platoon by platoon: C-1, ready to go; C-2, got a few problems; C-3, serious problems; C-4, hopeless. The students would stagger back to Benning after that all-night operation, take a shower, have a hot meal, and then head for this final lecture, anticipating a much-needed snooze in an air-conditioned classroom.

My approach was to project the readiness form on a screen and go over it, block by block, computation by computation, on and on, trying to keep the students awake long enough to pound the importance of the report into their befogged skulls. When students began to doze off, they were to get up and stand against the wall. The instructor's effectiveness was judged by how few catatonic officer candidates wound up at the wall. In teaching the readiness report, the competition between Pawlik and me reached fresh heights of ingenuity.

One day, I had an inspiration. I ordered a plucked rubber chicken from a gift catalog and hid the chicken under the lectern. The students came trooping in, enameled helmet liners tucked under their arms, desperately trying to look alert. I gave the order "Take seats, gentlemen!" Within minutes, I could hear snoring. As the first student rose and headed for the wall, I fired a question at him. He roused himself and answered. "That's wrong," I said, seizing the chicken and swinging it over my head. "And your punishment is . . ." I let the chicken fly. The class scattered in all directions as this realistic-looking hunk of fake poultry sailed through the room. When they realized what I had thrown, the students laughed and stayed awake for another ten minutes. The chicken became a fixed part of my curriculum. Education and entertainment, I realized, are not unrelated.

At Benning, we lived a life not all that different from that of Levittown suburbanites of that era. Dad came home from the office. Mom reported the kiddie violations of the day and the latest household catastrophe. One afternoon, Mike, age three, fell out of a tree and landed on his head. After a race to the emergency ward, the doctor told us to take him home and wake him every hour to make sure he could regain consciousness. At about 3:00 A.M., the kid asked if we would please leave him alone so that he could get some sleep. Linda, a serious, thoughtful, and independent little girl, was becoming the apple of her father's eye. We lived in a neighborhood full of similar families, with similar numbers of kids, with similar joys—and similar fears, since a menacing cloud hung over this otherwise apple-pie landscape.

Since Columbus was the hometown of the infantry, thousands of officers and noncoms had left their families here while they went off to Vietnam. Casualties were now running well over one hundred a week. When a yellow cab pulled up to a house and the driver got out, you knew he was delivering a telegram from the Defense Department and Benning had another widow and a new family of fatherless children. The system was unintentionally brutal, and as casualties mounted, the services devised a more compassionate way to deliver the grim news. Casualty notification officers, usually local recruiters, drew the hardest job in the military, to go to the families of the fallen, to deliver the word, to comfort them, and to offer whatever help they could.

One day, walking through Infantry Hall, I heard a raucous voice from my CCNY days: "Hey, paisan!" I turned to see Tony Mavroudis, my Greek buddy from Queens. Tony was still following in my footsteps. He had also gone from ROTC into the regular Army. He had done a Vietnam tour, and he was just starting the career course while I was an instructor. Tony became a fixture around our house, and a great favorite of the kids. The genteel but perceptive Alma came to appreciate the diamond under the rough exterior.

One day, as Tony approached the end of his course, he told me that he had volunteered to go back to Vietnam.

"What's the hurry?" I asked. "We'll all be going again soon enough."

"Don't kid me," Tony answered. "If it weren't for Alma and the kids, you'd volunteer too." He was right; as infantrymen, we thought that was where we belonged.

By now, the war had dragged on for so long that an infantry officer like myself could count on at least two tours, a helicopter pilot likely three. My return was just a matter of time. Tony went sooner rather than later.

I had just finished tucking in my children one night several months afterward when the phone rang. Alma answered and said it was for me. One of my Pershing Rifles buddies was calling, which one I do not remember. I was too stunned. Tony Mavroudis was dead. I did what people do in such situations. I started asking about details. We grasp at what we can handle in the face of what we cannot. Tony had been leading his company down a trail when a firefight had broken out. He was killed instantly. I told Alma what had happened. We sat on the edge of the bed, dry-eyed, wordless. The house suddenly seemed emptier. That boisterous, warmhearted spirit had been taken from us in an instant. It would take me time to absorb the loss.

One evening not long afterward I told Alma that we had to talk. "I'll be leaving here soon," I said. We had been lucky so far. We had stayed at Benning almost three years, during a war. The Army was obviously clocking me for another Vietnam tour. "You've got to be ready for it," I said. "It's inevitable." Alma's face assumed that impassive expression that cloaks what she feels inside. There was another interim possibility, I told her. I was eligible for the Army Command and General Staff College at Fort Leavenworth, Kansas. The college marked a critical turning point in the lives of career officers. If the advanced course was our bachelor's degree, Leavenworth was a master's (and the National War College represented a Ph.D.). Not every major would be selected for Leavenworth. Army officers not chosen, and the odds were about 50–50, could still have a fulfilling career, but would level off probably as lieutenant colonels, or in unusual circumstances, as full colonels. But to make general officer, Leavenworth was an all but inescapable prerequisite. If not selected now, I would almost certainly be going back to Vietnam. Alma understood; there was nothing more to say, and so we went to bed.

On a spring afternoon in 1967, I had just finished teaching a class and saw the long-awaited Leavenworth list posted on a bulletin board. I called Alma immediately. I could hear the relief in her voice. Vietnam was off for the time being. I was going to the Command and General Staff College.

You can roughly judge where the American male is at any point in his life by what he is driving. In my day, swinging bachelor: Ford Mustang or Chevy Corvette; new husband: Volkswagen; young father: station wagon. As we packed up at Benning and prepared to drive to Leavenworth, I was about to make my next model change. I had watched sadly, six months before, as a Mr. Wayne Guest drove off with my beloved blue Beetle, sold for $400. Alma insisted that a family with two kids needed more space. Brand- and color-loyal, I showed up soon afterward not with a station wagon, but with a reasonable facsimile, a blue Volkswagen van that the kids loved. Alma drove it twice to the PX and declared, "That heap has to go." She was not about to pull up to the officers' club at Fort Leavenworth in a used miniature bus. Thereafter, the Powells made the automotive equivalent of moving from company to field grade. We bought our first new American car, a 1967 Chevy Bel Air, and, with Michael, four, and Linda, two, headed west, via our customary detour, Elmira Avenue in Queens.

We eventually reached the Missouri River at the Penny Bridge in Missouri, so called because, even in 1967, it cost a penny to use. We crossed over into Kansas and entered Fort Leavenworth. Instead of going straight to the garden apartment my old Gelnhausen mentor Red Barrett had found for us in the adjacent town of Leavenworth, I parked next to the post's Memorial Chapel. I found what I was looking for, a grassy sunken lane that ran down to the river we had just crossed. The pioneers had come up the Missouri on flatboats and then headed overland in ox-drawn Conestoga wagons to link up with the Santa Fe and Oregon trails. The rut in the earth that we were standing in had been worn by these wagons on their westward trek. A sense of the past has always moved me, and I wished my children were old enough to feel the pulse of history in this spot. Fort Leavenworth was founded in 1827, and every morning on the way to play war games and read military history, I felt thrilled to be walking along roads that had known the footsteps of George Armstrong Custer, Philip Sheridan, Dwight Eisenhower, George Patton, and other storybook soldiers.

Until now, the infantry battalion of a few hundred men had been my universe. Leavenworth's mission was to raise our vision above the horizon of a battalion-level infantry officer and give us an understanding of the larger canvas of warfare. For the first time, in concentrated form, I began dealing with artillerymen, tankers, engineers, signal corpsmen, quartermasters— the whole panoply of an Army in which people with jobs and outlooks as different as those of accountants and cowboys have to learn to mesh. By the time the course ended, thirty-eight weeks later, we were expected to know how to move a division of twelve to fifteen thousand men by train or road, how to feed it, supply it, and, above all, fight it.

My CCNY record notwithstanding, I had done well so far in my military education. But Leavenworth was in another league academically. Officers who had finished in the top third of the Infantry Officers Advanced Course might well find themselves in the bottom third here. I studied hard and did my homework. And by now I had learned how to outwit multiple-choice tests, which the Army favored because they were easy to grade and supposedly more objective than essay tests. I could spot the throwaway and trick choices, which usually left two plausible answers, giving you even odds of being right with an intelligent guess. We were graded on a 1-to-4 scale, and I started racking up 1's, the equivalent of A's, in all my courses. And I still had time for extracurricular interests, particularly gin rummy, which I learned to play from a hell-raising cavalry officer named Jim Amlong, and to which I became addicted. Every time we had a ten-minute break in class, and every lunch hour, out came the cards. Any free time not devoted to gin rummy I spent on the softball diamond, where, after my dismal performance as a kid player, I was developing a reputation as a long-ball hitter.

The morning of February 1, 1968, I came out of the bedroom, put on the coffeepot, and turned on the TV news. I was stunned. There on the screen were American GIs fighting on the grounds of the U.S. embassy and ARVN forces battling before the Presidential Palace in the heart of Saigon. The Viet Cong, supported by North Vietnamese Army units, had launched a coordinated strike against 108 of South Vietnam's provincial and district capitals. When I went to class that day, the atmosphere was one of disbelief, as if we had taken a punch in the gut. Fighting over the next few days continued to be fierce, and twenty-six days passed before Hue was liberated. By then, the lovely former capital where I had served lay in ruins, with at least 2,800 of its people executed by the enemy. The campaign had been launched on the eve of Tet, the Vietnamese lunar New Year, and thus found its name in history.

Judged in cold military terms, the Tet offensive was a massive defeat for the Viet Cong and North

Vietnam. Their troops were driven out of every town they had attacked, and with horrific losses, estimated at 45,000 of the 84,000 men committed. But, 137 years before, Clausewitz had said something still relevant: "If you want to overcome your enemy, you must match your effort against his power of resistance, which can be expressed as the product of two inseparable factors . . . the total means at his disposal and the strength of his will." It did not matter how many of the enemy we killed. The Viet Cong and North Vietnam had all the bodies needed to fling into this conflict and the will to do so. The North simply started sending in its regular army units to counter the losses.

The images beamed into American living rooms of a once faceless enemy suddenly popping up in the middle of South Vietnam's capital had a profound effect on public opinion. Tet marked a turning point, raising doubts in the minds of moderate Americans, not just hippies and campus radicals, about the worth of this conflict, and the antiwar movement intensified.

I disliked watching Americans demonstrating against Americans in wartime. Those of us who knew we were going back to Vietnam would do our duty undeterred by demonstrations, flag burning, or draft dodging. Politicians start wars; soldiers fight and die in them. We do not have the luxury of waiting for a better war. On March 31, 1968, while I was at Leavenworth, President Johnson told the country that he would not seek reelection. It was a statesmanlike gesture—as well as a pragmatic reading of the writing on the wall. Johnson saw a dangerously divided country that he could not hold together. Still, packing it in and going home to the ranch was not an option available to career officers, or to American draftees, for that matter.

Leavenworth was my first assignment where there were enough other blacks to form a critical mass. In class and in formal social situations, the college was completely integrated. Informally, however, black officers hung out together. We had our own parties, put on soul food nights, and played Aretha Franklin records. Nevertheless, we had made it this far up the ladder precisely because we had the ability to shift back into the white-dominated world on Monday morning. Leavenworth represented integration in the best sense of the word. Blacks could hang around with the brothers in their free time, and no one gave it any more thought than the fact that West Pointers, tankers, or engineers went off by themselves. That was exactly the kind of integration we had been fighting for, to be permitted our blackness and also to be able to make it in a mostly white world.

Five days after President Johnson dropped out of the 1968 presidential race, the Reverend Martin Luther King, Jr., was murdered. For me and my fellow black officers at Leavenworth, Dr. King's death was an abrupt reminder that across the Penny Bridge, racism still bedeviled America. Each of us had experienced enough racial indignities to understand the riots unleashed in black ghettos in the wake of the King assassination. We understood the bitterness of black GIs who, if they were lucky enough to get home from Vietnam in one piece, still faced poor job prospects and fresh indignities. However, we saw ourselves as professionals first, with our duty to our oath and our country. And because of the relative freedom in the military, the American dream was working for us. We had overcome humble origins, worked our tails off, achieved field grade, proved ourselves anyone's equal, and were building better futures for our children. We heard the radical black voices—Stokely Carmichael, Eldridge Cleaver, and H. Rap Brown with his "Burn, baby, burn!"—with uneasiness. We were not eager to see the country burned down. We were doing well in it. In later years, however, I came to understand that a movement requires many different voices, and the tirades of the agitators were like a fire bell ringing in the night, waking up defenders of the status quo with the message that change had better be on the way.

At Leavenworth I met a lot of officers with graduate degrees earned on Army time. It dawned on me that an advanced degree, along with my efficiency reports, citations, and decorations, would make me more competitive. When I discussed my post-Leavenworth future with my assignment officer at Infantry Branch, I mentioned my interest in the Army's Graduate Civil Schooling Program. This gruff soldier, a fellow major, pointed out that there was a war on. I was aware of that, I said, but it did not prevent others from applying to graduate school.

He looked over my college grades. "You don't seem like graduate school material to me," he said.

I felt a surge of anger, but managed to suppress it. "You're going to have to turn me down in writing," I said, "because I intend to try anyway."

I applied for the Army-financed graduate program, and, fortunately, my superiors took into account my record at Bragg, Benning, Gelnhausen, Devens, and Vietnam and my good grades so far at Leavenworth. I was approved. The next step was to take the Graduate Record Examination, and if I passed, to apply to grad school.

Late one winter evening, after Alma and the kids had gone to bed, I was in the kitchen studying for an upcoming exam on Tactical Infiltration. It was a dark, cold night and I could hear the wind beating against the window. Suddenly, a voice sent a shiver through me. The television was on in the living room, and I got up and went to it. There was my friend Tony Mavroudis, dead these many months, on the screen. I called Alma. She came out in her pajamas, and we watched the rest of the program in heavy silence. It was an NBC documentary narrated by Frank McGee entitled *Same Mud, Same Blood,* dealing with blacks in the military in Vietnam. And there was Tony, in jungle fatigues, with his street-smart logic, driving home the program's message. Race did not matter out here, Tony said. "It doesn't exist. . . . We're all soldiers. The only color we know is khaki and green. The color of the mud and the color of the blood is all the same." At the end of the program, McGee said, "Five days after we left him, Captain Mavroudis . . . was killed by an exploding land mine." Scholars could take pages to express the wisdom Tony had captured in a few blunt words. The loss of this friend hit me harder on this night than on the day I first heard the news.

I was coming out of a class in Intelligence Estimates when I ran into my faculty advisor. "Do you know how well you're doing?" he asked me.

"All 1's so far," I said.

"Well, you're damn near at the top of the class." I could well be the honor graduate, he pointed out, if I aced the final exam.

About a week later, I entered a classroom with a huge map of Europe covering the front wall. The final examination of the course was not multiple-choice. It required essay answers to hypothetical tactical problems. There was no right or wrong answer, just the instructors' evaluation of the appropriateness of our decisions. In the last question, we had to respond to an armored attack on our division's flank. My dilemma was whether I should try to out-psyche the test writers and give the answer I thought they wanted or should answer with what I really believed. I chose the latter. I kept my division on tactical defense, not counterattacking until I had better intelligence on the enemy's strength, deployment, and intentions. Good decisions, I reasoned, are based on solid information. Check the pool for water before you take a header off the high board.

I should have known better. On the last exam of the last day, Leavenworth's gung ho faculty would obviously want you to attack! attack! attack! I scored my only 2, still a respectable grade. At graduation, I ranked first among infantrymen in my class. But I came in behind an artilleryman, a talented major, Donald Whalen (who went on to become a brigadier general).

It would have been satisfying to be number one, but I still think my answer was as good as what the instructor wanted. It revealed a natural inclination to be prudent until I have enough information. Then I am ready to move boldly, even intuitively. That day at Leavenworth, I was only a student answering a hypothetical problem, and any casualties were only on paper. A time would come when my advice and decisions would be paid for in real lives. And when that day came, I would not change my approach. For me, it comes down simply to Stop, Look, Listen—then strike hard and fast with all the power you need.

Leavenworth was my introduction to a more cosmopolitan world. Other nations sent the cream of their officer corps to the U.S. Army Command and General Staff College. We studied together, ate together, and played together. Here was the first opportunity to get to know men with whom we might (and later did) plan combined military operations. One of my Leavenworth buddies was a Belgian army major, Joseph Charlier. The next time I saw him, he was chief of staff of the Belgian armed forces, and I worked with him in NATO. Thus are old-boy networks born.

The townsfolk adopted these foreign officers, so far from home, some separated from their families. They were invited by Kansans of every station to picnics, Thanksgiving and Christmas dinners, birthdays, and baptisms. Years later, when I was serving as National Security Advisor to President Reagan, we faced a minicrisis during the visit of the president of Pakistan, Mohammad Zia ul-Haq. When asked for the list of guests he would like invited to the White House state dinner honoring him, Zia said he wanted Ed and Dollie included. Ed and Dollie? It turned out that when Zia was a major studying at Leavenworth, Ed, a mailman, and his wife, Dollie, had just about adopted him. Zia was still filled with warm memories of his friends, and, consequently, a somewhat astonished Ed and Dollie were flown to Washington for dinner at the White House.

While we were at Leavenworth, Alma, baptized a Congregationalist, became an Episcopalian. She did so because we wanted to grow together spiritually as a family. Alma's confirmation, like everything in Leavenworth, occurred against a backdrop of history. The small Memorial Chapel commemorated the loss of 7th Cavalry troopers at the Little Bighorn on June 25, 1876. During Alma's confirmation, I studied the plaques on the chapel walls. One next to the front door contained the names of Lieutenant Colonel George A. Custer, his younger brother Captain Thomas W. Custer, and other officers who perished that fateful day. Other plaques were less historic but no less touching: "John Anthony Rucker, 2d Lieutenant . . . 6th Cavalry . . . drowned . . . attempting to save the life of a brother officer." They tell a joke at Leavenworth about a little boy at the chapel with his parents. He wants to know about the names on the plaques. "They died in service," his mother explains. "The eight-thirty or the eleven?" the boy asks.

The pleasant life we were living was about to end. My orders had come through for Vietnam. That day, when I came home from class, I caught sight of Mike, now five, careening around a corner on two wheels of his tricycle and Linda playing with the Carter twins, children of close friends. I called to my kids and swept them up in my arms. This parting was going to be far harder than the last one. And war was no longer the adventure I had eagerly set out on in 1962. I was a husband and father now.

I pushed such thoughts aside. Tony Mavroudis had been right. We were soldiers by profession, and Vietnam was where we were supposed to be.

I drove the family from Leavenworth to Birmingham, where Alma and the kids were to stay while I was gone. Alma's sister, Barbara, had been divorced, and the two sisters and their children, four cousins in all, would be living together in a rented house about a mile and a half from Alma's folks in Tarrant City. I liked the location; it seemed secure. And I liked the economy of the sisters' splitting the rent.

A few days before my departure, Alma had an idea. We were living in the New South. For the past four years, public accommodations had been open to all. Parliament House, the fanciest hotel in Birmingham, boasted a fine restaurant. "That's where I want us to go for our farewell dinner," Alma said. That night, I, in my best tailored Hong Kong suit from my first Vietnam tour, and Alma, stylish as always, walked into a dining room without another black patron in sight. Our entrance into once forbidden territory was slightly daunting. But what was the point of it all, the sit-ins, the marches, the battles in court and Congress, the martyrdom, the eviction of Jim Crow, if not to enjoy the fruits of everyday life so long denied us? We followed the maître d' to a table, and we were treated graciously.

Toward the end of dinner, I handed Alma an envelope.

"What's that?" she wanted to know.

"Just put it away in case," I said.

"In case of what?"

"In case something happens."

In the envelope were my instructions in the event I did not return from Vietnam. Alma was not one to flinch from reality. I had friends, Pershing Rifles brothers, pals from Gelnhausen and Devens, and infantry course classmates, who had already died in the war. We knew many Army widows at Fort Benning. We talked briefly about my wishes—for example, my wanting to be buried in Arlington National Cemetery. Then we went back to more pleasant conversation.

Part of the difficulty in contemplating my return to Vietnam was the mood of America. Losses in the war were perceived as if they were happening only to the military and their families, people unlucky enough to get caught up in a messy conflict; they were not seen as sacrifices shared by the country for a common purpose, as in other wars. As a career officer, I was willing to do my duty. But as far as the rest of the country was concerned, we were doing it alone. We were in a war against an enemy who believed in his cause and was willing to pay the price, however high. Our country was not; yet it took our government five more years to get us out.

We had to get up while it was dark and the kids still sleeping in order for me to catch an 8:30 A.M. flight out of Birmingham. This time, I let Alma drive me to the airport parking lot, although I did not want her to come any farther. We said our goodbyes in the car, and on July 21, 1968, I was on my way again to Vietnam.

6 ☆ *Back to Vietnam*

THE SAIGON I had known in 1962 now looked as if it had been trampled by a giant. Where before the streets had been full of pedicabs, now they were jammed with jeeps, staff cars, and Army trucks. Where previously the U.S. presence had been muted, GIs now swarmed all over the place. Quiet bistros had been displaced by noisy bars populated by B-girls catering to our troops. The charming colonial capital was encircled by American barracks, headquarters, storage depots, airfields, hospitals, even military jails. Saigon now resembled an American garrison town more than the Paris of the Orient. I could not wait to go up-country.

I arrived at Duc Pho on July 27, 1968, assigned to the resurrected World War II 23d Infantry Division, known as the Americal. I was to serve as executive officer of the 3d Battalion, 1st Infantry, 11th Infantry Brigade. The Americal's headquarters was in Chu Lai on the northern coastal plain. Duc Pho was about a half-hour helicopter ride farther inland and to the south.

Most armies are a combination of fighting machine and bureaucratic beast, and our beast had a long tail. My job as exec was to make sure the battalion had all the support it required to remain in fighting trim, and my duties included everything from ordering up ammo, to making sure the helos had fuel, to getting mail out to the troops. As soon as I arrived, my new boss, the battalion commander, Lieutenant Colonel Hank Lowder, a compact, feisty scrapper, handed me another assignment. I was to prepare for the Annual General Inspection, a task better suited to peacetime at Fort Devens than Vietnam in the middle of a war. Still, the Army took its inspections seriously. Hank Lowder wanted me to handle the administrative headaches in preparing for the inspection so that he would be free to concentrate on fighting the war. Consequently, while he led the troops in the field, I was at Duc Pho making sure that the fumigation schedule, troop inoculation records, and other endless reels of red tape were inspection-ready.

My situation reminded me a little of the Duke of Wellington during the Peninsular Campaign. Wellington is purported to have written to the British Foreign Office in London: "We have enumerated our saddles, bridles, tents and tent poles, and all manner of sundry items for which his Majesty's Government holds me accountable. . . . Unfortunately, the sum of one shilling and ninepence remains unaccounted for in one infantry battalion's petty cash and there has been a hideous confusion as to the number of jars of raspberry jam issued to one cavalry regiment, . . . This brings me to my present purpose, which is to request elucidation of my instructions. . . . 1) to train an army of uniformed British clerks in Spain for the benefit of the accountant and copy boys in London, or, perchance 2) to see to it that the forces of Napoleon are driven out of Spain?" In preparing for the annual inspection in Vietnam and in all my future service, I would think of Wellington's jam jars whenever the purpose of the mission seemed to get lost in bureaucracy.

Though Duc Pho was away from the main VC units, it was hardly a garden spot. The first thing I noticed, parked on the edge of the camp, was a "conex" container, the kind used to ship heavy equipment or household effects. This huge crate, I learned, was our backyard mortuary, used to hold Viet Cong dead until we figured out what to do with the bodies. The next thing I noticed was the odor, which almost knocked me out. Excrement was burned all day long in fifty-five-gallon drums, and the whole post smelled like a privy. The burning, like laundry, KP, and other menial tasks, was done by Vietnamese whom we hired. The workers' loyalty was supposedly checked out by the local village chiefs, though Lord knows how many people running around inside Duc Pho were moonlighting for the VC, including the chiefs.

We were ambushed regularly and took occasional rounds of mortar and rocket fire. Every morning the roads out of Duc Pho had to be swept for mines that the VC might have planted during the night. While high-tech warriors back at the Pentagon were dreaming up supersophisticated equipment for this task, our troops used a down-home remedy. The men filled a five-ton dump truck with dirt; the driver put it in reverse and backed down the road. If he hit a mine, it would blow off the tires and probably damage the rear end. But the truck could usually be salvaged, and the roads were cleared. We lost an occasional vehicle, but seldom a driver.

Besides getting Duc Pho in shape, I had to go out and make sure that field units were also ready for the annual inspection. We had several FSBs (fire support bases) and LZs (landing zones)—Dragon, Liz, Chevy—located throughout our area. Early in August, I got a helicopter and flew out to check out LZ Dragon. I had heard that its messing facilities were substandard. Bad chow proved to be the least of Dragon's problems. I had not expected to find stateside spit and polish. Still, what I discovered jolted me. As I stepped out of the helo, I practically stumbled over rusted ammo left lying around the landing site. Sanitation was nil, weapons dirty, equipment neglected, and the troops sloppy in appearance, bearing, and behavior. Seven years had passed since American advisors had first gone to Vietnam in force, and it was four years since the big buildup after the Tonkin Gulf Resolution. Still, the end was nowhere in sight, and deterioration of discipline and morale was obvious. I issued orders to get Dragon back into shape, told the officers I would be back to check on their compliance, and moved on to the next site.

These were good men, the same kind of young Americans who had fought, bled, and died winning victory after victory throughout our country's history. They were no less brave or skilled, but by this time in the war, they lacked inspiration and a sense of purpose. Back home, the administration was trying to conduct the war with as little inconvenience to the country as possible. The reserves had not been called up. Taxes to finance the war had not been raised. Better-off kids beat the draft with college deferments. The commander in chief, LBJ himself, was packing it in at the end of his term. Troops of the ally we had come to aid were deserting at a rate of over 100,000 a year. That flying statesman Nguyen Cao Ky had gone beyond air marshal to become South Vietnam's premier by age thirty-four, though by my second tour he had been reduced to vice president. Ky had married a young airline hostess who wore the same silk flying suit and trailing scarf as he did as they hopscotched around the country in his plane. Ky had said, "I have only one [hero]—Hitler. . . . But the situation here is so desperate now that one man would not be enough. We need four or five Hitlers in

Vietnam." This was the man for whose regime three, four, even five hundred Americans were dying every week in 1968. They were dying with the same finality as at Valley Forge or Normandy, but with little of the nobility of purpose.

Our men in the field, trudging through elephant grass under hostile fire, did not have time to be hostile toward each other. But bases like Duc Pho were increasingly divided by the same racial polarization that had begun to plague America during the sixties. The base contained dozens of new men waiting to be sent out to the field and short-timers waiting to go home. For both groups, the unifying force of a shared mission and shared danger did not exist. Racial friction took its place. Young blacks, particularly draftees, saw the war, not surprisingly, as even less their fight than the whites did. They had less to go home to. This generation was more likely to be reached by the fireworks of an H. Rap Brown than the reasonableness of the late Martin Luther King, Jr. Both blacks and whites were increasingly resentful of the authority that kept them here for a dangerous and unclear purpose. The number one goal was to do your time and get home alive. I was living in a large tent and I moved my cot every night, partly to thwart Viet Cong informants who might be tracking me, but also because I did not rule out attacks on authority from within the battalion itself.

Life at Duc Pho took crazy pendulum swings from the trite to the heartbreaking. One afternoon I was getting Coke and beer helicoptered out to the fire-

bases—a daily priority the exec dared not miss—
when Colonel Lowder sent word that he had run into
a stiff fight at Firebase Liz and needed help. I ordered
up a "slick," a bare-bones UH-1 helicopter, no seats,
just space and a couple of door guns, had it loaded
with 5.56mm rifle and 7.62mm machine-gun ammo,
and headed out over the treetops. We landed at Liz
near dusk and quickly unloaded. A grim-faced Lowder told me to take back nine of our casualties. The
vulnerability of a helicopter on the ground left little
time for niceties. The nine KHAs (killed by hostile
action, the Army's replacement term for KIA, killed
in action) were rolled into ponchos and loaded onto
the slick. As we took off in the half-light, I slumped
to the floor, facing nine recently healthy young
American boys, now stacked like cordwood. We
landed in darkness at an evac hospital, a MASH unit.
The tents were a hive of activity, with wounded being
flown in from all directions.

People in combat develop a protective numb-
ness that allows them to go on. That night I saw this
shield crack. Eventually, the bodies were taken from
the slick into the field hospital to be confirmed as
dead. Medical staffers unrolled each poncho and
examined the bodies with brisk efficiency, until the
last one. I heard a nurse gasp, "Oh my God, it's . . ."
The final casualty was a young medic from their unit
who had volunteered to go out to the firebase the day
before. Nurses and medics started crying. I turned
and left them to their duty.

Then it was back to bean counting for the annual
inspection. When it finally took place, we were exam-

ined by a scrupulous but fair officer, Lieutenant Colonel Carrol Swain, inspector general of the Americal Division. The battalion scored highest in the division, an achievement that meant more back at headquarters, I am sure, than to grunts counting the days until their tour was over.

On October 31, 1968, President Johnson called a halt to the bombing of North Vietnam. To those of us on the ground, these geopolitical stratagems were as remote as sunspots. While back at home the country seethed with controversy over the war, I do not recall a single discussion on its merits among my fellow officers all the while I was in Vietnam. Questioning the war would not have made fighting it any easier. If a bombing halt meant anything to us, it meant less pressure on the enemy and more grief for our men.

I got my picture in the newspaper, and it changed my life in Vietnam. The paper was the *Army Times,* and the photo had appeared in a story on my graduating class from the Command and General Staff College at Fort Leavenworth. Up in Chu Lai, Major General Charles M. Gettys, commanding the Americal Division, was reading a two-month-old issue of the paper and recognized me as an officer he had met briefly at Landing Zone Liz. On finishing the piece, Gettys told his staff, "I've got the number two Leavenworth graduate in my division and he's stuck out in the boonies as a battalion exec? Bring him up here. I want him as my plans officer."

A division commander has five major staff officers, the G-1 for personnel, the G-2 for intelligence, the G-3 for operations and planning, the G-4 for logistics, and the G-5 for civil affairs, involving relations with civilians. Of the five jobs, the G-3 is the most coveted, since operations are the reason why armies exist. The job usually goes to the fastest burner among lieutenant colonels in a division.

Gettys had already earmarked a hot property, Lieutenant Colonel Richard D. Lawrence, for his recently vacated G-3 spot. But it turned out that Lawrence still had three months to complete as an armored squadron commander, and Gettys found himself in need of a G-3 at once. And so, instead of starting off as plans officer, a G-3 deputy, I was picked by General Gettys over several lieutenant colonels for the G-3 job itself, making me the only major filling that role in Vietnam. Another officer had been considered as interim G-3 before me. But General Gettys's aide, Captain Ron Tumelson, had stuck his neck out with Gettys, telling the general the failings of his initial choice, a bold act that could have destroyed Tumelson's career. Gettys, to his credit, was persuaded by facts, and he took a chance on me, a major he barely knew. I never knew any of this until twenty-five years later when Tumelson wrote to me. The general's decision enormously influenced my career. Overnight, I went from looking after eight hundred men to planning warfare for nearly eighteen thousand troops, artillery units, aviation battalions, and a fleet of 450 helicopters.

The Americal was not a division in the usual organizational sense. Its lineage was honorable enough. It had originally been formed as the 23d Infantry Division in New Caledonia during World War II and christened the Americal—America plus Caledonia. The division distinguished itself in Guadalcanal, Bougainville, and the Philippines campaigns. Except for a brief resurrection in the mid-1950s, the Americal had been deactivated as of December 1945. The name was revived in Vietnam to stitch together three unrelated brigades from different U.S. locations, brigades that had not trained together or even arrived in Vietnam together. Once there, battalions within the brigades were arbitrarily shifted around the country like so many pieces on a checkerboard. The revived Americal lacked tradition, cohesion, and even any future. Once the war ended, the division would be dissolved. Even with these handicaps, it was a good division; but its reputation would be forever tarnished by one of the darker chapters in American military history at a place called My Lai.

Briefing is a performing art. You stand, pointer in hand, before maps and charts, and have a splendid chance to show your stuff, often to your seniors. Not long after taking over as G-3, I headed for the Chu Lai briefing room, located in a Quonset hut, with other map-toting, chart-laden staffers. Inside this functional structure were surprising touches—six plush general officer chairs and a backlit Lucite map board. This day, the Americal was to brief General Creighton Abrams, commander of all U.S. forces in Vietnam.

Abrams was a living legend, revered throughout the Army, the tank commander who punched his way through the German lines to relieve the surrounded 101st Airborne Division at Bastogne during the Battle of the Bulge. His boss at the time, General George Patton, told war correspondents that if they wanted to write about this officer they had better hurry—"He's so good, he isn't going to live long." Abrams was still with us, still all soldier, a man without a duplicitous bone in his body, and blunt as a punch in the nose. His aides had devised a system for decoding their laconic boss. A deep grunt? Abrams was satisfied. An abrupt groan? He was dissatisfied. And if Abe took the cigar out of his mouth, stand by for the blast of a blowtorch. One overworked briefer who had tried to peddle warmed-over intelligence to Abrams had been fired on the spot.

We could practically hear the tension crackling in the hut as we took our seats and waited. Within minutes, General Abrams strode in, and we flew to attention. A nervous General Gettys followed him. The two were longtime buddies, which did not seem to alleviate Gettys's anxiety.

All the briefers who preceded me were lieutenant colonels. Finally, Gettys stood up and said, "Major Powell will now brief." To prepare, I had called on my instructor training from Fort Benning, and my cramming techniques from Fort Leavenworth. I went through the Americal, battalion by battalion, explaining where every outfit was, its state of readiness, and what operations the troops were presently engaged in, and gave an extended forecast over the next several weeks. I used no notes. I had committed the information to memory.

When I finished, I turned to General Abrams and asked, "Sir, are there any questions?" He gave a grunt that I could not decipher as long or short, positive or negative, approving or rejecting. With the briefing over, he simply got up and walked out, with Gettys trailing after him.

A few minutes later, Gettys, having seen Abrams off, returned to the hut where we were milling outside, expectantly. He was grinning. "Abe's happy," Gettys said.

"He is, sir?" I asked. "How could you tell?"

"For one thing, he wanted to know, who's that young major?" Gettys said, putting an arm around my shoulder.

Back in Birmingham, on November 22, 1968, a Sunday morning, Alma was returning to the house she shared with her sister after spending the night at their parents' home. Dangling from the doorknob was a notice that she had a telegram, which she could pick up at the Western Union office. Alma called, but Western Union would not divulge the message over the phone. She went back to the Johnsons to pick up her father for moral support before heading into town to learn the contents of the telegram. It was from the Department of the Army informing her that her husband, Major Colin L. Powell, 083771, had been involved in a helicopter crash. Mail could be addressed to him at the indicated base hospital in Vietnam. Nothing more, and not a word about the nature of my injuries, except that they were minor.

. . .

The week before, Saturday afternoon, November 16, we had been flying west of Quang Ngai in General Gettys's UH-1H, a top-of-the-line helicopter, with only ninety hours logged in the air. The brightness of the day was reflected in the general's sunny mood. I studied him, dressed like any other GI, in jungle fatigues, soft cap, and canvas-and-leather boots, a rotund, amiable man, his broad face set in a smile. Gettys had reason to feel good. In this cat-and-mouse war, with rarely a decisive thrust, his ill-starred Americal Division had scored a clear victory. The day before, the 11th Infantry Brigade had uncovered twenty-nine North Vietnamese Army base camps, including a headquarters and a training post. The 11th had also captured a large cache of weapons and enemy documents. The battalion commander had ordered a landing site hacked out of the jungle, and that was where we were headed. General Gettys wanted to see the battalion's prize.

As we flew along the steep, encroaching hill-sides, the thought struck me that we had a lot of freight aboard one aircraft—the division's two-star commanding general; his chief of staff, Colonel Jack Treadwell (a Medal of Honor recipient); Captain Ron Tumelson, the general's aide; me, the division's G-3; and a four-man crew. I had thought earlier that maybe this landing would be better handled by a small slick piloted by one of those nineteen-year-olds with a safecracker's touch and plenty of experience in shoehorning helos into tight fits. But the general's pilot, Chief Warrant Officer James D. Hannan, was an experienced flier. This was his general, his helo, his landing, and he expected no problem.

We spotted a smoke grenade signaling the site of the hole chopped out of the heavy growth and headed for it. The pilot began his approach to the landing site, realized he was coming in too fast, backed off, and came at it again. On the second pass, he hovered, then began his descent. Bits of snipped-off branches and leaves swirled through the air as we moved down through the trees. Since I was sitting outboard, I could see how little clearance we had, about two feet at each end of the blade. I began to shout, "Pull out!" But it was too late. I watched the pilot struggling against a treacherous backdraft created by the trees, and then, *whack!* At a height of about three stories, the blade struck a tree trunk. One minute we were flying and the next we were dead weight, as the main rotor blades went instantly from 324 rpm to zero. The helo dropped like an elevator with a snapped cable. I reflexively assumed the crash posture, head down, arms locked around my knees. I listened to the engine's futile whine for what seemed an eternity before we smashed into the ground.

Standard procedure calls for getting away from the aircraft as soon as possible, before it catches fire. I released my seat belt and jumped out the door. Ahead of me was the helo's gunner, Private First Class Bob Pyle. We did not get far from the wreck before we realized that others were still on board, none of them moving. Pyle ran back to jimmy open the pilot's door. I climbed back into the hold, noticing for the first time a pain in my ankle. The engine was still grinding away, and smoke started to fill the helo. I found General Gettys, barely conscious, his shoulder at an odd angle and probably broken. I managed to release his seat belt, got him out, and dragged him into the woods. By now, several soldiers on the ground had joined us as we went back for the rest of the victims. I found Jack Treadwell and managed to pull him to safety. I climbed aboard again and heard the pilot moan as PFC Pyle struggled to free him. Ron Tumelson, the general's aide, was slumped over, his head trapped between the radio console and the engine, which had smashed through the fuselage as if it were an eggshell. Tumelson was covered with blood. I saw no sign of life and was sure he was dead. I managed to shove aside the dislodged console and free him. And then I heard him groan. I noticed a dent where the engine had struck his helmet, which had provided just enough protection to save him. I dragged him into the woods with the others. In the end, everyone was rescued, the most seriously injured being the pilot, who suffered a broken back.

When a commanding general's helicopter goes down, other aircraft materialize as if out of nowhere. I looked up to see a swarm of helos circling a landing zone that had not been big enough to accommodate even one without a mishap. Finally, they backed off and made way for a dust-off bird, a medical evacuation helicopter. One by one, we were winched up to the aircraft, swaying helplessly in the breeze, wondering if all eyes watching were necessarily friendly.

Back at the Chu Lai base hospital, x-rays revealed that, in addition to lacerations and bruises, I had a broken ankle. Ordinarily, that meant I would be evacuated. Army medical policy was to ship anybody with broken bones to Japan, since the dampness in our sector discouraged healing. The division, however, was not about to lose a recently acquired G-3 just because he had a cracked bone. The doctors put me in a cast, and I hobbled around as best as I could. I was not as sensitively impaired as my commanding general. General Gettys had been scheduled to meet his wife in Hawaii for R and R and complained to me, "Dammit, Colin, how's a man supposed to do what a woman expects him to do with his arm in a sling?"

My cast lasted a week before it started crumbling. I replaced it with an Ace bandage and went about my business. The doctors warned me that I was being foolish, but the ankle healed in about seven years. It only troubled me if I stepped off a curb at the wrong angle, which produced a sensation similar to being electrocuted. Fortunately, today, it gives me no trouble.

I was about to spend my second Christmas in Vietnam. During the holiday season, Chu Lai reeked of a strong, gamy odor. Gifts from home of smoked salamis and hams from the Hickory Farms mail-order company were all the rage. At first, they were heartily welcomed. Then they started to spill out of the mailroom and the huts and hooches until it seemed we were going to be overcome by smoke inhalation. I have not been able to eat a smoked anything since.

On Christmas Eve, my friends and I went to watch Bob Hope and the troupe he had brought to

212 · COLIN L. POWELL

entertain the forces, the stunning Ann-Margret, Les Brown (and—what else?—his Band of Renown), the pro football star Rosie Grier, and Miss World, Penelope Plummer. That was more like it, war as we remembered it from old newsreels. Afterward, we retired to the officers' club to listen to a Filipino rock group. I particularly remember their rendition of the Patsy Cline hit "I Fall to Pieces," which on Filipino lips had a charm of its own: "Arfo do PZs." And we drank too much. The helicopter pilots drank the most, especially those flying the next day. Many were on their second or third tours. Their casualty rate was high, and the highest risks of all were taken by the crews of the dust-off helos of the Medical Service Corps such as I had recently ridden. To pick up the wounded they had to hover in full view of the enemy and slowly corkscrew down. Every minute they could save resulted in lives saved. We had a near reverence for their courage. For their part, they faced their lot with black-humored fatalism, referring to fellow pilots who went down in flames as "crispy critters."

My distinction as the only major serving as a division G-3 inevitably had to end. Lieutenant Colonel Dick Lawrence completed his six months as a squadron commander and moved up to the G-3 slot Gettys had promised him. Gettys told me that he knew the situation was awkward, since I occasionally had had to overrule Lawrence while I was G-3; nevertheless, he hoped I would stay as Lawrence's deputy. I gladly signed on as his number two, and in the years that followed, Dick became another valued mentor to me.

. . .

Since by January 1969 I was halfway through my tour, I began thinking about my next assignment. I knew what I wanted. I had been approved for the Army's grad school program. The next hurdle was to pass the Graduate Record Examination. I managed to find an Arco-type study guide and, since Chu Lai offered few distractions, spent my evenings devouring this book. One drizzling Saturday morning, I crowded onto a slick that was taking a bunch of short-timers to Da Nang for their return home and made my way to a Quonset hut. There, with an unlikely-looking collection of would-be scholars, I took the test. A couple of months later I got word that I had done well, and I applied for admission to the George Washington University in Washington, D.C. GWU, just across the Potomac River from the Pentagon, had become something of a finishing school for the Washington military establishment. Many officers took degrees in international relations, which seemed appropriate. But at about this time, the Army began steering its personnel toward modern management so that it would have officers ready to enter the computer age. Consequently, I applied to the GWU School of Government and Business Administration, aiming for an M.B.A. This degree had an additional appeal. By now I had over ten years in the Army. And I figured that when my military career ended, I would be more marketable as an M.B.A. than as an expert in Western European political systems.

On January 22, 1969, Army charter flight P2102 touched down at Hickham Field, Hawaii, the military side of Honolulu International Airport. R and R, blessed R and R. I got off the plane, impatient to see my family yet afraid that it was too good to be true. I had arranged for reservations at the Halekulani Hotel, obtained plane tickets for the children as well as Alma, and had a rental car waiting. As I walked down a corridor into the terminal, I could see up ahead families leaning forward, straining to pick out a familiar face. Then I heard a wonderful shriek: "Daddy! Daddy! Daddy!" Little Mike, now almost six, with Linda, age three, toddling behind, came rushing toward me. Each one seized a leg and held on for dear life. The pressure of those small arms around me was one of the most joyous sensations I have ever known.

We did nothing very original over the next few days. We went to the beach. I tried to teach Mike to surf (as if I knew how). We saw the village where the movie *Hawaii* was filmed, and the zoo, and a dolphin show, and the blowhole where the blue waters of the Pacific spurt through the rocks in a timeless geyser. Alma and I went out alone just one night. We managed to find a baby-sitter and took in a luau at Fort De Russy. We went to the International Marketplace to hear Don Ho, who must have sung "Tiny Bubbles" to every soldier who ever made it to Hawaii on R and R. For weeks afterward, the lyric stuck in my mind ("Tiny bubbles, in the wine. Tiny bubbles make you feel fine . . .").

And then it was over. The last night, we put the kids to bed without any fuss, just as if they were home, and Alma and I sat out under the magical

Hawaiian sky. Vietnam was a million miles yet only a plane ride away. I did not talk about the past six months, and Alma did not ask. That is usually the way with career soldiers and wives. Alma, thank God, was not of that breed of service spouses who think they have been commissioned along with the husband and like to talk shop. They know who has been given an accelerated promotion and who has been passed over, who received the choice assignment and who was dead-ended. Alma never cared for that world of career politics. She made a home, raised the kids, kept me happy, and impressed everybody at every post at which we ever served.

What we talked about that night was the children. Mike had had to get used to me the first time I came home from Vietnam. Then, four years later, I was gone again. We were together here in Hawaii for only a few days, and I was leaving again. I was afraid of becoming a here-he-comes-there-he-goes father, and I counted on Alma to provide the extra parental ballast, which, from all evidence, she was doing nicely.

At midnight, an Army bus pulled up outside the hotel, and my brief taste of family life was over.

It was an afternoon in mid-March. I was in my office-hooch when I got word to expect a visitor from the inspector general's staff of MACV, Military Assistance Command Vietnam. In the Army, such news is about as welcome as learning that the IRS intends to audit you. The investigator turned out to be tight-lipped and noncommittal; he never explained the purpose of his visit. He used an old-fashioned reel-to-reel tape recorder as he took my name, rank, position, and duties in the division. No elaboration, just the questions fired off in a Joe Friday monotone. He then asked if I was custodian of the division's operational journals, and I said I was. He asked me to produce the journal for March 1968. I explained that I had not been with the division at that time. "Just get the journal," he said, "and go through that month's entries. Let me know if you find an unusual number of enemy killed on any day."

I sensed he knew what I would find. I started thumbing through the journal, and after a few pages one entry leaped out. On March 16, 1968, a unit of the 11th Brigade had reported a body count of 128 enemy dead on the Batangan Peninsula. In this grinding, grim, but usually unspectacular warfare, that was a high number. "Please read that entry into the tape recorder," the investigator said.

By now, both my curiosity and my guard were up. I asked if he would excuse me while I called the division chief of staff. "Cooperate with him," the chief of staff said firmly. The investigator asked me if I believed the journal accounts to be accurate, and I said they usually were. Then, as he prepared to leave, he asked if I knew Captain Ernest Medina. Yes, I answered, Medina was a member of my tactical operations center. The investigator said he was going to question Medina next. He left, leaving me as mystified as to his purpose as when he'd arrived.

I would not learn until nearly two years later what this visit was all about. By then, I was serving in the Washington area, and was called to appear before a board of inquiry conducted by Lieutenant General William Ray Peers at Fort Belvoir, Virginia. The board wanted me to give a picture of fighting conditions in the Batangan Peninsula in 1968. I knew it had been a hellhole, a rough piece of territory inhabited by VC sympathizers. The French in their day had been driven out of the Batangan Peninsula and stayed out. Every time we sent units there, we could expect dozens of traumatic amputations at the evacuation hospital from mines and booby traps sown by enemy guerrillas and sympathetic peasants, including women, even children.

None of which excuses what happened that March 16, 1968. On that date, a little over three months before I arrived in Vietnam, troops from the 11th Brigade entered the village of Son My on the South China Sea. A platoon headed by First Lieutenant William Calley herded hundreds of old men, women, children, even babies from the hamlet of My Lai into a ditch and shot them. Subsequent investigation revealed that Calley and his men killed 347 people. The 128 enemy "kills" I had found in the journal formed part of the total. A court-martial found Calley guilty of premeditated murder and sentenced him to life in prison. President Richard Nixon, however, intervened, and Calley's sentence was reduced to three years of what amounted to comfortable house arrest. Captain Ernest Medina was also tried on murder and manslaughter charges for permitting the death of some one hundred Vietnamese, but was acquitted. What the taciturn investigator had questioned me about that afternoon would be remembered as the My Lai Massacre.

My Lai was an appalling example of much that had gone wrong in Vietnam. Because the war had dragged on for so long, not everyone commissioned was really officer material. Just as critical, the corps of career noncommissioned officers was being gutted by casualties. Career noncoms form the backbone of any army, and producing them requires years of professional soldiering. In order to fight the war without calling up the reserves, the Army was creating instant noncoms. Shake-and-bake sergeants, we called them. Take a private, give him a little training, shake him once or twice, and pronounce him an NCO. It astonished me how well and heroically some of these green kids performed, assuming responsibility far beyond their years and experience. Still, the involvement of so many unprepared officers and noncoms led to breakdowns in morale, discipline, and professional judgment—and to horrors like My Lai—as the troops became numb to what appeared to be endless and mindless slaughter.

I recall a phrase we used in the field, MAM, for military-age male. If a helo spotted a peasant in black pajamas who looked remotely suspicious, a possible MAM, the pilot would circle and fire in front of him. If he moved, his movement was judged evidence of hostile intent, and the next burst was not in front, but at him. Brutal? Maybe so. But an able battalion commander with whom I had served at Gelnhausen, Lieutenant Colonel Walter Pritchard, was killed by enemy sniper fire while observing MAMs from a helicopter. And Pritchard was only one of many. The kill-or-be-killed nature of combat tends to dull fine perceptions of right and wrong.

My tour was to end in July 1969. Judged solely in professional terms, it was a success. Holding down the G-3 spot for the largest division in Vietnam, as a major, was a rare credit. My efficiency reports continued highly favorable. I received the Legion of Merit, and General Gettys awarded me the Soldier's Medal for my role in the helicopter crash rescue. That was Vietnam as experienced by the career lobe of my brain. And, for a long time, I allowed myself to think only on that side, an officer answering the call, doing his best, "content to fill a soldier's grave."

But as time passed and my perspective enlarged, another part of my brain began examining the experience more penetratingly. I had gone off to Vietnam in 1962 standing on a bedrock of principle and conviction. And I had watched that foundation eroded by euphemisms, lies, and self-deception. The pernicious game-playing that I had first detected in Gelnhausen had been exported to Vietnam during my first tour and had reached its full flowering during my second tour. Consider an expression like KHA, killed by hostile action. It removed some of the sting of the stark, more familiar KIA—killed in action—as though we did not want to upset the folks back home by what really happened in those rice paddies. The distinction was so meaningless that only self-deluding bureaucrats could detect it, and certainly not the poor KHAs. The Marines had fought throughout World War II and Korea as Marine Expeditionary Forces, MEFs. In Vietnam, they were refashioned MAFs, Marine Amphibious Forces. Why? "Expeditionary" raised images of men shipped overseas to fight and die, while you could be holding amphibious exercises off North Carolina. Who were we kidding, except ourselves? Years afterward, after I had become Chairman of the Joint Chiefs of Staff, the Commandant of the Marine Corps, General Alfred M. Gray, threw out that Vietnam-era obfuscation. Marines left the country on military *expeditions*. Al, to his credit, restored MEF to its old standing.

Readiness and training reports in the Vietnam era were routinely inflated to please and conceal rather than to evaluate and correct. Like the children of Lake Wobegon, everybody came out "above average." The powers that be seemed to believe that by manipulating words, we could change the truth. We had lost touch with reality. We were also deluded by technology. The enemy was primitive, and we were the most technologically advanced nation on earth. It therefore should be no contest. Thus, out of the McNamara shop came miracles like the "people sniffer," a device that could detect concentrations of urine on the ground from an airplane (brought to you by the same people who later came up with Agent Orange). If the urine was detected in likely enemy territory, we now had an artillery target. But woe to any innocent peasants or water buffalos that happened to relieve themselves in the wrong place. The people sniffer was of a piece with McNamara's Line, a series of electronic sensors strung across the country that were going to alert us whenever an enemy force began moving down the Ho Chi Minh Trail, an idea stillborn.

The Legion of Merit I received? It might have meant more to me in a war where medals were not distributed so indiscriminately. I remember once, as division G-3, attending a battalion change-of-command ceremony at one firebase where the departing CO was awarded three Silver Stars, the nation's third-highest medal for valor, plus a clutch of other medals, after a tour lasting six months. He had performed ably, at times heroically. He was popular with his men. Yet, the troops had to stand there and listen to an overheated description of a fairly typical performance. Awards were piled on to a point where writing the justifying citations became a minor art form. The departing battalion commander's "package," a Silver Star, a Legion of Merit, and Air Medals just for logging helicopter time, became almost standard-issue. You accepted the package because everyone else did. These wholesale awards diminished the achievements of real heros—privates or colonels—who had performed extraordinary acts of valor. I remember looking at the faces of the troops the day of the three Silver Stars and thinking, this is insane, and we have brought these young soldiers here to witness the insanity. What lessons are we passing on to them? That bull works? A corrosive careerism had infected the Army; and I was part of it.

Dark episodes like My Lai resulted, in part, because of the military's obsession with another semi-fiction, the "body count," that grisly yardstick produced by the Vietnam War. The 11th Infantry Brigade had actually been awarded a Special Commendation for 128 "enemy" killed at My Lai, before the truth came out. The Army, under Pentagon pressure to justify the country's investment in lives and billions, desperately needed something to measure. What military objectives could we claim in this week's situation report? A hill? A valley? A hamlet? Rarely. Consequently, bodies became the measure. But body counts were tricky. The press knew precisely the casualties on our side. They simply counted the caskets going out. Twenty caskets, twenty KHAs in the latest firefight. What do we have to show for it? How many of the enemy fell? Finding out was not easy. The VC and NVA did not use caskets. They were also skilled at breaking off contact and taking their dead with them. We might have used weapons captured as a measure. But you have to produce the weapons, and reporters can count. Enemy bodies did not have to be brought back. Every night, the company would make a tally. "How many did your platoon get?" "I don't know. We saw two for sure." "Well, if you saw two, there were probably eight. So let's say ten." Counting bodies became a macabre statistical competition. Companies were measured against companies, battalions against battalions, brigades against brigades. Good commanders scored high body counts. And good commanders got promoted. If your competition was inflating the counts, could you afford not to?

The enemy actually was taking horrendous casualties. But it made little difference. As one military analyst put it, divide each side's casualties by the economic cost of producing them. Then multiply by the political cost of sustaining them. As long as your enemy was willing to pay that price, body counts meant nothing. This enemy was obviously prepared to pay, and unsportingly refused to play the game by our scorekeeping. We were forever trying to engage the NVA in a knockout battle—a Vietnamese Waterloo, an Iwo Jima, an Inchon—but the NVA refused to cooperate. No matter how hard we struck, NVA troops would melt into their sanctuaries in the highlands or into Laos, refit, regroup, and come out to fight again. We had our sanctuaries too, stretching from the South China Sea all the way back to the U.S.A. The two forces joined to kill each other between the mountains and coastal plains of Vietnam. Every Friday night, our side toted up the body count for the week, then we went to bed and started all over again the next day.

At the end of my first tour, I had guessed that finishing the job would take half a million men. Six years later, during my second tour, we reached the peak, 543,400, and it was still not enough. Given the terrain, the kind of war the NVA and VC were fighting, and the casualties they were willing to take, no defensible level of U.S. involvement would have been enough.

I remember a soldier, while I was still battalion exec, who had stepped on a mine. One leg hung by a shred, and his chest had been punctured. We loaded him onto a slick and headed for the nearest evac hospital at Duc Pho, about fifteen minutes away. He was just a kid, and I can never forget the expression on his face, a mixture of astonishment, fear, curiosity, and, most of all, incomprehension. He kept trying to speak, but the words would not come out. His eyes seemed to be saying, why? I did not have an answer, then or now. He died in my arms before we could reach Duc Pho.

I recently reread Bernard Fall's book on Vietnam, *Street Without Joy*. Fall makes painfully clear that we had almost no understanding of what we had gotten ourselves into. I cannot help thinking that if President Kennedy or President Johnson had spent a quiet weekend at Camp David reading that perceptive book, they would have returned to the White House Monday morning and immediately started to figure out a way to extricate us from the quicksand of Vietnam. In the years between my first and second tours, the logic of Captain Hieu's explanation—the base is here to protect the airstrip, which is here to supply the base—had not changed, only widened. We're here because we're here because . . .

War should be the politics of last resort. And when we go to war, we should have a purpose that our people understand and support; we should mobilize the country's resources to fulfill that mission and then go in to win. In Vietnam, we had entered into a halfhearted half-war, with much of the nation opposed or indifferent, while a small fraction carried the burden.

I witnessed as much bravery in Vietnam as I expect to see in any war. I am proud of my service in the Americal Division. We had our bright moments and outstanding soldiers. Another officer who served in that division was a lieutenant colonel named

H. Norman Schwarzkopf. Norm Schwarzkopf, I, and so many others who went on to major military responsibility must have carried away something useful from the experience. I am proud of the way American soldiers answered the call in a war so poorly conceived, conducted, and explained by their country's leaders. Dozens of my friends died in that war. As small a circle as the CCNY Pershing Rifles lost its third member in Vietnam in 1968, John Young. All this heroism and sacrifice are precisely the point: you do not squander courage and lives without clear purpose, without the country's backing, and without full commitment.

I particularly condemn the way our political leaders supplied the manpower for that war. The policies—determining who would be drafted and who would be deferred, who would serve and who would escape, who would die and who would live— were an antidemocratic disgrace. I can never forgive a leadership that said, in effect: These young men— poorer, less educated, less privileged—are expendable (someone described them as "economic cannon fodder"), but the rest are too good to risk. I am angry that so many of the sons of the powerful and well placed and so many professional athletes (who were probably healthier than any of us) managed to wangle slots in Reserve and National Guard units. Of the many tragedies of Vietnam, this raw class discrimination strikes me as the most damaging to the ideal that all Americans are created equal and owe equal allegiance to their country.

In time, just as I came to reexamine my feelings about the war, the Army, as an institution, would do the same thing. We accepted that we had been sent to pursue a policy that had become bankrupt. Our political leaders had led us into a war for the one-size-fits-all rationale of anticommunism, which was only a partial fit in Vietnam, where the war had its own historical roots in nationalism, anticolonialism, and civil strife beyond the East-West conflict. Our senior officers knew the war was going badly. Yet they bowed to groupthink pressure and kept up pretenses, the phony measure of body counts, the comforting illusion of secure hamlets, the inflated progress reports. As a corporate entity, the military failed to talk straight to its political superiors or to itself. The top leadership never went to the Secretary of Defense or the President and said, "This war is unwinnable the way we are fighting it." Many of my generation, the career captains, majors, and lieutenant colonels seasoned in that war, vowed that when our turn came to call the shots, we would not quietly acquiesce in halfhearted warfare for half-baked reasons that the American people could not understand or support. If we could make good on that promise to ourselves, to the civilian leadership, and to the country, then the sacrifices of Vietnam would not have been in vain.

On June 15, 1969, with a few weeks left in my tour, I received a letter from the George Washington University. I had been accepted for the fall class in the School of Government and Business Administration. Earlier in the day, I had been out at one of the LZs, watching a rifle company return from patrol. The troops wearily climbed the hill, leaning into the weight of the rucksacks on their backs, M-16s slung in front of them, another day crossed off. That was another irony of the war in Vietnam. When the calendar hit a certain date, you just walked away from it.

On my return to the States, Alma and I had planned to spend a few days by ourselves before joining the kids and my in-laws in Birmingham. We arranged to stay in Atlanta, where Alma was to pick me up at the airport. I had written ahead telling her what hairdo, what kind of dress, and what colors I hoped she would wear, orange and yellow. I had nourished a fantasy in my imagination, and I wanted it fulfilled when I stepped off that plane. Alma did not fail me. We drove into town and checked into our hotel. That night, I fell asleep unfashionably early. Try as she might, Alma could not keep me awake. She kept tugging at me, saying I had to watch television because the astronauts were walking on the moon! It was July 20, 1969. I was exhausted, not just from jet lag, but deep in my bones, sleeping off the emotional and physical fatigue of a year in Vietnam. We managed to spend a day and a half by ourselves, and by then Alma knew what I wanted more than anything else, to get home to see my children.

7 ★ *White House Fellow*

WHEN I HUNG up my uniform and started classes at the George Washington University in Washington, I was reentering a world I had been out of for eleven years. I had lived in the cocoon of the military, wearing its uniform, guided by its rules, and associating almost exclusively with its members, since leaving college. Now I was, for all practical purposes, living as a civilian.

Alma and I immediately started house hunting. We had never owned our own home. So far, we had lived in transient military quarters, camped on the doorsteps of friends and relatives, or rented apartments on the fringes of Army posts. We had no fear over what we were about to do; it was just a question of which mansion we chose. During my tours overseas, we had managed to put away nearly $8,000. Back in Birmingham, the finest homes went for $30,000 to $35,000, well within our range. We found a real estate agent and started hunting through the northern Virginia suburbs where military families tend to gravitate. After about the tenth cramped three-bedroom look-alike, I asked the agent, "Is this what thirty-five thousand dollars buys around here?" Welcome, he told us, to the world of Washington real estate. A friend tipped us off to a new bedroom community, called Dale City, going up in Woodbridge, Virginia. Not particularly prestigious. Not much distinction between the houses. And every last tree had been bulldozed. But the developer was offering space, blessed space—five bedrooms, three baths—all for $31,520. We bought in Dale City, at 14605 DeSoto Court, on a VA mortgage for $20 down and $259 a month.

Soon the word was out on the New York telegraph: "You hear? Colin's bought himself a big new house—in Washington, D.C." "So soon?" "Can he carry it?" We had barely moved in before the relatives descended to see the house, to check on Colin's judgment, and, as long as they had a place to stay, to tour the nation's capital.

I underwent a crisis of confidence during my first semester at GWU. The Army had allotted eighteen months for me to complete an M.B.A. in data processing. I checked in with my department chairman before starting classes, a fine gentleman, Dr. Jack McCarthy. As Professor McCarthy leafed through my college record, I heard him mutter, "Hmm, no math, hmm, no statistics, hmm, no economics." He picked up a phone and got in touch with the Infantry Branch. I heard McCarthy say that he saw nothing in my academic past that would suggest success in pursuing an M.B.A. My heart sank, until he added, "At least not in eighteen months." He went on, "Yes, I know. Fine record at the Infantry School, Command and General Staff College, but they're not graduate school." Give Major Powell two years and two summer schools and there was hope for him, McCarthy recommended. Fortunately for me, the Army approved.

It was true; I was rusty at academic scholarship. I found the work daunting, and was not relieved by the fact that, at age thirty-two, I was the oldest student in most classes. Even the half-dozen other officers going through with me had an edge; they were administrative and finance types to whom economics and computers were already familiar terrain. As the professors plunged us into courses such as statistical analysis and calculus—I had already flunked the latter at CCNY—they might as well have been speaking Swahili to me. I began to experience the Impostor Syndrome. What am I doing here? I don't belong here. They made a mistake in admitting me.

Between classes, students hung out at the student union cafeteria, where we drank coffee and played cards. And there I made a discovery. In the class of the blind, the one-eyed student is king. Not only my fellow officers but most of the business majors were as bewildered as I was. My proctor, Dr. Marvin Wofsey, Professor of Management, took me aside and lifted my spirits. He had complete faith in me, he said. And, to my astonishment, my first-semester grades were straight A's.

That was how it went, until I struck a reef, a course called Computer Logic. For the final exam, we were to draw a flow chart of a software program showing how the computer made decisions. I was back again trying to visualize a cone intersecting a plane in space. I pulled a D in the midterm examination but managed to salvage a B in the course, probably through divine intervention.

I was eagerly scanning the *Army Times* those days to see who was going to be promoted to lieutenant colonel. I was on the promotion list, but my sequence number had yet to come up. I was anxious to make the jump not only professionally but financially. It meant a boost from $12,999 to $16,179 per annum at a time when I was taking home about $900 a month and sweating out that $259 mortgage payment. Early in July, I opened the *Army Times* and there were the numbers of those who would be promoted to lieutenant colonel next month, and my number appeared. It was not an early promotion this time; still, I was doing fine, a couple of years ahead of the pack. I managed to track down a captain at the Military District of Washington and asked him how I went about getting formally promoted. "Damned if I know, sir," he said.

I thought there ought to be some ceremonial fuss. I solved the problem by assembling the troops in the family room at 14605 DeSoto Court. Alma was out, and I was baby-sitting. I sat on the floor amid a jumble of toys while Michael Powell, now age seven, pinned a silver leaf on my sport shirt. The witnesses were Linda, five, and our most recent arrival, Annemarie Powell, watching with minimal interest from her infant seat.

Annemarie had been born two months before, on May 20. I remember vividly the day Alma came home from the hospital with that tiny bundle. I used a movie camera I had picked up at a PX in Vietnam for $10 to record the moment for posterity. As Alma got out of the car, Mike rushed up, excited and curious. Linda took a perfunctory peek at the newest princess, spun on her heels, and left, a fairly common sisterly relationship that would last for the next twenty years.

I thought Annemarie was absolutely beautiful. And since graduate school gave me plenty of free time, I liked carrying her in my arms up and down DeSoto Court, waiting for our neighbors to come out and admire her. We now had three healthy, handsome children and decided not to strain the world's population further.

. . .

That fall, I was back at GWU, a professional soldier in college at the height of the antiwar movement. It was an odd sensation, passing by fraternity houses where sheets painted with the peace symbol and antiwar slogans fluttered from windows and soapbox orators condemned the war I had fought in. As I walked around in my chino slacks and sport shirt, I felt like a disguised plant in the enemy camp. My brushes with the protesters were peripheral, however, since there were few flag burners among M.B.A. candidates taking courses such as Marketing Management and Business Accounting. Like me, my classmates were less concerned with politics than with boning up for the next exam and finishing their master's theses. They were the yuppies of tomorrow, though the term had yet to be coined.

In my final semester in grad school, Washington exploded. On April 24, over 200,000 opponents of the war swarmed over Capitol Hill to pressure Congress to get us out of Vietnam. I followed the smell of tear gas all the way from GWU to the Capitol. There I watched "Vietnam Veterans Against the War," hundreds of them, flinging their ribbons and medals at the building. I understood their bitterness. Since I had left Vietnam, over five thousand more Americans had died in that muddled conflict. But my heart could never be with these demonstrators. I still believed in an America where medals ought to be a source of pride, not shame, where the uniform should be respected, not reviled, and where the armed forces were an honorable part of the nation, not a foreign body to be rejected by it.

. . .

I did not bother to attend my graduation that May. Given the antiwar mood on campus and my status as a married man with three children, I felt no need for pomp, circumstance, or further protests. I picked up my degree at the dean's office. In two years of graduate school, I had earned all A's and the lone B in Computer Logic. My mentor, Dr. Wofsey, urged me to stay on for a Ph.D., which the Army might well have underwritten. But I had a pretty clear picture of myself. I was a good student, but no scholar, and a soldier before a student. I was eager to get back to the Army.

The Pentagon forms part of that interlocking web of power, comprising the White House, the Congress, federal agencies, the courts, journalists, and lobbyists, referred to as "inside the Beltway." I reported with my M.B.A. to the Pentagon in July 1971, assigned to A-Vice, the office of the assistant vice chief of staff of the Army. The holder of that position, Lieutenant General William E. DePuy, was a physically small yet dominating figure who had forged a reputation as one of the toughest generals to come out of Vietnam, famed for firing people left and right. He once explained the reason behind his severity: "I watched incompetent commanders get young Americans killed in World War II." He told new arrivals, "You may be competent on your terms, but if you're not competent on my terms, I'm going to get rid of you. You may do well somewhere else, but it won't be under me."

By now, President Nixon had started withdrawing U.S. forces to "Vietnamize" the war. As this withdrawal went on, a *sub rosa* document began influencing military thinking, a survey conducted by the Army War College in Carlisle, Pennsylvania, of 450 lieutenant colonels, nearly all of whom had served in Vietnam. The survey results were like dynamite. The respondents blasted the Army for not facing its failures. The most devastating attack was on the integrity of the senior leadership. The officers surveyed indicted phony readiness reports, rampant careerism, old-boy assignments, inflated awards, fictitious body counts—the whole facade of illusion and delusion. Their leaders had let them down, and they said so. As the final report put it: "There is widespread feeling that the Army has generated an environment that rewards relatively insignificant, short-term indicators of success, and disregards or discourages the growth of long-term qualities of moral strength. . . ."

The authors of the report did not try to find scapegoats outside the Army: "There is no direct evidence that external fiscal, political, sociological, or managerial influences are the primary causative factors of this less than optimum climate. Neither does the public reaction to the Vietnam War, the rapid expansion of the Army, nor the current antimilitary syndrome stand out as a significant reason for deviations from the level of professional behavior the Army acknowledges as its attainable ideal." The Army had created its own mess, and the report made no bones about who was ultimately responsible: "Change, therefore, must be instituted from the top of the Army."

The Carlisle survey leaked out and raised a ruckus. It was not, however, brushed aside. It was acted on by generals like William Westmoreland, George Forsythe, Bernard Rogers, Creighton Abrams, Walter "Dutch" Kerwin, and Bruce Palmer. My new boss, General DePuy, stood in the front rank of these reformers. He was not happy with our doctrine, structure, or leadership or the ethical climate of the Army in the wake of the Vietnam debacle. He had nothing but disdain for the careerist games that had infected the military. This three-star general had assigned himself no less a task than remaking, or at least rethinking, the role and structure of the entire U.S. Army. To do so, he had gathered around him the sharpest lieutenant colonels he could find, and had set them up as his personal brain trust.

I fully expected to spend my time in A-Vice installing computer systems, since that was the main skill the Army had sent me to grad school to learn. Our lives, however, turn on chance. On reporting to the Pentagon, I was interviewed by a brigadier general heading the Management Information Directorate. He kept me waiting half an hour, then kept calling me "Fowler," even after I politely corrected him. All he wanted to talk about was Washington real estate and the money to be made in it. I was resigned to my fate. Given the education the Army had financed, I glumly concluded that here was where I belonged.

I was rescued by an impressive officer, Major General Herbert J. McChrystal, Jr., who ran the Planning and Programming Analysis Directorate, a part of

DePuy's elite. I was summoned to the third floor, sixth corridor, "Army Country," to see McChrystal's deputy, Colonel Francis G. "Goose" Gosling. Gosling told me he had studied my record and did not think I should be drawing computer flow charts. I ought to be up here helping General DePuy design tomorrow's Army. The choice was between a pompous, inconsiderate time server and men of vision. I went from Gosling's office directly to Infantry Branch and begged to be saved from the clutches of the former and delivered into the hands of the latter. The Infantry Branch went along. Thus, the Army was spared an almost certainly mediocre computer hacker, and I was exposed at a key point in my career to the Army's best and brightest.

I was assigned a cubicle and, after a time, began working with General DePuy himself. As often happens, the reputation proved more fierce than the man. Bill DePuy simply could not stand the slipshod or the second-rate, and as long as that was not what you delivered, he treated subordinates well. He thought I showed communicating ability and put me to work on his speeches.

One day early in 1972, I was invited to attend a hush-hush meeting in the general's office. He was seated at one end of a long conference table with a handful of officers, including Herb McChrystal; my immediate superior, Colonel John P. Chandler; and a sharp office neighbor, Lieutenant Colonel A. A. "Tony" Smith. The door was closed, voices subdued, atmosphere clandestine. DePuy quickly got to the point. The Army's pullout from Vietnam was accelerating. The failure of the war had soured the country on the military. Congress was tightening military spending. We had to look reality straight in the eye, DePuy warned, and anticipate the worst. After more bleak analysis, he said, "Powell, I want you to take a couple of bright guys, go off into a corner, and start thinking the unthinkable. I want you to figure out how we would structure a five-hundred-thousand-man army."

We were all astonished. Considering that in Vietnam alone the military had had 543,000 troops at the height of the war, considering that there were 1.6 million presently in the Army, considering that it had not been as small as 500,000 since 1940, this reduction seemed draconian. Was this the strength the general expected to emerge? someone asked. No, he said, but it was the force he wanted to be ready for, just in case. Security was vital. Not a word of what was said this day was to go beyond this room.

I went off to my corner, working principally with Tony Smith, and we designed an absolute rock-bottom force called the "Base Army." Inevitably, our work leaked to senior officers. Terror struck the Pentagon. Suppose the country came to believe that it *could* actually get by on a 500,000-man army? Military life could become stark. The Base Army was shelved and never saw the light of day.

Still, no experience is ever a total loss. Just as the Army retrenched in the wake of Vietnam, all of the armed forces would have to contract after the Cold War ended. When I faced this reality as Chairman of the Joint Chiefs of Staff, I had already completed my graduate education in force-cutting twenty years before under Bill DePuy.

General DePuy taught me something invaluable about holding on to one's core of individuality in a profession marked by uniformity and the subordination of self. We were flying back late one night from a speech the general had delivered at Fort Leavenworth. We were alone in a small Air Force jet, one of those moments when rank dissolves and two men are just atoms in the universe. This head-to-toe soldier, this military paragon, was telling me that an officer had to withhold a part of himself from the service. "Never become so consumed by your career," he told me, "that nothing is left that belongs only to you and your family." We had to keep some part separate and inviolable. "Don't allow your profession," he concluded, "to become the whole of your existence." I remember thinking at the time of something the staff had observed. None of us had ever seen the inside of General DePuy's home. Now I understood why.

In some degree, I was already living by Bill DePuy's philosophy. Few of my Pentagon companions knew that I served as senior warden of St. Margaret's Episcopal Church of Woodbridge, or that I taught fifth-grade Sunday school there. These activities began soon after we had settled into Dale City. One day, Alma and I had been driving around, reconnoitering the new neighborhood, when we spotted, on a hill, a simple Episcopal church. It was called St. Margaret's, the same name as my boyhood Bronx church. We became communicants of St. Margaret's. I worked my way up from junior to senior warden, Alma became president of the altar guild, and Michael and Linda served as acolytes. Like Luther and Arie before us, we helped organize church bazaars, pancake suppers, and the thrift shop. I became an ecclesiastical financier, soliciting the congregation as head of the every-member canvass, our church fund-raising drive.

I once tried to sell the church. Our priest, the Reverend Rodney L. Caulkins, was a popular pastor, and his flock was growing so fast that St. Margaret's was practically bursting at the seams. The church sat on twelve acres of prime suburban real estate, which a developer wanted to buy to put up a shopping center. He offered us a handsome price. Father Caulkins and I knew that with that kind of money, we could build a bigger, better church somewhere nearby to accommodate the congregation's growth. The vestrymen approved the sale. The parishioners voted yes. The bishop approved. The developer came up with the earnest money. But just as I was attached to the old 1928 prayer book, we had members attached to the old church, though "old," in a burgeoning suburb, is a relative term. St. Margaret's, an A-frame structure, had been built only ten years before. An elderly parishioner owned a small piece of land that we needed for access to Route 1 to make the property commercially viable, and the old-timers got to her. They won her promise not to sell the parcel and thereby outmaneuvered the Young Turks. The opponents' clinching argument was that they would never follow St. Margaret's to a new site. They would shift to Pohick near Mount Vernon, which boasted an Anglican church dating from George Washington's time. Score one for the traditionalists. No sale for Powell and the preacher. St. Margaret's is still at its old location and still thriving.

One summer, the vestrymen decided to go on a retreat at a conference center near Richmond. Quiet contemplation and the luxury of examining the meaning of life were new to me. I enjoyed it, and so did the others, until, more quickly than expected, we were soul-searched out. On the second night, one of the brethren said, "Anybody got a deck of cards?" Thus was born the St. Margaret's poker club, a biweekly game that started for pennies and reached a point where a plunger could drop $10 in a night. The poker club made Father Caulkins uncomfortable and sparked a theological debate. Was cardplaying a proper pursuit for vestrymen? More important, should we cut the pot with the church? In the end, we decided to respect the separation of church and state. There was no split.

At this time, I was driving a rusty white 1963 Chevy Bel Air, bought from Alma's uncle Charles Smith for $88. Alma hated to be seen in this junker. One Sunday morning, I got up early and went to People's Drug Store and bought a can of white latex house paint. Before anybody was up, I had the job done. I woke up Alma and brought her outside. She was thrilled. The car looked new. You had to come within six feet before you could see the brushstrokes.

Shortly afterward, the poker club volunteered to paint Father Caulkins's rectory. The day was hot and muggy. We had brought beer along to salve parched throats. I was painting away in the back of the house when I noticed it was suspiciously quiet out front. I went to take a look, and there were my fellow vestrymen slapping red paint on my white car! They had finished a door and a half before I caught them. I blithely went on driving the new two-tone; but Alma would have none of it. There was nothing to do but give the Chevy a second coat of People's latex white.

During this period of our lives, we crystallized as a family in our own right, without the props of the military. We turned to public schools instead of on-post schools; we shopped at civilian stores, not the PX; and we lived in our own home, not military housing. And at the heart of this life stood our church. I was following in my father's footsteps, counting the collection and depositing it in the bank; Alma was following in her and my mother's foot-steps, working on rummage sales and the altar guild. I watched Mike and Linda assisting at mass, and saw myself in my cassock waving the incense burner before the altar on Kelly Street. The tradition had been passed to the next generation, from one St. Mar-garet's to another, like an endless stream.

One day I was wandering through the corridors of the Pentagon when I heard a voice call out, "Come over here. I want to talk to you." I turned to see a black colonel. At that time, you could circle the Pentagon's five rings all day long without seeing any black offi-cers, much less a full colonel. I went over to a stocky, distinguished-looking man who spoke with direct authority. "How come you haven't checked in yet?" he asked.

"Checked in? To what, sir?" I answered.

He introduced himself as Bobby G. Burke, gave me his address, and said, "You and your wife be at my home Saturday night. Eight o'clock." With that, he left. That was my introduction to the Rocks.

Roscoe "Rock" Cartwright had been a black brigadier general, following in the paths of Generals B. O. Davis and Daniel "Chappy" James. Cartwright and his wife had been killed in the crash of a commercial jetliner shortly before I reported to Washington. A group of black officers in the Washington area had taken a leaf from the white power structure; with Bob Burke as their leader, they had formed an old-boys network. Originally, they called themselves the No Name Club. But after Rock Cartwright's death, they had rechristened themselves the Rocks.

Alma and I met them and their wives that Saturday night at Colonel Burke's home. Most of the officers were older than I was. Most had peaked professionally, lacking the breaks early on that I was now getting. Still, they wanted to help young black officers up the career ladder, give them the inside dope on assignments good and bad, tell them about commanders able or incompetent, and talk up promising candidates to the right people. The Rocks also went to colleges to pass on their experiences to promising black ROTC cadets. They awarded an annual prize to the best ROTC cadet at historically black colleges. And sometimes they did nothing more than provide a sympathetic ear. They had bloodied their heads against the walls of prejudice, and now they wanted the next generation to climb onto their shoulders and reach the top.

The spirit of the Rocks appealed to me. They looked out for me along the way, and, in turn, I have tried to spot young black military talent and help these officers realize their potential. Blacks have probably looked after each other better in the military than in almost any other American institution, and I think we offer a model to the rest of the black community.

The Rocks had good times too. Our major social event has been the annual Soul Food Dinner, or, as Alma calls it, "the heart attack special." The social life was the same as at Fort Leavenworth, people getting together out of an affinity, in this case, cultural, and no different from bowlers or dentists enjoying each other's company. When blacks go off in a corner for their kind of music or dancing, I'm tempted to say to my white friends, "Don't panic, we're just having fun."

There may be one moment in our lives we can look back on later and say that, for good or ill, it was the turning point. For me, that day came in November 1971, while I was still in General DePuy's office. A major in the Infantry Branch called to tell me he was sending over an eight-page application for me to fill out by that weekend. An application for what? I asked. For a White House Fellowship. I had no idea what he was talking about, and after he explained, I said that I was not interested. I was already in one of the most prestigious and promising offices in the Pentagon. I was not looking for a detour. Besides, the idea of my becoming a White House Fellow seemed farfetched, especially since, at thirty-five, I was right up against the program's age limit.

The major made clear that Infantry Branch was not asking me. It was ordering me. The then Secretary of Defense, Melvin Laird, had been displeased because so few military candidates were applying, and consequently the branch had combed the personnel files looking for prospects. I had been drafted. I filled out the forms, provided the required references, met the deadline, and promptly forgot about the matter. I was one of over fifteen hundred applicants.

The White House Fellows program had been the brainchild of John W. Gardner, while he was serving as Secretary of Health, Education and Welfare. Gardner's idea was to expose young comers, particularly from the private sector, to the federal government at the highest level. The goal was to give future American leaders a better appreciation of how public policy was shaped and how their government operated. Gardner had sold his idea to President Lyndon Johnson, and by now the White House Fellows program had been under way for seven years. Alumni eventually included CEOs of major corporations, leaders in the professions, outstanding academics, and a healthy sprinkling of military officers. The program proved so effective that some Fellows, having had a taste of Washington, did not want to leave. They ran for Congress or managed to come back through appointments to high-level federal posts.

The key question on the application asked why we wanted to be White House Fellows. I did not particularly want to be one. Nevertheless, I had given the best answer I could. Because of the controversy over Vietnam, the American military had become alienated from its own people, which struck me as unhealthy in a democracy. Consequently, along with learning how the government worked, I wanted the civilian world to see that military officers did not have horns. How far that gulf had widened was brought home to me in June 1972 when CCNY abolished ROTC. The old drill hall, my home for four years, was torn down. From a high of fourteen hundred students, only eighty-one turned out for ROTC in its final year, as interest in the military hit rock bottom. This collapse saddened me, and not only because of sentimental associations. In a country where civilian control of the military is fundamental, I found it unfortunate to have this source of citizen officers reduced.

A few weeks after applying for the White House Fellowship, I received word that I had survived the first cut. I was one of 130 applicants invited to be interviewed. I had to start taking this program seriously. Subsequently, the list was pared to thirty-three finalists, and I was still in the running. The pressure was on. Word had leaked out to the clan that "Colin is going to the White House!" "That's right. Gonna help the President." What if I failed now? I could hear the murmuring: "What do you suppose he did wrong?" "This is a scandal for the family."

On a May afternoon, I boarded a bus with the other finalists in front of the old Civil Service Build-

ing, headed for Airlie House, a posh estate near War-
renton, Virginia, that had been converted into a convention center. There we were to be prodded, poked,
and pinched for the next three days in the final selection process. Seventeen of us would survive. On the
bus we were handed an information packet that
included biographies of each candidate, our first
opportunity to size up the competition. I took a seat
and was flipping through the packet when a young
black man sat next to me. He introduced himself as
James E. Bostic, Jr., from South Carolina. I glanced at
his résumé—first black to get a Ph.D. from Clemson
University, in chemistry. At age twenty-four,
youngest of the White House Fellow finalists. "What
am I doing in this league?" I said to Bostic. He looked
at me, apparently considering my rank and advanced
years, and seemed to be wondering the same thing. I
learned on the ride out that Jim Bostic was one of several children from a poor Southern family, most of
whom worked as laborers. Somebody had spotted
something special in Jim, and mentors, black and
white, had helped him fulfill a potential that might
easily have withered from neglect.

Once we were installed at Airlie House, the
atmosphere fell somewhere between a fraternity rush
party and a police interrogation. We were scheduled
into a rotating series of interviews where we faced
"commissioners," who were impressive and occasionally tough. Their caliber is suggested by one
whom I remember vividly, Milton Friedman, Nobel
Prize winner in economics. Their questioning was
deliberately provocative, designed as much to judge

our poise and character as to find out what we knew. I remember one young candidate cooing, "Dr. Friedman, I was so impressed by *A Theoretical Framework for Monetary Analysis.*" "Really," Friedman said. "What was it about it that impressed you?" Dead silence. The poor guy had apparently not prepped for this moment beyond learning the titles of Friedman's books.

The final interview took place on a Sunday evening. The directors had devised a fairly fiendish way of delivering the verdicts. Sometime in the middle of the night, a note would be slipped under our doors telling us if we had made the grade. In the meantime, we were free for some unstructured sociability. Among the other military candidates, I had become friendly with Bob Baxter, John Fryer, Don Stukel, and Lee Nunn, Jr., from a distinguished Kentucky political family. All of us were accustomed to being graded, and we had faced tests more lethal than being judged for a high-class internship. And so we stayed up late partying, and by the time I got back to my room, there was the note. "Congratulations! It gives me great pleasure to inform you that you have been selected by the President's Commission to serve as a 1972–73 White House Fellow. Sincerely, Arthur E. Dewey, Director."

The next morning, we reboarded the bus for a visit to the White House, for most of us a powerful and moving first. When the visit ended, it was back to planet Earth. I got into my '63 Bel Air for the long drive back to Dale City. On the corner of Pennsylvania Avenue and 18th Street, I saw a little boy lost, Jim

Bostic, who had also been picked, standing alone apparently with no place to go. I scooped him up and brought him home, where he and my family promptly hit it off. Jim went on to a brilliant business career with the Georgia-Pacific Corporation. I served as best man at his marriage to Edie Howard, the daughter of a military trailblazer, Colonel Edward Howard, who had graduated from West Point in 1949, soon after the services were racially integrated. Jim Bostic became the younger brother I never had, and we have remained fast friends for over twenty years.

As I prepared to begin the fellowship, I said my goodbyes to General DePuy, General McChrystal, and other friends on the A-Vice staff. If good things were to come out of the Army over the next several years, they would result, in no small measure, from the vision and drive of the remarkable DePuy and his team. I can suggest the quality of the people around him by noting that some of the lieutenant colonels in his orbit went on to make four-star general. They included Max Thurman, the soldier par excellence, a thinker and leader before whom we all stood in awe, who became commander in chief of the Southern Command; Lou Menetrey, who became commander of U.S. Forces in Korea; Fred Mahaffey, on his way to becoming the Army Chief of Staff until felled by a brain tumor at the age of fifty-two; and Carl Vuono, who did become Army Chief of Staff.

I knew where I wanted to spend my year as a White House Fellow—at an agency whose very name would cause most eyelids to droop, OMB, the Office of Management and Budget. I knew from my M.B.A. courses and my time in the Pentagon that budgets are to organizations what blood is to the circulatory system. And OMB had its hand on every department's jugular. It is one of the least understood yet most powerful federal agencies in Washington.

At OMB, I was interviewed by a small, wiry, engaging dynamo named Frank Carlucci, the deputy to the director, Caspar Weinberger. Carlucci was already making his mark among Beltway insiders. As a young career Foreign Service officer he had been stabbed while helping to put down a riot in Zaire. Later, the versatile onetime diplomat had helped salvage a foundering relief effort when floods struck Pennsylvania.

I was accepted as the OMB White House Fellow and soon met another member of the Weinberger team, William Howard Taft IV, a grandson of the twenty-seventh President of the United States. Taft, Weinberger's executive assistant, was not the sort of person I had encountered in the Army. Will was an erudite figure, as interested in the classics as in the machinations of government.

I spent the first four months parked in an OMB branch outpost, the New Executive Office Building, as contrasted to the main offices in the Old EOB, the magnificent nineteenth-century fortress next to the White House. I started out performing a makework job that actually turned out to be stimulating, even useful. President Franklin D. Roosevelt once observed that the federal bureaucracy was a huge beast: you kicked it in the tail and two years later it felt the sensation in the brain. Nothing had changed in the intervening years. President Nixon would issue directives and no one knew what, if anything, happened after his orders left the Oval Office. I was given the job of finding out.

A woman came into my life at that point who considerably enriched my stay at OMB, Velma Baldwin, the director of administration. White House Fellows assigned to OMB came under Velma's wing. No place to park your car? Velma found this newcomer a spot in the prestigious courtyard of the Old EOB, where I had the nerve to park the housepainted Chevy. Feel left out of serious department business? Velma would get you into key meetings. Need a travel advance? Velma found the money. The greatest service Velma performed for me, however, was to point out that in every agency there was somebody just like her, a career administrator who knew in what pockets the funds were hidden, how you hired somebody without being strangled by Civil Service red tape, and where the bodies were buried. These people, Velma explained, would still be in place long after the last cockroach died. Thanks to Velma Baldwin, I got to know her powerful counterparts in every cabinet-level agency, and had a catbird's view of how the government worked, or failed to work.

Not long after my arrival, Weinberger left OMB to head the Department of Health, Education, and Welfare, where he sharpened the cost-cutting reputation as "Cap the Knife" that he had earned as Governor Reagan's budget director in California. Carlucci also went to HEW as Weinberger's deputy, and Will

Taft as counsel. I had only brief exposure to these men at the time. But they were going to change my life.

In the game of musical chairs that followed Weinberger's and Carlucci's departure, Fred Malek became deputy director of OMB. Malek was a West Point and Harvard Business School graduate who had made a fortune rescuing a failing tool company in South Carolina. He had earned an earlier reputation in the White House personnel office as a hatchet man. Malek had cemented his status as the administration's kneecapper by going to the Department of the Interior and telling Interior Secretary Walter Hickle, who had fallen from favor, to be gone by sundown. When a secretary called saying, "Mr. Malek is on the line," it was like hearing the Mafia tell you that the money was due by midnight and no excuses.

Malek had been one of my interrogators at Airlie House. I dropped Fred a note congratulating him on his appointment, told him that I was working in the bowels of OMB as a White House Fellow, and asked that he let me know if I could be of any assistance. Almost immediately, he phoned, asking me to stop by his office. Fred was hawkish-looking, lean, erect, soft-spoken yet decisive. I was soon installed as his special assistant in an office in the Old EOB overlooking Pennsylvania Avenue, and became his gatekeeper. If you wanted to see Malek, you had to see Powell first.

Fred was not much interested in the departmental pulling and hauling that produce the federal budget. What he really wanted was to gain control over the bureaucracy for the White House. The people elect a President to run the country, but Presidents soon discover that they don't necessarily control the machinery of government. Their wishes are often thwarted during that two-year lapse between the kick in the beast's butt and the sensation in its head.

Fred went about gaining control of the government in a way that opened the eyes of this fledgling student of power. Just as OMB is the nerve center of the federal bureaucracy, the budget and personnel offices are the nerve centers in individual departments. Fred started planting his own people in the key "assistant secretary for administration" slots in major federal agencies. Let the cabinet officials make the speeches, cut the ribbons, and appear on *Meet the Press.* Anonymous assistant secretaries, loyal to Malek, would run operations day to day, and to the Nixon administration's liking.

I learned much in Professor Malek's graduate seminar. For example, Fred wanted to breathe fresh life into OMB by getting rid of layers of career bureaucrats and replacing them with new "management associates," young Harvard, Stanford, and Wharton hotshots. Fred, however, had a space problem. He called me into his office one day and explained his strategy and my role. Thereafter, I started phoning agency officials, explaining that I was calling on behalf of Mr. Malek with good news. Their power was about to be broadened. A function currently being handled by OMB was going to be transferred to their agency. Wonderful. More positions equal more funding, which equals more power, music to any bureaucrat's ear. Whoa! Let me explain.

You are getting only the function and the bodies. OMB is keeping the positions and funding. (We needed to keep these slots and salaries for Malek's young stars.) "But where can we put the people you're sending us?" the administrators would plead. "We don't have jobs for them. We haven't budgeted funds for them." "Mr. Assistant Secretary," I would say, "Fred Malek has every confidence that between attrition and some imagination on your part, you will work something out." Soon the unwanted OMB bureaucrats were gone, their offices and titles freed up, and Malek's youngbloods moved in. Out of that experience emerged one of my rules: you don't know what you can get away with until you try.

In January 1973, the White House Fellows gathered in an anonymous downtown office used by the CIA. The great adventure of the Fellows' year was to be a winter trip to the Soviet Union followed by a trip to Red China the following summer. While we waited to be briefed, jokes flew back and forth about microfilm concealed in imaginative apertures and the likeliest defectors in our group. The actual briefing by a CIA operative turned out to be tame. Instead of giving us intelligence targets and instructing us in the use of microdots, he merely warned us against bugged rooms, tapped telephones, and overly pliant Russian ladies.

The White House Fellows were looked after by Lieutenant Colonel Bernard Loeffke, a combination shepherd/chaperon/tour guide, a man who remains indelible in my memory. Bernie Loeffke had been born in Colombia of an American father and a Hispanic mother. He combined perfect military bearing with dark good looks and had a résumé in technicolor. Bernie was a West Pointer, a former White House Fellow himself, a master parachutist, a pilot who taught himself to fly, a physical fitness freak, a scuba diver, an Olympic-class swimmer, and a man who practically inhaled foreign languages. He had picked up three Silver Stars, four Bronze Stars, and a Purple Heart in Vietnam, which was remarkable even by the inflated standards of that era. Bernie was to lead us on our trip that winter behind the then still formidable Iron Curtain.

Our memories of the bitterness of the Cold War have already faded considerably. But when I first set foot on Soviet soil in the winter of 1973, the ground was still hard with suspicion and distrust. We entered in February at Khabarovsk in eastern Siberia, north of Vladivostok, on a flight from Japan. The first Russian I met was Alla Fedorova, our Intourist guide, who spoke impeccable American English and was rather attractive. Part of her attraction grew out of the novelty and mystery of someone from the other side, a dark-haired Russian and, we assumed, KGB.

We were put up at a no-star hotel in Khabarovsk. I have only fleeting impressions of this dour, dingy city, with its forests of cranes, derricks, and smokestacks, permanently leaden skies, and cold that felt like ice water poured down your back. We were not allowed to approach people, and they became uneasy if we tried.

Our first night at the hotel, the Russians chose to entertain us with a movie on seal hunting. As soon as the auditorium turned dark and the film started, Bernie Loeffke whispered to me, "This is a bore. Let's go." We managed to slip away, but stayed inside the hotel, since we had been warned not to leave. I don't think we would have if we could. The temperature outdoors was forty below zero.

We followed the sound of music to some sort of club in the hotel. Inside there appeared to be the entire senior officer corps of the Soviet Eastern Siberian Command, in uniform, with wives and girl-friends. Bernie and I stood in the doorway in our blue business suits with little American flag pins in our lapels, looking as if we had stumbled into the bear's cave. The music stopped. Every head in the place turned toward us. Bernie spoke in Russian to a waiter: "A table for two, please." The waiter looked petrified. His fear and the silence in the room were quickly explained. Our KGB handlers had tracked us down and were standing behind us. We were no doubt unaware, they explained, that the seal hunting film was not yet over. Perhaps we would like to see the end.

The next day we boarded the Trans-Siberian Railroad for Irkutsk, the old Siberian exile city. My most powerful first impression of the Soviet interior was its endlessness. We rode that train for three days and still had not reached a destination less than halfway across the country. The first day we spent watching a Dr. Zhivago landscape unfold before us, the limitless horizons of Siberia, slim white birches and herds of reindeer, which we observed while sipping sweet tea from glasses.

The second night, Bernie said, "This is boring. Let's see how the other half lives." We slipped back to what seemed to be a third-class carriage full of bundled-up peasants. Bernie introduced us as Americans, and their faces lit up. "Ah, our brave allies in the Great Patriotic War. Our comrades in defeating the fascists." They began passing around vodka bottles. No sooner had we started to enjoy ourselves than our friends from the state security apparatus showed up again. They were sure we would be more comfortable in our first-class car, a superior product of East German industry. On the way back, we passed a compartment where I saw off-duty customs officials leafing through a familiar-looking magazine and laughing bawdily. When we got back to our car, we learned that one of the White House Fellows had had his copy of *Playboy* confiscated as obscene material not allowed in the Soviet Union.

We made an interim stop at another military outpost, the city of Chita. At the time, the tension crackled along the nearby border between the Soviet Union and China. We were allowed out of the train to stretch our legs, but not permitted into town. And we were not to take any pictures. We heard the whistle blow, warning everybody to reboard. Bernie made a quick head count, realized two of the Fellows were not back, and alerted Alla Fedorova. She disappeared, and the next thing we saw from the train window was a half-dozen uneasy "passengers" pacing an otherwise empty platform. Not until our missing friends showed up did these Russians board the train. And that was how the rest of our KGB detail blew its cover.

Approaching Irkutsk, we skirted Lake Baikal, the largest body of fresh water on the Eurasian land-mass. The shore was ringed by factories. I learned, after the Cold War had ended, that the pollution from those plants had killed off some of the world's richest fisheries. Apparently, profit-seeking capitalists were not the only threat to the environment.

The immensity of Russia struck me all over again after our day in Irkutsk. Besides the three days on the train, it took another seven hours to fly to Moscow. By now, Alla, who had started out as merely attractive, looked ravishing. The flight was our first experience with Aeroflot, and it had some of the quality of early barnstorming. The plane was barely heated, and as we walked down the aisle, one passenger's foot went through the floor into the baggage compartment. We were a bit curious when the aircraft was towed to the end of the runway with the cockpit still empty. When the pilots did arrive, they did not rev the engines to test them as is usually done. They simply took off, full power, like a MIG-19 fighter zooming up to intercept an intruder into Soviet airspace. The towing, we learned, was intended to save fuel. And the rocket takeoff was indeed performed by former MIG-19 pilots no doubt nostalgic for the good old days.

For someone who grew up during the fifties, whose first military assignment had been facing the Red Army across the Fulda Gap, who had spent two tours fighting the communists in Vietnam, there was something eerie about standing, during the Cold War, in the heart of what a future American President would call the "evil empire." Much of American life for the previous twenty-five years had been defined by this adversary. American budgets, politics, weapons, foreign policy, science, research, and domestic priorities and the lives of millions of military-age Americans were influenced almost as much by what happened in Moscow as by what happened in Washington. And here I was, a member of the American military establishment, whose reason for being was to contain this giant, standing in Red Square and then being briefed by that elite of Soviet think tanks, the USA-Canada Institute, where they all seemed to speak American English and could probably give you the team standings in the National League.

I began to get a visceral feel for this country, one that comes from touching, feeling, and smelling a place rather than only hearing or reading about it. What I sensed was the common humanity of all people, including these Russians who were then supposed to be our mortal enemy. The people I met on the train, passed in Red Square, and rubbed elbows with at the GUM department store were not political ideologues. They were the Soviet equivalent of my own family, a mother buying groceries for supper, a tired father headed home after a hard day at the ministry mailroom, kids thinking more about the soccer prospects of Moscow against Kiev than about spreading Marxism globally.

At the same time, I also felt the immensity and power of this country, its terrifying capacity to intimidate its own people and its apparent ability to match whatever military might we could muster, weapon for weapon, system for system. What I could not see, from the superficial perspective the Soviets afforded us, was the fatal weakness that even then had to be undermining their system, dooming it to ultimate collapse.

We left Moscow for Sofia, Bulgaria, and experienced a marvelous sensation. We were still in the communist bloc, but all of a sudden there were vivid colors. We went to Warsaw and there was life. Coming out of the Soviet Union, even to these countries, was like going from black-and-white still photos to a movie in color. Our senses, deadened by the grimness of Soviet existence, came to life again.

In Warsaw, we visited the Year 2000 Institute, which was supposed to provide a vision of Poland's future, come the millennium. I never forgot the words of a professor who talked to the Fellows, a big, shambling man with a bemused look. "Look where God put Poland," he said. "Between Germany and the Soviet Union. Every generation, one or the other rolls over us. Sometimes both. We have been denied our Polish destiny." His words intrigued me. This communist certainly did not sound like someone ready to die on the barricades for the Soviet Union. I had a sense that he and his countrymen would love to be free of their "ally." A seed took root in my mind that day. Sixteen years later, when the communist bloc first began falling apart, I remembered the Polish professor, stuck my neck out, and predicted to an audience of high-ranking Army officers that, far from staying with the Warsaw Pact, these satellites would probably prefer to join NATO.

The White House Fellows program meant instant entree to people one did not ordinarily encounter at Fort Devens or Chu Lai. Back home, we were taken to Georgia to meet the governor. We had been permitted to bring our spouses, and as our motorcade headed out of the Atlanta airport, with Georgia state troopers on motorcycles leading the way, sirens wailing, and traffic halted in all directions, I gazed out the window and said to Alma, "Tall cotton."

The governor turned out to be a boyish forty-nine-year-old with a blinding smile. He sat us down and mesmerized the Fellows with his vision for Georgia and his grasp of national politics. My knowledge of Southern politicians at this point extended to Bull Connor, George Wallace, and the former Georgia governor, Lester Maddox, who liked to distribute ax handles to fellow bigots. The governor now before us represented the New South, and I remember thinking, this man is presidential timber. Three years later, Jimmy Carter became the country's thirty-ninth president.

I had a brief exposure during this period to Admiral Hyman G. Rickover, father of the nuclear submarine, irascible, unreasonable, an officer who could make strong men weep. A friend who had applied for the Navy's nuclear sub program once described to me his grilling by Rickover: "Why should I want you in my program? What makes you think you can drive a nuclear submarine? You don't look as if you know diddly-squat."

I had been invited to a swearing-in ceremony at the General Services Administration, at which Rickover was expected to speak. The admiral said only a few words, but I have never forgotten his message. Organization doesn't really accomplish anything. Plans don't accomplish anything, either. Theories of management don't much matter. Endeavors succeed or fail because of the people involved. Only by attracting the best people will you accomplish great deeds. Admittedly, Rickover's approach to handling people could be brutal—breaking them down so that he could build them back up to his specifications. That could never be my style. But there was no denying the force of his insight. Truth from the mouths of curmudgeons is truth all the same.

"It's like letting little children watch the sex act," Joe Laitin, the public relations director at OMB, once told me. Joe was explaining why he did not approve of the White House Fellows program. Along with Fred Malek, Joe had become another OMB mentor. At the end of the workday, with traffic backed up twenty-six miles from the Old EOB to my house in Dale City, I would hang around until it lightened, listening to Joe's bottomless fund of stories. He was Brooklyn-born, a former newspaperman who had become something of a movable institution in government PR circles. He had served for a time in the White House press office under Lyndon B. Johnson and regaled me with stories of how he told the President tales at night so that LBJ would go to sleep peacefully. He had once fed Johnson some made-up economic gossip, which the President leaked to the press, causing the stock market to go goofy for a session or two.

When Fred Malek first took over as deputy, he had wanted to fire Joe, and the Nixon administration's former headsman was not given to idle threats. I asked Joe if he had been worried at the time. "Let me tell you something," he said. "Every new guy who comes here wants to dump me. It happens every few years. Week one, let's get rid of Laitin. Week two, they learn that Laitin is a career official and not so easy to unload. By week three, they have gotten themselves into a public relations jam with the *Washington Post* or CBS and the old firehorse comes to their rescue. They start thinking, maybe this guy ain't so bad. By week four, they love me."

I asked Joe what he had against White House Fellows. I was a Fellow, and he and I got along fine. Joe explained. Democracy did not always function well in the light of day. Democracy is give and take. People have to trade, change, deal, retreat, bend, compromise, as they move from the ideal to the possible. To the uninitiated, the process can be messy, disappointing, even shocking. Compromise can make the participants look manipulative, unprincipled, two-faced. It was okay for me to witness this, Joe went on, because I was old enough and had experience. "But some of these bright-eyed kids start wandering around the West Wing and cabinet members' offices and they're horrified to find how things really get done."

The other side of the coin, Joe said, was that "some of them taste power before they can handle it. They get drunk on it." In their intoxication, they tend to overlook the fact that the law eventually checks unbridled power, and they can get into trouble. "Now, there's nothing wrong with sex," Joe went on, "but there is something immoral about having children watch it, until they know what they are watching."

Laitin's views are not far removed from the wisdom of our Founding Fathers. Men like Hamilton, Madison, and Jefferson recognized that we are imperfect beings. Consequently, they invented a government of separate powers and checks and balances—to control the imperfections in human nature. Joe Laitin understood that, but was not so sure the young White House Fellows could grasp it yet.

In the summer of 1973, I was in a village in China, a world that few Americans had ever seen, listening to the wizened local chieftain. We were on the final field trip of our White House Fellowship year. On July 23 we had arrived in Canton, where an endless river of bicycles glided noiselessly past us on immaculate streets. I was surprised that a city could be so huge, yet so clean and quiet. The Chinese took us to other major cities and the usual tourist stops—the Forbidden City, the Great Wall. At a primitive rural hospital we watched a woman undergo a twenty-minute thyroid operation while anesthetized by acupuncture. When it was over, she got up, drank a glass of lemonade, and walked out. In Shenyang, we visited a machine shop where it was hard to tell the men from the women in that age of padded, quilted, shapeless unisex dress. We learned that the workers put in a six-day week with an occasional holiday but no vacations and earned the equivalent of $52 a month, including foremen, supervisors, and all but top management. Despite conditions that would have sent American workers to the picket lines, they seemed content.

One of our guides on the Chinese trip was a fifty-four-year-old professor who had studied in the United States. Early in his career, he told us, he had worked only to gain wealth and position. He had filled his students with book learning, conditioning them to strive for individual success. Neither he nor they had possessed a speck of practical knowledge or social conscience. And then came the Great Cultural Revolution. Our professor was dispatched to the countryside, where for the first time, he said, he performed "honest labor." "Before that, I knew nothing. I could not even grow cotton. I, who had taught scholars, had to be reeducated by peasants." He spoke with a sublime smile. I heard a lot of gushing among the younger White House Fellows. My own experience with manual labor in a Pepsi bottling plant helped keep my enthusiasm in check.

What struck me about China, particularly after visiting the Soviet Union, was the absence of paranoia. Our Chinese guides seemed less frightened than their Soviet counterparts. They were not constantly searching our baggage, restraining our movements, or stopping us from taking pictures. Two distinctive threads, however, ran through the Chinese experience. You could ask an ordinary person in Beijing, Canton, Shenyang, or any village, "How are you doing?" and the answer was invariably a smile and "Fine. Under Chairman Mao we have a sewing machine, a radio, a bicycle." The thoroughness of thought control in so vast a country was frightening. The second iron rule was that Chinese officials would admit shortcomings, but never error.

One day when we were visiting along the Amur River, which runs between China and the Soviet Union, I asked our guide if we could see any military bases. He told me with a benign smile that it would be impossible, because peaceful China maintained no bases along this troubled border. In the course of a visit to a temple, we suddenly heard a deafening roar. We turned to see two Chinese MIG-19s streaking into the sky, apparently from a nearby airfield. "What was that?" I asked our guide, who continued to gaze ahead placidly and silently. "What was what?" he answered. End of discussion.

In the village where the wrinkled old chief spoke to us, he explained how he and his people had burrowed through a rock mountain practically with their bare hands to reach fertile soil on the other side. They had then lugged broken stones up the mountain to build terraces to hold the soil in place. Just as they finished, the rains came and washed away all they had accomplished. But, armed with the thoughts of Chairman Mao and the quotations from his little red book, they started over again, until they had built this bountiful community. The chief invited us to share a meal from the harvest of these terraces. The menu, as near as I could determine, was millet with a little gravy and an unidentifiable vegetable. It was plain fare, our host admitted, but nourishing, and, along with the wisdom of Chairman Mao, it would sustain us.

After the meal, he rose and said that he was sorry he had no gifts, but he wanted us to have a small rock with the date inscribed on it; the rock had been taken from a terrace and was given with the heartfelt friendship of his villagers. Colonel Loeffke jumped up and said that he had brought gifts for our hosts. With that, Bernie produced a shopping bag and started handing out buttons with happy faces, ball-point pens, Nixon inaugural pins, and other trinkets in a scene suggestive of the purchase of Manhattan from the Indians. The village chief said with an enig-matic smile, "You have given us so much, and we have given you so little. Please forgive us."

As the White House Fellows' year wound to a close, Fred Malek called me into his office. His television set was tuned to Senator Sam Ervin's Watergate investigating subcommittee. "This'll blow over," Fred observed. He wanted to talk to me, he said, about my staying on at OMB for another year. I knew by now that my initial reluctance to become a White House Fellow was the error of a greenhorn. When the Fel-lows discussed the power of the executive branch, it was with President Nixon. When we studied the leg-islative branch, it was with U.S. senators. When the subject was social programs, we talked to the Secre-tary of Health, Education and Welfare. In the foreign arena, we met with leaders of Japan, the Soviet

Union, China, Poland, Bulgaria, and West Germany. We had lunches and dinners every week with journalists like Eric Sevareid, Dan Rather, and Hugh Sidey. The aim of the program was to let us inside the engine room to see the cogs and gears of government grinding away and also to take us up high for the panoramic view. In all the schools of political science, in all the courses in public administration throughout the country, there could be nothing comparable to this education.

Still, I was ready to return to the Army. As a graduate student, a Pentagon desk officer, and a White House Fellow, I had been away from real soldiering for over three years. The Fellows program, particularly, had been a detour from a straight-line military career path, and I was eager to get back on track. I bore in mind the fate of an earlier Army Fellow who had made a big hit in the White House. He had been asked to stay on to work on domestic issues, which he did. And guess what? The Army did not promote him to full colonel. The White House put pressure on the Army, and eventually he was promoted. But an officer who had not yet commanded a battalion, who had missed a few other stations of the cross while basking in White House praises, who was passed over by his promotion board and advanced only through political pressure, was finished. He made colonel, all right—permanently.

That was not the path I wanted. The Army was my life. I thanked Malek for his invitation, but told him I was ready to leave. And despite Malek's optimism, the evidence that Sam Ervin and the Watergate special prosecutor were uncovering did not make the Nixon administration seem like a particularly seaworthy vessel. All I wanted was to cross over to the other side of the Potomac and find out what assignments the Pentagon had for a soldier eager to command troops again. I had not been in direct command since serving as a company commander at Fort Devens in 1962. For all practical purposes, I had been a battalion commander of Vietnamese troops during my first tour, though I was carried on the books as an advisor. But during my second Vietnam tour, I served solely as a staff officer. Now, as a lieutenant colonel, evaluated as qualified by Infantry Branch, I hoped for a battalion of my own.

In the spring of 1973, in those last days as a White House Fellow, I went to the Infantry Branch assignments office, where a fellow lieutenant colonel took down a loose-leaf notebook and opened it before me. Listed, by hand, were all the battalions in the Army, followed by three columns: Column A, indicating who was currently commanding the unit; Column B, who was slated to get the battalion next; and Column C, who was scheduled to command it after that. I went down Column B looking for blank spaces, since I wanted something immediately.

The process was not quite as simple as I am suggesting. In those days, office politics, the old-boy network, and favoritism could influence the assignment. If a commanding general, for example, wanted you in his division, that could clinch the deal. Today's system is more objective and less subject to external pressure. The Army locks a board of officers in a room with a stack of personnel records on microfiche. There is almost no way for someone to intervene on behalf of fair-haired candidates. And the board is big enough so that one member does not have undue influence. The board pores over these records, weighs strength against weaknesses, and does not come out until the best potential commanders have been identified. Since there are more qualified commanders than commands, some candidates will inevitably be disappointed. The odd thing is that the old system and the new produce about the same proportion of successes and failures. But at least with the modern method, the credit or blame lies with human fallibility, not favoritism.

I wound up slated for Korea, not through preference or pull, but because command of the 1st Battalion, 32d Infantry, 2d Infantry Division, Eighth Army, Korea, was one of the few blanks I found in Column B. The battalion was known as the Queen's Own Buccaneers, shortened to "the Bucs." The name reflected the battalion's roots in Hawaii, when ruled by Queen Liliuokalani in the 1890s.

The hard part was telling Alma where I was going. Korea was an "unaccompanied tour," which meant leaving her alone in Dale City for a year with three children, ages ten, eight, and three. My wife, a sensible woman, was not thrilled. "I'm asking you to make a sacrifice," I admitted.

Alma did not disagree. "But if this is what you want," she said, "if this is what you think is best for you, then do it."

Her support made it easier, but not easy. This marked the third time I would be absent from the life of my son, the second time I would be leaving Linda, and the first time I would be parted from Annemarie, at her most enchanting age. Having to leave my wife and children to go off to Korea was, at that point, the most painful thing I had ever faced.

The White House Fellowship ended, and I put on the uniform again. The people I had met during that year were going to shape my future in ways unimaginable to me then. But first, I was off to Korea, where an old soldier would teach me a unique brand of military leadership.

8 ☆ *"Go, Gunfighter, Go!"*

MY NEW COMMANDING OFFICER, Major General Henry E. "the Gunfighter" Emerson, had taken over the 2d Division at Camp Casey just a few months before I arrived in Korea. I got an early hint of what he might be like from my change-of-command ceremony. I was replacing Lieutenant Colonel Zeb Bradford, another officer also out of the DePuy staff, and a battalion commander who had done a first-rate job with the Bucs. Changes of command tend to be somewhat uncomfortable. There is only so much you want to hear about how the other guy ran his ship. I prefer the overlap to be brief, and in this case it was.

The morning of the ceremony, Bradford and I arrived at a nearly deserted parade ground. I had become accustomed in Germany and Vietnam to overblown hoopla at these events, a big turnout, and the shower of medals. But here, only a lonely-looking four-man color guard stood in the middle of the field. Five company commanders and their guidon bearers, representing the battalion's five companies, were spread out like solitary pickets. A handful of onlookers watched from the stands. "Gunfighter doesn't care to have the troops stand in the hot sun while a couple of colonels tell each other how wonderful they are," Bradford said to me. The sergeant major presented the battalion colors to Bradford, who handed them to me, and I returned them to the sergeant major. That was it. The whole business took less than thirty seconds. I started thinking I might like Gunfighter Emerson.

Soon afterward, I went to division headquarters to report to the general. He came bursting out of his office and seized my hand, which he pumped like a well handle. The man was about fifty, tall, rangy, with a great eagle's beak of a nose, craggy features, a hot-eyed gaze, and a booming voice. He never stopped pacing as he welcomed me. He had earned his nickname in Vietnam by carrying a cowboy-style six-shooter rather than a regulation .45 caliber pistol, and I noticed that he had a revolver engraved on his belt buckle. I was also aware that he had won a reputation there as a fierce fighter.

General Emerson scheduled a commanders call for this morning, and I stayed on to attend. As my fellow officers came in, the general introduced me, and we seated ourselves around the conference room. Emerson continued to pace. "Today's subject," he announced, "is marksmanship." He started off in a reasonable tone. As he went on, however, he warmed to his subject. Marksmanship was important! The pacing quickened. If marksmanship was neglected, soldiers would be unprepared! The eyes began to blaze. And if soldiers were unprepared, they would not win. And what the hell kind of leadership was that? Fists now pounding. The pattern was never to change all the while I served under the Gunfighter. A modest premise, mounting fervor, and an apoplectic windup. I observed his accelerating excitement on every subject from deploying helicopters along the DMZ to soldier correspondence courses. And his punch line was always the same, a vein-popping "If we don't do our jobs right, soldiers won't win!"

His performance before the troops was no different. The first time I witnessed it, we had assembled the entire division on the Camp Casey parade field. Gunfighter started off calmly. "Our mission in Korea is to maintain the armistice agreed to on July 27, 1953, between the United Nations and North Korea. Further, our mission is to come to the aid of our South Korean allies should that armistice be violated." As he spoke, Emerson's voice took on velocity. I heard one of the sergeants whisper, "Here he goes." Pretty soon, Gunfighter was shouting, "And if those North Korean sons of bitches ever cross that DMZ, we're gonna kick their asses!" By now, the eyes were flashing and the veins throbbed on his neck. "And if the Chinese throw a million troops across the border, we're gonna kick their asses too!" The troops caught the spirit and began shouting, "Go, Gunfighter, go!"

Emerson had inherited a tough command. Morale in the 2d Division when he took over was not high, and discipline was slack. I found it heartening to hear a leader sound off with spirit and show a will to change. This division could stand a little gung ho.

On just my second night in camp, I had gotten a taste of the division's condition. I was in my quarters, a metal half-Quonset with a shower, bed, desk, and smelly diesel heater, getting ready to hit the sack when I got a call asking me to come immediately to the provost marshal's office. The night was chilly with just a hint of the impending Korean winter in the air as I hurried down the hillside still buttoning my jacket.

I entered a small building just inside the camp gate, containing a desk for the MP sergeant and a couple of detention cells. I seemed to have walked in on a fight with a wildcat. An MP was trying to hand-cuff about 150 pounds of unadulterated fury while a half-dozen others warily circled this blur of arms and legs. A major, cool as ice, stood outside the ring. "Remember your training," he was saying. "If I told you once, I told you ten times, not one on one. Every-body on him!" With that, the other MPs piled on and subdued the culprit. At the bottom of the pileup, I glimpsed a small private, who, I was informed, was from my battalion.

As the MPs took him outside and wrestled him into the back of a van for transfer to the stockade in Seoul, the major explained the situation. The private was part of a gang that allegedly intended to murder

the camp provost marshal. He and his pals had created a deliberate ruckus in order to get arrested and
tossed into the cells. While there, they planned to
start another fight, and when the provost marshal
came to break it up, the scrapper I had just observed
was supposed to stab him with a long needle he had
managed to sneak through the body search. The last I
saw of the prisoner, he was shackled hand and foot,
kicking out the back window as the van pulled away.
This was my introduction to the drugs, racial tension,
and indiscipline plaguing the Army in Korea, without
even the distraction of a war as in Vietnam.

Today's all-volunteer Army has high standards.
It was not the case then. We were in transition from
the draft to the all-volunteer force. As we dragged
ourselves home from Vietnam, the nation turned its
back on the military. Many of our troops, in Army
shorthand, were "Cat Four," Category IV, soldiers
possessing meager skills in reading, writing, and
math. They were life's dropouts, one step above Category V, those who were considered unfit for Army
service. Today, about 4 percent of the Army is Cat
Four, while in those days the figure was closer to 50
percent.

General Emerson was determined to turn
around this slack, demoralized operation. He gave
the job his total attention, since Gunfighter was a
bachelor to whom the Army was wife and mistress.
He had begun a program for remaking the 2d
Infantry Division which he called "Pro-Life," not to
be confused with the antiabortion movement. Emerson's Pro-Life program, as he put it, "was to provide

the soldier opportunities to become a winner rather than a loser in life." Given Army conditions in Korea, I favored "pro" anything, within reason, though reasonableness was not always Gunfighter's long suit.

He was not a lone voice in his reforming zeal. In this transitional period, the Army was trying to make military life more appealing and to get rid of aspects that made people disinclined to stay in. Hated KP was eliminated. The Army went to a five-day week with weekends off wherever practical. Barracks were redesigned to end the hospital-ward look and to provide a private room and bath for every three soldiers. Almost none of these innovations, however, had yet reached Korea. Gunfighter, nevertheless, was determined to lift morale.

We were in this country because of a war that had ended twenty years before. The Korean War stands almost hidden in the shadows of the two wars that flank it, the drama of World War II and the agony of Vietnam. Yet, 54,000 Americans died in this conflict, heavier casualties proportionately for its three years than suffered during the nearly ten years of major U.S. involvement in Vietnam. And Korea was the war I pretty much grew up on. I was eight when World War II ended, and my memories are the sketchy recollections of a child. But I was in the impressionable ages of thirteen through sixteen when the older boys from Kelly Street went off to Korea. The GIs who fought there returned talking about combat in a primitive place where things moved by oxcart and the stench of dung was everywhere. Today, South Korea

is another Asian economic miracle producing everything from cars to VCRs to microchips. And when I
arrived, the impending economic miracle was
already beginning in a Seoul bristling with office
towers and humming with entrepreneurial energy. A
few miles beyond, however, the capital's sophistica-
tion yielded to thatch-roofed villages, small vegetable farms, rice paddies, and the ever-present oxen.

Camp Casey, where I was to spend the next
year, was about an hour's drive from Seoul, a strag-
gly succession of World War II Quonset huts stretching up a valley and climbing the surrounding
hillsides. The atmosphere was pure war zone, with
none of the softening amenities of a post where families live. We were about twenty-five miles from the
DMZ, the demilitarized zone forming the buffer
between North and South Korea. And the 2d Infantry
Division was there, to put it bluntly, to provide a
buffer of American flesh and blood.

We were there to obstruct a North Korean
attack. If and when that danger ever lifted, the Army
would pull out. Therefore, there was no need for
building costly frills. The Quonset huts were hot as
ovens in the summer and cold as charity during the
bitter Korean winter, which we were about to enter.
The Quonsets were heated by inefficient diesel-fuel
units that required a little carburetor valve to function. I found that many barracks were unheated for
lack of this small part, a situation reflecting the prevailing sloppiness on the post. When my supply clerk
ordered the valves, the maintenance battalion
brushed him off—"Out of stock." I went to the ware-

house myself and raised hell until I found the valves—near a stash of World War I gas mask canisters. The supply people, who could not find valves to heat barracks, said that they were keeping the nearly sixty-year-old canisters because they were afraid to throw them away. This was the environment Emerson was trying to change, and I was all for it.

On checking the battalion records, I was struck by the number of short-term AWOLs, men usually gone only a few hours. "Yobos," my executive officer explained. Yobos? Any eighteen-year-old who had had trouble getting a date in high school could have an apartment and a girl, a yobo of his own, in Tong Du Chon, the town next to Camp Casey, and for only $180 a month. The girls were provided by a combination madam-yenta serving the American garrison. Given the grim accommodations on post, the appeal of these menages was not hard to understand. And from a health standpoint, the arrangement was probably preferable to the widespread patronage of $10 prostitutes, who had driven the VD rate in Camp Casey to lofty heights, with repeat performers in some units propelling the rate to over 100 percent.

Tong Du Chon was a one-industry town, and the U.S. Army was the industry. Back home this was the era of Afros and black exploitation movies like *Shaft* and *Superfly.* Black soldiers were not permitted extreme Afros in the Army, but off duty, they sported every other superfly fashion—three-inch heels, wild suits and capes, outfits the tailors of Tong Du Chon could churn out almost overnight for $20. For the whites, cowboy hats, fancy-stitched boots, and denim shirts were the off-duty rage, and attempts to get away with longish hair.

On my first visit to Tong Du Chon, I strolled along a block jammed with sidewalk artists who seemed to be grabbing at my wallet. Finally, I understood through their pidgin English that they wanted to see my family photographs. I took out a snapshot of little Annie, and in twenty minutes, for $10, a painter produced an oil painting of my daughter—my Korean daughter, since no matter who these artists depicted, the aspect was always Oriental. Elvis Presley was the big draw for white troops in Tong Du Chon, Elvis painted on velvet in every pose and size. I wonder how many American family rooms are decorated with these portraits of the King, with almond eyes, kept by paunchy men now in their fifties.

Whole streets of Tong Du Chon were filled with brassware sellers offering candlesticks, ashtrays, plates, plaques, utensils—any object or shape into which brass could be beaten. I soon learned the source of the metal. We were conducting a night firing exercise that fall, first pounding the side of a hill with artillery and then sending in infantry to pepper it with small-arms fire. A red-star cluster went off signaling "cease fire." Immediately, the hillside twinkled with pinpoints of light. What was that? I asked. "Koreans," my exec informed me. Shadowy shapes emerged out of shallow holes and trenches and headed straight for the firing range. They carried flashlights, even candles, and started scavenging spent bullets, shells, and brass cartridge cases while they were still hot. Some got a head start by hiding in caves inside the impact area. This was the source of brass found in the shops of Tong Du Chon.

The second time my battalion went on one of these night exercises, I had to send the exec into a nearby village the next day to inform the chief that one of his people had been accidentally killed on the range. The chief's reaction was a matter-of-fact nod. These were desperately poor people, and they were ready to take lethal risks as the cost of doing business.

"You see, gentlemen, if you play football, you've only got twenty-two men on the field. Baseball, nine men plus the runners. Basketball, ten." General Emerson had brought us together one fall morning, and I was not sure where this commanders call was headed. "But we've got eighteen thousand men in the division," he continued. "And we want all of them to play. We want all of them to feel like winners. Pro-Life!" His solution was "combat sports."

Gunfighter went on to explain. We would start with combat football. Instead of conventional eleven-man teams, we would field whole units—first platoon against second platoon, maybe eighty men at once. We would play on the soccer field, and the objective was to get the football into the opponent's net. How? Any way you can, the general explained. Run it, throw it, kick it, pass it. And, to liven up the action, we would use two footballs at once. The rules? None. You can tackle, block, clip, blindside, anything. Referees? No rules, so you don't need any referees. And no penalties.

As soon as we started combat football, the division doctors were in an uproar. They were being flooded with orthopedic cases, some serious. They threatened to blow the whistle on Gunfighter. We instituted minimal rules. We put in a referee to stop play at least when both balls went out of bounds. We replaced combat boots with sneakers. We banned kicking, clipping, and punching. The troops loved combat football, at least the spectators did, and Gunfighter Emerson adored it.

In every successful military organization, and I suspect in all successful enterprises, different styles of leadership have to be present. If the man at the top does not exhibit all these qualities, then those around him have to supplement. If the top man has vision and vision only, he requires a whip hand to enforce his ideas. If the organization has a visionary and a whip hand, it needs a "chaplain" to soften the relentless demands of the others. In the 2d Division, the chaplain role was performed by Brigadier General Harry Brooks, the assistant division commander and the first black general under whom I served directly. Where Gunfighter was theatrical, impetuous, demanding, and unbending, Harry Brooks provided stability, coolness, and common sense. Brooks could steer combat football from total to only partial mayhem. Without the flywheel of a Harry Brooks, the laudable energy of a Gunfighter would have torn the division apart. I loved, admired, and learned from both men.

"Goooood morning, Camp Casey." The determinedly cheery radio voice woke me every day at 5:30 A.M.

Another of Gunfighter Emerson's Pro-Life antidotes to brawling, drug abuse, boozing, lechery, and trying to stab provost marshals was physical exhaustion. Consequently, we began the day with a four-mile run, to be completed in thirty-two minutes or less. "Last week's winner of the run was . . ." the announcer went on. "And today's temperature is . . ." Oh God, let it be ten below zero. If it was that cold, we did not have to run. One degree higher, and we still had to pry ourselves from our warm bunks and start running in air that frosted our lungs—up a sloping hill, then up a steeper hill, to the halfway point at Camp Hovey, located on a mountaintop, then back down to Camp Casey, all before breakfast. We ran the last two minutes at a sprint, hundreds of men yelling their guts out. The curious thing to me was that the same men who griped constantly about the run were all over me the minute we crossed the finish line wanting to know, "What was the time, Colonel? How'd we do? Did we beat the 72d Armored?" Gunfighter was on to something.

I had the only infantry battalion in a brigade of tankers. A couple of old Gelnhausen buddies, Clyde Sedgwick and Bill Wiehl, commanded the neighboring tank units. They made the run at a leisurely trot, while I went flat out, following the same cycle as my men—annoyance at getting up in the arctic cold, exhaustion halfway through the run, and exhilaration at the finish line. I was determined to have the 1st Battalion of the 32d Infantry win. I was not going to let a bunch of soldiers who rode around all day in mobile pillboxes beat infantrymen in a foot race.

We had troops called Katusas (KATUSA stood for Korean Augmentation to the U.S. Army), who could run forever. Our units were always under-strength. My battalion rated seven hundred men and I never had more than five hundred. We filled out the ranks with Koreans. They competed to join us, which got them out of their own units, and consequently we had the pick of the lot. The Katusas were among the finest troops I have ever commanded. They never showed up drunk or failed to show up at all. They were indefatigable, disciplined, and quick to learn. And they earned $3 a month, less than one of our men would blow on beer in a night in Tong Du Chon.

On the rare occasion when a Katusa got out of line, I simply went to his Korean noncom. "Sergeant Major, how are you today?" "Ah, Colonel, Sergeant Major is very well, thank you." "Sergeant Major, Private Kim seems to have a problem obeying orders." The insubordinate private would be gone within the hour, on his way back to the Korean army. If Private Kim was worth salvaging, he and the sergeant major might disappear behind the barracks, where Kim was made to understand the error of his ways. In similar disciplinary cases, an American soldier might write to his lawyer or congressman. Different cultures were at work, presenting different trade-offs in the contest between freedom and order, between the rights of the individual and the needs of the group. On balance, though it can be far less tidy and inconvenient to those in authority, I'll settle for our way.

· · ·

One winter day, Gunfighter summoned his commanders to tell us we were going into something called "reverse cycle training." We were to turn night into day. "After all," Gunfighter pointed out, "the North Koreans won't be fighting us nine-to-five." And so I took my battalion to the hills around the Imjin River, where we turned the clock upside down, breakfast at 8:00 P.M., compass course through the wilderness until a 1:00 A.M. lunch break, assembling and reassembling weapons and employing claymore mines and mortar fire in the "afternoon," from 2:00 A.M. to 7:00 A.M., dinner at 8:00 A.M., and attempted sleep from 9:00 A.M. to 3:00 P.M. We did this for ten-day stretches, trying to turn the circadian clock around, which, for certain constitutions, never worked. The meals at these ungodly hours literally made some soldiers sick, and we had to go back to serving at the same time other people ate. But Gunfighter was right. Wars assume irregular hours.

It was a crisp, clear winter day in December. The roar of artillery fire and crump of mortars were heavier than anything I had heard in two tours in Vietnam. I had the Bucs deployed on one side of the valley along the Rodriguez Range, ready to storm the hills on the opposite side. "Move out, Buccaneers," a sergeant shouted, and the men on point began to push toward the valley floor.

The North Koreans had not suddenly decided to break the twenty-year armistice. We were simply engaged in a "Gunfighter Shootout," an exercise involving live ammunition, and plenty of it, to come as close to simulating actual combat conditions as possible without drawing blood. We fired off hundreds of 81mm and 107mm mortar rounds and 106mm recoilless rifle fire against targets arrayed as advancing troops.

How had we come by all the firepower? one of my company commanders asked me. For a while the valley had echoed like D-Day. I said nothing. It would have been impolitic to explain. But Gunfighter did not want his division to mistake a few pops from our meager allowance of training ammo for actual combat conditions. We had fired off shells from our war reserve, a fact best not known to the North Koreans, or our superiors in Washington.

"Colonel Powell, you got to come down to C Company, pronto." The caller this Saturday afternoon was the company commander, a promising young officer who had not yet found that fine balance in handling his men between coercion and persuasion.

I hurried from my hooch to discover a small crowd at an intersection near C Company's rec room. The men parted to let me through. At the center stood a soldier, either drunk or doped up, brandishing a pool cue. His eyes were afire and his face contorted. "Somebody's gonna die!" he was hollering. "Somebody's gonna die! You put my buddy in jail. Nobody's gonna put me in jail. Somebody's gonna die first!"

"I called the MPs, Colonel," the lieutenant informed me. "They're on the way."

I nodded and started toward the assailant, maintaining a distance of one pool cue. "What are you gonna do, son?" I said. "Hit me?"

"Somebody's gonna die," he repeated.

I spoke gently. "Son, put the cue down."

"No, sir."

"Do you know who I am?"

"Yes, sir, Colonel Powell."

"I want you to put the cue down before you hurt somebody. I want you to put it down before somebody hurts you." I came closer. "You see, if you don't do what I tell you, all these men are going to whip hell out of you. Then, when they're done, you're going to the stockade for a year. What sense does that make? So put the cue down, and we'll have a nice talk."

His arm dropped, the pool cue dropped. And he started to cry. "Nobody understands. Nobody cares." Suddenly the homicidal maniac had become a confused, hurt kid.

We put him on restriction for a couple of weeks. Soon afterward, I passed him on the post and he threw me a snappy salute. "Colonel, how you doin,' sir." He grinned to some of his pals. "That's Bro P, Brother Powell, he's all right." And Bro P became my nickname, at least among the black troops, for the rest of the tour.

Some of the race friction at Camp Casey could be traced along musical fault lines. The whites wanted rock and country-and-western. The blacks wanted soul, Aretha Franklin, and Dionne Warwick. The issue got so testy that we summoned the Tong Du

Chon bar owners to division headquarters to see if we could work out a fair formula. They finally agreed that they would feature roughly seven "white" songs for every three "black" songs. As a result of this compromise, the whites were unhappy only 30 percent of the time and the blacks 70 percent.

The soldiers had worked out their own solution. White troops gravitated toward bars in a certain part of town and blacks to another. The line of demarcation became known as the Crack. A white crossed the Crack at as much peril to himself as a black trying to enter a white Birmingham bar before the Civil Rights Act. To Gunfighter, the situation was anathema. The idea that one group "owned" part of Tong Du Chon was unacceptable. The thought that an American soldier had to fear for his safety at the hands of other American soldiers was intolerable. "Racism is bad," Gunfighter told his assembled senior officers. "Race tension is not Pro-Life. I will not permit racism in my division." We half expected him to say, "Racism will end by zero seven hundred tomorrow morning."

Gunfighter had a plan. He had already ordered a special detachment of MPs to Tong Du Chon, he informed us. "And you gentlemen are going to walk every damn street in the Crack. You're going into dance halls, bars, any place of public accommodation. And if anyone is threatened or attacked, I'm sending in the Ready Brigade along with the MPs to clean out the place." With that, he gave us a tight smile and said, "Now you go and have yourselves a good time."

In one joint we ran into Father Gianastasias, a Catholic chaplain, who was dancing with a bargirl.

Some officers were taken aback. I was not. I knew Father G's MO. He went where he would find his flock. The kid with a problem who felt uneasy about going to battalion HQ could locate Father at the Kit Kat Klub, where the priest would match him beer for beer until the soldier felt comfortable enough to bare his soul. We had other chaplains who spent their time in their hooches studying St. Paul's Letters to the Corinthians. All very admirable, but it did not do much for troubled soldiers. And while his methods were unorthodox, we never heard a whisper that Father G ever violated his priestly vows.

I cannot say that our march on the Crack produced integrated bliss. We had not achieved that at home, much less in a honky-tonk town halfway around the world. But General Emerson's gutsy solution broke the color line. Thereafter, no group owned any part of Tong Du Chon. No vigilante code superseded the authority of the U.S. Army. We had shattered the mystique of the Crack.

Seeking racial harmony was no fleeting whim with Gunfighter. He went at it full throttle, as at everything else. One day, I learned that an Emerson favorite, an unusually capable officer whom he had recently elevated to a top position on the 2d Division staff, had referred to black troops as "darkies." I looked into it, and the charge turned out to be true. I thought it serious enough to bring to the attention of my superior, the brigade commander, who took the matter up to division. Gunfighter relieved the offending officer that afternoon, though I know the loss of an able subordinate was painful to him.

. . . .

White officers and noncoms could be tough on white troublemakers and shirkers, but many were reluctant to crack down on recalcitrant blacks for fear of being labeled racists. I had no such qualms, as in the case of a corporal whom I shall call Biggs. My command sergeant major, Albert Pettigrew, a soldier of the old school, came to me one day looking distressed. "Begging the colonel's permission," Pettigrew said, "I need to advise the colonel that we have a new man just transferred in from an artillery battalion up north, Corporal Biggs."

"So?"

"Corporal Biggs looks like trouble," Pettigrew said. "He's from that battalion where the CO got relieved because he lost control of his men. Biggs was the ringleader. Now he's got himself transferred here to Casey."

"Got himself transferred?" I asked. The resourceful Corporal Biggs, Pettigrew explained, had managed to have orders cut sending him wherever he wanted to go.

"I'd like to see this soldier," I told Pettigrew.

Soon Biggs was before me, a small, cocky-looking guy. "I'm really glad to be down here," he told me.

"Why?" I asked him.

Biggs informed me in a confidential tone that we had serious racial problems, but he thought he could handle them.

"Really," I said. "That's nice. But let me tell you the rules we go by in the Bucs." Biggs listened with bored courtesy as I explained how I ran my battalion.

The next thing I knew, Biggs was holding meetings of black troops behind the barracks, and proving a skilled organizer. He gave dire warnings of what white officers would do if blacks did not stand up to them. He used drugs to manipulate himself into a position of control. After three weeks of this provocation, I had Pettigrew bring me Biggs's file. After studying the file, I called the corporal to my office again. "How're you doing, Biggs?" I asked.

Biggs looked grave. "Sir, the battalion's got more trouble than I thought. I got here just in time. We ought to get together every day to talk things over."

"That won't be possible," I said.

"Why not?"

"You see, Corporal, there's a plane at Osan and you are going to be on it today. That plane is going to Travis Air Force Base in California, and when you get off, some people will be waiting with your discharge papers. And they're going to put you out the gate."

"You can't do that to me," Biggs protested.

"I've already done it. You're out of my battalion. Out of this brigade. Out of this division. Out of this man's Army. And you are unemployed."

I was on solid ground, since I had found enough misconduct in Biggs's record to support an "administrative discharge," a way to get rid of unfit soldiers for a miscellany of reasons. I called in Sergeant Major Pettigrew and two of my biggest, toughest NCOs to take the man away. Soon word went out to the battalion. "You hear what Bro P did? Whacked Biggs. That's right. Biggs is gone, man, gone. You don't mess with Bro P."

We had plenty of white problem soldiers. But proportionately we had more disciplinary problems with blacks. Less opportunity, less education, less money, fewer jobs for blacks equaled more antisocial behavior in the States, and these attitudes traveled. I also observed that black soldiers were less skillful at manipulating the system than white troublemakers. The blacks tended to be defiant, as if breaking the rules were a badge of black pride. Their attitude seemed to be "Take that," whereas the white offender's attitude was "Who? Little me, sir?"

Among the blacks, I had some of the finest soldiers and NCOs I have ever known. They had found in the Army a freedom in which they could fulfill themselves. I did not like seeing their proud performance tarnished by nihilistic types, a minority within a minority. What problem soldiers needed, like the kid with the pool cue, was someone to care about them other than a Biggs, with his siren song of self-destruction. I wanted to care for them positively. And, with all his excesses, so did Gunfighter.

One officer who had caught the Pro-Life religion was my immediate superior, the 1st Brigade commander, Colonel Peter G. Grasser. Grasser was an outstanding troop trainer, demanding yet able to win respect and affection. As winter deepened, the temptation was great for the troops to hibernate in their hooches or spend all their free time with their yobos, rather than engage in healthy outdoor activities. What the brigade needed, Pete Grasser concluded, was a skating rink to be ready by Christmas. Gunfighter heartily endorsed the plan. We put the troops to work finding the flattest piece of earth in Camp Casey and ringed it with sandbags to a depth of about six inches, sealed with rubber from fuel bladders. We had benches installed and cut fifty-five-gallon drums to use as fireplaces in which the men could toast marshmallows and roast chestnuts. Grasser ordered ice skates shipped in from God knows where, and bugged us daily about our progress. I could just imagine the sugarplum visions dancing in his head—soldiers gliding along the ice as Johnny Mathis sang "Chestnuts roasting on an open fire . . ." and Bing Crosby crooned "White Christmas," with booze, yobos, and B-girls in Tong Du Chon all but forgotten.

Finally, late one afternoon, the rink was completed, and the men filled it with water. We retired to the officers' club for drinks, waiting for the ice to form, which in Korea in December should not take long. At one point, I noticed a bunch of young lieutenants laughing slyly. My antennae always quiver when junior officers get a devilish gleam in their eyes. Soon they got up and left. I called to my exec at the other end of the bar. "Go and see what those guys are up to," I said.

He came back about a half hour later, red-faced either from the elements or from laughing himself silly. These lads had taken a fifty-five-gallon drum of antifreeze from the motor pool. The exec had caught them just as they were about to pour the stuff into Colonel Grasser's rink, which then would not have frozen at fifty degrees below zero. It made no difference. The rink hardened, but the surface resembled concrete and was unusable.

Gunfighter's favorite tool for promoting racial tolerance was the 1970 film *Brian's Song,* about the friendship between the black pro football player Gale Sayers and his white Chicago Bears teammate Brian Piccolo. We ran the movie in the post theater and followed it with a discussion. How far apart had these two men started? What divided them? What brought them together in genuine friendship? What lessons did their story have for the troops in Camp Casey? It was an effective tool. Gunfighter loved the movie and had it shown again and again. At one point, I counted that I had seen *Brian's Song* six times.

We got word one day that H. Minton Francis, head of the Pentagon's equal opportunity program, was coming to Camp Casey. Gunfighter was ecstatic. He wanted Francis to witness the troops watching and then talking about *Brian's Song.* My battalion drew the assignment. One problem! Most of my men were out in the field on training exercises, and most had seen the movie almost as often as I had. I came up with a plan to get us through the predicament. We would show the movie to about forty available troops in the battalion service club, where Gunfighter and Francis could observe the discussion in an intimate setting.

I had my staff pull together a roomful of men still available in the battalion area. I had timed it so that Gunfighter and Francis would arrive for the last ten minutes of the movie and the discussion period. We had just started running the film when I got an urgent phone call. Emerson's chief of staff, Colonel Paul Braim, was on the line. Gunfighter wanted my *entire* battalion watching the movie. I tried to explain why this was impossible. Maybe I did not understand, Braim said. Gunfighter wanted the movie and the discussion in a *full* theater, and he would be arriving in twenty minutes.

I stopped the movie and told the projection crew to set up in the post theater—and to get an ax from the firehouse en route in case the place was locked up. Every warm body in the area was to be dragooned to attend—asleep, awake, drunk, sober. I posted a couple of sergeants on the main road and told them to divert everybody they saw to the theater, no matter what battalion they belonged to. They found one guy in handcuffs being escorted to the jail by two MPs. All three were redirected to the theater. We managed to fill the house with bewildered troops by the time Emerson and Francis showed up.

I had just about enough time to place a few plants throughout the theater. When the film ended, one bright lieutenant spoke up on cue. "I think this film shows what people of different backgrounds can achieve when mutual respect, not race . . ." Gunfighter beamed. He and Francis stayed for about five minutes of this edifying talk and then left. I went onstage, thanked the men for coming, and told them they were now free to go about their business.

The whole thing had been another exercise in breaking starch, the kind of hollow effort I abhorred.

I felt like a fraud. Outside the theater, as I saw the men shaking their heads, I put my head down and started walking away. The first sergeant of the combat support company fell into step alongside me. "That was a hoot, sir, wasn't it?" he said.

"It was stupid," I blurted out. "I hate to see the troops do stupid things. I hate to be the one responsible for it."

He was quiet for a time. "Colonel Powell," he said, "don't worry. We don't know what that was all about. But the men know you wouldn't have cooked up anything that dumb on your own. They trust you. They won't hold it against you. We went along because you needed it. Relax, sir."

In all my years in the Army, among all the citations, medals, and promotions, I never appreciated any tribute more than I did the sergeant's words at that low point.

It was a cold April night, about 1:00 A.M. My battalion had been marching for four hours. The only sounds in the stillness were rifle butts slapping rhythmically against hips, leather boots thumping against the dirt road, and feet splashing through puddles. We had been on reverse cycle for a week, sleeping by day, training by night. Finally we had reached our destination. The exercise was over, and the exhausted, out-of-sync soldiers slumped to the ground, waiting to be trucked back to Camp Casey. I was particularly eager to return because the next day I was going home on leave. As I was sitting there, one of my officers approached with a message that the division lacked enough gas to transport the battalion back to camp. We would have to march the remaining thirty or so kilometers. The men wearily dragged themselves to their feet and started, too exhausted even to complain.

We were passing through a Korean village where the only sound was a dog howling in the night. My operations officer, Captain Harry W. "Skip" Mohr, dropped back from the head of the column to talk to me. "Sir," Mohr said with an excitement out of keeping with the weary mood, "we've got just a little more than twelve miles to go. If we kick the battalion into high speed, we can finish it in three hours and use this hike to qualify for the EIB." I had put the battalion through a punishing series of tests over the past three weeks. I was trying to qualify as many men as possible for the EIB, the Expert Infantryman's Badge, which is ordinarily earned by fewer than one infantryman out of five. We had already met the physical training requirement and the map reading, navigation, and other tests. The only remaining hurdle was completion of the twelve-mile hike in three hours. I looked back over the ragged column and said, "Skip, you've got to be kidding."

Mohr kept at it. "Sir, it's flat terrain until the last couple of miles. I know these men. They can do it."

One thing I had learned in the Army: you don't step on enthusiasm. The word went up and down the column to pick up the pace. The men fell into the rhythm like a train slowly picking up speed. Over the next couple of hours, parkas flew open, sweat trickled down faces in the frigid night, and the huffing and puffing of hundreds of men sounded like a peculiar wind. We faced one final, steep mountain leading into Camp Casey. I did not see how the men could make it. I myself had to stop every couple of hundred yards to take in gulps of air.

And then, up ahead, I heard a few isolated voices counting cadence in a Jody chant, then a few more, until the mountains rang with the battalion's singing. As we crossed the gate into the camp, the sergeants started whipping this herd into precision ranks. As we hit the paved road and passed division headquarters in parade-ground order, our raised voices woke up General Emerson. Gunfighter came out of his quarters in his bathrobe, beaming as the men passed in review. For me, this moment, in the middle of the Korean night, with seven hundred once bedraggled soldiers now welded into a spirited whole, was magical, one of the treasured memories of my life.

We qualified more men for the Expert Infantryman's Badge in our single battalion than were qualified in all three battalions of our neighboring infantry brigade. And the next day, I went home on leave, feeling as if I were leaving one family for another.

If it had been tough to leave the family for Korea the previous September, the separation after my ten-day leave was even harder. When I had left Alma to go to Vietnam in 1962, it was with the mind of a twenty-three-year-old off on an adventure. I was now thirty-seven. Professionally, the tour in Korea was the most satisfying so far. But the trip home showed at what price. I felt a confusion of emotions on leaving the house at Dale City, loss at missing out on beautiful moments in my children's growing-up, a touch of guilt at not bearing my share of the responsibility, and even a twinge of regret that they all seemed to be doing fine without me. If it had not been for people like Gunfighter, if it had not been for that other family waiting for me, going back to Korea would have been mere duty, unredeemed by any joy.

I returned in time for Gunfighter's latest enthusiasm, the Korean form of karate, tae kwon do. He brought in Korean army instructors to teach us the fine points. Everybody in the division was to perform tae kwon do every morning. Everyone was to join a team. Everyone was to earn a belt. And everyone was to wear the traditional tae kwon do white uniform. If you were going to do it right, Gunfighter said, you had to look right. Our G-4 (logistics) officer tried to explain that the U.S. government did not provide taxpayer funds for Korean martial arts attire. Gunfighter did not want to hear any nitpicking excuses. Soon every Korean tailor in sight was working day and night producing thousands of tae kwon do uniforms. I had progressed to a green belt when one day my driver landed a backward heel kick on my temple. My head exploded and I went down like a felled tree. I woke up to hear the driver moaning, "Oh my God! I killed the CO. I'm going to the stockade for sure!" I never made the next belt.

One morning at a commanders call, General Emerson announced, "Everybody in this division is going to be a high school graduate." Probably half of our troops were dropouts. Many had never succeeded at anything, never stuck to or completed a task, beyond enlisting in the Army or getting drafted. We were to find teachers, start classes, and prepare these men to take the GED, the General Educational Development program. And they'd damn well better pass.

We scoured the countryside, hired American wives whom some soldiers had brought to Korea at their own expense. We hired American civilians and assigned qualified officers and noncoms to teach. We set up classes in barracks, rec rooms, dayrooms, and supply rooms. From 3:00 P.M., when the men came in from field training, until supper, they were in class, studying English, math, science, and history. When the general asked what percent of our eligible soldiers were enrolled in the program and we reported 85 percent, he said, "Dammit, where's the other fifteen?" As Gunfighter saw it, the U.S. Army had entered into a contract with these young people. We had told them that the Army would make something of them, give them something useful to take back to civilian life. If they left without an education, they were headed back to the bottom of the heap.

While Gunfighter was promoting sound minds in healthy bodies, his division almost flunked the Annual General Inspection and did, in fact, fail the equipment maintenance phase. After reviewing the 2d Division's maintenance program, the inspector general concluded that it did not really have one. Emerson did not care. He was more interested in building men than in maintaining machinery.

His morale building could occasionally put a hole in a good night's sleep. I don't think Gunfighter knew rock and roll from a Gregorian chant, but he knew that the men missed rock concerts at home. So we had them, all night long, every couple of months, during which my quarters reverberated like a drum. One of the young lieutenants had an idea that tickled Gunfighter. In the States they had held Woodstock. Our all-night musical bashes were called Gunstock.

It was a day in spring. As I approached the brigade headquarters, I spotted a soldier wearing the Bucs crest coming out of the building. He was in dress greens on a post where just about the only time anybody wore anything but fatigues was to be court-martialed. He saluted, and, out of curiosity, I said, "What's up, son?" He had just been interviewed, he said, for Soldier of the Month. How had he made out? I asked. He had not made it, he said, looking disappointed. "I understand," I said. "The competition is stiff. Maybe next time."

"I'd have done better, sir, if I had more time to prepare," he said. That caught my attention. When had he gotten the word? I asked. This morning, he answered. I was furious, not so much because my battalion had missed out on an honor, but because sloppy staff work had turned this young man from a potential winner into a loser. Instead of recognition, he had experienced rejection. I patted him on the back and said I was proud of him anyway.

When I finished my business at brigade, I went back to my office and summoned Sergeant Major

Pettigrew. I wanted to know how we went about picking candidates for Soldier of the Month in the Bucs. It turned out to be hit-or-miss. "If we go into battle," I said, "we go in prepared. We don't send American soldiers into combat unprepared. I don't look at this situation any differently. This is the last time we're just throwing a kid into competition." I ordered Pettigrew to gather all his first sergeants and produce a system for finding the best soldier in the battalion every month—with plenty of time to groom him to meet the competition. We won Soldier of the Month the next five times in a row.

If you are going to achieve excellence in big things, you develop the habit in little matters. Excellence is not an exception, it is a prevailing attitude. My conviction—that you go in to win—was shaped in small encounters, such as going after Soldier of the Month. I was to carry that conviction throughout my career. If you are considering getting into Vietnam, Kuwait, Somalia, Bosnia, Panama, Haiti, or wherever, go in with a clear purpose, prepared to win—or don't go.

Officers of the rank of major and above got no medals under General Emerson. His explanation was characteristically blunt: "I don't believe in medals for senior officers. A field grade officer's job is to perform, and if you perform well, you'll get an outstanding efficiency report. And that's all you need. So don't waste your time writing up silly citations for each other. Don't waste the clerks' time."

Junior officers still got medals. NCOs too. And medals were showered on the other enlisted men. In

Emerson's view, these were kids who didn't quarterback the high school football team, didn't date the cheerleaders, didn't get elected to the student council, had never received enough recognition in their lives. He was finally going to make them winners at something. Newly arrived officers, on learning Gunfighter's attitude, were thrown off stride, particularly since his no-medal policy was so at odds with what they had known, especially in Vietnam. The result, however, was extraordinary. Soon medals did not matter. The bloated citations, the artificial pressures, disappeared. We just got on with our jobs. Some grumbling continued. Promotion boards were still going to take decorations into account for people who had served elsewhere, under commanders other than Gunfighter Emerson. But having observed the abuses in Vietnam, and believing that reform has to start somewhere, I supported Gunfighter's guts and wisdom.

In the fall of 1974 my tour was winding down, and my career might have fallen into jeopardy had General Emerson been a lesser man. The September evening started out civilly enough, with a farewell party for me at our cubicle-size Bucs battalion officers' club. As it turned out, Lieutenant Colonel Robert Newton, commanding a sister unit, the 2d Aviation Battalion, was also celebrating his departure. And so we joined forces and headed for the airmen's Mile-High Club. Membership was acquired by consummating the act of love in an airplane aloft, or by making a credible claim to the achievement, since witnesses were hard to produce.

After a few rounds, our combined group now headed for the more staid division officers' club. Our arrival coincided with a new social initiative. Single American women lived in Seoul, mostly teachers and civilian employees of the military, and the division staff had invited some of them up to Camp Casey. The intent was to demonstrate that civilized officers were not necessarily limited to Eighth Army headquarters. The women might find equally desirable dates, even prospective husbands, at Camp Casey.

And then our party barged into the O-club. What happened next is perhaps best conveyed in the after action report prepared by the club manager, Major Raymond H. Wagner: "Upon entry into the main bar, there were two officers sitting on top of the jukebox. I told them to get off . . . they refused. . . . The division G-1 indicated there might be trouble between the 2d Aviation Battalion and the 32d Infantry. . . . It was at this time that four or five officers grabbed LTC Powell and attempted to throw him over the bar. This resulted in a general free-for-all. . . . Fifteen to twenty officers were involved. . . . One unidentified officer was thrown over the bar, causing breakage to bottles. . . . It became a verbal match as to infantry versus aviation capabilities. The language used was hardly what could be considered in good taste as there were women at the far end of the bar. . . . One officer picked up the patio tables and threw them over the ledge, followed by the willful destruction of all the glasses they could find. . . . The swinging doors at the bar entrance had been destroyed. The Foosball game had been turned upside down. LTC Newton offered very little if any assistance in maintaining order. LTC Powell seemed to have control of his officers. . . . It is my judgment that the incident was provoked by members of the 2d Aviation Battalion. . . . My recommendation would be to change the name of the Mile-High Club to the Adolescent Club. . . ."

The next morning, while my head was still throbbing, my exec brought me a freshly typed letter from the deputy post commander, Lieutenant Colonel Chumley W. Waldrop, detailing damages to the club of $411.40 to be paid by my unit and the 2d Aviation Battalion, payment due by 1600 hours. I called Bob Newton—he answered sounding as if he were speaking through wool—and I reported the situation. "A fair apportionment of the damages," I added, "would be a hundred dollars from my guys and the rest from yours." In his fogged state, Newton did not argue.

Ordinarily, I had breakfast with the troops in the battalion mess hall. This morning I thought it prudent to breakfast at the division mess to gauge General Emerson's mood. Gunfighter must have noticed that several of his officers sported shiners, bruises, and puffed lips. He said nothing. But I detected on his seamed face a bemused smile. We paid our end of the damages, and that was the end of this puerile caper.

It is a different Army today. Such improper behavior, while not in the same league as the Tailhook affair and involving no women directly, would likely have resulted in disciplinary action and ruined careers, including my own. Once word leaked out to some crusading journalist, the brawl would probably pop up in a major newspaper or on TV news and might cost Emerson his neck too. But Korea was then an almost forgotten front. Nobody paid us much attention. We had few women in the Army, and very few stationed at an outpost like Camp Casey. Our behavior, admittedly, was occasionally animal house. But a certain stretch of the rules and common sense provided a practical solution to the misbehavior of lonely, bored men. Years of dedicated service were not destroyed for moments of foolishness.

Right to the end, Gunfighter had surprises in store. In my last days, he called me in and said he wanted my battalion to try out a new sport, combat basketball. It did not sound quite as lethal as combat football, until he started describing the game. We would put twenty men on each side. The objective, as in the conventional game, would be to get the ball through the hoop. But instead of just passing and dribbling the ball, you could advance it by kicking it, rolling it, or tucking it into your gut and plunging ahead like a fullback. Blocking and tackling were also permitted. And to give more fellows a chance to shine, we would again use two balls.

It sounded crazy to me, but it fit General Emerson's athletic philosophy. Conventional team sports, with their rigid regulation, favor stars. But in any-thing-goes, no-holds-barred sports, finely developed skills become marginal. The ninety-six-pound weak-ling can trip the all-county six-footer as easily as anyone else. In combat football, everyone's a quarterback. In combat basketball, everyone's a forward, a guard, a center. Gunfighter's goal was maximum participation. We inaugurated combat basketball in a big Quonset hut with steel beams arching down to the hardwood floor. I took no chances and posted an ambulance and medical team by the exit, which proved a wise precaution when players began bouncing off the girders. (I could imagine the possible outcome: "The Secretary of the Army regrets to inform you that your son, while slam dunking, was . . .") One single episode of mayhem ended combat basketball.

Gunfighter wanted me to extend my tour, and for a flicker of a moment, it was tempting. But the pull of my family at this point was too strong, and a coveted next assignment awaited me. I did, however, feel a deep sense of fulfillment as this tour drew to an end. My two previous field commands had been at the company level and had lasted only a few months each. They had left me with a sense of uncertain achievement. In the intervening eleven years, I had performed other worthwhile assignments, but they did not satisfy my reason-for-being. What I lived for was to be an able commander of infantry. I might tell myself that I was, but after the Korean tour, I felt it in my bones. All self-doubt had vanished.

I knew better than to expect any elaborate fanfare on turning over my command to my successor. I left Korea with less ritual than when I arrived. We were out on maneuvers on Rodriguez Range, and when the day's work was done, I shook my successor's hand, passed him the colors, wished him well, climbed into a helicopter for the ride back to Camp Casey, and flew home. No medals. No speeches. Gunfighter was as good as his word, however. He skipped the fireworks, but he gave me an excellent efficiency report, including a conclusion that I was general officer material.

I can easily put that man's occasional excesses into perspective. In the end, results are what matter. While I served under General Emerson, AWOLs in the division dropped by over 50 percent. Reenlistments jumped by nearly 200 percent. And while impetuous youths might occasionally punch each other out, racially related brawling practically disappeared. Gunfighter went on to make three stars and to command XVIII Airborne Corps before he retired. Many of his initiatives, hatched in the isolation of Korea, would probably not have withstood the scrutiny of the new Army, the Judge Advocate General's Office, the press, or the Medical Service Corps back in the States. Yet, I found this man inspiring. He had an instinct for knowing what gave soldiers pride, especially the rank and file who had rarely tasted any in their lives.

Gunfighter remained true to himself in every circumstance. After he got the big job with the big house as commander of XVIII Airborne Corps, he decided that such an elevated post required a wife. He recalled the name of a fine woman from a prominent family whom he had once met. He found her, romanced her, and proposed, in rapid succession. Alma and I were among the wedding guests at Fort

McNair. Chaplain Gianastasias was brought in to conduct the ceremony. Father G gave a lovely homily drawn from the wedding at Cana, weaving into his remarks his service with Gunfighter in Korea. As soon as the priest started down from the pulpit, the general, to the astonishment of the guests, started up the steps. "Did you hear that?" he exclaimed from the pulpit. Everyone in the church sat stunned. The groom went on. "Did you hear what that fine man of God just said about Korea? Yes, he was with me, a key part of our Pro-Life program." With eyes blazing and veins throbbing, Gunfighter proceeded to give as rousing a Pro-Life speech as if he were addressing the 2d Division instead of his wedding guests, with only the profanities omitted. His refined, artistic bride had not realized that she was marrying an Army corps, not just a man.

Had it not been for a Tom Miller and Red Barrett in Germany, a Bill Abernathy and Cider Joe Stilwell at Fort Devens, a Charles Gettys in Vietnam, a Gunfighter Emerson in Korea, I would have left the Army long ago. These men gave our lives a flavor, a spice, a texture, a mood, an atmosphere, an unforgettableness. I realize, looking back on that period over twenty years ago, that my service in Korea marked the end of an age. We were moving from the old Army to the new, from draftees and enlistees to an all-volunteer force of unprecedented standards, from an Army with few women to an Army with many. It was the end of the hard-drinking, hell-raising, all-male culture in which I had grown up. No longer would hundreds of men march through the post, throaty voices raised in profane Jody chants (I don't know, but I've been told, Eskimo [anatomy] are mighty cold. . . . Give me your left, your right, your left . . .). As one of my pals put it, it was "our last chance to be old-fashioned infantrymen before the lace-curtain Army took over."

Was the old Army better than the new? It was not. Today's force is superior, as proved in operations like Just Cause in Panama and Desert Storm in the Persian Gulf. And I do not forget the bad, which I have inventoried in some detail. In fact, I vowed to myself that I would never say in my retirement, "That's not the way we did it in the old days." Yet, late at night, when my thoughts drift, I fondly recall those days. I savor the intense camaraderie, the irrepressible characters, the coltish high spirits. And I recognize that thirty years from now, today's lieutenants and captains will have gone gray and will mistily recall their "old Army." I am proud to be part of the leadership that created the new Army just as I am proud to have been part of the old one that had to change. I came home from Korea having served the happiest year of my military career, in many ways because of what was and can never be again.

Just before I left Korea, I had bundled up all the letters Alma sent me. One of them I had read at the time with no particular reaction. But I have reread it since with a sense of wonder. On August 13, 1974, Alma wrote: "I feel we are on the verge of something exciting. I somehow don't feel that we will settle into a comfortable rut living out our lives in Dale City with you coming and going to the Pentagon. . . . I don't know what is in store for us, but something big and exciting will happen."

9 ☆ *The Graduate School of War*

WHILE I WAS in Korea, five generals had met in Washington to select Army officers to attend the service war colleges. I was lucky enough to be selected. The Army, Navy, and Air Force all have prestigious institutions, but the likelihood was that I would go to the Army War College. The president of the selection board was one of my mentors, Lieutenant General Julius Becton. Becton decided instead that I should go to the National War College at Fort McNair, in Washington, D.C. The NWC, the Harvard of military education, was open to about 140 students yearly, with equal attendance from all the armed forces as well as civilians from the State Department, the Central Intelligence Agency, and the U.S. Information Agency. Becton was an NWC graduate.

When you are in Korea on twelve-mile marches and bellowing Jody chants, the National War College seems as remote as the stars. I had been crouching in the mud on a Gunfighter Shootout when I got word that I had been chosen for NWC. I returned to the States in September 1974 at a strange interlude in our national life. The month before, President Nixon had resigned in the wake of the Watergate scandal, and just as I got home, Nixon's successor, President Gerald Ford, pardoned Nixon. I remembered Fred Malek's words on Watergate when I had decided not to stay on with the administration and had gone instead to Korea: this will all blow over.

NWC classes would not start until August 1975, and so I was temporarily assigned to the Pentagon, where I expected to mark time for nine months. William Brehm, assistant secretary of defense for manpower, reserve affairs, and logistics, had other ideas. "Colonel Powell," Brehm said, almost as I came through the door, "we're in hot water with Congress. We're supposed to produce an annual projection of the military's manpower needs. And we've been late for the last few years. I don't care how you do it, but your job is to get the report in on time."

For the first time, I began working with career Pentagon civilians, under Irving Greenberg, a thoroughgoing professional. A new challenge for me, but old to these hands, was to try to get the four services pulling together, since our report to Congress had to cover the manpower each service thought it deserved. As I began my task, I found that the Air Force had the fastest reaction time, not surprising from the youngest service and from people used to supersonic speed. The Marines Corps, the smallest service, fought as if its every manpower position was a battleground. The Navy was the most cautious about revealing its intentions. And the Army performance? Solid, dependable, but not all that imaginative.

Experiencing interservice rivalries firsthand turned out to be an important education for me. A time would come when juggling these competing interests would become almost my full-time job. This initial exposure introduced me to an eternal paradox: the rivalry among the services produces both the friction that lowers performance and the distinctiveness that lifts performance. The challenge then, now, and forever is to strike the right balance.

I worked like a dog those months, as John Brinkerhof, my immediate boss, and I went through endless drafts. It was a happy day for me when we submitted the report to Congress—ahead of time— and I could head for the National War College.

What pleased me about attending NWC, as much as the career significance, was that I did not have to uproot my family. We could go on living in Dale City as I commuted to NWC at the historic Washington Arsenal at Fort McNair. There is a majesty about the 1907 building where the college is located. From the grand entrance, you step into a marble three-story rotunda, encircled by balustraded galleries and crowned by a Spanish-tiled dome eighty feet high. The place has a hushed aura, something like the Lincoln Memorial. It was near this site that the Lincoln assassination conspirators were hanged, and the ghost of one of them, Mary Surratt, is said to haunt a nearby building.

At the college we were subjected to nothing so mechanical as multiple-choice questions. In fact, we took no examinations. The courses in history, politics, diplomacy, and military theory were designed for intellectual stimulation and growth rather than the mastery of technical material. Mornings we attended lectures in an auditorium resembling the medical school amphitheaters you see in nineteenth-century paintings. Our teachers were diplomats, academics, chiefs of the military services, writers, top people in every field. We were introduced to the great military thinkers and their ideas—Mahan on sea power, Douhet on airpower, and Clausewitz on war in general. In the afternoon, we had a choice of electives in subjects such as Futuristics, Media Impact on National Security, and Radical Ideologies.

It was a good time to be at the NWC. In the wake of Vietnam the soul searching—the what-went-wrong syndrome—created a lively ferment. A teacher who raised my vision several levels was Harlan Ullman, a Navy lieutenant commander who taught military strategy. So far, I had known men of action, but few who were also authentic intellectuals. Ullman was that rarity, a scholar in uniform, a line officer qualified for command at sea, also possessed of one of the best, most provocative minds I have ever encountered. Ullman and his fellow faculty members enabled me to connect my worm's-eye experiences to an overview of the interrelated history, culture, and politics of warfare.

That wise Prussian Karl von Clausewitz was an awakening for me. His *On War,* written 106 years before I was born, was like a beam of light from the past, still illuminating present-day military quandaries. "No one starts a war, or rather no one in his senses should do so," Clausewitz wrote, "without first being clear in his mind what he intends to achieve by that war and how he intends to achieve it."

Mistake number one in Vietnam. Which led to Clausewitz's rule number two. Political leaders must set a war's objectives, while armies achieve them. In Vietnam, one seemed to be looking to the other for the answers that never came. Finally, the people must support a war. Since they supply the treasure and the sons, and today the daughters too, they must be convinced that the sacrifice justifies the cost. That essential pillar had crumbled as the Vietnam War ground on. Clausewitz's greatest lesson for my profession was that the soldier, for all his patriotism, valor, and skill, forms just one leg in a triad. Without all three legs engaged, the military, the government, and the people, the enterprise cannot stand.

In my world, thus far, social life had centered on contemporaries in rank, maybe a notch above or a notch below, plus neighbors and relatives. Harlan Ullman knew no such boundaries. On one occasion, Harlan and his British-born wife, Julian, invited Alma and me to meet some of their friends at a dinner in their Georgetown townhouse. The guest of honor was to be Vice Admiral Marmaduke G. Bayne, president of the National Defense University, which included both the National War College and the Industrial College of the Armed Forces. In my circle, lieutenant commanders did not ordinarily hobnob with admirals, yet Harlan Ullman did. The admiral was friendly enough, but a flicker of puzzlement crossed his face when we were introduced. He had come expecting to meet Lewis Powell, associate justice of the Supreme Court, not a student from his own school.

At the NWC, wives were permitted to audit the elective courses, and Julian Ullman often came to hear Harlan lecture. She and I usually sat together. On drowsy Washington afternoons, it was not always easy to stay awake listening to "lessons for us today from the Punic Wars." Years later, after I had become deputy national security advisor, the Ullmans came to my fiftieth birthday party, and when it came time for me to make a little speech, I called Julian, with whom I shared the same birthday, to my side. I put my arm around her, and confided to the guests that while I was a student at the war college, she and I had slept together, adding, after an agonizing pause, "during her husband's lectures."

In February 1976, midway through the NWC, I received an accelerated promotion to full colonel. Many thoroughly respectable military careers top out at that grade, and I wondered how much further mine would go. The military then operated on a rigid career principle—up or out. The system was hard, competitive, and more ruthless than civilians probably realized. Those who did not make the next grade did not simply mark time in place. If passed over more than once for promotion, an officer had to retire to make way for the next generation. The competition got stiffer at every level. Of one hundred career lieutenants starting out, perhaps only one would make brigadier general.

I always tempered my career expectations with caution. Yet, soon after that accelerated promotion to colonel, I received more good news. After the war college, I was to take command of the 2d Brigade of the 101st Airborne Division at Fort Campbell, Kentucky. I was the youngest in my war college class to make colonel and one of only two Army officers in the class chosen for brigade command. In Korea, I had led a battalion of 700 men. Next, I would be commanding three battalions, totaling over 2,500 men. With all the caution in the world, I could not add up this evidence—National War College, accelerated promotion, upcoming command—without concluding that I might have a future at the senior level. I might make general. Still, there was a long way to go.

I was excited that after the war college I would be joining the 101st Airborne Division, "the Screaming Eagles," a storybook outfit. The 101st had been formed in mid-1942, along with the 82d Airborne Division, from the merger of five parachute regiments of the deactivated 82d Motorized Division. In the famous photograph of General Eisenhower saying farewell to paratroopers with blackened faces just before D-Day, he is talking to the men of the 101st. The 101st jumped into Holland in Operation Market Garden, immortalized in the book and movie *A Bridge Too Far.* When Bastogne was surrounded during the Battle of the Bulge, it was the 101st's commander, Brigadier General Anthony McAuliffe, who issued the legendary reply when the Germans demanded surrender: "Nuts." The 101st added to its fighting reputation in Vietnam.

And then I hit a mine. I was supposed to replace Colonel Fred Mahaffey, the fastest of fast burners, another DePuy protégé, the officer most of us expected to become Army Chief of Staff someday (until his untimely death). Major General John Wickham, commanding the 101st, called to inform me that Mahaffey was being promoted to brigadier general and would be leaving the 2d Brigade right away. Mahaffey's early departure meant that Wickham would have to fill my slot with someone else, since he could not wait another two months until I graduated from the war college. I was distressed. I was also not ready to give up.

The National Defense University had a policy that you could not leave the course early. Air Force Major General James Murphy was president of the National War College, under the university's president, Admiral Bayne. I went to Murphy and explained that if I could not leave early, I was going to lose this command and have to get back in the queue. Murphy was sympathetic, but reiterated the policy. I would have to finish my classes, go on an out-of-country field trip, and come back for graduation.

I saw a crack of daylight. Since I had made field trips abroad to Russia and China as a White House Fellow, maybe I could make a field trip more profitably elsewhere. How about Fort Campbell—home of the 101st? "Hmm," Murphy said. "You just might do that, then come back to present your final report and graduate with your class."

I contacted General Wickham and asked him to hold my command open. I hurried to Infantry Branch to pull a little sleight of hand, but hit another roadblock. They could not let me assume command on temporary duty while I was on permanent duty with the war college. Okay, I said, then assign me to Campbell permanently and make my return to the war college temporary. Velma Baldwin of OMB would have been proud of me, and Fred Malek too.

I brought my solution back to General Murphy. "Just one thing," he said. "Would you mind leaving your jump boots and 101st patch at Campbell when you come back? We don't have to flaunt our arrangement." I went out to Campbell without the family, took command, came back six weeks later, and graduated from the NWC.

In those days, the rule for Washington-area real estate was, what goes up just keeps on going up. We sold the house in Dale City, after living there for seven years, for about twice what we'd paid for it. Alma was ready for a change, and now that her husband was a bird colonel with a brigade, we should rate Army housing approaching elegance.

As usual, we drove—kids and all—from Washington to Fort Campbell, this time in a monster Chrysler, which I'd bought from a war college classmate, Bill Bramlett, for $50 and which averaged seven miles per gallon. Fort Campbell is in rural country astride the Kentucky-Tennessee border, about an hour north of Nashville. We followed directions to Cole Park, where the residences of the commanding general and brigade and battalion commanders were located. On the way in, we passed a rustic masterpiece, a log cabin mansion, General Wickham's home. Alma's eyes lit up. We passed a small Capehart home, named for the U.S. senator who sponsored military housing legislation. We passed another Capehart, and another and another, all the same. Alma's eyes narrowed. These, it turned out, were the brigade and battalion commanders' houses. We stopped before 1560 Cole Park, the house assigned to us. The three kids sprang from the car like tigers released from a cage and started exploring the outdoors while Alma and I went indoors.

"Nice," Alma said. "Same house we had at Benning with the hardwood floors, dishwasher, and air conditioning when you were a captain, except here we've got linoleum floors, no dishwasher, and no air conditioning, and now you're a colonel. Colin," she asked, "when are we going to get one of those fancy houses you promised?"

"Soon," I said.

John Wickham was the kind of officer whom gruffer types like to denigrate as a "political general" because he had served in the Pentagon as military assistant to two Secretaries of Defense, James Schlesinger and Donald Rumsfeld. Wickham faced another prejudice—he had gotten a command that ordinarily went to an aviator. I met him at division headquarters, a short, wiry man with steel-gray hair and a quiet, confident demeanor. I was surprised at how agilely Wickham moved. In Vietnam, the Viet Cong had thrown a satchel charge into his bunker; he was torn up so badly that he spent over a year in Army hospitals. John Wickham had paid his dues and was every inch a soldier.

Wickham's assistant division commander, Brigadier General Weldon C. Honeycutt, my immediate boss, had been a classmate of mine at Fort Leavenworth. "Tiger" Honeycutt was a born warrior who had come out of Vietnam a hero and who may have been the most profane man in the Army, where the competition is fierce. "Powell," he greeted me when I first reported in, "besides Leavenworth, I don't know shit about you, but welcome to the 101st anyway. Best son-of-a-bitching division on God's green earth." He sat down and left me standing as he reviewed the division. "We've got three infantry brigades," he said. "Yours is dead-ass last. You got Kinzel"—Lieutenant Colonel Arthur Kinzel—"the best battalion commander out here, running your 501st Infantry. But your 502d and the 506th are at the bottom of the heap. So fix 'em. Now get your ass outta here."

Thank you, sir. If this had been my first exposure to the Tiger Honeycutts of this world, I might have been upset. The Army, however, was full of them. They provided the pepper that stings, but spices as well. Colonel Ted "Wild Turkey" Crozier, General Wickham's chief of staff, was another memorable figure. His nickname derived from a spiritous product that he favored and from his explosive enthusiasms. He had been sent by the Pentagon to Fort Campbell presumably to ride out his time to retirement in serenity. Instead, he had gotten the key chief of staff job and continued to live up to his reputation. At Campbell, John Wickham provided the vision. Honeycutt and Crozier applied the lash to get the

crew to comply. Fortunately, we had two officers fulfilling the chaplain role, Brigadier General Chuck
Bagnal, the assistant division commander for support, and Colonel Arthur Lombardi, an old-timer
who ran day-to-day post operations. While the
enforcers ranted and raved, Bagnal and Lombardi
spoke with calmness and reason. While the others
raised hackles, these two smoothed feathers. With
vision only, you get no follow-through. With
enforcers only, the vision is realized but leaves a lot
of wreckage. Good chaplains pick up the pieces and
put everything together again. At Campbell, fortunately, we had all three roles filled.

The 101st had a unique mission, helicopter-borne
assault, and General Wickham was its apostle. The
division was the only air assault unit in the world
combining light infantry battalions and helicopter
battalions to move them swiftly around the battlefield. We were airborne, but not paratroopers. And
we certainly were not heavy armor. Consequently,
we took flak from both sides. Any airborne troops
who did not jump were "legs," the paratroopers'
term, not intended as a compliment. Any soldiers
who flitted around in anything as flimsy as a helicopter would not last five minutes on a battlefield,
said the heavy armor people. Our mission, John
Wickham believed, was to prove both sides wrong.

"Reforger" was the upcoming show that fall of 1976.
It stood for "Return of Forces to Germany," an
annual exercise through which the United States

assured our NATO allies that we could rapidly reinforce the Continent. This year, the 101st was to carry out Reforger, and I was hoping to go back as a colonel and brigade commander to the haunts where I had served as a lowly lieutenant eighteen years before.

Two of the 101st's three brigades were to go on Reforger and one would be left behind for stateside duties. To my bitter disappointment, my brigade, the 2d, had already been designated to stay home. I moped for half a day and then decided that we were not going to listen to the other two brigades' war stories when they got back. We were going to have our own little surprise.

Air assault school is to the helicopter forces what jump school is to paratroopers. I decided to qualify as many of my soldiers as possible at the school, starting with me. So far, none of my fellow infantry brigade commanders had been able to pass the physical training test to get into air assault school. I presented myself to the noncoms who ran the test, did my push-ups, squats, pull-ups, ran the obstacle course—and flunked the last by a tenth of a second. I went back a week later sufficiently primed to pass the test. At age thirty-nine, I felt like an old man trying out for college football, rappelling out of helicopters and making twelve-mile forced marches as the senior officer among about one hundred enlisted soldiers.

After I had earned my air assault badge, I gathered my battalion commanders, company commanders, and staff and made an announcement. "Some of you are not air-assault-qualified," I said, pointing to my new badge. "On October 30, we are going to be photographed together, and anybody in that picture without the badge will be out of the picture in this brigade as far as I am concerned."

I went to my three chaplains and told them to enroll in the air assault course too. To make it easier for them, I locked up the chapel, except on weekends. Chaplains belonged with the troops, I suggested, and the troops did not always frequent the chapel. The Baptist chaplain objected. He had not entered the Army to play commando, he advised me. If he expected to comfort my troops, I said, he was going to complete air assault school along with every other officer. He grudgingly complied and broke his leg during the first week. After an appropriate interval, I asked him when his cast was coming off. "Why?" he asked. "So you can finish the course," I answered. He got himself transferred to another brigade.

Six weeks later, the rest of the division returned from Germany, having had a successful exercise. General Wickham was impressed by our accomplishments in his absence—particularly the 100 percent air assault qualification among my officers. Since he did not want my brigade to feel like Cinderella, he had Ted Crozier lean on me to put my men in for awards for outstanding achievements. I submitted a few names. But I was of the Gunfighter Emerson school. Inflation debases currencies and medals. I had my own reward in the lesson learned. If you get the dirty end of the stick, sharpen it and turn it into a useful tool.

. . .

My folks came to Fort Campbell to celebrate Thanksgiving in 1976. Mom enjoyed catching up on her grandchildren and helping Alma in the kitchen. But Pop had come to Fort Campbell to see and be seen. I bundled him up in a black coat with his ever-present fedora and had my driver take us all around the post in a jeep. Since Luther had never heard a gun fired in his life, I took him to an M-16 rifle range so that he could see what his son did for a living. We had drinks at the officers' club. We went to the division boxing matches with General Wickham. Luther sat in the front row as if he had never sat anywhere else, and he chatted with Wickham as if he had known generals all his life.

I wanted to give Mom and Pop another taste of the world I lived in. My brigade still used the old-fashioned company mess halls, and that was where the Powell family went for Thanksgiving dinner. We took our places at the CO's table and the cooks served us turkey with all the trimmings. I looked around at one point, and Pop was gone. I spotted him in the kitchen talking to the cooks, shaking hands, telling them what a fine meal they had put on. Then he started table-hopping through the mess hall, like Omar Bradley mixing with the troops before an invasion. What impressed me was my father's total aplomb. He was never daunted by rank, place, or ceremony. Luther Powell belonged wherever Luther Powell happened to be. On his last night with us, Pop sidled up to Alma in the kitchen and whispered, "Colin's going to be a general." Alma asked how he knew. He had been talking, Pop said, to General Wickham.

The next day, I drove my folks to the Nashville Airport. As we headed for the terminal, Pop, for once, made no fuss about my carrying his bags. His step was slower, his face a little drawn. My father was growing old. And it shocked me.

The admirable General Wickham had a few passions, one of which was thermostats. These were the days of the energy crisis and rocketing oil prices. The general had promulgated one inviolable rule: thermostats in every building on post were to be set at sixty-eight degrees. It is a civilized temperature if you are in a modern, well-insulated, evenly heated structure. The men of the 2d Brigade, however, were in World War II, two-story, uninsulated barracks heated by one oil furnace in a corner of the first floor. If your bunk was near the furnace, then you received the promised sixty-eight degrees. But the farther away you were, the less correlation there was between the thermostat setting and the temperature. And it gets cold in Kentucky in the winter.

Every night, the division duty officer spot-checked, and if anybody had touched the thermostat, the brigade commander had to report personally to General Wickham to explain why he could not enforce a simple order. I have never felt quite so foolish as I did standing before the commanding general of the 101st Airborne Division explaining why the thermostat in one of my barracks was discovered at a tropical seventy-three degrees.

The men and officers now became engaged in a battle of wits. These soldiers were ready to die for their country in wartime, but they were not prepared to freeze to death for it in peacetime. They continued to raise the setting. We had steel ammo boxes nailed over the thermostats and put locks on the boxes. First the men began jimmying them open. When the perpetrators of this crude gambit were caught and punished, the more cunning types managed to have keys made.

Most officers were college graduates, some with advanced degrees, the products of the Command and General Staff College, even the National War College, the heirs of Washington, Grant, Lee, Pershing, Eisenhower, and Patton. Were we to be out-maneuvered by privates and corporals? Apparently yes, because as the winter wore on, something peculiar occurred. The thermostats remained at sixty-eight degrees, yet the men stopped complaining. Those even in the remotest reaches of the barracks were warm as toast. Spring approached before we solved the mystery. Some electrical genius had figured out that by sticking a straight pin into the wiring at an undetectable place, you could short out the system and, in effect, free the furnace from control by the thermostat. Even if the duty officer found the barracks hot as the equator, the thermostat still showed sixty-eight degrees. When the heat became uncomfortable, out came the straight pin, until the temperature dropped. Everybody was happy, from General Wickham to the thinnest-blooded private in the farthest, draftiest corner of the barracks.

Officers have been trying for hundreds of years to outsmart soldiers and have still not learned that it cannot be done. We can always count on the native ingenuity of the American GI to save us from ourselves, and to win wars.

Every afternoon, I walked a fixed route, at the same time, through the streets of my three battalions, deliberately letting myself be ambushed. I had lifted a leaf out of Father Gianastasias's book. Go where your flock is. It did not take long for the soldier with a gripe, the noncom with a problem, to figure out where he could waylay the brigade commander for a private minute or two. Good NCOs and junior officers understood what I was doing. I was not breaking the chain of command. They knew that I would never agree to anything in these curbside sessions that would undermine their authority. If anything, my outdoor office hours gave them a chance to blow off steam too.

Mike and I were playing pitch and catch behind the house in Cole Park one day when he volunteered that he liked it at Fort Campbell. "All the kids are like us," he said. "Everybody's mom and dad do the same thing." His words were a relief to me. I grew up in the same neighborhood with the same kids well into my college years. One attraction of Dale City had been that even though I was gone part of the time, my family stayed in the same home and the children stayed in the same school system. Service parents worry about the effect on their children of constant uprooting. And here was my son telling me that the move was fine, that the common experience of the fathers made for a comfortable common ground for the kids.

Life was good at Fort Campbell, although we had to do a little restructuring. We found only a tiny Episcopal congregation, without an organist for the hymn-singing or a cross for the processions. Alma and I worked with the Episcopal chaplain to find other communicants on the post, many of whom had slipped into the inactive reserve. We sat down over several nights and wrote notes, inviting them to get active again. We located a pianist and a processional cross and conscripted our kids once more as acolytes. The congregation began to grow, and we found our faith anchored once again. But we were never able to recapture entirely the spirit of St. Margaret's after we left Dale City.

My kids attended on-post schools operated under the authority of the federal Department of Health, Education and Welfare. We had a school board, and I was appointed board president by General Wickham, which put the Powell children on the spot. Not only was their old man the brigade commander, he was also the guy who hired, fired, and paid their teachers.

My kids were turning out to be good students, including Annemarie, who began first grade at Fort Campbell. Mike became the star catcher on the junior high baseball team, which allowed me to bask a bit. Linda showed an aptitude for music. At first we rented a flute for her from the school. She progressed quickly, and the teacher recommended that Linda have a flute of her own. Ever the dutiful father, I scanned the "For Sale" section of the *Post Daily Bulletin* and parted with $25 for a used flute. Linda was appalled. Alma was appalled. So was the flute teacher. This instrument leaked more air than a '72 Vega with 100,000 miles. We bought her a better flute. She continued to excel, and the flutes improved. She topped out, fortunately, before we reached the $25,000 gold top-of-the-line model.

More important than flute lessons, Linda received the greatest educational gift at Campbell, a teacher who made a difference. Betty Querin taught sixth grade and possessed the rare capacity to communicate with budding teenagers. The middle child often occupies an anomalous position between the firstborn and the baby, and Linda found that with Betty she could share her innermost feelings. This teacher awakened my daughter intellectually, and to this day they remain close. Every child deserves at least one Betty Querin.

We rarely know what our children think of us, what, from the flood of childhood impressions and memories, stands out and what fades. Recently, the photographer Mariana Cook did a book on fathers and daughters and asked Linda and Annemarie to provide an observation to accompany our photograph. Linda wrote: "My father is a gentle man, but, as a child, I remember being a little afraid of him— he was so big. He rarely raised his voice, but when he did, my heart would drop through my stomach. But I also remember once weaving a pink-and-white net around my bicycle as decoration so that as I picked up speed it would trail color behind me. The net got caught in the spokes and I went flying over the front of the handlebars. I sat stunned and crying on the asphalt. My father appeared from nowhere, scooped me up, held me close, and carried me home." I did not remember the incident, but she never forgot.

Annemarie wrote in the same book: "Dad is the smartest person I have ever known. He always wins at Trivial Pursuit. He's always been frank with me when it was necessary. He looks great in a tux or his dress blues. His successes never surprise me; they just make me proud. He's the best mechanic in town. I have always had the secure feeling that he could and would take care of us, no matter what."

Who am I to quarrel with my daughters' judgments, especially regarding mechanics?

Where the children are concerned, I never believed that possessions could buy love, popularity, respect, or accomplishment. Consequently, I have always been careful about giving them money. They received an allowance of $2 a week when they reached age twelve. They wanted for nothing; but they were taught not to want too much. And on the big holidays, Christmas and birthdays, they got the big presents.

When Mike reached his teens, I thought it was time to give him some grounding in the facts of life. The way I handled the matter was direct, but I am not sure how courageous. I stopped by his room one night and handed him a paper bag with a book in it entitled *Boys and Sex.* "What's this?" he asked. "Read it," I answered, "and let me know if you have any questions."

As each of my children reached age sixteen, I wrote him or her a letter trying to pass along what I hoped was wisdom, or at least the benefit of my right choices and mistakes. Mike was first, and I wrote, among other things, "You now begin to leave childhood behind and start on the road to manhood. . . . you will establish definitively the type person you will be the remaining fifty years of your lifetime. Temptations will come your way, drugs, alcohol, opportunities for misbehaving. You know what is right and wrong, and I have confidence in your judgment. . . . Don't be afraid of failure. Be more afraid of not trying. . . . Take chances and risks—not foolhardy actions but actions which could result in failure, yet promise success and great reward. And always remember that no matter how bad something may seem, it will not be that bad tomorrow."

I watched with fascination what each side of the family contributed to the character of our children. Alma's folks and mine could not have been more different. Mike and Linda, when they were small, lived with the Johnsons while I was in Vietnam. We managed to visit my parents "on the way" no matter in which direction of the compass we were traveling. The Johnsons were not much for emotion. They lived disciplined, austere lives. They were voracious readers. They read to the children, and reading tends to be contagious. From them, my kids absorbed a sense of discipline and a respect for learning. From the Powell side, the children absorbed a love of life. They met funny, irreverent characters, people who laughed, deep from the belly, without restraint, people who played as hard as they worked. Let's have a party. Let's have a song. Let's dance. I enjoyed watching both strains blossom in my children.

From the day Pop pulled up to 952 Kelly Street with a 1946 Pontiac, I began a love affair with cars. I loved to drive them, but what went on under the hood might as well have been magic. In Dale City, I lived next door to a fellow who would listen to me gripe about my car problems and say, "Check the voltage regulator," which would have been fine if I'd known what it was. I bought a Chevy manual, and little by little I began demystifying the gizmos under the hood. Pretty soon I was changing my own oil!

Across the street, another Dale City neighbor rebuilt Volkswagens as a hobby. A Volks had been my first car. I still had a soft spot for them even after family expansion forced me to sedans and station wagons. I started hanging around, handing tools to this guy, learning more. By the time I reached Fort Campbell, I could adjust the timing on the distributor, solder a radiator, and trouble-shoot the electrical system. While I enjoyed sports, they never became obsessions, no doubt because of my modest athletic ability. But automobiles had a special appeal. In my professional life, whether in field commands or desk jobs, I was always dealing with unpredictable human beings, their foibles—and mine. The situation compounded as I rose in rank and responsibility. Cars, unlike people, lack temperament. When working on them, I was dealing not with the gods of the unknown, but the gods of the certain; not the gods of abstraction, but the gods of the concrete. If something malfunctioned in the engine, and I proceeded logically, I could identify the problem and fix it, the only area in life where I had that kind of control. I found these mechanical puzzles absorbing and relaxing. I had found my true hobby.

Alma found her avocation at Fort Campbell. This was the first post where her husband was a commanding officer and where her relationship to the wives was somewhat analogous to my relationship to my officers. She became the mother figure to the younger women. She plunged into volunteer work at a time when the women's liberation movement had taken off and some feminists disparaged unpaid hospital work, bake sales, and fund drives. That attitude, Alma believed, overlooked the singular nature of military life. Husbands of service wives might leave on a moment's notice. When or if they were coming back was never certain. "If we don't get to know each other now," Alma would say, "how can we help each other through the tough, lonely times?" Beyond their immediate value, the traditional volunteer activities were providing just what the feminists championed, sisterly support.

It had been only two years since I had bade farewell to the old Army in Korea. At Fort Campbell, we were almost, but not quite, into the new Army. The new jargon was coming into vogue. It was during this period that the old mess hall gave way to the "dining facility" and the old mess sergeant became the "dining facility manager." The post laundry became the "Installation Fabricare Facility." I almost gagged.

The new all-volunteer force was to be evaluated by modern management measures—reenlistment rates, AWOL rates, drunk-driving rates, annual physical fitness rates, medical appointment show-up rates, and delinquency rates on supply store accounts. Every month, each brigade, battalion, and company got a printout reporting how well it was doing compared to other units. You needed these statistical measures to judge comparative performance in a huge organization like the Army. But numbers alone cannot measure factors like morale, leadership, and that feeling that a unit is combat-ready. Gunfighter Emerson could not have focused on a printout of these statistical indicators if you held a pistol to his head.

I had long since learned to cope with Army management fashions. You pay the king his shilling, get him off your back, and then go about doing what you consider important. If, for example, you are going to judge me on AWOL rates, I'm going to send a sergeant out by 6:30 A.M. to bloodhound the kid who failed to show up for 6:00 A.M. reveille. The guy's not considered AWOL until midnight. So drag him back before then and keep that AWOL rate down. I vigorously set out to better every indicator by which my brigade was statistically judged. And then went on to do the things that I thought counted.

I detected a common thread running through the careers of officers who ran aground even though they were clearly able—a stubbornness about coughing up that shilling. They fought what they found foolish or irrelevant, and consequently did not survive to do what they considered vital.

Once, however, I violated my own rule. The new Army, sensibly, had decided to curb excessive drinking. We had too many alcohol-fogged performances, too many families wrecked by drink, too many people killed in alcohol-related car crashes. Wickham rode this one hard. If a soldier was picked up for driving under the influence, he and his sergeant, company commander, battalion commander, and brigade commander were all to report to Wickham or Tiger Honeycutt and give an explanation. Then Wickham upped the stakes. Any officer caught driving under the influence was to receive an Article 15 proceeding, nonjudicial punishment that could mean a ruined career. MPs were posted outside the officers' club to pounce on any officer suspected of having had one too many.

I called in all my officers. I was going to save them from themselves by creating what amounted to a job action. "The club's off-limits," I announced. "No Happy Hour. No Italian-night dinner with wine. No O-club at all. Not for the 2d Brigade." As I said this, you could have heard a cork drop.

Receipts at the club took a nosedive. Chuck Bagnal, the assistant division commander who ran Fort Campbell's clubs, asked if I had lost my mind. "We can't have it both ways, sir," I said. "You can't have MPs parked outside waiting to nab my officers while another part of the Army is selling drinks for a quarter at Happy Hour."

Within a couple of weeks, I had Wild Turkey Crozier on my back. "Powell," he said, "you can't put the club off-limits to your brigade."

"I'm already doing it," I said, and repeated my sermon on hypocrisy. The Army could not condemn behavior with one hand and promote it with the other.

"Bullshit!" Crozier explained. "Back off."

I knew that I had played out this hand. I had fought the good fight, but did not want to make it my last fight. You cannot slay the dragon every day. Some days the dragon wins. I reopened the officers' club to my brigade. But I also made sure that my officers understood the consequences of anything more than one social drink. The MPs stopped lurking outside; and in time Happy Hour became a thing of the past in the Army.

I had an adjutant, Major James D. Hallums, whose duties included running the brigade sports competitions, which at Fort Campbell were red-hot. "Sir, we can take the division boxing championship," Hallums told me one day. We had a sergeant in the brigade known as Hammering Hank, he said, a near pro with a lot of experience in coaching boxing teams. I told Hallums to go ahead. Never step on enthusiasm.

Soon he was back with a conspiratorial smile. Not only was the 2d Brigade team looking strong, but Hammering Hank had scouted the competition, and not one outfit at Fort Campbell had a featherweight, the 120–125-pound class. All we had to do was field a fighter and we could win the division featherweight championship strictly with byes. That was true, I agreed. But I pointed out that we did not have a featherweight.

"Colonel," Jim went on, "do you remember that kid from the 506th who kicked in almost a thousand dollars for the United Way Drive, Pee Wee something?" I certainly did. Most of the troops contributed $1. This soldier's donation had been so out of line that I had told Hallums to bring him to my office so that I could see if he was all right. His name was Rodney "Pee Wee" Preston and he turned out to be a shy little guy who might weigh 120 pounds soaking wet. He explained his philanthropy by telling us that the Army took care of all his wants, and therefore he should do all that he could to help others.

"Let's get Pee Wee for our featherweight," Hallums said.

"Has he ever boxed?" I asked.

What difference did it make, Hallums replied. He wasn't going to fight. He was just going to draw byes.

Hallums managed to persuade Pee Wee to join the boxing team. His most persuasive argument was that Pee Wee would not have to go with his battalion on jungle training exercises in Panama—the soldier had an obsessive fear of snakes. Even though Pee Wee was not going to fight, Hammering Hank proved to be a coach of integrity and insisted that Pee Wee had to train along with everyone else.

The boxing tournament began, and our strategy worked. Pee Wee drew byes at one level after another until he was headed for the 101st Airborne Division featherweight championship, without, so far, having had a glove laid on him. In the championship matches, our fighters went up against the division's

Support Command. The commander of the Support Command, on to our little scam, had scoured his ranks and also discovered a featherweight. Consequently, when Pee Wee stepped into the ring that night, a Panamanian kid resembling a miniature Roberto Duran climbed into the opposite corner. This lad bounced around, snorting like a bull, pumping warm-up uppercuts like pistons. Pee Wee, in the meantime, stood in his corner looking like a lamb at the slaughterhouse. As Hallums and I watched from the first row, I turned to Jim and said, "The deal's off. I am not going to be an accessory to murder." I went to Pee Wee's corner and told him that this was not in his contract. He did not have to fight.

"Oh no, sir," he said. "I have to. The whole 506th's here."

Which was true. Pee Wee's battalion was present in force and in combat fatigues, since they were going directly from the fight to maneuvers in Panama, which Pee Wee had escaped. I was not sure whether they had come to laugh or cry.

The bell sounded for round one. The Panamanian bounded to the center of the ring and began hitting away as if Pee Wee were a punching bag. I winced. Pee Wee did what Hammering Hank had taught him. He kept his arms in close to his body while his gloves protected his face. He kept circling to his left, taking the pounding, until the bell sounded, ending round one. Pee Wee had not thrown a punch, but he was still standing and apparently unhurt. Some modest cheering went up from our side. "Attaboy, Pee Wee! Hang in there, kid!"

Round two, a carbon copy of round one. The Panamanian pummeled Pee Wee. Pee Wee kept his guard up, circled, and never punched. But I noticed that his opponent had slowed down toward the end of the round, as though the sheer effort of beating on Pee Wee had tired him. End round two. By now the cheering for Pee Wee had become loud and enthusiastic. We could see his opponent in his corner shaking his head, grumbling about something to his trainers. Hammering Hank, in the meantime, kept begging Pee Wee, "Just throw a punch, kid. Just one. Any punch!"

Round three, the final round. The two boxers came out of their corners, the Panamanian sluggishly. It was becoming clear that this guy knew how to box, but was out of shape. Out of nowhere, Pee Wee hit him with a right to the jaw. The Panamanian's arms dropped and the guy quit! The place went crazy. The whole brigade was screaming, "Pee Wee! Pee Wee!" The referee declared a TKO. Pee Wee had become the legitimate featherweight champion of the 101st Airborne Division. His battalion descended on him, hugging him, kissing him, carrying him on their shoulders.

Frank Capra could not have done better. Although Capra would have yelled, "Cut! Print it!" at this point. Pee Wee, however, as division champ, now had to go to Fort Bragg to fight the featherweight champion of the 82d Airborne Division for the XVIII Airborne Corps championship. There I had the pleasure of sitting with my old boss, the present commanding general of the corps, Gunfighter Emerson. I told Emerson the story of Pee Wee. His eyes shone and he kept saying, "Dammit! Dammit! Dammit! You hear what this man is saying? You hear what that boy's accomplished?"

This night, Pee Wee again managed to hang in gamely for all three rounds but was outpointed and lost on a decision. Gunfighter nevertheless had to meet Pee Wee. We found him in the locker room, where the general pumped his hand until I thought it was going to break off. "By God, son," he gushed, "you're what it's all about! You're the real champ!" Pee Wee was, in fact, the incarnation of everything Gunfighter believed, the little guy who, if given half a chance, could for one shining moment become a winner.

Sixteen years later, as I was retiring as Chairman of the Joint Chiefs of Staff, Katie Couric of NBC interviewed me in the Pentagon for my last profile in uniform. I told her the Pee Wee story as an example of inspiration. She was intrigued and managed to have her crew track him down. (At first they found the wrong Pee Wee, Mike Caruthers, another boxer in the brigade with the same nickname.) She had Pee Wee Preston interviewed for the program. He was now a metalworker in Shelbyville, Illinois, married, and with two kids. If those kids ever asked, "What did you do in the war, Daddy?" Pee Wee had quite a story.

One day I got a call from Gunfighter's staff telling me that the old soldier was about to retire, and XVIII Airborne Corps was going to put on a big show.

Emerson had personally requested me to command the troops for the parade. I begged off. Fort Bragg was the home of the 82nd Airborne. Even though the 101st was part of Emerson's corps, the paratroopers of the 82d would not appreciate having someone from the 101st come over to lead their troops. Ten minutes later an aide was on the phone again. "The general said, 'Tell Powell to get the hell down here.' " It sounded like the Gunfighter to me.

I went to Fort Bragg and started whipping these brawny paratroopers into marching trim, much as I had done as a drill team leader at CCNY. On the appointed day, thousands of people were in attendance and Gunfighter stood on the reviewing stand, shaking every hand in sight and slapping every back. I was standing before the troops at parade rest when I saw him gesture for me to come over. He thanked me for taking charge of the parade and said he had something special he wanted me to do. When he gave the word, I was to order the officers to do an about-face, so that they would be facing the troops from about eight inches away. I started to question him about this novel command, but he told me not to worry. I went back and managed to get the word passed along to the other officers on parade.

The ceremony began with speeches and awards honoring Emerson. When the time came for Gunfighter to speak, he could barely compose himself. He began weeping, repeating himself, and summoning the names of long-dead comrades. He paused at one point, looked straight at me, and shouted, "Now!"

"Officers—and officers only—" I ordered, "about face!" There we stood almost nose-to-nose with the soldiers, wondering what was supposed to happen next.

Then Gunfighter bellowed from the reviewing stand, "Officers, salute your soldiers!"

It was a moving gesture, pure Gunfighter Emerson, and in its simple symbolism said everything that had to be said about armies and about who, in the end, most deserves to be saluted.

After my experiences in Korea, I was highly sensitive to the Army's racial environment. One of my early acts at Fort Campbell was to call in my executive officer, Lieutenant Colonel Henry B. "Sonny" Tucker, and tell him I wanted to meet the NCO handling equal opportunity and affirmative action. Sonny, a big, casually powerful Alabaman, eyed me strangely, but said he would produce the man.

Tucker ordinarily had a wonderful way of handling soldiers and their problems, which I could overhear through our adjoining office wall: "Come here, son, you make my colonel unhappy, you make me unhappy. So let's see how fast you can make us both happy again." Somehow, problems disappeared overnight. But this time nothing happened. Two days later, I repeated that I wanted to see the EEOC noncom. "We're looking, we're looking," Sonny assured me. If he could not find the man, how much importance could the brigade be giving to this subject? After my third demand, Tucker brought in a fat, listless sergeant wearing low-quarter shoes and white socks. He was on limited duty because of a leg injury, and coasting out his last months before retirement. I dismissed the man and then tore into Sonny Tucker. This guy was a dud. What kind of attention were we giving this mission?

"Calm down, Colonel," Sonny said. "We don't have to waste a crackerjack sergeant on this problem. We haven't had a racial complaint in the brigade in months."

I started poking around, asking questions, testing Tucker's report. He turned out to be right. While we had not achieved perfect racial harmony, the present Army nowhere near resembled the one I had left in Korea. The reason was largely the all-volunteer system. By now, draftees were long gone. And the current recruits, white or black, were doing well in everything, including race relations, mostly because they were better educated and in the Army by choice. I nevertheless recruited a top-notch equal opportunity NCO to make sure things stayed that way.

I also pressured Sonny about attendance at high school equivalency courses. "Most of these soldiers are already high school graduates," he informed me. What about our classes in English as a second language? "We don't take recruits anymore who don't speak English," Sonny explained patiently. It was becoming a better Army, maybe not as much fun as the Army of my sentimental reveries. But then, fun was not its reason for being. The post-Vietnam reforms were taking hold. The Army was rebuilding itself with a restored sense of pride and purpose.

. . .

I was happily immersed in commanding troops when in February 1977 I received a call to come to Washington. A new administration had been inaugurated on January 20, one for which I had voted. I had been impressed on meeting Jimmy Carter when I was a White House Fellow. But my vote was more influenced by a belief that, after the ordeal of Watergate, the country needed a fresh start. I was still voting absentee as a permanent resident of New York City and had not enrolled in a party, nor have I ever.

I had been summoned to Washington to be interviewed for a National Security Council job by Carter's National Security Advisor, Zbigniew Brzezinski. Here we go again, I thought, off the career track, and I did not want it. I went to see John Wickham first, who was not only my superior officer but an operator skilled in the Washington labyrinth. "Go," Wickham said. "At least you have to talk to him."

I was doing something that I loved to do and needed to do—validate myself once again as a true infantry officer. I had managed to make the transition from the old to the new Army without too much culture shock. I hated the idea of leaving again so soon. I had served with other divisions, but the 101st, so full of legend, had captured my heart. When I had taken over the brigade, I had been handed a special coin, another 101st tradition. Whenever a fellow member of the division challenges you to produce the coin, you do, or you buy the drinks. I have never been successfully challenged. From brigade command to chairman, that coin was always in my wallet.

344 · COLIN L. POWELL

And, frankly, I was hoping to become chief of staff of the 101st Airborne Division after I gave up brigade command. I could learn a lot more about soldiering by doing that job for the wise John Wickham. But for now, I was off to Washington, hoping against hope that I could escape the Beltway vortex and stay with the division.

A few days later, I found myself back in a familiar haunt, the Old Executive Office Building, where I had worked as a White House Fellow at OMB. The OEOB has an aura of quiet power with its endless pillared, silent corridors. History practically seeps out of its walls. At the beginning of World War II, this building had housed the Department of State and the War Department, until the Pentagon was built. This day, I treated the buttoned-down staff in the OEOB to a rare sight, an Army colonel in jump boots, bloused pants, and greens. I was making a statement. I am a brigade commander, 101st Airborne, and happy where I am. You've got the wrong guy. I made my way up a wide curving staircase to the third-floor location of the National Security Council. I was ushered into an ornate nineteenth-century office where I met Dr. Brzezinski, a man with sharply planed Slavic features and an intense manner. With him was his deputy, David Aaron. Dr. Brzezinski asked me to take a seat, which I did, flat-footed, with the boots on prominent display.

After showing surprising familiarity with my past, particularly the White House Fellowship, Brzezinski got down to business. "We're looking for a soldier who knows how to operate at this level.

Frankly, we'd like you to run the NSC's defense program staff," he said.

It sounded like a golden opportunity. I told him I was flattered, but not interested. "I'm not even halfway through my command," I said. "I really don't want to leave Fort Campbell. And this work you're describing isn't me. I don't know anything about it."

Instead of dampening Brzezinski's enthusiasm, my resistance only whetted it. "That's exactly what we want," he said. "Not an academic, but someone who can bring us fresh thinking."

I continued to demur, saying, "I'd rather stay with the troops."

By now, David Aaron's expression and his line of questioning seemed to be saying, what is this guy with combat boots doing here anyway? He says he doesn't want the job. Let's not waste any more time on him. Yet, my reluctance continued to fan Brzezinski's ardor. He seemed fascinated that anyone could resist the siren song of White House power. Finally, he said, "Let's leave it this way. When you're closer to the end of your command, we'll talk again. It may not be the job we're discussing now. But we want you."

I had started to leave when Brzezinski added, "Before you go, I want you to meet the fabulous team we've put together." I spent the rest of the afternoon moving from office to office along the third floor, much of the time listening to frighteningly naive arms control proposals, which were to fall flat as Kansas when later presented to the Soviets.

When I got back to Fort Campbell, General Wickham was eager to hear about the trip. "Colin, you didn't take this job," he said, "but they'll be back, or somebody else will. You're not going to have a conventional Army career. Some officers are just not destined for it."

I quickly put Washington behind me, went on with the training exercises, the boxing matches, the pleasures of command. I had inherited one crack battalion and two that were becoming so. My goal was to make all three tops before I left.

"You'd better have that thing looked at, sir," Sonny Tucker said. The way my exec fussed over me, I did not need parents. The "thing" Sonny was concerned about was a growth that had appeared one morning on the left side of my neck. It did not hurt, but it did not go away. It just kept getting bigger.

I went to the post hospital, where one of the examining physicians said, "We don't know what it is, but it could be cancerous." He explained that they would have to perform a needle biopsy, and then cut out the mass. If the biopsy proved cancer-positive, he said, "we'll have to go all the way to your throat. You may wake up not speaking."

I was forty years old, the father of three children, in the prime of my personal and professional life, and I was scared. Within days, they had me in the operating room. Alma stood vigil. So did Sonny Tucker. I remember him looking at the doctor as if to say, "You mess up my colonel and I'm gonna bust your arms."

I did not have a malignancy. After the biopsy, the doctors clamped the incision and let it heal, which it did, inside out, leaving me with a dimpled scar on my neck. It looks like a bullet wound, and since I am a combat veteran, people assume it is a wound. If they ask, I tell the unheroic truth. I smoked in those days, but became increasingly uneasy after this experience. Today, I'm no longer a smoker.

As my command of the 2d Brigade wound to a close, Dr. Brzezinski, good as his word, again asked me to come to Washington. I wondered if John Wickham's prophecy was proving right.

A NEW CHALLENGE—NATIONAL SECURITY ADVISOR TO THE PRESIDENT

In the Rose Garden on November 5, 1987, the day I was announced as President Reagan's choice to be the new National Security Advisor. Cap Weinberger (left) has just stepped down as Secretary of Defense and Frank Carlucci (right) has just been announced as his successor. Weinberger and Carlucci played crucial roles in carrying out Reagan's vision for a restored and proud military force. The legendary Senator John C. Stennis, former chairman of the Senate Armed Services Committee, is in the rear.

**In the Oval Office with President Reagan, July 1988.
Apparently we had something to laugh about just
before beginning a meeting.**

I flew overnight from Geneva to meet with President Reagan at his ranch in the Santa Ynez Mountains outside Santa Barbara, California, on November 25, 1987. I have just briefed him on the INF Treaty, which Secrctary Shultz had concluded with the Soviets the day beforc in Geneva.

SUMMIT MEETING WITH GORBACHEV

A tense moment in the Kremlin on May 30, 1988,
during the Moscow summit. Presidents Reagan
and Gorbachev are debating a last-minute change
Gorbachev wants to make to the final summit
communiqué. We were just about to adjourn to the next
room for the two presidents to exchange the instruments
of ratification for the INF Treaty, which would begin the
destruction of nuclear weapons, reversing the Cold War
arms race. Secretary of State George Shultz is on the far
left. Jack Matlock, the U.S. ambassador to the
Soviet Union, is on my right.

Tending to the press in the back of Air Force
One on the way home from the NATO summit
on May 3, 1988. Marlin Fitzwater, the
President's outstanding press secretary, is
hovering over me in shirt sleeves.

IN THE THICK OF OUR ARMS-CONTROL PLANNING

The National Security Planning Group discusses an arms-control issue in the White House Situation Room in 1988. Clockwise around the table from President Reagan: George Shultz, Secretary of State; Jim Baker, Secretary of the Treasury; Jim Miller, Director of OMB; Howard Baker, Chief of Staff; me; Bill Graham, Science

Advisor to the President; Ken Adelman, Director of the
Arms Control and Disarmament Agency; Admiral Bill
Crowe, Chairman of the Joint Chiefs of Staff; and
Frank Carlucci, Secretary of Defense. Against the back
wall are Assistant Secretary of State Rozanne Ridgway
and Ambassador Paul Nitze.

The Joint Chiefs of Staff at the time of Desert
Storm. Left to right: Admiral Frank Kelso, Chief
of Naval Operations; General Carl Vuono,
Chief of Staff of the Army; me; Admiral David
Jeremiah, Vice Chairman of the Joint Chiefs of

Staff; General Al Gray, Commandant of the Marine Corps; General Merrill "Tony" McPeak, Chief of Staff of the Air Force. We were a close-knit team with one job: help Norm Schwarzkopf win a war.

DAVID KENNERLY

Swamped by marines and sailors aboard the amphibious ship U.S.S. *Wasp,* off the coast of Somalia on my birthday, April 5, 1993, during Operation Restore Hope. Pocket-sized cameras have converted the armed forces into an army of paparazzi photographers. I loved every minute of it.

AND IN THE GALLEY

A potato-peeling contest with my Soviet counterpart, General Mikhail Moiseyev, while visiting the galley aboard one of our ships in San Diego harbor in 1990. Guess who won . . .

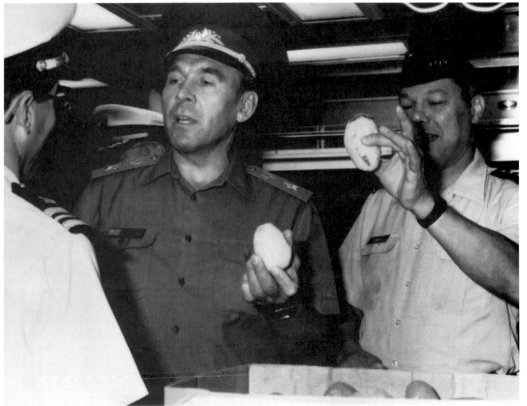

SADDAM HUSSEIN INVADES KUWAIT AND WE PLAN OUR RESPONSE

With General H. Norman Schwarzkopf outside the Pentagon on August 15, 1990. We are waiting for President Bush to speak to a large crowd of Pentagon employees. Desert Shield has been under way for ten days and Norm would soon leave for Saudi Arabia to command the large force that was assembling in the Gulf.

BRIEFING THE PRESIDENT ON DESERT SHIELD

The date is September 24, 1990. I am briefing President Bush on the status of the two options available to him to deal with the Iraqis—sanctions or war. Others, left to right: Secretary of Defense Dick Cheney; National Security Advisor Brent Scowcroft; and Chief of Staff John Sununu.

Norm Schwarzkopf's war room in Riyadh, Saudi Arabia. At the table, left to right: Paul Wolfowitz, Undersecretary of Defense for Policy; me; Dick Cheney; Schwarzkopf; Lieutenant General Cal Waller, deputy commander in chief of CENTCOM; and Major General Bob Johnston, CENTCOM Chief of Staff. Standing just behind us: Lieutenant General Walt Boomer, Marine Component Commander; Lieutenant General Charles "Chuck" Horner, Air Component Commander; Lieutenant General John Yeosock, Army Component Commander; Vice Admiral Stan Arthur, Navy Component Commander; and Colonel Jesse Johnson, Special Operating Forces Commander.

At the White House in January, 1992, heading to the Mansion from the Rose Garden, with President Bush and Secretary of Defense Dick Cheney. Admiral David Jeremiah, the very able Vice Chairman of the Joint Chiefs of Staff is in the rear between Bush and Cheney.

"FIRST WE'RE GOING TO CUT IT OFF, AND THEN WE'RE GOING TO KILL IT"

DEPARTMENT OF DEFENSE PHOTO/R. D. WARD

I wasn't aware of how often I used the "six gun" method of calling on reporters at Pentagon press briefings on the Gulf War until "Saturday Night Live" strung together about ten similar shots and added gunfire sound effects.

With our troops in the Gulf during Operation Desert Shield. Dick Cheney and I would spend time with Schwarzkopf and his staff, then fan out to visit units. The troops were glad to see us and they did wonders for our morale, too. They were the best and brightest of American youth.

PEOPLE AND PLACES

Visiting a school science lab in Annapolis in 1991.

In front of the Buffalo Soldier statue at Fort Leavenworth on the day of its dedication in July 1992. This black 10th Cavalry trooper, with "U.S." on his collar, eagles in his button, a coat of blue, and a rifle in hand, was every bit the equal of his white comrade and deserving of the same benefits of citizenship. He and thousands like him made the way easier for me.

Alma and I being received at an audience with Pope John Paul II in 1983.

At the Vietnam Veterans Memorial on Memorial Day, 1991, I talk to PFC Patrick McElrath, who was seriously injured in Panama during Operation Just Cause.

In my office with the Harlem Globetrotters in March 1991. I needed help to spin the ball on my index finger.

FAMILY ALBUM

**Alma, sponsor and mother of the U.S.S.
Kearsarge, kisses her ship after christening her
with a bottle of champagne in Pascagoula,
Mississippi, in 1992. We took pride in the role
of *Kearsarge* as the mother ship for the rescue of
a downed pilot, Captain Scott O'Grady, in
Bosnia in June 1995.**

**With Lieutenant Mike
Powell in Germany in
early 1986. His military
career was ended a year
later by a terrible
jeep accident.**

The most important people in my life in 1987, Annemarie, Mike, and Linda with Alma. Mike is slowly recovering from his accident and has to lean against the chair to stand up.

Powell family photo taken in Secretary Cheney's office just before my welcoming ceremony as the new Chairman of the Joint Chiefs of Staff on October 3, 1989. Left to right: Dick Cheney; Norm and Marilyn Berns, my brother-in-law and sister; my son, Mike; Alma; me; daughters Linda and Annemarie; and my daughter-in-law, Janc, holding our grandson, Jeffrey.

WORKING WITH PRESIDENT CLINTON

Above: President Clinton leaving the Pentagon after visiting us, with Secretary of Defense Les Aspin, right, on April 8, 1993. He met with the new civilian leaders of the Department of Defense and the Joint Chiefs of Staff.

Below: In the East Room of the White House on September 19, 1994. President Jimmy Carter, Senator Sam Nunn, and I have just returned from Haiti, where we persuaded the illegal Haitian military government to step down and accept the arrival of U.S. forces and the return of President Jean-Bertrand Aristide. President Clinton is briefing the press on the results of our mission.

MY LAST SALUTE IN UNIFORM

Retirement day at Fort Myer, Virginia, September
30, 1993. Alma and I salute as the national anthem
is played. My only regret is that
I could not do it all over again.

THE JOURNEY CONTINUES

**On the speaking circuit in retirement. I am
preparing to speak to fourteen thousand people
waving American flags at the Bakersfield Business
Conference in Bakersfield, California,
in the fall of 1994.**

Part Three

THE WASHINGTON YEARS

10 ★ In the Carter Defense Department

ALTHOUGH I SERVED most publicly during the Reagan-Bush years, I actually cut my teeth on national security during two and a half years in the Office of the Secretary of Defense during the Carter administration. In May 1977, I again went to Washington to meet with Zbigniew Brzezinski at the National Security Council. He told me that the job I had initially been offered, running his defense program staff, had been filled by Victor Utgoff, who now needed an assistant. I found the offer highly resistible, since I had already rejected the top job. Still, turning down the White House does not come easily to a soldier schooled in obedience. This time, I told Brzezinski that I needed to think the matter over.

While I was in Washington, I got another call, this time from the Pentagon. I was to see someone named John Kester, who had a title a mile long, "Special Assistant to the Secretary and the Deputy Secretary of Defense." I had my sources in the building, and I used them to get a line on Mr. Kester. I learned that he was an ambitious, driving young lawyer, close to the Defense Secretary, Harold Brown, and that Kester's hard-nosed style had ruffled feathers all over the Pentagon.

Kester's huge office was on the E-Ring, the Eisenhower Corridor, and right next to the Secretary of Defense's office. He was indeed young, at thirty-eight two years younger than I, not always the desirable relationship between a prospective superior and subordinate. And John Kester was brash. He made clear that he and the deputy secretary of defense, Charles Duncan, ran this show for Secretary Brown. And Kester made no bones about his position as a de facto chief of staff who was determined to gain control over this sprawling bureaucracy and ride herd on the Joint Chiefs of Staff. Kester had created a four-person team of military officers to help him, and he wanted me to run the unit as his executive assistant.

So far, in this first encounter, Kester had done all the talking. Finally, it was my turn. "How did you happen to send for me?" I asked.

"I checked you out," Kester replied, "and I heard a lot of good things." He had access to a nomination book profiling a half-dozen Army officers, including me, who had been considered for the job of junior military assistant to the Secretary of Defense. The assignment, however, went to Air Force Colonel Carl Smith, who was to cross my life at critical points in the future. Kester had used this book to recruit for his own military assistant. He had been particularly impressed by my White House Fellowship and my having been a Vietnam veteran and field commander.

"I checked you out, too, and everything I heard was not so good," I said with a smile. He appeared amused by my bluntness. A good sign; he was not looking for a yes-man. We finished the interview and I went back to Fort Campbell.

I now had two high-level job offers, neither of which I wanted. I had had enough off-track assignments. My hope still was to move up from brigade commander to chief of staff of the 101st Airborne and have Washington forget about me. On my return, General Wickham, as an alumnus of the Defense Secretary's office, wanted to hear the latest gossip from the E-Ring. He also made clear that I was not going to become his chief of staff. Of his brigade commanders, I was junior and not an aviator, a key qualification for this assignment. "Besides," Wickham said, "I know the system, and the Army is not going to pass up an opportunity to have one of its people in either of those key jobs." However, he did not want to influence me as to which one I should favor.

For that advice, I called another trusted friend, Carl Vuono, a fellow DePuy protégé recently promoted to brigadier general and now working for the Army Chief of Staff, General Bernard Rogers. "Carl," I said, "I lean toward the Defense job. I'm not eager to leave the Army again. But I'll go wherever the chief thinks it best." Carl checked with General Rogers, and the answer came back: we want Powell in Kester's operation. Kester and Rogers had been toe-to-toe on several turf issues, and Rogers may have seen some advantage in having an Army man in Kester's operation. After expressing my regrets to Zbigniew Brzezinski, I went to work for John Kester.

The family returned from Fort Campbell to the Washington area, and we contracted to have a home built in Burke Center in Virginia's suburban Fairfax County, a move which swallowed up all the profit we had made on the Dale City sale. Our new home was closer to the capital. "Close-in" is the magic phrase in Washington real estate. In those days, every mile nearer to town added about $10,000 to the price of a house.

A brigade commander at Fort Campbell has about as much idea of what shapes defense policy as a Chevy dealer in Kansas knows what happens inside the General Motors boardroom. I was in for an education. John Kester installed me in a small office outside his suite. From that vantage point, I watched him, a tall, lanky man who stayed that way through disciplined jogging and who spoke in a high-pitched voice that belied his authoritative manner. I was intrigued by Kester. Though plain of speech and style, he was something of a Renaissance man. Classical music purred in his office. I occasionally heard him on the phone speaking French. He was widely read and wrote so clearly and in such a lively style that you would never suspect he was a lawyer and government official.

Kester was a player. I soon observed that all significant Pentagon power lines ran through his hands. The Secretary, Harold Brown, a physicist, a former Johnson administration Air Force Secretary and director of defense research and engineering, and most recently president of the California Institute of Technology, made the final decisions; but Kester had so arranged it that nobody or no piece of paper got to Secretary Brown without going through him first.

There are in-boxes, there are out-boxes, and with Kester there was limbo. I was talking to John one day as he flipped through a paper that an assistant secretary of defense had submitted to Harold Brown for a decision. Kester flung the document into a box behind him. Limbo. A few days later, the author of the memo called to ask about its fate. John's secretary stalled him. Mr. Kester was out of the office. Mr. Kester was on another line. Mr. Kester was in conference with the Secretary. The document was still in Mr. Kester's briefcase. The document had been temporarily mislaid. More days passed before Kester finally allowed the distressed official to see him about the fate of his paper. John went off on a tangent. Had this fellow hired the very able candidate that John had sent to him? The man mumbled excuses, and finally saw the light. He was sorry; he had not had time to get around to it. He would see the man right away. That was wise, Kester said. And that afternoon, the languishing memo came out of limbo and went sailing into the Secretary's office. That was the Kester style, punishment and reward, one for you and one for him (and sometimes two for him).

On another occasion, John announced that no promotions above GS-13, the middle management range, could be made in the Office of the Secretary of Defense without Brown's (read Kester's) approval. On still another occasion, he ordered that nobody in the Pentagon could hire an outside consultant without his say-so.

As a career soldier and a colonel, I stood in awe of three-star and four-star generals. John Kester did not. Not only had he gathered civilian promotions into his hands, but he went after senior military promotions as well. No longer would lists for brigadier and major general be signed pro forma by Secretary Brown. Kester would carefully review them. John also changed the service chief's traditional prerogative of recommending generals and admirals for promotion to three and four stars. Past practice had been for the chiefs to submit a single name for each opening. No, Kester said, they must now submit two candidates, and the Secretary of Defense would choose. The chiefs were not happy. General Rogers had informed one general that he was going to have him promoted to four stars and give him FORSCOM, command of all Army forces in the United States. Kester stepped in and said, oh no, give us the required two nominations, which Rogers did. Defense Secretary Brown, Secretary of the Army Clifford Alexander, and Kester then reviewed the candidates' qualifications in their own good time, while Rogers fumed. Finally, Secretary Brown made the decision, and it was not Rogers's choice.

Shortly afterward, I was summoned to Rogers's office, where I proceeded to serve as a punching bag. "This is the worst personnel experience I've had in thirty-five years of service," Rogers said, venting his annoyance over Kester. "I cannot understand how some civilian special assistant can override the judgment of the Army's senior general."

When he finally stopped to take a breath, I spoke up. "Sir, I understand your frustration," I said, "but Kester is just trying to make clear that these positions belong to Secretary Brown, and he has to have a choice." Rogers, of course, knew that, and he cooled down. When he dismissed me, he acknowledged, just as he had when he first assigned me to the job, that my loyalty remained with Kester, even when decisions went against the Army.

Kester had gained control over the flow of people, paper, and promotions in America's huge defense establishment. His approach was as direct as the man himself. Rewards for good little boys and girls and punishment for naughty ones. He sought and exercised power not for his own ego—John's ego needed no stroking—but because he believed he was best serving the interests of his boss and the Carter administration.

Kester was the political horse in a troika. The other two members were Tom Ross, assistant secretary of defense for public affairs, and Jack Stempler, assistant to the secretary of defense for legislative affairs, the department's liaison with Congress. Every morning, Secretary Brown held a meeting of his closest staff in his office. I sat at the back of the room, like a fly on the wall, next to a grandfather clock that chimed solemnly every half hour. The Secretary of Defense clearly needed these players. Harold Brown was brilliant, one of President Carter's best appointments; but this physicist-intellectual preferred paper to people. I always had the impression that Brown would be just as happy if we slipped his paperwork under the door and left him alone to pore over it or to work out theorems. If his wife, Colene, wanted to have dinner with her husband, she often had to come to the office, where Harold nibbled and scribbled his way through a pile of papers in a tiny, hieroglyphic scrawl.

Harold Brown had earned his Ph.D. at Columbia University. Jack Stempler's degree in practical politics came from the back streets of Baltimore. One morning, the Secretary opened the meeting muttering about a congressman who had angered him. The man was a hypocrite, Brown complained. He told you one thing one day, then voted the opposite way the next. "I refuse to have anything more to do with him," Brown announced.

"All right, Harold," Stempler said, "you've got that out of your system. Feel better now? But the congressman happens to be one of the people's elected representatives, and you need his vote on the Armed Services Committee. You've got to kiss him. You've got to love him. In fact, I want you to have lunch with him tomorrow."

Brown groaned.

And if that did not win the congressman's heart, John Kester chimed in, we'll put a military base in his district on the hit list.

On another occasion, Secretary Brown was upset by a story in the *Washington Post* that he thought was unfair. "I'm writing a letter to the editor," Brown declared.

"Not on this one," Tom Ross, the PR man, said. "They'll love that. It's just what they want you to do to keep the story alive. Harold, when you wrestle with a pig, the pig has fun and you just get dirty." Still, Brown insisted he was going to write. "Harold," Tom went on, "just take the hit. Never get into fights with people who buy ink by the barrel."

I sat there taking my notes and thinking that if the National War College had been my classroom in military politics, I was now out doing field work.

As Christmas 1977 approached, I got in touch with my sister, Marilyn. She and her husband, Norm, had finally had it with the snows of upstate New York and had moved from Buffalo to southern California. I urged them to come East for the holidays. For the past year, I had watched the change in my father. The man who had fussed over his little plot of land like a plantation owner now preferred sitting indoors all day. The man who could talk the birds out of the trees went silent for hours on end. I thought it wise to get the whole family together this year at Elmira Avenue. It turned out to be a happy but muted Christmas. One thing was obvious—Pop had slipped from ringmaster to spectator.

A couple of months later, early in 1978, I went home to accompany my mother on a visit to Pop's doctor. The doctor went straight to the point. Pop had cancer of the liver. It was terminal, maybe a year, probably less. My mother took it hard. When we were alone, she cried inconsolably. She and my father had contained their feelings toward each other for so long that I was surprised by the flood of emotion. I now found myself on the shuttle from National Airport to La Guardia in New York almost every weekend as Pop continued to decline.

I arrived at Elmira Avenue on Saturday, April 22, to see Pop, who was now bedridden and occupying my old room. The hospital could do nothing more for him, and the doctors had sent him home.

The bed he lay in had a sentimental significance for me. I had bought it with an employee's discount while I was working at Sickser's, the first serious contribution I had ever made to furnishing our home. On the dresser were the two photographs Pop always had nearby, Marilyn at her high school graduation and me as a second lieutenant in Gelnhausen.

Mom and Miss Bell, still a boarder, were changing Pop's sheets. He had become incontinent. It shook me. That proud man lay there helpless, while two women changed him and his son stood watching from the doorway. As they turned over his naked body, my mother said, "Will you look at that. I'm seeing more of him now than in all the years we were married." I started laughing. Mom started laughing, Miss Bell burst out laughing too, and I saw a flicker of a smile cross Pop's lips. The moment captured the irrepressible Jamaican family spirit, humor in the face of joy or sorrow. Tears rolled down my cheeks.

After they had cleaned Pop, plumped his pillow, and sprayed the room, the women left us alone. I talked to him, my words followed by awkward silences. I kept talking. Finally, Pop struggled to focus his eyes. He was trying to say something. I leaned forward. "Colin," he whispered, pointing toward his head, "there's nothing up there anymore." They were the last words I ever heard him utter. The following Saturday, he died. The formative figure in my life was gone.

Mom, while grieved by her loss, did not let it interfere with a practical streak nurtured over a lifetime of penny-pinching. We had settled Pop's estate, all but his '64 Chevy. I asked if I might have it. Of course, Mom said, and gave me the car, for $400.

John Kester served two masters, Secretary of Defense Brown and Brown's deputy secretary, the number two man in the Pentagon, Charles Duncan. Though a Democrat, Duncan had all the credentials of a country-club Republican. His business background had been capped by the presidency of Coca-Cola, he possessed wealth, and he combined shrewdness and charm. He ran the department day-to-day and handled the three service secretaries. He had a particular gift for handling defense contractors and politicking on the Hill.

Duncan's military assistant, Major General Joe Palastra, was, like me, a DePuy alumnus and an infantryman. "I hate this job," Palastra told me more than once. Joe enjoyed working for Duncan, but he chafed at any Pentagon duty and was never really happy unless he was in the field with troops. Joe had recently been promoted to major general and was in line for a division command. Duncan, however, was not going to let Palastra go until he had a suitable replacement. The military assistant's job rated at least a brigadier general. Palastra expected that I would soon be on the list, and this possibility fired his imagination. The next thing I knew, Joe was asking if I would like a break from the daily grind. In October, Deputy Secretary Duncan was making a trip to Iran, Saudi Arabia, Kenya, and Egypt. I could go with him. The trip was already wired with Kester and Duncan, he said. I sensed that I was being set up for an audition. Palastra the warrior had become Palastra the matchmaker.

Iran was America's bulwark in the Middle East. It occupied the center of the oil crescent. And Iran stood in the way of the Soviet Union's historical hankering for a warm-water port on the Persian Gulf. Ruling Iran was America's staunch ally, Shah Mohammad Reza Pahlavi, a man who was beloved by his people, so we believed, and was leading them into the modern age. To support his reign, the United States had stuffed Iran with modern weaponry. The ostensible purpose of Duncan's trip was to gauge how well these arms were being integrated into Iran's armed forces. But there had been rumblings of late. A fanatical Islamic fundamentalist, the Ayatollah Khomeini, in exile in Paris, was calling for the overthrow of the Shah. Duncan was also going to Iran to see how well our ally was holding up.

We flew to Tehran on October 23, 1978, and were greeted by the head of the U.S. Military Mission to Iran, Major General Philip Gast. There I met my first Iranian generals, bemedaled, proud, imposing, all speaking excellent English. After a lavish meal of lamb served at the officers' club, we mounted a reviewing stand to watch a parade of Iran's crack troops, the "Immortals," in tailored uniforms, berets, and gleaming ladder-laced boots, men who performed with much shouting and martial flair. The Iranian officer next to me explained, "Their loyalty is total. The Immortals will fight to the last man to protect the Shah."

We visited Isfahan, an exotic city of the ancient world, and watched the centuries blur as a formation of one of the world's most modern fighter planes, the F-14, which we had provided to the Iranian air force, streaked over the lovely Lutfullah mosque. During another feast, hosted by local officials, I heard a familiar rat-tat-tat sound coming from the street. It sounded like machine-gun fire, but our hosts played dumb.

We next visited the airfield at Shiraz, where the F-14s were based, an installation as sophisticated as any in the United States. I took aside a young American Air Force captain who was training the Iranians. How good was this air force really? I asked him. At first, he was uneasy. Then it came pouring out. "You've got two men in the F-14s," he said, "and two social classes." The pilots, he explained, came from the Iranian upper crust. They could take off, perform the flashy high-speed, low-level passes, and get the plane back on the ground. "But, hell, Colonel," he said, "I could teach you that stuff in a week." The one who really mattered in an F-14, he continued, was the WSO, the weapon systems officer. The WSO operated millions of dollars' worth of the most advanced aeronautical technology on earth, including the plane's attack systems. This critical though less glamorous function, however, was relegated to *homofars,* the equivalent of warrant officers, barely educated men from the humbler classes. "It'll take a couple of generations before those guys have any real grasp of what they're doing up there," the captain told me. "Until they do, all you'll see flying around here is half an airplane." As the F-14s continued to roar overhead with flawless precision, I wondered, was this show the aeronautical equivalent of breaking starch?

Later that night, I came down to our hotel lobby to meet Secretary Duncan. We were supposed to attend a formal dinner that the Iranian air force was hosting at the commandant's quarters. A beautifully uniformed escort officer met us, apologized profusely, and said that we would not be able to leave the hotel. Fighting had broken out between fundamentalist mobs and the police. The streets of Shiraz were not safe.

The next day, we took off for Saudi Arabia. I looked at those gleaming F-14s arrayed on the hardstand, and I thought of what the American instructor had told me. I thought of the turmoil in the streets the night before, and I began to wonder; had Charles Duncan and I seen the inside of Iran, or only the shell?

We were in a briefing room at a Saudi Arabian fighter base at Dhahran listening to the commander instruct his pilots when the door flew open and a Saudi officer wearing a flight suit and a checkered scarf strode in. He was only a major, but something about his presence sucked up all the authority in the room. He was introduced to Duncan and me as "Major Bandar." I was meeting my first Saudi royal, Prince Bandar Bin Sultan, son of the minister of defense and aviation, nephew of King Fahd, and a man who would eventually become the oil kingdom's ambassador to the United States.

About a year after this first encounter, Bandar was living in Washington and attending the Johns Hopkins School of Advanced International Studies. We started playing racquetball together at the Pentagon Officers Athletic Club, he and I against Charles Duncan and General David Jones, then Chairman of the Joint Chiefs of Staff. I remember Prince Bandar coming out of the POAC after our first game. He had a gym bag slung over his shoulder. He flicked it off with a shrug, and an aide materialized out of the woodwork and caught it. The prince extended his hand into empty space, and pulled it back with a Coke can in it. It is good to be a prince, I thought. In the years to follow, we would often work together, and the vast social gulf between us began to shrink until the familiarity between the kid from the South Bronx and the prince from a royal palace approached the outrageous and the profane.

The 1978 trip abroad with Charles Duncan included a stop in Kenya, my first visit to Africa. Exotic as it seemed, the continent did not exert the pull I expected. My black roots were in West Africa, and that emotional experience lay in the future.

Less than three months after the trip, on January 16, 1979, the Shah was driven from his country. I saw in the *Washington Post* photos of the naked bodies of executed generals who had been our hosts, stretched out on morgue slabs. The *homofar* class went over to the Shah's enemies. The Immortals had not fought to the last man. They had cracked like a crystal goblet on the first day of fighting. My suspicion of elites and show horse units deepened. Keep looking beneath surface appearances, I reminded myself, and don't shrink from doing so because you might not like what you find. In the end, in Iran, all our investment in an individual, rather than in the country, came to naught. When the Shah fell, our Iran policy fell with him. All the billions we had spent there only exacerbated conditions and contributed to the rise of a fundamentalist regime implacably opposed to us to this day.

Nothing further was said about a change in my status after Duncan and I returned from our trip. Then, one day in December 1978, as Charles was passing by my cubicle, he gave me a wink and a wave before disappearing into Kester's office. A minute later, John buzzed me to come in. I found both men wearing Cheshire-cat grins. "Congratulations," John said. "You've made brigadier general." Before I had a chance to absorb the news, Duncan added, "And I want you to come to work as my military assistant."

Promotion from lieutenant colonel to full colonel is a step up. From colonel to brigadier general is a giant leap. I did not take this promotion coolly. I acted more like a kid on Christmas morning. We brought my mother to Washington for the promotion ceremony. Aunts, uncles, and cousins also flooded to Burke Center. Our home turned into a madhouse. Mom was nervous as a bride, constantly bugging Alma to help her fix her hair, iron her dress, and approve her wardrobe until you would think she was getting the star.

The formal promotion ceremony for me and Colonel Carl Smith, Secretary Brown's military assistant, was held on June 1, 1979, in the elegant dining room of the Secretary of Defense. I walked into a room full of family and friends from past posts, even ROTC. Charles Duncan, now my boss, did the honors for me, and with great grace. The one gaping hole was Pop. Still, I felt that he was up there somewhere strutting among the other souls saying, "Of course, what did you expect?"

Secretary Brown's protocol officer at the Department of Defense, Air Force Lieutenant Colonel Stuart Purviance, presented me with a framed quotation by Abraham Lincoln. It seems a telegraph operator at the War Department had informed the President one day that the Confederates had captured a bunch of horses and a Union brigadier general. The operator was surprised when Lincoln expressed more concern over the horses. Lincoln supposedly explained, "I can make a brigadier general in five minutes. But it's not so easy to replace one hundred and ten horses." That was the quote Purviance had framed for me. On the back, Stu had taped an envelope marked: "Not to be opened for ten years." I obeyed his wish. When I did open the envelope in 1989, the note inside read: "You will become Chief of Staff of the Army." I smiled to myself. At that point, I had become Chairman of the Joint Chiefs of Staff. The framed utterance by Lincoln has followed me to every office I have occupied since, the perfect cure for a swollen ego.

368 · COLIN L. POWELL

After the formal ceremony, we had a Powell first, a catered affair for over 150 guests at home. Mom thought it was a terrible extravagance. She and the relatives had always done the cooking for family celebrations, but she adapted herself admirably to the luxury. The promotion made me, at age forty-two, the youngest general in the Army. My children were beaming. My relatives were beaming. I was beaming. And I hoped Alma was beaming. This really would be a coup, since I was always kidding her about her controlled enthusiasm in the face of my victories, large or small. When I told her I had graduated number two at Leavenworth, she'd said, "That's nice, but I always expect the best of you anyway." An unawed wife is also good for keeping your hat size constant. This night at Burke Center, however, Alma *was* beaming.

A rite of passage for new generals was to attend "charm school," a series of orientations beginning with a welcome by the Army Chief of Staff, then General Rogers. Fifty-two of us gathered in a Pentagon conference room to hear words that I have never forgotten. After congratulating us, Rogers put everything into perspective. "Let me tell you how keen the competition is at this level," he began. "All of you could board an airplane and disappear over the Atlantic tomorrow, and the fifty-two colonels we'd replace you with would be just as good as you are. We would not be able to tell the difference. Furthermore, many of you have to accept that you have had your last promotion. So do your best, and let the future take care of itself." Half of us would make major general. At most, ten of us would make lieutenant general. And maybe four of us would make four stars.

He was proud of us, he said, and he expected us to do well. But he also warned of the tests of rank. "Some of your careers will stall out," Rogers said, "because you think the star puts you above the rules, and you become little tin gods. Some of you will top out because you can't handle the responsibility. Some of your careers will falter because your wives start acting as if they got the promotion. I am not speaking hypothetically," Rogers went on. "Everything I am saying will happen to somebody in this room."

With that, he wished us Godspeed and good luck. As the years went by, most of the new generals in that class fulfilled Rogers's expression of confidence. But I also saw his prophecies borne out by others.

Charles Duncan and I had become fast friends. We played racquetball almost every day, we traveled the world together, and on one or two occasions, we had been known to take a drink together. One night, as I was getting ready to leave work, he asked me to stay awhile. The Carter administration was in upheaval. President Carter had recently retreated to Camp David, discovered a malaise in the country, and resolved to renew the nation's battered spirits. Part of the renewal included shaking up his cabinet to remove, among others, Joseph Califano, Secretary of Health, Education and Welfare, and James Schlesinger, Secretary of Energy.

I sat down on the couch in Duncan's office and waited to hear what he wanted. "Colin," he began, "I'm leaving. The President wants me to take over the Department of Energy." I was sorry to hear this but, frankly, saw a ray of sunshine breaking through. Here was my chance to escape the front office and go back to the Army. Charles went on, "And I want you to come with me." I had been sidetracked before, but this was going over the cliff. As I started to object, he raised his hand. It was all set. He had already cleared the matter with the new Army Chief of Staff, General Edward "Shy" Meyer. Duncan promised that he would let me go as soon as he had his feet wet at DOE. I had no choice but to accept.

Also joining the DOE transition team was the general counsel for the Department of Defense, Deanne Siemer, a tough player to whom I offer the ultimate accolade: she was a match for John Kester. Deanne was supposed to reorganize the entire Department of Energy, while I set up its front office. And I had an unwritten duty. Since I had managed to stand up to this juggernaut at Defense, I was now to provide a shock absorber between Siemer and Duncan at DOE.

The transition team also included a sharp, ambitious lawyer named Bernard Wruble, who was to make a permanent contribution to my philosophy. One day we were having a particularly fiery debate, and another DOE lawyer went off in a sulk when his position was demolished. Wruble walked over to him and said, "You forgot what you learned in law school. Never let your ego get so close to your position that when your position goes, your ego goes with it." Those words stayed with me.

For the first time since I had manned the bottling machine at the Pepsi plant in Long Island City, I found myself in a purely civilian job. The Department of Energy was a patchwork of the old Atomic Energy Commission, the Federal Energy Regulatory Commission, and three other once independent agencies. They behaved like stepchildren from different marriages forced to live together and not happy about it. Congress, however, loved the new arrangement. DOE was going to save Western civilization by supporting experimental energy schemes in congressional districts all over the country—solar windmills, solar mirrors, gas from coal, oil from shale. The quest for energy independence was a golden wand wafting federal funds over the land.

My job in organizing the front office really involved deciding who stayed and who had to go. I was assigned this always unpleasant task so that Secretary Duncan would not come out as the heavy. Thankfully, after two and a half months, Duncan had as firm a grip as he was ever going to get over this bureaucratic jury-rig. I had done my part and told him that I was eager to leave. Duncan was gracious about releasing me. Parting from DOE was easy. Leaving Charles was hard. Our personalities meshed. We both believed that you work hard, play hard, and take the job seriously, but not yourself. He awarded me the Secretary of Energy's Distinguished Service

Medal, and when he pinned it on, there were tears in his eyes and mine.

The DOE episode marked the first time I ever saw my name in a national news magazine. In its September 3, 1979, issue, *Newsweek* described me as one of Harold Brown's "whiz kids," brought to DOE to wage, in the energy field, "the moral equivalent of war." Wow!

My hopes for a return to the Army were torpedoed. W. Graham Claytor, Jr., previously Secretary of the Navy, had moved into Duncan's spot as the number two man at Defense, and Claytor asked me to become his military assistant, working alongside Navy Captain Jack Baldwin, a superb officer who was Claytor's current assistant. Because Claytor came out of the Navy side of the Pentagon and already had one naval military assistant, Army Chief of Staff General Shy Meyer saw it as a tactical advantage to have an Army man at Claytor's elbow. My escape route had been sealed.

Graham Claytor was sixty-seven years old, a gentleman of the old school with an occasional cantankerous streak. He had graduated from Harvard Law School, clerked for a Supreme Court Justice, and become a powerful Washington lawyer, but scored his greatest success as an executive running the Southern Railway. Trains were his passion. He had accumulated a priceless collection of toy trains, many dating to the nineteenth century, and he had them displayed from floor to ceiling all over his Georgetown home. My first exposure to Claytor had occurred while he was still Secretary of the Navy and I was working for Duncan. The aircraft carrier U.S.S. *Saratoga* was scheduled to be overhauled, at considerable cost, and the Navy had analyzed the issue exhaustively, concluding that the most economical place for the job was the naval shipyard in Norfolk, Virginia. Claytor, as Secretary of the Navy, concurred in the recommendation. Vice President Walter Mondale, not always the mild gentleman of his public persona, heard about this decision and called Duncan to say that there apparently had been a misunderstanding. He had promised the people of Philadelphia, during the 1976 presidential campaign, that the *Saratoga* would be rebuilt in their shipyard. So make it happen.

Duncan, a realist, called me in and said, "I want you to disappear somewhere and come back with a rationale for overhauling the ship in Philadelphia rather than Norfolk." Since I had no naval and less shipbuilding experience, this was going to be an exercise in creative writing for me. I did the best job I could, and a few days later handed Duncan a single-spaced, three-page argument for rebuilding the *Saratoga* in Philadelphia.

The next thing I knew, Graham Claytor came barging in, 16-inch guns blazing, flinging my report on Duncan's desk. His naval experts had made a professional judgment of the best yard in which to rebuild the *Saratoga,* he said. And he supported their conclusion. He was Secretary of the Navy, and he did not expect to be overruled. "I'm the one," Claytor said, "who has to go before the House Armed Services Committee and argue this flip-flop after I've already recommended Norfolk." Duncan managed to calm him down. They were men of the world, Charles said. They understood the game. And the administration wanted Philadelphia.

Claytor grumpily snatched back my paper, returned to his office, and told his Navy analysts to come up with a recommendation the exact opposite of their first conclusion. The Virginia delegation in Congress got word of what was happening and cried foul. And, as he had feared, Claytor had to go up to Capitol Hill and defend the department's new position. I was astonished. He made the case for sending the *Saratoga* to Philadelphia so persuasively that you could not imagine rebuilding the ship anywhere else. Never let your ego get so close to your position that when your position goes under, your ego goes with it. Graham Claytor, an old lawyer, knew this. Vice President Mondale was on the bridge when the *Saratoga* sailed into the Philadelphia yard.

Thursday, April 24, 1980, was a clear, sunny day in Washington. I arrived at the office at my usual time, 7:00 A.M. Graham Claytor was already there, looking preoccupied. As the morning wore on, I could feel tension mounting along the Eisenhower Corridor. Claytor kept slipping out of meetings and into Secretary Brown's office, keeping me at arm's length. "The Secretary doesn't want any military assistants in on this," he kept saying, whatever "this" was. I drove home that night as much in the dark as any other commuter.

The next morning at 7:00 A.M., a knot of early birds gathered around a television set in the deputy secretary's office as President Carter, his face ashen, explained what had happened the day before. An attempt had been made to rescue the fifty-three American hostages seized by Iranian "students" and held captive in the American embassy in Tehran for the past five months. The mission, the President said, had failed. "It was my decision to attempt the rescue operation," Carter went on. "It was my decision to cancel it when problems developed. The responsibility is fully my own."

It took a while longer for the details to dribble out. The operation, designated Desert One, involved eight Navy RH-53 helicopters and six C-130 Hercules transports with a force of commandos aboard drawn from the four services; most of them were Army paratroopers. They had set out for Dasht-e-Kavir, the remote Great Salt Desert in Iran. The plan was to have the helicopters fly next to another staging area near Tehran. Agents on the ground, working for the United States, were to provide trucks to bring the commandos from the helicopters to the American embassy, where they would attempt to overpower the guards. The helicopters would fly out of their hiding place, land at the embassy compound, pick up the freed hostages, and take them to transport planes at a seized airfield nearby from which they would be flown to freedom. The planners had figured that six of the eight helicopters, minimally, were necessary for the success of the mission. But mechanical malfunctions knocked out two helos before the rendezvous in the Great Salt Desert could occur, and a third suffered a hydraulic failure on arrival. Upon getting this news, the President aborted the mission. Though a technical failure at this point, Desert One was not yet a publicly known embarrassment or a human tragedy. That was still to come. As one surviving helicopter maneuvered to get into a refueling position for the return flight, its rotor struck the fuselage of a C-130. Both aircraft burst into flames. Ammunition exploded. Eight men were killed outright and four more severely burned.

I had never heard a whisper about Desert One. Yet, I had had enough experience in helicopter operations in Vietnam, Korea, and the 101st Airborne to be surprised at the way this operation had been conceived and conducted. Helicopters are notoriously temperamental. For a mission this demanding of men and machines, far more than eight helos should have been launched to make sure that six would still be airworthy to carry out the demanding second leg of the mission. Desert One also erred in counting on a "pickup" team drawn from all four services and brought together just for this mission in which men from one service flew helicopters of another. Weaknesses in the chain of command, communications, weather forecasting, and security further contributed to the failure. There can be no question of the bravery of the men who headed out into the Iranian desert. But more than bravery was required. Consequently, the mission failed, and men paid with their lives. Colonel Charles Beckwith, the Delta Force commander, said it best: "You cannot take a few people from one unit, throw them in with some from another, give them someone else's equipment, and hope to come up with a top-notch fighting outfit."

I would remember Beckwith's words in the future when it became my responsibility to plan combat operations at the highest levels. You have to plan thoroughly, train as a team, match the military punch to the political objective, go in with everything you need—and then some—and not count on wishful thinking. I would have rated Desert One's chances of success at a hundred to one, foolhardy odds for a military operation. And the failure may well have fatally wounded the Carter presidency.

I also felt that the handling of this affair had been a public communications fiasco. I blew off steam by writing a facetious "Guide for Handling Disasters" that went as follows. Release facts slowly, behind the pace at which they are already leaking out to the public. Don't tell the whole story until forced to do so. Emphasize what went well, and euphemize what went wrong. Become indignant at any suggestion of poor judgment or mistakes. Disparage any facts other than your own. Accuse critics of Monday-morning generalship. Finally, accept general responsibility at the top, thus clearing everybody at fault below.

Our civilian leaders eventually recognized the need to forestall future Desert Ones even before the military did. Several years later, in 1987, against the opposition of the Defense Department, Congress enacted legislation creating the Special Operations Command (SOCOM) under a four-star general, to provide the planning, coordination, and supervision lacking in Desert One. In Just Cause, the mission to restore democracy to Panama, and in the 1991 Gulf War we were to find out how well this overhaul worked.

I continued working for Graham Claytor for the next eight months. I liked and admired all my Pentagon bosses, Kester, Duncan, and Claytor. Consequently, I approached election day in 1980 with mixed feelings. I had supported Jimmy Carter in 1976. This time, I could not. The Carter administration had been mauled by double-digit inflation and the humiliating spectacle of the Americans held hostage in Iran. Desert One had been a military and psychological disaster. The record on national security, admittedly, was not all bad. During Harold Brown's watch, work had begun on nearly all the weapons systems that matured by the time of the Gulf War. A Brown subordinate who deserved major credit for this pioneering was William Perry, director of research and engineering, who later became Secretary of Defense himself. But on the whole, the vibrations coming out of the Carter White House were not comforting to the military profession. Dropping the B-1 bomber was wise, but other force cuts were so damaging that the Army Chief of Staff, General Meyer, went before Congress complaining of a "hollow Army," thus handing the Reagan forces a potent campaign issue. Carter withdrew the meat cleaver and started to build up the country's defenses, but it was too late. By then, the December 1979 Soviet invasion of Afghanistan had made his administration look naive in its expectations of a harmonious era of East-West relations in which we could drop our guard.

The case of Master Sergeant Roy P. Benavidez epitomized for me an insensitivity toward the military during this time. Benavidez had earned the Army's second-highest decoration, the Distinguished Service Cross, for valor in Vietnam, where in 1968 he had saved the lives of eight trapped Special Forces troops, in the course of which he was wounded nine times. Years later, after additional evidence of his bravery was reviewed, Benavidez's award was upgraded to the Medal of Honor. This highest military decoration was traditionally presented by the President, which would have given a boost to the battered ego of the armed forces at the time. But President Carter never got around to pinning the medal on Benavidez.

That November 1980, I checked my absentee ballot for Ronald Reagan and mailed it back to New York. I knew officers who did not vote in presidential elections in order to remain politically pure, depriving themselves of registering a preference for their commander in chief. That was going too far for me. I also split my ticket. I had no hesitation about crossing party lines as my way of expressing nonpartisanship.

Ronald Reagan was elected handily. At the Pentagon, we now waited for the other shoe to drop. Who would be the next Secretary of Defense? Soon after the election, a Reagan transition team showed up at the department. Old career hands warned me that the transition would follow a predictable course. Victorious Young Turks would fan out to assigned offices, making a few peremptory courtesy calls on leading lame ducks, but otherwise treating them as if they had leprosy. After all, they were the opposition. They had lost. What could they know? The newcomers would be attracted to the disgruntled in the department, those just waiting to tell them how terrible the previous administration had been. Since these complainers had not gotten along with the losers, the transition team would assume that they must know what they were talking about. Little thought would be given to why the grumblers had fared poorly. Every gripe would be taken at face value. Out goes the baby, the bathwater, and the bathtub.

The first Reagan wave to hit the Pentagon beaches was led by William Van Cleave, heading the Defense Transition Team. Van Cleave and his band prowled the corridors finding all kinds of misdemeanors and felonies and were impatient to poke into classified military plans. They prepared fat transition books of issues to be resolved, failings to be fixed, people to be dumped. At this point, a new Secretary of Defense had not yet been named, and Mr. Van Cleave and company were working in splendid isolation.

Finally, the other shoe fell, and a shudder went through the Pentagon. Caspar Weinberger, his reputation honed in the Nixon Department of Health, Education and Welfare as "Cap the Knife," was to be Secretary of Defense. We tried to comfort each other.

At least Weinberger was known as a strong manager. He was close to Ronald Reagan. His knife might make the department leaner, but also tougher and more efficient.

Van Cleave and his transition team happily presented the Secretary-designate their blueprint for a new, improved Pentagon. Weinberger quickly showed his management style. He asked Van Cleave when he would finish his work. The following June, he replied. Weinberger thanked Van Cleave and told him his services were "no longer required." Van Cleave had fallen victim to the same psychology the outgoing administration had suffered from him. He was not Weinberger's man. What could he know?

Early in January 1981, Weinberger's own advance party arrived. One member was Richard Armitage, a Naval Academy graduate and recent member of Senator Robert Dole's staff. Armitage was in his mid-thirties, big, bald, brassy, built like an anvil; he looked as if he could step into the ring next Saturday at the World Federation of Wrestling. I was one of the people he talked to about the transition. I learned that Armitage had spent six years in Vietnam, which gave us much to talk about, and that he pumped iron every morning, which gave us less to talk about.

I was told one day to give a hand to another newcomer, Weinberger's director of political appointments. The title suggested a grizzled Republican former state chairman or a defeated GOP congressman who needed a job. I was introduced instead to a young woman in her mid-twenties, Marybel Batjer, the daughter of a Nevada judge. She had worked for

California's Bechtel Corporation, as had Cap Weinberger. Ms. Batjer's political mentor was Senator Paul Laxalt, Republican from Nevada. Despite her youth, she struck me as bright, capable, and mature beyond her years.

One thing could be said for the newcomers, especially Armitage and Batjer. Unlike the previous transition know-it-alls, they were shrewd enough to realize that a new broom may sweep too clean. They discovered a base of knowledge in the department worth preserving. They recognized that some people actually knew what they were doing and need not be fired on the spot. They willingly sought help from older hands, instead of stumbling around in the corridors of their own ignorance.

Because Weinberger had once been director of the Office of Management and Budget, and because I had served my White House Fellowship there, I was dispatched one evening, shortly before the inauguration, to bring him to the Pentagon to look over his new office. The lobby of his hotel was filled with prosperous-looking Republicans, flushed with victory, eagerly awaiting the inaugural festivities. I had myself announced from the desk and went up to Weinberger's room. The Secretary-designate opened the door. He was dressed impeccably but soberly, his manner somehow formal yet warm. He greeted me with a kind of Victorian cordiality. He flattered me that he remembered me from OMB and said that he was delighted we would be working together again. While honored, I wondered what those words might augur for my hopes of going back to the Army.

That was what Alma wanted too. She pointed out something of which I was unaware: I was much more relaxed, much more a man in his natural habitat, much more fun in straight military assignments. In the Army, I was working with a band of brothers who shared backgrounds, memories, and values. The political assignments were far more frustrating and tension-ridden. There was a comparison with working on cars. You could fix things more easily under the military hood than in the messier gearboxes of politics. And while assignments abroad had kept me away from my family for long periods, working in the Office of the Secretary of Defense had almost the same effect. I was gone before my children were awake and came home after they had gone to bed.

On January 20, 1981, I arrived at the office early as usual. The executive suites were empty. An unnatural quiet had settled over the Eisenhower Corridor. Passing the torch from one administration to another leaves a brief vacuum in the halls of power. A few days before, I had chatted with Graham Claytor as he cleared out his desk. He and the rest of the Democratic Defense appointees had fought the good fight and lost. Yet, I had a sense that they were not devastated by Carter's departure, at least not from the national security perspective. I liked and admired Graham Claytor and was going to miss him. He was soon back on his favorite track, becoming president of Amtrak, and deserved much of the credit for saving the country's rail passenger service.

On his last day in the Pentagon, Claytor held a small awards ceremony. At the end, he shook my hand and said, "Colin, don't be surprised if you end up as Chairman of the Joint Chiefs of Staff someday." I remember thinking that it was a nice compliment, but an unlikely prophecy.

11 ★ *The Reaganites—and a Close Call*

I WAS WALKING past the Secretary of Defense's office just after the inauguration when a familiar figure with the compact, wiry frame of a wrestler (which he had been) stepped into the hallway. He wore no jacket and his shirtsleeves were rolled up, very un-Pentagon. "Mr. Carlucci," I said, "welcome to the department."

He stopped. "Oh, yeah, Colin Powell," he said with a smile. "I remember you from OMB. Good to see you again. You're going to be my military assistant, I understand."

In the years since we had been together at OMB, Frank Carlucci had become an inside-the-Beltway star. He had served as ambassador to Portugal between 1975 and 1978, a time when the administration was worried about that country swinging from a rightist dictatorship to communism. Carlucci had enabled the United States to steer a subtle center course until Portugal could find its own way to democracy. He had been number two more often than Avis, deputy at OMB, undersecretary at HEW, and deputy director at the CIA. He was now waiting out Senate confirmation as Weinberger's number two at Defense. His talents had been recognized and employed by both parties, which tainted him in the eyes of some conservative purists. To them, Carlucci had committed an especially grievous sin. During the Carter administration, he had served in the CIA under Admiral Stansfield Turner, whose name provoked rage on the right for Turner's wholesale firing of covert operatives. White House politicos did not want Carlucci at Defense, nor did powerful Senator Jesse Helms. But Weinberger did want him, and purists be damned. As I had observed in Weinberger's handling of Bill Van Cleave, the Secretary, with his polished, Old World manner, had a will of steel. Also, as part of this portable entourage, Weinberger had brought William Howard Taft IV to Defense as his general counsel, the position Taft had filled for him at HEW.

"Mr. Secretary," I said to Carlucci, "let me know what I can do for you."

"For one thing, don't call me Mr. Secretary," he said.

"Okay, I'll stick to Mr. Carlucci," I responded.

"Not Mr. Carlucci either, and certainly not Mr. Ambassador. Just call me Frank."

I finally accepted that behind closed doors it would be Colin and Frank. "But," I added, "don't embarrass me by forcing me to call you Frank in front of all these generals. They are *never* going to call you Frank openly. This isn't HEW. You're running the armed forces of the United States, and we don't call our bosses Jim Bob, or Freddie, or Frank."

Carlucci was finally sworn in on February 4 over Helms's objections in a deal that brought Fred Iklé, a stainless conservative, to the department as undersecretary of defense for policy. Carlucci took over Graham Claytor's old job and office. And I remained in place, now as Carlucci's senior military assistant.

The man so modest in forms of address enjoyed playing the consummate insider. One day when Carlucci kept referring to "Cap" in an unlikely context, I finally said, "Weinberger?" No, Frank explained, he meant Carlos Andrés Pérez, charismatic president of Venezuela. I was amused by the contrasts between his style and his substance. Frank could be planning Machiavellian machinations while changing the diaper on his baby daughter, Kristin, whom he brought to the Pentagon on Saturdays when his wife, Marcia, was tied up with her job.

"I want you to go to the Wehrkunde with me," Carlucci informed me a few days into the new administration. The Wehrkunde was a conference held in Munich every February and sponsored by a German publishing magnate, Baron von Kleist. Heavy-duty papers with titles like "A New Strategic Paradigm for Europe" were delivered. National security wonks hungered to go to the Wehrkunde.

"Fine," I told Frank. "I'll have the Air Force lay on a plane."

"No," he said, "just get us a couple of seats on a commercial flight."

I did as Frank asked, and we trotted out to Dulles Airport. There we waited while our departure was delayed for hours because of an engine breakdown. Frank eyed his watch nervously. We finally boarded, and Frank took his first-class seat, to which, by rank, he was entitled. I kept on moving. "Where you going, Colin?" he asked. "I only rate coach, Frank," I said. Consequently, we could not work together during the flight. And we lost another day of work coming back by accommodating ourselves to the airline schedule.

I no sooner got back to my office than General Robert "Dutch" Huyser, commander of the Military Airlift Command, pulled me by the ear. "That was dumb," Huyser said. How could he provide secure communication when we were off flying Pan Am? How could he safeguard top-secret documents? The next time we bypassed military aircraft designated for official travel, it was off with my head. Frank finally agreed, and we started using military planes.

One thing soon became apparent about the Reagan administration: the World War II generation was back in the saddle. The President's military screen credits may have been modest—hc made training films on the Hollywood front—but the war was a defining experience for him, and he liked to dwell on it. Cap Weinberger had risen from private to captain in the Pacific theater, serving under General Mac-Arthur. There he had met his wife, Jane, an Army nurse. He too was shaped by that era.

One morning in a staff meeting, Weinberger mused to Carl Smith and me, "I'm puzzled. Are you all in the military or not? I seldom see officers on my staff in uniform." We explained that wearing civvies had become common during the early seventies to make it appear that fewer military personnel were serving in Washington. Weinberger harrumphed and said, "If you're in the military, you wear a uniform." The word went out, and that was that.

"There's something that bothers a lot of us around here," I told Carlucci one day. I explained how we had been unable to get President Carter or Secretary Brown to present Master Sergeant Roy Benavidez the Medal of Honor he had earned. Benavidez had performed his gallant deeds in 1968; it was now 1981. "It would mean a lot to us to see this hero get his due," I said. The idea leaped like a spark from Carlucci to Weinberger to the White House. Reagan's image maker, Michael Deaver, seized on the possibilities. A Hispanic-American, neglected during a Democratic administration, was finally to be honored by a Republican President. Pull out all the stops.

The scenario chosen was for President Reagan to come to the Pentagon. The ceremony was to be held on February 24, 1981, in the huge center courtyard, with the whole Pentagon invited. Ordinarily, a military officer would read the citation and the President would hang the medal around the recipient's neck. Reagan looked over the citation and said, "This is something I'd like to read," pointing out that he had had some experience with scripts. He thus became the first President ever to recount the heroic deeds personally before bestowing the nation's highest military honor. Even more than inauguration day, that afternoon marked the changing of the guard for the armed forces. We no longer had to hide in civvies. A hero received a hero's due. The military services had been restored to a place of honor.

More substantial proof that a new era had dawned came as the new administration took over the defense budget. Ronald Reagan had run on a strong defense platform and against the "hollow Army" that General Shy Meyer had deplored. Even though the final Carter budget, which the Republicans inherited, increased defense spending by over 5 percent, word went out from Weinberger's office asking the service chiefs how much more they needed. This was Christmas in February. This was tennis without a net. The chiefs began submitting wish lists. The requests initially totaled approximately a 9 percent real increase in defense spending. I sat in the Secretary's office with Frank Carlucci and heard words I had never expected to hear in my life. That was not enough. Weinberger ordered the chiefs back to the drawing boards. They went from their wish lists to their dream lists, pulling out proposals they never expected to see the light of day. The latest figures went to the Office of Management and Budget, and the word came back, not enough. OMB's conclusion was based on no strategic analysis; the Reagan White House was simply telling the Pentagon to spend more money. The military happily obeyed. Manna, they realized, does not fall from heaven every day.

Weinberger managed to up the inherited Carter budget by 11 percent, or $25.8 billion, the pattern for the foreseeable future. We had not embarked on a pointless spending spree. After successive lean years, the armed forces were in poor shape. The glamour investments—research for sophisticated weapons, primarily—had been well funded. But the bread-and-butter expenditures that support the services and that make military life tolerable had been neglected. The forces were like a tumbledown house with a BMW parked in the driveway. The Reagan budgets funded pay raises, spare parts, training, modern communications centers, repair facilities, child-care centers, family housing, dental clinics—items that in many cases had been neglected since World War II. And Congress readily approved these increases. The once-feared Cap the Knife had become, to his critics, Cap the Ladle. Those of us on the inside, however, knew that the services were undernourished. We needed a ladle to restore the country's military strength, purpose, and pride.

Late in February, in my capacity as Carlucci's gatekeeper, I made an appointment for the new Secretary of the Army, John O. Marsh, Jr., to see Frank. Jack Marsh was a thoughtful, soft-spoken former Virginia congressman whom I knew only slightly. I had no idea what his business was that day with Carlucci, but when he came out, he led me into the hallway. There, the mild-mannered Marsh tossed me a hand grenade with the pin pulled out. "Colin," he said, "I'd like you to consider resigning from the military. I'd like you to become undersecretary of the Army." He added that he had just checked out the idea with Carlucci and the White House personnel office and had a green light.

Though stunned, I understood what was going on. I had a reputation for being able to move the Pentagon bureaucracy. More to the point, Marsh also hoped to place a qualified minority executive in a senior political position in an organization composed almost 40 percent of minority soldiers. I told Marsh I would have to sleep on this one.

I ordinarily spared Alma my days at the office. But this decision would change both our lives so radically that I had to have her opinion. We did not lose much sleep over it. I was a forty-four-year-old brigadier general with a good future. The Army was my life. Resigning and taking a political appointment would confirm everything I wanted to spike—the suspicion, sometimes in my own soul, that I was becoming more politician than soldier. Alma agreed 100 percent. And a plunge into the uncertain waters of political appointments made her uncomfortable. The next day, I thanked Marsh for the honor, but turned him down.

The day after Marsh's offer, I went in to see Carlucci. I liked working with him, but, by now, I had been in the front-office suites for nearly four years. "Frank," I said, "I want to go back to doing what brigadier generals are supposed to do."

"Yeah, sure, we'll get around to it," he answered and then proceeded to unload a bundle of new assignments on me.

At the end of the day, before going home, I liked to stretch out and talk shop with now Rear Admiral John Baldwin, Carlucci's other military assistant. One March evening, Baldwin said, "Colin, you'll never get out of here."

"Why not?"

"First, Carlucci has no incentive to let you go. He's happy with you. He's not military. He doesn't understand our need not to stay away too long. He's just getting you in deeper and deeper."

"And the second reason?" I asked.

"Your real boss is Shy Meyer, and he would prefer to keep you here."

Jack Baldwin's words rang out like a fire bell in the night. The next morning, I went into Carlucci's office again and said, "Frank, I've got to go."

"Yeah, yeah, we'll talk next week."

By early spring, however, by constantly badgering Carlucci, I managed to pull it off. General Meyer proved unexpectedly understanding. He assigned me as assistant division commander for operations and training, 4th Infantry Division (Mechanized), Fort Carson, Colorado. The ADC job is an apprenticeship for command of a full division. I could not have chosen better myself. I began telling my friends about my good fortune. To my surprise, many whose judgment I valued did not share my enthusiasm, including Major General Dick Lawrence, under whom I had served as deputy G-3 in the Americal Division in Vietnam, and Julius Becton, who had steered me to the National War College, both of whom were members of the armor fraternity.

"Colin," Lawrence told me, "I would give anything not to see you going to Fort Carson." Why? I wanted to know. He had "bad mojo," uneasy vibes, Lawrence said, because of the 4th Mech's commander, Major General John W. Hudachek. He knew

Hudachek, and the guy was, well, difficult. "He shouldn't have been given a division," Dick said. Julius Becton called me to express similar reservations. I was also warned of potential problems involving my new commanding general's wife. I was not discouraged. I was eager to get back to the troops. And I had always gotten along with my commanders, good guys like Red Barrett and tough guys like Tiger Honeycutt.

I had come to admire the rare Carlucci mix, tough and energetic in pursuing his goals, yet thoughtful and kind in his dealings with people. I continued to be impressed by his lack of ego. Frank Carlucci did not need people scattering petals before him. He threw a farewell party at which he awarded me the Defense Distinguished Service Medal, and we parted as close friends.

The last people I said goodbye to before heading out to Fort Carson were Rich Armitage and Marybel Batjer. Rich was about to become assistant secretary for international security affairs. The man cussed like a sailor and spoke sense in simple declarative sentences. I understood him and he understood me. We had connected immediately. I had made not simply a service friend or a job friend, but a friend of the heart. And Marybel, who probably could not have distinguished an admiral from a doorman before she came to the Pentagon, displayed a native shrewdness at sizing up people, a talent invaluable in someone handling political appointments. The three of us had informal channels reaching into almost every corner of the Pentagon, the only way to tap into the stream of information flowing beneath the department's formal reporting system. And almost every day, we exchanged this useful intelligence. I did not know it then, but this relationship would endure and become invaluable for the rest of my career.

For a lad from the South Bronx whose idea of a view was to stand on an apartment house rooftop and see Brooklyn, the site of Fort Carson was intoxicating. The post is situated at a point where the Great Plains collide with the Rocky Mountains. Pikes Peak and Cheyenne Mountain, towering like twin thrones, are visible from Fort Carson. "There's too much sky," Alma had said on the drive out. "Where did it all come from?" And she missed the trees. I knew what she meant. The vast, treeless prairie and the Rockies somehow dwarfed a person.

Colorado Springs is a handsome city built on the fortunes of nineteenth-century gold-mining barons. The present gold mines are three major military organizations, of which the prize is the U.S. Air Force Academy north of town, with its airy architecture and four thousand of the brightest young men and women in the country in its cadet wing. NORAD, the North American Air Defense Command, is located inside Cheyenne Mountain and also at nearby Peterson Air Force Base. NORAD monitored the skies for enemy bomber and missile strikes and operated the forces to intercept attackers. NORAD's natural setting is so magnificent that many Canadians and Americans who served there come back to the area to retire.

South of town is Fort Carson, home of the 4th Infantry Division (Mechanized), the blue-collar brother-in-law. The 4th Mech made a hellish racket with its guns; it chewed up the landscape with its tanks and unleashed thousands of libidinous nineteen- and twenty-year-olds onto Colorado Springs. The division also pumped more money into the local economy than the other two organizations combined and, consequently, was welcomed, even loved a bit, like a rough, self-made millionaire uncle.

Three flat ranch houses had been built on top of a bare hill on the edge of the post, one for the commanding general, one for the assistant division commander for operations and training, my job, and one for the ADC for support. The houses provided living space but no charm. Alma was still not about to get the home she had dreamed of for a general's lady.

On my first day at Fort Carson, I walked up to the second floor of a modern, fifties-style headquarters building and had a conversation with my predecessor, Brigadier General Grail L. Brookshire. Afterward, my new aide, Captain Fred Flynn, took me across the hall to meet my new boss commanding the 4th Mech, Major General Hudachek. Both Brookshire and Flynn, I had noticed, had been strangely reticent about the man. I entered a large office, the walls covered with the usual plaques and power photographs, the windows affording a panoramic view of the parade ground and the Rockies. There I met a stocky officer of medium height with close-cropped hair and a serious aspect. Hudachek greeted me with a brisk no-nonsense handshake and got down to business. His main interests were training and management. My responsibility would be training. He spoke forcefully and intelligently on the subject, without wasting words. The programs he had in place impressed me. After ten minutes, he made clear that the conversation was over. As I left, I thought, this guy sure knows his stuff. I can learn from him. I also noticed that no smile had crossed his lips during this first encounter. Jack Hudachek was clearly not a Red Barrett, a Charles Gettys, or a Gunfighter Emerson.

The mission of the 4th Mech was to fight the communist-bloc armies on the battlefields of Europe. My experience, particularly with tanks, had been scant. And so I set out to qualify myself as an expert gunner on an M-60A1 tank. As division ADC, I did not have to do this. But coaches who have never played lack a certain credibility. I began my training under a trio of tough tanker sergeants who were respectful, but unawed by my single star.

It was my first day on the qualification course, and I was performing as tank commander, training the main gun on a target one thousand meters off as we barreled over what appeared to be flat terrain. Suddenly, the tank nosed down. Realizing that we had hit a dip, I furiously elevated the main gun tube, but too late. I heard a sickening scrape. The tank came to a halt.

Certain things simply are not done. You don't spit into the wind. You don't mount horses from the right side. You don't run ships aground. And tankers never stick their main gun tube into the dirt or run out of gas. Infantrymen believe that tankers will urinate in the fuel tank rather than be caught empty. And tankers elevate the gun tube *before,* not after, going into a decline.

The sergeant looked at me with weary patience. "Sir," he said, "we've got to take a break and check the tube." We bore-sighted it. Luckily the tube was not bent. We swabbed it out and were soon on our way again. By the third pass, I was nailing the target, and I qualified as expert tank gunner.

I was not naive enough to give myself too much credit. A tank crew assigned to instruct a general is rarely a pickup team. I had been propped up by a crack gunner, loader, and driver. Nevertheless, I enjoyed displaying the expert's badge on my desk. And few experiences are more exhilarating than racing along at thirty miles an hour with fifty tons of iron under you.

We were trying to figure out how much practice ammunition a tank crew had to fire to become proficient. One thing we knew was that Soviet crews fired about one-tenth as many rounds in training as American crews did. The cost differential was tremendous. Every time we fired from a tank, it cost the taxpayers from $200 to $1,000, depending on the type of round. And each of our crews fired approximately one hundred rounds a year. The Army's training technicians had designed simulators and devices like video games that would allow our crews to become proficient using less live ammo. We wanted to find out what combination of actual firing and the use of training devices produced the best performance. One tank battalion was given the maximum number of rounds. Another got fewer rounds. Another got fewer rounds still and more time on the simulator-trainers. The acid test was to take these differently prepared battalions out to the major qualification range, give them the same number of rounds, and see which did best.

The answer turned out to be "none of the above." The battalions that did best were those with the best commanders. A good commander could motivate his men to excel under any conditions. "We're gonna win even if they give us one lousy round" was the winning attitude. The new technologies were adopted, and they did make a difference. But we never lost sight of the reality that people, particularly gifted commanders, are what make units succeed. The way I like to put it, leadership is the art of accomplishing more than the science of management says is possible.

General Hudachek's leadership style was that of a tough overseer. The job got done, but by coercion, not motivation. Staff conferences turned into harangues. Inspections became inquisitions. The endless negative pressure exhausted the unit commanders and staff. The 4th Mech was a capable ship, but not a happy ship. Given his customary dour mood, I was astonished one day when the general came bounding into my office and said, "Powell, you're doing a great job. I'm going to put in a special report and see if you can't make the next board." The selection board for major generals was about to meet, and while I was one of the junior brigadiers in my class, a special report could give me an early shot at two stars. Hudachek called in his aide, a captain named Philip Coker, to set the report machinery in motion.

In the end, the special report came to nothing. The personnel office informed us that an officer had to be in his assignment at least sixty days, which I had not, to receive special consideration. Nevertheless, I appreciated Hudachek's effort. It seemed to say that despite his prickly personality, if you did the job right, he would treat you right.

I seemed to be the Episcopal missionary wherever my family went. Soon after our arrival at Fort Carson, I poked around to find out where our congregation met. I was informed that Episcopal services were held Sundays at 9:00 A.M. in the *Catholic chaplain's office*! The following Sunday we walked down the side aisle as the Catholics filed into the chapel for mass. We made our way to the office in the back, where eight folding chairs had been set out. We sat down, and half an hour later, the Episcopal priest showed up, a lieutenant colonel in the Chaplain Corps. He passed around a hymnal that I had never seen before and began the service. Two women strummed guitars accompanying what sounded to me more like a folk song than a hymn. I tried to get into the spirit as best I could, but yearned for the old-time religion.

After the service, I went up and introduced myself to the priest, who turned out to be Colin P. Kelly III, son of the American hero of World War II. "I've got a question, Father Kelly," I said. "How have you pronounced your first name all these years?" "Coh-lin," he said, which was an Irish variant, and considered incorrect by the British, who said "Cah-lin." I explained how I had started out British-style but had yielded to peer pressure as a kid after his father became a household name. And then I asked, "Why do we hold our service in a Catholic priest's office? Why don't we have our own church?" There were too few Episcopalians, he said. I suggested that if the setting were more appealing, we might attract more. I knew that the old World War II barracks complexes of the kind we had at Carson contained wooden chapels. "Please find us one of those, Father," I said. I also asked him to consider replacing the folksy *Songs of Living Waters* hymnal with something containing the old anthems like "A Mighty Fortress Is Our God." He eventually found us a chapel and the service took on a more traditional flavor.

We had one child out of the nest by now. Just before we left for Fort Carson, my son, Mike, had graduated from Lake Braddock High School in Burke, Virginia. Mike had come out with us to Fort Carson that summer, but by August he was off to the College of William and Mary in Williamsburg, Virginia. I never tried to tell him what he should do with his life. But I did try to guide Mike. For the previous year, I had ridden herd on him to get his college applications submitted on time. I had fussed over his essays like a schoolmarm. He had been accepted at West Point and had also won a four-year Army ROTC scholarship, either of which would be a blessing for our family fortunes. I was pleased when he chose the College of William and Mary. The service academies are prestigious, and I was proud that he had been accepted to West Point. Still, I suspected that Mike would get a more rounded preparation for life in a school more broadly focused than a military academy. And should he settle on a military career, the old man had not done all that badly with his geology major and an ROTC commission.

That year, Linda entered Cheyenne Mountain High School in Colorado Springs, her third high school in three years. Somehow the uprooting did not seem to affect her. She was on her way to becoming a National Merit Scholarship finalist. We enrolled Annemarie, now eleven, in a Catholic school, the Pauline Memorial Academy. We liked the discipline the nuns provided, though they could do little to control her irrepressible nature. Annemarie became a cheerleader. She fell in love with ice skating (certainly not an inheritance of her Southern mother or Bronx father), and she took classes in the Olympic-style rink located in the Broadmoor Hotel, where she glided like a swan.

Alma expected to be as active in volunteer work at Carson as she had been on previous posts. While in Washington, she had served as president of the Armed Forces Hostess Association, which performed a popular service for families facing the anxieties of moving all over the globe. A sergeant's wife, for example, could come to the offices of the Hostess Association in the Pentagon, and learn all about schools, hospitals, rents, and just about everything from the temperature to local religious activities at her husband's next post. At Fort Carson, Alma was hoping to put her old audiology skills back to work at the post hospital. She was surprised, however, to run into a wary resistance among other wives to getting involved in volunteer work. We were soon to find out why.

I started hearing complaints from fellow officers that we had a co-commander at Fort Carson. While General Hudachek rode herd on his subordinates, the wives reported that Mrs. Hudachek did the same on them. The Hudacheks were a devoted couple, and the general had made his wife his partner in running the post. Ann Hudachek served prominently on all the advisory councils he had set up to oversee the commissary, the PX, the child-care center, everything. She obviously had a deep commitment to the welfare of the soldiers under her husband's command and to their families. The rub was the brusque way both Hudacheks went about their roles. I became the lightning rod for these grievances. Finally, I decided, yes, pay the king his shilling, and the queen too, if necessary. But the situation at Fort Carson had gone too far. I had been watching it for four months and saw morale sagging. I believed that I had a responsibility to act.

An ADC is a division commander on training wheels. By Army custom, I was at Fort Carson to soak up the skills and mores for division leadership. Some commanding generals are happy to delegate broadly to their ADCs while they sit back and watch. Hudachek stood at the other end of the continuum. I had a sense that he would have been just as happy if his two ADCs disappeared. He ran the division, and we were permitted to study at the master's knee. Which did not make what I set out to do any easier—or wiser.

Tom Blagg, the chief of staff, sat outside Hudachek's office and under his thumb. I told Tom that the division had serious problems, and I wanted to talk to Hudachek about how we might fix the situation.

"Colin," Tom said, "don't do it."

"Why not?"

"Because," Tom went on, "it's not a problem Hudachek can discuss or even admit. I'm warning you—you won't help him. And you might hurt yourself."

Tom was no fool, and only a fool would dismiss his counsel. Still, I had managed to navigate in some of the trickiest currents of the Pentagon. I was sure I could handle a talk with Hudachek. "Tom, I don't have any choice," I said. "I would be neglecting my duty if I ducked this one."

The next morning I leaned into the general's office. "Sir," I said, "when you're free I'd like to have a word with you on some training matters and about the wives."

"Busy," Hudachek said. I went back to my office.

Toward the end of the day, his secretary informed me, "He's free now."

"What is it?" Hudachek asked as I came in.

I went over a few diversionary training items. Then I started tiptoeing into the minefield. "Sir, I think we could do more with the wives. They are not as involved as they should be." The response was a blank stare. I pushed on. "Ann has wonderful ideas. She wants to do so much for the troops and their families." Still, a stony silence. "I think we need to find a way to pursue her interests with a little more participation by the other wives." The conversation did not end, or even develop. It just withered.

I no sooner got in the door that night than Alma said, "What did you do?"

"Did I do something?"

"Ann Hudachek called about an hour ago and asked me over for a cup of tea. 'Alma,' she told me, 'I'm so sad. The general and I are really fond of you and Colin. We thought we could at least count on you two.' " Obviously, Hudachek had called his wife about my visit as soon as I left his office. Strike one? I nevertheless continued going about my duties, relishing my work with the troops, trying to put post gossip, suspicion, and intrigue behind me.

While I was at Fort Carson, the Army was engaged in a hot debate about how best to check on unit readiness. The traditionalists favored the Annual General Inspection. I had been a battalion exec on my second Vietnam tour when we had to carry out one of these exhaustive reviews in the middle of a war. To me an inspection once a year was the spring cleaning approach to preparedness. Beat the rugs, wash the curtains, clean out the attic and the cellar. Look great the day the inspector arrives and hope you don't fall apart afterward. And, should the enemy attack, pray that they do it just after the inspection when you are in peak form, because two weeks later you will be back to your bad habits.

The new school of preparedness preached that inspections should be an ongoing process, instead of one gigantic exercise in breaking starch. The proponents favored hitting a company here, a company there, unannounced, until over the course of a year a whole division would be inspected. Every unit would have to be on its toes for twelve months rather than just two weeks out of the year. Not surprisingly, unit commanders favored the old system. Nobody welcomes a surprise attack on an unprepared position. I, however, was a convert to the new thinking. While the debate was under way in the Pentagon, I tried to extend it to Fort Carson. I told Jack Hudachek that this was the way to go. He heard me out, but was not buying. Strike two?

One afternoon, after I had been with the division for about nine months, the commanding officer of one of the brigades showed up at my office wearing a troubled frown. I asked him in and closed the door. He told me that a sergeant in one of his battalions had come to him charging that the man's commanding officer had become sexually involved with the sergeant's wife. Such conduct is devastating to morale and taken seriously in the Army. As the experienced officer that I thought I had become, I should have turned the matter over for investigation to the post lawyers or the Criminal Investigation Division. Instead, I decided to look into it myself. I told the brigade commander to bring the suspect battalion commander to me. My hope was to find out if the guy did it, and if so, to advise General Hudachek that the officer be relieved of command and transferred. In short, hand the boss a solution instead of a can of worms.

But the script went haywire. The officer denied all. I now had no choice but to take Hudachek the worms. "Fine. Thank you," was all he said. "I'll take care of it." He then did the professional thing: he turned the matter over to the lawyers and the CID. The subsequent investigation nailed the officer, down to motel receipts for his trysts. Hudachek never called me in again on this matter, never discussed it, never pointed out that I might have handled it better. Just "Thank you. I'll take care of it." Strike three?

By May 20, 1982, I had completed my first year at Fort Carson. The man who ten months before had wanted to put my name before the major general selection board called me into his office. "Sit down," Hudachek said. He was a chain-smoker, and the cigarette trembled in his hand as he handed me a two-page document. This was my annual efficiency report. My future hung on these pages. When I finished reading it, I said, "Is this your considered judgment?" He nodded. "You realize the effect it will have," I said. "This report will probably end my career." Oh, no, Hudachek protested. I was coming along fine, he assured me. And he would be rating me again next year. "The next report will take care of you," he added. Unconvinced, I excused myself, got up, and left.

Army efficiency reports are written in code words. If you don't know the code, you cannot crack the meaning. For example, one box reads, "Promote ahead of contemporaries." Another reads, "Promote with contemporaries." And a third, "Do not promote." The choices seemed clear enough. But by now, these reports had become so inflated that you needed to have box one checked to remain in the running. Hudachek had checked me in box two. Damaging, but not lethal. The narrative evaluation, however, was nearly fatal. He had praised my performance solely as a "trainer." My command potential was ignored. I had not been sent to Fort Carson to become a trainer, but to qualify as a division commander. I had attended divisional prep school, and in his judgment, had flunked.

Still, Hudachek did not have the last word. He was the "rater." My report still had to be completed by a "senior rater." That officer was Lieutenant General M. Collier Ross, deputy commander of Forces Command, a man over two thousand miles away in Atlanta, Georgia, whom I had met exactly once. Two weeks later, I opened an envelope from FORSCOM with a certain trepidation. General Ross repeated Hudachek's praise of my ability as a "trainer" and added, "He deserves full consideration to be a principal *staff* officer in a major command headquarters. The rater considers this more Colin's forte than command at this time and I concur. . . ." The words were damning enough, but Ross also had to check a set of blocks. Block one meant top of the heap, block two, some risk to promotion, and block three, forget it. Ross gave me a block three. This was the *coup de grâce*. Yet, I could not blame General Ross. He had no real knowledge of my performance other than Hudachek's opinion. At least, Alma got a promotable rating. "Powell has a truly gracious wife," Ross had written, "fully capable of representing the Army and supporting her husband wherever he may be as- signed."

I went to bed that night with my head in a whirl. This was the worst professional judgment passed on me in twenty-four years in the Army. Bernie Rogers had warned at charm school that 50 percent of us were not going to make two stars. I now knew which half I fell into. At GOMO, the General Officer Man- agement Office in the Pentagon, young lieutenant colonels who move generals around would look at this report and think, this walk-on-water soldier has finally been punctured. Powell turned out to be just a political general. Can't hack it in the field. Shy Meyer would see the report and shake his head; Colin's been away from the troops too long. And the next promotion board would look at an unblemished record until now, and wonder, what happened to this guy? I slept poorly that night.

The next morning, however, I went into the office and I felt fine. Just as I had learned on that hillside in Vietnam after witnessing my first death in battle, things always look better in the morning. I am capable of self-pity. But not for long. I stopped in to see Tom Blagg and told him what had happened. "I warned you," Tom said. The trouble had begun with my going to Hudachek about the wives, he believed. To which I added, yes, and arguing with Jack about annual inspections, and my handling of the officer involved with the sergeant's wife. That one drove the nail into the coffin. I had blown it, I told Tom. Still, I had no regrets. I had done what I thought was right. Hudachek had done what he thought was right and graded me accordingly. I was not going to whine or appeal, get mad at Hudachek, or go into a funk. I would live with the consequences.

I went on enjoying my duties. But part of my brain started disengaging itself from the Army. One night I sat down at my desk at home and retooled my résumé for the civilian market. I was not going to hang around until forced to retire. Just the year before, I could have been undersecretary of the Army!

It was an odd time for me, one foot still in the service, the other ready to step out, but where? I thought I would give GOMO a call to make sure I was going to stay at Fort Carson for another year. I got in touch with a lieutenant colonel, who said, "Funny you should call; we were just about to get in touch with you. We'll call back tomorrow." Don't call us, we'll call you—it always sounds like a brush-off. Now I was totally in the dark. Was this going to be good news or the ax? I spent another uneasy night.

I was in the field watching a tank gunnery exercise when my aide shouted over the roar of the firing
that GOMO was trying to reach me. I drove back to
headquarters and put through a call to the Pentagon.
General Hudachek was leaving, I was informed,
going off to Korea to be chief of staff of the Eighth
Army. Major General Ted Jenes was coming out
from Fort Leavenworth to replace him. So far, none
of this directly concerned me. The colonel at GOMO
went on. I would not be staying at Fort Carson, he
said. In August, I was going to be assigned to Fort
Leavenworth to take over Jenes's job as deputy commanding general of an operation called CACDA,
Combined Arms Combat Development Activity.

I hung up the phone suspended somewhere
between hope and bewilderment. Jenes was a two-
star. The job he was vacating and that I was going to
was a two-star slot. Either the folks at the Pentagon
had not seen my latest efficiency report or I had been
brought back from the dead.

On an afternoon toward the end of July, Alma and I
headed for the conference room down the hall from
General Hudachek's office. The brigade commanders, battalion commanders, division staff officers,
and their wives greeted our entrance. I had often
served as buffer, lightning rod, and father confessor
between these officers and our commanding general.
We had managed to create an able, if not always a
happy, ship. My old pal Tom Blagg was gone by now,
replaced by a new chief of staff named Bill Flynn.
Flynn delivered a gracious speech and presented me

with the division's going-away gift, a statue of a cowboy in chaps sculpted by a prominent Western artist, Michael Garmon. I followed with my own farewell speech. All the while these festivities were going on, Jack Hudachek remained twenty feet away, behind his closed office door. The party broke up, Alma went home, and I returned to my office to pack up a few things.

"The general will see you now." I turned to see Hudachek's secretary standing in my doorway. As I went in, he mumbled something that sounded like "Best of luck." Same to you. He handed me a plaque with the division seal glued on it. We shook hands perfunctorily, and I left. A parade had marked my arrival at Fort Carson, but I departed without banners or bugles.

As I prepared to go to Fort Leavenworth, I was still not sure what Mother Army was up to, but I began to believe that my career had not crash-dived. I had done some poking around and learned that not only was I going into a two-star job with one star on my shoulder, but the new position had provided a launch pad to higher rank for all its previous incumbents. I learned how I had been rescued from oblivion. General Richard G. Cavazos, commander of FORSCOM, was the superior of General Ross, the senior rater on my efficiency report. Cavazos, a hero during the Korean War, was an Army legend. When this officer talked about what it meant to be a soldier, to offer your life in the service of your country, he brought grown men to tears. The deeply conscientious Cavazos kept a close eye on all division commanders in FORSCOM, and he had come out to Fort Carson occasionally to look over the Hudachek operation.

After the last such trip, Cavazos had flown back to Atlanta with Julius Becton. As Becton later reported the conversation, Cavazos had told him that he was concerned about Hudachek's division. "Did you notice anything in that conference room today?" Cavazos had asked Becton. "The only one who dared say anything in Hudachek's presence was Powell. The rest of them were terrified." Cavazos was not in my rating chain; his deputy, Ross, had rated me. But in the Army there are rating systems and there are rating systems. Until you become a general, the promotion machinery is fairly formal. There are not that many generals, though, so an informal network operates at that level. Chats over drinks at the officers' club, phone calls, the gossip mill, the old bulls sniffing the air and figuring out what is really happening become as important as efficiency reports. What this inner circle had apparently concluded was that, yes, Powell got into trouble at Carson. However, he had done what he thought was right, and had risked putting his head in a noose. He probably needs to watch his mouth and his step. In the end, however, it came down to the fact that the generals knew the officer being rated and they knew the officer who had rated him. My future was not foreclosed.

At this time, I received a letter from a White House Fellowship alumnus, Tom O'Brien, who worked at Harvard. Tom asked if I was interested in a job as the university's director of financial programs.

What I knew about academic finance would fit on a dime. Yet, it was nice to be wanted, particularly after the close call. Given the new assignment, however, I could tear up my civilian-tailored résumé and turn down the Harvard nibble. I was going back to Fort Leavenworth, fourteen years after I had attended Command and General Staff College there, and glad of it. Shortly after the family arrived at Leavenworth, the new major general promotion list came out; I was on it and could expect to be promoted within a year.

My new job at Leavenworth was vital to the Army, but would not sound particularly thrilling to laymen. Under its latest reorganization, the Army had divided U.S.-based forces into two commands. Forces Command, FORSCOM, controlled the units and prepared them for war. Training and Doctrine Command, TRADOC, developed war fighting doctrine and operated training facilities to provide the trained troops to FORSCOM. A prime TRADOC objective was to make sure the different schools—infantry, armor, artillery, and air defense, for example—trained their forces to fight as a team, rather than solo performers. TRADOC had created an organization to promote that objective, the Combined Arms Combat Development Activity. I was now CACDA's deputy commander, under an energetic three-star general, Jack Merritt. I quickly found myself caught up in an assignment near to the heart of my old mentor, General John Wickham, designing a lighter-equipped, smaller infantry division for faster battlefield mobility, particularly useful in Third World conflicts.

One of the historic houses at Fort Leavenworth was 611 Scott. Built in 1841, it had originally been the sutler's place, the PX of those days. Generals William Tecumseh Sherman, Philip Sheridan, and George Armstrong Custer had all lived under this roof. The impetuous Custer, according to legend, left from this house when he set out for the Little Bighorn. And the ghost of Mrs. Sheridan still haunted 611 Scott. Sheridan had left the unhappy woman behind when he went off on a trip to Chicago, and she died while he was gone. Thereafter, her spirit supposedly never left the house. Today, 611 Scott is a ten-thousand-square-foot gleaming white mini-mansion set above the Missouri River. The dining room easily seats forty. The grounds are beautifully landscaped, and a handsome gazebo rises on the front lawn. This was now our home. Alma finally had her mansion. And I, at long last, was redeemed in her eyes.

The latest family move meant we had to uproot the girls again and plunk them down in new schools. It took Annemarie her usual day and a half to get settled and start showing up with friends. Whatever pain and frustration the disruption inflicted, she confided and confined to a little diary she kept.

By now, Linda was attending her fourth high school, a little disruptive for any teenager. Leavenworth High School, however, had more black students than her earlier schools, which led to a formative experience in her life. Linda's high school drama department had decided to stage an anthology of scenes from several plays. The black girls, including Linda, had chosen something from *For Colored Girls Who Have Considered Suicide / When the Rainbow Is Enuf.* The content is fairly rough for high school students, and their choice sparked a furor. A week before the performance, the administration canceled the black segment.

I promised my angry daughter that I would read the play. Apart from the jarring fact for a father that his daughter had been cast as a prostitute, I thought the work was strong and honest. I called the principal and expressed my opinion. Linda wrote an editorial for the school paper attacking the cancellation. The administration stuck by its decision, but made one concession. During the part of the performance when the scene from *Colored Girls* would have been presented, the black students would be allowed to discuss with the audience the issue of the cancellation.

I told Linda that we had both gone through the chain of command, and Army-like, it was now her responsibility to abide by the decision. On the last night of the performances, however, Linda had a surprise in store. During the discussion period, she stepped forward and said, "I think you might like to see what we have been talking about." She then proceeded to perform her part. After initial astonishment, the audience burst into applause. I do not know if Alma and I have ever been prouder. We thought, however, that we were only observing a girl's brave gesture. Instead, we were witnessing a young woman choosing her destiny. Linda was determined to become an actress and never looked back.

· · ·

One afternoon in September, I slipped out of a marathon briefing on Army communications and came home early. "Colin," Alma said, "you need a haircut." I had not done that well at the post barbershop and managed to dredge up from my memory a shop in the black section of Leavenworth that I had patronized fourteen years before. I drove downtown, and there was the shop, just as I remembered it, down to the striped barber pole in front. Inside, faded pinups advertising ancient hair tonics covered the wall. Dog-eared magazines littered a rack, and the place had that unique barbershop fragrance. The shop was empty except for a barber older than his posters.

He put down his newspaper and waved me to a chair. "Welcome, General," he said, introducing himself as "Old Sarge" and draping a striped sheet over me. As he snipped away, I studied the photographs over the mirror, black generals, including Rock Cartwright, Julius Becton, Roscoe Robinson, Emmet Paige, and Harry Brooks, all from the generation just ahead of me. The barber handed me a small red-covered diary. "I'm going to ask you to sign my book when we're done," he said. The cover was stamped "1959." I started thumbing through it, studying the signatures, caught up in the parade of familiar names. His little red book read like black military history. Early signatures were mostly of majors, then a few lieutenant colonels, and in more recent years, a comforting number of more senior officers. And then I stopped short. There, in 1968, I found "Colin Powell, Major, USA." I had no recollection of signing the book.

"You don't remember me," Old Sarge said, "but I remember you."

He held up a hand mirror so I could see the back of my head. I nodded my approval. He removed the sheet and shook it out. I fished out a pen and signed the book, this time as "Brigadier General Powell." "What's your name again?" I asked.

"Jalester Linton," he said, "10th Cavalry, Buffalo Soldiers."

I was not only reading black military history, I was shaking its hand. We got to talking about all the sites on the post named for fabled soldiers of the past, like Grant Avenue and Eisenhower Hall. I asked Old Sarge if anything at Leavenworth commemorated the Buffalo Soldiers. "Well," Linton said, "there's 9th and 10th Cavalry avenues." I had never heard of them.

I became curious about the history of the Buffalo Soldiers. I started reading everything I could lay my hands on. What I learned filled me with pride at the feats these black men had achieved and with sadness at the injustices and neglect they had suffered. Blacks had fought in just about all of America's wars. They served to prove themselves the equal of white soldiers, which was precisely why some whites did not want blacks in uniform. My reading led me to the words of Howell Cobb, a Confederate general, who advised Jefferson Davis against arming blacks. "Use all the negroes you can get for . . . cooking, digging, chopping and such," Cobb said. "But don't arm them. If slaves will make good soldiers," he warned, "our whole theory of slavery is wrong." Frederick Douglass put it another way: "Once you let the black man get upon his person the brass letters 'U.S.,' let him get an eagle on his button and bullets in his pocket, and there is no power on earth which can deny he has earned the right to citizenship in the United States."

In 1867, Congress officially put that eagle on the buttons and put bullets in the pockets when it created four black regiments. For twenty-two years, a white officer, Colonel Benjamin H. Grierson, commanded one of them, the 10th Cavalry. When Grierson finally bid goodbye to his troops, he said, "The valuable service to their country cannot fail, sooner or later, to meet with due recognition and reward." Ninety-five years later, it was too late for reward, and I did not see much recognition of the Buffalo Soldiers either.

I read about the fate of Lieutenant Henry O. Flipper. Imagine a child born into slavery, yet possessing the grit to get himself admitted to the U.S. Military Academy in 1873, just ten years after Emancipation. Every black cadet before Flipper had been shunned, reviled, and ultimately hounded from West Point. Flipper took it all for four years without breaking and graduated in 1877. He was sent out West in 1878 to join Troop A, 10th Cavalry, the first black officer ever assigned to the Buffalo Soldiers. Three years later, bigots in uniform framed him on a charge of embezzling from commissary funds. A court-martial found Flipper innocent of that charge, but guilty of "conduct unbecoming an officer and a gentleman." He was given a dishonorable discharge, his military career in ruins by age twenty-five. The resilient Flipper nevertheless managed to carve out successful careers as a mining engineer, author, and newspaper editor. But the stain on his honor obsessed him, and he spent the final years of his life fruitlessly trying to clear his name. The finding of the court-martial was finally reversed in 1976 through the determined efforts of a white schoolteacher from Georgia named Ray MacColl.

During the court-martial, Flipper's attorney had put the question squarely: "Whether it is possible for a colored man to secure and hold a position as an officer of the Army?" My own career and that of thousands of other black officers answered with a resounding yes. But we knew that the path through the underbrush of prejudice and discrimination had been cleared by the sacrifices of nameless blacks who had gone before us, the Old Sarges and Henry Flippers. To them we owed everything.

Not long after my visit to the barbershop, I was jogging past the post cemetery and came upon an abandoned trailer park. Nothing was left but crumbling concrete platforms and an intersection of gravel roads. There I saw a leaning, weather-beaten street sign marking 9th Cavalry Avenue and another marking 10th Cavalry Avenue. I was still upset when I got back to my quarters. I took a shower, went to my office, and called in the post historian, retired Colonel Robert von Schlemmer. "Is that the best we can do?" I said. "Two dirt roads in an abandoned trailer park?"

"Sir, you're right," von Schlemmer said patiently. "But before you blow a gasket, you should know what I went through just to get the Buffalo Soldiers even that recognition."

"Fine," I said, "but where do we go from here? I want something more appropriate honoring the memory of those men."

"I'll tell you what," he said. "If you'll take the lead, I'll get the Leavenworth Historical Society behind you, and we'll throw in some seed money, maybe five thousand dollars. But you've got to figure out what you want to do."

I had been thinking about it all morning. "Leavenworth is full of equestrian statues," I pointed out. "I'd like to see a statue here honoring the Buffalo Soldiers. It ought to stand on the bluff overlooking the Missouri, with the cavalryman facing west, headed toward the future."

Five thousand dollars was not going to produce much of a statue, von Schlemmer warned. The first thing I was going to have to learn was how to raise money.

I believed I had a duty to those black troops who had eased my way. Building a memorial to the Buffalo Soldiers became my personal crusade. I called in Captain Phil Coker, Hudachek's former aide, whom I had brought from Fort Carson. "You're 10th Cavalry, aren't you?" I asked Phil. Yes, Coker said, he had been part of the squadron at Fort Carson, obviously long after the 10th had been integrated, which occurred during the Korean War. "You're going to immortalize your old outfit," I told him. "You're going to dig up the history of the Buffalo Soldiers." Coker went at it as if we were talking about *his* ancestors. He scoured the archives while I started looking for money. Those troops had suffered second-class treatment after serving as first-class fighting men. I was determined that the Buffalo Soldiers were finally going to go first-class.

John Wickham came back into my life while I was at Fort Leavenworth. In the spring of 1983, Wickham was about to become Army Chief of Staff. He called me from Washington to say that he had drawn up a list of thirteen of the brightest lieutenant colonels and colonels he could find. He asked me, as a brigadier general, to lead them on a one-month crash study to find out where he ought to be taking the Army over the next four years. Since I was the fourteenth officer, he called the enterprise Project 14.

It was now nearly a dozen years since the U.S. withdrawal from Vietnam, and the Army was almost completely recovered from the trauma of that conflict. On May 27, 1983, we turned in the Project 14 report, recommending to Wickham some modest course corrections. The one point we underscored was that the Army could not stand another Desert One fiasco. The Army exists to win battles and wars, not just to manage itself well. If we expected to restore the nation's confidence in us, we had to succeed in the next test of arms.

I flew to Washington to brief General Wickham and his staff on the final report. Afterward, as the two of us walked back to his office, I took the opportunity to seek his counsel about something troubling me. Wickham's predecessor, General Shy Meyer, had assured me that he intended to keep me at Leavenworth for two years, then put me in line for a division command, which I wanted more than anything. But during this trip to Washington, I had heard disquieting rumors. "I hear I'm being considered to replace Carl Smith as Weinberger's senior military assistant," I told Wickham, hoping against hope that he could knock the report down.

"That's right," Wickham said. "Pete Dawkins's name is up too. But I think you're better suited." It was hardly the answer I wanted. Dawkins, my long-ago classmate at the Infantry School at Fort Benning, was still the Army's golden boy, the exemplar of exemplars. "I'm all for Pete Dawkins for the job," I said. "I've only been out of the Pentagon for twenty-two months. I've paid my dues. I've already served as military assistant to three deputy secretaries. General, don't let this happen to me again." I feared being branded permanently as a military dilettante, I told him. Wickham remained noncommittal, and I got out of town and back to Kansas as fast as I could.

Carl Smith, Weinberger's current military assistant, had been promoted to brigadier general with me on the same day four years before in Harold Brown's office. Two days after my return to Fort Leavenworth, Carl called. Secretary Weinberger wanted me to come back to Washington for a chat, Carl said, adding, "Colin, I'm getting out of here even if I have to stick it to an old buddy to do it."

A few days later I was walking down the familiar E-Ring to the Secretary's office. As I entered, Weinberger rose and shook my hand warmly in his gentlemanly manner. "Colin," he said without wasting words, "you know General Smith wants to leave. Do you want his job?"

"No, Mr. Secretary, I'm happy where I am. But," I added, "I'll serve wherever I'm sent."

"I expected you to say no less," Weinberger answered. "I would have been disappointed if a soldier didn't prefer the field." We chatted a few more minutes and parted, with me still praying for deliverance by Pete Dawkins.

Before I could get out of the building, Carl Smith found me. I had the job, he informed me with evident relief. Within minutes, Wickham confirmed the news. "We haven't had an Army man in that spot since I left in 1976," he explained. "And we want it. But don't worry. I'm arranging a house for you at Fort Myer, Residence 27A, two minutes from the Pentagon and a fine place. And when you come back here, it will be with your second star."

Still, I had to go back and tell Alma that after less than a year, it was goodbye to Fort Leavenworth and the beloved house of history.

I particularly regretted leaving the Buffalo Soldiers project unfinished. I had been able to light a fire under it, and I did not want that fire to go out. I had a black civilian on my staff whom I trusted implicitly, Alonzo Dougherty, who was also an officer in the Kansas National Guard. "Lonnie," I said, "you know what this project means to me. I'm turning it over to you. I'll continue to do whatever I can, long distance. But I am counting on you to keep it alive here." Dougherty agreed to carry on.

. . .

On June 29, 1983, one of the last days of my
CACDA tour, I stood in Grant Auditorium and Lieutenant General Carl Vuono, now deputy commander
of TRADOC, pinned that second star on me. The
promotion to major general was welcome enough
professionally. Emotionally it meant that I was
finally out of purgatory. I had taken a gut wound and
had survived. It would not be wise, however, to run
that risk again.

After eleven all too short months, the Powell
family left Fort Leavenworth and reluctantly headed
back to Washington.

12 ★ *The Phone Never Stops Ringing*

OVER THE PREVIOUS two months I had become a light
sleeper. I heard the phone this night, September 1,
1983, on the first ring. Alma passed the receiver
to me as if in a trance, without waking up. I glanced
at the red readout on the clock radio: nearly midnight.

"General Powell, this is the DDO"—the deputy
director of operations. He was calling from the
National Military Command Center, which monitors
the globe around the clock. The DDO and I had
become frequent nocturnal communicators of late.

"Got a problem," he informed me. "A Korean jetliner out of Anchorage en route to Seoul has dropped off the radar screen."

I would have to decide whether I should wake up the Secretary of Defense and give him this news fragment. "Do you have anything more?" I asked.

"That's all for now," he said. "The plane just left the scope."

I lay there in the dark, deciding what to do, imagining Seoul Airport, with anxious families wondering why the delay. I phoned the Secretary. If the jet had gone down in the Pacific, we might want to call out U.S. forces for a search-and-rescue mission. Cap Weinberger sounded as composed in the middle of the night as at noon at the Pentagon. He asked me to keep him informed.

As soon as I hung up, the phone rang again.

"General." It was the duty officer again. "It looks okay. We just got a report that the plane probably made an emergency landing."

I passed this word along to Weinberger. Still, I could not get back to sleep. My instincts kept nagging me. You do not lose and find airplanes that casually. I had just started to doze off when the duty officer called a third time.

"Sir, Burning Wind intercepted some odd traffic between the Soviet Air Defense Command and one of their fighter pilots. The Korean plane may have violated Soviet airspace." Burning Wind was an air intelligence operation we carried out over the Pacific using RC-135 reconnaissance planes.

"What are you suggesting?" I asked.

"Don't know yet," he answered. I knew we were both feeling the same foreboding. Could the Soviets have shot down a commercial jetliner full of civilian passengers?

That is how a tragedy unfolds in the Pentagon—not in the neat, complete paragraphs of newspapers or the rounded sentences of TV correspondents, but in fragments. Finally, enough information dribbled in for the Secretary of State, George Shultz, to issue a statement at 10:45 that morning saying that a Soviet fighter plane had, in fact, shot down a Korean airliner. "The United States reacts with revulsion to this attack," Shultz said. "Loss of life appears to be heavy. We can see no excuse whatever for this appalling act."

The initial Soviet response was a flat denial. When that story was punctured by the truth, the Russians said the plane had intruded into Soviet airspace and that they had tried to direct it to the nearest airfield, but the pilot just kept on flying. Finally, the Soviets admitted they had shot down the plane, but claimed it was on a "deliberate, thoroughly planned intelligence operation," directed from the United States and Japan.

It would be years before the whole truth came out, after the collapse of the Soviet Union tore away the veil of state secrecy. Korean Air Lines flight 007, en route from Alaska to Korea, had accidentally drifted 360 miles off course and had in fact flown over Soviet airspace twice, first over the Kamchatka Peninsula and then over the island of Sakhalin. The pilot sent up by the Soviet Air Defense Command to intercept KAL 007, Major Gennady Osipovich, flying a Sukhoi-15 fighter, reported that the intruder was using navigation lights and the flashing anti-collision beacon commonly employed on commercial night flights. Osipovich had also flown along the right side of the jet (how close we do not know) for a closer look. The Soviet pilot, who had logged at lcast a thousand interceptions against American military aircraft and knew their outlines as well as his own plane's, claimed he did not recognize the Boeing 747 as a commercial jetliner. He dropped back, locked his radar on the target, and when given the order, shot down KAL 007 just as the plane was exiting Sakhalin and about to reenter international airspace. Osipovich fired two missiles. One struck the tail; the other tore off half of the left wing. It took twelve minutes for the stricken plane and its 269 passengers to plunge into the ocean at a speed of several hundred miles an hour.

Why did the Soviets shoot down an innocent civilian aircraft? The best answer appears to be that the then Soviet leader, Yuri Andropov, was trying to buck up sloppy military discipline and had promulgated a tough new "Law on the State Border." Thereafter, intimidated Soviet military officers had carried out the law's requirements like unthinking robots.

During the Cold War, almost no event stood in isolation. Every occurrence had to be forced into the matrix of East-West confrontation. The Russians had tried to pass off KAL 007 as a spy plane, adding falsehood to a tragic blunder. From our side, I watched Cap Weinberger and George Shultz wrestle for policy dominance on this issue. Weinberger saw the incident as a morality play, with the Soviet Union performing its role as evil incarnate. He argued that Shultz should cancel an upcoming meeting in Madrid with the Soviet foreign minister, Andrei Gromyko. Shultz took the position that we could condemn to our heart's content, but we should not let this incident, however tragic, derail negotiations with the Soviets to further our mutual interests. President Reagan did a bit of each. He called the Soviet behavior "an act of barbarism born of a society which wantonly disregards individual rights and the value of human life." Yet, he wanted the Shultz-Gromyko talks to go forward.

The downing of KAL 007 occurred less than two months after I had taken over my new job as military assistant to Weinberger. I drew some useful lessons from the incident. Don't be stampeded by first reports. Don't let your judgments run ahead of your facts. And, even with supposed facts in hand, question them if they do not add up. Something deeper and wiser than bits of data inform our instincts. I also learned that it is best to get the facts out as soon as possible, even when new facts contradict the old. Untidy truth is better than smooth lies that unravel in the end anyway. Avoid putting a spin on a story that subsequent revelations may discredit (the trap the Soviets fell into). Be prepared to see an international event expand—or contract—for political ends apart from its intrinsic meaning. And finally, in a world bristling with engines of destruction, don't be surprised if they explode from time to time.

Five years later, in 1988, when I had become National Security Advisor, we faced a similar situation when we had to explain to the world why the American cruiser U.S.S. *Vincennes* shot down an Iranian airbus, killing 290 passengers and crew. It was a tragic blunder. We said so and released the facts publicly as fast as possible.

I had received that initial phone call on KAL 007, not at Quarters 27A, which we were supposed to occupy at Fort Myer, but at Quarters 23A, a small house across the street from the unending noise and bustle of the officers' club. We had been bumped from the grander digs we had been promised by a higher-ranking officer. I set aside a small room in the new house as my secure communications center, and the bundles of wires running into it made the place look like ganglia under a microscope. Chesapeake and Potomac telephone crews were forever at the house, repairing, replacing, reconfiguring, until Alma knew them all by their first names. And the phones never stopped ringing from the day we moved in.

I was now working with a Weinberger team much changed since I had left back in 1981. Frank Carlucci had departed government service at the end of 1982 to become president of Sears World Trade, Inc. A businessman, Paul Thayer, replaced Frank as deputy for a time; but Thayer ran into legal difficulties and had to resign. Will Taft replaced Thayer as the second in command of the Defense Department. Along with sharp judgment honed as general counsel, Will had a special qualification. He was one of a handful of people who enjoyed Weinberger's total confidence and who could influence the headstrong Secretary's views.

I had inherited from my predecessor, Carl Smith, a gem in his secretary, Nancy Hughes, smart, level-headed, tactful, and possessed of a priceless gift, the capacity to anticipate a boss's thinking. Nancy, with brief interruptions, would work for me to the end of my military career. You don't tamper with perfection.

While I had been on Harold Brown's staff, I used to sit inconspicuously against the back wall of his office taking notes during staff meetings. As Weinberger's military assistant I made a symbolic leap. Weinberger held his meetings punctually at 8:30 A.M. I should say "held court," since he was far different from the cerebral and solitary Brown. Brown tolerated a tight little circle, though he would rather have been alone. Weinberger liked to be surrounded by an entourage. Brown preferred get-it-over-with informality. Weinberger enjoyed meetings displaying ritual and structure. He presided from an overstuffed pale blue armchair. To his left, in another armchair, sat his legislative affairs assistant. To his right, on a couch, sat his public affairs assistant, while I sat at the other end. Across a coffee table, facing the Secretary, sat his deputy and general counsel. The seating of principals remained as fixed as a constellation in the heavens, even as the meeting grew. Fred Iklé, the number three official in the department, soon wanted in. Weinberger said fine; and Iklé managed to claim the empty middle seat on the couch. If his boss, Iklé, was in, Rich Armitage wanted to attend. Weinberger agreed. Others asked to come. Why not, Weinberger said. Their assistants wanted to come too. Weinberger concurred. The morning meeting grew so large that five minutes before, enlisted receptionists started hauling in chairs from neighboring offices like movers from Allied Van Lines. This gathering was an affirmation of Robert Ardrey's *Territorial Imperative.* You staked out your turf the way tigers do when they urinate on trees. Your scent had to be stronger than someone else's or you would be elbowed aside. Neither the jungle nor the upper reaches of government have any unclaimed space. It is already taken, or seized by the stronger.

The only real issues covered at these meetings were media hot potatoes and pending legislation reported by the public relations and legislative assistants. After they had had their say, Weinberger would go around the room, calling on everyone. The only ones who spoke at length were those who did not understand the game. I always had plenty to discuss with the Secretary, but not before a crowd. The staff meeting served one useful purpose, however. It stroked the participants' egos and made them feel part of the team. Afterward they could return to their own staffs in the glow of reflected glory. "The Secretary just told me . . ." they could say. Or better still, "I just told Weinberger . . ." The big tent was a technique I adopted myself in the future.

I had received an early education in the style of my new boss on one of my first days on the job. On July 26, 1983, I had arrived at about 6:30 A.M. and was flipping through the *Early Bird,* the Pentagon's overnight news summary, when an item plucked from the *Washington Post* caught my eye. The Navy had established a "Wound Laboratory" at the Bethesda Naval Hospital in Maryland to train medical students in the treatment of battlefield injuries. They were to practice on dogs that had been anesthetized, then shot. Alarm bells started going off in my head. I had visions of Americans learning that Lassie or Snoopy had been sacrificed to military medical experimentation. I called my counterpart in the Secretary of the Navy's office, Captain Paul David Miller. Secretary Weinberger was going to want to know what this was all about. Paul told me that nobody was available at Bethesda this early. "I'll get you something later in the morning," he said. I told him he'd better give me something now. The Secretary was due any minute. A vote on the placement of MX missiles was the hot issue this morning, and the Secretary had scheduled early interviews with all three networks. Miller passed along what little information he had.

I had barely hung up when Weinberger came through the door. His first words were "What's this about shooting little dogs?" (The Weinbergers owned a collie named Kiltie.)

"Sir," I started to explain, "it's important when Marines are in combat situations . . ."

"Put a stop to it," he said.

"Sir, this kind of medical research is helping . . ."

"Tell the Navy it's over. The program is canceled. They are not even to consider it. Is that clear?"

I called Miller back, transmitted the order, and got a lot of disbelieving "but-but-but." I told him that

I would explain later. For now, we had to get the Secretary down to the Pentagon broadcast studio on the second floor and wired up for his first appearance on the *Today* show.

The world could have been on the brink of nuclear extinction, but Bryant Gumbel's first question was about the *Washington Post*'s dog story. No such thing could happen, Weinberger answered coolly. He had already given orders canceling any such program, if indeed one ever existed. His other interviews led off with the same question, and in every case, the Secretary assured the nation that the military would not be shooting little dogs, for whatever allegedly good purpose.

Weinberger's reaction that day had been intuitive. He had not called for a blue-ribbon panel of surgeons, psychiatrists, veterinarians, and People for Ethical Treatment of Animals to masticate the issue. He had recognized instantly, in a nation of pet lovers, that whatever the scientific premise, this idea would not fly. And so he killed it on the spot. Mail came pouring in. Phone calls jammed the Pentagon switchboards. Editorial writers sang Weinberger's praises. Weinberger was a hero. I had learned a lesson from a master in public relations. Certain matters are sacrosanct. Also, you can face the messiest public issue and, if you tackle it head-on and quickly, you can move a liability to the asset column.

One September morning, Weinberger informed me on his arrival that I should prepare myself for hot-weather travel. We were going to Central America, my first trip abroad with him. On September 6, we

departed from Andrews Air Force Base aboard a
DC-9 with "The United States of America" emblazoned across the fuselage; the plane was part of the
89th Airlift Wing, which operates the government's
VIP fleet. As we boarded, I noticed among the party,
including Rich Armitage and fourteen reporters, a
new face, a confident junior staffer who quickly
made clear that he represented the National Security
Council. From the moment we were airborne, he
started worming his way into Weinberger's presence,
though the Secretary's formal facade usually kept
outsiders at arm's length. As we worked around a
small conference table, preparing ourselves for meetings with three Central American chiefs of state, our
newcomer, assertive and well informed, deferred to
no one but Weinberger, apparently seeing himself as
the second-ranking dog on this sled. Who is this guy?
I wondered. I looked him up in the trip book, which
contained itineraries, maps and bios that our staff had
prepared. There he was: Oliver L. North, Major,
USMC.

Secretary Weinberger and his wife were extremely
close, and he always wanted Jane along on his foreign trips. For spouses, official travel means constant
exposure to unfamiliar faces, a stream of polite
chitchat, and smiles so fixed that they almost have to
be pried off at night. Jane Weinberger was a more
private person than her husband, a warm, intelligent
woman, one-on-one, who had little enthusiasm for
her public role. Weinberger often invited other
spouses along as companions for Jane. On Septem-

ber 22, we were scheduled to begin another trip, this one around the world, and Weinberger insisted that Alma come along under "invitational travel orders," which made her an official member of the party. I thought it might be stretching a point to bring the wife of the Secretary's chief horse holder, dog rob-ber, and gofer, but Weinberger insisted. Alma came, and the first night she expressed her puzzlement to me. Was she a tourist? Excess baggage? What exactly was she supposed to do?

As the trip progressed, her role emerged. Alma became a handy go-between. She could tell hostesses things that Jane Weinberger could not—for example, that the Secretary's wife was overtired (Jane was just beginning to suffer painful osteoporosis), and per-haps the tour of the Etruscan ruins might be cut short. Jane felt comfortable with Alma, and after the last receiving line had folded and the last formal dinner ended, they would unwind, comparing notes on the day's doings before turning in.

I always left Alma off the foreign trip passenger lists. Weinberger always put her on. "Mr. Secretary," I said on one occasion, "there is really no basis for Alma to come this time."

"Nonsense," he replied. "A unique addition to the traveling party. I wish for her to come. Say no more about it."

Alma had found her niche. She was Jane's lady-in-waiting.

On October 13, we learned that Judge William Clark, the President's current National Security Advisor, a man struggling in a job for which he had little bent or taste, was stepping down to become Secretary of the Interior. Clark, along with Weinberger, was part of the Reagan California crowd. Clark's replacement was an outsider who filled Weinberger with apprehension. Clark's deputy, a former Marine lieutenant colonel now in his mid-forties, was Robert C. "Bud" McFarlane. McFarlane was not the sort of man whom Weinberger could regard as a peer. McFarlane had, furthermore, an infuriating manner of expressionless noncommitment. "Hmmm. Thanks for calling. Have a nice day," he would respond to the Secretary's phone calls, behavior which drove Weinberger mad. Bud McFarlane replaced Judge Clark as National Security Advisor on October 17.

McFarlane's most visible subordinate turned out to be the brash Marine from the Central American trip, Ollie North, now a lieutenant colonel. North was fast becoming a legend, the guy you went to to get things done. North displayed remarkable imagination and energy, but every now and then, strange things happened. One day, one of my assistants came to my office and said, "General, Colonel North wants a permit to carry a gun."

"Why does he need a gun around the National Security Council?" I wanted to know.

"People are out to get him," my assistant said.

"Who?" I asked.

"He didn't say."

Ollie North's personal security had nothing to do with the Secretary of Defense. Let the Navy figure out if he needs to be armed in the Old Executive

Office Building, I said, since Marines come under the Navy Department.

On October 23, six days after Bud McFarlane became National Security Advisor, I received another middle-of-the-night call from the National Military Command Center. This time there was no question about alerting Weinberger immediately. A terrorist truck bomb had struck a U.S. Marine barracks at the airport near Beirut, Lebanon. Again, the news came out in dribbles. Each time, I had to convey the mounting horror to a Defense Secretary who I knew was squeamish about death. On taking over his Pentagon office, Weinberger had gotten rid of a portrait of James Forrestal, the first Secretary of Defense, who had taken a suicide plunge from the Bethesda Naval Hospital. Weinberger replaced Forrestal's picture with a rosy Titian on loan from a Washington museum. This night, each of my calls was like a physical blow to the Secretary. Eighty bodies pulled out. A hundred. A hundred and fifty. In the end, the toll reached 241 Marines dead. A near-simultaneous terrorist attack at a barracks in downtown Beirut killed seventy-seven French soldiers.

Our Marines had been stationed in Lebanon for the fuzzy idea of providing a "presence." The year before, in June 1982, the Israelis had invaded Lebanon in one final push to drive out PLO terrorists. This move had upset the always precarious Middle East balance. The United States, consequently, was attempting to referee the withdrawal of all foreign troops from Lebanon. The Marines had been deployed around the Beirut airport as what State Department euphemists called an "interpositional force." Translation: the Marines were to remain between two powder kegs, the Lebanese army and Syrian-backed Shiite units fighting it out in the Shouf Mountains. Weinberger had opposed the Marines' involvement from the start, but lost the policy debate in the White House to McFarlane and Secretary of State George Shultz.

I was developing a strong distaste for the antiseptic phrases coined by State Department officials for foreign interventions which usually had bloody consequences for the military, words like "presence," "symbol," "signal," "option on the table," "establishment of credibility." Their use was fine if beneath them lay a solid mission. But too often these words were used to give the appearance of clarity to mud.

On August 29, before the airport truck bombing, two Marines had been killed by Muslim mortar fire; on September 3, two more, and on October 16, two more. Against Weinberger's protest, McFarlane, now in Beirut, persuaded the President to have the battleship U.S.S. *New Jersey* start hurling 16-inch shells into the mountains above Beirut, in World War II style, as if we were softening up the beaches on some Pacific atoll prior to an invasion. What we tend to overlook in such situations is that other people will react much as we would. When the shells started falling on the Shiites, they assumed the American "referee" had taken sides against them. And since they could not reach the battleship, they found a more vulnerable target, the exposed Marines at the airport.

What I saw from my perch in the Pentagon was America sticking its hand into a thousand-year-old hornet's nest with the expectation that our mere presence might pacify the hornets. When ancient ethnic hatreds reignited in the former Yugoslavia in 1991 and well-meaning Americans thought we should "do something" in Bosnia, the shattered bodies of Marines at the Beirut airport were never far from my mind in arguing for caution. There are times when American lives must be risked and lost. Foreign policy cannot be paralyzed by the prospect of casualties. But lives must not be risked until we can face a parent or a spouse or a child with a clear answer to the question of why a member of that family had to die. To provide a "symbol" or a "presence" is not good enough.

The Beirut bombing was soon followed by our invasion of Grenada on October 25. The Caribbean island had fallen under control of a young Marxist, Maurice Bishop, whose regime was building a jet runway with Cuban aid; the strip was going to be made available to the Soviet Union. Then Bishop was assassinated, and the chaos following his murder threatened nearly a thousand American medical students studying on Grenada.

We attacked with a combined force of Army paratroopers, Marines, and Navy SEALs. It should have been easy enough to take over a country of 84,000 population defended by a Third World militia of about two thousand poorly armed troops and a Cuban construction battalion. Yet, it took most of a week to subdue all resistance and rescue the medical students. The invasion was hardly a model of service cooperation. The campaign had started as a Navy-led operation, and only at the last minute was Major General H. Norman Schwarzkopf, then commanding the Army's 24th Infantry Division (Mechanized), added to Vice Admiral Joseph Metcalf's staff to make sure someone senior was on board who understood ground combat. Relations between the services were marred by poor communications, fractured command and control, interservice parochialism, and micromanagement from Washington. The operation demonstrated how far cooperation among the services still had to go. The invasion of Grenada succeeded, but it was a sloppy success. I was only a fly on the wall at the time, but I filed away the lessons learned.

Weinberger was a man of stubborn principle. His critics would have said "stubborn" period. He would battle like a lion against any cabinet peer or antagonistic congressman. But he could not bear to cross probably the most pliable man in the administration, President Reagan. Weinberger's attachment and loyalty to the President were total and visceral. He disliked causing discomfort to the man he idolized. Consequently, when Ronald Reagan was persuaded to put Marines in an untenable position for an imprecise purpose in Beirut, Weinberger would not confront him on the issue.

While Weinberger never hesitated to battle with George Shultz and others in White House policy disputes, he hated any unpleasantness involving his own workaday staff. I could not get him to fire a driver who was so drunk when he went to pick up the Weinbergers after a Thanksgiving holiday that he greeted them with "Happy Easter."

Cap Weinberger was a man who worked grooves into his life and then stayed in them. I would arrive in my office by 6:30 A.M., and at exactly 6:58, Weinberger's driver would inform me by car phone that the Secretary would arrive in two minutes. On the dot, Weinberger stepped from his private elevator, followed by the driver, lugging an old-fashioned lawyer's briefcase with a big metal clasp on top. Weinberger headed for the Pershing desk, an elaborately carved walnut piece over nine feet long, formerly belonging to General John "Black Jack" Pershing, commander of the American Expeditionary Force in World War I. Weinberger unloaded the briefcase of its homework, papers that would launch multimillion-dollar defense purchases, make people admirals or generals, or send surface-to-air missiles to anticommunist guerrillas. The briefcase empty, Weinberger sat down and, for a few seconds, simply gazed ahead, as if bracing himself for the day ahead. He next buzzed in the CIA courier who delivered the President's Daily Brief, a heavy vellum report containing the cream of overnight intelligence. I preferred the *Early Bird* with its compendium of newspaper stories. In the evening, Weinberger packed up the ancient satchel and adjusted his chair so that it fit flush, exactly centered, against his desk. He tapped his foot on the base of the chair, signaling the end of the workday. The ritual was unvarying.

Weinberger's outward gravity concealed an impish wit and unexpected quirks. My job, and hence my borrowed power, was to control the Secretary's time, the one commodity he could not stretch. Consequently, I was in and out, conferring with him a dozen times a day. One morning, I surprised him reaching for something from his top right-hand drawer. Before he could close it, I spotted the contents. The drawer was full of chocolates, candy kisses and chocolate bars, treats I subsequently discovered that he munched on when no one was around. The Secretary of Defense was a closet chocoholic. On another day, when I surprised him polishing off a Hershey bar, he said, "Colin, the only real power I exercise in this building is that I can order the kitchen to prepare a chocolate dessert when I entertain important guests."

My duties had no specific definition and ran from Weinberger's strategic advisor to bag carrier. On one occasion, I had to retrieve his tuxedo from home so that he could change in his office for a soiree. I stood there briefing him on the evening's event while he emptied his pockets, the contents of which revealed an unexpected side to this formal man. Out came a little stub of a pencil. He had carried it, he explained, since he was a child. An Australian halfpenny emerged, a memento of his wartime courtship of his wife in the Pacific. "I'm always more comfortable with these around me," he explained shyly.

Like Harold Brown and John Kester, Cap Weinberger was a cultivated man. His tastes ran to the classics in literature and music. We bought him a small clock radio with a cassette player, and he worked when alone to the accompaniment of Bach and Beethoven. I found the cultured side of the man appealing, something not found in that many infantrymen; and at times, I felt my own cultural inadequacy. But, if anything, my reading habits got worse during this period. By the time I got home at 9:00 P.M., I might get two pages into a good book before I dozed off.

Weinberger also had a taste for pomp. Long before my return to the Pentagon, the CIA had reported that Libyan hit men were en route to the United States to assassinate the President and other American leaders. It was a false alarm, but, among other measures, sentries in service dress uniform were posted outside the suites of the Secretary and the deputy secretary. We wound up with twelve useful men and women working in shifts assigned to an essentially useless duty, since the Pentagon had perfectly adequate civilian police. When I took over as military assistant, with the assassination threat long since proved only a rumor, I wanted to end the guard detail. Weinberger would not hear of it. He loved having these strapping troops, the American equivalent of the Tower of London's Beefeaters, posted outside his doorway. He saluted the sentinel on duty whenever he left the office and saluted again whenever he came back.

Frank Carlucci had once counseled me that wise subordinates picked their fights with Weinberger selectively. "If it's small potatoes," Frank had warned, "don't waste your energy. Even if he's dead wrong. Save yourself for the serious stuff. And even then you'll probably hit a stone wall." Weinberger could indeed be obstinate, as I was to find out in the case of "Star Wars."

On March 23, 1983, about four months before I had returned to the Pentagon, President Reagan delivered a major policy speech announcing that the United States intended to pursue a "Strategic Defense Initiative." The President had been persuaded by the Joint Chiefs of Staff and other advisors that we could create a defensive shield in space, controlled by satellites and capable of destroying incoming Soviet missiles. The President immediately grasped that such a shield could change the nuclear equation. The present situation was a balance of terror, Mutually Assured Destruction, MAD. You destroy us, and we will destroy you. But if, because of this shield, *they* could not destroy *us,* then the huge nuclear arsenals still growing on both sides made no further sense.

Immediately following the President's SDI speech, Senator Ted Kennedy branded the idea a "reckless Star Wars scheme," a term which, because of the wildly popular movie, stuck. This phrase scared the hell out of people with the prospect of nuclear megabursts going off in the heavens and radioactive debris raining down to earth. I am not ideologically liberal or conservative, but I believe the liberal community made a serious mistake by ridiculing this concept out of hand as unwise even if it could be done. The real problem, I think, was that

Ronald Reagan's critics could not bear the thought that he had proposed a major conceptual breakthrough in the nuclear stalemate.

Weinberger became more Catholic than the Pope on the subject of SDI and served as the administration's point man in hearings on the Hill. Onc day, on his way to testify before Congress on the subject, Weinberger sought to defuse Star War fears by asking the Pentagon's head of research and engineering, Richard De Lauer, if the x-ray lasers that would destroy Soviet missiles would be powered by nuclear explosions. "Is it a bomb?" Weinberger asked De Lauer. That was how you generated the laser beams, De Lauer explained, by detonating a nuclear device in space.

"But it's not a bomb, is it?" Weinberger asked, looking for semantic elbow room. De Lauer found a useful euphemism: "No, not a bomb, it would be a nuclear event." Thereafter, Weinberger in congressional testimony and elsewhere refused to admit that SDI required a nuclear blast. He would begin rolling two No. 2 yellow pencils between his fingers, a Captain Queeg talisman indicating that his mind had gone into combat mode. He preferred the word "generator" to "bomb."

Technically he was wrong. And I feared that in his obstinacy he would look evasive. When the two of us were alone in his office, I tried to explain. "Mr. Secretary, a nuclear device does have to explode in space to generate the enormous energy required to make the system work. The power is not supplied by Con Edison."

"Generates energy, you say," he repeated with satisfaction. "Then you agree with me. It is not a bomb. It's a generator."

After a time, I realized that there was method in his stubbornness. As long as he never yielded on this point, no headline could ever scream, "Weinberger Confirms Nuclear Bombs in Space: Kennedy Demands New Star Wars Hearings."

I soon understood why Weinberger was not over-awed by Congress. Members often displayed a well-developed talent for hypocrisy. We endured torrents of righteous wrath from lawmakers shocked by Weinberger's budget requests. But the same guy whipping us on the floor one day would be on the phone the next, begging us to add to the Pentagon budget some vaguely military program for a community college in his district. As one committee chairman put it to me, no matter how high-flown the debate, at the end of the day, he had to have one vote more than 50 percent, or no budget passed. And what swung votes was what some people called pork and others called national defense. I soon understood the difference. Pork was national defense spending in another member's district.

It was not easy to stand up to members of Congress, since we needed their votes. But the line had to be drawn somewhere. Once, while serving as Weinberger's military assistant, I got a call from Congressman Charles Wilson of Texas. Charlie Wilson was a defense stalwart and a particular rainmaker in winning aid for the mujahedin who were fighting the communist regime and Soviet forces in Afghanistan. Charlie had earlier called our Legislative Affairs Office to arrange military transportation for a trip to the region. He wanted to bring along his girlfriend. He had, quite correctly, been turned down. He then called me. He complained about nitpicking bureaucrats, and knew I would straighten them out. I was well aware that Wilson was a vote we counted on, and I took a deep breath before answering. "Charlie," I said, "that's unauthorized use of government aircraft. The Secretary cannot approve it."

What was I, he demanded, anti-bachelor? "I'm damned if I'm going to travel all over the world without the company of a pretty lady." My answer was still no.

"Suppose I just show up at the airport with her?" he asked.

"The pilot will refuse to fly her," I said, "and you shouldn't put an officer on the spot like that." He blew more smoke and hung up.

I was disappointed a few days later to get a letter from Congressman Wilson reminding me that he would still be around if I ever came up for three stars. I wrote him and said, "Please do what you think is right and I'll keep trying to do what I think is right." What he thought was right was to cut three C-12 attaché aircraft from the next defense budget, making no pretense about why he was doing it. Open vindictiveness was not going to hurt a good ole boy from a safe east Texas district.

The girlfriend episode marked my first serious run-in with a member of Congress, and I came away with this conclusion. You can afford adversaries, but not enemies. Today's adversary may be tomorrow's ally. I managed to remain friends with Charlie and to accommodate his substantive requests. And we continued to get his vote on key issues. Sometime after the airplane incident, at a formal dinner, I met Charlie's girlfriend, a stunner. "See what you cost me," he said. He had a point.

My boss was a good man to be on the right side of, but he was the wrong man to cross. Richard Perle, a determined Cold Warrior, had come into the department as assistant secretary of defense for international security policy. Perle, known around the building as "the Prince of Darkness" for his unremitting anti-Soviet stance, had brought with him a kindred soul, a bearded and brash former congressional staffer named Frank Gaffney. I watched Gaffney's debut at a Weinberger staff meeting. He lectured the Secretary on the evils of softness toward the Reds and referred to the four-star Chairman of the Joint Chiefs of Staff, General John Vessey, as "Jack." After the meeting broke up, Weinberger took me aside. "Who is that young man?" he asked. "What is his name?" I told him, but for the following year, no matter how often Frank Gaffney surfaced, he remained to Weinberger the man without a name. I gave Perle's protégé a course in bureaucratic table manners, and Weinberger was eventually able to utter "Gaffney," even eventually to nominate him for a higher post. But second chances with Cap Weinberger were rare.

. . .

Early on, I accompanied Weinberger when he went to the White House for a meeting he had to attend in the Situation Room. I waited outside until he and the President came out and headed for a small nearby office for a private chat. It was the first time I had ever seen Ronald Reagan up close. Weinberger gestured me to come forward and introduced me to him. What struck me as the President took my hand and gave me a melting smile was a radiance the man generated. He was perfectly attired, not a hair out of place, the tie knotted just so, the snowy white shirt looking as if he had just broken starch. We exchanged a few pleas-antries, and he and Weinberger turned to the business at hand. What stayed with me after this brief first brush was the paradox of warmth and detachment Reagan seemed to generate simultaneously, as if there could be such a thing as impersonal intimacy.

I was a juggler trying to keep the egos of three ser-vice secretaries, four service chiefs, the Chairman of the Joint Chiefs, and other Pentagon pashas all in the air at once. They expected instant access to the Sec-retary, who did not always welcome their attentions. Dealing with them was the toughest part of the job, and not everyone applauded my performance. One Pentagon powerhouse tried to get me fired. John Lehman, Secretary of the Navy, was probably the ablest infighter in the building. Lehman would never budge an inch in the competition among the services. To him, the Navy position was always the Alamo. Not content to run the Navy, Lehman was forever pressing on Weinberger his ideas for running the entire defense establishment. Weinberger did not enjoy Lehman's aggressiveness, and I had to play the heavy, keeping him at bay. Not surprisingly, Lehman blamed me for depriving the Secretary of the benefit of his brilliance. He went around the building claiming that I was not serving the Secretary, but ingratiating myself with the Joint Chiefs of Staff to guarantee my future. His displeasure reached a point where he went to see Will Taft and urged Taft to have Weinberger get rid of me. Will jokingly told me of the incident. I was not amused. I called Lehman's military assistant, Paul Miller, and told him that if his boss was displeased with my performance, he ought to tell me to my face, not try to sandbag me. Nothing changed. Weinberger continued to resist Lehman. Lehman continued to blame me. And I did not get fired. In the course of these clashes, however, I did pick up from John Lehman's vocabulary a new twist on an old bromide: "Power corrupts; but absolute power is really neat."

My father had already passed away, and so had Alma's mother, in 1972. As we entered 1984, Alma was about to lose her father and I my mother. R. C. Johnson died in Alma's arms on February 5, 1984, at the age of eighty-one. I had started off as a suspect son-in-law, a soldier, and possibly worse, a West Indian. By the time R.C. died, I had overcome these demerits and could affectionately kid this sober educator, get him to take a rare drink, and tease him about tools somehow migrating from my toolbox into his.

I took on the responsibility of wrapping up R.C.'s estate. I had gone through the Birmingham house and rounded up the arsenal of guns he had accumulated in drawers, closets, and the basement. I put the weapons in the trunk of my car and took them back to Washington. Jim Brooks, who ran the message center for the Secretary of Defense, was a gun collector and wanted to see what I had brought back. Jim was interested in a Smith & Wesson .38, a couple of Magnums, and an old Japanese army rifle of my own. He bought the pistols, and finally we got down to the rifle. During one lunch hour, we went to the parking lot so that I could show him the piece, stowed in the trunk of my car. Jim looked it over and said he would think about it and left. I had put the rifle back into the trunk when a patrol car pulled up. Out came an officer from the Department of Defense police force.

"Is this your car?" he said.

"Yes," I answered.

"Please open the trunk."

I started to explain about the gun collection.

"Open the trunk, please," the cop said.

I opened it to reveal a weapon that would have been obsolete even when the Japanese bombed Pearl Harbor.

"Come with me," he said, taking my rifle.

"Look, I'm Major General Powell," I said. "I'm Secretary Weinberger's military assistant."

"Please come with me, sir." He tried to lock me in the caged-off backseat. I refused. I told him, as they say in the movies, that I would go quietly, but I intended to ride up front.

We entered the police station in the basement of the Pentagon, where a sergeant sat behind a desk ready to book people and read them their Miranda rights. I was not looking forward to this scene. Suddenly, a police lieutenant appeared. "General, what are you doing here?" he asked.

"I think I'm being arrested," I said.

"I'll take over," he told the patrolman. And turning to me, he said, "You can go back to your office, sir. I'll see that your rifle is returned."

When I got back, my secretary, Nancy Hughes, explained what had happened. A vigilant secretary on the fourth floor of the Pentagon, up in Air Force country, had seen two people down in the parking lot handling a rifle. Terrorists! She had immediately called the police. The savvy and tactful Nancy got wind of what was going on and notified a man called Doc Cooke.

The Secretary of Defense ran the department, but David O. "Doc" Cooke ran the building. Formally, Doc was deputy assistant secretary of defense for administration. Functionally, he was the chief fixer. Need to kick somebody upstairs who was not doing his job? See Doc Cooke. Want a private bathroom worthy of your rank as assistant secretary? Doc can install it. Can't get a parking place in the prestigious River Entrance lot? Try Doc. Need to spring a major general who is about to get busted? Doc's your man. His power was formidable, this Godfather of the Pentagon. Doc was the one player whom even crafty John Kester had been unable to outwit. Doc had all the understanding of the military bureaucracy of a Navy captain, which he had been, and the wiles of a lawyer, which he was. Without Doc Cooke, the Pentagon would not open in the morning. No one else would know where the keys were. Doc and Nancy had arranged my release without bond, bail, or further embarrassment.

My mother died a hard death. She had had a heart attack five years before. She survived only to get cancer, requiring a mastectomy. Then she had a second heart attack. Toward the end, as with my father, I found myself flying up to New York almost every weekend. Even in her constant suffering, her spirits never flagged. When she knew there was no hope, she uttered the typical Jamaican sucking sound followed by the untranslatable "Chuh!" "Chuh, Colin, you just put me out there, throw some ivy over me, and forget it." I thanked God for Ida Bell, by now a twenty-five-year boarder in my mother's home. Miss Bell had helped my father during his terminal illness. Now she was doing the same for my mother. I will always be indebted to Ida Bell.

Maud "Arie" Powell died on June 3, 1984. The week before, knowing the end was near, I had driven the whole family to New York for what I sensed might be the last visit. It touched me, the closeness that bound my wife and all three children to my mother. The kids all called her "darling," a pleasing sound they had picked up because that was what she called them.

My father had been the formative figure in my life. The role of my mother was no less important. I absorbed from her as well lifelong habits of hard work and self-discipline. She had never stopped working until incapacitated. Yet the necessity to earn a living had never interfered with her perfect mother love. I never understood how she could work so hard away from home every day, yet never allow my sister or me to feel anything but mothered. Parents are a luck of the draw. With my mother and father, I could not have been luckier.

The funeral service was held at St. Margaret's, our old family church in the South Bronx. By now, the modernists had taken over. All that had meant so much to me, the imagery, the poetry, the liturgy, had been changed. The church had adopted a new service, and the present young priest at St. Margaret's had taken modernism to the extreme, rendering God genderless and ordinary. I knew my attachment to the forms of the past was more emotional than intellectual. But I found it disconcerting to discover that the rock of faith I was raised on could move. My mother received a unisex, low-key, nontriumphant burial service. I do not recall hearing the word "God" mentioned once. I found myself whispering, "Don't worry, Mom. We'll do something better later, because this is not the way you would want to go."

Cap Weinberger was an avid Anglophile. His manner, speech, and appearance, his patrician never-apologize-never-explain attitude, had a certain Englishness, minus the accent. Consequently, when the Secretary received an invitation to take part in the famed Oxford Union debates, he could not resist. The students had invited him to compete against an

Oxonian Marxist professor, E. P. Thompson, on the issue "Resolved, there is no moral difference between the foreign policies of the United States and the Soviet Union." American embassy officials in London, on learning the news, begged the Secretary not to do it. The Oxford students were heavily leftist, capable of vocal abuse, and unimpressed by anybody. Such an argument could not be won, the embassy staff argued, and a loss would lead to embarrassing stories in the European media. Prime Minister Margaret Thatcher, staunch ally and friend of the Secretary, urged him to reconsider. It was unseemly for an American Secretary of Defense to take part in a venture involving unavoidable risks and a doubtful prize, the opponents argued. Their arguments only hardened Weinberger's resolve.

We left Andrews Air Force Base late in the evening of February 27, 1984, and arrived in London early the next morning. Weinberger was busy with other matters and, I noticed, had given his debating notes only a cursory glance during the flight. That evening I accompanied him through the halls of the Oxford Union, walking past portraits of prime ministers whose own debating skills had been perfected here. I took my place and watched my man mount the stage to argue the "con" position carrying his No. 2 pencils. The students in the packed house reminded me of Romans at the Colosseum waiting for a Christian to be thrown to the lions. Professor Thompson had a formidable reputation as a debater.

What we had forgotten in the hurly-burly of running the department was that our chief had been a former television talk show host, a book reviewer, and a highly paid lawyer. His peroration that night was masterful. Were the Western and Soviet systems different? "I leave you with one thought," he concluded. "When you leave here tonight, there will be no midnight knock at your door." By a close margin, he won. Weinberger was as excited as I have ever seen this emotionally contained man. Though his victory was clear-cut in our eyes, we had taken out a little insurance. The way the debate winner is determined at Oxford is by counting how many people leave via the "pro" exit and how many by the "con." We made sure that every member of our security detail and every staffer and secretary left via the "con" exit.

I knew that Weinberger, for all his outward self-possession, had been deeply troubled by the tragic bombing of the Marine barracks in Beirut. I did not realize how deeply until a singular draft document came out of his office. He asked me to take a look at it and circulate it to the administration's national security team. Weinberger had applied his formidable lawyerly intellect to an analysis of when and when not to commit United States military forces abroad. He was put off by fancy phrases like "interpositional forces" and "presence" that turned out to mean putting U.S. troops in harm's way without a clear mission. He objected to our troops being "used" in the worst sense of that word. He had come up with six tests for determining when to commit American forces.

Weinberger's antagonist, George Shultz, was dismissive of Cap's approach. I had watched the irony of their squabbling for months. The Secretary of State was often ready to commit America's military might, even in a no-man's-land like Lebanon. What was the point of maintaining a military force if you did not whack somebody occasionally to demonstrate your power? On the other side was the man responsible for the forces that would have to do the bleeding and dying, arguing against anything but crucial commitments.

Not only did Weinberger want to sell his guidelines inside the administration; he wanted to go public that summer. We started considering possible speaking platforms, but White House political operatives nixed any such controversial speech until the presidential election was over. After Reagan's reelection, Weinberger addressed the National Press Club on November 28. I went with him to hear him describe the tests he recommended "when we are weighing the use of U.S. combat forces abroad." (1) Commit only if our or our allies' vital interests are at stake. (2) If we commit, do so with all the resources necessary to win. (3) Go in only with clear political and military objectives. (4) Be ready to change the commitment if the objectives change, since wars rarely stand still. (5) Only take on commitments that can gain the support of the American people and the Congress. (6) Commit U.S. forces only as a last resort.

In short, is the national interest at stake? If the answer is yes, go in, and go in to win. Otherwise, stay out.

Clausewitz would have applauded. And in the future, when it became my responsibility to advise

458 · COLIN L. POWELL

Presidents on committing our forces to combat, Weinberger's rules turned out to be a practical guide. However, at the time of the speech, I was concerned that the Weinberger tests, publicly proclaimed, were too explicit and would lead potential enemies to look for loopholes.

In May 1985, I was invited to speak at the ROTC commissioning ceremony at the College of William and Mary. Twenty-seven years had passed since I had stood in Aronowitz Auditorium at CCNY to receive my own second lieutenant's bars. Among the cadets I was to commission this day was Michael Powell. When it came time for me to administer the oath, I instructed the cadets to do an about-face so that they were looking out at the audience of parents and loved ones, a gesture I had appropriated from Gunfighter Emerson's retirement parade. When it was Mike's turn to come across the stage, he got an embrace along with his commission, a powerful moment of continuity for father and son. In the audience, besides Alma, were Mike's sisters, Linda, a William and Mary sophomore, and Annemarie, soon to be a freshman there. I like to think that Thomas Jefferson, an uneasy slaveholder, would have appreciated the Powells' getting a first-rate education at the college from which he graduated.

As a just-commissioned second lieutenant, Mike wanted to take a new car to Fort Knox for his basic training in armor, his assigned branch. I tried to persuade him to wait until he got to Germany, where he was going eventually, and where he could buy a

European car. No way. Mike had had enough of my hand-me-down Volvos, especially after the night when he had to steer while I towed a broken-down Volvo on the end of a rope for ninety miles from Richmond to our house, a hair-raising experience for the towee. Enough of Pop's penny-pinching. Mike wanted a new Honda now. I took him to a Honda dealer and introduced him to the art of the deal. To Mike's utter humiliation, I spent three hours haggling with five salesmen and two managers. But in the end, we got our price.

By now, I was buying Volvos presumably dead and bringing them, like Lazarus, back to life. People started seeking me out for my Volvos. Others happily gave me their moribund models. I would fix them up, slap $99 worth of Earl Scheib paint on them, and resell them. Business became brisk. I even tried to get a dealer's license, but the state of Virginia would not consider Fort Myer a legitimate business address. Over the past ten years, over thirty Volvos have passed through my hands. If only Sweden awarded a Nobel Prize for recycling its cars.

A large part of my day in the Weinberger office involved going through correspondence addressed to him to decide what required his personal attention. The document dated June 17, 1985, was a stunner, a draft National Security Decision Directive (NSDD) entitled "U.S. Policy Toward Iran," printed on White House letterhead, addressed to Weinberger and Secretary of State George Shultz, and classified top secret. Our copy of the eight-page NSDD was also marked "Sec Def: Eyes Only for You." Weinberger nevertheless expected me to screen everything. As I read through the NSDD, I realized what it represented: Bud McFarlane, the current National Security Advisor, was making a bid for Kissingerian immortality. Kissinger, former holder of the job McFarlane now held, had demonstrated, along with President Nixon, the conceptual audacity to think the unthinkable, to open a door to Communist China that America had kept shut for a generation. The NSDD proposed opening a dialogue with Iran to include sending U.S. arms to the Iranian government of the Ayatollah Khomeini, a regime that had held fifty-two Americans hostage for over a year, that the United States had formally declared a terrorist state, that President Reagan had said the United States would never deal with, that the United States had boycotted and was urging all its allies to boycott as well, and that was linked to the bombing deaths of 241 Marines in Beirut? Could anything be more audacious? I shot this document in to the Secretary with a suggestion that Rich Armitage also take a look at it. I was eager to hear Weinberger's reaction.

When the memo came back, I felt proud of my boss. Across the cover memo Weinberger had written: "This is almost too absurd to comment on. . . . It's like asking Qaddafi to Washington for a cozy chat," referring to Libya's anti-American strongman.

Normally, Weinberger found Bud McFarlane about as communicative as a stone, one reason he disliked dealing with him. But after this dismissal of his brainstorm, McFarlane asked for an appointment with Weinberger. I watched the usually phlegmatic Bud make an earnest pitch to Weinberger, who sat behind his Pershing desk with a "show-me" impassivity. This bold initiative could win over Iranian moderates, McFarlane argued. It could get us back into Iran before the Soviets filled the power vacuum we had left there; and it could achieve the release of seven American hostages currently held in Beirut.

"The only moderates in Iran," Weinberger answered, "are in the cemetery." It was foolish to expect good faith in obtaining the release of hostages from the same regime that had countenanced their seizure. The Khomeini regime, he told McFarlane, was equaled in evil only by the Soviet Union. As McFarlane left, Weinberger turned to me and said that he hoped we had heard the last of this nonsense. George Shultz at State had condemned the arms deal with equal force; it was one of the few areas where he and Weinberger agreed.

It was Weinberger's habit to keep a record on little white pads of what happened during his day. The notes ranged from entries like "McFarlane meeting on NSDD" to "Call the vet for Kiltie." As he completed a pad, he put it into the middle right-hand drawer of his desk. When the drawer was filled, he stored the pads in a closet. He once told me he had followed this practice for years. Did this small mountain of notes constitute a "diary"? As a result of McFarlane's arms-for-hostage plan and the subsequent Iran-contra scandal, the question would one day have legal implications for Caspar Weinberger— and for me.

. . .

One afternoon that summer, John Wickham, now Army Chief of Staff, called me on his hot line. He had some news. I was supposed to put in two years as military assistant, and the time was just about up. Consequently, I was expecting orders, and Wickham's news was good indeed. I was going to be sent to Germany to take command of the 8th Infantry Division (Mechanized). I was to replace Major General Charles W. "Bill" Dyke, one of the Army's most dynamic officers. I went home to Fort Myer that night floating on air. I was going to leave the Beltway behind to return to real soldiering and, after nearly twenty-seven years, go back to Germany. In a subsequent trip to West Germany with the Secretary, I took the opportunity to drop in on Bill Dyke for a briefing. I could not wait to take over the division.

My euphoria lasted three weeks. Wickham came down to my office, which struck me as a bad sign. "Colin," he said, "I have no doubt about your ability to command."

"Yes, but . . ." I said.

"But Secretary Weinberger has been talking to me. You have the man's total trust. He relates to you in an extraordinary way. You play as vital a role here as you would in any field command. I'm afraid I've come with good news and bad news."

I did not need tea leaves to guess the bad news.

"I can always find another division commander," Wickham went on. "And the Secretary needs you here. So, you'll be staying. The good news is that in about a year, we'll give you a full corps, without your going through a division command."

Wickham left, and I went in to find the Secretary nibbling on a chocolate bar. He greeted me like a father who has just prevented a foolish son from running away from home. "Then it's decided. You'll stay," he said. "And next year, instead of one division, you'll have two." People like the Secretary understood the politics of defense. But they do not always understand the culture of the Army. My skipping a division and going directly to a corps would not necessarily elicit admiration from my peers. Some, in fact, would resent this move and mutter, quite rightly, about "politics." Wickham had assured me that I was different, and could pull off the move without enraging the old bulls. I was not convinced. I still remembered the White House Fellow who had been promoted to colonel through political pressure, which effectively finished his military career. For the next year, however, I would be commanding nothing but a desk outside the Secretary's office.

Every morning I received a black plastic case stamped "Top Secret" containing the choicest intelligence winging around the world and intercepted by our electronic eavesdropping enterprise, the National Security Agency. Vice Admiral Arthur Moreau, the assistant to the Chairman of the Joint Chiefs, came to me one morning with an odd revelation. The Secretary's office was not getting some of the most curious traffic that the NSA plucked out of the air. On his own hook, Art had decided to share this withheld material with me. What I read amazed me. Foreign intermediaries were, for a price, evidently cooking up arms deals between Reagan administration officials and the alleged Iranian "moderates." McFarlane's initiative, evidently, was very much alive. The content of the messages was startling enough, but what troubled me just as much was why the Secretary's office should be cut out of the loop.

I started showing the intercepts to Weinberger. Each time he called McFarlane, trying to find out what was going on, the National Security Advisor remained close-mouthed. Finally, an exasperated Weinberger summoned me one day and said, "Colin, who are we getting these messages from?" I explained that they were bootlegged to us by Admiral Moreau, who got them from the NSA.

"Indeed," Weinberger said. "And don't I control the National Security Agency?"

He did, I said. It was under the Department of Defense. The NSA's director, Lieutenant General William Odom, was Weinberger's subordinate. "Would you call General Odom," Weinberger said, "and remind him who he works for?"

I phoned Odom as soon as I got back to my office and asked him what was going on. I sensed the discomfort of a man being tossed between two reefs. McFarlane's NSC, using the authority of the White House, had instructed Odom to give these intercepts the narrowest circulation, excluding the Secretary of Defense. We straightened that matter out in a hurry.

Weinberger continued to rail against the Iranian arms deal, which appeared to have attracted the sleaziest sort of rug merchants. Still, loyalty to the President remained the dominant element in Cap's mind.

The proposed arms deal was a bad idea. But at the time, it was bad policy, not a criminal act liable to bring down the presidency. Senior officials cannot fall on their swords every time they disagree with a President. And this scheme looked, at the time, as if it would die of its own foolishness anyway. But we underestimated the President's support for the plan or the determination of the NSC staff to pull it off.

The greatest appeal of the arms deal to Ronald Reagan was the possibility it offered of freeing the hostages. Their families came to the White House and followed him on his speaking trips. Their appeals affected him. He wanted the hostages freed, and was willing to take political risks to do it. I myself believe that hostages taken by terrorists represent individual tragedies, and we must do what we can to obtain their freedom. Nevertheless, hostage taking and terrorism cannot be allowed to drive foreign policy decisions. Ransom, however euphemized, is still ransom and should never be paid. Giving in to hostage takers and terrorists can only demonstrate to them that their weapons work.

Early in December 1985, Bud McFarlane decided to resign as National Security Advisor. We were hardly encouraged by his likely successor. I was with Weinberger in Europe for a NATO meeting when he took a call from William J. Casey, head of the Central Intelligence Agency. Casey was upset, Cap told me after he hung up. Admiral John Poindexter, McFarlane's deputy, was the leading candidate to replace Bud. "He's not up to it, Cap," Casey had said. Poindexter lacked the depth and breadth the job demanded. Casey wanted Weinberger to use his influence with the President to help him derail Poindexter's appointment.

I had dealt with John Poindexter and had my own opinion of his suitability. He was brilliant, but in a narrow, technical sense. Poindexter would rather communicate with a colleague next door by computer than talk to the person face-to-face. I had to call him one day to discuss a troublesome story on the front page of the *Washington Post.* "I don't read the *Washington Post,*" he informed me.

"You don't have to agree with what you read," I said. "Often I don't either, but you have to know what papers like the *Post* and the *New York Times* are saying to operate in this town."

"I don't read the *New York Times* either," John answered.

Weinberger did put through a call to the White House. "Mr. President," Weinberger said, "I understand Bud has left and that you're planning to go with John Poindexter. Bill Casey has called me, and Bill doesn't think John is up to the job. So Bill asked me to call you." I watched Weinberger nodding as President Reagan apparently gave his reasons for sticking with Poindexter. Weinberger closed saying, "Mr. President, if you're comfortable with John, I'm sure we'll all get along just fine."

In mid-December 1985, Weinberger had two issues to discuss with British Prime Minister Margaret Thatcher, the super-secret F-117 Stealth fighter and a military cellular phone system. The British had developed a phone system called Ptarmigan, and the French had a similar system called Rita. Both were well ahead of anything we could develop for years. Consequently, the Army had taken bids from these two allies to buy one of their cellular systems off the shelf, a $4-billion-plus deal. It fell to Weinberger to explain to Prime Minister Thatcher why the British had lost the contract to the French. I accompanied him to Britain, and as he prepared to leave the American embassy for 10 Downing Street, Weinberger said, "Colin, I think you should come with me. I'll want good notes on this matter." Our ambassador, Charles Price, accompanied us.

We were admitted to Mrs. Thatcher's receiving room, a quiet, comfortable place with two couches facing each other, a scattering of easy chairs, and a blazing fireplace. We were greeted by the PM's private secretary, Charles Powell, who pronounced his name "Pole." The prime minister, perfectly coiffed, came in wearing a suit that managed to look both feminine and businesslike.

Cap Weinberger started easing his way into his unpleasant task, talking first about the F-117. He had barely opened his mouth when the PM cut him off.

"My dear Cap, I want you to know how very, very distressed I am by this shabby business of the Ptarmigan," Mrs. Thatcher began. "Nothing you can say will convince me that there wasn't dirty work at the crossroads. We've been cheated. Do you hear me? Cheated. And don't try to tell me otherwise."

The two admired and liked each other, especially after Cap's vigorous support of Thatcher in the

Falkland Islands War. He remained stoic as she continued the mantra of "dirty work" and "cheating." When she stopped long enough to catch her breath, Weinberger started explaining the U.S. decision, but the PM cut him off at the knees. "The French!" she said, as if the word were an epithet. Those awful people had obviously done something improper. "I'm sure they did not play fair." She turned to me. "Don't write that down, young man." Her opinions of the French and her expressions of disappointment with her American cousins continued unbroken for ten more minutes. Finally, Weinberger tried explaining again, patiently, sensibly. "But Cap," she said, like a schoolteacher upbraiding a pupil, "I say there was dirty work at the crossroads! Didn't I tell you not to tell me otherwise? Haven't you been listening?"

The performance was fascinating to the spectator. Not so pleasant for the target, I suspect, from the wilted look on Weinberger's face. Margaret Thatcher was every bit the Iron Lady of her public image, certainly one of the most formidable leaders I have ever met; and I had seen her swing her famous verbal handbag right at Weinberger's head.

Every time we thought the Iran-arms proposal had a stake through the heart, Weinberger would return from the White House to report that it had risen. After one such return, he asked me to figure out how, if the Israelis gave the Iranians arms from their stocks, we might replenish them. I went to Hank Gaffney, in the Defense Security Assistance Agency, the Pentagon office that sold and supplied arms to other nations, and I asked him to prepare a memo describing the legal implications of various transfers. Reflecting Weinberger's lack of enthusiasm, I asked Gaffney to accentuate the negative. The response came back that the proper way to carry out a replenishment was through the Arms Export Control Act, which would require notification of Congress as to both the immediate and ultimate destination of such arms transfers. This was precisely the information that the NSC did not want to reveal. I gave the memorandum to Weinberger just as he was headed for another White House meeting, hoping that this time we had a stake that would kill the beast.

On January 17, 1986, the President signed a top-secret "Finding of Necessity," declaring that the covert sale of arms to Iran was in our country's interest. The scheme was still foolhardy, but now legal. Illegality, in what came to be known as the Iran-contra affair, grew out of other elements, namely the diversion of funds to the Nicaraguan contras and perjured testimony given by participants before Congress. The day after the President signed the finding, Weinberger was told to start implementing it. He directed me to arrange for the transfer to the CIA of 4,000 (later raised to 4,508) TOW missiles, an antitank weapon. The TOWs were to go to the CIA under a federal law called the Economy Act, which allowed government agencies to transfer material to each other. This stratagem was legal as far as the Army was concerned. The TOWs were then to be transferred by the CIA to Iran.

Weinberger supported the indirect approach because he felt that the clandestine supply of weapons to another country was the CIA's line of work, not his department's. "I want nothing to do with the Iranians," Weinberger told me. "I want the task carried out with the department removed as much as possible." We treated the TOW transfer like garbage to be gotten out of the house quickly.

I called General Max Thurman, now vice chief of staff of the Army, and asked him to make the TOWs available to the CIA. I told him nothing more. I had known for months that the arms plan was kicking around. But it was not until the moment Weinberger directed me to carry out the transfer that I knew the President had definitely decided to go ahead with it and send the weapons to Iran.

Soon after delivery of the first batch of TOWs, I got a call from a worried Lieutenant General Arthur Brown, director of the Army staff. "We don't know where this stuff is going," Brown said, "but it sure as hell isn't staying with the CIA. The Army general counsel has advised us that you should be aware that if arms in that amount are going to a foreign country, Congress has to be notified."

"Put all that in a memo," I told Brown. On getting his memo, I decided that the course of wisdom was to draft a memo of my own to Poindexter repeating the legal requirement that Congress must be notified if these arms went to a foreign country. I showed the memo to an unhappy Weinberger. Precisely what he had warned against was coming home to roost, the risking of the administration's credibility in a reckless cause. I handed the memo to Poindexter personally at the weekly breakfast meeting the NSC chief held with Weinberger and George Shultz. What we did not know was that Poindexter and company did plan to notify Congress—in the last week of the Reagan administration, three years off. Timely congressional notification might have blown this scheme out of the water.

Throughout the early months of 1986, I operated in a twilight zone, carrying out my job while at the same time planning to leave it. My daily routine would have made no sense as a job description. I might start out the day deciding which memoranda Weinberger should see and finish the day editing the Secretary's next speech. In between, I would stroke a disgruntled chief's ego, arrange to have the parade ground reseeded, and integrate the Secretary's dining-room staff, which consisted entirely of Filipino waiters and must have looked like raw racism to our foreign visitors.

Most of my tasks and a thousand and one phone calls would evaporate with time. But I did leave one mark. The Secretary's office is located in the Eisenhower Corridor of the Pentagon. I have always felt a special affinity for Dwight Eisenhower, a war hero who did not have to bark or rattle sabers to gain respect and exercise command, a President who did not stampede his nation into every world trouble spot, a man who understood both the use of power and the value of restraint and who had the secure character to exercise whichever was appropriate. It was Ike, for example, who had resisted pressure to intervene in Vietnam when the French went under at Dienbienphu. I admired him as a soldier, a President, and a man.

The corridors in Army, Navy, and Air Force country were decorated like mini-museums, while the Eisenhower Corridor was hung with a few pictures. Ike's hall, I believed, should honor his memory more dramatically. Weinberger, a lover of history and tradition, concurred. Doc Cooke was the man I went to see to push through my plan to remake the corridor. Doc found the money in some budgetary cookie jar, gave me his talented staff artist, Joe Pisani, and we went to work. For months, the corridor, draped with drop cloths, looked like a Jackson Pollock retrospective. The hammering and sawing seemed to go on forever.

Midway through the project, Marybel Batjer dragged me out into the hall. Were we opening a bordello? she wanted to know. The corridor commemorating the architect of victory in Europe was being painted fingernail pink.

"Does this look right to you?" I asked the foreman.

"We don't pick 'em, General," he said. "We just slap it on."

It turned out the paint number had been transposed on the work order, and the hallway had to be redone. In the meantime, some wiseacre hung a sign in the corridor: "Powell's Pizza Parlor, Opening Soon."

Nine months after the work first began, John D. Eisenhower, the late President's son, presided over the dedication of the refurbished corridor. We had found an old sign reading "Buying Station—The Bell-Springs Creamery," from the creamery where Ike worked eighty hours a week as a boy. We displayed his West Point yearbook, opened to his photo with the inscription "Daredevil Dwight, the Dauntless Don. . . . He's the handsomest man in the Corps." Among the glass display cases were mementos of the military career of the Allied leader who gave the fateful "go" for the invasion of Normandy. From the exhibits you could trace Ike's life from Abilene, Kansas, to the White House. The corridor today is an attraction on the Pentagon tour and a lasting source of pride to me.

On March 25, I sat with Alma in probably the most stately setting in all Washington, the Diplomatic Reception Room at the Department of State, which Weinberger had borrowed for my farewell dinner. I accepted the tribute as a mark of friendship and the almost sonlike relationship I enjoyed with Weinberger. The next day, Cap personally presented me with the third star that went with my new job as a corps commander.

My breaking away had required the intercession of Will Taft. After all my pleading failed, Will had gone in and finally persuaded Weinberger to sit down and pick a replacement for me. Weinberger's new military assistant was to be Vice Admiral Don Jones. By this time, I did not care if they picked Bectle Bailey. I just wanted out.

Faithful John Wickham proved as good as his word. I was off to command V Corps in Germany.

The assignment stirred powerful emotions in me. I was returning to the place where I had begun my military career commanding forty troops; I was now to command 75,000.

As an additional farewell treat, Weinberger took me along on Air Force One when President Reagan went to Grenada to receive the thanks of the island's people for the October 1983 U.S. invasion that threw out the communists. It was my first trip with the President, and as I sat in the rear of the plane, with stewards passing drinks and snacks, watching my individual TV screen, I thought, this is a pleasant way to travel. Later, Weinberger took me forward to the private cabin for a photo op with the President. Ronald Reagan's greeting was so cordial that I could not tell if he actually remembered me or if I was experiencing the standard Reagan seduction. The President was wearing the customary snowy white shirt and perfectly knotted tie. But his jacket was hanging up and he wore jogging pants to save the crease in his trousers.

I have never witnessed an outburst of mass emotion to match the President's welcome in Grenada. The island's population was about 84,000 people, and all of them seemed to have been packed into the sports stadium. Ronald Reagan was introduced as the liberator, the Messiah, the savior, and the crowd went wild. He gave a masterful speech, greeted by a thunderous ovation. Yet, I observed what I had noticed in him before, a certain professionalism, as if the directions read, "Crowd cheers," and he accepted it as part of the script.

. . .

Two years and ten months—and a lifetime had passed. I left the Pentagon with the warmest feelings toward the man I had served. Cap Weinberger had his little quirks, but at the core, he was a great fighter, a brilliant advocate, a man who, like his President, set a few simple objectives and did not deviate from them. He projected strength, unflappability, and supreme self-confidence. Yet I will never forget a revealing moment in a near-empty 707 in the dark of the night somewhere over the Mediterranean. It happened in October 1984 on the final leg of one of those draining capital-to-capital marathons. We had done business in Italy, Tunisia, Israel, and Jordan. In the Sinai, we had been caught in a lung-infecting mist that frequently blankets the area. None of our party was feeling well, least of all Weinberger. Sitting in a cabin up forward were Rich Armitage and I on one side and Weinberger on the other. We could barely see in the dark. We thought he was asleep. But then that deep voice broke the silence. We always looked on the Secretary as unshakable. Yet, he was saying, to himself, it seemed, "This is a lonely life. You make real enemies but few real friends. It exhausts a man in body and spirit. I try to serve the President as faithfully as my strength permits. But gratitude does not always come easily to him or his wife." He paused for a moment as though he suddenly realized how nakedly he had revealed himself to us. He went on, "I can speak to you two. I trust you." Finding that this seemingly indomitable man shared the same anxieties as the rest of us made him more, not less, admirable in my eyes. But this was a face we were permitted to see only on that one occasion.

Weinberger's more customary dogged certainty was both the man's strength and his weakness. During his years in the Pentagon, the world had shifted, but Weinberger had not. His calls for ever-increasing defense spending started to sound like a stuck whistle. And he eventually lost Congress's attention. He hated to let go of the "evil empire," even as it was starting to dissolve before our eyes. Yet, when he was right, it was at precisely the right time. To Weinberger and Reagan we owe the resurgence of the United States as a respected and credible military power, after the debacle of Vietnam and the fiasco of Desert One. I readily give credit to the Carter-Brown era for getting much-needed modern weaponry on the drawing boards. But had it not been for the Reagan-Weinberger buildup, that is where most of those weapons would have wound up—on the drawing boards. Possibly the greatest contribution the Reagan-Weinberger team made was to end the long estrangement between the American people and their defenders. During this time, the rupture was healed, and America once more embraced its armed forces.

On March 16, I left the Pentagon to prepare for my new assignment. I saluted as I passed the sentinel in front of Weinberger's office (whom I had never managed to dislodge). I turned in my true badge of status, my River Entrance parking permit. I have never felt anything but pride at serving my country. This day, I walked taller than ever. And it may have been my imagination, but it seemed to me that during the Reagan-Weinberger years, everyone in the military started standing taller too.

13 ★ *"Frank, You're Gonna Ruin My Career"*

I FACED TAKING over V Corps with confidence tinged with a touch of anxiety. It was ten years since I had been in command of the 2d Brigade, 101st Airborne Division, at Fort Campbell. In my previous field assignment, I had been an assistant division commander under Jack Hudachek, where I had not exactly emerged as George Patton. And I still felt uneasy about skipping a division command and going directly to a corps. I was determined to prove that I was an able commanding general and not a Pentagon-bred political general.

I had hoped to assume command in April, but the officer I was replacing, Lieutenant General Robert L. "Sam" Wetzel, was in no hurry to cut short his own tour, since after this command he would be retiring. I therefore did not report to Germany until June 1986. I spent the intervening months getting back up to speed at combat schools. Alma and I also studied German eight hours a day, five days a week, for three weeks. I had a slim edge over her, a C and a D in the language at CCNY, and my earlier tour in

Germany, where I picked up a vocabulary consisting mostly of *Bier und Schnitzel.* German irregular verbs did not entrance Alma, and I practically had to hold a gun to her head to get her to go to class.

Worse was yet to come. Because of the terrorist threat in Germany in those days, we both had to take a course called Defensive Driving, at a stock-car track in West Virginia. They had us barreling around the track taking curves at eighty-five miles an hour, practicing how to elude terrorists. We were taught how to spin the car around at breakneck speed and wind up going in the opposite direction, like a Mafia getaway driver. The final test involved ramming a car blocking a road. You had to hit it just right to knock it out of the way without destroying your own car or killing yourself. Alma did not graduate with honors and did not much care.

I went to West Germany first, and shortly afterward, Alma, Linda, Annemarie, and our cat, Max, flew into the Rhine-Main airport to be met by Second Lieutenant Michael Powell. While in ROTC, Mike had gone through jump school and air assault school, just as I had, though he wound up as a tanker rather than an infantryman. He was now on active duty serving as scout platoon leader, 2d Armored Cavalry Regiment, VII Corps, stationed in Amberg.

Came the day for the change of command, July 2, 1986. V Corps assembled on the headquarters parade grounds with American and West German government and military officials on the reviewing stand. The Wetzels, Sam and his wife, Eileen, arrived, and we exchanged a few words of greeting.

Wetzel and I inspected the troops, the V Corps colors were turned over to me, and command formally changed hands. The king is dead. Long live the king.

In one sense, not much had changed in the quarter century since my last West German tour. When I had first arrived in Gelnhausen in December 1958 as a twenty-one-year-old second lieutenant, Dwight D. Eisenhower was President of the United States and Nikita Khrushchev the Soviet premier. Twenty divisions of Soviet and communist-bloc troops faced five U.S. divisions, plus our Allies' forces, across the border between East and West Germany. Two years before, the Soviets had crushed the freedom fighters in Hungary. One year after my departure, they had put up the Berlin Wall, and subsequently they stamped out bids for freedom in Czechoslovakia and Poland. East and West then stood virtually warhead to warhead. As I took over V Corps, in 1986, four American divisions and nineteen Soviet divisions still confronted each other over a border bristling with even deadlier weaponry. On our side, we had replaced old M-60A3 tanks with sophisticated M-1s, obsolete M-113 personnel carriers with new Bradley Fighting Vehicles, and aging tactical nukes with more accurate and devastating models.

Yet, much had changed. For the past two years, Mikhail Gorbachev, a new Soviet man, age fifty-four, energetic, dynamic, preaching the openness of glasnost and the reforms of perestroika, had ruled the Soviet Union. Margaret Thatcher, no pushover, had said that Gorbachev was a chap we could do business with. The previous November, President Reagan and the Soviets had held their first summit at Geneva. Reagan had annoyed Gorbachev by insisting on pressing ahead with SDI. Still, they were negotiating arms reductions and trying to reduce the possibility of nuclear annihilation.

I was, however, a soldier, not a politician, and my present mission was to be prepared to engage Soviet forces the instant they advanced across that weave of valleys forming the Fulda Gap, the same role I had had as a young lieutenant a quarter of a century before.

V Corps headquarters was located in Frankfurt and occupied one of the largest buildings in all Europe, the Abrams Complex, named in honor of the late Army Chief of Staff General Creighton W. Abrams, whom I had briefed long ago in Vietnam. It had been constructed in the 1920s by the renowned German architect Hans Poelzig, to house the main office of the I. G. Farben Petrochemical Company. For a time after World War II, General Eisenhower ruled as Supreme Allied Commander Europe from the suite I was to occupy. The building's lobby was an art deco masterpiece, mucked up, however, by a greasy snack bar and other commercial concessions. At the time of my arrival, magnificent leaded glass windows were about to be taken out to vent the hamburger grill.

As I moved into my new office, a Gothic cavern, the first thing I did was set on my desk a photograph of a man in his mid-forties with a broad smiling face and wavy hair, wearing army fatigues. He looked like a steelworker, the kind of guy you might want to have a beer with in a Pittsburgh tavern. I wanted his picture before me because this man was my opponent, General Colonel Vladislav A. Achalov, commander of the Red Army's eighty-thousand-man 8th Guards Army, positioned across the Fulda Gap.

My division commanders were older than me and had more time in service. Major General Orren R. "Cotton" Whiddon ran the 8th Infantry Division, which had almost been mine the year before. Whiddon was a lanky, self-confident Texan who knew his business. The 3d Armored Division was commanded by Major General Tom Griffin, who went way back with me to the Infantry Officers Advanced Course at Fort Benning. Backing me as deputy corps commander was my National War College classmate Major General Linc Jones. Colonel Thomas White, an architect of post-Vietnam fighting doctrine, had also just joined V Corps, commanding the 11th Armored Cavalry Regiment. And I had a crack chief of staff in Brigadier General Ross W. "Bill" Crossley. I had brought from the States Sergeant Major William Nowell, as command sergeant major, the senior non-commissioned officer in the corps. I was counting on Nowell to serve as my pipeline to the morale and needs of the troops.

Immediately after the change of command ceremony, I had Bill Crossley gather the team together at the V Corps officers' club, once the I. G. Farben workers' canteen. I knew that whatever I said this day would reverberate over the corps telegraph before sunset, and that this first impression of the new corps commander would stick. I told the commanders that I had two top priorities—war-fighting and steward-ship. V Corps' reason for being was to whip Achalov's 8th Guards Army, if and when the time came. Every scout on the front line and every mechanic in the rear was here for that purpose. As for stewardship, the word had an almost holy ring for me. The American people had spent a lot to make the corps combat-ready. We had to make sure that not a dollar was wasted. They had also entrusted their sons and daughters to our care. The one thing that would guarantee trouble for a commander, I promised, was not tending to the well-being of soldiers and their families. What I had to say this day did not differ from what I had been taught at Fort Benning over a quarter of a century before: accomplish the mission and look after the troops. Back in the States, the night before my son, Mike, had shipped out for Germany, I had leaned over him after he had gone to bed, given him a fatherly kiss, and told him to look out for him-self *and to take care of his soldiers.*

I also wanted to give the commanders some understanding of the kind of leader I was. "I fit no stereotype," I said. "I don't chase the latest manage-ment fads." Vogue phrases such as "power down" and "centralized versus decentralized management" were not part of my vocabulary. I would give each of them whatever help was needed to get the job done. Sometimes I would hover over them; at other times, I would give them a long, loose leash. One technique was not right and the other wrong. The situation would dictate which approach would best accomplish the team's mission.

Command *is* lonely, I said, and that was not just a romantic cliché. Sharing a problem with the boss, in this corps, would not be seen as weakness or failure, but as a sign of mutual confidence. On the other hand, they did not have to buck every decision up to me. "I have a wide zone of indifference," I said. "I don't care if you hold reveille at five-thirty or five forty-five A.M. And don't ask me to decide."

I explained my idea of loyalty. "When we are debating an issue, loyalty means giving me your honest opinion, whether you think I'll like it or not. Disagreement, at this stage, stimulates me. But once a decision has been made, the debate ends. From that point on, loyalty means executing the decision as if it were your own."

This particular emperor expected to be told when he was naked. He did not care to freeze to death in his own ignorance. "If you think something is wrong, speak up," I told them. "I'd rather hear about it sooner than later. Bad news isn't wine. It doesn't improve with age." I would not jump in too early if they could still handle a problem. But I did not want to find out when it was too late for me to make a difference. "And if you screw up," I advised, "just vow to do better next time. I don't hold grudges. I don't keep book.

"I will give you clear guidance as to what I want," I continued. "If it's not clear, ask me. If after a second and third explanation you still don't get it, there may be something wrong with my transmitter, not your receiver. I won't assume you are deaf or stupid." The worst thing was for subordinates to labor in ignorance in order to conceal their confusion and wind up doing the wrong thing. "If you ever leave my office and don't understand what I want, just march right back in and ask," I said.

I told them that I would fight for everything they needed to perform the mission. "If we don't have it in Frankfurt, I'll go to USAREUR"—U.S. Army Europe. "If they don't have it, I'll go to Washington. But I will back you all the way."

I told them that if, as commanders, they found themselves in a fight with my staff, I was predisposed to take their side. The staff existed to serve them. "If, however, I find that any of you are dumping on my people without good cause, you can bet I'll come to their rescue."

I explained that during these first few weeks, I expected to visit all ten West German communities where the corps was stationed. "You'll be advised the first time I come, since I'll want to meet your senior officers, the *Bürgermeister,* and other local officials. My wife will visit clinics and child-care centers and get to know your wives." But after that first round, my visits would be on short notice, "just enough time to let you get the coffee table dusted and the underwear picked up. I'm not trying to play 'gotcha.' But it's the only way for me to learn what's really going on." I was reflecting my continuing distrust of the Annual General Inspection syndrome of preparedness. I knew that planned visits always produce a flurry of wasted effort: "The smell of fresh paint and the sight of whitewashed walkways is a sure sign of an insecure commander," I told them.

"I'll be frank," I said. "From time to time, I'm going to make you mad as hell." Making people mad was part of being a leader. As I had learned long ago, with John Pardo and the losing drill team, an individual's hurt feelings run a distant second to the good of the service.

Finally, I attempted to convey the deep love I had for the Army. "The Army is to be enjoyed, not endured. Have fun in your command. Don't always run at a breakneck pace. Take leave when you've earned it. Spend time with your families. I don't intend to work on weekends unless it's absolutely necessary. And I don't expect you to do it either. Anyone found logging Saturday or Sunday hours for himself or his troops had better have a good reason. Remember, this could be your last command, and it's probably mine. So let's enjoy it."

Just a couple of days after my arrival, like the pull of a magnet, I made a sentimental journey back to Gelnhausen. I took only my aide, Bruce Scott. On my arrival, we drove to the familiar Coleman Kaserne and parked in front of D Company's barracks. The company commander met us and escorted me to the orderly room, all the while giving a running commentary on the company's current doings. I barely heard a word. I was lost in reverie, a lieutenant, unaccountably wearing a general's uniform, surrounded by old memories and faces from the past, Tom Miller, Red Barrett, Sergeant Edwards.

.   .   .

Once again, my family had to be resettled. Linda went back to William and Mary, and with Mike in the Army, that left three of us. We moved into the corps commander's quarters and enrolled Annemarie in the American dependents' Frankfurt High School. Our house resembled a checkpoint at a hostile border crossing. It was eight miles from my office in a sub-urb called Bad Vilbel and consisted of two cramped stories served by one orderly. One bathroom had been converted into an armor-plated sanctuary in which we were to lock ourselves until rescued in case of a terrorist attack. The house was encircled by barbed wire, and in front stood a guardhouse with one-way glass from which MPs scanned our resi-dence twenty-four hours a day. Home sweet home.

Watching the general's house all day struck me as the height of boredom for teenage soldiers (other than catching an occasional glimpse of Annemarie sunbathing). To help break the monotony, I took one of the guards with me on a helicopter ride to Grafen-wöhr. I asked him what the guys at the barracks had told him to ask me when they learned that he was going to travel with the corps commander. He gulped. "Go ahead, son," I urged him. "Don't be afraid."

"Well, sir," he said, "it's the jogging." I fre-quently took a run across the countryside, and as soon as I started, an MP or two in jogging togs would pop out of the guardhouse and run discreetly behind me. "The guys," the corporal went on, "wondered if you knew that on our weekends off, the provost mar-shal always picks guys to suit up and wait in the guardhouse in case you go for a jog."

I said nothing, but this was just the kind of overkill that I hated. Some poor soldier, on his supposed free time, had to sit all day in a cell on the off chance I might run for twenty minutes. Admittedly, security was a problem. Terrorists had bombed the Frankfurt PX the month before my arrival. But I always ran different routes at unexpected times, and terrorists depend on regularity. I waited a few days in order not to give away my source, and then I told the provost marshal to knock it off. I could take care of myself. If I got shot, it would not be his responsibility. He looked unconvinced.

For security, I had an armor-plated white 380 SE Mercedes. Staff Sergeant Otis Pearson, a black soldier from rural Alabama, became my driver. Otis, tall, lean, handsome, and taciturn, had, like many young men, used the Army to overcome a rough upbringing. The Army was now his family, and he soon became part of the Powell family too. Otis had driven for my predecessor, Sam Wetzel, an avid sportsman, well connected to the German upper crust and an occasional guest at handsome hunting lodges. Consequently, Otis had spent a lot of time hauling dead animals out of the woods for Wetzel. Neither the crowd Wetzel traveled with nor his favorite pastime appealed to me. I preferred racquetball and auto repair, both of which were right up Otis's alley. Soon after my arrival, I bought an almost new BMW 728, which we worked on together. My idea of fun was to come roaring out of the garage at Bad Vilbel like Batman and have the BMW up to 105 miles an hour on the autobahn before my guards could figure out what had happened.

. . .

While the West Germans enjoyed the security of 75,000 V Corps troops stationed between them and the Soviets, they would have been just as happy if we had stayed in our barracks until war broke out. Tanks and personnel carriers chew up roads, and our armored columns barely left room for a Volkswagen. Our helicopters made a dreadful racket and were constantly interfering with air traffic at civilian airports. We were particularly unpopular with the "Greens," the German environmentalists who were strong in the states of Hesse and Rhineland-Pfalz, where V Corps was stationed.

One morning I got a call from the 3d Armored Division commander, Major General Tom Griffin. The Greens had planted a hundred young trees during the night right down the middle of our tank driving range. "General, I'm just gonna flatten 'em," Griffin told me.

"Hold on, Tom," I said. One does not casually run over trees in Germany. Instead, we dug them up and replanted them in our housing area. Griffin then arranged an Earth Day–type celebration. We invited local politicians, the press, and the Greens, although the Greens ignored our invitation. We, nevertheless, thanked them for helping to improve our landscape. As I had learned in the Weinberger dog-rescue operation, with a little imagination you can turn a knock into a boost.

I can still recall how proud I felt back in 1958 when Captain Tom Miller assigned me to guard that 280mm atomic cannon—until I lost my .45 pistol in the course of the mission. In those days, at my pay grade, I gave no thought to the wisdom of using nuclear weapons in the field. It was simply "Yes, sir!" Airborne Ranger! Twenty-eight years later, I was in the command center with my senior officers war-gaming an 8th Guards Army attack. My G-3, Colonel Jerry Rutherford, was at the map board with a pointer explaining that if the enemy crossed the Haune and the Fulda rivers heading toward the Vogelsberg mountains, they would then be into the valley of the Main River. From there the terrain was flat, giving them a clear shot all the way to Wiesbaden and the bridges over the Rhine River. NATO forces would be cut in half, and the enemy could swing north all the way to the English Channel. "So our last defensible position is the Vogelsberg range," Rutherford explained, "and at that time it may be necessary to ask for release of nukes."

"Give me the plan," I said.

"We'll hit 'em with Lances and AFAPs"— artillery-fired atomic projectiles. "The radius of effect will be just enough to close the roads without affecting our own troop movements."

"What about civilians?" I asked.

"There won't be any civilians."

"Where did they go?" I wanted to know.

"The plan is for the Germans to stay put, in their villages, out of the way of our strikes. We'll just hit wooded areas."

"Let's think for a minute," I said. "You're a German civilian. You've just heard over the emergency broadcast system that the Russians are coming, and you should stay put so you don't get in the Americans' way. What do you really think is going to happen? You know damn well. Every BMW and Volks in Hesse and Rhineland-Pfalz is going to be stuffed with everything, including the family schnauzer, and headed west."

We were not talking simply about dropping a few artillery shells at a crossroad. No matter how small these nuclear payloads were, we would be crossing a threshold. Using nukes at this point would mark one of the most significant political and military decisions since Hiroshima. The Russians would certainly retaliate, maybe escalate. At that moment, the world's heart was going to skip a beat. From that day on, I began rethinking the practicality of these small nuclear weapons. And a few years later, when I became Chairman of the Joint Chiefs of Staff, I would have some ideas about what to do with tactical nukes.

I was settling in comfortably. My every need was anticipated by Bruce Scott, my aide, and Judi Reaume, my able secretary, who had served several V Corps commanders before me and who knew where all the land mines were buried. A ballroom just a few feet from my second-floor office had been converted to a racquetball court, and I kept in shape playing every day against other officers and Otis, my driver.

I quickly grew fond of the Abrams Complex and was eager to undo the disfiguring we had perpetrated. I had the post engineers locate the original 1928 design and flew Joe Pisani over from the Pentagon to undertake a redesign similar to what he had done in the Eisenhower Corridor. The lobby started to look again as it had in the days of the Weimar Republic. I saved the glorious curved leaded-glass windows from being removed to make way for the hamburger grill vent. The restoration continued and was seen through to completion by my successor, Lieutenant General Jack Woodmansee.

Nevertheless, it required two successors beyond Woodmansee before another of my intentions was realized, finding and returning a lovely statue of a nude woman that had once graced a courtyard behind the headquarters. The lady had been banished in 1947 at the insistence of the fuddy-duddy wife of an American colonel.

I found it deeply satisfying to see how the budget victories won by the Pentagon were being translated into tangible improvements in Germany. Thanks to the Reagan-Weinberger buildup, modern equipment rolled into the corps, and the troops' quarters became more livable. By now, the all-volunteer Army was fully in place, and we were getting the best-educated enlistees in history. I had to smile when my commanders complained that their strength levels had dropped below 98 percent. How soon they forgot the Cat Fours, the lowest-level acceptable recruits, so prevalent just a few years before, and the days when force levels often dropped below 70 percent. I was not eager to commit troops to battle. But if that day came, Comrade Achalov and his Red divisions would face a helluva foe.

Marybel Batjer sent me week-old copies of the *Washington Post,* but somehow I could no longer get worked up about Beltway tempests. I loved what I was doing, and had not looked back at Washington once since leaving.

My immediate boss was a distinguished officer, General Glenn Otis, commander of all U.S. Army forces in Europe and a NATO commander as well, heading the Central Army Group. Otis had two American corps under him, my V Corps and VII Corps, where my son, Mike, served. VII Corps was commanded by Lieutenant General Andy Chambers. My taking over V Corps meant that both corps were commanded by black three-star generals. The heartening thing is that no one took any notice, proof of how blind to race the Army had become and a nice corrective to European misperceptions about American race relations.

Despite living in a semifortress, our family was happy in Frankfurt. Except during field exercises, the workday usually ended at five. I finished with a game of racquetball, went home, had dinner, did a little paperwork, and relaxed. The phone was not constantly ringing in the middle of the night with the DDO reporting the latest international firestorm. By comparative standards, I had jumped from the frying pan into the easy chair. I whiled away my happiest free time tinkering with my 1982 BMW with the help of Otis.

Social demands were fairly heavy, however, and I was often on a dais with a *Bürgermeister* or snipping a ribbon at a German-American culture center. Alma belonged to at least four women's organizations with names as unpronounceable as *Steubenschurzgesellschaft*. But it was pleasant to have others performing for me my old roles as gofer and horse holder. Whenever a fund drive began, I was expected to make the first symbolic contribution. Whenever the O-club held a charity auction, Alma and I were expected to make the first bid.

And when the annual blood drive came along, the corps medical officer wanted me for the first drop. I went with him to the hospital, trailed by photographers from the corps newspaper. A young medic put the cuff around my arm to take my blood pressure. He looked puzzled, took it again, and then once more. He went to the medical officer, who came back and took the reading himself. The doctor canceled the photo op and my role in the blood donation drive. The years of middle-of-the-night phone calls and fourteen-hour days in Washington had evidently taken their toll. I had moderately high blood pressure. I was put on medication and have continued it ever since, with the pressure nicely under control.

Though we were in the same country, we did not see much of Mike. Most of our contact was via letters, and Mike's news took me back to my own days as a young officer. He wrote that one night, while on border outpost, his troop commander had gotten drunk and passed out. The phone rang, and since the officer was feeling and hearing nothing, Mike had to take the call. The squadron executive officer at the other end of the line, suspecting something, demanded to know why the commander could not come to the phone. Mike had to tell the truth. The next morning the commander was relieved of duty. It had been a tough call for Mike. He had done the right thing, though some of his contemporaries, out of misguided loyalty to their superior officer, criticized him.

I felt particularly close to Mike when he told us about experiencing his first death in the field. My first experience had occurred when that stray shell at Grafenwöhr tore apart a tent full of young Americans. An M-113 armored personnel carrier had rolled over a soft shoulder and crushed one of Mike's men to death during a late-night exercise. Mike shared his anguish in a long letter to me. As a father, I ached to jump in and help. But I knew that a soldier had to live through and learn from these experiences essentially alone. There is no profession in which life-and-death responsibility is placed on younger shoulders than in the military, and Mike was growing up fast. The accident also reminded Alma and me, as if we needed reminding, that even in peacetime, soldiering is dangerous work. And parents are never entirely free of anxiety.

Reports coming to me through the grapevine indicated that Mike was doing exceptionally well and had a chance of becoming troop executive officer after making first lieutenant. He had made his choice. He too wanted to make the Army his life. It pleased me that he had reached this decision on his own.

. . .

In the early fall of 1986, we were visited by a congressional delegation. I had a fairly standard pitch for such visiting firemen. This particular group included a forty-five-year-old four-term Republican congressman from Wyoming whom I had never met before, Richard B. Cheney, then a member of the House Permanent Select Committee on Intelligence. I was aware that Cheney, when he was only thirty-four, had served as White House Chief of Staff under President Gerald Ford. Rather than put on the usual dog-and-pony show, I took the group into my private office. I picked up the photograph of General Achalov from my desk. "This man is the reason V Corps is here," I began. Achalov, I explained, had started out as a paratrooper, smashed his legs in a jump a few years ago, and switched to heavy infantry. "He is younger than I am," I went on. "He has had more training." The man was a military thinker who had written a half-dozen articles on European land warfare. I had read them all. He commanded eighty thousand troops, more men than I had, and his soldiers were just as well trained and armed as mine. They were just sixty-six miles from where we were sitting. "The forces I command, nevertheless, can stop them," I said. "We might not be able to hold back successive divisions, which are backed up practically to Moscow. But we can stop Achalov."

Congressman Cheney was reticent and asked few questions. What he did ask, however, knifed to the heart of the issue, and I recognized that I was in the presence of an exceptional mind. I could not have known then that in the years to come the two of us would be bound closely, facing not potential but real enemies.

One of the spoils of World War II that the American Army inherited from Hitler's Third Reich was a private railroad train embodying the magnificence of a bygone age. The train had a fully equipped kitchen, a staff of stewards, and a lounge area and slept six passengers. It was available to senior American commanders in Germany. Alma and I had become close friends of Ronald Lauder and his wife, Jo Carol. Ron had served as a deputy assistant secretary of defense while I was in the Pentagon and was now American ambassador to Austria during a testy time when the Nazi-tainted Kurt Waldheim had been elected president. That fall, I decided to enjoy a touch of grandeur absent in the subway-riding days of my youth. I invited the Lauders and their two daughters, Jane and Aerin, to come to Frankfurt to join us on the train for a journey to Berlin. Ron, a man of considerable means, approved of this mode of travel, but I disappointed him in Berlin by my cheeseburger palate and acceptance of wine served in screw-cap bottles. In our subsequent friendship, we worked out a division of labor. Ron picks the restaurants and the wine, and I enjoy them.

While I was immersed in running V Corps in Germany, those clandestine NSA messages I had brought to Weinberger's attention in Washington finally uncoiled spectacularly in the Iran-contra affair. On

November 1, the world learned, from *Al Shiraa,* a Beirut magazine, that the United States had been secretly selling arms to Khomeini's regime, despite President Reagan's pledge never to deal with terrorists. I had played a part in getting the Army's TOW antitank missiles transferred to the CIA, which then shipped them to Iran. Then came the next shocker, revealed by Attorney General Edwin Meese on November 25. The Poindexter-North operation had jacked up the prices of weapons sold to Iran and siphoned off the profits into private bank accounts to fund help for the Nicaraguan contras. I had not known of this diversion, nor had the President, the cabinet, or Congress. Poindexter resigned and President Reagan dismissed Ollie North.

The President now had to appoint a new National Security Advisor, and I heard through the Armitage-Batjer back channel that Frank Carlucci was the leading candidate, a wise choice. I was immediately wary, however, when Judi Reaume called out that Frank was on the line. I congratulated him, but his first words made my heart sink. "Colin, you've got to come back. I've taken over a mess and I need you to help me clean it up. I want you to be my deputy."

"Frank, I didn't make the mess," I said. "You can find a dozen guys to do that job as well as I can." I pointed out to Carlucci my thin credentials. "Why don't you pick one of your friends from the Foreign Service?" I asked. "Or what about Jon Howe?"—the sharp admiral who had replaced me as Carlucci's military assistant at Defense. "Jon's already been a policy planner at the State Department," I pointed out.

498 · COLIN L. POWELL

"I'm not looking for a foreign policy expert," Carlucci said. "I'm looking for someone who knows how to make things work. I need what you did for Cap and me, someone who can impose order and procedure on the NSC."

"Frank, I'm finally back in the real Army," I pleaded. I told him that I did not want to leave until I had proved I was an able corps commander. I did not want to be the guy who ran a company for a couple of months, a battalion and a brigade for a year, skipped a division, and ran out on a corps after just five months. And after the experience with Poindexter and North, I could not believe the country would stand for another military man in the NSC.

"We need you, Colin," Frank went on. "This is serious. Believe me, the presidency is at stake."

I played my last card. "You know I had a role in this business." I described my arranging for the delivery of the TOWs under President Reagan's Finding of Necessity.

"I'll have Justice and the White House lawyers look into it," he said.

"Frank, you're gonna ruin my career," I told him.

"We'll talk again," he said and hung up.

Like a man fallen overboard grasping for a life ring, I called General Wickham. He was sympathetic but gave me the old line: "I told you long ago, Colin, you may not be destined to be a commander. It's your decision, but I believe you should do what they ask you to do." He added, however, that he would see that if I took the post, I could still come back to the Army as soon as the crisis passed. I knew he meant

it, but Wickham was due to retire. His replacement
might not take the same accommodating attitude. If I
took this job, I feared it would probably mark the end
of my Army career. Still, the pressure mounted. Soon
Cap Weinberger was on the line. "Colin, I'm sure
you'll do what's right in this hour of the President's
need," he said.

Two days later, Carlucci called again. He had
checked out any potential legal problems regarding
the TOWs, and I was clean. I became blunt, as I saw
the last exit closing. "There is only one way I can
make this departure honorable, the only way I'll be
able to face my fellow officers," I said. "It can't come
from you, Frank. It has to be a request directly from
the commander in chief. That's the one thing my
world will understand."

"Okay," he said.

Two days passed and nothing happened. I dared
hope that I had dodged the bullet.

On December 12, Alma and I had just come
home from a Christmas party and were sitting in the
kitchen when the phone rang. I picked it up and
heard the commanding voice of a White House operator. The President was calling. Ronald Reagan came
on the line and spoke in an intimate, homey tone,
hoping, gee, he had not called at an inconvenient
time, and gee he wasn't used to giving orders to generals. He started going down the "talking points"
(prepared by Ken Adelman, head of the Arms Control and Disarmament Agency, who was helping Carlucci with the NSC transition). What a pleasure it had
been to have me along on that inspiring trip to

Grenada, the President said. He knew what a fine job I was doing with V Corps. He knew how much the command meant to me. He knew how happy Alma and I were in Frankfurt. It would only be a detour in my military career, but it was critical for the country that I come home. He needed me to help Frank Carlucci straighten out the mess at the NSC.

"Yes, sir," I answered. "I'll do it." I had no choice.

"God bless you," he said.

My appointment as deputy assistant to the President for national security affairs was announced on December 18, 1986. I went back alone to Washington for a few days to arrange for quarters, buy a car, and enroll my daughter, Annemarie, in the school she had been pulled out of just five months before. And I met briefly with Frank Carlucci about the job we faced at a rudderless, drifting, demoralized NSC. I returned to Frankfurt in time for a chaotic Christmas with our house torn apart by the movers, and formally gave up my command of V Corps on the last day of 1986.

I had commanded V Corps for just over five months. Had I stayed for a full tour, I might have had a shot at promotion to four stars and command of all U.S. Army forces in Europe. I had taken over a crack corps from Sam Wetzel, and my team had made it even better. Two initiatives that I had set in motion paid off soon after I left. V Corps won the next two major NATO competitions, the Boselager Cavalry competition, which the United States had never won before, and the Canadian Army Cup tank competition, which we had not won recently, even with the M-1 Abrams tank, the best in the world. These competitions may mean little to the layperson, but in NATO this was the equivalent of winning the World Series and the Super Bowl in one season. My successor, Jack Woodmansee, was kind enough to call me at the White House and share the credit. But I sure wish I had still been in Germany to watch the trophies being presented.

On January 2, 1987, I found myself wearing one of my old civilian suits and sitting in the West Wing of the White House in a cubicle about the size of the bathroom in my V Corps office. Next door, in an airy, prestigious corner office, sat my new boss, or rather my old boss in his new job, Frank Carlucci, now National Security Advisor to the President. The White House was eerily quiet. The President, along with much of the staff, was still not back from the Reagans' holiday vacation in California.

Frank and I were asking ourselves the same question: What do we do now? Our situation was similar to taking over a demoralized battalion where the commanding officer has just been relieved, or inheriting a losing team after the coach has been fired, or acquiring a company recently looted by its officers. Ken Adelman, Marybel Batjer, and Grant Green, Carlucci's former military assistant, had already come over to the NSC to help Frank through the changeover. Adelman had the hardest job, sandblasting the old staff down to bare metal before returning to his job at the Arms Control and Disarmament Agency. What Carlucci and I had to do was rebuild almost from the bottom up.

I was still trying to figure out how my phones worked when a hearty, nasal voice called out, "Is he in there?" Suddenly, my doorway was filled by a tall, lean, exuberant figure, hand extended. "George Bush," he said. "Want to welcome you to the White House. So glad you and Frank have come over. Going to make a *grrreat* team." At this point, I was still, in my mind, an infantry general, and the Vice President of the United States had just popped in to greet me on my new job. I felt like a bonus-baby rookie welcomed by one of the club owners. The Vice President and I were even going to share the same bathroom, I learned. This was something to tell Alma tonight.

The National Security Council had been created in 1947, the year the old War Department, Navy Department, and other services were folded into one Department of Defense. Its charter was brief and not particularly instructive: to advise the President "with respect to the integration of domestic, foreign and military policies relating to national security." In plain English, a lot of different agencies and people compete for the President's ear where war and peace are concerned, and consequently he needed a "referee," a body with no ax to grind that would present to him, balanced and unbiased, the views of each contender, along with the National Security Advisor's own position. A good advisor was an honest broker. Henry Kissinger had taken the office to the heights of power, eclipsing the State Department and running China and Soviet policy directly out of his West Wing office. When he became Secretary of State, he held on to the NSC post for a while to make sure no one could do the same to him.

Under McFarlane, Poindexter, North, and company, the NSC had gone off the rails. The situation was not entirely their fault. They worked for a President who did not like to step between his powerful cabinet members and make hard choices. They worked for a President who said he wanted the hostages freed and the contras kept alive and did not much concern himself with details as to how it was done. Consequently, the NSC had filled a power vacuum and had become its own Defense Department, running little wars, its own State Department, carrying on its own secret diplomacy, and its own CIA, carrying out clandestine operations. The result had been the Iran-contra fiasco.

I had my first fight the first day. Carlucci had always hated dealing with speeches and sent me to represent the NSC at a senior staff meeting where a draft speech for the President on the defense budget was being reviewed. Pushing the draft was chief speechwriter Tony Dolan, a scrappy former investigative reporter, a Pulitzer Prize winner, now occupying the far-right stall in the Reagan speechwriting stable. I asked if the speech was not a bit shrill. Dolan jumped up and delivered a finger-pointing tirade on my microscopic credentials to critique anything beyond an infantry manual. I understood what was going on. The new kid on the block was being tested. I held my ground, but this was going to be an even tougher neighborhood than the Pentagon front office.

A few days later, after the President had returned, Carlucci poked his head into my doorway. "Come on," he said, "we're going to brief him." Senator John Tower was heading an investigation of the Iran-contra affair, and one failing he had encountered in the White House was the absence of any record of what the National Security Advisor or his staff had said to the President and what he had agreed to. My duty, Carlucci explained, was to close that gap. "Feel free to speak out," he said, "but your main job is to take notes on what I tell him and what he decides."

As we entered the Oval Office, the President was being briefed on other matters by his Chief of Staff, Donald Regan. On our arrival, the President rose, smiled warmly, and moved to an armchair to the left of the fireplace. He apologized again for taking me out of Germany. Vice President Bush came in and took the armchair to Reagan's left. Carlucci sat on a couch. I sat at the other end. On another couch across from us sat Don Regan. The President started off by telling a joke (which, I learned, was standard procedure). My eyes went to his feet, where I spotted something odd. How could his shoes, besides being mirrorlike, have none of those creases across the instep caused by normal wear? On this and every other occasion, his shoes always looked as if they were being worn for the first time.

After going over world events of the past twenty-four hours, Carlucci got to the immediate challenge, how we intended to rebuild the NSC from the wreckage of Iran-contra. "First, Mr. President," Carlucci said, "we've gotten rid of Ollie North's office. We're taking the NSC out of covert operations." He explained further that I would be conducting a review of all current covert operations being conducted by the CIA. "We've come up with four tests," Frank continued. For every such operation we were asking: (1) Is it legal? (2) Do we know what it is supposed to achieve? (3) Is it achieving its objective? (4) If this operation should suddenly appear on the front page of the *Washington Post,* would the American people say, "Aren't we clever little devils," or would they say, "What a bunch of boobs"? If a program could not pass these tests, Carlucci said, we would recommend its elimination. "And," he concluded, "we're hiring a lawyer, Paul Stevens, to make sure everything we do is kosher."

At this first briefing, President Reagan listened carefully and asked a few questions, but gave no guidance. This became the pattern almost every morning when we briefed him. We would lay out the contrasting views of various cabinet officers and Congress and wait for the President to peel them back to get at underlying motives. It did not happen. Most unnerving, when Carlucci presented options, the President would say little until Frank gave his recommendation. And then the President would merely acknowledge that he had heard him, without saying yes, no, or maybe. Frank and I would walk down the hall afterward with Frank muttering, "Was that a yes?" We eventually assumed that the President knew we had balanced competing views and had given him our best judgment. He evidently felt it unnecessary to do more than acknowledge what we would be doing in his name. That, at least, was our optimistic interpretation.

The President's passive management style placed a tremendous burden on us. Until we got used to it, we felt uneasy implementing recommendations without a clear decision. Would the decision hold if criticized later by one of the losers? Would the President recall it? One morning after we had gotten another decision by default on a key arms control issue, Frank moaned as we left, "My God, we didn't sign on to run this country!"

Carlucci noticed that between us we had inherited five secretaries. My principal secretary was a capable, gracious woman named Florence Gantt who had been at the NSC for over twenty years. I asked Florence why we needed so many secretaries. Because, she explained, in the past the staff tended to work twelve- and fourteen-hour days, and weekends too. I discussed the situation with Carlucci, who said, "Transfer two of them." We could do enough damage working reasonable hours. It was the around-the-clock fanatics who had driven the administration to the brink of ruin. And that was how we worked, out by 7:00 P.M., occasionally in on a Saturday, and never in on Sundays. Carlucci was capable of slipping off for tennis at 3:00 P.M. on a Friday and not coming back at all. And he could still make sounder decisions and cover more ground than the previous midnight moles. We were going home at a more civilized time. But it was not in the nature of these jobs to conform to regular hours. I brought work home and was soon back to the Weinberger pace. The good old days of Frankfurt were behind me.

The faithful John Wickham had arranged a temporary Georgian mansion for us at Fort McNair on the Washington Channel, the handsomest Army residence we had yet occupied. The first time the family approached it, Annemarie threw up her arms in her best Scarlett O'Hara impersonation and said, "I swear I'll never be poor again!" All very splendid, except that Fort McNair was cut off from the world. Every time Alma needed a spool of thread, she had to drive over the 14th Street Bridge. The place was so quiet I called it Menopause Manor. And worst of all, there was no garage where I could tinker with my cars. We were just as happy when Wickham got us a more modest house at bustling Fort Myer. This was going to be the third family move in less than a year.

On February 26, the Tower Commission released its report on the Iran-contra affair. It depicted President Reagan as confused and uninformed and found that his hands-off management style was the reason he did not know what was going on in his own presidency. The Tower Report became our owner's manual. We did what it recommended. Carlucci issued an order that the NSC was not to become involved in operations. We advised Presidents; we did not run wars or covert strategies. We had a Defense Department and a CIA for those roles.

With the issuance of the report, pressure built up for the President to give the American people his explanation of Iran-contra, which, so far, he had resisted doing. Landon Parvin, a veteran speech-writer, was brought in, and, at Carlucci's instructions, I worked with Parvin on what was to be the definitive Iran-contra address.

The Tower Commission had come down hard on Cap Weinberger and George Shultz for not being aggressive enough in finding out what Poindexter's NSC was up to. This was an unfair rap. I vividly remembered sitting in Weinberger's office and hearing him rail against the idiocy of the arms deal. I had helped him try to limit the Defense Department's role to minimum compliance with NSC requests and instructions. And I knew that Weinberger, as well as the rest of us at Defense, had no knowledge of the most illegal aspect of the affair, the diversion of Iranian arms sales profits to the contras.

Learning that I was involved in preparing the President's speech, Weinberger let me know that he hoped his role could be clarified. Since he and also George Shultz had opposed the scheme, I tried to get the President to say something exonerating these two reluctant players. We came up with suggested language for the President: "As a matter of simple fairness, however, I must say that I believe the [Tower] commission's comments about George Shultz and Cap Weinberger are incorrect. Both of them vigorously opposed the arms sales to Iran, and they so advised me several times. The commission's statements that the two Secretaries did not support the

President are also wrong. They did support me despite their known opposition to the program. I now find that both Secretaries were excluded from meetings on the subject by the same people and process used to deny me vital information about this whole matter." In the last draft of the speech that I worked on, this language clearing Weinberger and Schultz was included.

On March 4, President Reagan addressed the nation on television from the Oval Office, probably the least pleasant speech he ever delivered. "A few months ago," the President began, "I told the American people I did not trade arms for hostages. My heart and my best intentions still tell me that's true, but the facts and evidence tell me it is not. As the Tower Board reported, what began as a strategic opening to Iran deteriorated, in its implementation, into trading arms for hostages. This runs counter to my own beliefs, to administration policy, and to the original strategy we had in mind. There are reasons why it happened, but no excuses. It was a mistake."

The paragraph letting Weinberger and Shultz off the hook, however, wound up on the cutting-room floor. President Reagan's political advisors killed it, believing the passage diluted the main message, the President's willingness to accept full responsibility. I was unhappy about the omission. Ten days later, in his weekly Saturday radio broadcast, however, the President did at least say that Secretary Shultz and Secretary Weinberger "advised me strongly not to pursue the initiative."

Ronald Reagan had made his public *mea culpa.* But in his heart of hearts he remained pure. For the rest of his term, we learned to avoid the subject like poison ivy. Once anybody accidentally hit the trip-wire, Reagan would launch into a twenty-minute monologue on why the deal had not been arms-for-hostages; and how did we know there were no Iranian moderates?

Three issues dominated the NSC. First was the changed East-West dynamic created by Mikhail Gorbachev. Next was the muddle in Central America made even muddier by the Iran-contra revelations. And finally there was the Middle East, where Iran and Iraq were still warring and endangering the free flow of oil through the Persian Gulf, and where American hostages were still held captive in hiding places in Lebanon, despite the arms given to Iran.

To perform our NSC role, we had to add to the alphabet soup that drives citizens outside the Beltway crazy. Since the NSC was responsible for pulling together positions from several departments and agencies for the President's consideration, we needed a coordinating body, and created the PRG, the Policy Review Group. We put together an outstanding collection of subcabinet officials. Rich Armitage attended from DOD, which for me was like having my brother and bodyguard present. From State, Mike Armacost, the undersecretary for political affairs, attended. A career foreign service officer, Armacost had also been a White House Fellow, and we had known each other for years. The JCS was represented by Lieutenant General John Moellering and later by Vice Admiral Jon Howe. Howe, who replaced me as military assistant to Carlucci, also served at the State Department as director of political military affairs and as Vice President Nelson Rockefeller's national security advisor. The CIA was represented by Dick Kerr, the agency's number three man. Don Gregg, Vice President's Bush's advisor on national security, also attended. Others were added, depending on the issue on the table. But the above group was the core. We all knew each other well and knew the Washington ropes and snares.

Just ten days after my arrival, on January 12, the Persian Gulf became the PRG's first order of business. All departments were informed that henceforth only one channel of communication existed between the United States and Iran, the State Department. No more arms hustlers or James Bondian NSC staffers bearing cakes and Bibles (as Ollie North had done on a secret trip to Tehran) were to speak for the United States. We also made clear that Iran would not get so much as a slingshot from America while the arms embargo lasted. And since the free flow of oil from the Persian Gulf was as crucial to us as blood pumping through an artery, Iraqi and Iranian threats to Kuwaiti oil tankers would be met. We advised the Kuwaiti government that the United States was willing to respond to its request to put its tankers under U.S. flags, thus placing the vessels under America's protection. What we were trying to create, which had not existed before, was a policy that everybody understood and agreed on. Because the President was so passive, a few people had previously made end runs around his authority unknown to others.

Because Weinberger and Shultz were continually scrapping, we often had more fights than coopera-tion. Carlucci and I wanted clear positions that the cabinet helped shape, that the President blessed, and that the Congress understood.

When, for example, a few months later, the U.S.S. *Stark* was accidentally attacked by an Iraqi Exocet missile in the Persian Gulf, we had a policy in place, so that we did not have to explain to Congress why the ship was there in the first place. The attack had been a tragedy, costing the lives of thirty-seven American sailors; but it was a tragedy that had occurred in the course of an overall coherent goal—to keep the oil lanes open. When a Kuwaiti tanker carrying a U.S. flag hit a mine in the Gulf we could manage the resulting flap because the incident hap-pened in the context of the same policy—to keep the oil flowing. Such coherence had been missing previ-ously and had led to the Iran-contra debacle. The Policy Review Group became our instrument for achieving a broadly understood and agreed-upon for-eign policy within the administration.

The next big question was what to do about the contras, who were still fighting the Marxist Sandinista government in Nicaragua. The back-door aid to the contras that Ollie North had arranged to get around a congressional ban had created the messiest part of the Iran-contra affair. But that fact did not detract from the justice of the contra cause. How to deal with the con-tras, however, produced a fault line that split the administration right down the middle, even among those who supported them. George Shultz at State saw the contras as useful for keeping pressure on the Sandinistas to come to the bargaining table, where we hoped to persuade them to democratize their country and stop exporting communism. Cap Weinberger saw the contras in a romantic vein, like the mujahedin fighting the Soviets in Afghanistan. To him, these Nicaraguans were freedom fighters deserving of our full support in a serious bid to throw off the Marxist yoke in Managua.

I like to get my truth from the ground level. In this case, the best source was a man named Alan Fiers, head of the Central American Task Force at the CIA, who was responsible for getting weapons, ammunition, transportation, food, and medical supplies to the contras. At one PRG meeting, I asked Fiers, "How large a force could the contras ultimately field?" Maybe fifteen thousand men tops, he said. "Is there any hope that this force can come out of the hills and beat the Sandinista army?" Not a chance, Fiers said. "Is there any possibility the Nicaraguan people will rise up to support the contras?" Unlikely, Fiers answered. That settled it for me. The contras were a card to play in pressing for a negotiated solution; but not a solution themselves.

We had recruited a fiery anti-Castro Cuban, José Sorzano, to guide us on Latin American affairs. José addressed me as *mi general,* reminding me that Latin Americans had over two centuries of practice with this salutation.

To give me a better feel for the contras, José arranged for me to meet with several of their leaders who were being supported by the CIA in Miami. I found a mixed bag. Colonel Enrique Bermúdez, military commander of the contras, impressed me as a true fighter ready to die for his cause. Others were just unregenerate veterans of the corrupt regime of Anastasio Somoza, who had found themselves on the wrong side when the Sandinistas took over. "Gucci *comandantes*," someone dubbed them. But in the old days of East-West polarization, we worked with what we had.

Working with José Sorzano and two White House legislative aides, Dave Addington and Alan Kranowitz, I became the chief administration advocate, trying to win enough congressional support to keep the contras afloat. Every few months, Congress had another contra-funding bill before it. We had little trouble winning support for nonlethal aid. And I could count on staunch bipartisan support for lethal arms aid from congressmen like Representatives Bob Michel and Mickey Edwards and Senators David Boren, Warren Rudman, and Ted Stevens. But among most Democrats, it was next to impossible to get approval for weapons and ammunition.

One night, during a conference committee debate on still another bill, I found myself getting nowhere trying to convince the Democratic side that you did not summarily cut off aid to men fighting for democracy in the middle of the fight. "Let me tell you a story," I said. "I've been in the jungle. I've been where the contras are now, except that it was in Vietnam in 1963. You can't imagine how desperately we waited for that Marine helicopter to supply us every two weeks. Our lives, not just our comfort, hung on that delivery. It's no different for the contras today." This was not some foreign policy seminar we were conducting in a fancy air-conditioned room, I pointed out. "We're talking about whether men who placed their trust in the United States are going to live or be left to die." The room became still, and some of the Democrats nodded. Within an hour, we had almost worked out a deal. We took a break to give both sides a chance to caucus.

On our return, I noticed Ted Stevens and Warren Rudman lagging behind, whispering to each other. After we were seated again in the conference room, I was about to tell Democratic Congressman Dave Obey that we had an agreement when Ted Stevens jumped up and said he could not go along unless the Democrats also agreed to a new date by which Congress must consider additional aid to the contras, a demand previously turned down by the Democrats. Rudman shouted that he agreed with Stevens, and the two of them started walking out. At that point, everyone wanted to go home, and so the Democrats wearily conceded. After the meeting, I was rounding a corner in the Capitol with Stevens and Rudman when both men broke out laughing. Their walkout had been a performance, and it had worked. They said I was too "nonpolitical" to have been cut in on the game. I may have been a graduate student at the Pentagon and White House. But at Congressional U., I was still a freshman.

Overarching all other concerns was our relationship with the Soviet Union. Our defense strategy and budget were almost wholly a reflection of Soviet capabilities and intentions as we read them. The size and state of the Red Army were the measures against which we built our forces. Our choosing sides in conflicts around the world was almost always decided on the basis of East-West competition. The new Soviet leader, Mikhail Gorbachev, however, was turning the old Cold War formulas on their head. Gorbachev appeared to be more intent on solving the Soviet Union's internal failings than in embarking on fruitless adventures from Angola to Afghanistan. He had little interest in continuing to pick up the tab for huge Cuban and Nicaraguan deficits. Only by reducing East-West tensions could he cut the Soviet Union's voracious defense spending and turn the country's resources to crying civilian needs. Consequently, by late summer of 1987, Gorbachev had shown a willingness to negotiate away intermediate-range nuclear forces—INF missiles. That meant eliminating the Soviets' SS-20 missiles and for us, the Army's Pershing II missiles and the Air Force's ground-launched cruise missiles. Ronald Reagan was operating from a position of political and military strength. From this posture, he had the vision and flexibility, lacking in many knee-jerk Cold Warriors, to recognize that Gorbachev was a new man in a new age offering new opportunities for peace. The prospects brightened that we could get an INF treaty; and that meant that for the first time since the dawning of the atomic age, a class of nuclear weapons would be destroyed.

While we were tackling global issues at the NSC, the country's attention was riveted to the joint congressional hearings on the Iran-contra affair, which started on May 5 and were drawing audiences like a soap opera. During the hearings, the country witnessed the extraordinary performance of Ollie North, who had been cast by the committee as villain, but brilliantly managed to emerge as an appealing patriot for at least half the viewers. I was not one of them. However well-intended his motives, North, along with Poindexter and others, had used the weapons sales to raise money for purposes prohibited by the elected representatives of the American people. He had done so in a way that avoided accountability to the President and Congress. It was wrong.

I was not called to testify by the congressional investigating committee, but on June 19 I did give a deposition to committee lawyers concerning my role in helping arrange the transfer of the TOWs to the CIA. I met in the White House Situation Room with Arthur Liman, chief Senate counsel, and Joseph Saba, staff counsel for the House of Representatives. They were most interested in finding out why the Department of Defense had transferred the TOWs to the CIA rather than directly to Iran. I repeated Secretary Weinberger's reasoning. "He did not see it as something that was the Defense Department's role—the transferring of weapons to a country such as Iran. To the extent that such a transaction was going to take place, it should be handled by elements of the government that are able and agree to handle such transactions."

Offhandedly, Liman said, "Maybe I should know this, but did the Secretary keep a diary?"

"The Secretary, to my knowledge, did not keep a diary," I answered. "Whatever notes he kept, I don't know how he uses them or what he does with them." I had never seen anything that would meet the common understanding of a diary. But I alluded to "notes," because I remembered the little white pads Cap kept in his desk drawer. I had never read these jottings, so I did not think that they should be characterized by me as a diary. I expected the lawyers to press me with follow-up questions, but they went on to other matters. The notes were not a secret. *Time* magazine later printed a picture of Weinberger packing them on his last week in office. They were subsequently placed in the Library of Congress and not destroyed or spirited away.

I hoped this session would mark the end of my involvement in this affair. However, those notepads would surface again as Lawrence Walsh, the independent counsel, prolonged his investigation of Iran-contra ad infinitum. In 1991, four years after my first interview, the independent counsel's staff reviewed the pads at the Library of Congress. They concluded, erroneously in my view, that Cap had not been truthful when he said that he did not know that Hawk missile parts had been shipped to Iran in the fall of 1985, prior to the President's formal authorization in January 1986. The staff questioned me at length on entries in the pads, which I was now permitted to read for the first time. Weinberger's lawyer, Bob Bennett, then asked me to give a deposition on the matter. In that deposition, I made one casual reference to the notepads as a "diary."

Bingo! That did it. The independent counsel figured he had caught me in a contradiction. Four years before, I had said Weinberger did not have a diary to my knowledge, though I had made the allusion to notes. Now, having seen those notes and having been questioned on them by the prosecutor's staff, I had referred to them as a diary. That was sufficient offense for Walsh to write me up in his final report.

When that report came out on December 3, 1993, it said that I, too, "was privy to detailed information regarding arms shipments to Iran" during 1985. Dead wrong. I knew of *proposals* to ship missiles at the time. I did not know that shipments had actually been made until sometime in 1986, after President Reagan signed the Finding of Necessity authorizing the deal with Iran. "Powell's early statements regarding the initiative were forthright and consistent," the report concluded. It went on to say, ". . . but some were questionable and seem generally designed to protect Weinberger. Because independent counsel had no direct evidence that Powell intentionally made false statements, however, these matters were not pursued." I was furious at the implication. I was not to be judged on whether or not I actually made false statements. Walsh simply implied that I did and dropped the matter, leaving the unfair and unfounded conclusion. I was not alone. Rich Armitage and others received similar unjust treatment.

But at least the report ended Iran-contra for me. The independent counsel, however, was tough on Weinberger. He was indicted, though President Bush pardoned him just before leaving office. Along with many others, I had spoken to the President recommending the pardon. Weinberger was a proud and honorable man. His indictment was a disgrace. This was the man who, from day one, had branded the scheme of arms for hostages as "absurd." He fought it every step of the way and only stopped fighting when President Reagan made the decision to go ahead. Instead of being praised, he was quibbled to death by an out-of-control independent counsel with unlimited time and money at his disposal. The charge against Cap Weinberger was a travesty of justice.

Frank Carlucci left the PRG meetings almost entirely in my hands. Having suffered through endless, pointless, mindless time-wasters for years, I had evolved certain rules for holding meetings. First, everyone got a chance to recommend items for the agenda beforehand, but I controlled the final agenda, which I distributed before the meeting. Once a meeting started, no one was allowed to switch the agenda. Everyone knew that the meeting would last exactly one hour. The first five minutes and the last ten minutes belonged to me. In those first five minutes, I reviewed why we were meeting and what had to be decided by the end of the session. For the next twenty minutes, participants were allowed to present their positions, uninterrupted. After that, we had a free-for-all to strip away posturing, attack lame reasoning, gang up on outrageous views, and generally have some fun. Fifty minutes into the hour, I resumed control, and for five minutes summarized everyone's views as I understood them. Participants could take issue with my summation for one minute. In the last four to five minutes, I laid out the conclusions and decisions to be presented as the consensus of the participants. Then it was over. Those disapproving of the outcome could go back home and complain to their bosses, who could appeal to Carlucci. This approach seemed to work.

Late in May, the family returned to William and Mary for Linda's graduation. On the way home, Linda told us that she was dead serious about an acting career. All our children had been active in school dramatics; but a profession? The lottery offered better odds. Linda also screwed up the courage to ask if I would support her through acting school. Much to her astonishment, I am sure, I agreed. But then, what is a father but a banker provided by nature? Linda enrolled in a two-year program at the Circle in the Square Theatre School in Manhattan. I found it strange that one of my children was going back to the New York roots I had willingly left nearly thirty years before.

I returned to my office on the afternoon of June 27 just as Lieutenant General Andy Chambers, still commanding VII Corps in Germany, phoned me. I was happy to hear from Andy, but wondered what he wanted—was it to talk about my son, Mike? I was right, and it was bad news. "Mike's been badly hurt," Andy said, adding quickly, "but he's not going to die." He gave me the sketchy details. Mike and another lieutenant, Ulrich Brechbuhl, had been riding in a jeep driven by an enlisted driver, Specialist Boese. The jeep went out of control on the autobahn and flipped over. Mike was thrown out, and the vehicle landed on him before rolling to a halt. The other two men had suffered only minor injuries. I would soon be getting a call from the Army hospital in Nuremberg with details on Mike's condition. It is futile to try to recapture one's reaction to such news, with part of the mind reeling, the other part struggling to figure out what to do. I told Florence Gantt that I was going home to break the news to Alma. Florence immediately started arranging to get us to West Germany.

Alma was in the kitchen unloading the dishwasher when I arrived, and she asked what had brought me home so early. I told her. At first she was quiet, and then I saw that steely resolve take over her expression. How soon, she wanted to know, could we see Mike? I would have a strong partner to lean on in this hour of trial, probably stronger than she would have.

Grant Green, executive secretary of the NSC, had already alerted his wife, Ginger, about Mike's accident. The Greens were among our closest friends, and Ginger, a lawyer, dropped everything to come to the house, helping us wait out the next desperate hours. Finally, the call came from the hospital. Mike had suffered a broken pelvis and serious internal injuries. His condition was critical. That evening, thanks to Florence and the Air Force, we clambered over the payload of a C-5 cargo plane up to a tiny compartment behind the cockpit and flew to West Germany.

. . .

We found Mike in intensive care, looking terribly bloated, but smiling, thanks to the painkilling morphine. The pelvis carries blood vessels that, in Mike's case, had been ruptured. He had been given eighteen units of blood, twice the body's normal supply. The swelling resulted from thirty pounds of fluid accumulated in his system from the transfusions. The Army's surgeon general in Europe, Dr. Frank Ledford, had come down from Heidelberg, and after our visit with Mike he took us into a small room to explain our son's condition. Mike would need pelvic surgery of a kind still in the experimental stage. His other major injuries included a severed urethra. His recovery would take four to six months, Dr. Ledford said. The extent of his recovery was unknowable at that point.

Not until months afterward did we learn through a friend of Mike's exactly what had happened after the accident. The three Americans in the jeep had initially been taken to a German hospital. There, Lieutenant Brechbuhl, who spoke German, heard a doctor say, "There's nothing we can do for this one," referring to Mike. With that, the lieutenant leaped off the examining table and said, "No. You can't leave him. Call the American hospital, right away." And that was how Mike had wound up in Nuremberg, in desperate condition but holding on to life.

I had to return to Washington the next day, while Alma remained at Mike's side. A couple of days afterward, the hospital became a bedlam. A shell had exploded during a field exercise, killing two soldiers outright, and ambulances full of injured men arrived at the hospital. One soldier whom Alma saw brought into Mike's ward had lost both legs and most of his fingers. As she watched the medical staff stretched to the breaking point, Alma volunteered to help. The staff put her to work at the desk, answering phones and directing visitors. General Otis later awarded her a citation for her contributions during the emergency.

Within four days of the accident, Mike was in Walter Reed Army Medical Center in Washington. There he was examined by Dr. Bruce Van Dam, perhaps the best orthopedic surgeon in the military and certainly one of the finest in the country. Dr. Van Dam was thoughtful and professional. He explained to Mike that he and the chief urologist would be performing procedures rarely attempted. As he was leaving, he added, "You know your military career is over, don't you?" Mike had not known, or had blotted it out of his thoughts.

Alma was there at the time, and Mike kept saying, "I want to talk to my dad. Get me my dad." I got to the hospital as fast as I could, and for the first time since this ordeal had started, I saw my son demoralized. "I don't know what else I can do," Mike kept repeating. "I always expected to make the Army my life. What am I going to do now?"

On my way out, I spoke to Dr. Van Dam regarding Mike's shattered career. "I wish you had shared that news with me first," I said.

He was understanding but firm. "I'm sorry, but this is the reality," the doctor said. "It had to be faced sooner or later."

The night of the first operation was terrible, most of all for Mike, but for the rest of us too. The pelvis, the doctor had told us, would heal by itself, but in a crippling, disfiguring way unless the surgery worked. A plate had to be bolted to the back of the pelvis and a rodlike contraption bolted across the front literally to hold Mike together. Afterward the pain would be unbearable, we were warned. And the amount of morphine necessary to kill pain at that level would kill the patient.

After the operation, we were permitted to see Mike, who was a mass of tubes, with the morphine he was permitted barely reducing the agony. Alma busied herself in the room. But the three-star general, the great coordinator, facilitator, administrator, never felt more useless in his life. Just when I thought I could not endure witnessing my son's ordeal any longer, a pert nurse came bounding into the room. "Hi," she said. "How we doing here? Let's cut back on this morphine. That's enough of that. You're going to be all right." She moved to the rods and screws sticking out of Mike's body. "Let's see how this Erector set is doing," she said, as she tightened the nuts with a Sears Craftsman wrench. Her name was Barbara Cilento, and something about her brisk, upbeat competence made us think everything was going to be all right. She reminded me of one of my own preachments, "Perpetual optimism is a force multiplier." In the Army we were always looking for ways to multiply our forces. And a positive outlook was one way. This time I was on the receiving end of the optimism, and it worked.

Mike would have to undergo several more operations. Still we were grateful to skilled physicians, like Dr. Van Dam and Drs. Stephen A. Sihelnik and David G. McLeod, who brought our son from a point where his life had been written off to putting him on the road to recovery. And we rank, along with those M.D.s, Barbara Cilento, R.N. She became Mike's angel of mercy, and, we thought for a time, maybe a budding romance as well.

For the next six months, Alma's life and mine centered on the hospital. I got there as often as I could between NSC crises. Our son was on the mend, partly through excellent medical care, but as much because of some unbreakable fiber within him in which we took enormous pride.

One challenge in guiding Reagan foreign policy was to help the President rule with his head as well as his heart. By the fall of 1987, Middle East terrorists now held nine Americans captive. For all the near destruction of his presidency, Reagan would have gone for another hostage-freeing scheme at the drop of a Hawk missile. He was moved both by compassion and an awareness of the damage done to Jimmy Carter's presidency by a hostage crisis. Carlucci and I worked on the President to tone down his public utterances about the kidnappings, not because the kidnappings were not cruel, which they were, but because the attention and publicity were exactly what made hostage-taking effective and led our enemies to seize more people. To put the matter into some kind of perspective, we pointed out that just as many Americans were lost on the streets of Washington every week to urban terrorism. We could not let our foreign policy be driven by the political karate of a handful of zealots.

Similarly, the POW/MIA issue came up regularly. And again the President was moved, particularly by able leaders like Anne Mills Griffiths, who had a brother missing in action and who headed the respected National League of Families. But MIA families were also manipulated by con artists fabricating evidence and raising money under false pretenses for their own enrichment. It helped keep the issue in proportion to remember that there had been approximately 78,750 MIAs in World War II, 8,100 in Korea, and 2,230 in Vietnam. I knew that often a booby trap made from a bomb or a fighter plane exploding would produce an "MIA" about whom, sadly, we would never learn anything further. Despite this awareness, I believe that we must keep pressure on the Vietnamese, Laotians, and Cambodians until we have the fullest possible accounting for all of our MIAs.

In early November, Cap Weinberger informed the President that he intended to resign as Secretary of Defense. Jane Weinberger's osteoporosis and other ills had worsened. The Secretary had spent seven grueling years on the job. This year marked the second time that Congress had resisted Weinberger's budget boosts, and the White House had not backed him. He still had the President's personal loyalty, but Weinberger's standing with Nancy Reagan, never strong, had continued to slip, no small setback in this administration. The pragmatic First Lady viewed Weinberger, with his unremitting hostility toward the Soviet Union, as swimming against the tide. In the chronic Weinberger-Shultz feud, she increasingly took Shultz's side, which pained Weinberger. He was enough of a performer to recognize an exit line. He asked the President to relieve him as Secretary of Defense.

The search for a new Secretary was short. Will Taft, Weinberger's able deputy and close confidant, was a candidate. But the call went once again to Frank Carlucci, whose performance in every national security department made him a perfect fit. Taft would stay on as Carlucci's deputy secretary.

With Carlucci going to the Pentagon, I saw an opening for me to try to return to the Army. That is, until Chief of Staff Howard Baker cornered me one morning and led me into his office. "If we offered you National Security Advisor to the President," he said, "would you take it?"

"Howard," I answered, "after Poindexter, you can't possibly put another active duty officer in as head of the NSC. You'll be crucified."

"The President can appoint anybody he wants," Baker said. "What I'm asking is, what will you say?"

It is not easy to say no to a President, and I had probably played out all my Army options by now anyway. "If offered, I would accept," I said.

On October 16, the NSPG, the National Security Planning Group, the inner circle of the NSC, met in the White House Situation Room. Frank and the

President entered and sat down. Frank passed me a note. "Done," it read. "He is delighted with you." The President himself never spoke to me about the job, never laid out his expectations, never provided any guidance; in fact, he had not personally offered me the position or congratulated me on getting it. After ten months in the White House, I was not surprised. That was the Reagan way, and I was honored by the confidence he had in me.

On November 5, 1987, a sunlit day with a hint of autumn crispness in the air, we filed into the Rose Garden. The President expressed the nation's gratitude to Cap Weinberger for making the country strong again. He pointed out the superb qualifications of Carlucci as Weinberger's successor. And he then announced that Lieutenant General Colin L. Powell would succeed Carlucci as the President's National Security Advisor. Alma and my daughters were there; but what brought the mist to my eyes was the presence of my son, who had gotten out of his hospital bed, put on a suit, and stood, with the aid of crutches, for the first time since his accident.

Over the previous ten months, I had been delegated so much responsibility as deputy that I felt fully confident about handling the top NSC job. I was the sixth Reagan appointee in that position, which someone referred to as the administration's Bermuda Triangle. And I was determined to be Reagan's last National Security Advisor. I confess that I also felt along with the pride a certain burden to prove myself as the first African-American to hold the position. As the columnist Carl Rowan put it, "To understand the significance of Powell's elevation to this extremely difficult and demanding post, you must realize that only a generation ago it was an unwritten rule that in the foreign affairs field, blacks could serve only as ambassador to Liberia and minister to the Canary Islands."

Before I could be formally appointed, a hitch developed. Several influential people did object to having an active-duty officer heading the NSC. Critics included Admiral Crowe, Chairman of the Joint Chiefs of Staff; Alexander Haig, President Reagan's first Secretary of State and once the deputy at NSC himself; and Brent Scowcroft, also a former National Security Advisor, to President Ford. I myself had told the *New York Times* in an interview that the National Security Advisor should be a civilian political appointee. Democratic Senator Tom Harkin of Iowa had, in fact, proposed legislation (S. 715) prohibiting an active-duty officer from being National Security Advisor. Passage of this bill would pose a real headache for me.

The post of National Security Advisor did not require Senate confirmation. But as a three-star general, I would have to be confirmed for any job in order to hold on to my rank. If I dropped back to two stars, I could be appointed without Senate confirmation. But I was not eager to be demoted in the Army so that I could be promoted in a civilian post. A bit of suspense hung over my future.

14 ☆ National Security Advisor
to the President

ON DECEMBER 18, 1987, I got a call from Senator Sam Nunn's secretary telling me to make sure that on the next afternoon I watched C-Span, the cable TV channel that, among other things, covers Congress. When the time came, I was curious, and a little anxious. After the Iran-contra fiasco, Nunn, powerful chairman of the Senate Armed Services Committee, had become strongly opposed to having military officers serve as the President's National Security Advisor. By now, I had moved from the deputy's cubicle to the grand West Wing corner office recently vacated by Frank Carlucci, and hoped nothing I heard on C-Span was going to require my departure.

The next afternoon, I turned on the office television set, and there was Nunn, in his earnest drawl, bashing away: "A military officer knows that his next promotion depends on the Secretary of Defense and the top generals and admirals in the Pentagon," Nunn was saying. ". . . any active-duty officer who serves in that position may be subject to an inherent conflict between his responsibilities to the President and his own professional future in the service. Assignment of a military officer to this senior, sensitive position also raises serious questions about the civilian control of the military." But suddenly, Nunn took a 180-degree turn: "Why, then, make an exception now?" he asked, and proceeded to answer his own question. ". . . I believe that this is a rather unique set of cirumstances." He pointed out that only about a year remained in the Reagan administration and "we have had considerable turmoil in the office of the National Security Council." We needed continuity, Nunn said. Consequently, he was willing to support confirmation of this particular nominee.

"Will the gentleman yield?" The C-Span camera turned to Republican Senator John Warner, the ranking minority member on the Armed Services Committee. Warner too had said it was a bad idea to put a soldier in this highly political spot, but praised "the unusual distinction that this fine officer has brought to the nation and himself."

Nunn moved that my nomination be approved, and I was subsequently confirmed by the Senate. Within minutes, Nunn and Warner were on the phone laughing like schoolboy pranksters, asking if I had enjoyed the performance. Of course, I was pleased. Not only had the exception in my case been a compliment, but Senate approval allowed me to keep the NSC position and still hold on to my three-star rank.

While I felt up to the job, what had happened in this soldier's life was still dizzying. Ten years before, I had thumped down the corridors of the Old EOB in my jump boots to tell Zbigniew Brzezinski, then National Security Advisor, that I felt no qualification for and wanted no part of his operation. And now I had the job that he and Henry Kissinger before him had held. I was no longer someone's aide or number two. I would be working directly with the President, the Vice President, and the secretaries of State and Defense, who formed the NSC. I was to perform as judge, traffic cop, truant officer, arbitrator, fireman, chaplain, psychiatrist, and occasional hit man. And I would not only be organizing the views of others to present to the President; I was now expected to give him my own national security judgments. I had become a "principal," with cabinet-level status, if not the rank.

Around this time, I saw a story in the *New York Times* about New York City's new landmarks commissioner, Gene Norman, the same Gene I had played stickball with on Kelly Street, whom I had seen just once since he went off to join the Marine Corps over thirty years before. I invited Gene and his wife, Juanita, another Kelly Street alumna, to join Alma and me for lunch at the White House mess. We talked about another old pal who had recently resurfaced, Tony Grant, now a lawyer and corporation counsel for White Plains, New York. All the while we were laughing and carrying on, an unspoken undercurrent flowed: had all this really happened to a bunch of kids from Banana Kelly?

In the mess, Gene noticed something that had always bothered me. Nearly all the waiters in the White House mess were Filipinos. The mess was a wholly Navy-run operation; I had been successful in integrating waiters in the Pentagon, but I did not have any leverage in my new job to crack this monopoly.

The same held true for the White House ushers. They were mostly black, including those who served at formal dinners, creating an atmosphere suggesting a plantation in the antebellum South rather than the White House in the twentieth century. These jobs were practically handed down from father to son. They were prized. The ushers liked the situation just fine the way it was. And, no thank you, they did not need some upstart African-American general to break up a good thing in the pursuit of integration.

Though not yet formally confirmed, I had been filling the advisor's job on an acting basis since November 18, the day Frank Carlucci departed to take over at Defense. Just two days into the job, I had briefed a group of Knight-Ridder newspaper editors in the Roosevelt Room on the situation in Nicaragua. Among them was one black editor, Reginald Stuart, who so far had asked no questions. Finally his hand went up. "Being the first black person to occupy this position," Stuart asked, "what do you feel are the chances no one will try to undercut you in the post, or bypass you?" I managed to conceal my surprise—the brother was asking if I was a *token*!—and ticked off the facts: I had already been with the NSC for ten months; I had dealt with every issue from arms control to Bermuda tax treaties; I had already worked directly with the President and the secretaries of State and Defense. I was neither undercuttable nor bypassable. I am afraid I let my annoyance show.

Two weeks later, I attended a reception hosted by the Joint Center for Political Studies, a black Washington think tank, and spotted Stuart. I went up and said, "Man, why did you hit me with that one?"

He gave me an amused smile. "That's what every white guy in the room was thinking, but was afraid to ask. So I asked it for them."

In December, Mikhail Gorbachev was coming to Washington for the first time for his third summit meeting with President Reagan and to sign the treaty to eliminate intermediate-range nuclear force missiles. INF missiles had a range of about three thousand miles, which placed them between tactical battlefield nukes and intercontinental ballistic missiles aimed at targets like Washington, Moscow, New York, and Leningrad. INFs were the missiles that the Western Allies and the Soviets would hurl at each other in the event of war in Europe. In November, I traveled to Geneva with Secretary Shultz to work on the INF treaty and to prepare for the December summit. Shultz led the mission and did most of the talking at our sessions with the Soviets at the American embassy. I listened, observing the men around the table, beginning with Eduard Shevardnadze, Soviet foreign minister, handsome, silver-haired, with the expression and mild speech of an Anglican vicar.

The figure my eyes kept returning to was an older, small, spare, tough-looking soldier, Marshal Sergei Akhromeyev, first deputy minister of defense and, as chief of the Soviet general staff, head of all Soviet military forces. As I studied this "Hero of the Soviet Union," I continually had to reverse mental gears. Only a year before, I had been commanding

V Corps, whose sole mission was to hurl back Akhromeyev's armies, specifically the 8th Guards Army. Now I was National Security Advisor, engaged in negotiating agreements that should start to make V Corps and the Soviet 8th Guards Army obsolete.

That evening the Americans hosted a candle-light dinner for the Soviet team in the residence of the American ambassador. The conversation hit a lull at one point, and I leaned toward Akhromeyev. "Marshal," I said, "you must be one of the last World War II veterans still on active duty." (It was now forty-two years since V-E Day.)

The marshal nodded. "I am the last of the Mohicans," he said. I laughed, surprised at his familiarity with James Fenimore Cooper. "Oh, yes," he said, smiling, "many Russians of my generation have read Cooper and Jack London, Mark Twain, all your best writers."

I asked Akhromeyev what he had done during the war. He had enlisted in the Red Army at seventeen, he said, right off the farm. His unit was posted about thirty-five miles from Leningrad during the siege by the Germans, which lasted 890 days and cost 830,000 civilian lives alone from bombardment and starvation.

"For eighteen months," Ahkromeyev said, "I never set foot inside a building, even when the temperature went to fifty below zero. I was out of doors through two winters, never knew a warm day, always fighting, always hungry." The room was silent as he spoke. "And such loss of life. Eight out of ten boys my age died during the war. Only I and one other from my high school class of thirty-two survived."

I felt two reactions to the old marshal's story—
admiration for the courage of a fellow soldier and
recognition of how hard it must be for Akhromeyev
to accept that so much blood had been shed, not only
to save Russia, but to preserve the false god of Marxism. He understood the need for change and supported perestroika. But he and Gorbachev both clung
to reforming, not abandoning, the old faith.

Before going to Geneva, I had had to make a key
decision: who was going to replace me as NSC
deputy and run the store during my absences. I had
been closely associated with Cap Weinberger, a former Secretary of Defense. I was just as close to the
current Secretary, Frank Carlucci. And I was a military man. I needed to spike any perception that the
NSC was a wholly owned subsidiary of the defense
establishment. I found just the man, John D. Negroponte, off in the unlikely outpost of assistant secretary of state for oceans, the environment, and
international organizations. Negroponte, a career
Foreign Service officer, had the management style I
liked, toughness applied in an easygoing manner, a
rare combination. And as a State Department career
officer, John would help dispel the perception that I
was Defense's man. I made a few other changes in
the team Carlucci and I had put together. Paul
Stevens moved up from legal advisor to be my executive secretary, and Nick Rostow took over the legal
job. Roman Popadiuk became my press assistant.

In the military, we are constantly judging
human material, placing and replacing personnel. By
now, I had developed Powell's Rules for Picking

People. What I looked for was intelligence and judgment, and most critically, a capacity to anticipate, to see around corners. I also valued loyalty, integrity, a high energy level, a certain passion, a balanced ego, and the drive to get things done. Academics and subject specialists are valuable for their expertise. But, above all, I needed people to help me make the NSC trains run on time.

After the Geneva trip, I flew to California and went to the Reagans' ranch in the Santa Ynez Mountains above Santa Barbara, where the first family was spending Thanksgiving and where I was to brief the President on the now completed INF treaty. I was surprised at the modesty of the ranch house, small and lacking even central heating. I entered and found President Reagan in a plaid shirt, jeans, and boots, a man clearly in his element. And hovering, just within our peripheral vision, was Nancy Reagan, never missing a word. The President beamed as I reported the deal we had made with the Soviet Union, and with reason. He was the first American leader to begin dismantling nuclear weapons.

The White House staff was booked into the Biltmore Four Seasons in Santa Barbara, and when I got back there from the ranch, the President's press secretary, Marlin Fitzwater, cornered me. "It's time to lose your virginity," Marlin said. He wanted me go to the nearby Sheraton Hotel to brief the White House press corps on the INF treaty and other issues covered at Geneva. I was to speak "on background," which meant I was about to become one of those anonymous "senior administration officials" quoted in news accounts.

The White House press corps can be a carnivorous lot, and I braced myself for this first exposure by relying on the techniques drilled into me thirty years before at the Fort Benning Infantry School instructors course—how to stand, move, use the hands and the voice (never cough or shift your feet); how to organize your thoughts (tell 'em what you're gonna tell 'em, tell 'em, then tell 'em what you just told 'em). Communication is still communication, whether to a class of OCS students or to Sam Donaldson.

I nevertheless felt as if I were approaching a minefield as I went to the mike, explained the treaty and other issues, and opened the floor to questions. The air was quickly filled with the Sanskrit of arms control—"encrypting telemetry," "throw weights," "multiple independently targetable reentry vehicles." My confidence grew as I managed to get wood on every pitch. The questioning turned to two sites agreed to by us and the Soviets for verifying disarmament, Magna, Utah, and Votkinsk, Siberia. Which one was preferable? a reporter asked teasingly. "Given my druthers, I'd take Magna," I said. Votkinsk was quite a desolate place. But, I promised, "We will make sure CNN gets there." They began laughing. I started not only to act relaxed, but to feel relaxed. By the end of the conference, I felt positively warm toward these folks. I was like a child who has not yet seen any tigers in the jungle and therefore concludes there aren't any.

On this first outing, however, I did pick up a few useful press pointers. I realized that the interviewee is the only one at risk in this duel. The media report only stupid or careless answers, not stupid or unfair questions. Also, when reporters ask a follow-up question, you're headed for trouble—so break off, apply power, gain altitude, or eject.

I looked anxiously at my watch this November morning. I had a roomful of Russians in my office, the advance delegation for the Gorbachev-Reagan summit. Unlike their dapper new leader, this group still wore suits that looked as if they had been tailored by State Garment Factory #2, Minsk. My life was now consumed by the thousand and one logistical preparations a summit meeting demands. This morning, I was trying to sell the Russians on helicoptering Gorbachev in from Andrews Air Force Base so that he could get a panoramic view of Washington. "*Nyet,*" they said, concerned about security. Gorbachev must come in by motorcade.

Weeks before, I had committed myself to a Veterans Day luncheon speech before the women of the James Reese Europe Post #5 of the American Legion Auxiliary at the Howard Inn near Howard University. Outside my window, an early, heavy snow was falling. It probably made the Russians feel at home, but presented a problem for me, since a sixteenth of an inch of snow is sufficient to paralyze Washington. I had asked Florence Gantt to call the good ladies of Post #5 to find out if they intended to cancel the lunch. Oh, no, they were expecting General Powell.

There was, for me, something touching about these women, many of them widows of black GIs who had fought in the segregated services of World War II, still meeting to honor their men. Therefore, I left the Russians in the middle of a summit planning session to skid and slide my way up to the Howard Inn, where I was greeted by my hostess, the Reverend Imagene Stewart, and my audience, nine elderly ladies in a room set up for two hundred. To my astonishment, the television cameras of C-Span were there, which magnified my impact somewhat, since C-Span ran my speech to the nine ladies three times, nationwide.

Subsequently, this appearance spawned a continuing relationship between me and my hostess's homeless facility, the House of Imagene. Once after I ran a Pentagon clothing drive for her she sent me a note: "Don't send me any more old clothes. I need suits to dress up these folks for job interviews!"

With or without me, the Soviet advance party was having a good time. On their first night at the Madison Hotel, they hit the minibars in their rooms to the tune of $1,400. We asked the hotel management to stop restocking the bars. I was also playing referee between the KGB and our security agencies. The Soviet team had arrived with all kinds of electronic equipment. And when Gorbachev came, they would bring their own nuclear release system, the equivalent of our "football," carried wherever the President went. The National Security Agency, our eavesdropping outfit, was licking its chops for permission to move its intercepting gear onto the White House grounds. The CIA wanted a shot too. Spooks spying on spooks spying on spooks. Anybody walking across the White House lawn wearing a pacemaker during the summit would be lucky not to be microwaved.

The security chief for the Soviet advance party was a senior KGB deputy minister, Vladimir A. Kryuchkov, who asked to see me. When our Secret Service found out that I intended to let a top KGB official into the West Wing of the White House, they panicked. There was no telling what Kryuchkov might be up to. How do we know what's in his shoes? Suppose he tries to plant a bug? Suppose he sticks a pin mike into your sofa? "Fellas," I said, "I don't think the Soviet security chief for summit meetings makes his own drops. What are you going to do when Gorbachev comes, strip-search him in the East Wing?" I assured them that as soon as Kryuchkov was gone they could sweep my office down to the bare walls.

Kryuchkov had wanted to see me, he said, "to make absolutely sure of the safety of Comrade Gorbachev." I outlined the security arrangements, and he nodded approvingly. "Yes," he said, "we have been much impressed by your Secret Service. We could learn from them," and he added, "just as you could learn from us." He then gave me a sly smile and said, "We are pleased too to see so many new employees at our hotel. The FBI headquarters must be depleted."

Less than a year after his visit to the White House, Vladimir A. Kryuchkov became head of the KGB.

. . .

The mistake Ronald Reagan's liberal critics made was to assume that because he was a conservative and because he supported a huge defense buildup, he was some sort of dude-ranch warmonger. Wrong. Ronald Reagan was a visionary, dreaming of reversing the threat of nuclear annihilation. That was what the INF treaty was all about. That is what SDI was aimed at. The SDI "umbrella" was intended to make nuclear weapons obsolete. The science of SDI (or Star Wars, as its critics insisted on calling it) was mind-boggling, but the strategy was fairly elementary. The present situation was tantamount to two enemy soldiers each in his foxhole armed with a hand grenade. If you throw yours to destroy me, I'll still have time to throw mine to destroy you. Mutual Assured Destruction, MAD. In order to give himself an edge, soldier #1 gets a rifle. Seeing this, soldier #2 gets himself a rifle, and on and on. This is known as an arms race. SDI was intended to break the circuit. President Reagan saw SDI as a shield as contrasted to a sword. If we have a shield on our left arm, we don't need such a massive sword in our right hand. And the more secure we feel behind the shield, the smaller the sword needs to be. The SDI shield was designed not to destroy people, only to protect them.

The President loved the shield image, although it was a bit exaggerated. The actual strategic edge of SDI was that while it could not stop all enemy missiles, it could destroy enough so that the Soviets could not be sure they could deliver a nuclear knockout punch. Therefore, SDI would render the continued nuclear buildup futile. Reagan had offered to share SDI technology with the Soviets, an offer they never believed. And many of our planners did not believe Reagan meant it either, though I knew that he was sincere. Only when the Soviets also felt secure, the President reasoned, would they be ready to shorten their nuclear sword. That was the visionary in the man. But Gorbachev took the position that missiles were cheaper to build than supersophisticated shields, and therefore the Soviets could just keep building them to overwhelm whatever defense we constructed. That argument omitted the economics of the equation. We had the money to go either route, SDI or more missiles, while, economically, the Russians were hurting. At the Reykjavík Summit in 1986, Gorbachev had shown himself willing to trade off a major portion of the Soviet strategic arsenal, if we would abandon SDI, which showed that while he pretended to dismiss it, he actually feared the new technology. We knew he would come to Washington in December still fighting SDI. And we knew that Reagan would stick by it.

A few days before Gorbachev's arrival, I was briefing the President on the summit agenda when he interrupted to show me two small boxes. He opened them and, with a smile, held before me two pairs of gold cufflinks depicting figures beating swords into plowshares. Like many of his inspirations, the cufflinks had been given to him by a California pal. The President was going to wear one pair the day of Gorbachev's arrival and give the Russian leader the other pair at their first one-on-one meeting in the Oval Office. I pointed out that I did not think the Russians wore French cuffs. He was not deterred. On this and subsequent days, we had a lot of homework to cover; Gorbachev was going to be sharp. Yet, every time I went in to brief the President on summit issues, he also brought up the cufflinks. The disarmament and economic issues would eventually be dealt with, he knew. But he also wanted personal symbols that bonded the two men who were to resolve them.

With just days to go, I asked Soviet Ambassador Yuri Dubinin to come over to my office as soon as possible. I had a problem, and so did he. Dubinin, a big, white-haired, usually affable man, looked miserable as I explained the dilemma. Sweat glistened on his brow. Mrs. Reagan was furious, I told him. She had extended invitations to the Soviet leader's wife, Raisa Gorbachev, to tea, to lunch, to whatever she preferred. And after repeated inquiries by our staff, we had heard nothing back, not a yes, a no, not even an acknowledgment that the invitations had been received. Tom Griscom, the White House communications director, my cochair in planning the summit, a wit and popper of ego balloons, observed, "What is this, animal house? A food fight between two First Ladies?" Knowing Mrs. Reagan's iron will, I told Dubinin that we were on the verge of jeopardizing a cordial summit meeting if she did not get a simple, civil response, and damn quick.

"Colin," Dubinin said, shifting uncomfortably, "it is a delicate situation. Mrs. Gorbachev is . . ." His words petered out. I understood all about demanding First Ladies. Still, I told him, "Get cracking if you do not want to screw up this summit over something so silly. Why don't you crank up that new KGB fax of yours and get us an answer, quick." Twenty-four hours later we received a cabled acceptance from Raisa Gorbachev, decision-making at the speed of light by Russian standards. She agreed to tea.

Yes, I knew a bit about strong-minded First Ladies. But I still had more to learn. My staff and I had choreographed the treaty-signing on the first day to get the summit off to a dramatic start. We had selected 11:00 A.M. as the hour. Ken Duberstein, an energetic, politically savvy young Brooklynite, was the President's deputy White House chief of staff, and I sent Ken the suggested schedule. He later phoned me to say that the signing had to take place at 1:45 P.M. Not possible, I said; that would foul up the entire day. Ken repeated, 1:45 P.M. I told him maybe 11:30, or at the very latest, noon. Duberstein insisted on 1:45. His behavior was so arbitrary and out of character that I said, "Kenny, what's so special about one forty-five?" He would not give me a straight answer, but neither would he budge. We had to bend the schedule all out of shape to accommodate this inexplicable demand.

Some weeks later, Duberstein finally told me the reason. And that is how I became one of a half-dozen people in the White House to learn the secret. Now the whole world knows that Nancy Reagan consulted an astrologer to decide where and when the President should conduct the business of the United States; and this California seer, Joan Quigley, had decreed that the stars were right for a favorable signing of the INF treaty at 1:45 P.M.

Nancy Reagan's interest in astrology was not out of step with a quasi-mystical streak in the President himself. He had been much affected by what had happened at Chernobyl. If an accident in a Soviet nuclear power plant could spread radioactive poison over so much of the globe, what would nuclear weapons do? The President had learned that the name Chernobyl derived from a Russian word meaning "wormwood." Because of wormwood's harsh taste, the plant is mentioned in the Bible as a symbol for bitterness. The President's train of thought ran from Chernobyl, to wormwood, to rancor, to Armageddon. He told us that what had happened in that city was a biblical warning to mankind.

December 7 came, Gorbachev landed, and we were sticking nicely to the script: arrival of the general secretary on the south lawn of the White House; a brief one-on-one meeting with the President in the Oval Office; Reagan's eager presentation of the cufflinks, which Gorbachev pocketed with a simple "Thank you." The two leaders then led their delegations to the East Room for the signing of the INF treaty. "For the first time in history," President Reagan said, "the language of 'arms control' was replaced by 'arms reduction.' " We had laid out two leather-bound copies, blue for the United States, red for the Soviet Union, which Reagan and Gorbachev signed, a little past 1:45 P.M.

It was now time for substance over ceremony. Gorbachev still wanted to derail SDI, and he wanted to make a pitch for economic aid for his country. We wanted the Soviets out of Afghanistan and wanted Jews to be free to leave the Soviet Union. I had arranged for the principals and immediate staff to meet in the Oval Office at 2:30 P.M. But the State Department wanted so many people included, American and Soviet, that, at the last minute, George Shultz asked to move to the much larger Cabinet Room. My antennae started quivering. Sudden changes threw Ronald Reagan off his form. Unwisely, I yielded to Shultz.

When everyone was seated in the now jammed Cabinet Room, the President invited Gorbachev, as his guest, to speak first. I started jotting down my impressions as the Soviet leader spoke from his handwritten notes: "Bright. Fast. Quick turning radius. Vigorous. Solid. Feisty. Colorful speech." Gorbachev was tossing off terms like "MIRV" and "depressed trajectories" and the throw weights of SS-12s, -13s, -18s, and -24s, like one of Ken Adelman's wonks in the Arms Control and Disarmament Agency. At one point Gorbachev said, "I am aware you are getting ready to produce new chemical weapons at your facility in Pine Bluff, Arkansas." He even knew that these weapons would be fired from 155mm artillery shells, which I did not know. The President listened with a fixed, pleasant expression. Suddenly, he interrupted to say he had a story. We knew that he kept a stack of Russian jokes on file cards, most of the gags fed to him by the American embassy in Moscow. Gorbachev yielded the floor.

"An American professor was in a cab on his way to the airport for a flight to the Soviet Union," the President began. "It turns out the cab driver was a student. 'When you finish your studies,' the professor asked him, 'what do you want to do?' 'Don't know,' the cabbie said. 'I haven't decided yet.'

"At the other end of the flight the professor was taking a cab into Moscow and struck up a conversation with the Russian driver. He was a student too. So the professor asks what he's going to do when he finishes school. 'Don't know,' the cabbie says, 'they haven't told me yet.' That," the President said amiably, "is the basic difference between us."

As he finished the story the Americans wanted to disappear under the table, while Gorbachev stared ahead, expressionless. This was his third meeting with the President, and by now he knew Reagan's style. He evidently considered getting what he wanted more important than being offended; he turned again to the agenda, as if he had heard nothing.

The President's performance continued to reveal his thin preparation. On diplomatic questions, he would turn to Shultz and say, "Well, George, you might want to say a word about that." On military matters, he turned to Carlucci: "Frank, I'm sure you would like to address that point."

After the meeting ended, our side retreated to the Oval Office. George Shultz couragcously said what had to be said: "Mr. President, that was a disaster. That man is tough. He's prepared. And you can't just sit there telling jokes."

The President knew the session had not gone well and took the scolding in stride. But he was not devastatcd. "Well, what do we do now?" he said.

The President and Gorbachev had another working session scheduled for the next morning. I was determined not to repeat the mistakes of today, part of which I accepted as my fault. "The first thing we're going to do is stay in the Oval Office," I said. George Shultz now agreed. "And the next thing, Mr. President," I said, "is to get you a better set of talking points." Ronald Reagan's ego was not going to benefit from any further lecturing this day. He was hosting a state dinner for Gorbachev in the evening, and I suggested he might want to go back to the residential quarters to get ready. I assured him we would have everything prepared for him by morning.

As the meeting ended, Shultz still looked distraught, as though we had suffered a first-round knockout. I suggested we all take a deep breath, buckle down, and fix the problem. I went back to my office and had Florence Gantt round up Fritz Ermath, Bob Linhard, and Nelson Ledsky of my staff. As soon as they arrived, I gave them the classic five-paragraph Army field order: Situation: serious; we lost the first engagement. Mission: retake the initiative. Execution: counterattack by preparing the President better for the next day. Logistics: three or four pages of tightly written talking points to be prepared by this staff. Command and control: here in this room, with approval of the talking points by the Secretary of State. "I'll see you around midnight," I said, "after the state dinner."

The event went swimmingly, with Ronald Reagan doing the thing he seemed born to do, speaking warmly, convincingly, wittily—and he was well prepared. I got back to my office a little before midnight to the usual chaos of crash projects, men in rolled-up shirtsleeves, ties pulled down to half mast, women's hair disheveled, people hunched over texts messy with scribbled edits, half-empty foam cups of cold coffee and plastic spoons littering desks, secretaries clicking away at word processors, printers spewing out the latest draft. I looked over the current version and said, "Good. But not good enough." I gave some course corrections and went home to grab a few winks. I was back in the West Wing by 5:00 A.M. The staff, now draped over chairs and couches, looked bleary-eyed. Ermath handed me the latest version of the President's talking points. I glanced at my watch. Shultz would be over by 7:00 A.M. for his shot at our work. "One more time," I said, giving a few new directions. They roused themselves and sat down again around the conference table.

Shultz came in on the dot, and I showed him what we had. "I think it's good," George said, "but let me take it back to the department. My people need to have a look."

"Better make it fast," I said. "I still have to brief the President, and he sees Gorbachev at eleven A.M."

The President looked refreshed and relaxed as I reviewed the talking points with him. They were laid out double-spaced, like a script. The pages covered SDI, arms control, regional conflicts, human rights, and economic aid. He behaved as if yesterday had never happened. My own mood was determinedly upbeat. Things always look better in the morning. Perpetual optimism is a force multiplier, even for Presidents.

"Good stuff. I've got it, I've got it," the President said, nodding as we went over the talking points.

He was sitting in an armchair next to an end table. I opened the drawer to the table and slipped the three pages into it. "After we have the official opening ceremonies," I went on, "we'll be coming back here to the Oval Office." Gorbachev's aide (a sinister-looking KGB official whom Griscom had dubbed "Dracula") would open his briefcase and hand Gorbachev a steno pad with the handwritten notes. "That's when you casually take your talking points out of this drawer," I told the President. "Just make sure, sir, that you speak first."

Later that morning, the President greeted Gorbachev on his arrival at the White House, and the two men and their staffs then went to the Oval Office. We had the photographers in for a photo op, then settled down to business. Gorbachev already had his steno pad in hand. I looked to the President, who was drawing his notes from the end table. He began talking naturally and persuasively. He noted that yesterday had been a proud day. As the general secretary himself had said, however, the two of them still had much to do. He was encouraged by the Soviets' willingness to limit ballistic missiles to between 4,800 and 5,100 warheads. Offensive missiles had kept the peace for over forty years, but our peoples deserved better. That was the purpose of SDI. It would improve world stability by removing any incentive to strike first in a crisis.

The scene was playing perfectly, with the President setting the course we wanted the discussion to take. All the while, I eyed Gorbachev and again recognized what a quick study the man was. He knew in an instant what we had done to reverse yesterday's direction. When the President finished, Gorbachev started talking, flipping through his pad. He soon abandoned it and was giving a fact-filled presentation out of his head, displaying total command of his material. He stated his still strong objections to SDI. Contrary to distortions in the U.S. press, Gorbachev said, the Soviet Union was not developing its own SDI. But if the United States wanted to proceed down that path, that was our business. The Soviet Union, however, would have a response. But his main thrust remained positive, to continue the search for agreements to reduce nuclear arsenals.

The talk went on for over an hour and a half. Shultz, Carlucci, and I occasionally had to backstop the President on details. Though Gorbachev was clearly superior in mastery of the issues, there was not a trace of condescension in his manner, none of this business of Vienna in 1962, when Nikita Khrushchev had bullied a young, inexperienced President, John F. Kennedy. Gorbachev's attitude was more like Margaret Thatcher's. The British PM also stood heads above Ronald Reagan in absorbing and articulating complex issues. But both she and Gorbachev recognized in Reagan the qualities that had won over Americans in two presidential elections. The man was not only President, but in many ways the embodiment of his people's down-to-earth character, practicality, and optimism. Wise fellow heads of state recognized this fact; more cynical leaders did not. And Mikhail Gorbachev was nobody's fool.

. . .

The morning of December 10 was dreary and drizzly, as crowds gathered on the White House south lawn for Gorbachev's departure. Gorbachev, however, was as sunny as a politician who has just won a primary, which, in a sense, he had. Gorbachev had stopped his motorcade on 16th Street, on the way from the Soviet embassy to the White House, and started working the crowd, with great success, establishing, as we later learned, that he was more popular outside than inside the Soviet Union. We still, however, had one big, dangling detail to settle—the Soviets wanted a ceiling of 5,100 ballistic missiles, and we wanted 4,800. We had to resolve this difference before we could move from the INF treaty to a START treaty to limit strategic long-range nuclear systems, the weapons designed to be lobbed over the ocean at each other's cities.

We were huddled with the Soviets in the Cabinet Room arguing over the allowable number of ballistic missiles, while the Reagans and Gorbachevs were waiting for us to finish so that they could begin the departure ceremony on the rain-soaked south lawn. Finally, Carlucci suggested to Akhromeyev that we split the difference on the missiles at 4,900. Our team went to the President, who accepted the recommendation after Shultz and I assured him it was a good deal. I experienced the same sensation Carlucci had expressed earlier. Ronald Reagan trusted his people. He was going to take your advice, so you had better be right. The President once signed a photograph of me briefing him one day in the Oval

Office with the inscription "If you say so, Colin, it must be right," indicating a level of trust that could be a little frightening.

Gorbachev also agreed to the compromise limit, and on that rainy Washington afternoon, the world continued to become a safer place.

In January 1988, we entered the last year of the Reagan administration. It began on an interesting note for someone like me who had come out of the wings and onto the national stage barely one month before. I received copies of an exchange of notes between Senator Ted Stevens of Alaska and Vice President Bush. Just after Christmas, Stevens had written:

> Dear George,
>   I am really impressed with Colin Powell. In my judgment, he should be on your "short list" for potential vice presidents.

A few days later, on January 5, 1988, Bush answered:

> Ted,
>   You are right about Colin Powell. A class guy in every way.

A nice compliment, but not exactly concurrence; and Bush never said anything about the matter to me.

Democracy was triumphing in Latin America that season, but not in Nicaragua under the Sandinistas or in Panama under Manuel Noriega. I had known for some time that the Nicaraguan contras were never going to march through Managua, banners and rifles raised aloft in victory. They were not strong enough. Still, they were our leverage to keep the Sandinistas at the negotiating table, a tactic that was working. The two sides had entered into initial agreements the previous August. I believed that in order to keep the pressure on, we had to continue to supply arms to the contras, not through the back door, but with Congress's approval. I was still spending some of my most frustrating days trying to sell a contra arms package. As February approached, we almost had a deal. If only the Republicans would agree to a few minor concessions, we could win the Democratic swing votes we needed. I had not reckoned, however, with the character of House Minority Whip Dick Cheney, whom I had briefed back at V Corps in Frankfurt. Cheney would not agree to any more concessions. He preferred losing on principle to winning through further compromise. Consequently, on February 3, the administration proposal went down to defeat. A month later, we had to settle for a less desirable deal to hold the contras together, just barely, with more nonlethal aid.

On February 19, I flew with Secretary of State George Shultz to Finland en route to Moscow, where we would plan the next summit meeting, to be held in the summer. By now, Shultz and I had become close. He was one of the most distinguished public officials I had met, and the more I knew him, the more impressed I became. I admired Shultz not only for his intellectual powers, but for the way he determinedly managed to put the substance into Ronald Reagan's vision. We met every morning at 7:00 A.M. in my office along with Frank Carlucci; and we three worked as a team rather than as heads of competing bureaucracies. In this administration, George Shultz was the single minister of foreign policy, and I made sure that the NSC staff understood that and backed him all the way.

On this trip, we stayed in Helsinki at the lovely Kalastajatorppa Hotel to shake off our jet lag before going on to face the Soviets. Shultz graciously gave a dinner at the hotel for our traveling party of about fifteen, where we turned out to be intensely interesting specimens to a group of Japanese tourists at the next table.

As our group started to break up, the Japanese swarmed around us with their cameras. They wanted to have their pictures taken with the famous man. Shultz and I primped ourselves a bit; but the Japanese were circling someone else. The celebrity they wanted to pose with was Charles Redman, the State Department's assistant secretary for public affairs. Redman was the one who went before TV cameras every day to brief the press. Redman was the one the Japanese recognized from their own television. We had entered an age where TV images formed perceptions, and these perceptions eclipsed reality. I was going to see this distorting phenomenon increasingly at work in our foreign policy deliberations.

. . .

When we got to Moscow, I met with a figure right out of Cold War history, Anatoly Dobrynin, Soviet ambassador to the United States in the eras of Khrushchev, Brezhnev, Andropov, and Chernenko. Dobrynin must have been made of cork. He had survived all these hard-line communist regimes and was still a senior advisor to Mikhail Gorbachev in the era of glasnost and perestroika. We had spent the day at Osobnyak, an old czarist mansion, now a guesthouse belonging to the Foreign Ministry, working with Dobrynin and Eduard Shevardnadze on the upcoming summit.

At the end of the day, Dobrynin sidled up to me and said he thought we ought to have a little chat, just the two of us. His driver took us in a Zil limousine to a massive grand hotel across the Moscow River from the Kremlin. The lobby was almost deserted, and I asked Dobrynin, "What kind of place is this?" "For the big guys," he said, in his comfortable American English. "Politburo, KGB." We took an elevator to the fourth floor, where Dobrynin led me into a private dining room. One did not ordinarily travel to the Soviet Union for the cuisine, but this meal was sumptuous. And it was served by a set of twins, briskly efficient young Russian women.

Dobrynin had a big, open, avuncular face and a disarming manner. I was on my guard. "Colin," he said, as we ate, "you must understand what's going on here. Gorbachev is the first lawyer we have had running this country since Lenin. That is a more critical point than you realize. A society run by bureaucrats issuing diktats can't function, because there is no recourse to these apparatchiks. There is no remedy for reform. Gorbachev is trying to make this a nation of laws instead of a place run by party hacks." Dobrynin went on to point out that the new leader's approach to the military was unprecedented. "He's driving the generals crazy," Dobrynin said. "Gorbachev says, 'Why do you tell me we have to have this weapon or that weapon just because the Americans have it? I'm not out to conquer the Americans. So tell me why do we need this for our own security?' " Nobody had ever questioned the military before, Dobrynin said. In the past, the military always got anything it wanted.

He asked me to try to see what Soviet imperialism looked like from their side. "You are always beating up on us about Cuba, Cuba, Cuba," he said. "Do you know who gave Cuba to us? You did. Castro was a revolutionary, not really a Marxist. He came to the United Nations. He stayed in the Hotel Theresa in Harlem. Your government ignored him, made him a pariah. So he dropped into our laps.

"You beat up on us constantly over Nicaragua," he continued. "But all we will give the Sandinistas is enough to defend themselves. Not enough to bother their neighbors. In the future, you won't see us so quick to join somebody else's revolution." Those days were ending, Dobrynin went on. No more foreign adventures that cost the Soviet Union billions of rubles and returned nothing but despotic regimes and bad relations with the United States.

What Gorbachev wanted, Dobrynin continued, was to fix the Soviet Union at home. The new regime wanted to move toward free markets. But the switch was not easy. "You take bread," Dobrynin said. "We subsidize the cost. It's so cheap that it's more economical to feed pigs bread than slop. It costs more for the plastic to wrap it in than for the bread itself. We know this is insane. We know it can't go on much longer. But you don't just cut off a bread subsidy after sixty years. Then we would really have another revolution." Gorbachev, he said, had also tried to impose higher taxes to make the country more fiscally responsible, "But then you run the risk of killing off any entrepreneurial spirit."

I knew I was listening to an old pro, a diplomat as smooth as prerevolutionary silk. Still, I did not automatically discount what Anatoly Dobrynin told me. I went back to my hotel and wrote down every word I could remember.

On March 1, President Reagan was in Brussels to meet with the other fifteen NATO heads of state. The changes shaking the Soviet Union were rattling all our old comfortable assumptions. German Chancellor Helmut Kohl, whose country was the likely battleground in any East-West war, wanted further agreements to reduce tactical nuclear weapons, like our Lance missiles with a range of sixty miles. At home, the Reagan administration was under pressure from people who wanted to know, with the Soviet threat reduced, why we were still spending almost four times as much per capita on defense as our average NATO partner.

The NATO leaders sat around a huge circular table at the Brussels headquarters with their staffs occupying satellite chairs behind them. President Reagan was to be the last of the sixteen to speak. At the end of the first day, as his turn approached, and after hearing his predecessors burbling over Gorbachev, I was not sure the notes we had prepared for Reagan were adequate. At the next break, I went to him and whispered, "Sir, your notes are really not good enough, and I apologize. I'm afraid you're going to have to wing it."

He looked at me pleasantly. No panic. "Okay," he said. He was to follow Canadian Prime Minister Brian Mulroney, who began by saying he knew a little about living next door to a superpower too. Mulroney then compared the three-thousand-mile undefended border between his country and ours to the bristling border between the Eastern bloc and the West. That armed frontier represented the past, he said. The U.S.–Canadian model must represent the future. Mulroney was eloquent, and he helped steer the day away from the Gorbamania that had dominated so far.

Finally, it was President Reagan's turn. He spoke about what we were trying to achieve with the Soviet Union. He covered our goals and expectations simply and convincingly. He spoke without notes, and his words obviously moved the other heads of state. Ronald Reagan was a more complex man than the one-dimensional figure his critics tried to paint. On this day, he again showed his grasp of the historic changes taking place in our relations with the Soviets; and he conveyed his beliefs in homey, uniquely Reaganesque terms. He was confident and comfortable in his own skin, more than anyone I have ever known.

. . .

As we were coming out of the NATO session, Chris
Wallace, of NBC News, asked to interview me. "I'd
like to get some background off-camera first, if you
don't mind," Wallace said. I agreed and briefed him
for a good fifteen minutes. "Let's go on camera now,"
he said, which we did for a twelve-minute taped
interview. During that time, I told him that the talks
were going fine, although some disagreement was
inevitable when so many leaders met. After the interview, he asked me follow-up questions, off-camera,
for another ten minutes. Altogether I had talked to
Wallace for well over half an hour, and I was happy
to get back to my room to grab a little rest.

I must have dozed off when I was jolted awake
by the phone. It was someone from the press office
back in the White House wanting to know if I realized what I had done. I did not know what the caller
was talking about. I was informed that I had disagreed publicly with the President and had shot him
down on network television.

I immediately went to Marlin Fitzwater's press
center and had the staff bring up the taped *NBC
Nightly News* on a monitor. Wallace and his crew had
caught the President coming out of the meeting, and
Chris had asked him if there had been any disagreement among the NATO partners over the continuing
Soviet threat. The President had said he had never
seen such harmony. Wallace asked the President if
they had disagreed about anything? "No," Reagan
said, as the camera cut away from him and back to
Wallace. "But even some of his own advisors dis-

agreed about that," Wallace continued. And there I was on camera saying, "Where you have sixteen nations, all each sovereign, certainly there will be differences and there will be heated debate and discussion from time to time." These were the seven seconds plucked from over a half hour of substance I had given the guy.

Shortly afterward, I ran into Wallace and told him, "Chris, that was a cheap shot."

He remained unfazed. "I needed an angle," he said. "And if that's the worst that ever happens to you, you're lucky."

By now, I was well aware that this jungle had tigers. Back in Washington, I briefed the press on Panama on April 5, my fifty-first birthday. I was asked about a leaked account that we might consider kidnapping Manuel Noriega. And I replied with one of my new rules for handling the media: "I don't discuss options." As the conference neared an end and I was about to get off with my skin still intact, I suddenly felt someone's teeth sink in. The Reverend Jesse Jackson had recently delivered his advice on Panama, and a reporter asked me, "Is it proper for Jesse Jackson to involve himself in foreign affairs?" I instantly understood the game. This reporter was saying, "Won't you please take a shot at Jesse so we can get the brothers arguing and make some news?"

"I am an admirer of the Reverend Jesse Jackson," I said, "and I appreciate his, as well as anyone's, opinions." Translation: "You ain't gonna get me and Jesse bashing each other for your entertainment."

More lessons in the care and feeding of the media. You do not have to answer every question put to you. They get to pick the questions. But you get to pick the answers. And I learned the hard way from the Chris Wallace encounter to aim beyond the audience of one who is asking the question. Shape your answer, instead, to the audience of millions who will be watching you on the tube.

Sometimes breaking starch for appearance's sake reaches global levels. The Kuwaitis wanted us to sell them Maverick air-to-ground missiles and F/A-18 aircraft from which they could be launched. AIPAC, the American Israeli Political Action Committee, the major lobby of the American Jewish community, had beaten back a sale of Maverick missiles to Saudi Arabia about a year before. AIPAC also officially opposed the sale of the planes to the Kuwaitis. I sensed, however, that AIPAC was not looking for another knock-down-drag-out fight with the Reagan administration. "It's not the plane we object to so much," an AIPAC official confided to me, "but the Maverick missiles they carry." There were two types, he knew, a smaller D model and a bigger G model. The Saudi sale that AIPAC had successfully blocked involved D-model Mavericks. "We have to be consistent," the AIPAC official said. "We opposed the Saudis on the D model. So we have to oppose the Kuwaitis on the same basis."

I listened, puzzled. "You realize the G can do all the damage the D can do, plus a hell of a lot more, don't you?" I said. "Yet you won't oppose the sale of F/A-18s if they carry the bigger G model?"

"We need to be consistent," he repeated.

The Kuwaiti crown prince, Saad Al Abdullah Al-Salim Al-Sabah, was in town to try to close the sale. I went to the prince's hotel suite to join Rich Armitage and Robert Oakley of my National Security Council staff, who were explaining to his highness the problem with the sale. I described to the prince the difference between the D and G Mavericks. We could not sell him F/A-18s with the smaller D-type, but I thought we could sell the plane with the more destructive G-type, I pointed out. The prince asked me to repeat. I did, as he and his advisors looked at each other as if to say, "And they call us mysterious." He asked if they might withdraw for a private consultation.

When the Kuwaitis came back, the prince said, yes, they would be willing to buy the F/A-18s and the G-model Mavericks with the bigger bang, if I would write out and sign this arrangement. I figured they feared that nobody would believe the deal otherwise. I agreed.

Everyone was happy. AIPAC had blocked the sale of D-model Mavericks to the Kuwaitis, just as it had to the Saudis, thus saving face. The Kuwaitis got a mystifying windfall. And the aircraft and missile manufacturers had a big sale. The moral? It can probably be found somewhere in *Alice in Wonderland*.

While the President had the final cut on all speeches, I had initial White House approval on those touching on national security. The draft before us this day, to be delivered on April 21 to the World Affairs Council of

Western Massachusetts in Springfield, had been shep-
herded by Tony Dolan, chief of the hard-line speech-
writers and a master of the Reagan voice. Ronald
Reagan wanted to continue moving away from confrontation and toward cooperation with the Soviet
Union. But behaving like a pushover is not a good
bargaining tactic. Dolan therefore wanted some bite
in this speech. Furthermore, the President was a conservative, and the country was going into an election
year. Reagan would not be running himself, but the
administration was determined to hold on to its conservative base and hand it to the next Republican candidate. The speech, consequently, had been written as
an old-fashioned West-versus-East stem-winder to
anchor the Republican right wing before the Moscow
Summit. I was a shade apprehensive about the diplomacy of it, but from a hard-nosed political standpoint,
I reckoned the strategy made sense.

On April 22, the day after the President delivered the speech, I was with George Shultz in the
Kremlin, in the Hall of St. Catherine, a magnificent
czarist chamber with high ceilings, ornate yellow-
and-white walls, and massive crystal chandeliers
shimmering above. Across the table from us sat
Mikhail Gorbachev, face grim, voice tight, hand
chopping the air, condemning the tough speech President Reagan had given in Springfield twenty-four
hours before. "I have to believe," he said, "that there
is backward movement and an attempt to preach to
us." Otherwise, how to explain Reagan's old-style
Soviet-bashing? "Is this summit going to be a cat-
fight?" he asked.

I noticed how Gorbachev had prepared himself for his attack. He did not have his steno pad today. In front of him was an empty file folder on which he had written all across the front, the back, and the inside, starting out horizontally and ending up scribbling diagonally down into the corners. I could picture the scene the night before: "Comrade Chairman, here are your briefing papers for tomorrow." Short pause while Gorbachev leafs through them and throws them aside. "This rubbish has been overrun by events. I'll do it myself."

During our meeting, the Soviet leader pointed out that Richard Nixon had recently criticized the INF treaty. "Nixon has taken a break from the labor of writing his memoirs to take part in political debates," Gorbachev noted sarcastically. "The dead should not be allowed to take the living by the coattails and drag them back to the past." We should resist people "who want to put sticks in the spokes of Soviet-American normalization." What was he to make of this renewed belligerency? Was this a return to the old politics, or was President Reagan simply playing to the American right? Very perceptive, Mikhail, I thought.

The dressing-down went on for a full forty-five minutes, including the translation. In the beginning, I had worried about the price we had paid for the Springfield speech. But I began to sense that Gorbachev too was playing to his own constituencies represented by the Soviets around the table. He could not let his nation be pummeled without appearing to strike back.

George Shultz had been out of town while the Springfield speech was being cleared. He had never seen it, and he was a little stunned by Gorbachev's harangue. Shultz, however, wisely ignored the browbeating and when Gorbachev stopped at last, proceeded calmly to the agenda. Gorbachev's tone changed. The Russian began describing his objectives under perestroika and glasnost. He was going to reform this lumbering giant of a nation. He was going to make the Soviet Union efficient. He was going to make it responsive to market forces. He was going to change the Communist Party. He was going to change the USSR in ways we never imagined. He was saying, in effect, that he was ending the Cold War. The battle between their ideology and ours was over, and they had lost. He looked directly at me, knowing I was a military man, and said with a twinkling eye, "What are you going to do now that you've lost your best enemy?"

That night, back in my hotel room, I thought over this extraordinary day, and I felt a conviction deep in my bones. This changed Soviet line was no ruse to disarm us. This man meant what he said. Lying there in bed, I realized that one phase of my life had ended, and another was about to begin. Up until now, as a soldier, my mission had been to confront, contain, and, if necessary, combat communism. Now, I had to think about a world without a Cold War. All the old verities we had lived by were now as misleading as an out-of-date timetable.

After Moscow, George Shultz went with Eduard Shevardnadze for a visit to the Republic of Georgia, and I headed home, with a stop en route in London to update Prime Minister Thatcher. Again I was ushered into her sitting room, where we talked for almost an hour. As I was getting ready to leave, I mentioned one last Gorbachev line. "He told us, Madame Prime Minister," I said, " 'I am going to do as much as I can for as long as I can. I will make it irreversible. And then someone else will come and replace me when I've worn myself out.' "

"Oh, dear boy," she said, with a dismissing wave, "don't believe everything you hear. Why, even I say things like that from time to time."

Back home, the intelligence and policy communities were having a hard time coping with the changes in the Soviet Union. CIA Soviet specialists told me about an upcoming meeting of the Communist Party Central Committee at which, this time for sure, the hard-liners would hand Gorbachev his head. The meeting was held, and afterward Gorbachev fired a dozen or so generals and hard-liners. I felt sympathy for our Kremlinologists. The world they had studied and had known so well for forty years was losing its structure and rules. With all their expertise, they could no longer anticipate events much better than a layman watching television.

I had seen what was happening up close and began to pay less and less attention to the experts. George Shultz also started to ignore CIA Soviet assessments. The evidence was increasing that Gorbachev was dead serious about wanting to end the economic burden of the arms race, dump Soviet puppet states onto Western bankers, and get out of the wars-of-liberation business. Our professionals were reluctant to predict a future bearing no resemblance to the past. They thought Gorbachev would fail, and he did. They did not think he would fail from the left for not being revolutionary enough, but instead from the right for abandoning the Soviet dream, now turned nightmare. Our foreign policy and intelligence community was losing its archenemy; as the old joke goes, "What will all the preachers do when the devil has been saved?"

On May 6, the student of yesteryear who preferred drilling in the field house to sitting in his college classes was on the dais at Clemson University in Clemson, South Carolina, about to be awarded an honorary doctorate. Jim Bostic, my White House Fellowship classmate and virtual younger brother, was now a successful executive with the Georgia-Pacific Corporation. Jim had also become one of Clemson's alumni jewels, and had nominated me for the degree. Nine days later, I was at William and Mary to give the commencement address and receive another honorary Ph.D. I told my audience that this was my frequent-flier payoff for all the checks I had sent and would continue to send to the college. Mike had been class of '85, Linda class of '87, and Annemarie was entering William and Mary that fall. Next, I was invited to be commencement speaker at her graduation from Washington and Lee High School in Arlington, Virginia. Around this time, I phoned my Aunt Nessa Llewellyn. She had seen me on TV, she said, advising the President, getting those fancy degrees. "Lord," she said, "how all these pickaninnies done well!"

. . .

On a hectic afternoon in May, one of my aides poked his head in my doorway and said, "Charlie Wick's people want to know which elevator he goes up, does he turn right or left when he gets out, where will the light switch be when he goes into his room?" Along with preparing the substantive issues, we were handling the logistics headaches of the upcoming Moscow Summit. Charles Z. Wick, a close Reagan California friend, was now director of the U.S. Information Agency; and while my staff was swamped trying to make arrangements for over eight hundred people to go to Moscow, Charlie's staff seemed to take up 40 percent of our time.

I called Wick and said, "Charlie, if you want to go to Moscow, your guys had better not make another phone call to this office." Charlie immediately called off his auxiliaries. This is what goes on behind the drama of summit headlines.

Ronald Reagan was always looking for the homey touch, some way to break through suffocating protocol to camaraderie. He wanted to call Gorbachev by his first name. "You know," the President said, "when I first met the Western leaders at the economic summit, I said, 'My name's Ron.' And in a few hours it was 'Ron' and 'Brian,' and 'François' and 'Margaret.' "

We batted this cosmic issue back and forth between the White House and the State Department. George Shultz said he thought that using first names was a good idea. Rozanne Ridgway, his assistant secretary of state for European affairs, disagreed. It was too early, Roz argued. Don't force the intimacy. I sided with Roz. Glasnost or not, we were still dealing with a tough customer. Besides, it struck me as unseemly. Gorbachev was young enough to be Reagan's son, and I was sure he would be uncomfortable calling the President of the United States "Ron." As it turned out, during the summit, when Reagan did hazard "Mikhail" a couple of times, Gorbachev always came back with "Mr. President."

We were going to Moscow with high hopes. On May 15, the Soviets had started to pull their troops out of Afghanistan. And during this summit, we expected to complete the nuclear arms reduction breakthrough. Reagan and Gorbachev had already signed the INF treaty. In the meantime, it had been approved by the Supreme Soviet Presidium, but still had to be ratified by the U.S. Senate. We expected approval, but not without a fight from conservatives, Republican and Democrat. The treaty was bitter for these people to swallow because we would have to give up some weapons and because a residue of distrust of the Soviet Union persisted. I became part of the administration's sales staff, trying to promote the treaty to Senate hard-liners and fence-sitters.

On May 28, the day before our arrival in Moscow, while the presidential party was sloughing off jetlag in Finland, we got word that the Senate had ratified the treaty.

The next day, as Air Force One began to descend on Moscow, I made my way to the President's private cabin. He had about thirty speaking occasions scheduled during this summit, and I wanted to go over the talking points for events on his immediate arrival. This was my last chance to catch him before he left the plane. I entered the cabin to find him sitting alone, looking out the window as we descended low enough to make out houses and farms on the Russian landscape.

"Look, there's almost no traffic," he said, barely acknowledging my presence.

"Mr. President, I wondered if you have any questions about your cards for the arrival statements," I said, sitting down next to him. I started going over the cards, but he was not listening to me. By now, the flaps were dropping, the wheels were coming down for the landing, and I was getting panicky, especially when the President finally turned to me and said, "What were you saying?"

He was not concerned about my anxieties. He was finally seeing the "evil empire." During the previous summit, he had wanted to fly Gorbachev across America so that he could show him our bustling highways and the factories pouring out consumer goods. To Ronald Reagan, the almost empty Russian roads symbolized the failure of communism. They reinforced his conviction that he had to help Gorbachev turn Soviet society in our direction.

Once we got on the ground and he stepped before the cameras and microphones, he was, as usual, letter-perfect.

During the first one-on-one meeting between Reagan and Gorbachev, the Soviet leader handed the President a draft statement. He suggested they include it when the time came to issue the final communiqué. Reagan read it and liked it. The language seemed unobjectionable: ". . . the two leaders believe that no problem in dispute can be resolved, nor should be resolved, by military force." And "Equality of all states, noninterference in internal affairs and freedom of sociopolitical choice must be recognized as the inalienable and mandatory standards of international relations." The President asked the staff to consider Gorbachev's proposed language.

I, as a relative newcomer, saw nothing particularly dangerous in the statement. But the old Soviet hands in our delegation went through it like a bomb disposal unit defusing a booby trap. George Shultz and Roz Ridgway urged the President to say no. The statement was code language giving our unintended blessing to the Soviets to hold on to the Baltics— Lithuania, Latvia, and Estonia—which we still did not concede as belonging to the Soviet Union. Underneath the appealing phrases, the statement said, essentially, what is yours is yours and what is ours is ours, and let's stay off each other's turf.

The matter had been set aside while we turned to other issues and memorable summit spectacles: Ronald Reagan at Spaso House, the American ambassador's residence, listening to Russian dissidents courageous enough to come here and describe the oppressions they had suffered; the American President talking to students at Moscow University under a gigantic bust of Lenin; the President who had labeled the Soviet Union the "focus of evil in the modern world" standing shoulder-to-shoulder in Red Square with Mikhail Gorbachev.

Then, during the last working session in St. Catherine's Hall, Gorbachev again shoved the suspect statement across the table to the President and urged him to accept it. The session was to end in minutes. Next door, in St. Vladimir's Hall, a crowd had gathered and the media were setting up for coverage of the signing and the exchange between the two leaders of the INF treaty instruments of ratification.

Gorbachev pointed out to Reagan that this was the same language he had suggested when they met the first day. The President had liked it then, so why not sign now? The pitch was high, hard, right past the staff, and aimed at the President's head. Reagan looked uncomfortable, which he was in improvised situations. Gorbachev suggested he talk the matter over with his advisors one last time.

The Russians went to their corner and we went to ours like seconds in a heavyweight match. What was so bad about this innocuous statement? the President asked. He and Gorbachev were getting along so well. Weren't we here to promote peaceful relations? We repeated the arguments against, which the President accepted with a disappointed shrug, as we rejoined the Soviet group, where Gorbachev stood waiting and smiling. Reagan told Gorbachev that he did not have the support of his advisors. Gorbachev turned to us, the smile vanishing. What was the problem? Shultz explained our position. None of these objections made any sense, Gorbachev shot back, practically boring a hole through Reagan with his stare.

Until this moment, I had seen myself largely as an administrator, the guy who made the NSC trains run. I was not Henry Kissinger or Zbigniew Brzezinski, with their Ph.D.s and international relations backgrounds. But I did not like the inconclusive, teetering nature of this last-minute debate. The matter called for closure. Looking at Gorbachev, I said that this was not an issue to be resolved on the spur of the moment. He had his political problems at home, and we had ours. Our mutual interests would not be served if the President took back something that could divide his supporters at home. I spoke evenly and coolly, deliberately intending to cut off further discussion. Our advice to President Reagan was that he should not agree to this statement, I said.

Everyone was silent. Gorbachev looked around the circle. If this was what the President's generals think, so be it, he said. With that, he led Reagan out of the room, saying, "Come, people are waiting for us." They headed toward the lights and cameras in St. Vladimir's Hall, where they signed the ratifying documents.

The previous December, in Washington, the two leaders had agreed on the INF treaty. Now, both their nations had agreed. The destruction of intermediate-range weapons could now begin, 1,500 on their side and 350 on ours—not so many, perhaps, given the total size of the arsenals, but a momentous beginning.

The mood aboard Air Force One was jubilant exhaustion as we flew out of Moscow. We had worked like dogs, and the President had made history. Someone had discovered that today was the birthday of Jim McKinney, who ran the White House Military Office and who had performed logistics miracles on the trip. The plane's stewards somehow managed to produce a birthday cake to celebrate the event. I went forward to the private compartment and asked the President and First Lady to join us. We all gathered around and sang "Happy Birthday" to Jim. Several people seized the occasion to congratulate the President on his Moscow triumph. The plane was filled with White House aides whose sweat behind the scenes had made his victory possible. The moment cried out for the President to thank them and to say, "I couldn't have done it without you." But he simply acknowledged the praises and said nothing more. Nor did Mrs. Reagan thank us.

By now I had come to know Nancy Reagan quite well. I knew that her love of Ronald Reagan and her devotion to him were total. She protected his well-being and his presidency. She comforted him and brought him joy. If she went away for a few days, we could see the President get out of sorts as he pined for her. Ronald Reagan was incomplete without his Nancy and she without him. She could be difficult, as she watched out for her man. She could be tough with people when the President could not. She was criticized and feared to some extent, but her role was vital. By the end of his administration she and I would become friends, a friendship that has grown with the years.

But that day, on the plane, I was surprised that neither the President nor the First Lady expressed gratitude for what their staff had done for them. I finally concluded that their silence did not indicate ingratitude. It just did not come spontaneously. A few days after we returned, when it was suggested to him, the President sent us all thank-you notes and commemorative gifts.

· · ·

One weekend in July, my son, Mike, came to my office with a surprise. He was going to marry a young woman named Jane Knott, whom Alma and I knew and liked very much. Nevertheless, our reaction was mixed. On the one hand, this development marked Mike's continuing recovery after, by now, fourteen surgical procedures to reconstruct his pelvis and repair internal injuries. He had moved from wheelchair to crutches to cane. Most promising, Mike had gone to work in the Pentagon as a specialist in Japanese affairs. Nevertheless, the idea of an interracial marriage made Alma and me uneasy, despite the happy nearly forty-year marriage of my sister, Marilyn, to Norm Berns. I stress the word "uneasy"—we were not actually opposed. The older generation knows what the younger generation may still have to learn. Making a marriage work is tough enough even under ideal conditions. You do not need to make it tougher.

Mike had first dated Jane, a Navy captain's daughter, years before, while they were students at William and Mary. They broke up after a time, and, I suppose, both families felt relieved. But after Mike's accident, the courtship revived. The sensible next move was for the families to get to know each other. Alma and I invited the Knotts over to our place at Fort Myer for dinner. The atmosphere was stiff at first, until we started rediscovering an old universal truth: people are individuals first, not racial stick figures. When you come into personal contact with people, you are going to like them or not, respect them or not, depending on what they are, not what their pigmentation is. And by the end of the evening, the Powells and Knotts were getting along fine.

That summer, the Army and the Navy were in a battle royal. U.S. military forces are divided into ten major commands led by CINCs (standing for "commander in chief" and pronounced "sink"), all four-star officers. One such commander, the CINC for CENTCOM, was about to retire. CENTCOM, Central Command, covered parts of the Middle East and Southwest Asia. The Persian Gulf nations, however, did not want American bases on their soil; consequently, CENTCOM was headquartered at MacDill Air Force Base in Florida, served by a staff of seven hundred and able to call on U.S. units all over the world.

Choosing the right CINC for CENTCOM was critical. If you had to put your finger on the hottest part of the globe, it would likely come down in CENTCOM's domain. So far, the job had alternated between Army and Marine officers. Since the present commander, Marine General George Crist, was about to wrap up his tour, the Army expected its turn next. The Navy, however, since it now had forces in the Gulf escorting reflagged Kuwaiti tankers, thought it was high time a Navy admiral got CENTCOM. The Joint Chiefs of Staff were split down the middle. The Army and Air Force wanted an Army man, and the Navy and the Marines wanted an admiral. The chairman, Admiral Crowe, broke the tie, three to two, voting for the Navy man. The decision was now in the hands of the Secretary of Defense, Frank Carlucci.

The Army's candidate was Lieutenant General H. Norman Schwarzkopf, fifty-five, a burly, brilliant, volatile, six-foot-three bear of a man whom I had first come to know a few years before as a Fort Myer neighbor. We had never served together and were not close, but I knew his reputation as a superb troop leader. I was also aware of both the brilliance and the explosiveness that produced the apt nickname, "Stormin' Norman." As National Security Advisor, I was not formally in the personnel assignment loop; yet I had strong opinions about who should get CENTCOM, especially after long talks with my Pentagon confidant Rich Armitage. We agreed that having the Navy run military forces in a region where navies were few, weak, and insignificant made little sense. More important, CENTCOM had been designed as a rapid deployment task force to fight land battles in the desert region. The job clearly belonged to a soldier or Marine, not a sailor. And we had confidence in Schwarzkopf. I made my strong preference known to Carlucci. Frank himself was not keen on having an admiral at CENTCOM and overruled the JCS recommendation. And that is how Norm Schwarzkopf came to obtain the command that would propel him into history.

On August 16, while I was on the road, my secretary, Florence Gantt, showed me a message from one of my NSC Latin American experts back in Washington, Jacqueline Tillman. "Please tell *mi general*," it read, "that his ever alert, sharp-eyed staff immediately noticed he was nowhere to be seen when the President boarded Air Force One out of New Orleans. . . . Naturally, wild rumors are sweeping the halls of the third floor of the OEOB."

I was in New Orleans at the time with the President, who had gone there to make his final speech as party leader to the Republican National Convention before turning over the reins to the 1988 presidential nominee, Vice President George Bush. This was my first convention, and I thoroughly enjoyed the combination of circus and democracy. I also had a tiny bit part.

The previous December, Senator Ted Stevens had sent the note suggesting me to George Bush as his possible running mate. That, however, was a private communication. Earlier in the year, Howard Baker had found himself on a television show being questioned about a lack of racial diversity in the Republican Party. By contrast, the Democrats had Jesse Jackson emerging from their ranks as a national political figure. Baker, political to his fingertips, saw an opening when he was asked about Republican vice presidential prospects. He threw my name into the pot. When I saw him later, I said, "Howard, why did you do that?" He answered with that oh-shucks Tennessee drawl, "I just thought it was a good idea." Baker's mention stirred several pundits, including George Will, Charles Krauthammer, William Raspberry, and Clarence Page, to write about me as a VP prospect. On the political Richter scale, this attention ranked below a boomlet. Still, at the convention, some of my friends had a little fun with the idea. I was sitting in the stands when I heard people laughing and smiling around me. I turned to see some White House pals holding up a sign proclaiming, "Bush/Powell '88."

After President Reagan's convention speech, the staff had gone out to the airport to fly to California, where the President planned a brief vacation. TV cameras filmed the entourage as it reboarded Air Force One. It was then, when my Washington staff failed to see me board, that Jackie Tillman had sent her message. Where was Colin? Amid all the speculation about George Bush's running mate, the staff began wondering, is he staying behind with Bush in New Orleans? Could it be? The answer was far less exciting. I had boarded the plane by the rear door.

On the airport tarmac, just before we took off, Bush had revealed his choice of running mate to Ronald Reagan: Senator Dan Quayle of Indiana. At the time, the choice of me, or a dozen other long shots, could not have been any more surprising. My fifteen minutes in the national political spotlight was fun; it was flattering. It also embarrassed me a little. And Vice President Bush certainly never said anything to me on the subject.

I got a call from the President's secretary, Kathy Osborne, late one afternoon that spring of 1988. "General Powell, I've got a man on the line," she said. "I know he's an old friend of the President, but I think you should talk to him first. He says he's been in touch with Mr. Ghorbanifar about releasing hostages."

God help us. Here was one of our recurring headaches. We had two rules around the White House: we did not negotiate with terrorists, and we did not talk to the President about every harebrained idea that came down the pike for freeing the hostages. And here was an old California pal who wanted to talk to him about one of the charter phonies in the arms-for-hostages scam, a man with three dates of birth, three passports, and six aliases, a former source dropped by the CIA as an "intelligence fabricator and a nuisance," a man who flunked every CIA lie detector test he ever took and who got only his name and nationality right on one of them, and a man who had almost destroyed Ronald Reagan's presidency two years before. I thanked Kathy for alerting me and told her that, yes, I would take care of the gentleman.

I could not get rid of him. From then on, this businessman was forever on the phone telling me excitedly of Ghorbanifar's latest strategy. He knew Ghorbanifar was on the level, he said, because he had been a guest in the man's Paris penthouse. He once reported that Ghorbanifar had paid half a million dollars of his own money to get the hostages released. We should be working with him, the President's friend advised.

I started out reasonably, explaining to the old Californian why he should not deal with Manucher Ghorbanifar, and why he must not bother the President on this matter. The friend, however, could not resist this opportunity for adventure. The calls kept coming all summer and into the fall. Finally, in October, I asked him if he might be coming to the Washington area soon; I needed to talk to him. He was on the next plane. We arranged to meet in the lobby of the Watergate Hotel on a Sunday morning. I took Barry Kelly with me, a CIA official who was my intelligence director on the NSC. We met a dapper, elderly man and escorted him to a remote corner.

"Sir, you are playing a dangerous game," I said. "You are dealing with one of the world's leading sleazebags." I let Kelly read him the rap sheet on Ghorbanifar. Then I said, "You aren't going to free any hostages. You are only going to harm your friend, Ronald Reagan." I stuck my finger under his nose. "When I leave here, I am going back to the White House, and I am going to instruct the telephone operators to disconnect you if you ever call again. You are forcing me to turn you into a nonperson. Don't make me do it."

It apparently worked. We heard no more from him.

Mike Powell and Jane Knott were married on October 1. I kidded my son about postponing his honeymoon so that he could accept a speaking invitation. Strange priorities for a red-blooded American youth, I said. The speech, however, meant a great deal to Mike. Frank Carlucci had asked him to speak at a ceremony honoring handicapped employees at the Department of Defense, where Mike was now working. Alma and I went to the Pentagon auditorium with our new daughter-in-law and Dick and Eleanor Knott, her parents. We had no idea what Mike intended to say. We watched him, supported by his cane, make his way slowly to the rostrum.

He began to speak in a clear, firm voice. He likened the struggle of the handicapped to combat. He described his feelings in the hospital as the painkillers were reduced and the stream of visitors, cards, and flowers began to dwindle. He spoke of the day when two rehabilitation therapists told him, bluntly, that the easy part, being sick, was over, and the hard part, making his broken body work again, was about to begin. The next morning, he said, "I looked in the mirror. My hair was a mess, dried out by medication. I had lost a great deal of weight. My face was colorless and unshaven. I stood supported by my crutches with a catheter coming out of my stomach. I stood trembling, and I began to cry, uncontrollably. I was at the lowest point of my entire life. This war was real, and I was losing." Mike went on to describe how he went from rock bottom that day to fight back to his present renewal of hope, the war that every handicapped person has to fight, and little different from the struggle of a soldier wounded in battle. "The power of human will is amazing," he concluded. "It lifted me from a bed; it stood me up from a wheelchair; it handed me a cane; and it has allowed me to walk through life again."

Tears were streaming down my face. I glanced at Alma and Jane, who smiled. We did not have to exchange a word. The pride was in our eyes.

That fall, the heavy lifting in the White House appeared nearly over. The spotlight had swung to

George Bush and his campaign for the presidency against the Democratic nominee, Governor Michael Dukakis of Massachusetts. Since his first hearty greeting on my arrival in the White House nearly two years before, I had come to know Bush well. I had studied his behavior in Oval Office meetings with the President, where he said little, preferring to give his advice to the President privately.

During one of my early days as deputy, I had met his wife, Barbara. I had gone to a luncheon given for the visiting French minister of defense at the French embassy and found myself seated next to her. "Mrs. Bush," I said, "how are you today?"

"Fine," she answered, "and call me Barbara."

"My mother would never have allowed me to do that," I said.

"I'm not your mother," she told me. "Call me Barbara." She spoke with warmth, but with an unmistakable firmness. And from that moment on, Barbara and I began a close friendship.

It was not until I had worked with George Bush for nearly a year and a half that I saw a different man from the unobtrusive figure in Oval Office meetings. It occurred over Panama. On February 4, 1988, the U.S. Justice Department had indicted Manuel Noriega, the Panamanian dictator, for drug trafficking and racketeering. The United States imposed sanctions against Panama. Thereafter, the political situation in that country continued to deteriorate. In March, Noriega put down an attempted coup. His PDF, the Panama Defense Force, started roughing up the opposition and making mass political arrests.

President Reagan accepted Frank Carlucci's advice that we send more troops to Panama, an unsubtle hint of what might happen to Noriega. Over the next several weeks in Washington, a hawks-doves debate see-sawed over how best to deal with this tinhorn tyrant. We knew one thing: Noriega was worried about the indictment. It offered us our most powerful leverage in prying him from power. Secretary of State Shultz came up with a proposal in which I concurred: if Noriega would get out of Panama, the United States would lift sanctions against his country and drop the indictment against him.

On a Sunday afternoon in May, I called the Vice President to brief him on this proposal. It was not the most wholesome deal, I admitted, but we had to keep our eye on the objective, which was to get this thug out of power, and try to bring democracy to Panama. The Vice President had no problem with this initiative, he told me.

A couple of days later, he came back from a trip turned completely around. He had been to California and had spoken to the Los Angeles police chief, Darryl Gates, who told him that dropping the indictment would be a serious mistake. Nailing Noriega was a law-and-order issue, and the Shultz deal would do a terrible disservice to thousands of police officers laying their lives on the line every day in the war against drugs.

At a meeting that weekend in the President's second-floor residence, Bush did something none of us had ever seen him do before. He argued with the President directly in front of the rest of us. The deal was bad, bad, bad, and the President should not go through with it, Bush insisted. Reagan, I must say, was unmovable. "Ummm, George, that's interesting," he said, "but I think it's a deal worth taking." And that was that. No counterargument. No raised voice. Just "No."

The next day, outside his office, with his nose about one inch from mine, and punctuating his arguments with his finger in my chest, Bush told me the Noriega proposition stank. "I have never been so sure of anything in my life, and I will do whatever I have to do to kill this deal," he promised. I had not been chewed out so professionally since my Gelnhausen days. In the end, we did offer the deal to Noriega, but it fell through. We would have to deal with him some other way. From this incident, however, I learned two things about George Bush. First, here was a far tougher man than I had seen before; and second, do not assume you are home free with Bush after the first reading.

On November 9, after the presidential election, the White House staff held a simple ceremony in the Rose Garden to welcome the victorious George Bush back from the campaign trail. Afterward, I was returning to my West Wing office, and since we were next-door neighbors, the Vice President and I walked together. "Well, Mr. Vice Pres—excuse me, Mr. Pres—Mr. President-elect. What should it be now?" I asked. Bush laughed and said he did not know.

When we got to his office, he said, "Come on in. Let's chat for a bit. I need an update on what's been happening." I gave him a quick survey of the international scene. When I finished, he said, "You're one of the few people in the White House I want to consider for the new team. I have some options I hope you'll think about. Jim Baker would like you as deputy secretary of state"—which confirmed where Baker was going. "Or you can have the CIA. Or you can stay on as National Security Advisor for a while, until you decide what you want to do."

"I'm flattered," I said, "but I'm certainly not owed anything."

"No, no," Bush said, "we want you. Take some time. Think it over."

That night I stopped by Carl Vuono's house at Fort Myer. Carl's brilliant career had culminated in his rise to the top as the four-star Army Chief of Staff. He led me to his upstairs study at Quarters 1, where I told him about my conversation with the President-elect. I added that the Army certainly did not owe me anything either and, with the NSC job coming to an end, this might be the time for me to retire. I had thirty years in, and I was getting interesting offers from the private sector. One retired military gray eminence had recently stopped by to tell me he was leaving the board of a major corporation and thought I would make a good replacement. When he told me the five-figure salary I would get just for sitting on a board, I was staggered. "Carl," I said, "I've been away for a while, but what I really want is to stay in the Army, if there's a job for me."

Carl is a no-nonsense guy and came right to the point. Forget this business about being away too long, he said. My standing with the Army college of cardinals was still good. He wanted me back, and the Army wanted me back. In fact, he said, he had a job for me, commander in chief of Forces Command, FORSCOM, responsible for all Army field forces based in the United States, almost one million troops, including National Guard and Reserve units.

When I got home, I did what I usually do when faced with a personal decision: I drew up a balance sheet. I put "Stay" on the left side and "Go" on the right side, since staying in the Army or going out were my only intentions. I did not want to go to the State Department as number two. It would be a demotion. And I did not want to be the nation's chief spook at the CIA. That was not me. And there was no point lingering at the NSC, since I knew Bush had his own man in mind, the able Brent Scowcroft. I wound up with nineteen reasons on the "Stay" side and only a few on the "Go" side, which came down to "new career, make some money." After mulling the matter over for a couple of days, I went in and told Vice President Bush that I wanted to return to the Army, a decision which he accepted graciously. Immediately afterward, at our regular morning briefing, I told President Reagan what I had decided. "FORSCOM is four stars, isn't it?" he asked. Yes, I answered, the Army's highest rank. "Good, good," he said.

The man who had done so much to shape my life, Frank Carlucci, and so much to save the Reagan-Bush presidency by rehabilitating the NSC after Iran-contra, was leaving too. After all Frank had done, I thought his departure as Secretary of Defense was not handled gracefully. He got a phone call from one of Bush's aides, who informed Frank that the President-elect's choice to replace him, former Senator John Tower, was about to be announced to the news media. My old friend Will Taft agreed to stay on at Defense, running the department during Tower's confirmation proceedings (which turned out to be protracted and unsuccessful). I was delighted when the Bush administration later rewarded Taft's talent and loyalty by naming him U.S. ambassador to NATO.

In the dying weeks of the Reagan administration, I could feel the pressure subside. I accepted engagements I ordinarily would have had to pass up. In mid-November, I was attending a dinner at the National Academy of Sciences honoring the dissident Soviet physicist and Nobel laureate Andrei Sakharov. I was about halfway into the meat course when a security man slipped me a note from George Shultz. Shultz needed to see me right away. The State Department was just across the street, and so I walked over and took the elevator to the seventh floor. George was behind his desk in his office, a small gem of Early American style. With him were Ambassador Roz Ridgway and his assistant, Charles Hill. They greeted me, and George explained the urgency of his call. He had been notified by Yuri Dubinin, the Soviet ambassador, that Gorbachev was coming back to the United States. We all gave out simultaneous weary sighs.

"He's going to address the UN, and he wants to see the President one more time," Shultz said, handing me Dubinin's communication.

I read it. "And obviously Gorbachev wants to meet the next President," I said, handing back the message. I suggested that we needed to remind Mikhail Gorbachev that in this country we had only one President at a time.

The next morning, we briefed President Reagan on Gorbachev's trip. He was willing to meet Gorbachev again, but at this late stage of the game the meeting was not to be treated as a summit.

Gorbachev was going to address the UN on December 7, approximately three weeks away. Shultz thought he had an inspiring place for the President and the Soviet leader to meet. Since Gorbachev would be in New York to address the UN, why not use the Metropolitan Museum of Art, and give this Soviet man a taste of American culture? As a native New Yorker, that did not strike me as such a hot idea. A meeting at the Metropolitan, with the motorcades and entourages of the two world leaders running around Manhattan, would practically paralyze the city. As we shopped George's idea around, the Secret Service complained that this site presented serious security headaches. The advance people claimed that the Met would create a logistics nightmare. They had a better idea—Governors Island, in New York Harbor. That site would not tie up anybody. The island was just a short hop from the UN via the East River, and security would be a cinch. Shultz still did not like the idea, but gave in to the White House stage managers.

As the planning went forward, I called Ambassador Dubinin to hammer home one point. This was not to be a meeting on substance. It was too late for anything in the Reagan administration and too early for the Bush administration. No deals. No initiatives. No eleventh-hour surprises pulled on the old leader going out or the new leader coming in. Also, on this occasion, Ronald Reagan was still President, and George Bush, though President-elect, would be there only as Vice President.

On the day of Gorbachev's UN appearance, the President's party waited on Governors Island for the boat that would bring the Soviet leader to us. We had taken over the residence of the admiral commanding the First Coast Guard District for the occasion, and while we waited, we monitored a stream of messages on Gorbachev's progress: his arrival in the UN General Assembly Hall to thunderous applause; and his speech, which impressed us. On their own, with no quid pro quo from the West, Gorbachev announced that the Soviets were going to cut their armed forces by 500,000 men.

At one point, Vice President Bush asked me to step out with him into the garden, where the foliage was now brown and withered. He had been unusually jittery ever since Gorbachev had asked for the meeting. He and Brent Scowcroft, who would soon succeed me as National Security Advisor, were concerned that Gorbachev was going to try to put one over on the new kid on the block. Bush was looking for reassurance from me that there would be no bolts from the blue today. "Mr. Vice President," I said, "I have gotten all the assurances I can from the Russians, short of putting words into Gorbachev's mouth. But he certainly knows our feelings. And the President is prepared to knock down anything they try to float on short notice."

Our lookouts reported that Gorbachev's boat had been sighted. The President's party gathered in front of the admiral's house to greet the Soviet leader, Ronald Reagan out front, his face ruddy and glowing, his hair blown by a stiff wind.

The lunch was warm and intimate. With no contentious matters on the agenda, the President was in his element. He told Gorbachev that he was leaving office with only one mission unaccomplished. He had not been able to reinstate the horse cavalry in the Army, and he loved horses. Nothing was better for the inside of a man, the President said, than the outside of a horse. Had he known the President's wishes, Gorbachev answered, he could have helped. The Soviet Union was full of horses, which started him reminiscing about his own boyhood experiences on a farm.

I was looking at my watch like a coach with a one-point lead praying for the clock to run out before any last-minute fumbles. And then George Bush spoke. He had said nothing until this moment. "We're a nation of investors," the Vice President said. "An investor wants to know what things are like today and is even more interested in the prospective situation. So, Mr. General Secretary, what assurance can we give an investor about conditions in the Soviet Union three or four or five years from now?"

Gorbachev laughed. "Mr. Vice President, even Jesus Christ could not answer that question." President Reagan smiled at the reference to the Savior. In spite of all the talk of godless communism, Reagan had told us often that he thought Gorbachev might have a religious streak, although it seemed to me that he was only using Russian idiom.

There was no doubt in my mind that this meeting, for all the goodwill between Reagan and Gorbachev, had been engineered by the Soviets to get a close-up look at the next American leader, a conviction confirmed by Gorbachev's next words. Looking straight at Bush, he said that he knew what Bush's advisors had been telling him. He knew that skeptics still thought he was playing some kind of game, trying to lull America so that the Soviet Union could take advantage of us. Mr. Bush, he said, would soon learn, however, that he had no time for games. He had enough troubles of his own at home. "In 1985," he said, "when I said there was going to be a revolution, everybody cheered. They said, yes, we needed a revolution. But by 1987, our revolution was on, and the cheering began to die down. Now in 1988, the revolution still goes on, but the cheering has stopped." He still had to continue his revolution, he said, not for our benefit, but for his country. I had watched this man over the past fourteen months, and there was no doubt in my mind that he meant what he said.

The final photo op at Governors Island had three men posing for the cameras on a small jetty with the Statue of Liberty and the New York skyline in the background, Reagan, Gorbachev, and Bush, the past, present, and future.

· · ·

I had received several presents from Gorbachev during our encounters, but the one I prized most was a
shotgun with a beautifully engraved metal breech.
Since the gun was no doubt worth more than $180, I
had to turn it in to the General Services Administration
for appraisal. I could then have first crack at buying it
back. Otherwise, it would go on the auction block.
The GSA must have had Sotheby's price the gun. I
would have been better off with a pawnshop appraisal.
Nevertheless, I wanted the weapon. I swallowed hard
and wrote out a check, hoping Alma would be none
the wiser. But in going over our checking account, she
came across the stub, and she confronted me: "Colin
Powell, twelve hundred dollars for a silly shotgun!"

My daily life in the West Wing amounted to constant
decision-making and then passing along my recommendations, issues ranging from where best to hold a
summit in New York to helping craft nuclear disarmament treaties at the summit. By now, I had developed a decision-making philosophy. Put simply, it is
to dig up all the information you can, then go with
your instincts. We all have a certain intuition, and the
older we get, the more we trust it. When I am faced
with a decision—picking somebody for a post, or
choosing a course of action—I dredge up every scrap
of knowledge I can. I call in people. I phone them. I
read whatever I can get my hands on. I use my intellect to inform my instinct. I then use my instinct to
test all this data. "Hey, instinct, does this sound
right? Does it smell right, feel right, fit right?"

However, we do not have the luxury of collecting information indefinitely. At some point, before we can have every possible fact in hand, we have to decide. The key is not to make quick decisions, but to make timely decisions. I have a timing formula, $P = 40$ to 70, in which P stands for probability of success and the numbers indicate the percentage of information acquired. I don't act if I have only enough information to give me less than a 40 percent chance of being right. And I don't wait until I have enough facts to be 100 percent sure of being right, because by then it is almost always too late. I go with my gut feeling when I have acquired information somewhere in the range of 40 to 70 percent.

January 20, 1989, a Friday morning, inauguration day. I was sitting in my little office at home at Quarters 27A, Fort Myer, since I had not been invited to the inaugural ceremonies. No reason why I should be, since I was part of the departing old guard. The phone rang. It was Ken Duberstein, who had succeeded Howard Baker as White House Chief of Staff.

"I'm coming over to pick you up," Ken said. "I think we should be with the President in his office on his last day."

I had enjoyed working with Ken and was going to miss him. In the fourteen months that he had run the White House staff, he had achieved the smoothest, most congenial operation I had seen during the Reagan years. I ran the national security shop. Tom Griscom, as the public communications chief, oversaw the speech, press, and other information activities. And Ken directed the whole show. The three of us managed to do our jobs with few collisions and a touch of fun. At one point, my staff kept pressing me to get approval for a National Security Council seal for our stationery. Duberstein did not want the NSC to be identified separately from the White House. Nevertheless, he and his staff showed up one day at my office to present a seal. It was a little stuffed seal with a bracelet dangling from its neck that read "National Security Council staff." And that ended our ego trip. Unlike some personality combinations I had known running the White House, our group proved that you could do a job without friction, even with pleasure, if you could get beyond the ego game. And Ken Duberstein deserved most of the credit for that atmosphere.

On that last day of the administration, Ken picked me up and we arrived at the White House a few minutes before 10:00 A.M. I stopped by my office first. On the day before inauguration, the White House maintenance staff had come through the West Wing taking down every picture, cleaning out every desk, emptying all the files. With everything freshly painted and scrubbed and the sofa pillows fluffed, I felt like an intruder in my own office. I did not dare sit on anything. The room was now a neutral space suspended between me and my successor, Brent Scowcroft.

I went to the Oval Office and found the President sitting behind his desk, wearing a black suit with a striped tie, as impeccable as ever. With him were Duberstein, Marlin Fitzwater, Kathy Osborne, and Jim Kuhn, the President's personal assistant. The office was strangely naked, already stripped of any personal traces of Ronald Reagan. As we chatted, the President placed his last call. It was to Bonnie Nofziger, the wife of his political consultant Lyn Nofziger; the Nofzigers' daughter, Sue Piland, was terminally ill, and the President was calling to express his concern to the family. He got off the phone, and started reminiscing about the Yellow Room, his favorite in the residential quarters of the White House. Someone suggested he carve his initials on his desk. He laughed and said he had already removed the "kickboard" as a souvenir. "I left a note for George in the desk drawer too," he said.

The President turned to me. "Oh, Colin," he said, "what should I do about this?" He pulled from his pocket the nuclear authentication code card he had carried all these years.

"Hold on to it, sir," Kuhn said. "You're still President. We'll turn it over after the swearing-in.

"Mr. President," he continued, "it's time." He let the press photographers in for the last photo op. They took several group shots of us standing behind the President, who was seated at his desk. The photographers then positioned themselves behind a sofa, cameras aimed at the door leading to the Rose Garden. "Now, Mr. President," Jim said. Action. Camera. Reagan got up and headed for the door, with that familiar athletic spring in his step. As he reached the doorway, he turned around and took one last look back. And that is the image the cameras captured and sent out to the world of the end of an era.

As the President left for the Capitol, I went back home to catch the inauguration on television. Just as the ceremony ended, I remembered that I had to call somebody at the office. I picked up my private White House line and it was already dead.

I had just completed the most crowded, momentous year of my life. I was leaving the White House with two problems nagging at me, the unsolved issue of Manuel Noriega in Panama, and the contras, still hanging by a thread, while a Marxist regime ruled in Nicaragua. Yet, I had also taken part in the historic turning point in the second half of this century, the seismic changes occurring in the Soviet Union. I had worked closely with major world figures. And I had helped shape the Reagan policies that reversed the race toward nuclear Armageddon. The best part for me had been working directly with Ronald Reagan. He may not have commanded every detail of every policy; but he had others to do that. The editor and author Michael Korda once wrote a perceptive definition: "Great leaders are almost always great simplifiers, who cut through argument, debate and doubt, to offer a solution everybody can understand. . . ." That description fit Ronald Reagan.

The man had been elected President twice by knowing what the American people wanted, and even rarer, by giving it to them. What he gave us was inspiration and pride, described best in, of all places, the *New York Times,* not ordinarily a bastion of Reagan support. In the lead editorial on the President's last day in office, the *Times* noted: ". . . he remains to the end, both amazing and comfortable." The editorial cited a key to the President's secret, sticking to his guns on a few fundamental themes—"strengthen defense and cut taxes." The piece also caught the essence of the man. "President Reagan," the *Times* noted, "has come across as something like Professor Harold Hill," from Meredith Willson's 1957 hit, *The Music Man,* about the dream merchant who comes to town and promises, "River City's gonna have her Boys' Band—as sure as the Lord made little green apples. . . ." Harold Hill, the *Times* said, made the children of River City "swell in pride in their will, unity and potential. Ronald Reagan has done that for America." The piece was entitled "Exit the Music Man." The show happens to be my favorite, and I thought the tribute was apt.

I was now leaving the service of this remarkable man, content with the job I had done, but eager to return to my first love, the uniform, the troops, the Army.

Part Four

★

THE
CHAIRMANSHIP

15 ★ One Last Command

EVERY TIME I sat down in the FORSCOM conference room at Fort McPherson, Georgia, I faced a
legendary pacifist. Shortly after I took over there as
commander in chief, I put up a framed poster of
Martin Luther King, Jr., given to me by Mrs. King,
and inscribed with Dr. King's words: "Freedom has
always been an expensive thing." I wanted the
poster there to remind me, and everyone who sat in
that room, of the leading role the Army had played
in defending freedom and advancing racial justice.
On one of my last nights in the White House, at a
reception in the East Room, a black usher had come
to me and said, "Sir, I was a private in the Army in
World War II, the old segregated Army. I never
thought I would see the day when a black general
would be in this house. I just want you to know how
proud we all are."

"I appreciate that," I said, "but you don't have it
quite right. I'm the one who's proud of what all of
you did to pave the way for the rest of us."

I once quoted Dr. King's words in a speech to
the National Association of Black Journalists to
express the idea that freedom is expensive and must
be defended. I got a cool reception and took some
editorial flak. I was probably stretching a point by
trying to connect the champion of nonviolence to the
military profession, and I never used the line again.

Since I had served in the White House during the 1988 presidential election, people in Atlanta, and elsewhere, occasionally asked how I felt about the Willie Horton television spot used against Michael Dukakis, the Democratic candidate. Horton, a black convict, had raped a woman and stabbed a man while on a weekend pass from a Massachusetts prison during the time Dukakis was the state's governor. Was the ad depicting this incident racist? Of course. Had it bothered me? Certainly. Republican strategists had made a cold political calculation: no amount of money or effort could make a dent in the Democratic hold on the black vote, so don't try. Some had gone even further—if the racial card could be played to appeal to certain constituencies, play it. The Horton ad served that purpose. It was a political cheap shot.

I nevertheless tried to keep matters in perspective. I had been given responsibility at the highest level in a Republican administration. National Security Advisors to Presidents are not chosen as tokens. The job is real, demanding, and critical. Never in the two years I worked with Ronald Reagan and George Bush did I detect the slightest trace of racial prejudice in their behavior. They led a party, however, whose principal message to black Americans seemed to be: lift yourself by your bootstraps. All did not have bootstraps; some did not have boots. I wish that Reagan and Bush had shown more sensitivity on this point. I took consolation, nevertheless, in the thought that their confidence in me represented a commitment to the American ideal of advancement by merit.

The late Whitney Young, when he was director of the National Urban League, used to commute from his suburban Westchester County home to his office in Manhattan. And as the train approached the 125th Street station in Harlem, Young would ask himself, should he get out and demonstrate, or should he continue on downtown? Young appreciated the role of the movement's hell-raisers. But he stayed on the train, concluding that what he did downtown to promote jobs for blacks in American corporations was a better use of his talents. The crusade for equal rights requires diverse roles, just as an Army needs clerks and cooks along with airborne Rangers.

On assuming command of FORSCOM, I had reached the nation's highest military rank, four stars. I had been National Security Advisor to the President. My career should serve as a model to fellow blacks, in or out of the military, in demonstrating the possibilities of American life. Equally important, I hoped then and now that my rise might cause prejudiced whites to question their prejudices, and help purge the poison of racism from their systems, so that the next qualified African-American who came along would be judged on merit alone.

I am also aware that, over the years, my career may have given some bigots a safe black to hide behind: "What, me prejudiced? I served with/over/ under Colin Powell!" I have swallowed hard over racial provocations, determined to succeed by surpassing. Had I been more militant, would I have been branded a troublemaker rather than a promotable black? One can never be sure. But I agree with Whitney Young. I admire the shock troops who marched, sat in, and demonstrated, *and* I admire the job makers who rode past 125th Street. I further admire those who serve by making an example of their lives. And I salute the countless thousands of ordinary African-Americans who, day in and day out, go to work, support their families, and are, along with Americans of all races, the backbone of this country.

As commander of FORSCOM, I now had under me a quarter of a million active duty troops and another quarter of a million reservists, and I presided over the training of almost half a million National Guard soldiers. I was constantly on the road, dropping in on these forces from Florida to Alaska. I came to know well the generals commanding every division. What I discovered far exceeded our most optimistic expectations from the Reagan-Weinberger buildup. We had a well-trained and well-equipped force in a high state of combat readiness. But to fight whom, and where? With the Cold War fast thawing, I found our commanders still fixated on a battle between us and the Soviet Union. I had been in a position to observe firsthand the cracks in the Soviet monolith. I had sat across from Mikhail Gorbachev in Moscow and Washington and on Governors Island and heard him acknowledge defeat in the Cold War. I had watched Gorbachev unilaterally chop the Soviet military by half a million men. I had seen our old enemy cooperate with us in achieving peaceful settlements in Angola and Namibia and in the war between Iran and Iraq.

Some of my fellow officers foresaw the need to change course. My mentor John Wickham had created light, fast-moving divisions for operations unrelated to the Soviet threat. Army Chief of Staff Carl Vuono was anticipating the tough transition from the fat budgets of the past to inevitable shrinking funds for the military in the future. And a few others glimpsed what was happening. But for most of the American military establishment, it was as if our principal adversary had taken a U-turn and headed home, while we were still bracing for a head-on collision. I decided to use the pulpit of FORSCOM to deliver a dose of reality. A perfect opportunity presented itself when my old boss at the Combined Arms Combat Development Activity at Fort Leavenworth, General Jack Merritt, invited me to speak at a seminar sponsored by the Association of the United States Army, the service's trade union, which Jack headed. I accepted, but warned Jack that what I had to say might not go down well with the Army leaders or defense contractors who attended these shindigs.

On May 16, at a hotel in Carlisle, Pennsylvania, near the Army War College, I stood before enough three- and four-star generals to form a galaxy and enough tycoons to arm half the world. I gave a speech entitled (with a bow to Yogi Berra) "The Future Just Ain't What It Used to Be." I pointed out that in spite of the vast changes staring us in the face, there were still those who saw Gorbachev as a Machiavellian schemer trying to trick us into letting our guard down. No, I said, the real explanation for his behavior was "Soviet domestic and foreign impotence and failure. The Soviet system is bankrupt, and Gorbachev is the trustee." I described those areas where Gorbachev's government had helped promote peace and said, "As a public and military matter, our bear is now wearing a Smokey hat and carries a shovel to put out fires. Our bear is now benign." I had intended this speech as a wake-up call, and nobody had dozed off; I could feel the tension in the room.

I had two more ideas in my prepared text that I had crossed out, restored, and crossed out again. No reporters were present that day, and if I could not speak bluntly to my colleagues now, when could I? And so, back in 1989, I predicted: "If tomorrow morning we opened NATO to new members we'd have several applications on our desk within a week—Poland, Hungary, Czechoslovakia, Yugoslavia, maybe Estonia, Latvia, Lithuania, and maybe even the Ukraine. In fact, members of the now public opposition parties in Soviet Georgia actually debated last week whether their region's future should include nonalignment or membership in NATO." My observations seemed about as likely to this audience as my predicting that we would join the Warsaw Pact. "The Soviet military machine," I went on, "is still as big, bad, and ugly as it ever was. That fact hasn't changed. But I believe it will." What did that mean for the U.S. Army? The American people would still support a strong defense. But "the kind of growth we had in the early eighties is a thing of the past. You can count on it." For the future, "we've got to spend wisely and well." We had to put a hard question to ourselves before others put it to us: "Do we need this item?" And when the answer was no, we had to say no. Our challenge, I said, was to accept that we had to retrench, yet continue to maintain "the best damned Army in the world."

I could not immediately judge the audience reaction. People stand up and cheer when they hear what they want to hear rather than what they ought to hear. But Jack Merritt said afterward, "Colin, that's powerful stuff. It belongs in *Army* magazine." The speech was reprinted in the magazine, where it was pounced on by a retired Army major general, Henry Mohr, a columnist for Heritage Features, an arm of the conservative Heritage Foundation. Mohr sent me a courteous but disbelieving letter, saying: "You may be interested to know that a planning conference in which I participated a few weeks ago on 'National Strategy for the 1990s' came to a much different conclusion than yours. The net assessment of key participants (including the personal views of a representative of the CIA) was that the Soviet Union will emerge in the early 1990s from its ongoing 'reorganization and modernization' much stronger militarily than it is today."

It was going to take more than one wake-up call by one CINC to shake up a military conditioned by forty years of Cold War.

My travels and talks around the country had another purpose that was going to pay off in the future. I was able to judge, up close, the talents of men like Norm Schwarzkopf, now running CENTCOM in nearby Tampa, Florida. My FORSCOM deputy, Lieutenant General John Yeosock, an old National War College softball teammate, doubled as commanding general of the Third Army, working out contingency war plans with Schwarzkopf. I watched tough Lieutenant General Carl Stiner drive the XVIII Airborne Corps to peak fighting trim at Fort Bragg. At Fort Lewis, Washington, I was much impressed by the commanding officer of the 9th Infantry Division, an artilleryman with a curious background. Major General John Shalikashvili had been born and raised in Warsaw. His mother was the daughter of a czarist general, and his father had left the Soviet Republic of Georgia to serve in the Polish army and later in the German army during World War II (in the Nazi Waffen SS, it was later discovered, unknown to John Shalikashvili). Shalikashvili had not come to the United States until he was sixteen and had entered the Army as a draftee. I remember concluding at the time that there was no limit to this officer's potential. As we moved away from the Cold War, I was judging teammates for hot wars much closer than I imagined.

In peacetime, when a corps, a division, or a battalion is well run, the commanding officer has, frankly, a picnic compared to the dawn-to-dusk pressures of a place like the NSC. At FORSCOM, I had good people working for me. I set out a clear command philosophy. Once again, I could lead the good life: home by 5:30 P.M.; racquetball with my old V Corps driver, Otis Pearson, whom I had transferred to Atlanta; a fine Victorian mansion, Quarters 10, as the CINC's residence; and time for Alma and me to enjoy our new status as grandparents. Jeffrey Michael Powell had been born to Jane and Mike just before our move to Atlanta.

I'd enjoyed many perks in my job as National Security Advisor, but no home-to-work transportation was authorized by Congress in my new post. So there I was, running a million-person operation and driving to work in a gasping, gas-guzzling sixteen-year-old Chrysler station wagon which left oil puddles in front of FORSCOM's brand-new $40 million headquarters. But once I got to the office, Otis could legitimately chauffeur me around to my official appointments in a gleaming government-issue Mercury.

The Chrysler was my everyday workhorse for lugging tools, spare parts, and kids to college. But by now I was deeply involved in my love affair with old Volvos. One was a 1967 Model 122 with a balky twin-carbureted engine. When something went wrong that I could not figure out right away, I would retreat to my study in Quarters 10 and pull out the manual. I would sit there, schematics of the fuel and electrical systems spread out in front of me, and through the process of elimination trace the problem. When I had eliminated every explanation but one, I would go back to the garage and say, all right, you little SOB, I've got you. I cannot exaggerate the satisfaction it gave me to analyze and solve a car problem by reading a book. For me it was like hitting a hole in one or bowling 300 was for other guys.

My idea of a good time is to disconnect every wire, tube, hose, cable, and bolt of an engine, unhook the driveshaft from the transmission, sling a chain around the engine, hook the chain to the rafters, and winch the engine out of the hood, as I stand there, grease-stained and triumphant. I enjoy best working in solitude. I do not like having buddies drop by to kibitz. And that is how I spent much of my free time in Atlanta. I cannot see that my particular passion makes any less sense than hitting dimpled balls, fuzzy balls, or seamed balls.

One day in early summer I got word that Dick Cheney, the new Secretary of Defense (after John Tower's nomination had fallen through), wanted to see me. As National Security Advisor, I had worked closely with Congressman Cheney, who was then House minority whip, responsible for rounding up Republican votes for Reagan administration policies. Cheney had not yet been to FORSCOM and wanted to stop by to be briefed on his way back to Washington from visiting CENTCOM and the Special Operations Command, SOCOM, also in Tampa. I went out to Atlanta's Charlie Brown Airport to pick him up and brought him back to my headquarters, where my staff presented a briefing on the state of the country's strategic ground reserves, which I commanded. Then we went to Quarters 10 for lunch.

He was the same Cheney I had first met in V Corps and worked with on the Hill, incisive, smart, no small talk, never showing any more surface than necessary. And tough. This man, who had never spent a day in uniform, who, during the Vietnam War, had gotten a student deferment and later a parent deferment, had taken instant control of the Pentagon. His congressional friends had apparently warned him that if he did not put his brand on the

Defense Department right away, the generals and admirals would eat him alive. In his first week on the job, he publicly slapped down the Chief of Staff of the Air Force, General Larry Welch, at a televised press conference because Welch had discussed MX missile deployment options with Congress. The public chewing-out—"it's inappropriate for a uniformed officer," Cheney had said—ended with an ominous "Everybody's entitled to one mistake." Welch, I knew, had been done wrong. His talks with the Congress had been okayed by Cheney's then deputy, Will Taft, and Brent Scowcroft, the current National Security Advisor. I had spent enough time in this game to recognize the move. Cheney had seized an early opportunity to say, I am not afraid of generals or admirals. In this job, I run them. He had made his point. But Welch also showed his mettle. A powerful group of retired Air Force officers wanted to go after Cheney's scalp. Larry told them to back off. "I've been shot at by professionals," this veteran Vietnam fighter pilot told them. "Let's get on with our work."

I was fairly sure Cheney had not stopped in Atlanta only for a briefing on FORSCOM training. But during our conversations, this closemouthed man gave no hint of any other reason why he might have come. My message to him was that I was content where I was.

That June, I got a call from David Wallechinsky, a writer for *Parade* magazine, the newspaper supplement that goes to almost every American home on

Sunday. "General, your life is a great American story," David said. "Poor minority kid from the South Bronx rises to high office in the White House, earns four stars." *Parade* wanted to profile me, probably for the edition coming out the week of July 4. I was to get the cover story, mug shot and all. I agreed, and Wallechinsky came down with Eddie Adams, the Pulitzer Prize–winning photographer who in the Vietnam War took the unforgettable picture of the South Vietnamese police chief executing a Viet Cong officer in the street during the Tet offensive.

    Parade finished the story; yet the Fourth of July came and went without its appearing. In the meantime, the purpose of Dick Cheney's drop-in began to come into focus. In September, Admiral Bill Crowe's second term as Chairman of the Joint Chiefs of Staff would end. Unexpectedly, Crowe declined nomination for another two-year term. He did, however, have a strong candidate to succeed him, his vice chairman, Air Force General Robert Herres, a superb choice. A half-dozen other names were also bandied about in the press, including mine. The succession sweepstakes was on, though nobody, including Cheney, had said a word about the job to me. And I was not seeking it. The way I read the tea leaves, Herres was a shoo-in. My thinking was that I would serve out my assignment at FORSCOM and possibly be a candidate for Army Chief of Staff when Carl Vuono retired. And, conceivably, I might have a shot at the chairmanship when Herres retired. Or I just might retire after FORSCOM. I had over thirty years in, and there were still attractive private offers out there.

On Sunday, August 6, I flew up to Baltimore for Carl Vuono's annual commanders conference of senior Army generals. It was a sport-shirt-and-docksiders, let-your-hair-down affair, held this year at Belmont House, an estate-turned-conference-center outside the city. I looked forward to the next three days. I would be among my fraternity—Carl as Chief of Staff; Butch Saint, a friendly rival, now CINCUSAREUR, commanding our Army forces in Europe; Norm Schwarzkopf from CENTCOM; and a dozen others whom I had grown up with in the service. We were going to brainstorm where the Army ought to be headed, my favorite subject.

That morning, coming up on the plane, I had seen a story in the *New York Times* headlined "Scramble on to Succeed Chairman of Joint Chiefs of Staff." The reporter, hunting for an angle, had written that I had been keeping in touch with Secretary Cheney through "frequent letters." Dead wrong. I had sent one quarterly report to Cheney, as required of all CINCs.

We were into the last day of the conference when at about 2:00 P.M. I received a note. Secretary Cheney wanted me to call him. I slipped out of the room, trying to look inconspicuous while all eyes followed me. Cheney had already left his office, but fifteen minutes later, with the conference ended, I got another message: would I come to the Pentagon right away. Vuono gave me a knowing wink and said, "I'll fix you up with a helicopter."

I picked up Alma and off we went. At the Pentagon helipad, we were met by a driver with a van. When we reached the Pentagon's River Entrance, I asked Alma to wait while I, dressed in loafers, chinos, and a polo shirt, went in to see the Secretary of Defense. Cheney greeted me with a smile, oblivious to whether I was wearing casual clothes or something out of Gilbert and Sullivan. He is that kind of man. He wasted no time. "You know we're looking for a chairman," he said. "You're my candidate." He then ticked off my qualifications in his judgment. I knew my way around the Pentagon and the White House. I had the required military command credits. I understood arms control, an item high on the Bush agenda. And he thought he and I could get along. He asked me how I felt about the job.

"Of course, I'm flattered," I said. "And, obviously, if you and the President want me, I'll take it and do my best. But you know I'm happy in Atlanta and not looking to move." Unspoken was my genuine concern. This would be a tough assignment. I was the most junior of the fifteen four-stars legally eligible for the chairmanship. My fourth star had been on my shoulder for barely four months, and several of the senior candidates had far more impressive military credentials.

George Bush evidently had similar reservations, since Cheney next said, "The President wonders if your appointment would be a problem for you with the other, more senior, generals and admirals."

I knew I could count on Vuono's support, and I had good relations with the other service chiefs. "I'm not worried about that," I said. Never let 'em see you sweat.

"Fine," Cheney answered. "I'm going to recommend you. But, as you know, it's the President's decision."

I said nothing to Alma until we were in the Learjet headed back to Atlanta. "Here we go again," she said.

The next day, Wednesday, August 9, Cheney called to say the President had approved his recommendation; I would succeed Bill Crowe. The President wanted me back the next day for a Rose Garden announcement. I flew to Washington that night. Alma chose to remain in Atlanta, where she had a prior commitment. My daughters, Linda and Annemarie, were also tied up, so Mike stood in the Rose Garden with me on August 10 as President Bush congratulated Bill Crowe for his outstanding performance as chairman and then announced his intention to nominate me to be the twelfth Chairman of the Joint Chiefs of Staff.

I had six weeks to detach from FORSCOM and prepare for Senate confirmation. Over the next few days, each of the chiefs and the major four-star commanders checked in to offer their congratulations and support, which I was certainly going to need. The President's concern had been answered.

I ran into one more hurdle. On the day my nomination as chairman was announced, I was in my office receiving congratulations from friends when a young lieutenant wearing rubber gloves appeared in the doorway. The Army takes drug abuse seriously and looks for drug users through random urinalysis testing. My number had come up. I excused myself and took the test. I passed.

Parade came out with a cover story on me the Sunday after my announcement. The timing seemed to indicate that someone at the magazine had an inside track on the chairmanship. Actually, *Parade* lays out its issues weeks in advance, and in this case, well before I was the President's choice. Either David Wallechinsky's instinct or luck was right on. The story did produce one surprising side effect. Wallechinsky had been looking for a human-interest angle, and my secretary in Atlanta, an able Army sergeant named Cammie Brown, tipped him off that I kept motivational sayings under the glass cover of my desk. David called and asked if I would read him some of them, which I did: "It ain't as bad as you think. It will look better in the morning," "Check small things," "Be careful what you choose. You may get it," and other lessons life had taught me. He collected thirteen of these thoughts and ran them in the *Parade* article as "Colin Powell's Rules." I began getting hundreds of requests for the rules from all over the country, to a point where I had to have them printed in quantity on cards. In case readers are still interested, the rules are included in the back of this book.

Three days after the announcement of my nomination as chairman, I was yanked back, suddenly and sadly, to the roots of my calling. Ronnie Brooks, my model, mentor, and inspiration during the days of the

CCNY Pershing Rifles, died of a massive heart attack at the age of fifty-four. I flew up to the Metropolitan Baptist Church in Albany, New York, and spoke at Ronnie's funeral, praising this good man, his courageous wife, Elsa, and the three fine sons they had raised. As I looked at my other PR pals present, Roger Langevin and Gabby Romero among them, I could not help being struck by the randomness of life. Had I never met the inspiring Brooks, the perfect cadet who preferred to become a civilian chemical researcher, would my life have taken the course it did?

Just two weeks after the Japanese attack on Pearl Harbor, Prime Minister Winston Churchill came to Washington with the "Chiefs of Staff Committee," the heads of British land, sea, and air forces. This body, which had existed since 1923, coordinated His Majesty's soldiers, sailors, and airmen's fight against the Axis powers. The United States had no comparable body to work out combined operations with the British, and so President Franklin Roosevelt created a "United States Joint Chiefs of Staff," representing the Army, the Army Air Forces, and the Navy. Admiral William Leahy, Roosevelt's confidant and assistant, presided over the group and served as liaison to the President. Leahy carried the title "Chief of Staff to the Commander in Chief of the Army and the Navy." The U.S. Joint Chiefs of Staff became the organization that led us through World War II.

In 1947, a permanent Joint Chiefs of Staff was established by act of Congress, and in 1949, the position of chairman was created. General Omar Bradley became the first to occupy the position. This remained the structure that ran the U.S. military for almost forty years, with occasional amendments to the law. The Marine Corps Commandant, for example, was authorized to participate in most JCS deliberations in 1952 and became a full member of the JCS in 1978.

The system was seriously flawed. Each chief, except the chairman, was the head of his own service yet also expected to vote against service parochialism in the national interest. It was a tough balancing act. The chiefs had trouble going "purple," the metaphor used in the Pentagon for mixing green, blue, and white uniforms. The deck was stacked against the very thing these dual-hatted leaders were supposed to achieve, "jointness," the word we use in the military to describe teamwork. Yet, almost every great military campaign of the modern era has been a joint effort—General Ulysses Grant's joining with the Union Navy to move down the Mississippi and split the Confederacy; MacArthur's brilliant landing at Inchon during the Korean War; and the greatest combined enterprise of all, D-Day. Jointness in our time was more often produced out of the necessity of the moment rather than built into the machinery.

The JCS also had the responsibility to provide military counsel to the Secretary of Defense and the President. But it had to be *consensus* advice, not separate opinions. Almost the only way the chiefs would agree on their advice was by scratching each other's backs. Consequently, the sixteen-hundred-member joint staff that worked for the JCS spent thousands of man-hours pumping out ponderous, least-common-denominator documents that every chief would accept but few Secretaries of Defense or Presidents found useful. The tortuous routines worked out for processing this paper flow would have done credit to a thirteenth-century papal curia—successive white drafts, buff drafts, green drafts, and finally the sanctified red-striped decision paper. These failings in the JCS were more than bureaucratic. In my judgment, this amorphous setup explained in part why the Joint Chiefs had never spoken out with a clear voice to prevent the deepening morass in Vietnam.

The flawed arrangement persisted until General David Jones, the ninth chairman, spoke up in frustration in 1982 just after he retired. Jones recommended that the JCS Chairman become the "principal" military advisor to the Secretary of Defense and the President and be given greater authority over the staff serving the chiefs. Shy Meyer, while Army Chief of Staff, wanted to do away with the Joint Chiefs entirely and replace them with a National Military Council whose members would have no responsibility for their particular service and could therefore devote their full energies to coordinating the armed forces. These proposals sparked a debate that resulted in Senator Barry Goldwater and Congressman Bill Nichols sponsoring and winning passage of the Defense Reorganization Act of 1986, commonly referred to as the Goldwater-Nichols Act.

This act, for the first time, gave the Chairman of the JCS real power. As "principal military advisor," he could give his own counsel directly to the Secretary and the President. He was no longer limited to presenting the chiefs' watered-down consensus recommendations and then whispering his personal views. The chiefs, however, were still advisors and encouraged to give their counsel and even disagree with the chairman. Goldwater-Nichols also placed the sixteen hundred people on the Joint Staff under the chairman, not the multiheaded corporate body of chiefs. Even with this reorganization, the chairman was not in the chain of command, but the Secretary of Defense could require that military orders go through him to the field commanders, which Cheney had done.

Bill Crowe had been the transition chairman, since Goldwater-Nichols went into effect in the middle of his watch. Assuming I was confirmed, I would be the first full-term chairman to possess Goldwater-Nichols powers. I was formally confirmed by the Senate on September 20 to become the youngest officer, the first African-American, and the first ROTC graduate to fill this office. The immigrant's son from the South Bronx now occupied the highest uniformed military post in the land. If only Colonel Brookhart at the CCNY drill hall could see me now.

I went to bed on October 1 content, but weary. Bill Crowe's term had ended at midnight the day before, and this Sunday had been my first day in the chairman's job. I had gone to my new office that morning in the practically deserted Pentagon just to look around and drop off some things. Crowe had kept a colorful collection of military headgear on the bookshelves covering the entire wall behind his desk. He had taken the hats, and the shelves were empty. I made a mental note to call my old Gelnhausen buddy Bill Stofft, now the Army historian, and ask him to send me the green-bound World War II histories. Later, when I did call, Bill's assistant asked me how many books I wanted. I told him, "Thirty-five feet worth."

The windows of the chairman's office had been painted over for security purposes, since they were just a few feet from the busy main Pentagon River Entrance where the shuttle buses stopped. The paint denied me a stunning view across the Potomac River to the Capitol. I could not see the sailboats plying the Tidal Basin or even the Pentagon parade ground. That too had to change. The answer Doc Cooke's people eventually hit on was one-way, bulletproof Mylar. I could look out, but employees lined up for the buses could not look in. Over the years, I found myself in an ideal position to watch the daily human drama, from little cabals of Pentagon officers to lovers arranging trysts.

On that first day, I placed on my desk the marble set with the Schaeffer pens that I had won at Fort Bragg in 1957 for being "Best Cadet, Company D," and that has been on every desk I have ever occupied. I also intended to hang my going-away present from the FORSCOM staff, a Don Stivers print entitled "Tracking Victorio," depicting the 10th Cavalry Buffalo Soldiers on patrol against an Apache warrior. And I intended to put up the framed Lincoln letter that Stu Purviance had given me when I got my first star, the one in which the President said it was easier to make new generals than to replace lost horses.

That afternoon, Alma and I went to a family party in Washington thrown by my cousin Arthur S. "Sonny" Lewis, that extraordinary man who had gone from an enlisted Navy career to ambassador to Sierra Leone after picking up degrees at Dartmouth. My sister, Marilyn, and brother-in-law, Norm, and aunts, uncles, and cousins came from all over. We had a double-barreled celebration—my new job, and Mike and Jane's first anniversary. All the fun and warmth of my Jamaican boyhood came flooding back, and the party went on to the last tot of rum. Alma and I got to bed at about midnight at Wainwright Hall, the VIP motel at Fort Myer where we were staying while the chairman's quarters were being refurbished for us. I had been asleep only a couple of hours when the phone rang.

16 ☆ "Mr. Chairman, We've Got a Problem"

I HAD BEEN chairman of the Joint Chiefs of Staff just over twenty-four hours when the Joint Staff operations officer, Lieutenant General Tom Kelly, woke me up to alert me to a coup brewing against the Noriega regime in Panama. I could expect a call in a few minutes, Kelly told me, from General Max Thurman, who had just taken over in Panama as CINC SOUTHCOM, commander in chief of the Southern Command.

Welcome back to the big leagues.

Though Max Thurman had been in his job only a day longer than I had been in mine, it was reassuring having him in Panama during a potential crisis. Max was a legend, considered one of the smartest, toughest officers in the Army, a hardworking bachelor who appeared to have no interests outside of his job and who, because of his compulsiveness, had acquired the affectionate nickname "Mad Max."

Noriega had been on and off my radar screen over the past six years. I had first met him on the trip to Latin America with Cap Weinberger in September 1983, when Ollie North had been so conspicuous a part of our party. During that visit, we had held a pro forma meeting with the new puppet president of Panama, Stanford-educated Ricardo de la Espriella; and then we went to meet the country's real ruler, Brigadier General Manuel Antonio Noriega, chief of the PDF, the Panama Defense Force, in his headquarters building, the Comandancia. I found Noriega an unappealing man, with his pockmarked face, beady, darting eyes, and arrogant swagger. I immediately had the crawling sense that I was in the presence of evil.

Noriega had been on the payrolls of the CIA and the Defense Intelligence Agency going back twenty-five years. He had also cut deals with Cuba, Libya, and other intelligence customers, and he permitted the KGB to operate freely in Panama. You could not buy Manuel Noriega, but you could rent him. We ourselves were using him as a conduit to get arms to the Nicaraguan contras in their guerrilla war against the Sandinistas. I remember thinking at the time of this first encounter how odd it was to be treating a thug like a respected national leader. Two years later, in 1985, when I met him again, we were still giving Noriega the kid-glove treatment. On this occasion, Weinberger had invited him to the Pentagon after Noriega promoted himself to four-star general. He was not, of course, the only despot honored at the Pentagon. Another I recall was President Mobutu of Zaire. But again, we had our uses for Mobutu, in his case, to funnel arms to anticommunist rebels in Angola. Cold War politics sometimes made for creepy bedfellows.

Noriega played a cunning hand. He kept on the good side of Director of Central Intelligence Bill Casey by supporting anticommunist covert operations in Nicaragua. He occasionally shut down minor drug operations to satisfy the U.S. Drug Enforcement Agency while raking in millions by laundering Colombian drug money. Noriega, however, began to overplay his hand. His complicity in the PDF murder of his leftist enemy Hugo Spadafora in 1985 had drawn a flock of investigative reporters to Panama and brought down the wrath of Senator Jesse Helms. And by February 1988, Noriega's drug deals had provided enough evidence for grand juries in Miami and Tampa to indict him. This was the indictment that George Bush, as Vice President, had told me we must not bargain away.

I had been National Security Advisor at the time and had to referee a debate over the wisdom of indicting a "friendly head of state." We had gotten ourselves into a box. The administration had allowed the indictments go forward, yet we were still paying Noriega. The Drug Enforcement Agency had even awarded him a letter of commendation. The administration finally took a clear stand on Noriega. All U.S. agencies were to drop him. He could not be under criminal indictment and on the payroll at the same time.

After the indictment, the Panamanian people took to the streets to demonstrate against Noriega, assuming that the United States was now ready to help them get rid of this crooked caudillo. Noriega responded by dumping yet another puppet president, Eric Delvalle, and replacing him with Manuel Solis Palma, the education minister. George Shultz began pushing for aggressive action to remove Noriega, including U.S. military intervention. Frank Carlucci, then Secretary of Defense, and Admiral Bill Crowe, Chairman of the JCS, disagreed. As detestable as Noriega was, they argued, we could not justify the use of U.S. forces to remove him. Though it may surprise some people, the military is not necessarily eager to apply force to achieve political ends, except as a last resort. The intellectual community is apt to say we have to "do something," and diplomats fire off their diplomatic notes. But in the end, it is the armed forces that bring back the body bags and have to explain why to parents. President Reagan had never really considered an invasion of Panama short of a direct provocation. He believed that the United States should avoid looking like the "gringo" bully, invading just because we did not like the way the Panamanians handled their internal affairs. And there was no serious communist threat lurking there.

I had thought all along that if we ever did get involved in Panama, dumping Noriega would not end the problem. His power base was the PDF. When we got rid of Noriega, another PDF goon would rise up to take his place. And so far we had not seen a man on a white horse to replace him and his henchmen. As National Security Advisor, I spent several PRG meetings trying to find a PDF officer a cut above Noriega or a Panamanian civilian leader who could survive PDF opposition. At one point, the CIA's operations director told me that the agency might have found a savior, a bona fide anti-Noriega liberal who might help bring down the dictator. Who was this paragon? I wanted to know. He was Eduardo Herrera Hassan, I was told, Panamanian ambassador and military attaché to Israel, then on the outs with Noriega.

The CIA spirited Herrera out of Tel Aviv and brought him to Washington, where I met him in my White House office. He turned out to be handsome, charming, and slick. Herrera said all the right things against Noriega, though he suffered from the I-I-I syndrome. The words "freedom" and "democracy," however, never passed his lips. He was most concerned about the welfare and future of the PDF. I concluded that Herrera was a smoother Noriega. Herrera returned to Israel, but Noriega got wind of his trip and fired him. The CIA brought him back to the United States and supported him in case he might still prove useful.

As the Reagan era came to an end in January 1989, President Bush inherited the Noriega problem. The strongman continued to show his contempt for democracy by roughing up the political opposition and making mass political arrests. He stopped the elections of May 1989 when his opponent, Guillermo Endara, seemed to be winning, and Noriega had his PDF toughs beat up Endara's vice presidential candidate in full view of American TV cameras. By the time I became Chairman of the JCS in the fall of 1989, Noriega's ouster and replacement by a democratic government was gaining priority in the Bush administration, and President Bush's personal distaste for the dictator had not diminished.

In the wee hours of October 3, as promised, Max Thurman followed up on Tom Kelly's earlier alert to give me a fuller briefing. The uprising, he said, had been planned by a PDF officer, Major Moises Giroldi Vega, and was supposed to begin in about six hours, at 8:30 that morning.

"What do we know about Giroldi?" I asked Max. "Does he have any allies? Are any units on his side? What does he want from us?"

"We don't know anything about him," Max said. As for his motive, Giroldi appeared to represent disgruntled unpaid PDF soldiers. His coup seemed to be a job grievance more than a blow for democracy. And he was not asking us for anything yet.

"Are we trading one Noriega for another?" I asked Max.

"Could be," he responded, though it was tough to know, given the scant information we had.

I asked Max to keep me informed and then phoned Secretary Cheney. This was a key call, the first time I would be carrying out the JCS Chairman's responsibility to provide military advice to the Secretary of Defense. I was impressed by Cheney's coolness as I woke him up and told him what we knew. I passed along Max's and my view that we did not have enough information to commit ourselves to Giroldi. Cheney agreed and then called Brent Scowcroft, who also concurred and so advised President Bush.

The next morning, 8:30 came and went without a coup. Max called to report that Giroldi had apparently run into logistics problems and had postponed his move until later in the day.

Later that morning, I went to the White House to meet with the President and his national security team. I called Max Thurman directly from the Oval Office, got the latest word, and then told the President what Thurman now knew. Giroldi commanded the PDF's 4th Infantry Company, which provided security for Noriega's headquarters in the Comandancia. He had helped Noriega put down the most recent attempted coup, and the two men were personally close. Noriega was the godfather of one of Giroldi's children. Giroldi was asking us to use U.S. troops to block access to the Comandancia so that PDF units outside the city could not come to Noriega's rescue. He had no intention, however, of turning Noriega over to us. He had the odd notion that Noriega would accept his fate and retire peacefully to the country. He was taking no chances, however, about the safety of his own family. He had asked U.S. officials in Panama to provide sanctuary for them.

The whole affair sounded like amateur night, and Cheney, Thurman, and I still agreed that the United States should not get involved. All of the President's other advisors concurred, although we were a little uneasy that if Giroldi failed, we might be accused of passing up an opportunity to get rid of Noriega. President Bush, however, had made up his mind. Giroldi had still said nothing about democracy. And we would not support him unless he made a commitment to restore civilian rule.

This was my first opportunity to see the Bush team in action, and I was surprised that critical deliberations were taking place with no preparation or follow-up planned. The PRG system that Frank Carlucci and I had created had been dismantled by the new team. Brent Scowcroft, a sharp player, later diagnosed the problem and reimposed order by reincarnating the PRG as the Deputies Committee, chaired by Bob Gates, his deputy. But all that was in the future. On this day, the Oval Office debate was a free-swinging affair, and the freest swinger of all was the President's Chief of Staff, John Sununu. Sununu did not suffer fools gladly, or smart folks either, for that matter. He cut people off in midsentence and pursued his pet tangents, a behavior, I noticed, which did not seem to bother the President. Bush listened, spoke little, and made sense when he did talk. He repeated that the plotters had to express a clear intention to restore democracy "or we don't commit." He then brought the meeting to a close. I went back to the Pentagon, staying in constant touch with Thurman.

At one point during this tense day, I went to Cheney's conference room and set eyes on someone I had never expected to meet. The Secretary was hosting the new Soviet minister of defense, General Dimitri Yazov, and with Yazov was General Colonel Vladislav A. Achalov, former commander of the Soviet 8th Guards Army, which faced my V Corps in Germany. Cheney introduced us, and we smiled at each other across the table with evident irony, two soldiers who had once studied how to kill each other. "General Achalov," I said, "you know, I used to keep your picture on my desk in Frankfurt."

He gave me a crafty smile and said, "Yes, and I kept your picture on my desk."

Night fell, and the last word out of Panama was that the Giroldi coup would take place the next day. Game called on account of darkness.

The coup did take place the next morning. Giroldi held Noriega in the Comandancia, but then did not know what to do with him. We instructed Max Thurman that he could take custody of Noriega only if he was offered to us by the conspirators. But Thurman was not to initiate action to seize him. Noriega, in the meantime, showed no sign of wanting to retire to his hacienda. Instead, he picked up his phone, called loyal subordinates in Panama City and in Río Hato, seventy-five miles away, and arranged his own rescue. By early afternoon, Noriega had managed to talk Giroldi into giving up, and the coup, such as it was, collapsed. The whole thing had lasted just five hours.

After reporting the debacle to the White House, Cheney and I walked out to the River Entrance parade field. With one crisis already under my belt, it was time for the official ceremony marking the beginning of my chairmanship. I did not find this an auspicious start, but I had learned a few things already: Cheney was cool and solid; the Joint Staff was a fast-moving, professional organization; and President Bush, while tolerating the noisy swirl of advisors around him, saw through to the essence of issues and made sound decisions.

Giroldi was finished. Noriega soon ordered that he be executed, but the U.S. fallout from Giroldi's failure was just beginning. Democrats and Republicans in Congress began jumping all over the administration for blowing a supposedly golden opportunity to dump Noriega. Senator Jesse Helms led the pack. Cheney and I had to go up to the Hill and listen to second-guessers berate us for not coming instantly to Giroldi's aid, as if this Brand X plotter were the next Simón Bolívar. I consoled myself with the words of Clausewitz: "The vividness of transient impressions must not make us forget that such truth they maintain is of a lesser stamp." And few events could have been more transient than the coup of Major Moises Giroldi Vega. I remained convinced that we had made the right decisions.

Thurman and I had received quite a baptism. We compared notes and determined that if we ever were forced to act in Panama, we would recommend getting rid of the PDF. Max began to develop a plan to do just that.

The Saturday after the failed coup, I was helping Alma get us settled into our new home, Quarters 6, the chairman's residence, when Bob Woodward of the *Washington Post* called. Woodward was doing a story on the failed coup for the Sunday edition and said he just wanted to check a few facts and give me a chance to give my interpretation of what had happened. Woodward had the disarming voice and manner of a Boy Scout offering to help an old lady cross the street. He assured me that anything I said would be on "deep background," which is one step in anonymity beyond "a senior administration official said today . . ." So far, news stories recounting my role in the Panama coup had painted me as the fair-haired boy who had fallen flat on his face. Consequently, I was not averse to getting my version of events across in a newspaper of note. I agreed to talk to Woodward.

His story the next day was not inaccurate, but neither was it helpful. The experience reminded me of posing for what you think is going to be a reasonably flattering photo, only to find out that the photographer has chosen to print the shot of you with your mouth hanging open. Nevertheless, I continued dealing with Woodward, though Alma warned me to handle with care.

Over the next two months, rumors of more coups floated out of Panama. They came to nothing, but

Thurman accelerated his contingency planning. An existing plan, code-named Blue Spoon, was beefed up to include taking out the entire PDF as well as removing Noriega. Under the revised Blue Spoon, thirteen thousand troops of the U.S. Army South and supporting units in Panama would be reinforced by another ten thousand troops of the XVIII Airborne Corps from the United States. Lieutenant General Carl Stiner, commander of the XVIII Airborne Corps, would command the joint task force. If we did attack, this force was to seize all PDF installations, put down PDF resistance, and help bring the legitimately elected Endara government to power. Blue Spoon further included a raid by Delta Force to rescue an American citizen, Kurt Muse, a CIA source who had been placed in solitary confinement in Modelo Prison by Noriega for spying. Noriega had threatened that if the United States moved against Panama, Muse would be killed instantly. With Secretary Cheney's approval, we quietly began to infiltrate additional equipment and units into Panama.

Quarters 6 on Grant Avenue at Fort Myer is a stately home, and living there was a little like living in the White House. Alma and I had big, fashionably appointed public rooms for entertaining on the first floor and lived in an apartment on the second floor. The difference from the White House was that our apartment was tiny, just big enough for the two of us with hardly enough room for an overnight guest. I spent my free time there in a small study with a TV set and a secure phone.

I was sitting in the study on Saturday evening, December 16, 1989, when I got another call from Tom Kelly. "Mr. Chairman," Kelly said, "we've got a problem." As usual, the first details were sketchy. I learned only that a U.S. Marine had been shot in Panama. Soon afterward, I was informed that four officers in civvies had driven into Panama City for dinner, where they ran into a roadblock near PDF headquarters. It was Panama's annual armed forces day, and I suspect that a lot of the PDF soldiers had been drinking and carousing. At the roadblock a group of these soldiers tried to yank the Americans from their car. The driver hit the gas and started to pull away. The PDF fired, and Marine Lieutenant Robert Paz was hit and died soon afterward.

The situation grew worse as the night wore on. A Navy officer, Lieutenant Adam J. Curtis, and his wife, Bonnie, who had witnessed the shooting, were detained by the PDF and taken to a police station for interrogation. Curtis was roughed up and threatened with death. Mrs. Curtis was forced to stand against a wall while PDF soldiers pawed her until she collapsed.

I reported all this to Cheney, and we considered whether we had an unignorable provocation. He informed the White House, and a meeting was set with President Bush for the next morning.

That Sunday was hectic. I went first to the Pentagon to check with Thurman on Saturday's events. Although our officers had taken a wrong turn and had blundered into the roadblock, the PDF's behavior was still inexcusable. Moreover, the shooting represented an increasing pattern of hostility toward U.S. troops. "How's Blue Spoon proceeding?" I asked. "Rehearsed and ready to go," said Max. I called the leaders of the Transportation Command and the Special Operations Command and told them to be ready to move, then went to Cheney's office for a 10:00 A.M. meeting. In the room were Paul Wolfowitz, undersecretary of defense for policy; Pete Williams, the assistant secretary for public affairs, in my judgment the best in the business; and Bill Price from the NSC. We went over the options. By the time Cheney ended the meeting, Wolfowitz and Price were still not sure we had a "smoking gun" justifying military intervention. Cheney asked me to stay behind. When we were alone, he asked, "What do you think?"

"Max and I both believe we should intervene to protect American citizens," I said. "Besides, Noriega's not a legitimate leader. He's a criminal. He's under indictment." I told Cheney, however, that I wanted to hold off my final recommendation until I had a chance to talk to the chiefs.

"Okay," Cheney said. "I'll set the meeting with the President for this afternoon."

Panama was the first major foreign crisis of the Bush administration. It also presented the first serious test of the chairman's new role under Goldwater-Nichols. In the past, the chiefs had voted to achieve a consensus that the chairman could carry to the Secretary of Defense and the President. Now, I was the principal military advisor. The chiefs had great skill and experience. They were the ones who provided the trained and ready forces to the CINCs. I was not likely to ignore their wisdom. But now, as chairman, I was no longer limited to a messenger role.

Back at my office I asked Tom Kelly to have the chiefs meet me at Quarters 6 at 11:30 A.M. I did not want all that horsepower coming to the Pentagon on a Sunday morning. They were sure to be spotted by the press, setting off all sorts of alarms. Soon they began arriving from church and home. I made coffee, and we sat down in the library on the first floor. "Sorry you lost a man," I said to Al Gray, the Marine Corps Commandant. Gray nodded grimly. Tom Kelly and Rear Admiral Ted Sheafer, my intelligence officer, briefed the chiefs. After we had talked over the military options, I gave them my judgment. "Paz's killing can't be overlooked. Blue Spoon is a good plan. We're ready, and I think we should go with it. But I want your views."

Carl Vuono, the Army Chief of Staff, Carl Trost, the Chief of Naval Operations, and Vice Chairman Bob Herres all agreed. Larry Welch, the Air Force Chief of Staff, still debated if we had sufficient provocation, but soon concurred. Al Gray wondered if we needed to move as quickly as Blue Spoon required. Al knew that the plan, as it stood, contained only a minor role for the Marines. He wanted time to bring Marine amphibious units to the party. "Al," I said, "Max has a solid plan, ready to go, and we're not going to delay it or add anything unnecessary." Al understood, and in the end, Blue Spoon had the unanimous support of the chiefs.

It was a strange time to plan for war. Sunday afternoon, December 17, I was hurrying down a festively decked corridor of the White House, Tom Kelly at my side, lugging his map case, when our way was blocked by Christmas carolers in eighteenth-century costume. We shook hands with them, exchanged holiday greetings, and continued on up to the Bushes' private apartment on the second floor.

The President was sitting in his pensive pose, slouched, chin resting on his chest, chewing his lower lip. He wore slacks and a blue blazer with red socks, one marked "Merry" and the other "Christmas." He had called in Dick Cheney; Jim Baker, now Secretary of State; Brent Scowcroft and his deputy, Bob Gates; and Marlin Fitzwater, the press secretary. John Sununu was not present, which promised a little less blindsiding.

Cheney led off with a review of what had happened in Panama and described our proposed response in general terms. He then turned the stage over to me to explain the military plan. Tom Kelly uncovered his maps, and I began to brief, using a pen-sized laser pointer that threw a beamless red dot on the map. The disembodied dot seemed to amuse the President.

Except for Cheney, the others were hearing an expanded Blue Spoon plan for the first time. I started off with our prime objective: we were going to eliminate Noriega *and* the PDF. If that succeeded, we would be running the country until we could establish a civilian government and a new security force. Since this plan went well beyond "getting Noriega," I paused to make sure that this point had sunk in, with all its implications. No one objected.

I went into the military details. We would use the forces in place, which we had been quietly beefing up to a current total of thirteen thousand troops. That number, however, was not enough. Thurman and Stiner had a strategy to strike at every major PDF unit and seize all key military installations. Army Rangers would parachute onto the main barracks at Río Hato, west of Panama City, and take out the PDF companies used to put down past coups. Our Air Force's new F-117A Stealth fighter would be employed for the first time in combat to support the Rangers. Paratroopers of the 82d Airborne Division would fly in from Fort Bragg and drop on objectives east of the city. More infantry from the 7th Infantry Division would be flown in from Fort Ord, California, to extend our control of the country and to help restore law and order. U.S. troops already stationed in Panama would seize the Comandancia and objectives in the city proper; and Navy SEALs would take the airfield where we knew that Noriega kept his "getaway" plane. Special Forces units would search for him, a tough assignment, since we had not been able to track him day to day. A Marine company in Panama was set to secure the Bridge of the Americas over the Panama Canal, and the Delta Force had the mission to rescue Kurt Muse, the CIA source held in Modelo Prison across the street from the Comandancia. The Blue Spoon force would total over twenty thousand troops. I predicted that within hours of H-Hour, Noriega, captured or not, would no longer be in power and we would have created conditions that would allow the elected Endara government to come out of hiding and take office. I finished my briefing pointing out that "the chiefs agree to a man." Then the questions began flying.

George Bush sat like a patron on a bar stool coolly observing a brawl while his advisors went hard at it. Brent Scowcroft's manner had an irritating edge that took getting used to, but his intelligence was obvious and his intent admirable. He wanted to leave the President with no comfortable illusions: "There are going to be casualties. People are going to die," Scowcroft said. The President nodded, and let the debate roll on.

Jim Baker believed we had an obligation to intervene; that was why we maintained military forces, to meet such obligations. He could not resist mentioning that the State Department had urged intervention for some time. Scowcroft kept my feet to the fire. "Suppose we go through all this and we don't nab Noriega? That makes me nervous." That was possible, I said, since we did not know where he was. Suppose he escaped into the jungle? That too could happen, and it was an easy place to hide. Brent hammered away at casualties. Numbers, he wanted. Numbers. I said I could not be specific. Obviously, people were going to get hurt and die, soldiers and civilians, I said. A lot of real estate was going to be chewed up. We could anticipate chaos, especially in the early stages.

The key issue remained whether we had sufficient provocation to act. We had reasons—Noriega's contempt for democracy, his drug trafficking and indictment, the death of the American Marine, the threat to our treaty rights to the canal with this unreliable figure ruling Panama. And, unspoken, there was George Bush's personal antipathy to Noriega, a third-rate dictator thumbing his nose at the United States. I shared that distaste.

The President himself pushed me on casualties. "Mr. President," I said, "I can't be more specific."

"When will we be ready to go?" he asked.

"In two and a half days," I replied. "We want to attack at night. We're well equipped to fight in the dark, and that should give us tactical surprise."

The questions continued, thick and fast, until it started to look as if we were drifting away from the decision at hand. I could see Tom Kelly, in his first meeting with this group, growing uneasy. But then Bush, after everyone had had his say, gripped the arms of his chair and rose. "Okay, let's do it," he said. "The hell with it."

Back at the Pentagon, I called Max Thurman and other key commanders and spoke again to the chiefs. D-Day was set for December 20, and H-Hour at 0100.

A few weeks earlier, Cheney had called me to his office alone. "You're off to a good start as chairman," he said, offering me a seat. "You're forceful and you're taking charge. But you tend to funnel all the information coming to me. That's not the way I want it." He went on to say that he expected information from numerous sources. He had me dead to rights. Information is power. He knew it as well as I did. And I had tended to control it. I told him I understood, as long as we both recognized my obligation, as his senior military advisor, to give him my counsel. Matters could get choppy if he were to operate on military advice or information of which I was unaware. "Fine," he said, "as long as we understand each other . . . Colin." The slight hesitation let me know that the relationship was still familiar but that I was being shown my place in it.

I eventually became accustomed to the man's manner, so different from that of the paternal, courtly Cap Weinberger. Cheney was a cerebral Wyoming cowboy, used to wide-open spaces where one did not have to deal with many people. He was a conservative by nature and in his politics, a loner who would take your counsel, but preferred to go off by himself to make up his mind. And he was supremely self-confident, or the next best thing, he managed to give that impression. Here was someone else who had learned never to let 'em see you sweat. I enjoyed working with a master of the game.

As D-Day approached, I told Tom Kelly to make sure Cheney got every scrap of information about Blue Spoon. I still preferred to brief the Secretary myself, or at least be present while he was briefed. But over the next feverish forty-eight hours I would not have time, and after our recent discussion I certainly did not want Cheney to feel cut off from any source. He began vacuuming up data. How many men in a squad? What equipment do SEALs carry? Why do Rangers jump from five hundred feet? He wanted to have it all by H-Hour, and I understood why. When the dust settled on this invasion, I would still be an advisor; but he and the President would have to bear the responsibility.

In one of my several phone conversations with Max Thurman, I mentioned that Blue Spoon might be fine as a code name to hide an operation, but it was hardly a rousing call to arms when the time came to go public. You do not risk people's lives for Blue Spoons. We kicked around a number of ideas and finally settled on Max's suggestion, Just Cause. Along with the inspirational ring, I liked something else about it. Even our severest critics would have to utter "Just Cause" while denouncing us.

War planning is a mosaic of thousands of troubling details. The weather was turning bad, and icing conditions stateside were going to affect our ability to assemble the required airlift. Rules of engagement, the instructions to our troops as to when they could use deadly force, had to be approved. I had to tell Thurman to change the F-117A target list. We did not want to bomb Noriega's country villas in the hope he might be there and end up killing maids and children instead.

The last night before the invasion, sitting alone in the dark in the backseat of my car on the drive home, I felt full of foreboding. I was going to be involved in conducting a war, one that I had urged, one that was sure to spill blood. Had I been right? Had my advice been sound? What if the icy weather in the States hampered the airlift? How would we then support the troops already in Panama? What would our casualties be? How many civilians might lose their lives in the fighting? Was it all worth it? I went to bed gnawed by self-doubt.

When I got to the Pentagon early on Tuesday morning, December 19, I found that my Joint Staff, under its able director, Lieutenant General Mike Carns, and Max Thurman's SOUTHCOM staff in Panama were on top of things. Army Lieutenant General Howard Graves was skillfully merging our military plans with State and NSC political and diplomatic efforts. All loose ends were being tied up. We were "good to go." My confidence came surging back. My worries vanished, and I entered the calm before the storm.

That afternoon, with the country going to war in less than ten hours, I had a student named Tiffani Starks in my office asking me to explain why I had chosen a military career. The conversation was part of the girl's high school project to interview a "famous person." Earlier, I had had lunch with Thomas P. Daily, an Annapolis midshipman, the pay-off after my losing a bet on the recent Army-Navy football game. I went through these innocent encounters as scheduled to make my day look normal and thus protect the security of Just Cause.

After talking with Miss Starks, I slipped off to the White House for one last meeting. Jim Baker and the State Department had worked out a plan to spirit Endara from his hiding place just before H-Hour to Fort Clayton, home to U.S. Army South, where he would be sworn in as president. We did not yet have Endara's agreement to the plan and would not know if he would go along until later in the evening. Endara's participation was the last check-off point before the invasion. If we did not have him on board, President Bush would have to decide whether to go ahead without him or to abort the mission.

What about Noriega? the President kept asking. Were we going to nab him? Was this operation going to be branded a failure if we could not deliver Noriega's head? "Mr. President," I said, "we don't have any way of knowing where he'll be at H-Hour, but wherever he is, he won't be El Jefe. He won't be able to show his face." I also cautioned against demonizing one individual and resting our success on his fate alone. Still, a President has to rally the country behind his policies. And when that policy is war, it is tough to arouse public opinion against political abstractions. A flesh-and-blood villain serves better. And Noriega was rich villain material.

I was at home at 7:40 Tuesday night when Cheney called to say that Endara was on board. Just Cause could go forward. I went back to the Pentagon at 8:30, telling Alma only that I might not be home for a while. I did not elaborate. I was tired from the incessant tension of the previous days and grabbed a quick nap in my office. At 11:30 P.M. I joined Dick Cheney in the National Military Command Center, a maze of rooms jammed with computers, maps, radios and telephones, and action officers scurrying all over the place. Tom Kelly had recently carved out a crisis room in the middle of this jumble for me, my principal staff officers, and the Secretary of Defense. We sat there at a table with two large television monitors in front of us on which to receive situation reports from Panama. Behind us on another table were telephones, providing direct, secure lines to Thurman, Stiner, and their staffs in the headquarters at Quarry Heights in Panama.

Tom Kelly leaned over my shoulder. "The weather held us up," Tom said. "But all planes are in the air." They were headed to Panama from Pope Air Force Base, next to Fort Bragg, and bases around the United States. The press, we knew, had spotted the unusual air activity, but was reporting it as a show of force or a reinforcement operation. We had achieved strategic surprise. But now that our forces were on the way, it would be hard to maintain tactical surprise.

The Panama Defense Force had figured out by 9:00 P.M. that something was up, but was not sure what to do about it. PDF troops began firing around Fort Amador soon after midnight and mortally wounded an American schoolteacher. General Stiner decided to move up H-Hour by fifteen minutes, and at 0045 hours, December 20, troops of the 193d Infantry Brigade swept out of their barracks and down into the city to attack the Comandancia. Just Cause was under way. Reports dribbled into the crisis center in frustrating bits and pieces: "Delta Force landing on the roof of Modelo Prison. . . . Delta has killed the guards. . . . Delta Force in. . . . Kurt Muse out of his cell. . . . Delta Force leaving in helicopters from the roof. It's okay. No! The helo is taking fire. It's hit! It's coming down! No, it's going down the street . . . it's hit . . . it's down . . . they're okay. . . ." This rescue operation took six minutes that lasted an eternity.

Intense fighting erupted around the Comandancia. The PDF headquarters was soon in flames, and the fire spread to a neighboring shanty area. The Rangers landed at Río Hato, preceded by F-117As dropping two-thousand-pound bombs to stun Panamanian soldiers in the barracks long enough for the paratroopers to hit the ground. More Rangers and the 82d Airborne force began dropping over the Torrijos International Airport complex east of the city. The Marines took the Bridge of the Americas. On the Atlantic side, 7th Division and 82d Airborne troops entered the city of Colón against stiff opposition. The PDF was putting up a better fight than expected, though our casualties were light. The biggest loss, so far, was sustained by Navy SEALs attacking Punta Paitilla Airport, where four of them were killed in a poorly conceived attack. We had made the mistake of assigning the SEALs, however tough and brave, to a mission more appropriate to the infantry.

Almost every report coming into the crisis center corrected the previous report, confirming the old adage "Never believe the first thing you hear." Sitting in that small room in the National Military Command Center, I felt as if I were on an emotional roller coaster. Combat, especially night fighting, is organized confusion. Journalists, historians, and Monday-morning quarterbacks can never fully appreciate the opportunities for error facing people who have to make life-and-death decisions in the midst of chaos with limited, even wrong, information. Cheney sat there that night quietly observing his first war. He kept asking sharp, relevant questions, and every hour or so he moved into the next room to report on a secure hot line to Scowcroft and the President. The chain of command was clean and clear. The President talked to Cheney; Cheney talked to me; and I talked to Max Thurman, who talked to Carl Stiner. Thurman and Stiner were the pros on the scene, and our job in Washington was to let the plan unfold without getting in their way.

At 7:40 the next morning, the President went on television to explain to the American people why we had invaded Panama. The cameras then shifted to the Pentagon, where, at 8:30, Cheney spoke first, describing in greater detail the provocations that had led to the invasion. Then it was my turn to explain the military operation.

During that night, while the fighting was still raging, I had left the crisis center and had gone to an adjacent room to think through what I wanted to say when I faced the public and the press. Army Major Ray Melnyk, an operations officer on Tom Kelly's staff, had prepared briefing maps and charts for me. I sent them back because they were full of military jargon, suitable for Fort Benning, maybe, but not helpful in explaining to the American people what their sons and daughters were doing in Panama. Melnyk quickly drafted simpler maps, and I spent the next hour memorizing the missions, the units, and our twenty-seven targets.

That morning, on television, after Cheney spoke, I explained every detail down to the last platoon assault. I reminded the audience that this was an ongoing campaign. Most of our objectives had been taken, but we expected continued resistance from PDF remnants and paramilitary units, called "Dignity Battalions," mostly street gangs armed by Noriega. So far, we had lost only four soldiers, but we should expect more casualties. My intention was to convey a sense of calm and confidence that we knew what we were doing. The reputation of the American armed forces was on the line. Desert One, the bombing of the Marine headquarters in Lebanon, the messy Grenada invasion, and the shootdown of the Iranian airliner had all contributed to skepticism about the U.S. military and its leadership. I remembered our Project 14 advice to General Wickham six years earlier—we have got to win cleanly the next time.

I took questions from the reporters, and right off the bat they wanted to know about Noriega. If we did not catch him, what was the point of invading Panama? I responded, "We have now decapitated him from the dictatorship of his country." Wouldn't it make life miserable for the U.S. forces down there, a reporter asked, if Noriega was still running around in the Panamanian wilds? "It's been some years," I answered, "since Mr. Noriega . . . had been living in a jungle. He's used to a different kind of lifestyle, and I'm not sure he would be up to being chased around the countryside by Army Rangers, Special Forces, and light infantry units." Another reporter persisted: could we really consider Just Cause successful as long as we did not have Noriega in custody? "The operation is a success already," I said, "because we cut off the head of that government, and there is a new government that was elected by the Panamanian people." Still, it would be more convincing, I knew, if we could produce the head.

When I got back to my office the phone was ringing. It was Alma. "You were pretty good," she said. My sternest critic had given me a passing grade.

By the next day, most of the fighting was over, except for scattered skirmishes with the Dignity Battalions. Noriega, however, still eluded us. We brought in more infantrymen from the 7th Division to comb the countryside and run down the remainder of the PDF. These troops went from town to town shouting "boo," which convinced the once feared PDF detachments to surrender. We packed Panama City with more troops to maintain order. We put up temporary housing for Panamanians displaced by the fighting and fires that had burned down several blocks, particularly around the Comandancia.

President Endara had been sworn in a few hours before H-Hour and was now in the Presidential Palace. Twenty-four Americans gave their lives in Panama to achieve this victory for democracy. My private estimate to Cheney had been that we would lose about twenty troops. Our armed forces had acquitted themselves superbly, although we had made some mistakes. We did not plan well enough for reintroducing civil government. Our press arrangements produced recriminations on both sides. We were slow in getting the press pool to Panama and to the action. Pete Williams, the Defense Department spokesman, tried to compensate by sending a commercial airliner to Panama loaded with a couple of hundred reporters whom we could not properly accommodate. Consequently, the press ate us alive, with some justification. In the future, I knew, we needed to do a far better job.

Yet things had happened on the press side during Just Cause that tested to the limit my customary support of the media. On the second day of the invasion, I watched President Bush during a televised press conference. He was visibly upbeat after the quick success of Just Cause. The President could not know that as he was giving occasionally smiling answers to reporters, the networks were simultaneously showing on split screens a transport plane at Dover Air Force Base, Delaware, unloading the bodies of the first American casualties. The effect was to make the President look callous. Sensational images, but cheap-shot journalism.

I was angered when the press started trying to direct the war as well as cover it. Near the center of Panama City stood a radio tower. Every armchair strategist knows that you have to knock out the enemy's capacity to communicate. And look at that, the U.S. military had foolishly left this transmitter operating, broadcasting prerecorded Noriega propaganda. The White House started taking flak from the press over the still-standing tower. And I started taking flak from Brent Scowcroft. I told him that the tower was not bothering us, and we did not yet have troops in that part of town to take it. We did not want to knock the tower down anyway, because President Endara would need it in a day or so. No dice. The press heat was too great and the tower had to go. I told Thurman and Stiner to destroy it. They were mad as hell at being overmanaged from the sidelines and for being ordered to take a pointless objective. But soon, Cobra attack helicopters were shooting missiles at the girders, not unlike my old Vietnamese buddies shooting down trees with a rifle.

After the first night at the crisis center, we were back in our offices. I got another call at the Pentagon

from Brent Scowcroft telling me that several correspondents were trapped in the Marriott Hotel in
Panama City. "We've got to put troops in to rescue
them," Brent said.

"They're in no danger," I pointed out. "I've
checked the situation. They're safe in the basement
of the hotel. The fighting will soon sweep right past
them."

I thought I had convinced Brent until I got a second call. He was taking terrific presssure from
bureau chiefs and network executives in New York.
"We've got to do something," he said.

"We shouldn't do anything," I reiterated. "We've
got a perfectly competent commander on the ground.
He's got a plan, and it's working." Were kibitzers supposed to direct the fighting in Panama from executive
suites in Manhattan? I reminded Brent that there were
35,000 other American citizens in Panama, and we
were trying to ensure the safety of all of them. Only a
few minutes passed before Cheney called. There was
no discussion. Do it, he said. No more arguments.

Again, I reluctantly called Thurman and Stiner.
"I hate to tell you this," I said as I explained the situation. "But get those reporters out, and I'll try to
keep Washington off your backs in the future."
Stiner sent in units of the 82d Airborne to storm the
Marriott. On the way, they ran into a stiff firefight.
We got the reporters out, but the 82d took casualties,
three GIs wounded, one seriously, and a Spanish
photographer was killed by American fire while
covering the rescue.

I told Cheney that I did not want to pass along
any more such orders. "If the press has to cover a

war," I said, "there's no way we can eliminate the risks of war." Cheney called Scowcroft and asked him not to issue any more orders from the sidelines. This was a new, tough age for the military, fighting a war as it was being reported. We could not, in a country pledged to free expression, simply turn off the press. But we were going to have to find a way to live with this unprecedented situation.

Early on Christmas Eve, I was in my garage trying to relax by pulling the engine on one of my Volvos when my cellular phone started ringing. My exec, Tom White, was calling with the news we had been hoping for. I let out a whoop and a holler and ran back into the kitchen. "They found Noriega!" I shouted to Alma. Our troops had been searching for him for days in hideouts and hinterland villages. We had missed him on the first night while he hid in a whorehouse. Noriega had just sought sanctuary, Tom had told me, in the Papal Nunciatura in Panama City. He had called the papal nuncio, Monsignor Sebastian Laboa, and asked to be picked up in a Dairy Queen parking lot near San Miguelito. There the strongman was found waiting in a dirty T-shirt, shapeless Bermuda shorts, and an oversize baseball cap pulled low over his all too recognizable face.

My relief was even greater ten days later on January 3, when Monsignor Laboa persuaded Noriega that the game was up and that he should turn himself over to the Americans. The Vatican looked on Noriega as an accused criminal with no legitimate claim to political asylum. As soon as the Panamanian people learned that Noriega was in U.S. custody, they started dancing in the streets. Until then, they had been afraid that he might yet return to power.

I flew to Panama in early January for a firsthand look and to visit the troops. While with the 82d Airborne, commanded by Major General Jim Johnson, I was carried away. "Goddam, you guys did a good job!" I said. Fred Francis of NBC caught my outburst on camera, and I made the evening news. Anyone fearing a moral decline in this country may be heartened to know that the Joint Staff mailroom was soon flooded with complaints about the chairman's language.

Our euphoria over our victory in Just Cause was not universal. Both the United Nations and the Organization of American States censured our actions in Panama. Reports circulated of heavy civilian casualties. Some human rights organizations claimed that the invasion had resulted in thousands of Panamanians killed. At the time, Max Thurman's SOUTHCOM staff estimated Panamanian casualties in the low hundreds. Subsequently, the House Armed Services Committee carried out a thorough investigation, which estimated that three hundred Panamanians were killed, of whom one hundred were civilians and the rest members of the PDF and the Dignity Battalions. The loss of innocent lives was tragic, but we had made every effort to hold down casualties on all sides.

A CBS poll conducted soon after the installation of President Endara showed that nine out of ten Panamanians favored the U.S. intervention. President George Bush had been vindicated in a bold political decision. Generals Thurman and Stiner and all the troops under them had achieved a victory for democracy with minimal bloodshed. The American people supported the action and were again proud of their armed forces. We had a success under our belt.

The lessons I absorbed from Panama confirmed all my convictions over the preceding twenty years, since the days of doubt over Vietnam. Have a clear political objective and stick to it. Use all the force necessary, and do not apologize for going in big if that is what it takes. Decisive force ends wars quickly and in the long run saves lives. Whatever threats we faced in the future, I intended to make these rules the bedrock of my military counsel.

As I write these words, almost six years after Just Cause, Mr. Noriega, convicted on the drug charges contained in the indictments, sits in an American prison cell. Panama has a new security force, and the country is still a democracy, with one free election to its credit.

17 ★ *When You've Lost Your Best Enemy*

I MAY OWE one of my best pieces of work as Chairman of the JCS to the unlikely figure of Arnold Schwarzenegger. I had managed to whip myself into good physical condition at FORSCOM. But now, back in the Beltway pressure cooker, I was starting to get out of shape. One night I found myself sitting next to Arnold at a charity dinner and confessed that I had relapsed.

"You need a Lifecycle," Arnold said. "I'll send you one."

"I can't take anything from a contractor or a manufacturer," I pointed out.

"You won't have to," he answered. "Consider it a personal gift from me." A stationary bike with computer-controlled resistance soon arrived, and I now started my day working out on it as soon as I got up at 5:30 A.M. I did some of my clearest thinking during the half hour on the Lifecycle.

I was pumping away on a Saturday morning, November 4, some weeks before the Panama operation, when I started to crystallize what I really wanted to accomplish as chairman. I saw it as my main mission to move the armed forces onto a new course, one paralleling what was happening in the world today, not one chained to the previous forty years. As soon as I was out of the shower, I went to my study and started jotting down thoughts on purple-bordered notepads. The color had been chosen deliberately to symbolize that the chairman belonged to no individual service.

What I was hatching amounted to analysis by instinct. I was not going on intelligence estimates, war games, or computer projections. And I intended to avoid the still rather ponderous, paper-churning machinery of the Joint Staff. My thoughts were guided simply by what I had observed at world summits, by my experience at the NSC, by what I like to think of as informed intuition. I was going to project what I expected to happen over the next five years and try to design an Army, Navy, Air Force, and Marine Corps to match these expectations. I wrote at the top of the pad, "Strategic Overview — 1994."

I wrote down what I foresaw in the Soviet Union: "Rise of opposition parties, Western investment, market pricing, and Gorbachev still supreme authority." (You can't win 'em all.) I predicted Soviet military budget cuts of 40 percent, manpower cuts of 50 percent, a cap on naval shipbuilding—in short, a Soviet force intended strictly for a "defensive posture." And then I really stuck my neck out: by 1994, "No Soviet forces in Eastern Europe"; "Warsaw Pact replaced"; "East Germany gone"; all Eastern-bloc countries "neutral states with multiparty systems." I also wrote, regarding Germany, "reunified," and Berlin, "undivided." In South Africa, I anticipated by 1994 a "black majority government," and in Latin America, "Cuba isolated, irrelevant." Of course, trouble spots would persist, and I identified them as "Korea, Lebanon, the Persian Gulf, Philippines." I made another heading, "Potential U.S. involvement," and under it listed two places, "Korea, Persian Gulf."

I began matching these projections to a commensurate strength and structure for the U.S. military. And here, going almost entirely on gut feelings, I wrote, "From a 550-ship to a 450-ship Navy, reduce our troop strength in Europe from 300,000 to between 75,000 and 100,000, and cut back the active duty Army from 760,000 to 525,000." The Marines, the Air Force, and the reserves would be cut as well.

These levels would be tough to sell to Cheney. He was still a hard-liner and not ready to bet on a "kinder and gentler" Soviet Union. But he was also savvy, and not long out of Congress, where he had sensed the mounting political pressure to cut back on defense spending and declare a peace dividend. Cheney had already approved a budget for the next fiscal year that reflected real reductions in spending. But we had pasted that budget together without any overarching strategic vision. Early on, the Bush administration commissioned a major study, National Security Review No. 12, to come up with a new strategy. But NSR 12 was being drafted by career bureaucrats and few administration appointees. The study team did not have a vision or practical political guidance from the President and his NSC team. The principal value of this study seemed to be to provide the administration with a defense against critics of inaction—NSR 12 is looking into that, the White House could say. But NSR 12 came up short, a bland work, full of generalities and truisms, doomed to the dustbin.

Meanwhile, Congress, independent national security think tanks, and self-styled freelance military experts were blanketing the town with proposals. We had to get in front of them if we were to control our own destiny. Paul Wolfowitz, the undersecretary for policy, and his new team began to work. I was determined to have the Joint Chiefs drive the military strategy train, so I had scoped out certain ideas, even if they represented hunches more than analysis. I wanted to offer something our allies could rally around and give our critics something to shoot at rather than having military reorganization schemes shoved down our throat.

After the weekend in which I had done my solitary brainstorming, Otis drove me to work in the chairman's Cadillac. My mind was so afire with ideas that I hardly heard what Otis was talking about, until he extended an arm into the backseat holding a Beretta pistol. He assured me he had obtained legal permission to carry a gun, and that as my driver-bodyguard, he ought to be armed.

Once in the office, I turned on the tape player and went over my jottings one more time with the help of a little subliminal Mozart. Then I called in Lieutenant General George "Lee" Butler and Major General John "Dave" Robinson, directors of the Joint Staff responsible for strategy and budgeting respectively. They and their aides had already done some work on restructuring. I gave Butler and Robinson my rough notes from the weekend and told them to recast them as briefing charts. And I wanted the graphics within two days. The title of this slide show was my own, "Strategic Overview — 1994," but I paraphrased a subtitle from Mikhail Gorbachev, "When You Lose Your Best Enemy."

Although I had been chairman for only a month at this time, I had cautioned the chiefs that change was inevitable and had shared my thoughts with them. These were bright, sophisticated men who could see what was happening in the Soviet Union. But each of them, as the head of a service, ran a huge bureaucratic institution with a massive investment in the past. And each chief naturally preferred to have force reductions fall more heavily on the other guy. Within the JCS, only the chairman and vice chairman could assume bureaucratic neutrality. After years of watching the chiefs, I knew that they would not willingly contribute more than loose change as the collection plate was passed. They would practically have to be mugged, and preferred to be mugged to prove to their institution that they had fought the good fight before the budget ax fell.

The Army and Air Force were the most vulnerable. They had the most invested in fighting an air-land battle in Europe against the Red Army, a battle that was almost certainly never going to be fought. Army chief Carl Vuono and Air Force chief Larry Welch knew that they would have to cut deeply, but not as much as I had in mind.

The Navy was next in line for a substantial whack, since its major mission was to protect the Atlantic sea-lanes so that we could get to Europe to fight World War III. Part of the rationale for the Navy's aircraft carriers was to project power ashore against an invading Red Army, a role fast becoming obsolete. The Chief of Naval Operations, Admiral Carl Trost, who had only eight months left on his watch, was not disposed to give up much naval power just because the Army and Air Force might be losing their enemy. Trost argued that the Soviet navy was still growing and, until intelligence reports showed otherwise, the American fleet should not be shrunk drastically.

The Marines were on somewhat firmer ground. With justification, they presented themselves as the nation's "911" response force, with or without a Soviet Union. General Al Gray, the Marine Commandant (a colorful guy who chewed tobacco in our meetings), would fight to the death against anything beyond a symbolic nick in the size of the Corps. Yet, the Marines had also benefited from the Reagan buildup, which had been aimed at the now fading Soviet threat. The Marine Corps would have to take its hits too.

There was no way I could get group consensus. The chiefs also knew, however, that with the new Goldwater-Nichols authority, I did not need consensus. I could give my recommendations to the Secretary of Defense and the President on my own. Still, realistically, I knew that we had to shape the new military as a team.

A few days later, on November 10, the most brutal symbol of communist oppression, the Berlin Wall, cracked open, with the East German government's acquiescence. East Germans came pouring through for a taste of freedom. The most hard-shelled anticommunist had to see that the old order was not simply changing; it was falling apart. On November 14, I took a deep breath and submitted my strategic overview to Secretary Cheney. He did not embrace it on the spot, but gave me a fair hearing. If our defenses had to be chopped back, Cheney too wanted his hand, not some outsider's, guiding the ax. He was also concerned that in a few weeks Bush was heading to a summit meeting with Gorbachev in Malta and did not have a strategic concept for the future. After examining my charts, he said, "All right. We'll take this to the President."

I went back to my office and told the staff to have a clean set of charts ready by the close of business, since the Secretary and I would be going to the White House the next day. They looked stunned, and I could understand why. In the past, sea changes far less radical than what I was proposing took years rather than days to work their way through the Joint Staff labyrinth.

The next day, as we entered the White House Situation Room, Cheney displayed an uneasiness I had not seen before. Until now, he and Bob Gates, Scowcroft's NSC deputy, had both been saying that the hard-line communists might well knock off Gorbachev and restore the bad old days. Now Cheney was letting his chairman make a pitch to the President premised on just the opposite. Uneasy or not, I gave Dick credit. He was willing to test his bedrock beliefs against fresh evidence; and he wanted the President to have the same opportunity. The Situation Room this day held the heart of the Bush team: the President; his Vice President, Dan Quayle; John Sununu, the Chief of Staff; Secretary of State Jim Baker; Treasury Secretary Nick Brady; Brent Scowcroft; and Gates. Dick Darman, director of OMB, was also there, about to be thrown into cardiac shock—a defense team proposing *less* spending.

I made my presentation. The President listened but remained noncommittal. I had gained as much as

I hoped for at this stage; neither a green light nor a red light, but maybe a yellow light. Proceed with caution. President Bush posed two questions. What was the bottom line that we should present to the Soviets, and what should we expect in return? Since he was about to embark on the summit with Gorbachev at Malta within days, the questions were crucial. Cheney said that we would have answers for him before he left.

Carl Vuono had said that I could keep the chiefs in my corner by making sure of one thing—that I always kept them informed. I had just violated that rule. Although they were generally aware of my ideas, I should have given them the specific "Strategic Overview—1994" briefing before taking it to the President. My only excuse was the pressure of time. The next day, I gathered the chiefs in the "Tank," the flag-draped secure room in the Pentagon reserved for meetings of the Joint Chiefs. (The expression "Tank" derived from a tunnel the service chiefs had to pass through to reach their first meeting room in the Department of Interior building before the Pentagon was completed in 1942.) Alongside each chief's seat were the customary dishes of candy and dried fruit that some disdained and others devoured. I presented the same slide show I had given to the President the day before. I could see the raised eyebrows. I had blindsided them, not a mistake I intended to make again.

Before President Bush departed for Malta, Cheney and I recommended to him that he let Gorbachev know the changes we were contemplating. In return, he should press Gorbachev to withdraw Soviet troops from Eastern Europe rapidly and bring them home where they would not present an offensive threat. He should also press Gorbachev for greater reductions in Soviet defense spending and the end of Soviet support of Third World insurgencies.

I did not have to wait long before events began to vindicate my prediction of trouble spots. In late November 1989, after the failed Giroldi coup and before Just Cause, we had to respond to a coup against President Corazon Aquino of the Philippines. I have read former Vice President Dan Quayle's description of this uprising in his book, *Standing Firm.* "I was the one asking the questions, seeking the options and pushing for a consensus," Quayle wrote. "I can remember Larry Eagleburger [the acting Secretary of State] saying afterward that if I hadn't been there, we might not have stopped the coup in the Philippines. It was a great hour in the relations between our two countries, and a great moment for me personally." True enough, but there were a few rocky moments that evening.

On November 29, Cheney and I had just returned from a conference in Brussels. Cheney, exhausted and ill with the flu, went home and stayed there. I went to work the next day, returned home, and gratefully hit the sack soon after dinner. An hour later, the phone rang, and I was informed by Tom Kelly that a coup was under way in the Philippines headed by a General Edgardo Abenina. I went immediately to the National Military Command Center in the Pentagon, arriving just after 11:00 P.M. I entered a room designed specifically for dealing with such situations. It was small, low-ceilinged; my steps were muffled by gray carpeting. The room was cold, kept that way to aid the performance of the supersensitive electronic gear. We were using a new teleconferencing system that allowed people from various agencies to confer without leaving their buildings. This was the first time the system would be used in an actual crisis. I sat at a table facing five television monitors. On one I could see the White House Situation Room, with Vice President Quayle at the center of the table. Quayle was there because President Bush was in the air flying to Malta for his meeting with Gorbachev. The face of Larry Eagleburger at the State Department filled a second screen. On a third was Bill Webster, the CIA director, and on a fourth, Harry Rowen, assistant secretary of defense for international security affairs, who was upstairs in the Pentagon. I could see myself on the fifth screen. Next to me sat General Bob Herres, the vice chairman, who had also been a candidate for chairman. Herres was approaching retirement, but would be of enormous help to me down to his last day. Bob went home to get some rest after I relieved him so that one of us would be fresh in the morning. Also, by pure chance, the CINC for all our forces in the Pacific, Admiral Huntington "Hunt" Hardisty, was there too, having come from Honolulu to the Pentagon for budget talks.

President Corazon Aquino, I was informed, had reported that the presidential palace in Manila was being bombed and strafed by rebel planes. She had requested U.S. military intervention to stop the attacks. Eagleburger argued hard in favor of answering Aquino's appeal. "We sponsored this democratic government," he said, "and we have to respond." Sporadic reports kept arriving; there was gunfire here and there, and a possible need to rescue Aquino from the palace. But we were hearing more confusion than hard information.

Our ambassador in Manila, Nicholas Platt, reconfirmed an official request that we bomb an airfield under rebel control. Mothy old T-28s, World War II prop-driven trainers, based at this field, were the planes attacking the capital. Again, State was eager to respond. I called Dick Cheney to update him. He intended to handle his end this night from his sickbed, since he could reach the President's plane by secure phone. I also suspected that Cheney preferred to stay home rather than deal with Quayle on the monitor. It seemed to me that in military decision-making Cheney wanted to deal directly with the President.

The Vice President said he needed to contact President Bush soon with a recommendation. I had taken a media beating for holding back on the Giroldi coup in Panama in October. If I wanted to overcome any impression of indecisiveness, I should have plunged ahead now. But I was not about to be stampeded. I started asking questions. We could bomb the airfield, but did we know who we would be bombing? Who would we hit, rebels or loyalists? The State Department probably pictured a neat, surgical strike. Instead, I envisioned anxious young pilots flying their first combat missions, not precision-tooled automatons. My concern was that if we started shooting up planes on the airfield, we were inevitably going to kill people, and I warned the other teleconferees, "I can guarantee you that the Filipinos are going to blast us at their funerals, no matter which side we hurt." We were still, in some quarters, viewed and resented as former colonial masters.

Before we did anything rash, we needed more on-site information. I wanted to talk to Fidel Ramos, the Philippine defense minister, to get an eyeball account. It just happened that the American military attaché ordinarily posted to our embassy in Manila was also in the Pentagon this night, upstairs with Harry Rowen. This officer had a little black book with the phone numbers of all top Filipino defense officials. I told him to send it down to the command center, where I handed it to a Navy watch officer. "Just keep dialing," I told this officer, "until you get me a military officer at the top."

You might think, given the billions we spend on defense communications—direct lines, secure lines, scrambled lines, satellites—that my request would be a cinch. Instead, the Navy officer informed me, "I can't reach their guys with this hardware, General. I need a plain old telephone." In this supersophisticated center we did not have a single ordinary line. A sergeant popped up and said, "I can get you one, sir." Go to it, I said, and he started tearing up the floor panels to run a line in. Our resourceful sergeant quickly produced a functioning commercial telephone.

In the meantime, I described to Quayle and the others a plan that Hardisty and I had devised: have our F-4 Phantom jets stationed at Clark Air Force Base buzz any T-28s daring to come onto the runway at the rebel-held airbase. In short, scare hell out of them. If any of these planes started to take off, fire in front of them. And if any took off, shoot them down. I concocted a phrase to include in the order to convey the desired sense of menace. Our aircraft were to demonstrate "extreme hostile intent." I called Cheney, who agreed. He contacted Air Force One and called me back within ten minutes to tell me we had the President's approval. In short, we had a clear line of authority for graduated military action, commander in chief to Secretary of Defense through me to the appropriate military units. "Go," Cheney said.

While all this was happening, Dan Quayle had also called the President's plane, and just as I was about to have Hardisty transmit the order for the F-4s to take to the air, Andrew Card, John Sununu's deputy, came up on the screen and said, "Hold up— the Vice President is getting new instructions from Air Force One." I already had instructions from Air Force One! I waited uneasily before calling Cheney back to tell him of the crossed wires. This was untidy crisis management. On my screen, I saw Quayle come back into the Situation Room wearing an unconcerned expression. "I've talked to the President," was all he said.

"Does that mean we can go?" I asked.

"Oh," he replied. "I thought you already had."

I turned to Admiral Hardisty and gave him the go order. For a few hairy minutes I had been in the uncomfortable position of serving two masters, a prescription for confusion. The F-4s were launched. They buzzed the airfield repeatedly, and no Filipino pilot took off to see what would happen next.

Finally, after dialing for nearly forty minutes, the Navy watch officer managed to locate Fidel Ramos, the Philippine defense minister, and his chief of staff, General Renato De Villa. They told me that the situation was dicey, but under control. Bombing? Who was asking us to bomb anything? Don't bomb, we were told. Within hours, the coup collapsed without our getting further involved and without the F-4s shooting up anybody or anything. And we learned that there had indeed been forces loyal to President Aquino at the airfield. A few days later, General Abenina, the coup leader, said, "We were about to take over the government. Then the U.S. warplanes appeared. We simply cannot hope to win against the stronger power of the United States Air Force."

The night the coup ended, I left the Pentagon feeling good. I had applied Clausewitz's teachings, or Weinberger's Maxim No. 3, and my own rule in forming military advice: take no action until you have a clear objective. We had applied restrained, proportionate, calibrated force, linked to a specific goal. And it had worked.

A few days later, Dick Cheney was well and back in the saddle. After a morning staff meeting, he asked me to stay behind. "That went reasonably well," he said of the Philippine episode. "But don't worry, you will never be put in that situation again. From now on, the channel of communication will be clear at all times. You can be sure of that." I could read between the lines. There had evidently been a discussion at the White House as to how instructions from the President would be passed in a crisis.

When I read Dan Quayle's book, I could understand why, after the media drubbing he had taken over the previous months, he wanted to look presidential. And he did perform well in the Philippine situation. But when it was over, his aides put a spin on the story that exaggerated Quayle's role. The *Los Angeles Times* reported, ". . . it was a chance to shine and one that [Quayle] seized with gusto."

With the Philippine crisis resolved, and Just Cause ended in Panama, we could get back to redesigning the armed forces. In February 1990, Secretary Cheney would have to submit a defense budget for fiscal 1991–1992, and I hoped to use the time in between to win his support for my plan to reshape the force. What I had shown him and the President thus far had been influenced by my experience years before in Bill DePuy's operation when we had tried to project the smallest Army that could still meet our world responsibilities. This time around, I came up with a label, the "Base Force," to describe such a minimum level for all the services. The question now was how far below present levels we could safely set that base. I was thinking in terms that I knew would jar the JCS—15 percent, 20 percent, even 25 percent.

. . .

After three stimulating months as chairman, I was finally getting into a comfortable routine. I wanted a congenial atmosphere in the chairman's office. I favor a light touch with my associates, which you can achieve only with those in whom you have absolute trust and who do not mistake an easygoing style for lax standards. I like staff members who take their work seriously, but not themselves. I like people who work hard and play hard. I long ago concluded that organization charts and fancy titles count for next to nothing. I told my staff that they should go in and out of my office without exaggerated ceremony. I was well on my way to achieving this atmosphere by surrounding myself with able, compatible souls who did not lose their cool even when I was bouncing off the walls. And since I am not one of those managers who believe the new broom has to sweep clean, I happily retained a gem from my predecessor, Admiral Crowe, to handle media relations, Colonel F. William Smullen.

I next took a look at the directors of the Joint Staff. These were two- and three-star admirals and generals who ran a large staff and worked directly for the chairman and not the Joint Chiefs. The chairman's more powerful position made the Joint Staff an attractive assignment. More to the point, Goldwater-Nichols had made service in a joint position a criterion for promotion to higher rank. Consequently, I had no trouble recruiting first-rate talent. The Joint Staff became the finest military staff anywhere in the world.

I think it is important for a boss to be frank about his temperament and work habits so that people working for him have a chance to understand and adjust. I warned the staff that when I am preoccupied, I can be short-tempered over interruptions or questions. In high-pressure situations, I tend to snap into a single-minded mode. I become intense, focused, oblivious of the world around me. On those days, I might walk into the office without so much as a hello. If my executive officer brought me some issue not immediately relevant, I might growl and tell him to keep out of my way. I advised the staff not to overreact to these mood swings. Ride them out, and I would soon be back on an even keel.

The more senior I became, the more precious became my time, the one commodity I could not stretch. I developed some simple rules: the staff was not to commit me to any meeting, speaking or social engagement, trip, or ceremony without my approval. Not even for five minutes. And when I did schedule a meeting, it was to start on time. People who keep other people waiting are being inconsiderate. I react to waiting for people who show up late about as patiently as I do to a taxi meter clicking in stalled traffic. And my office was to return phone calls promptly.

I instituted Kester's law on signatures. John Kester taught me that every time I put my name to something, I created a legal document. Consequently, no one should sign anything for me but the most innocuous paper. I knew of bosses who allowed their secretaries to sign their names to correspondence of substance, a practice I never permitted. Kester also taught me that a dated document became even more legal. Consequently, no pre- or postdated signings. I sign only on the actual date on the document.

I ordered my staff not to prepare any "bedbug" letters for my signature. The expression originated with an old story about the New York Central Railroad. A passenger writes to the railroad's president reporting his outrage at being bitten by a bedbug in his Pullman bed. A letter of apology comes back from the president of the railroad explaining the lengths the company went to to ensure that such things never happened, and assuring the passenger that it would not happen again. The passenger reads the letter feeling pretty good until a little scribbled handwritten note from the president to his secretary falls out of the envelope: "Send this SOB the bedbug letter."

My staff might get a letter from some citizen with a gripe and draft a form reply for me saying, "Thanks for your concern, but these things happen"; or "Sorry, wrong department." I would scrawl across the top, "Find out the problem and see if we can fix it. And if we can't, tell the writer who can. But no bedbug letters."

As chairman, I stuck by my old maxim to check small things, reinforced long ago at Pathfinder school when I had discovered the sergeant's static line unconnected. Checking small things achieves two purposes. It reveals to the commander the real state of readiness in contrast to a surface appearance of readiness. And a general's attention to detail lets the soldier far down the chain know that his link is as vital as the one that precedes or follows.

In running the large Joint Staff, I relied on techniques picked up from Brown, Weinberger, Carlucci, and others over the years. Every morning at precisely 0831 hours I entered the Joint Staff conference room for an 0830 meeting. My principal staff officers, mostly two- and three-star generals and admirals, about twenty in all, knew that they had one minute to avoid being considered late. I abolished the formal briefing format used by previous chairmen, which kept the graphics staff up all night running off charts. I went around the table and had the generals and admirals tell me what was going on in their area. If the honest answer was "nothing," that was what I wanted to hear, without any penalty for this straight response. The meeting lasted from five to thirty minutes. I used it to check signals and launch the day, rather than to resolve issues. The meeting also had another more important purpose. I wanted the staff directors to check me out. Was I mad? Was I in a joking mood telling old war stories? Was I passing out compliments or "dammits"? I always tried to be upbeat, especially if something was going bad and we faced trouble. The boss's mood infects the organization. The worst situation is when no one knows what the leader's mood is. My staff could tell first thing in the morning. By the same token, I could detect the same in them. When you meet with people every day, you learn to read them at a glance, you know who has a problem, who needs help or bucking up, who is expecting a butt chewing. The morning meeting was meant for team building. The serious work was done in small groups around a little round table in my office.

In bureaucracies, small matters can have large symbolic value. One day, Al Gray, the feisty Marine Corps Commandant, pointed out that a document had gone to the Secretary of Defense over my signature on Joint Chiefs of Staff stationery. "If you're going to send out stuff in the name of the chiefs," Al said, "we all have to okay it, and I never saw that piece of paper before it went up." Al was right.

Under Goldwater-Nichols, I was principal military adviser. I did not have to take a vote among the chiefs before I recommended anything. I did not even have to consult them, though it would be foolish not to do so. But I needed a symbolic gesture to make the point of the chairman's independence. I ordered a batch of stationery that had "Chairman, Joint Chiefs of Staff" printed across the top. I threw out the old stationery and with it threw out forty years of JCS bureaucratic tradition. I was not the pipeline for the composite opinions of the chiefs. I was speaking for myself to the Secretary and the President. A one-word change in a letterhead made that clear and legitimate.

I initiated a couple of other new techniques for doing business. Increasingly, I had the chiefs meet alone without any staff officers or notetakers present. Not very good for historians, but a great way to encourage candor. I also preferred meeting with the chiefs in my office instead of the Tank, which carried the baggage of the old corporate body. I also stopped putting out fixed agendas for the JCS meetings. The chiefs did not mind, but their staffs did not like it. Without an agenda, they did not know what papers to prepare for their bosses before the meetings. As a result, the chiefs did not come to my office loaded with positions that they felt they had to defend. They actually had greater freedom in speaking their minds. Since we no longer voted, they did not have to go back to their bureaucracies and defend a vote. Some will no doubt dispute me, but I believe this new style gave the chiefs more clout than they had enjoyed as a more formal body. If I bought their ideas, I was ready to take them to Cheney and advocate them as strongly as my own. In this way, their advice got real consideration, rather than the almost automatic dismissal accorded to the ponderous, toothless consensus reports of the past.

At the time we were brainstorming a reshaped military at home, I had a chance to see up close what shape our old adversary was taking. Jack Maresca, our ambassador to the Conference on Security and Cooperation in Europe, was involved in organizing a CSCE seminar designed to defuse East-West tensions. It was unprecedented. The military chiefs of the NATO nations *and* the Warsaw Pact countries *and* nonaligned European countries were going to meet in January 1990 at the Hofburg Palace in Vienna, where the Congress of Vienna had taken place in 1814 to redraw the map of Europe after the defeat of Napoleon. Maresca asked me to attend the seminar, and I agreed.

Entering the gilded conference hall on January 16, I took my place at a huge U-shaped table and saw across from me a man I would have spotted as a soldier even if he had not been in the uniform of a Soviet general. He was Mikhail Moiseyev, who had replaced Sergei Akhromeyev as chief of the Soviet general staff. What a switch—Akhromeyev, in his seventies, World War II vintage, small, grandfatherly; and Moiseyev, fifty-one, big, energetic, forceful in manner and bearing.

In my remarks, I wanted to make a point that I thought had been lost ever since history had thrust the United States into superpower status. With all our power, it was still not easy being a military figure under our political system. "I was required to take an oath to support and defend the Constitution of the United States," I pointed out. And I explained that this document "looks at the military and, in particular, at my service, the Army, as a necessary but *undesirable* institution, useful in times of crisis, and to be watched carefully at all other times."

I pointed out further that from our country's birth, the American people had resisted the idea of a standing army. One author of the Constitution recommended a limit of two thousand troops. And I quoted George Washington's response: "An excellent idea— if only we can convince our collected enemies to maintain no more than an equivalent amount." And I pointed out that I, as chairman with my four stars, was not the highest-ranking military figure in America.

That person was the commander in chief, the President, a civilian. And I reminded this audience of allies, adversaries, and potential enemies of the fundamental purpose of American arms: "The American people have insisted that when we have to raise armies, their posture must be defensive and the rationale for their size must be relentlessly examined. As I sit here today, my Congress is at home thinking up ways to shrink our Army. This is the way it is in a democracy, and I would want it no other way."

I had tried to set a tone of conciliation and nonbelligerence. Therefore, I was eager to see what approach the new chief of the Soviet armed forces would take when Moiseyev's turn came to speak. I was disappointed. He sounded like the Soviet counterpart of America's knee-jerk Cold Warriors. Out came all the stock, stale, confrontational clichés, all neatly printed in a bound booklet his aides distributed. Moiseyev took questions after his speech and came off like a recorder spouting canned Kremlin tapes. I was concerned because I had stuck my neck out claiming that the world had become a different place, while Moiseyev's performance said that little had changed.

I whispered my concern to Ambassador Maresca. I needed to get to know this man better, I said, to see if there was anything more here than an old Soviet warhorse. Maresca arranged a small private dinner in his Vienna apartment for that evening. I took with me Tom White, my executive assistant, and Peter Afanasenko, a superb Russian interpreter from the State Department.

When our guest came through the door that night, I thought maybe we had the wrong man. All the bluster was gone. Moiseyev seemed warm and relaxed. We sat down to dinner, and he quickly demonstrated that at least one thing still worked in the Soviet Union, the intelligence system. "You entered the Army in 1958?" he said.

"Yes," I answered.

"And so did I. You were married in 1962?"

"Yes," I answered again.

"And so was I. You have a son, and he was commissioned in the Army?"

"Yes," I said.

"I too have a son in the army." Then Moiseyev wagged his finger at me and said, laughing, "But I have accomplished all this at fifty-one, while you are almost fifty-three!"

That broke the ice. As the vodka flowed, the atmosphere continued to warm up. Moiseyev told us about his boyhood in Siberia, where his father had been a gandy dancer on the Trans-Siberian Railroad who never missed a day no matter how low the temperature dropped. His mother still lived in their hometown in Siberia. Only when the subject of the Baltics came up—the United States still regarded them as occupied nations—did I glimpse the old Soviet belligerence and this man's toughness. He had lost seven uncles in World War II, Moiseyev said, soldiers who died liberating places like Latvia, Lithuania, and Estonia from the Nazis, and now they hated the Soviet Union?

Toward the end of the evening, he and I had become two old infantrymen swapping war stories. I felt comfortable enough to start raising some questions. "We all know the Soviet Union's in the midst of change," I said. "What's the point of peddling that old threadbare party line?" He also knew that the Soviet armies were going to pull out completely from bases in the bloc countries. "Why don't you do it faster?" I asked. "Because the children have to finish the school year," he said. The answer was so perfectly understandable from one soldier-parent to another that I burst out laughing. I do not know if any of my advice got through that night, but as we parted, Moiseyev threw a bear hug around me and said, "I feel like I have known you all my life." For my part, I felt that I had met someone hovering between an old-fashioned communist adversary and a new army buddy.

Room 2118 of the Rayburn Building, the hearing room of the House Armed Services Committee, has a plaque in front of the dais that reads:

U.S. CONSTITUTION—ART I, SEC 8
THE CONGRESS SHALL HAVE POWER . . .
TO RAISE AND SUPPORT ARMIES . . .
PROVIDE AND MAINTAIN A NAVY . . .
MAKE RULES FOR THE GOVERNMENT AND
REGULATION OF THE LAND AND NAVAL FORCES.

I assume the plaque is there in case anyone does not understand who, in matters of defense, controls the pocketbook. On February 1, Cheney and I were in Room 2118 to defend the proposed Pentagon budget for 1991–92. In the past, determining what we needed militarily had been easy. Lay out the Soviet threat and come up with whatever was required to meet it. But with the Soviet military shrinking, we faced a likely stampede by members of Congress arguing that there was no threat, hence no need for a large military. "Peace Dividend" had become a fashionable phrase. Since we did not need so many guns, we could start shifting money to schools or housing or crime prevention. The day before, President Bush had delivered his State of the Union message, and in it he had reflected the changed world by proposing the first deep cuts in American troops in Europe.

Cheney and I went before the House and Senate armed services committees to promote the Bush defense budget as proof that the administration was responding to the new world climate. Yet, as we left Capitol Hill, we knew that unless we came up with an overarching strategy to guide reductions, the Pentagon's political enemies were likely to come after us with a chain saw. Consequently, while still not embracing my Base Force concept, Cheney urged me to continue to refine it.

Inside the Defense Department and in talks to members of Congress, I began promoting a rationale for the Base Force, a shift from a solely *threat-based* force to a *threat- and capability-based* force. We might not face the old threat from the Soviet Union, I said, but we had to maintain certain fundamental capabilities. For example, we might no longer have a specific airlift requirement to move X million tons of matériel to Europe to meet a potential Soviet invasion. But we still needed the *capability* to move huge stores to unpredictable trouble spots around the world. We might no longer face the 8th Guards Army across the Fulda Gap, but we still needed the *capability* to project power elsewhere. I proposed forces capable of performing four basic missions: one to fight across the Atlantic; a second to fight across the Pacific; a contingency force at home to be deployed rapidly to hot spots, as we did in Panama; and a reduced but still vital nuclear force to deter nuclear adversaries.

I made some early converts among my colleagues. Norm Schwarzkopf understood what I was after, and so did General Jack Chain, heading the Strategic Airlift Command. Another powerful ally was General Jack Galvin, SACEUR, commanding all NATO as well as U.S. forces in Europe. The Joint Chiefs were coming along. Yet, I was astonished by the death grip of old ideas on some military minds. The Navy kept arguing for more aircraft carriers. Why? Because it knew that the Soviet Union was building more carriers. How did it know? Because satellite photographs taken years before showed a keel plate laid down in a Sovict shipyard. Obviously, the keel was for a carrier, and therefore Soviet carriers were still coming on line. I argued with Navy bosses that it made no sense to believe that the Soviet Union was pulling out of its old empire in Eastern Europe, yet building a navy to rule the seas. Today, the Russians are selling their aircraft carriers for scrap.

I was rethinking other verities too. I remembered, in the Weinberger era, sitting in the Tank with my old mentor John Wickham, the Army Chief of Staff, for a briefing on a new artillery weapon, the Copperhead, which could be guided electronically to a target. Wickham argued, "With accuracy like this, we don't need to have messy tactical nuclear firepower on a battlefield." The nukes were like an old-fashioned artillery barrage, laying down a blanket of random destruction in order to destroy anything under it. The new smart weapons were more like accurate rifle fire.

Shortly after I became chairman we faced a problem with a certain nuclear artillery shell. It was not as safe as we wanted. Consequently, the Army had performed a vasectomy on these rounds, rendering them sterile by gas injection. Then the nuclear bomb builders solved the safety problem, and they wanted to reverse the vasectomy. That struck me as foolish. At a time when we were dismantling huge intermediate-range nuclear missiles, why should we be putting money into refitting small tactical nukes of questionable value? My argument ran into a stone wall. The Army did not want to give up its battlefield nuclear firepower. Hard-line Pentagon civilian policymakers opposed me too, including Dick Cheney. Still, I was becoming more and more convinced that tactical nuclear weapons had no place on a battlefield.

On February 18, I stood on a stage at the George Washington University's Charles E. Smith Center, with the sensation of decades whirling by. The last time I had been on this campus was twenty years before, in the spring of 1971, winding up work on my M.B.A. At the invitation of Stephen Trachtenberg, GWU's new president, I was back, the recipient of an honorary degree and commencement speaker at the winter graduation ceremony. I began by pointing out that this was my second GWU degree and that this one had cost the government a lot less. The serious point I wanted to register was the unimaginable change that had swept the world since I had left the campus. When I was a GWU student, I pointed out, Nelson Mandela had been a convict in a South African prison. A few days ago, Mandela had finally been freed. And before the year was out, Mandela would address a joint meeting of the U.S. Congress. When I was a grad student, 600,000 Soviet troops had been stationed in Czechoslovakia. Now a playwright and former dissident, Václav Havel, was the Czech president. When I was at GWU, studying business administration, the Warsaw Pact armies had been running offensive maneuvers designed to carry them all the way to the Atlantic. Now the pact was a shambles. I reminded the audience that in 1947, George Kennan, the diplomat-historian, had counseled that if we contained communism, the system would eventually fall of its own weight. Kennan had been proved right. "The Soviet system shuddered and stopped," I said. "And now we are watching it collapse."

After the ceremonies, as I was getting into my car, I stopped for a moment and thought about the day I had walked from Smith Center to Capitol Hill, tear gas burning my eyes, to watch hundreds of Vietnam veterans fling their medals at the Capitol. While

I was a GWU student the largest mass arrest in America's history had taken place, with over thirteen thousand antiwar protesters jailed in Washington. At the time, I had felt deeply depressed about the public's attitude toward my profession. We had managed to turn that situation around. The challenge now was to maintain our restored respect. And matching today's force to today's realities, I felt, was key.

Praise the Lord. A long shot was coming in. Not that Alma and I had ever doubted the talent of our daughter Linda. But the laws of theatrical supply and demand work against even the most gifted. Yet here we were on a March evening, all dressed up, headed for Lisner Auditorium at the George Washington University to watch Linda performing with a road company in *Play to Win,* the story of Jackie Robinson breaking the color barrier in baseball. Linda had a lead, as Jackie's wife. She was marvelous. And she was getting paid!

About this time, Linda got another break. She went out to California for a month to film a summer replacement series. While there, she was invited to dinner at the home of Arnold Schwarzenegger and his wife, Maria Shriver. It was a thrill for Linda, getting an inside peek at Hollywood life. But she decided Hollywood was not quite real and preferred to come back and pursue her career in the East. Frankly, I was relieved.

Dick Cheney urged me to keep pushing ahead with the Base Force, though he still reserved judgment. As part of my missionary work, I granted separate interviews on May 3 to two journalists covering the Pentagon, Michael Gordon of the *New York Times* and R. Jeffrey Smith of the *Washington Post*. I admitted to both that I had a tough internal selling job. I told Smith, "What I'm trying to put across to the department is that the military threat *is* different." Smith kept pressing me for a hard-news peg, saying my story so far was too soft. What size cuts was I proposing? he asked. I resisted being specific, but Smith persisted. Finally, I relented and said, "Somewhere in the neighborhood maybe of twenty to twenty-five percent." On May 7, in a front-page story, the *Post* reported that "the nation's top military officer" predicted a restructured military could lead to "a 25 percent lower defense budget." I was surprised at the fuss my remarks caused, not only in the *Post*, but later in the *New York Times* and all other major newspapers, and even in *The Economist* of London.

Jim Baker, the wily Secretary of State, called to congratulate me, which suggested I might be in trouble. And I was concerned about Cheney's reaction. He too had publicly proposed cutting the Pentagon budget, but by only 2 percent a year over the next six years after taking inflation into account. Dick Cheney was not a boss who enjoyed being contradicted. When we met the day of the *Post* story, Dick said only, "Pretty good piece." As the day wore on, however, second opinions started rolling in. I learned through the Pentagon grapevine that the chiefs were unhappy; my cut recommendation had been too specific. Conservative Republicans on the Hill asked

Cheney how they could defend the President's budget when his own chairman was saying to slice even deeper. Our NATO allies complained. How could they go to their parliaments asking for serious defense spending when the United States was ready to cut so deeply?

The next day the Secretary summoned me to his office, wearing the Cheney frown. "We have to talk about what you told those reporters," he said.

"Yes, sir."

"I have to know if you support the President. I need to be sure you're on the team."

I was taken aback. I made the cautionary count-to-ten before answering. "Maybe I spoke out prematurely," I said. But what I had told the reporter was the writing on the wall. I regretted causing him a problem by speaking out of turn, I said, "but there can't be any question about my being on the team." It was a tense moment, and the air was crackling. We both, however, knew enough to pull back from the brink. And we continued work on the Base Force, and to achieve the 25 percent reduction.

Seven years had passed since I started the campaign to erect a statue at Fort Leavenworth to honor the Buffalo Soldiers. Just before leaving that post, I had passed the torch to Alonzo Dougherty, an Army civilian official and now a National Guard brigadier general. Lonnie did what he could, but without much support or money the project languished. Then Commander Carlton Philpot, a black naval officer, reported to Leavenworth as an instructor at the Command and General Staff College. Philpot became enthralled with the Buffalo Soldiers project. He took charge of the moribund effort and breathed life back into it. Philpot was not content with a statue of a soldier on horseback. He wanted a park with a reflecting pool *and* the statue. He wanted a foundation established to raise money for a Buffalo Soldiers Museum and to finance educational programs in black military history. Philpot contacted me and asked me to reenlist in the campaign. How much money would his plan take? I asked. "Half a million," he said. I gagged, but agreed to see what I could do.

Walter Annenberg, the wealthy publisher of *TV Guide,* was a former ambassador to the Court of St. James's. I had become friends with Walter and his wife, Lee, through my trips to California during the Reagan years. I wrote to Walter and told him about our dreams for Fort Leavenworth. He called back and said that the kind of memorial we were talking about could not be accomplished with $500,000; it would take more like $850,000. It was not the news I wanted, but Walter did agree to give the project an initial $250,000, if we could raise a matching sum.

I became a part-time fund-raiser. Money began to come in—$25,000 from cousin Bruce Llewellyn; $50,000 from Zachary Fisher, a remarkable New York philanthropist and friend of the military. After a few months, Walter called again. He hated loose ends, he said. What was happening to the Buffalo Soldiers campaign? I explained our modest progress. He believed in this project, he said, and wanted to see it move ahead. He was sending the fund a check for $250,000. We could worry later about the matching funds.

Thanks to Walter's jump start, I was able to travel to Fort Leavenworth on July 28 for a groundbreaking ceremony. I stood in an empty field where the barracks of black cavalrymen once rose, while a band played and flags fluttered. Among the dignitaries at the ceremony were Lieutenant General Leonard Wishart, the Leavenworth commanding general, Commander Philpot, and Brigadier General Dougherty. But the stars that day were Sergeant Major William Harrington and First Sergeant Elisha Kearse, both ninety-five years old, authentic Buffalo Soldiers who had served long ago in all-black regiments. As I shook their gnarled hands, I felt connected to my past, to Lieutenant Flipper, and to blacks who fought on the Western plains and charged up San Juan Hill, all but invisible to history. As we drove the ceremonial shovels into the ground, the story of those two old soldiers was a hole in history about to be filled.

Quarters 6 is a substantial brick structure with a wide veranda, set on Grant Avenue in Fort Myer's historic district. The house was built in 1908 at a cost of $19,202 as a duplex to accommodate the families of two lieutenants. In 1961, Quarters 6 was remodeled as the residence of the Chairman of the Joint Chiefs of Staff. Behind Quarters 6 were two garages, where I parked my Volvos and worked on them. I also managed to persuade neighbors to let me store more of my adult toys in their garages.

I enjoyed bringing foreign guests to Quarters 6 for lunch or dinner. Afterward, I took them outside, where America's history lay spread before us. Standing on a broad lawn overlooking the Potomac River, I could point out the Capitol, the Jefferson Memorial, the Washington Monument, and the Lincoln Memorial, and attach a little history lesson to each site. There was just one glitch. A young tree stood right in the middle, marring the panoramic view. And it was still growing. One day, I summoned my aide at the time, Major Tim Livsey. "Tim," I said, "that tree has to go."

Livsey looked stricken. "Sir, you don't really mean to cut down a tree?" He ticked off the opponents I would be taking on—the post engineers, public affairs officers, and budding environmentalists. And suppose the *Washington Post* got wind of the story, he warned.

"That tree is only going to get bigger until it destroys one of the finest views of Washington," I said. "Tell the post engineers to have it removed."

The Fort Myer post engineers decided, just to be contrary, I think, to schedule the tree removal for Earth Day! Shades of the plan to shoot little dogs to carry out wound research. Once the deed is done, how do you explain that you cut down a tree on Earth Day? I made a strategic retreat and let the matter rest.

A few weeks later, I called in Livsey again and laid out my strategy. The post engineers were to cut down the tree, pull the stump, and lay sod over the scar. And get it all done in an hour, I told Tim. The next morning, when Otis arrived to drive me to the Pentagon, I told him to wait a few minutes while I wandered out onto the lawn. The view across the Potomac was magnificent, unobstructed. I looked down at the thick grass and could barely make out where the tree had stood. Nor did anyone else seem to notice it was gone. Surprise, stealth, and swiftness have historically been key elements in successful campaigns.

August 1, 1990, began conventionally enough. Up at 5:30 A.M., worked out on the Lifecycle, had my standard breakfast, raisin bran, a banana, orange juice, and coffee. Arrived at the Pentagon before 7:00, where I received the usual overnight briefing from the CIA analyst waiting for me in the outer office.

This was, however, to be no ordinary day. In one respect, it should be triumphant. For the previous eight months I had been shepherding the Base Force through the bureaucratic maze, fighting reluctant chiefs and service secretaries and gaining key support from Paul Wolfowitz, the tough-minded undersecretary of defense for policy, who had reached conclusions similar to mine through his own analysis. Dick Cheney, who kept an open mind throughout, despite early doubts, finally approved the concept. The chiefs were mostly on board. Admiral Dave Jeremiah, my new vice chairman, was a strong fellow advocate. At times, I had been discouraged by setbacks and had almost given up hope. But the day Dick, Paul, and I briefed President Bush and won his approval, the Base Force became the administration's position. The President was going to Aspen,

Colorado, the next day, August 2, where he would meet with the British prime minister, Margaret Thatcher, and give a speech at the Aspen Institute Symposium announcing his new strategy and the Base Force as the new shape of America's armed forces. The changes envisioned were enormous, from a total active duty strength of 2.1 million down to 1.6 million. The strategic heart, the four forces I urged, had survived intact. The plan the President was going to propose would effectively mark the end of a forty-year-old strategy of communist containment, a strategy that had succeeded. We had won. The next day, Cheney, Wolfowitz, and I were to go to Capitol Hill to start selling the Base Force to the armed services and appropriations committees.

Also, this day, I had asked Norm Schwarzkopf to come up from CENTCOM headquarters to brief the chiefs and Cheney in the Tank on alarming rumbles along the Iraq-Kuwait border.

I went through the usual ceremonial hoops in a chairman's day, a photo op with one of the Joint Staff colonels getting his first star, and observing a parade in front of the Pentagon for President Gnassingbe Eyadema of Togo. Later, I went to Blair House for a luncheon honoring Eyadema. The State Department liked having black African leaders meet prominent African-Americans and milked these occasions for all they were worth.

I plowed through the rest of the day, and was home by 7:00 P.M. for dinner. Afterward, I retired to my study to go through an aviator's bag full of paperwork. A few minutes before 8:00 P.M., the secure

phone rang, rarely the harbinger of good news. Mike
Carns, director of the Joint Staff, was calling to tell
me that Saddam Hussein had just sent the Iraqi army
across the border into Kuwait.

18 ☆ *A Line in the Sand*

SADDAM HUSSEIN'S invasion of Kuwait occurred about
nine months after I had projected, in my "Strategic
Overview—1994," that Korea and the Persian Gulf
were the two world hot spots likeliest to involve U.S.
forces. The Iraqi army had made me uncomfortable
ever since Iraq and Iran ended their bloody eight-year
war in 1988, while I was National Security Advisor.
Once Saddam, with an army over one million men
strong, no longer had Iran to worry about, I feared he
would look for mischief somewhere else.

Iraq was nearly $90 billion in debt after the war.
As a proportion of its gross national product, it was a
sum that made the U.S. deficit look prudent. Saddam
blamed Kuwait and the United Arab Emirates (UAE)
for preventing Iraq from working its way out of this
Grand Canyon of a hole. They had thrust a "poisoned
dagger" into Iraq's back by busting the oil quotas set
by OPEC, the Organization of Petroleum Exporting
Countries, thus driving prices down and reducing
Iraq's income. Kuwait, he further charged, had
siphoned off $2.5 billion in oil from the Rumaila
field, which the two countries shared. And he cov-

etously eyed two Kuwaiti-held islands, Warba and Bubiyan, which blocked his access to the Gulf. The Kuwaitis were not Arab brothers, but "greedy lap-dogs" of the West.

On a trip in early July 1990 to Tunisia, Egypt, and Jordan, I found these states optimistic about finding an "Arab" solution to Iraq's financial problems. However, when I went on to Israel I found the Israelis less sanguine about Saddam's intentions. The trip had not been all work. In Jerusalem my counterpart, Lieutenant General Dan Shomron, the Israeli chief of staff, threw a party for me, at which I surprised the guests with some Bronx-acquired Yiddish. Word got out that I even conducted a private meeting with Prime Minister Yitzhak Shamir in Yiddish; not true, but too good to deny.

Back in Washington, during the third week in July, Rear Admiral Mike McConnell, my Joint Staff intelligence officer, came to the office and spread satellite photos on my desk. "The Iraqis have deployed three divisions near Kuwait's border, about thirty-five thousand men so far," McConnell told me, as he traced the startlingly clear images. He could identify the force as part of the Republican Guard, Saddam Hussein's elite troops, who were equipped with hundreds of modern Soviet-made T-72 tanks. Saddam's deployment near the border was ominous. But what did it represent? Intimidation? Pressure? Invasion? How far was he ready to go?

By July 24, I was concerned enough to call Norm Schwarzkopf at MacDill Air Force Base in Tampa. If the United States got involved militarily in the Persian Gulf, it would be in Norm's court. As CINC of CENTCOM, he was responsible for our military activities in South Asia, the Horn of Africa, and critical parts of the Middle East. We discussed the continuing Iraqi buildup, by now four divisions and over 100,000 troops. Arab leaders kept telling us not to worry. Arab brothers did not war against each other. Nevertheless, I told Norm, "I want you to come up with a two-tiered response." Tier one should provide for a range of retaliatory options "if Saddam commits a minor border infraction." But if his intentions turned out to be more ambitious, "I want to see a second-tier response, how we'd stop him and protect the region."

"I'll get started," Norm said. He already had a leg up on the problem. CENTCOM had grown out of the Rapid Deployment Joint Task Force created during Jimmy Carter's presidency to deal with a possible conflict between our then friend, Iran, and the Soviet army. An enormous amount of time and money had been spent on a bizarre U.S. response to stop the Russian army from ever coming through the Zagros Mountains of northern Iran. After the fall of the Shah, Iran went from friend to enemy, and the likelihood of the Soviet Union heading toward the Persian Gulf seemed far-fetched. CENTCOM, consequently, had turned its attention to the threat Iraq posed to its smaller neighbors.

Military men look for three surefire clues that an enemy force is preparing to attack. Is it moving its artillery forward? Is it laying down communications? Is it reinforcing its forces logistically, with stocks of fuel and ammunition? By July 31, all three conditions were present in southern Iraq. I called Schwarzkopf again. "I want you," I said, "to come up tomorrow to brief Cheney and the chiefs on your assessment of the situation and your contingency plans."

It was the next day that I attended the Blair House luncheon for President Eyadema of Togo. After lunch, I had Otis whip me back to the Pentagon. I was impatient to return for Schwarzkopf's briefing, scheduled for 2:00 P.M. I arrived at the Tank at about the same time as Dick Cheney. The chiefs rose, and we took our places. Cheney had me lead off. I quickly turned the floor over to Schwarzkopf, whose robust six-foot-three-inch frame and force of personality filled the room. Norm gave a sobering ninety-minute survey.

"What do you think they'll do?" Cheney asked.

"I think they're going to attack," Norm said. He thought it would be a limited attack to seize the Kuwaiti part of the Rumaila oil field and Bubiyan Island. He did not think Saddam intended to swallow all of Kuwait and topple the ruling family. On that note, the meeting ended.

Earlier, Dick Kerr, deputy director of the CIA, had given us the same judgment. The Bush administration, however, seemed intent on keeping out of inter-Arab squabbles. During a meeting with Saddam Hussein, five days earlier, our ambassador to Iraq, April Glaspie, told him, ". . . we have no opinion on the Arab-Arab conflicts like your border disagreement with Kuwait." Afterward, the ambassador sent a cable to Washington urging that the United States "ease off on criticism" until Iraq and Kuwait could settle their dispute themselves. In a subsequent message to Saddam, President Bush cabled that his administration "continues to desire better relations with Iraq." We had Arab states saying nothing was going to happen, and the United States saying that if anything did, it was not our concern.

Several suggestions had surfaced in the State Department and the Pentagon as to how we might deter the Iraqis. One was to speed up the aircraft carrier *Independence,* already headed to the Persian Gulf. Al Gray, the Marine Corps Commandant, had suggested sending Marine Prepositioned Squadron ships already loaded with Marine equipment that were presently stationed at Diego Garcia in the Indian Ocean. These moves, however, would be invisible and have no deterrent effect unless we publicly announced the purpose behind them. At that stage, the administration had not considered warning Iraq, and Cheney and I were reluctant to get out in front of the White House. The only action we had taken had been to fill a request from the UAE for two U.S. Air Force tankers to help conduct air surveillance, not a move likely to strike terror into Saddam Hussein.

By now, I regretted our earlier political and military inaction, although it was not clear that Hussein would be deterred by token moves. After Schwarzkopf's briefing, as Cheney and I were leaving the Tank, I said, "Dick, this is serious. We can't ignore what's going on. I think the President should get off a tough message to Saddam today. Even call him, but try to scare him off." Dick was as concerned as I was and began touching bases at the NSC and State to prepare a protest. But it was too late. Before we could fire a diplomatic warning shot, eighty thousand of Saddam's Republican Guards were across the border rolling toward Kuwait City.

The President called a full NSC meeting for 8:00 A.M. the next day. Schwarzkopf was already back in Tampa. I asked him to jump on a plane and bring his maps and plans to the White House meeting. This was Norm's first chance to see the senior policy crowd in action, and I wanted him to get a feel for the people with whom he was likely to be working. It was quite an introduction. The talk was disjointed and unfocused. As much time was spent discussing the impact of the invasion on the price of oil as on how we should respond to Saddam's aggression. The overhanging question was Saddam's next move. Would he stop at taking Kuwait or strike Saudi Arabia next? Should we seek sanctions? Just how far were we prepared to go? Before the meeting, the President had been asked by reporters if he intended to send troops, and he had replied, "I am not contemplating any such action."

The tier-one response having been overrun, Norm made his White House debut describing his contingency plan for defending Saudi Arabia. Still the discussion did not come to grips with the issues. I am uncomfortable with meetings that do not arrive at conclusions, and as I saw this one about to end, I tried to get clearer guidance. "Mr. President," I asked, "should we think about laying down a line in the sand concerning Saudi Arabia?" Bush thought for a moment, then said, yes, we should. But the fate of Kuwait was left unresolved. Bush left immediately for Aspen, Colorado, to meet with Prime Minister Thatcher and give the speech we had labored over so long laying out his new national security strategy, incorporating the Base Force. Cheney, Paul Wolfowitz, and I went to supersecure Room S 407 in the Capitol to pitch the Base Force to leaders of the Defense Department's congressional oversight committees. But all we heard was, yeah, sure, right. But what's going on in Kuwait?

On Friday, after the President returned from Aspen, he called the NSC together again in the Cabinet Room. "It sure has been some twenty-four hours," he said, as he took his customary place at mid-table. "Doing fine so far, though. Prime Minister Thatcher and I see eye-to-eye. I expect we can get our friends to support joint political and economic action in the Gulf." He was particularly pleased that one old mold appeared to have been broken. Mikhail Gorbachev had not treated this crisis as another East-West confrontation, with the Soviet Union willy-nilly lining up behind its onetime friend Saddam. The day before, the UN Security Council had voted 14–0 to condemn the invasion and demand immediate and unconditional Iraqi withdrawal from Kuwait, and the yea votes included the Soviet Union.

Bill Webster, the CIA director, gave us a bleak status report. "The Iraqis," he said, "are within eight tenths of a mile of the Saudi border. If Saddam stays where he is, he'll own twenty percent of the world's oil reserves. And a few miles away he can seize another twenty percent. He'll have easy access to the sea from Kuwaiti ports. Jordan and Yemen will probably tilt toward him, and he'll be in a position to extort the others. We can expect the Arab states to start cutting deals. Iran will be at Iraq's feet. Israel will be threatened." Saddam Hussein, Webster concluded, would become the preeminent figure in the Persian Gulf.

"We've got to make a response," Brent Scowcroft said, "and accommodating Saddam is not an option."

"You can't separate Kuwait from Saudi Arabia," Cheney added. "When the Iraqis hit the Saudi border, they're only forty kilometers from the Saudi oil fields. We have the potential here for a major conflict."

Larry Eagleburger, deputy secretary of state, sitting in for Jim Baker, urged, "We ought to go for a Chapter 7 from the UN," which would authorize military force and economic sanctions.

"I've already been on the phone with the Arab leaders," the President said. He had talked to President Mubarak of Egypt, King Hussein of Jordan, and King Fahd of Saudi Arabia. "They still tell me they can find an Arab solution." He sounded unconvinced. "But whatever we do, we've got to get the international community behind us."

Cheney turned to me to review military options. Again, I went over the Schwarzkopf plan for defend-

704 · COLIN L. POWELL

ing Saudi Arabia. I described the units we could put into the Gulf region in a hurry. I was reasonably sure that the Iraqis had not yet decided to invade Saudi Arabia. I was also confident that they did not relish a war with the United States. "But it's important," I said, "to plant the American flag in the Saudi desert as soon as possible, assuming we can get their okay." We did not want our inaction to embolden Saddam further.

Cheney and Eagleburger agreed. Scowcroft had taken this position within hours of the invasion. "We're committed to Saudi Arabia," the President said. We could start alerting units to be prepared to defend the country.

I then asked if it was worth going to war to liberate Kuwait. It was a Clausewitzian question which I posed so that the military would know what preparations it might have to make. I detected a chill in the room. The question was premature, and it should not have come from me. I had overstepped. I was not the National Security Advisor now; I was only supposed to give *military* advice. Nevertheless, I had wrestled with the politics and economics of crises for almost two years in the White House, in this very room. I had participated in superpower summits. More to the point, as a midlevel career officer, I had been appalled at the docility of the Joint Chiefs of Staff, fighting the war in Vietnam without ever pressing the political leaders to lay out clear objectives for them. Before we start talking about how many divisions, carriers, and fighter wings we need, I said, we have to ask, to achieve what end? But the question was not answered before the meeting broke up.

Later that day, President Bush and Scowcroft spoke with Prince Bandar, my old racquetball partner, now Saudi ambassador to the United States. They wanted Bandar to understand the threat his country faced and to know that we were prepared to come to its aid. Afterward, Scowcroft called Cheney at the Pentagon. Bandar was coming over, he said, and we were to give him another dose of reality. On his arrival at Cheney's office, Bandar played his usual American-ized, jaunty fighter-pilot role, drinking coffee from a foam cup and stirring it with a gold pen. Ordinarily, we addressed each other in terms bordering on the obscene, with my printable favorites including "Bandar the Magnificent" and "Bandar, you Arab Gatsby," while he called me "Milord." This day we did not kid around. As we sat at Cheney's small round table, I traced on reconnaissance photos the Iraqi forces prac-tically on Saudi Arabia's doorstep. Bandar studied them, an unlit cigar clenched between his teeth, but he said nothing.

"We're ready to help you defend yourselves from Saddam," Cheney said.

Bandar gave us a look of bemused skepticism. "Like Jimmy Carter did?" He was referring to an ear-lier crisis in which President Carter had come to Saudi Arabia's aid with ten unarmed F-15 aircraft.

"Tell Prince Bandar what we are prepared to do," Cheney said to me.

"We'll start by bringing in the 1st Tactical Fighter Wing," I began, "*and* the 82d Airborne, *and* a carrier." I kept adding follow-up units.

Bandar's interest quickened, and he interrupted me. "What's that add up to?" he asked.

"All told," I said, "about one hundred thousand troops, for starters."

"I see," Bandar said. "You *are* serious."

"We suggest you urge King Fahd to accept our offer to protect the kingdom," Cheney concluded. Bandar left, assuring us that he was on his way to report what we had advised.

After he was gone, Cheney brought up our earlier meeting with the President. "Colin," he said, "you're Chairman of the Joint Chiefs. You're not Secretary of State. You're not the National Security Advisor anymore. And you're not Secretary of Defense. So stick to military matters." He made clear that I had taken liberty for license. I was not sorry, however, that I had spoken out at the White House. What I had said about giving the military clear objectives had to be said.

Publicly, the President kept his counsel on the Iraqi invasion. All that he had told the American people so far was, "We're not discussing intervention. . . . I'm not contemplating such action." That was where matters stood, from Friday until Sunday afternoon.

In the meantime, the President went to Camp David in Maryland's Catoctin Mountains. On Saturday morning, the national security team followed. The centerpiece was to be a Schwarzkopf briefing in depth on what we could do to defend Saudi Arabia— troops required, deployment, armament, the air strategy. I watched the President nodding as this big, bluff, articulate, reassuring soldier spoke. When Norm finished with Saudi Arabia, he added a postscript: "Now, if you want to eject the Iraqis *and* restore Kuwait it is going to take . . ." He then reeled off additional troop requirements running to the hundreds of thousands and a timetable taking eight months to a year.

It was a muggy, drizzly Sunday afternoon. Cheney and Schwarzkopf were on their way to Jidda in Saudi Arabia to urge King Fahd to accept our offer of help. I was at home in my little study, feet on the desk, watching CNN as the President's helicopter landed on the White House lawn on his return from Camp David. A clutch of microphones had been set up, and the President approached them, walking into a fusillade of questions. The reporters kept pressing him on one point. Was he going to take military action? His face hardened. He began jabbing the air with his finger. "*This will not stand,* this will not stand," he said, "this aggression against Kuwait."

I sat upright. From "We're not discussing intervention" to "This will not stand" marked a giant step. Had the President just committed the United States to liberating Kuwait? Did he mean to do it by diplomatic and economic pressure or by force? Had a tail-end option suddenly become the front-end option?

Though we can never know what goes on in another person's mind, I had an idea of what had happened. After we had briefed him at Camp David, the President understood the resources at his disposal. He felt confident. His meeting earlier at Aspen, with the British prime minister, no doubt influenced him too. Eight years before, Margaret Thatcher had reversed an Argentine seizure of the

Falkland Islands. It also struck me that "This will not stand" had a Thatcheresque ring. The thought process, however, was pure George Bush. He had listened quietly to his advisors. He had consulted by phone with world leaders. And then, taking his own counsel, he had come to this momentous decision and revealed it at the first opportunity.

I turned off the television set and went to a map on my desk. I might have just received a new mission.

At 3:30 P.M. on Monday, August 6, Dick Cheney called me from Jidda. He had just left King Fahd, he said. "We've got his approval. I've informed the President. Start issuing orders to move the force."

Unleashing the American military leviathan is an awesome enterprise. We had already alerted the 82d Airborne Division at Fort Bragg, North Carolina, Third Army headquarters in Atlanta, and the 1st Tactical Fighter Wing at Langley Air Force Base in Virginia. But not one paratrooper was going anywhere until he could be airlifted by MAC, the Military Airlift Command, the armed forces' Federal Express. MAC is the air component of a sprawling land, sea, and air system called TRANSCOM, the U.S. Transportation Command, headquartered at Scott Air Force Base in Illinois and led by General H. T. Johnson, another classmate of mine at the National War College. He relayed Cheney's order to the 21st Air Force at McGuire Air Force Base in New Jersey and the 22d Air Force at Travis Air Force Base in California, our East and West Coast MAC nerve centers.

At any given moment, about 80 percent of MAC's planes are en route somewhere. When a high-priority order is flashed throughout the system, all other orders are canceled. A transport plane flying spare parts, say, to Ramstein, Germany, is now to land at the nearest terminal, unload, and head home. This activity is repeated all over the world. At Scott Air Force Base, a huge display board hitched to a computer system plots every single MAC aircraft. Scott knows what cargo is aboard, the fuel remaining, the plane's maintenance schedule, who is in the crew, and the amount of flight time left before each crew member has to be rested and replaced. Cheney's order was going to divert hundreds of planes from what they were doing and eventually head them toward a new destination, Saudi Arabia. The MAC fleet would zoom from 80 percent usage to 100 percent, putting aloft everything that could fly. Over sixteen thousand paratroopers of the 82d Airborne Division would start to board C-141s. Enough ammunition, spare parts, and maintenance equipment to support an entire wing of about seventy-two fighters would begin rolling aboard mammoth C-5 Galaxies. Flying tankers would take to the air to refuel F-15s headed toward the Persian Gulf. MAC would hire dozens of commercial air charters to round out the airlift. A winged armada was about to fill the skies over the Atlantic.

And security for this top-secret operation was blown completely.

The evening I relayed the order, a disbelieving Tom Kelly popped into my office. "They did it again!" Tom said. When so massive an airlift is launched, hundreds of classified messages fan out from the 21st and 22d Air Forces, alerting bases, supply depots, and terminals all over the globe. These orders at the lower level had gone out uncoded. This breach of security occurred at a time when the President was already furious over leaked covert operations. I blew up and started shouting, "Cancel the damn message! Cancel it!"

"Cancel it?" Kelly asked. "Do you want the flow to start or not?"

I gave up. I would have to ask Bill Smullen, my press officer, to check the newscasts and newspapers and pray that no reporter was at a key air base. But a sharp correspondent at the Pentagon, CBS's Dave Martin, broke the story. It was embarrassing. I nevertheless suppressed my irritation. It is next to impossible to keep so mammoth a move a secret for long. The Republic, I told myself, had survived worse.

The order to MAC went out August 6 at 8:45 P.M. By 9:45 the next morning the first loaded C-141 took off from Charleston Air Force Base in South Carolina.

We knew from CIA estimates that the Iraqis had at least a thousand tons of chemical agents. We knew that Saddam had used both mustard and nerve gases in his war against Iran. We knew that he had used gas on Iraq's rebellious Kurdish minority in 1988, killing or injuring four thousand Kurds. We briefly considered and then rejected sending over U.S. chemical weapons. The Iraqi chemical threat was manageable.

Our troops had protective suits and detection and alarm systems. In battle, we would be fast-moving and in the open desert, not trapped as civilians might be. A chemical attack would be a public relations crisis, but not a battlefield disaster. What to do about Iraq's biological capability, however, remained a more troubling question.

"Look, I'm not going to be briefing generals. I'll be talking to political leaders. So keep it simple. I don't want a fistful of charts. I want one chart." With those directions, given late in the evening of August 14, I sent my graphics staff, under Colonel Tim Lawrie, chief of the Joint Operations Division, back to the drawing board. The next day, President Bush was coming to the Pentagon for a briefing by the chiefs and to give a speech. I wanted to seize the opportunity to lay out a troop buildup schedule for the weeks ahead and let him know what decisions we would be needing from him at various trigger points.

The day before, I had gone to Tampa to see Norm Schwarzkopf. Norm had been antsy. "I need to know where the hell this operation is heading," he said. I understood his uneasiness. As chairman, I could live with a certain degree of fuzzy policy. But the CINC, the commander in chief who was going to Saudi Arabia to direct troops, ships, and planes, wanted clear-cut instructions. The answers would eventually emerge, but I needed to set the stage for the President to provide them.

The graphics technicians brought in a chart, simplicity itself, a line graph, the vertical axis show-

ing increasing troop strength, the horizontal axis pro-
jecting the weeks through December. My objective
was to plant a timeline in the President's mind. This
chart would let him know when he would have to
give us the word to reach certain troop levels.

I had only a fifteen-minute window of opportunity
between the end of the chiefs' briefing and the
speech the President was to give from the steps of the
Pentagon. Cheney arranged a meeting in his office
with only Bush, Cheney, Scowcroft, Sununu, and me
present. We sat at the round table, and Cheney let me
go ahead. I set copies of my chart before everyone.
"Mr. President," I began, "let me tell you how the
buildup is going." I pointed to the current date on the
chart and noted that as of this moment we had nearly
thirty thousand troops in Saudi Arabia. "Our current
mission is to deter and defend Saudi Arabia. Within a
couple of weeks we'll have completed the deterrent
buildup. We should have enough power to discour-
age Saddam from attacking, if that's what he has in
mind." As troops and equipment kept pouring in, I
pointed out, we would move from the deterrent to the
defensive phase, starting in early September. By
about December 5, I went on, we would have some
184,000 troops in place, and there would be no doubt
we could defend Saudi Arabia.

The President listened in his intent way, saying
little, as I took him through the operation, week by
week, also making clear its cost, $1.2 billion through
September 30 and $1 billion every month after that. I
pointed out that if we kept up the present pace, he

would have to begin calling up the reserves; and he would have to make that decision within about a week. "Sir," I said, "a call-up means pulling people out of their jobs. It affects businesses. It means disrupting thousands of families. It's a major political decision." And very soon he would have to activate a contingency plan called CRAF, the Civilian Reserve Air Fleet, which meant diverting commercial aircraft to military use.

Six days before, the United Nations Security Council had unanimously voted a trade embargo against Iraq. This prompted me to say, "If your goal is only to defend Saudi Arabia and rely on sanctions to pressure Saddam out of Kuwait, then we should cap the troop flow probably sometime in October." It would take a month or so for the pipeline to clear, producing those 184,000 troops by early December. We would also need to consider a troop rotation based on a six-month tour. "We've got about two months," I said, "to assess the impact of sanctions."

The President shook his head. "I don't know if sanctions are going to work," he said, "in an acceptable time frame."

If, then, he was thinking of driving Saddam out of Kuwait, assuming he could not be negotiated or sanctioned out, I needed to know some time in October, so that instead of letting the pipeline empty, we would keep filling it. There was something else we needed to know, I said. "If we are going to eject Saddam, is the objective only to free Kuwait or, while we're at it, to destroy his war-making potential at some level?" Each option required a different force level and affected the timetable. I made it clear that I was not expecting decisions now. The President had time to make up his mind. I was simply alerting him.

And, I was thinking to myself, do we want to go beyond Kuwait to Baghdad? Do we try to force Saddam out of power? How weakened do we want to leave Iraq? Do we necessarily benefit from a Gulf oil region dominated by an unfriendly Syria and a hostile Iran?

The President thanked us for the briefing and headed for the Pentagon River Entrance to a speaker's platform the White House advance team had erected overnight. In his remarks to a large Pentagon crowd, he thanked everyone for the preparations so far. And then he stated his goal: "The immediate, complete, and unconditional withdrawal of all Iraqi forces from Kuwait; the restoration of Kuwait's legitimate government." Norm and I glanced at each other. The President did not sound like a man willing to wait long for sanctions to work.

On August 17, Dick Cheney flew to Riyadh for further consultations with the Saudis. He had expressed no particular concern to me before leaving, but something must have happened when he found himself alone in his private cabin aboard the 707 high above the Atlantic. He called me at home over a secure radio telephone, sounding uncharacteristically agitated. "Colin," Dick said, "we've only got a few paratroopers over there, and a wing or so of aircraft, so far."

"I know," I said, "but the flow goes on."

"We don't have enough muscle there to stop anybody yet," he said. "Suppose all we do is provoke Saddam, push him to invade the Saudis? There isn't a damned thing we could do."

I knew that too. But there was no point in worrying him at this time. Here was a rare Cheney who needed reassurance. "Dick," I said, "remember what I told everybody when this thing first broke? We have to get some people and hardware in place right away as a signal to Saddam of our intentions. He doesn't want to fight the United States. I'm sure of it. That's why we had to get those early forces over there. That's the real deterrent, sticking the American flag in the desert and saying, 'Okay, do you want to mess with us?' "

"But if Saddam moves, we can't protect the Saudis," Cheney insisted. "Not yet, at least."

"If they were going to invade Saudi Arabia, they'd have done it by now," I answered. "Remember, Saddam's never had to extend himself before. He's always operated on interior lines of communication, against Iran, next door, and now against Kuwait. But Saudi Arabia's oil fields are another block away. He's never projected force that far across open, hostile desert. Relax, Dick." I went on in this vein for at least twenty minutes, hoping I was right. By the time I had finished, that confident, measured timbre had returned to Cheney's voice. Everybody needs a shoulder to lean on from time to time. And it was somehow reassuring to learn that the lone cowboy did too. He would do the same for me in the difficult months ahead.

. . .

The operation in the Gulf now had a name. Norm Schwarzkopf's staff and mine had kicked around a number of ideas. The image of a shield cropped up early. "Peninsula Shield"—too awkward. "Crescent Shield"—too Arabesque. Finally, we settled on a name we all thought had just the right ring. Cheney approved, and the mobilization in the Saudi sands to defend the kingdom thus became "Desert Shield." As we started to develop an offensive option alongside the defensive stance, Norm and I talked about how to differentiate the two. Desert Shield, Phase II? Norm suggested "Desert Storm." Stormin' Norman's storm. It was a natural, and we all went for it.

Schwarzkopf had by now set up headquarters in the Ministry of Defense building in Riyadh, the Saudi Arabian capital. He spent his days wrestling with the tangle of problems posed by putting a force in place to defend the kingdom. I spent my days funneling troops and equipment into the pipeline from the U.S. end. The service chiefs had the key roles. While their troops served under Norm, the chiefs bore primary responsibility for ensuring that these units were equipped and combat-ready. Since Schwarzkopf was the CINC with the priority, his fellow CINCs, world-wide, were backing him all the way.

By early September, the buildup was starting to reach mammoth proportions. Tens of thousands of troops were already in the Gulf region or on the way, streaming to airports and seaports all over the United States. The President had authorized the call-up of up to 200,000 reservists and guardsmen, and many volunteered even before the call. We could not have gone to war without them, and they were to perform superbly. Four aircraft carrier battle groups would soon be on station, supported by battleships and cruise-missile-firing submarines. Transport ships long in mothballs were reactivated. Hundreds of fighter planes, bombers, and cargo planes circled the Arabian Peninsula looking for places to land. The light infantry of the 82d Airborne and the 1st Marine Expeditionary Force would soon be joined by armored formations of the 24th Infantry Division sailing from Georgia and the 1st Cavalry Division from Texas. Huge bases had to be built in Saudi Arabia to receive this flood of troops and matériel.

In this early stage, we still did not know definitely if President Bush would resort to war to fulfill his "This will not stand" stance on the occupation of Kuwait. Nevertheless, we had to have contingent strategies ready for all options. Norm and his army component commander, Lieutenant General John Yeosock, my former deputy at FORSCOM, concentrated on devising a defense of Saudi Arabia. The Air Force staff quickly came up with an air campaign, the brainchild of Colonel John Warden, a brilliant, brash fighter pilot and a leading Air Force intellectual on the use of airpower. Before leaving for Saudi Arabia, Schwarzkopf had been impressed by Warden's work and arranged for him to brief me on August 11 on a plan called "Instant Thunder." "What I propose, General," Warden said, "is that we attack deep inside Iraq, knock out their command and control installations, transportation systems, production and storage facilities, and air defense networks." I was impressed too. Warden's approach could destroy or severely cripple the Iraqi regime.

But we also needed an air plan to help drive Saddam out of Kuwait, if it came to that. Schwarz-kopf and I asked Warden to expand his strategic plan to include tactical strikes against the Iraqi army deployed in Kuwait. Warden went to Saudi Arabia and worked directly with two Air Force generals, Lieutenant General Chuck Horner, Schwarzkopf's air component commander, and Horner's assistant, Brigadier General "Buster" Glosson. Warden's orig-inal plan would undergo numerous modifications and there would be much debate over targets, but his original concept remained the heart of the Desert Storm air war.

Schwarzkopf formed a ground-planning equiva-lent of Warden and his team called the "Jedi Knights," composed of bright Army lieutenant colonels. The Jedi Knights were closeted and told to come up with a contingency plan for a ground attack to kick the Iraqi army out of Kuwait.

In September I had to go to Madrid for a NATO meeting, and I decided to tack a trip to Saudi Arabia onto the front end. On September 12, at the Riyadh airport, I stepped out of an Air Force 707 and felt as if I had entered a blast furnace. The temperature was 105 degrees, and it was still early morning. At least I had had a good night's sleep on the plane. When I first became chairman, the Air Force had provided me with a C-135, a modified aerial refueling tanker with VIP accommodations suggesting a flying motel room. The problem was climate control, since between the floor and the ceiling the temperature ranged from arctic to equatorial. I was always wrapping blankets around my feet while my head sweated. And I usually came home with a cold. I asked the Air Force for something more temperate, and they started flying me in an old Air Force One, maybe no longer up to presidential standards, but not exactly no-frills transportation.

Norm Schwarzkopf had been in Saudi Arabia only a couple of weeks when I arrived. He now had the weight of the world on his shoulders, and it showed. I asked him about troop arrivals. A little ragged, he said. What about deployment of the enemy? We had them spotted practically down to the battalion level, he told me. He also set up a whirlwind tour for me, the 24th Infantry Division, the 1st Tactical Fighter Wing, the 1st Marine Expeditionary Force, the U.S.S. *Blue Ridge* (a command and control ship), and the battleship *Wisconsin.*

At this early stage, morale among our troops was high, but the desert was a bleak, forbidding world, hedged in by Muslim moral strictures uncongenial to GIs from the Western world. At one point, Prince Bandar warned me, "No Bibles." "Are you kidding?" I said. We were being inundated with Bibles from religious groups, and I could imagine the military trying to tell these folks, "The Arabs will take your sons, but not their Bibles."

"Saudi customs officials will have to confiscate the Bibles," Bandar insisted. We finally worked out a deal whereby we flew the Bibles directly to our air bases, while Saudi officials looked the other way.

Then Bandar informed me that no religious services could be held on Arab soil for our Jewish troops. "They can die defending your country, but they can't pray in it?" I asked.

"Colin, be reasonable," he answered. "It will be reported on CNN. What will our people think?"

We found a practical solution. We planned to helicopter Jewish personnel out to American vessels in the Persian Gulf and hold Jewish services aboard ship.

Bandar also worried about crucifixes. I told him our soldiers would be ordered to wear them inside and not outside of their T-shirts.

But what about these American women, with their bare arms and T-shirts, driving vehicles? There seemed no end to Arab sensitivities. Actually, our servicewomen provoked a mini social revolution. Saudi women saw them driving, and some started driving themselves. Since they were violating Islamic law, the women were arrested.

Bandar and I made one last gentleman's agreement. If any trouble grew out of sexual hanky-panky between an American and a Saudi, he would call me and we would be allowed to whisk the American out of the country and take appropriate disciplinary action ourselves before Islamic law clicked in. This likelihood proved to be the least of our worries. American troops in the region had less than usual rates of misconduct. I was proud of their discipline. But, frankly, part of the good behavior resulted from another Arab taboo: we had agreed not to allow our troops any alcohol in Saudi Arabia.

The big question on the troops' minds during my visit was rotation. How long before somebody else took their place? The issue went to the root of our commitment. Would the President wait out lengthy sanctions, which would require rotation? Or would he opt for an offensive, which likely meant staying in place for the duration? I wondered how long we could leave tens of thousands of restless young Americans there, baking in the sun, under Islam's prohibitions, wondering which way their government would go.

In Saudi Arabia, I witnessed the beginnings of a formidable force gathering as our allies started to arrive, the British first. The Gulf states committed forces, along with France, Canada, Italy, Egypt, Syria, and others eventually totaling twenty-eight nations. Countries unable to contribute troops helped finance the buildup.

We had been planning for this kind of war on a grand scale for years at NATO. But we had assumed it would be fought amid hills and forests against a Soviet enemy, not across sand dunes against an Arab foe. From the outbreak of the crisis I had spent much of my time with my NATO and other coalition counterparts or dealing by phone with them. Every nation had an equivalent of a JCS Chairman answerable to its political leaders, as I was answerable to Cheney and Bush. Luckily, the coalition allies who had much invested in this adventure had extraordinary defense chiefs. Marshal of the Royal Air Force Sir

David Craig of Great Britain and I became close. I had solid relationships with General Maurice Schmitt of France, General Domenico Corcione of Italy, General John de Chastelain of Canada, and General Dogan Gures of Turkey, whose country was providing bases for us.

Leading such a diverse force presented a challenge not unlike that which General Eisenhower faced as Supreme Allied Commander in Europe during World War II. Every country involved in the Gulf was sovereign and wanted assurances as to how its forces would be used. Very possibly, Norm Schwarzkopf's greatest single achievement was his extraordinary ability to weld this babel of armies into one fighting force, without offending dozens of heads of state.

Schwarzkopf was also a master at getting along with his Arab hosts. He had lived in the region as a young man and was a serious student of Arab culture. Big, profane Norm could sit and drink tea with Arabs and exchange courtesies for hours with the best of them. He became a favorite of King Fahd. Prince Khalid Bin Sultan, Bandar's half brother and an air force general, was appointed commander of the Arab forces and became Schwarzkopf's link to the royal family. Despite occasional flare-ups, the two of them worked together successfully. Khalid had the royal clout to get things done, and he was big and tough enough to stand toe-to-toe with Norm.

I returned home from my trip to Madrid and the Middle East on September 15, a Saturday night, looking forward to a quiet Sunday to shake off the jet lag. It was not to be. I woke up early the next morning and went to the kitchen for a cup of coffee. Alma was already at the table and pointed to the front page of the *Washington Post.* The headline was "U.S. to Rely on Air Strikes if War Erupts." It was the worst possible message at this time. The President was already being oversold on airpower. In one meeting he had told me, "Colin, these guys have never been seriously bombed. Bandar tells me a couple of bombs and they'll fold. Mubarak, Ozal in Turkey, they all tell me the same thing. We can knock 'em out in twenty-four hours."

I understood his impatience. He wondered how long he could keep the tide of troops flowing to a distant rampart, build an international coalition, and hold on to public support. Air strikes are so tempting, so swift, so seemingly surgical. We might be able to win a war by air, though, so far, no one had. "The trouble with airpower," I had warned the President, "is that you leave the initiative in the hands of your enemy. He gets to decide when he's had enough." We were planning a full campaign—air, land, sea, and space— to remove the decision from Saddam's hands.

The source for the *Post* story was General Michael Dugan, who had replaced Larry Welch as Air Force Chief of Staff just three months before. Dugan too had just returned from a trip to Saudi Arabia and had treated the traveling press to an on-the-record interview for hours on end, an act of supreme courage, but not too prudent. I had warned Mike Dugan twice before about statements he had made to reporters that did not square with administration policy. Within just ten days of Iraq's invasion of Kuwait, he had publicly claimed that air power could do the job. Among the things Dugan was quoted as saying in the *Post* article were that "airpower is the only answer that's available to our country"; that the Israelis had advised him "the best way to hurt Saddam" was to target his family, his personal guard, and his mistress; that Dugan did not "expect to be concerned" with political constraints in selecting bombing targets; that Iraq's air force had "very limited military capability"; and that its army was "incompetent." The *Post* piece ended by quoting Dugan as telling an F-15 squadron stationed in the desert, "The American people will support this operation until the body bags come home."

In a single story, Dugan had made the Iraqis look like a pushover; suggested that American commanders were taking their cue from Israel, a perception fatal to the Arab alliance we were trying to forge; suggested political assassination, which a presidential executive order forbade; claimed that airpower was the only option; and said in a lugubrious way that the American people would not support any other administration strategy. Dugan was not in the chain of command and should not have been commenting on operational matters anyway. His remarks had been an obvious grab for Air Force glory. It would have been difficult to pack more impolitic, indiscreet, and parochial statements into a single interview.

I tracked down Dugan in Florida, where he was attending a conference, and woke him out of a sound sleep. "Mike," I said, "have you seen the *Post*?"

"No."

"Then let me read you something." I went through the piece, item by item. He did not seem concerned.

I next called Cheney, who had not seen the *Post* article either. "We've got a problem," I told him. He would get back to me, he said, after he had a chance to read the paper.

Cheney called me right back. "That was dumb, dumb, dumb," he said.

"What do you want to do?" I asked.

"I'll brief Scowcroft, and then I'm going to take a walk along the C&O Canal," he answered.

I called Mike Dugan again, told him I had talked to Cheney, and braced him. Brent Scowcroft, I knew, was going to be on CBS's *Face the Nation* that morning, and a traditional part of that appearance for administration officials was to carry out damage control against negative weekend stories. "Stand by to have your butt chewed," I said. "And don't be surprised if it's on network television."

Mike answered only, "Right, yeah, I'm ready."

Scowcroft shot Dugan down, as expected.

At 7:45 the following Monday morning, I was working at my stand-up desk, going through the overnight intelligence reports, and watching commuters arrive through the one-way Mylar window when Cheney phoned. He wanted me to come up to join him and Deputy Secretary Don Atwood. I barely had the door closed behind me when Cheney said, "I'm going to fire Mike Dugan."

"Dick," I said, "can we talk about it?"

"I'm going to fire Dugan. I have lost confidence in him."

"Let's make sure the punishment fits the crime," I said. I watched Cheney's expression set like hardening concrete.

"As soon as you leave the room," he said, "I'm calling Dugan, and I'm relieving him." I assumed, correctly as it turned out, that Cheney had already obtained the President's approval.

With Cheney, there was never any doubt when you had hit the wall. My job now was to start thinking about a replacement, since Dugan would be out of his office before the sun set on the Pentagon. On an earlier trip to the Pacific, I had met General Merrill "Tony" McPeak, a lean-as-leather fighter pilot, fifty-four years old, bursting with energy and imagination. I had been warned that McPeak was a hip shooter, prone to fire off ten ideas in one burst, of which three might be good. Not a bad average, as ideas go, I thought. I recommended McPeak to Cheney and to Don Rice, the Air Force Secretary. He was their pick as well, and Tony became the new Air Force Chief of Staff. Dugan was being replaced by another airpower advocate, one, I hoped, who would be a tad more discreet.

Something was bothering me. On September 24 I went to Dick Cheney's office. "Dick," I said, "the President's really getting impatient. He keeps asking if we can't get the Iraqis out of Kuwait with air strikes."

"Yes," Cheney said. "He's concerned that time is running out on him." We both understood the President's restlessness, even though I had told him back on August 15 that he had until sometime in October to decide between continued sanctions or war. George Bush was investing enormous political capital in Desert Shield. His administration had come almost to a domestic standstill as the Gulf swallowed up his attention. And he did not think he could hold the international coalition together indefinitely.

"You know how Norm, the chiefs, and I feel," I said to Cheney. "We shouldn't go on the offensive until we have a force in place that can guarantee victory. And that's going to take time."

"So what do you want to do?" Cheney asked.

"Our policy now is to hope sanctions will work," I said. But I pointed out that by next month, the President had to decide whether to continue sanctions or keep building up to go to war. "I think we owe him a more complete description of how long-term sanctions and strangulation would work," I said. I thought we ought to lay out the advantages and disadvantages so that the President would have an alternative to going to war. "In the meantime," I said, "the buildup goes on." I had already discussed such an alternative with Baker and Scowcroft. Baker had been interested, but Scowcroft shared Bush's lack of faith in long-term sanctions.

"The President's available this afternoon," Cheney said. "We'll go over and you can lay it all out for him." I had time only to grab some handwritten notes before Dick and I went to the Oval Office.

It was a warm, drowsy autumn afternoon. The President was seated at his desk talking with Scowcroft and Sununu. Secretary of State Baker and the other members of the national security team were not present, since this was a spur-of-the-moment gathering and not an NSC decision meeting. I picked up a certain preoccupation in Bush's demeanor. I was not sure we had the President's undivided attention. He was meeting with President De Klerk of South Africa later that day and negotiating with Congress on a budget deal that would kill his "Read my lips; no new taxes" pledge.

"Mr. President," Cheney said, "the chairman has some thoughts for you." The President nodded for me to proceed.

"Sir," I began, "you still have two basic options available. The first is the offensive option." I walked him through the mobilization schedule. I also explained the air option we had in place, should Saddam attempt another provocation requiring our instant response. "I still recommend that we continue preparing for a full-scale air, land, and sea campaign," I said. "If you decide to go that route in October, we'll be ready to launch sometime in January."

But there was still the other option, sanctions. I described how we could maintain our defensive posture in Saudi Arabia while keeping sanctions in place. Even if we built up to an offensive force, we could always ratchet it back down to a defensive level. Containing Iraq from further aggression through our defensive strategy and strangling her into withdrawal through sanctions remained a live option. "Of course, there is a serious disadvantage," I conceded. Sanctions left the initiative with the Iraqis to decide when they had had enough. And history had taught us that sanctions take time, if they work at all. I was not advocating either route, war or sanctions, on this day. I simply believed that both options had to be considered fully and fairly. No decision would be required from the President for weeks.

When I finished, he said, "Thanks, Colin. That's useful. That's very interesting. It's good to consider all angles. But I really don't think we have time for sanctions to work." With that, the meeting ended.

In his book *The Commanders,* Bob Woodward paints a dramatic picture of this scene in the Oval Office. (He has it occurring "in early October.") Woodward has me wanting to steer the President toward a less aggressive course in the Gulf, but fearful to press my point hard enough because none of the other advisors present backed me. After his book came out, there was a lot of talk about Powell the "reluctant warrior." Guilty. War is a deadly game; and I do not believe in spending the lives of Americans lightly. My responsibility that day was to lay out all options for the nation's civilian leadership. However, in our democracy it is the President, not generals, who make decisions about going to war. I had done my duty. The sanctions clock was ticking down. If the President was right, if he decided that it must be war, then my job was to make sure we were ready to go in and win.

In early October, I found myself standing next to a Soviet general inside a missile silo at Ellsworth Air Force Base in North Dakota, with the missile targeted toward his homeland. I also took him into the secret recesses of NORAD, the North American Air Defense Command in Colorado, explaining how we would track his country's incoming missiles. I was squiring General Mikhail Moiseyev, chief of the Soviet general staff, around America in the midst of the Gulf buildup. The task was an intrusion, but necessary. In building the new harmony that we and the Soviets both wanted, personal relationships had become critical, especially given their cooperation so far in the Gulf crisis.

The warm feelings from my first Vienna meeting with Moiseyev had carried over. I liked and admired this man. Beyond the obligatory grand tour of American martial might, I also wanted Moiseyev to see everyday America, to feel it, to sense it, to touch it, to know the real strength of a free society. Besides, every time I took him to a military installation or showed him a weapons system, he looked bored stiff. "Yes, we have one too, only better."

On October 1, the day after Moiseyev and his wife, Galina Iosifovna, had arrived, I had rousted the general from the VIP quarters at Bolling Air Force Base and taken him to visit my favorite Washington sites. We had with us again as interpreter Peter Afanasenko, always a joy as a companion and a scholar of the Russian soul as well as the language. We began in the stillness of dawn at the Jefferson Memorial, since Jefferson is my special hero among the Founding Fathers. I particularly admired his modesty on assuming the presidency: "I advance with obedience to the work," he had said in his first inaugural, "ready to retire from it whenever you become sensible how much better choice it is in your power to make." And in the same message, he revealed a realism about public office that rang true to anyone who has been there: "I have learnt to expect that it will rarely fall to the lot of imperfect man to retire from this station with the reputation and favor which bring him into it."

I explained to Moiseyev the excerpts from the Declaration of Independence chiseled onto the southwest wall of the memorial. "Those words," I said, "launched the country I am going to show you."

Jefferson might seem an unlikely hero for me. As an African-American, I am aware of the contradictions in a man who could pledge in his second inaugural address, "Equal and exact justice to all men, of whatever state or persuasion," yet own slaves. We all are the products of our time, however, and as Jefferson once observed, people change, or else "we might as well require a man to wear still the coat which fitted him when a boy."

I next drove Moiseyev by the Washington Monument, which he barely glanced at, and then took him to the Lincoln Memorial, which clearly impressed him. He was most moved, however, at our last stop, the simple wall cut into the earth on the Mall, the Vietnam Veterans Memorial. I showed him how we could locate, by computer, the name of any of the more than 58,000 fallen, using my late friend Tony Mavroudis as an example. Moiseyev was quiet as we trooped along the wall. At the end he said, "We need to do more. We don't remember enough."

I knew he was not speaking of World War II, which is commemorated in practically every Russian village. He was thinking of the Soviet Union's own Vietnam, Afghanistan, which had cost over 13,000 lives and which his government blotted from public awareness as though it had never happened, leaving only the families of the dead to grieve. The visit to the wall brought us together as brothers in the profession of arms, no matter what flag we served, "content to fill a soldier's grave," as the old poem goes.

I took my guest to the Department of Veterans Affairs to give him a sense of what we did for those who had borne the battle. His eyes glazed over as VA officials described GI benefits and VA hospitals. But when we reached a display of prosthetic devices, we had his attention again. "We don't do enough," he repeated. "We should do more." The war in Afghanistan, with the heavy mujahedin use of mines and booby traps, had been hell on Russian limbs.

I took Moiseyev to the General Motors Buick, Oldsmobile, Cadillac Assembly Center in Detroit, Michigan, to give him a taste of American industry. Robert Semple, chairman and CEO of GMC, was our host, and when the tour of the assembly line ended, Semple escorted us to a test track, where the company had set out several late-model cars. All eyes went to a sleek red Corvette. Semple asked a GM driver to take Moiseyev and then me on a ride in the two-seater. I waved the driver off and said, "I'll take the general for a spin." Moiseyev and I got in. We had made a couple of turns around the track, and I had the Corvette pushing ninety, when Moiseyev gestured that he wanted to drive. I brought the car to a halt and we changed places. He bucked the six-speed sports car up to seventy and suddenly downshifted it to first, revving the Corvette to about 6,000 rpm. GGGrrrr!!! I hope this car never wound up on any dealer's lot.

At another point, Moiseyev and I were inspecting one of our ships in San Diego, and when we reached the galley, he decided to show off his proletarian credentials. A couple of cooks were peeling potatoes, and Moiseyev motioned for a peeler. He signaled me to take one, and proposed a race. We won the Cold War; but that day we lost the spud war. The champ was Moiseyev from Siberia over Powell from Banana Kelly.

Toward the end of the week-long visit, I hosted a dinner honoring Moiseyev and his wife at the Smithsonian Air and Space Museum in Washington. On our last night together, the Soviets threw a caviar-laden and vodka-drenched reciprocal dinner. By then, Galina, or Galla as we had come to know her, and Alma had become as close as the two old soldiers. Then it was time for us to take our friends out to Andrews Air Force Base for their flight back to Moscow. Alma and Galla rode in a limousine behind me and Moiseyev, and afterward Alma described Galla's conversation. During the stay, she had had a good introduction to the United States. "I do not envy anything I have seen in your country," Galla told Alma. "I am not jealous. I am just sad. We wasted seventy years. We lost the opportunity to do what you have done. And it will not be fixed in my lifetime."

. . .

On October 6, I called Norm Schwarzkopf in Riyadh over my secure phone. It was a beautiful system. The President's button was in the left-hand corner of the console and had a shrill, attention-demanding ring. Norm's button was in the right-hand corner, and all I had to do was punch it and his phone rang in Riyadh, easy as talking to the guy in the office next door. I asked Norm to send a team to Washington to brief the President on the offensive strategy we would use if we had to drive the Iraqis from Kuwait. Norm resisted: "I got no goddam offensive plan because I haven't got the ground forces." He still had only one corps, he pointed out. "I can't get there from here," he warned me.

I knew what Norm was worried about. All he had coming at this point were four Army divisions, a Marine division, an armored cavalry regiment, a British armored brigade, a French light brigade, a mixed Egyptian/Syrian force, and a collection of small coalition elements—all told, just over 200,000 troops. He would have enough to defend Saudi Arabia, but hardly enough to drive out an entrenched Iraqi army estimated at half a million men. Still, I needed to brief the President on what Schwarzkopf could do with what he had. And since he had maintained from the beginning that he would need more force to go on the offensive, I wanted to know how much more he required.

"Look," I told him, "your air plan is coming together nicely, and the White House needs to be briefed on it. I also need to show the bosses what the ground plan looks like, even if it isn't complete."

"All right," Norm said, "but I'd like to conduct this one myself." I told him no, his presence was far more important in Riyadh.

Schwarzkopf reluctantly dispatched a briefing team headed by Marine Major General Bob Johnston, his chief of staff. I wanted Cheney and the chiefs to hear the briefing before taking Johnston to the White House. We met in the Tank on the afternoon of October 10. Johnston reviewed the overall plan and then called on Brigadier General Buster Glosson to brief the air portion. Since Colonel John Warden had laid out the air plan for me in early August, Horner and Glosson had made it even more impressive, involving Navy, Air Force, and coalition aircraft and cruise missiles. The target list stretched from installations around Baghdad to the Iraqi trenches in Kuwait and all lines of supply and communication in between. The plan was bold, imaginative, and solid.

When Glosson finished, Lieutenant Colonel Joe Purvis from the School of Advanced Military Studies at Leavenworth, who was heading the Jedi Knights, briefed on the ground phase. This plan was based only on forces allocated so far. It involved three feints and a main attack. The Marines would feint an amphibious assault to hold down Iraqi divisions along the Kuwaiti coast. A second Marine feint would take place along the border between Kuwait and Saudi Arabia just in from the coast. The multinational coalition forces would conduct a third feint on the western end of the Kuwaiti-Saudi border. The main attack, consisting of all American divisions, would drive up the middle into the Iraqi main defenses with the aim of reaching a key road junction north of Kuwait City. We would be outnumbered and heading straight into the Iraqis' killing zones.

Schwarzkopf was right; it was a weak plan, and I could see why he had been reluctant to have it presented in Washington. He wanted two more divisions and a corps headquarters in order to do a better job. What surprised me was that Johnston and Purvis did not show what CENTCOM could do if it did have such a force. But even with only the one currently available corps, the plan was faulty. You do not send an outnumbered attacking force into the enemy's jaws. Furthermore, an obvious stratagem had not been addressed. Frontline Iraqi infantry were dug into Kuwait and therefore could not easily attack south. The Iraqi mechanized forces would not be likely to strike south into the endless Saudi desert if we attacked them on their right and from the air. The current plan made no attempt to exploit this vulnerable Iraqi western flank.

During the Tank briefing, Cheney asked a few perfunctory questions and left. He did not look pleased. I excused the briefers and discussed with the chiefs what we had heard. We held a common view: a better one-corps plan should have been prepared. Even so, any one-corps plan was too risky. I saw Cheney later, and he told me, "I may be a layman, but that strategy disappointed me."

He was right to feel that way, I agreed. But I reminded him, "We've just seen a first cut, and we've seen it under Norm's protest. We'll get something better. We've still got time."

The next day, Bob Johnston and his team presented the same briefing in the Situation Room to the President and what was now called the "Gang of Eight," President Bush, Vice President Quayle, Jim Baker, John Sununu, Brent Scowcroft, Bob Gates, Cheney, and me. The air plan continued to impress. But the reaction to the ground strategy was predictable. Scowcroft, a retired Air Force lieutenant general, jumped all over it. I pointed out again that Schwarzkopf had unveiled this plan under protest, and that we had time to come up with something better. In my own mind, I had concluded that Schwarzkopf's senior ground commanders had been so consumed with deployment and the defense plan that they had not given ground offensive planning their priority attention. I told the President that we would do better. He seemed relaxed. Bob Gates, however, was later heard to make a crack to the effect that "General McClellan lives," referring to the Civil War commander who would not budge because he never had enough troops, no matter how many Lincoln gave him.

I called Norm the next day, October 13, and gave him the reviews. The air briefing had gone well, but the ground strategy needed work. Then I said mischievously, holding the receiver away from my ear, "You know, some people are saying we've got a McClellan out there."

Norm took the bait. "You tell me what son of a bitch said that," he yelled. "I'll show him the difference between Schwarzkopf and McClellan!"

I felt slightly guilty. I had deliberately shoved the bayonet between his ribs to goad him into thinking harder about our ground offensive plan. After I hung up, I decided it was time for me to make another trip to Saudi Arabia.

Cheney kept assigning me last-minute tasks as I prepared to leave. "I want to know the high-side number for an offensive force," he said. "I want to know when Norm can give me a go for an attack." He had a third question, and I jotted it down in my notebook simply as "Prefix 5," my nuclear qualification code dating back to my Infantry Officers Advanced Course at Fort Benning in 1964. "Let's not even think about nukes," I said. "You know we're not going to let that genie loose."

"Of course not," Cheney said. "But take a look to be thorough and just out of curiosity."

I told Tom Kelly to gather a handful of people in the most secure cell in the building to work out nuclear strike options. The results unnerved me. To do serious damage to just one armored division dispersed in the desert would require a considerable number of small tactical nuclear weapons. I showed this analysis to Cheney and then had it destroyed. If I had had any doubts before about the practicality of nukes on the field of battle, this report clinched them.

Cheney's last words before I left for Saudi Arabia were: "Let's see an offensive plan with a little imagination this time."

By Monday, October 22, I was in the Saudi Ministry of Defense, sitting in Schwarzkopf's war room, five stories below ground. We gathered at a long table in the center of the room facing a wall plastered with map boards. Present were Norm; Lieutenant General John Yeosock, the Army commander; Lieutenant General Walt Boomer, the Marine commander; Admiral Stan Arthur, the Navy commander; Lieutenant General Chuck Horner, the Air Force commander; and Lieutenant General Cal Waller, CENTCOM's deputy commanding general. We talked a little about the one-corps offensive; it was still a loser and quickly set aside. The Jedi Knights had come up with a two-corps plan that would take advantage of our superior armored capability and the helicopter mobility of the 101st Airborne Division. This latest plan also took advantage of the exposed Iraqi western flank, but just barely. "Thanks," I said to the briefers, but after they left, I told Norm, "We've still got to do better."

Later that evening, he came to my suite at a resplendent guest palace made available by the Saudis. We talked about how we might better exploit the enemy's static position. The Iraqi army was just sitting there in Kuwait. The sea was to the east. Their own fortifications were to their south. In effect, they had trapped themselves. We talked about slamming the doors shut on the west and north and cutting off their lines of support. "We can use a heavy armored corps to roll fast and deep around the western flank," I said, "and we can send the XVIII Airborne Corps farther west and then north to block the Euphrates River Valley and cut off their lines of reinforcement and withdrawal." We continued trading ideas, sketching them out on stationery I found in a desk drawer. The strategy we were coming to required no genius.

The Iraqis' disposition of forces practically wrote the plan for us.

The next morning, we met again at Schwarzkopf's headquarters to flesh out our ideas of the night before. Norm repeated his request for a two-division corps from Europe. I agreed and said we would add a third division from the United States. We would also send another Marine division. I beefed up his request for additional fighter squadrons. Aircraft carriers? Let's send six. We had paid for this stuff. Why not use it? What were we saving it for? We had learned a lesson in Panama. Go in big, and end it quickly. We could not put the United States through another Vietnam. We could be so lavish with resources because the world had changed. We could now afford to pull divisions out of Germany that had been there for the past forty years to stop a Soviet offensive that was no longer coming.

"Norm," I said, "you've got to understand that the President and Cheney will give you anything you need to get the job done. And don't worry," I added, "you won't be jumping off until you're ready. We're not going off half-cocked." As I spoke, I saw the tension flow out of Schwarzkopf for the first time since I had arrived. As he later described this moment, "I felt as though he [Powell] had lifted a great load from my shoulders." And I went back to Washington feeling better than I had in weeks.

It was nearing 3:30 P.M., October 30, as Otis drove through the gate and pulled up before the West Wing entrance to the White House. I told him to let me off, then drive on farther and park. I played a little game on these occasions. The TV camera crews were usually gathered outside the gate. If I wanted news coverage of me taking maps into the White House, I removed them from the trunk myself. If I did not want to tip my hand, I had Otis drop me off, then discreetly bring me the maps inside the lobby.

Of all the times we had gathered in the White House since Saddam had grabbed Kuwait, this day was the most crucial. The President had pulled together the Gang of Eight, minus Dan Quayle, who was out of town. We had to resolve the fundamental question I had posed back in August and September: do we limit ourselves to defending Saudi Arabia and count on sanctions to squeeze Saddam out of Kuwait? Or do we gear up to drive him out? Defend or eject?

We met in the Situation Room, which pleased me. Gatherings in the Oval Office tended to take on a bull-session informality; between cups of coffee and people gazing out into the Rose Garden, it was harder to keep a discussion on track. This day, Brent Scowcroft led off, laying out the two options succinctly. "We're at a Y in the road," he said. If we took the route of ejecting the Iraqi army, that raised a critical question. Did we try to get a UN resolution authorizing the use of force? And if we could not get it, were we prepared to go it alone with other willing allies? Jim Baker was about to embark on a trip to Europe, and we discussed how much more help he could hope to enlist from our friends. We next went over the supersensitive need to keep Israel out of the fight. If the Arab states were to be held together against an errant brother, the one thing they would not tolerate was fighting alongside Israelis.

Eventually, the President said, "Okay, let's hear what Colin has to say."

I set my acetate overlays on an easel. I snapped on the pen-size laser. The President smiled. "I just got back from Riyadh," I began, "and I can report that the first phase of the mission is just about accomplished. We'll soon be in a position to defend Saudi Arabia. By early December, the last division, the last company, the last tent pole will be in place." I went into a detailed explanation of where every unit was posted, and how Norm intended to fight a defensive battle. After about ten minutes of describing the Saudi chessboard, I let a new overlay drop. "And here," I said, "is how we would go on the offensive to kick the Iraqis out of Kuwait." The President leaned forward. This was what he was waiting to hear. I described the air campaign, then the frontal supporting attacks into Kuwait to pin down the occupying Iraqi army, while a sweeping left hook against the western flank would cut off the Iraqis from the rear.

When I finished, Scowcroft asked, "What size force are we talking about?"

"We're approaching two hundred and fifty thousand for the defensive phase," I said. "But if the President opts for this offensive, we'll need a hell of a lot more."

"How much more?" Scowcroft asked.

"Nearly double," I said. "About another two hundred thousand troops."

"Whew," Scowcroft said, his gasp echoed by others around the room. I glanced at the President. He had not blinked. Dick Cheney added that he and the Joint Chiefs, whom we had briefed earlier, were all on board for the offensive plan.

President Bush asked again about airpower. "Colin, are you sure that won't do it?"

"I'd be the happiest soldier in the Army if the Iraqis turned tail when the bombs start falling," I said. "If they do, you can take the expense for deploying the ground forces out of my pay." But, I reminded the group, history offered no encouragement that airpower alone would succeed.

We considered issuing an ultimatum to Saddam by a certain date: get out or be thrown out. Jim Baker suggested February 1. "If we make the threat, we have to mean it," I said. "We have to be ready to go to war."

Again, the President nodded. He let the talk ramble a bit, as was his habit, and then he shut it off. "Okay, do it," he said. We had a decision. We would go to war in three months if sanctions did not work and the Iraqis were still in Kuwait.

Just after the midterm elections, on November 8, President Bush announced that another 200,000 U.S. troops were on their way to the Gulf, and he made their mission unmistakable: "to insure that the coalition has an adequate *offensive* military option." The howling in the Congress was loud. Was this George Bush, whom some people criticized as a "wimp," trying to prove his manhood by starting a war? The debate throughout the country started to take on the acrimony of the hawk-dove controversy of the sixties over Vietnam.

On November 29, the United Nations was scheduled to vote whether or not to sanction military force to get Iraq out of Kuwait. Resolution 678 displayed the usual fuzziness of documents written by many hands. Jim Baker had wanted plain language, arguing for "use of force." But the Soviet foreign minister, Eduard Shevardnadze, wanted something less naked. They compromised on "all necessary means." It did not matter. A bullet fired through a euphemism is still a bullet. The resolution passed the Security Council 12–2, with Cuba and Yemen voting no and China abstaining. History was made that day. If it came to war, the United States and the Soviet Union would not be antagonists for the first time since World War II.

The UN approval capped an extraordinary feat of diplomacy in this century, and the lion's share of the credit for this triumph belongs to George Bush, superbly aided by Jim Baker. By the time Resolution 678 was passed, a remarkable coalition had been welded together, mostly over the phone from the Oval Office. By now, thirteen NATO nations were contributing to the multinational force, including large contingents from the United Kingdom and France. Nearly all the Arab nations joined, with Egypt and Syria contributing a combined fifty thousand troops. Countries that had only just slipped out of the Soviet yoke came on board, including Czechoslovakia, Poland, and Bulgaria. Poor countries, like Bangladesh, Senegal, Somalia, and Zaire, had pledged what they could. Thirty-five nations were providing manpower, armaments, or money. All told, 200,000 coalition troops would be deployed alongside the Americans.

The UN resolution made clear that the mission was only to free Kuwait. However much we despised Saddam and what he had done, the United States had little desire to shatter his country. For the previous ten years, Iran, not Iraq, had been our Persian Gulf nemesis. We wanted Iraq to continue as a threat and a counterweight to Iran. Our Arab allies never intended to set foot beyond Kuwait. Saudi Arabia did not want a Shiite regime breaking off from Iraq in the south. The Turks did not want a Kurdish regime splitting off from Iraq in the north. We also knew that only a little more than half of the Iraqi army was committed to Kuwait. The rest was still in Iraq, able to maintain internal order and to fend off a still hostile Iran. In none of the meetings I attended was dismembering Iraq, conquering Baghdad, or changing the Iraqi form of government ever seriously considered. We hoped that Saddam would not survive the coming fury. But his elimination was not a stated objective. What we hoped for, frankly, in a postwar Gulf region was an Iraq still standing, with Saddam overthrown. The UN had given us our marching orders, and the President intended to stay within them.

I was amazed, given the forces and power now arrayed against Saddam Hussein, unmatched since

D-Day, that he still had not blinked. He had passed the sanctions exit, the defense-buildup exit, the offensive-buildup exit, and now the UN-authorization-of-force exit. And still he kept barreling down the highway to disaster. He had to know that he would lose, but as long as he could survive in power, he was apparently willing to pay the price for his Kuwait adventure in dead Iraqis. The President's instincts had been right from the start. As he told me on his return from a Thanksgiving visit to the troops, sanctions would not work. What we had to do was becoming inevitable.

I still believe that sanctions are a useful weapon in the armory of nations. They helped, for example, to hasten the meltdown of apartheid in South Africa. But sanctions work best against leaders who have the interests of their country and people at heart, because sanctions hurt the people and the country more than the leaders. The problem is that sanctions are most often imposed against regimes that have only their own interests and the retention of power at heart. And since these leaders are still going to have a roof over their heads, food on their table, gas in their tank, and power in their hands, sanctions rarely work against them. Saddam was the perfect example.

President Bush had taken to demonizing Saddam in public just as he had Manuel Noriega. "We are dealing with Hitler revisited," he said on one occasion, and described Saddam as "a tyrant unmoved by human decency." I suggested to Cheney and Scowcroft that they might try to get the President to cool the rhetoric. Not that the charges were untrue, but the demonizing left me uneasy. I preferred to talk about the "Iraqi regime" or the "Hussein regime." Our plan contemplated only ejecting Iraq from Kuwait. It did not include toppling Saddam's dictatorship. Within these limits, we could not bring George Bush Saddam Hussein's scalp. And I thought it unwise to elevate public expectations by making the man out to be the devil incarnate and then leaving him in place.

While the country faced the prospect of war that fall, war's reality was being driven home by a remarkable television event. Earlier in the year, I had been invited to a lecture on the Lincoln years that the Bushes had arranged at the White House. Afterward, I was standing in the East Room talking to a young man. "That period fascinates me," I said. "Really," this fellow said. "You know, I'm doing a television series on the Civil War. Would you like to see the tapes we've finished so far?"

That is how I first came to know of Ken Burns and his now famous documentary. My family was so moved by the tapes Ken sent that I told the President how we had been glued to the television set for hours. He asked to see them. I sent the tapes to the White House, and he and Barbara were so impressed that it took forever for me to get them back. After Ken Burns finished the series, he sent me a complete set. I gave the tapes to Cheney, who presented them to Norm Schwarzkopf as a 1990 Christmas gift. From the moment the program aired nationally on September 23, it held the country spellbound for five nights. "At least now people know what war is about," I said to Norm during one of our phone conversations. "It's damn good they do," he answered, as his own preparations accelerated.

Schwarzkopf later wrote that Ken Burns's *Civil War* renewed his determination to hold down casualties to the minimum. Thanks to Burns's artistry, millions of Americans understood that, yes, you went to war for high principles, but you should not go into it with any romantic illusions.

Norm Schwarzkopf, under pressure, was an active volcano. I occasionally found myself in transoceanic shouting matches with him that were full of barracks profanity. The cussing meant nothing. The anger passed, the mutual respect continued, and a deepening affection grew. I recognized the root of his rages. Blowing up acted as a safety valve for his frustrations. His subordinates took plenty of heat from him, yet remained fiercely loyal. However, his exasperations, which were real enough, he also vented upward, principally his conviction that his position and his needs were not always understood in Washington. Who was he going to rail against? The Secretary of Defense? The President of the United States? So he blew up at me.

I understood this; but Cheney occasionally required my reassurance that we had the right man in Riyadh. Dick is a man of plain style, and after his first trip to Saudi Arabia with Norm to sell King Fahd on asking for our help, he mentioned a couple of incidents to me that had bothered him. During the fifteen-hour flight to the Saudi capital, passengers had formed a line to get into the bathroom. According to

Cheney, a major had finally worked his way to the front, and when he got there, he called out, "General!" He had been keeping a place for Norm. On the same trip, Cheney said that he had seen a colonel on his hands and knees on the floor of the plane, pressing Schwarzkopf's uniform.

After that trip and on subsequent occasions, Cheney asked me about Norm. Most recently, he had said, "This is for all the marbles, you know. The presidency is riding on this one. Are you absolutely confident about Schwarzkopf?"

There was nothing particularly subversive about Cheney's question. Inevitably, reports of Norm's rough treatment of subordinates seeped back to Washington. Cheney dealt with Norm infrequently, while I was talking with him every day. Consequently, Dick relied on my judgment. I told him that my faith in Norm was total.

Still, a good commander always has a replacement in the back of his mind. People have heart attacks. They step in front of buses. A soldier takes a hit. Norm, under enormous pressure, was not immune. He had already come down with the flu a couple of times. Once, I had to insist that he go off and give himself a rest. For all his pyrotechnics and histrionics, however, Norm was a brilliant officer, a born leader, and a skilled diplomat in the region. He was the right man in the right place and I was happy to reassure Cheney from time to time.

On Monday, December 3, Cheney and I testified on Desert Shield before the Senate Armed Services Committee, a fairly tough sell, since Sam Nunn, the chairman, opposed going to war over Kuwait without giving sanctions a hard ride. Nunn reasoned that sanctions should be given as much time to work as they required, which seemed to me like entering a tunnel with no end. I reviewed the progress of the coalition buildup, and I gave a cold, hard appraisal of what we faced. Iraq was the fourth-largest military power in the world. Saddam's forces deployed in and around Kuwait numbered over 450,000 men, 3,800 tanks, and 2,500 artillery pieces; plus he had announced his intention to send another 250,000 troops. Also, hanging like a specter over the desert was the Iraqi biological arsenal and Saddam's feverish drive for nuclear capability. If war came, I had no intention of letting anyone on that committee think it was going to be a cakewalk.

That night, I flew to London with Alma. I had been invited by Winston S. Churchill, a member of the House of Commons and the grandson of Sir Winston, to address MPs and members of the British-American Parliamentary Group in the Palace of Westminster. The room where I spoke resembled a miniature Chamber of the House of Commons, and there I described the operations in the Gulf and the Base Force concept. As I spoke in this seat of Western democracy, the image of my mother and father, born as humble British subjects in a tiny tropical colony, flashed before me, and I wished they could see where fate had taken their son.

I was curious about the man I was to meet next, in office at this point for less than a week, and for whom I turned out to be his first foreign visitor. John Major greeted me, my executive assistant, Colonel Dick Chilcoat, the British secretary of state for defense, Tom King, and my counterpart, British chief of defense staff, Marshal of the Royal Air Force Sir David Craig, in a sitting room at 10 Downing Street. Major, at forty-seven, was boyish-looking and quite a switch from the redoubtable Mrs. Thatcher. Underneath the PM's mild exterior, however, I detected a steeliness. Major shot quick questions at me. How was the training going in the Gulf? How would the Iraqis respond to the air attack? How long would that campaign last? He cut off my answers as soon as he caught the drift and fired his next round. An aide came in and whispered in his ear. The prime minister had to leave. He ended the conversation cordially but briskly.

Underneath the high drama of preparing for war, the bizarre also went on. What, for example, did one horse in Minnesota have to do with our mobilization in the Persian Gulf? The wild card in this conflict was whether or not the Iraqis might resort to germ warfare. I assigned Brigadier General John Jumper to oversee our defenses against chemical and biological weapons, which Jumper did as head of a team dubbed "Bugs and Gases." One biological agent we believed the Iraqis possessed was botulinum toxin, one of the deadliest known to man. The only way to neutralize its lethal paralytic effects was through an antibody produced by one old horse named First Flight, stabled at the Veterinary College of the University of Minnesota. First Flight had so far produced some three hundred liters of antibody plasma, a valiant effort, but a drop in the bucket given the forces to be inoculated, now approaching half a million. Johnny Jumper and his team recruited another hundred horses to produce antibodies against botulinum toxin and to give First Flight a rest.

We hit other bumps on the road to readiness. Early in the buildup, the Saudis made a simple pronouncement. They were not going to allow any reporters into their country. That, we knew, could not stand. You do not send nearly half a million Americans, plus thousands of other nationals, halfway around the world to prepare for a major war and then impose a news blackout. We implored the Saudis to issue press visas. They grudgingly admitted a handful of correspondents. Some favorable news stories followed. Maybe, the Saudis reasoned, the Americans were right. And they then opened the floodgates to a point where handling the press crush, with some 2,500 correspondents eventually accredited, became a major headache for Norm Schwarzkopf.

Mail began clogging the arteries of war. As we approached Christmas, letters and packages to the troops swamped the military postal system. Everything imaginable and unimaginable arrived, insect repellent, suntan lotion, frozen pizzas, Christmas trees, wiffle balls, surgical gloves, Frisbees, Passover food, and lollipops (200,000 of them). Arnold Schwarzenegger begged me to let him send a planeload of Lifecycles and weight-lifting gear to keep the troops in fighting trim. I explained to Arnold that we were moving ammunition that week and would try to make room for his gift later, which we did.

The letters sent by schoolkids were touching but came in sufficient volume to sink a troop transport. Thousands of generic letters arrived with addresses like "Any Soldier USA." One had been sent by a schoolteacher who poured her heart out telling how proud she was of the troops. A hormonally hopped-up soldier wrote back describing in graphic detail how he would like to repay her kind words. She complained to the Defense Department, and we had to send a letter to the lad's commanding officer telling him to have his men knock off any further heavy breathing by mail.

The deluge reached a point where every day we were filling three and four C-5 Galaxies, those flying warehouses, just to accommodate mail and gifts to the troops. We tried to deliver everything, because it was as important to morale on the home front as it was on the imminent war front. American civilians were rallying around the troops as though they wanted to make up for the neglect during the Vietnam years. The explosion of yellow ribbons on trees, homes, jackets, and blouses recalled a national unity not felt since World War II.

We welcomed morale-building USO entertainers, but other visiting firemen became too much. Members of Congress on fact-finding trips began to show up at all hours, chewing up Schwarzkopf's priceless time to a point where Cheney had to go to the Hill and put a stop to it. We rationed congressional visits to one delegation per week.

Even in the grimmest of enterprises there are tension breakers. At one point, the tabloid *National Enquirer* ran a story headlined "Bush and Saddam Are Cousins" and offered genealogical "proof" that not only was George Bush related to the queen of England, but "Hussein and President Bush share a common ancestry dating back at least to the crusades." This news prompted the President to circulate a memo to the national security team that said, "No decisions I make will be affected by my relationship with Saddam Hussein. The Queen and I would have it no other way."

Lawyers got into the act. We could not complete a list of air targets until the Pentagon general counsel's office approved. In one preliminary list, we had targeted a triumphal arch celebrating Iraq's proclaimed victory over Iran in the eight-year war and a huge statue of Saddam, both in Baghdad. Colonel Fred Green, my legal advisor, came to see me with a battery of lawyers. They had gone over the list and approved everything except the arch and the statue. "Sorry, General," Fred said, "you can't touch them."

"Why not?" I asked, puzzled.

"You'd be bombing cultural landmarks of no military significance."

"Cultural landmarks! Gimme a break. I want to show his people Saddam's not out of bounds."

"Can't do it, General," Green said. "It would be like someone bombing the Lincoln Memorial or the Washington Monument. It contravenes international laws governing the conduct of war."

The arch and the statue were crossed off the target list. When I explained what had happened to

Cheney, he shook his head and muttered, "Lawyers running a war?"

We ran into unexpected problems in getting the sinews of battle shipped from U.S. and European ports to the Gulf. Some insurance companies demanded exorbitant premiums to cover commercial vessels sailing into a potential war zone. We had to beat them down or find cheaper coverage. The flow of manpower and matériel, nevertheless, was stupefying. In the first six weeks of Desert Shield, we brought in more tonnage than in the first three months of the Korean War. The lion's share of credit for this miracle of logistics belonged to a short, wiry dynamo named Gus Pagonis, an Army major general and the Desert Shield logistics chief. I had spotted Pagonis as a comer when he was still a lieutenant colonel. Nothing daunted the man. No shelter for the troops in the baking desert? Get the West Germans to provide the huge tents they used for festivals. Need still more shelter? Get the Saudis to lend the colorful tents they used for hundreds of thousands of Muslims making the annual pilgrimage to Mecca. Gus was stymied by only one obstacle, his rank. Commanders with more horsepower leaned on him to give their units priority, putting Gus in an impossible squeeze. Norm Schwarzkopf explained to me what Gus was going through, and our solution was to give Gus a third star, so that he had enough rank to match his responsibility.

Dick Cheney and I went to Riyadh on December 19 to size up the state of readiness and report back to President Bush. After we met with Norm and satisfied ourselves that all was proceeding on schedule, we visited the troops. At one stop, we stood alongside sleek F-117A Stealth fighters, surrounded by Air Force personnel and soldiers. Dick gave a talk both blunt and inspirational. The troops were going to stay here until Saddam left Kuwait, he said. "We can't say, okay, you can keep twenty percent of what you stole." Saddam had to leave or be driven out. In accomplishing the mission, however, our forces would get everything they needed, he promised. We were stinting on nothing. He asked if anyone had any questions for us. Such an offer would have been inconceivable in the Iraqi army, or in most armies, for that matter—ordinary soldiers given an opportunity to question their nation's top defense officials.

A pilot asked me about airpower. "Airpower will be overwhelming," I said, "but in every war, it's the infantrymen who have to raise the flag of victory on the battlefield."

"How long is it gonna take?" another GI asked.

"Wars are unpredictable," I said, "and I'm not a bookmaker or a fortune-teller. But I'll tell you this. We are not going to be bogged down." The President had already promised that the Persian Gulf would not become another Vietnam.

After the massing we had witnessed of planes, tanks, artillery, armored vehicles, ammo dumps, and hundreds of thousands of troops, I found it hard to believe that Saddam, at the last minute, would not fold. If he had any military men on his staff with an ounce of guts or sense, they would have to tell this nonsoldier, nonstrategist that his way was madness.

Still, madmen have ruled nations before and have pulled the roof down on their own people.

On Christmas Eve, immediately upon getting back from Saudi Arabia, Cheney and I flew to Camp David and were taken to rustic Holly Cabin. Already there were the President, Brent Scowcroft, and Scowcroft's deputy, Bob Gates. We sat before a roaring fire while Dick and I briefed the President on the readiness of coalition forces and the latest edition of the strategy. George Bush was under enormous pressure, and I could see it in his taut features. He was trying to balance Arab states, Israel, Western allies, the Soviets, Congress, and the American public, like a juggler spinning plates on the tops of poles, wondering how long he could keep everything in the air.

Between his impatience and Norm Schwarzkopf's anxieties, I had my own juggling act. Norm displayed the natural apprehensions of a field commander on the edge of war, magnified by his excitable personality. I had to reassure him constantly that he would not be rushed into combat. At the same time, the President was leaning on me: "When are we going to be ready? When can we go?" Dealing with Norm was like holding a hand grenade with the pin pulled. Dealing with the President was like playing Scheherazade, trying to keep the king calm for a thousand and one nights.

The discussion this day at Holly Cabin inevitably got around to casualties. No figure is harder to divine through the fog of war. The worst-case scenarios were frightening, our troops advanc-

758 · COLIN L. POWELL

ing against hundreds of thousands of entrenched Iraqis, a sea of mines between them and the enemy, ditches full of oil that were to be set ablaze as our men advanced, and hanging over our heads the unknowable elements of chemical and biological warfare. Military pundits all over town had their predictions, sixteen, seventeen, eighteen thousand. A respected think tank, the Center for Strategic and International Studies, produced a projection of fifteen thousand U.S. casualties. The grim guessing game turned grimmer when word got out that the Defense Department had ordered fifteen thousand body bags. Actually the order had nothing to do with Desert Shield. It was generated by a computer at the Defense Logistics Agency as a possible need over an indefinite future. Cheney had pressed Schwarzkopf, and Norm was no more eager than I to project the unprojectable. But he finally came up with a figure of five thousand casualties.

I completely rejected the highest estimates. They were extrapolated from old war game formulas in which the U.S. and Soviet armies would grind each other down in Europe. That was not our strategy. First, we planned to punish the Iraqi ground forces with an air offensive of an intensity the world had never witnessed. The air war was to be followed by a ground campaign employing not World War I–style infantry charges but swift, heavily armored units engaged in the left hook around the Iraqis' lightly defended Western flank. I resisted giving anything as slippery as casualty estimates to the President, and so far had managed to avoid specifics.

But, when pressed to the wall, I finally came in below even Schwarzkopf's estimate, at three thousand killed, wounded and missing.

Still a sobering figure, I thought, as I studied the President's face that Christmas Eve. From his questions and demeanor, I concluded that George Bush no longer wanted an Iraqi withdrawal from Kuwait. Over the past four months, Saddam's occupation had visited terror on the Kuwaitis—murder, theft, rape, the destruction of museums. If the Iraqis withdrew now, it would be with impunity for their crimes. A pullback would also mean that Saddam would leave Kuwait with his huge army intact, ready to fight another day.

We also talked that night about the controversy raging in Congress over whether to wait for sanctions to work or to go on the offensive. The President listened distractedly. Suddenly, his words brought us up short. "I'll prevail," he said, "or I'll be impeached." I interpreted this to mean that he had completely resigned himself to war. If he won, Congress's opinion would not matter; and if he lost, he was prepared to lose the presidency.

Cheney and I helicoptered back to Washington late that night, and I got home in time to spend Christmas Eve with my family. It was a subdued holiday. My thoughts were with the families who had loved ones in the Gulf region on the eve of war. My mood was not lightened when I called my sister, Marilyn, to wish her and her family a Merry Christmas and learned that she would have to be treated for breast cancer.

. . .

"Colin, I cannot tell you how difficult it is to tell you this." The caller was a British colleague, General Sir Richard Vincent, vice chief of the defense staff.

"Yes, Dick," I said. "What is it?"

"You see, Air Chief Marshal Patrick Hine met with the prime minister to brief him on the plan."

So far, no problem.

"After the meeting, Paddy turned his briefcases and laptop computer over to his executive officer . . ."

"And?" I held my breath.

"It seems the executive officer parked his car and did a bit of shopping . . . and the briefcases and the computer were stolen."

"What was in them?" I asked with a sinking heart.

"We've recovered the briefcases. No need to worry. But the hard disk in the computer may have contained the battle plan."

"When did this happen?" I asked, in disbelief.

"That's the second thing I dread telling you," Vincent said. "About a week ago."

"A week ago!" I said. "And now you're telling us!"

Most alarming, the British tabloids had gotten hold of the story. For the next few days, we held our breath. My press officer, Colonel Smullen, monitored the British and European media for signs that the information had fallen into the wrong hands. Nothing appeared. Our thief was either a patriot, not about to divulge the secrets of her majesty's government for personal gain, or a crook so out of touch he did not even read the news.

· · ·

Earlier in the year, Coretta King had invited me to be grand marshal for the parade in Atlanta marking the January 15 birthday of the Reverend Martin Luther King, Jr. Then the political weather started to change. Blacks, who represented approximately 11 percent of the U.S. population over age sixteen, represented 26 percent of U.S. troops in the Gulf. Obviously, casualties would hit them proportionately harder than whites. A *New York Times*/CBS poll that month showed that only half of blacks, compared to 80 percent of whites, supported the liberation of Kuwait.

Joe Lowery, of the Southern Christian Leadership Conference, whom I had come to know during my FORSCOM tour in Atlanta, called me. "Colin, you know I respect you, but . . ."

"But what, Joe?"

"There are those who think it might be inappropriate for a military man to serve as grand marshal for Dr. King's parade."

The last thing I wanted was to have anything mar an event honoring the memory of this human rights crusader. As it turned out, I now knew that I was going to be tied up in Washington on the date of the parade anyway, and so I pulled out.

On November 20, Democratic Congressman Ron Dellums from California and forty-four other members of the House filed suit in federal district court to prevent President Bush from initiating a war against Iraq without a congressional declaration. At about this time, Julian Dixon, a Democrat representing Los Angeles, grilled Dick Cheney and me, during one of our appearances on the Hill, about the high number of blacks in the war zone. Cheney answered the question, and Julian was ready to let the matter lie. But I wanted to clear up what I regarded as a serious misunderstanding. I said that I regretted that any American, black or white, might die in combat. But black fighting men and women, particularly in an all-volunteer force, would be offended to think that when duty called, they would be excluded on the basis of color. Go into the NCO club at Fort Bragg, I said. Tell the black sergeants there that we have too many of them in the Army. Tell them that they will have to stay behind while their white buddies go off to do the fighting. See what kind of reaction you get.

The military had given African-Americans more equal opportunity than any other institution in American society, I pointed out. Naturally, they flocked to the armed forces. When we come before Congress saying we have to cut the forces, you complain that we're reducing opportunities for blacks, I said. Now you're saying, yes, opportunities to get killed. But as soon as this crisis passes, you'll be back, worried about our cutting the force and closing off one of the best career fields for African-Americans. Do you want to have blacks in the military limited to the percent of blacks in the population, and throw the rest out? I don't think so. But you cannot have it both ways—favoring opportunity for blacks in the military in peacetime and exemption from risk for them in wartime. There was only one way to reduce the proportion of blacks in the military: let the rest of American society open its

doors to African-Americans and give them the opportunities they now enjoyed in the armed forces.

At about the time I was having these discussions, I was gratified by the words of Gary Franks, a
young representative from Connecticut, the only
black Republican in Congress. Franks came up to me
after I had briefed him and fellow freshman members
on the situation in the Gulf that January. "I want to
thank you for helping me get elected," Franks said.

"Me help you get elected?" I answered. "I don't
do politics."

He gave me a big grin. "In my district, it's
important for white voters to see that a black man can
be competent in something besides civil rights.
Thanks to you, they've seen a black man who could
cut it in a white world. And that helped me."

I appreciated what Franks said, since I too had
stood on the shoulders of blacks who went before me.

The President had begun a custom of inviting the
Gang of Eight to the White House after he returned
from Camp David on Sunday evenings. We gathered
there on January 6, 1991, and after dinner, he led us
into a small office he used in the residential quarters.
We had a decision to make, he said. In nine days the
UN ultimatum for Iraq to leave Kuwait would
expire. Secretary of State Baker was off to Europe,
where he was going to meet in Geneva with the Iraqi
foreign minister, Tariq Aziz, in a last-ditch attempt to
get the Iraqis to go peacefully and stave off war.
Also, in the week ahead, the House and Senate were
going to debate whether to grant the President

authority to go to war over Kuwait. Cheney thought opponents might defeat the resolution, and where would that leave the President? George Bush had said publicly that he welcomed the debate and was ready to run the risk that Congress might not approve. I myself favored having Congress take a stand. I had witnessed the contortions the government had gone through during Vietnam to avoid saying war is war ("killed by hostile action" instead of the blunter "killed in action," and other transparent dodges). I also knew that whatever Congress decided, President Bush was not going to back down. The decision he wanted to make this night was when to go to war. He turned to me. "Seventeen zero three hundred, Mr. President," I said—January 17, at 3:00 A.M. Riyadh time.

The early-morning H-hour for launching the air war had been agreed on for some time. Striking in the dead of night gave our fighter-bombers enough time to get in and out of Iraq in near-total darkness. The hour was also selected to minimize collateral damage, since most Iraqis would be at home, not on the street or at their jobs. The date, however, provoked a debate. The UN deadline expired on the 15th, Washington time. So why not strike at 0300 on January 16? someone suggested. To others, that looked too calculated, as if we could not wait to start dropping bombs. On the other hand, we did not want to wait too long after the deadline for fear of losing credibility and having fresh political obstacles thrown up by congressional opponents. About two days, I argued, seemed a reasonable compromise.

. . .

I found it interesting to contrast the moods of Schwarzkopf, the professional warrior, and Cheney, the resolute civilian, as the hour of battle approached. Norm continued to be edgy. He was the one with half a million lives depending on his judgment in the field. And he was testy by nature, short-tempered, doubtful that armchair strategists at home could grasp battlefield realities. The calm that descends on the eve of battle had not yet descended over Norm Schwarzkopf.

Cheney, after one brief lapse, had again become the picture of self-possession. As D-Day approached, I invited him down to my office for lunch. He had had a coronary bypass and was following a strict diet, enforced by his secretary. We rarely got together in a social setting, and this day I thought he deserved a culinary break while we talked. I asked Nancy Hughes to order cheeseburgers. We went over the target list one last time. He seemed to have memorized it. The man had become a glutton for information, with an appetite we could barely satisfy. He spent hours in the National Military Command Center peppering my staff with questions. How do tanks work? Patriot missiles? How do you put together an air plan? What does armored infantry do on a battlefield? How do you penetrate a minefield? He left his briefers drained. But at the end of the day, we had a civilian Secretary of Defense who knew what he was talking about militarily. By the end of this cheeseburger lunch, I considered Dick's education complete. My Joint Staff operations officer, Tom Kelly, organized a ceremony, and we presented Dick with a certificate stating that Richard Bruce Cheney was now an honorary graduate of all the war colleges.

Of course, the cool Cheney, in Washington, enjoyed a layer of insulation. The uneasy Schwarzkopf had to direct people to fight and die on the scene.

On January 15, as D-Day approached, I got an anxious call from my British counterpart, Sir David Craig. "Colin, do you still intend to bomb Iraq's biological installations?" he asked. I said that we did. "Bit risky that, eh?" Craig's concern was not baseless. Two days before, I had given the President our best military judgment. There was a risk in hitting these plants. The bombing would probably destroy any disease agents present. But it might also release them. It was a gamble, I told the President, but one we had to take. He was already agitated, and this added worry did not soothe him.

I remained less concerned over possible Iraqi use of chemical weapons. Our forces would be wearing protective clothing, and many would be in fast-moving shielded vehicles. But the biologicals worried me, and the impact on the public the first time the first casualty keeled over to germ warfare would be terrifying. We could not retaliate in kind, since we were a signatory to international agreements banning biological warfare. Still, we had to be prepared for Saddam's worst impulses. If we faced unconventional attacks, we had unconventional counterstrikes ready, even without resort to nuclear weapons. On the day the deadline was to run out, I started drafting a warning to Saddam. It read:

Only conventional weapons will be used in strict accordance with the Geneva Convention and commonly accepted rules of warfare. If you, however, use chemical or biological weapons in violation of treaty obligations we will:

destroy your merchant fleet,
destroy your railroad infrastructure,
destroy your port facilities,
destroy your highway system,
destroy your oil facilities,
destroy your airline infrastructure.

I saved the worst for last, and it was a bluff intended only to strike fear in him, an action that our lawyers would veto. If driven to it, I wrote, we would destroy the dams on the Tigris and Euphrates rivers and flood Baghdad, with horrendous consequences. I started circulating the message through channels, but time ran out before it could be cleared. Its meaning, however, was not lost on our side. We would fight a conventional war, unless Saddam drove us to other means, which would be swift and crushing.

As far as bombing biological arsenals and the attendant risk of unleashing rather than preventing a catastrophe, I told Sir David Craig, "If it heads south, just blame me."

President Bush had a knack for putting people at ease when they entered the Oval Office. A big grin, and "Hi, Dick, hi, Colin. Did you hear the one about the psychiatrist who . . ." There was no smile when we met on January 15, the day the UN deadline ran out. He barely acknowledged the arrival of the Gang of Eight. We took our usual places in the U of seats and couches in front of the fireplace, the President still occupying the armchair on the right which he had broken in for eight years as Vice President. I unbuttoned my uniform jacket, an unconscious gesture when I felt tense. Everyone seemed to take his emotional cue from the President. We were on edge, some speaking abruptly, others testily. We argued over the best response to a last-minute diplomatic brainstorm the French were pushing, and we went over the biological weapons threat one more time. We debated what the President should say in the speech he intended to make to the nation when the fighting started.

"I'm going to have to send General Schwarzkopf an execute order," I said, "if we are going to set this thing in motion." That sparked another heated discussion. According to the joint congressional resolution passed three days before (by 250 to 183 in the House and 52 to 47 in the Senate), the President was supposed to satisfy Congress that he had exhausted all efforts to get Iraq to comply with twelve UN resolutions before he could go to war. While the others were arguing about how to handle this requirement, I took out a yellow legal pad and started writing. When I finished, I interrupted the crossfire long enough to say, "Mr. President, maybe this'll do it." I read what I had written: "The Secretary of Defense has directed that offensive operations begin on 17 January 1991. This direction assumes Iraqi failure to comply with relevant

UN resolutions and that the President will make the determination required by Section 2 (B) House Joint Resolution 77. . . ."

When I finished, no one said anything. I took the silence to mean tacit approval. "After Dick signs it," I said, "I'll send the order to Norm later this afternoon." This handful of words would unleash a war.

Norm and I had a method for transmitting messages, a secure fax line, which we used when we wanted distribution kept to an absolute minimum. My executive assistant, Dick Chilcoat, would take the fax to a tiny communications center near my office, and at the other end, Norm's executive officer would take it off. Never more than four or five people saw a transmission. At 4:15 P.M. on January 15, I leaned into the doorway of Chilcoat's office next to mine and said, "Send the CINC the execute."

On the evening of January 16, the pre-battle calm descended over me. I was sitting in my office, shirt collar open, watching CNN. Once the dice have left your hands, there is nothing to do but watch how they come up. Not even small things remained to be checked. The battle was in the hands of the gods, particularly the arbitrary Mars. At 6:35 P.M., I was watching CNN's Bernard Shaw, Peter Arnett, and John Holliman, like current-day Edward R. Murrows, broadcasting from the ninth floor of the Rasheed Hotel, speculating over the meaning of sudden streaks of tracers exploding across the black, empty sky above Baghdad. I knew the answer. B-52 bombers, taking off from Barksdale Air Force Base in Louisiana hours before, had launched cruise missiles. Army Apache helicopters had crossed the border and shot up Iraqi early-warning radars. Young Americans were flying F-117A Stealth fighters from Saudi airfields and Navy A-6s from aircraft carriers. Tomahawk land attack missiles had been fired from our warships in the Persian Gulf and the Red Sea. Iraqi air defense emplacements were lashing out blindly over the Iraqi capital. It was January 17 in the Middle East. The air phase of what Saddam Hussein had called "the mother of all battles" had begun.

I had no doubt we would be successful. We had the troops, the weapons, and the plan. What I did not know was how long it would take, and how many of our troops would not be coming home.

19 ★ Every War Must End

I WAS UP most of the night of January 16–17, on the phone constantly, watching television out of the corner of my eye as we conducted our first war while it was being broadcast live from the enemy capital. Just after 5:00 A.M., Washington time, Schwarzkopf called me with his first summary report of the air campaign. Norm was too much the professional to be carried away by the first blush of victory, but he was hard pressed to conceal his excitement. "We got off eight hundred and fifty missions," he told me. "We clobbered most of the targets." Iraq's key biological weapons and nuclear sites had been hit hard. The Iraqis' western air defense system was knocked out. Supply dumps were in flames. Two Scud missile launching sites had been struck. "The ITT building in downtown Baghdad is glowing," he said, "and we've blown down one of Saddam's palaces."

That was the good news. I waited apprehensively. "What about losses?"

"Colin," he said, "it's incredible." It appeared so far that only two aircraft were down, while we had anticipated losing as many as seventy-five planes in this first strike. Our F-117A Stealth fighters, used in action only once before in Panama, slipped through the Iraqi air defenses like ghosts. Iraqi antiaircraft gunnery proved wild and ineffectual. And Saddam's air force barely got off the ground. That is how the war went throughout the first day, almost unopposed success.

Air traffic control alone was an astonishing feat. The first night, seven hundred coalition combat aircraft hit Iraq. Cruise missiles were launched in combat for the very first time. One hundred and sixty flying tankers circled the skies to refuel this aerial armada. The task of controlling these swarms of fighters, bombers, tankers, and missiles made Chicago's O'Hare look like a county airport.

After the initial strikes, I watched a TV reporter shove his microphone in front of a young fighter pilot just back from his first combat mission, helmet tucked under his arm, hoses dangling, face sweat-streaked, hair matted. After answering the reporter's question, the flier started walking away, then he turned back to the camera and said, "I thank God I completed my mission and got back safely. I thank God for the love of a good woman. And I thank God I'm an American and an American fighter pilot." I sat there, melting. This was the military I wanted the country to see, not the old stereotyped dropout from nowheresville, but smart, motivated, patriotic young Americans, the best and the brightest.

The euphoria of the first day actually created a problem. Reports by CNN's Wolf Blitzer from the Pentagon made it seem as if all that remained was to organize the victory parade. I called Pete Williams, the Defense Department's spokesman. "Pete," I said, "tell Blitzer and these other press guys to cool it. This is the beginning of a war, not the end of a ball-game." In this age of instant information, people tended to expect instant results. Over the next few days, the mood shifted quickly from euphoria to a funk. Why hadn't we won yet? Was something wrong? The truth was that, in spite of heavy punishment, the Iraqis had not shown the slightest sign of caving in, despite the expectations of the most fervent air power apostles.

On the morning of the 22nd, I went upstairs to see Secretary Cheney. "Dick, we've got to get this thing into perspective," I said. At this point, the American people had seen on television only staff briefings out of Saudi Arabia and the Pentagon. So far, no senior administration official had explained how the war was going. "Somebody should be doing that," I said.

"We'll hold a press conference tomorrow," Dick decided.

I then called my chartmakers and had them put together some graphics. Along with a detailed briefing on the operation, I also wanted a sound bite that would capture the essence of this campaign.

Late that afternoon, I was sitting at my desk jotting down phrases and running them through my mind, getting ready for the press conference. I tried out one combination that went: "We are going to cut off the Iraqi army and neutralize it." No. Cut it off and "attack" it. Maybe. Cut it off and "destroy" it. Closer, but I was still dissatisfied. I wanted something forceful, unmistakable and short. The vice chairman, Admiral Dave Jeremiah, my indispensable right-hand man, always looking out for me, stopped by the office. "Dave," I said, "I want you to hear something I've written. 'Here's our plan for the Iraqi army. First, we're going to cut it off, and then we're going to *kill* it.' "

Dave looked a little uncomfortable. "Sounds a bit stark," he said. "Are you sure that's what you want to say?"

Bill Smullen came in to discuss the press conference arrangements, and I repeated the line. Smullen's eyes widened. "Is that too strong?" I asked.

"It doesn't leave any room for misunderstanding," Bill answered.

The next day, at 2:00 P.M., Cheney and I faced the press in the briefing room on the second floor of the E-Ring. Dick led off with brief comments, and wrapped it up saying that Saddam Hussein "cannot change the basic course of the conflict. He will be defeated." He then turned the stage over to me.

I explained the battle plan. We were using our airpower first to destroy the Iraqis' air defense system and their command, control, and communications to render the enemy deaf, dumb, and blind. We then intended to tear apart the logistics supporting their army in Kuwait, including Iraqi military installations, factories, and storage depots. And then we would expand our attack to the Iraqi forces occupying Kuwait.

My presentation was deliberately understated and unemotional. And then I delivered the punch line. "Our strategy in going after this army is very simple," I said. "First we are going to cut it off, and then we are going to kill it." Those words led the press coverage on television that evening, and in the papers the next day. They achieved what I wanted. They let the world—and particularly Iraq—know our war aim unmistakably.

As I went over the charts to describe bomb damage, I said, "I've laundered them so you can't really tell what I'm talking about because I don't want the Iraqis to know what I'm talking about." And I added with a smile, "But trust me." The reporters seemed amused and did not press me further.

As the air war continued, I dealt less than frankly with the media on one occasion and later regretted it. Norm Schwarzkopf, briefing from Riyadh, had become a comforting television presence, big, confident, witty. At one press conference, Norm ran a video of one of our smart bombs streaking toward four cylindrical objects. As the screen filled with one of those Nintendo images of an exploding bull's-eye hit, he announced that four Scud missile launchers had just been blown away.

Or had they? Rear Admiral Mike McConnell, my intelligence chief, came to me about an hour later. "Mr. Chairman, we've got a problem," Mike said. "We don't think those were Scuds. We think they were four Jordanian fuel trucks pulled up at a rest stop."

"Where'd you get that?" I asked.

"A captain, an analyst, on Schwarzkopf's staff," McConnell said.

"So have the captain call General Schwarzkopf and tell him they made a mistake."

"Nobody over there is going to tell Norm Schwarzkopf he made a mistake," McConnell said.

"Then how the hell is he supposed to know?" I answered. I pushed a button on my console. The CINC came on immediately. "Hey, Norm," I said, and I explained what McConnell had just told me.

The phone suddenly felt like a hot rock. "Not Scuds! Jee-zus! You think it's easy being over here undercut by a bunch of Washington chairwarmers? Can't I get any support from anybody?"

"Relax," I said. "We got the info from your own staff. Just have your intelligence people analyze the strike again, and we'll talk. Let's not argue about it."

Norm was soon back on the phone. "By God," he said, "those certainly were Scuds. That analyst doesn't know what he's talking about. He's just not as good as the others. But I'm telling you, I can't put up with much more of this crap, going on television, then having your guys second-guess me."

"Just trying to protect your credibility," I said. "It's a precious asset."

The next day our photo reconnaissance experts came to me with pictures that were hard to deny, four burned-out hulls of tanker trucks, certainly not Scuds. I let the story stand, without correcting it. Norm's burdens were so heavy and preserving his equanimity so important that I did not want to undercut him. But the truth will out, as it did when a CNN camera crew shot film of the destroyed vehicles from ground level. Another good media rule: better to admit a mistake than be caught in one.

The Scud was a cheap, crude, inaccurate Soviet engine of destruction. In chummier days, the Russians had provided the Iraqis with hundreds of these missiles, which had a range of less than three hundred miles and carried only a small payload. The Scud was the only offensive air weapon the Iraqis used. They boosted its range by welding two of them end to end, which produced a rickety, even more wayward contraption that could carry only a 160-pound warhead. If these Scuds struck within two miles of a target, it was considered a hit. However, cities present targets that size, and when Scuds began to fall on Tel Aviv and Haifa, the Israelis instinctively wanted to lash back. No Israeli government could be seen as failing to protect its people from an Arab attack. Yet if we were going to preserve the Arab end of the coalition, we had to keep the Israelis out of this fight. The Scud, a lousy military weapon, thus was proving, for the Iraqis, a useful political weapon, since the Israelis began planning to take over Scud hunting themselves.

On January 28, Cheney asked Paul Wolfowitz, the undersecretary for policy, and me up to his office. Three very determined Israelis would be there, he said: Rear Admiral Abraham Ben-Shoshan, the defense attaché at the Israeli embassy; David Ivri, their defense director general; and General Ehud Barak, deputy chief of staff. The six of us sat down around Cheney's table and listened to the Israeli's intentions—a combined air and ground assault into the western Iraqi desert to find and destroy Scud launchers. A daring plan, but disastrous politics for the coalition. I asked if I might talk to Barak alone, soldier to soldier. The two of us retreated to my office.

"These attacks are devastating to the morale of our people," Barak began. I countered, mentioning the performance of our Patriot missiles in downing Scuds. Not good enough, he answered. Some Scuds were still getting through, terrorizing the Israeli civilian population. "You must understand us," Barak went on. "It is hard for Israelis to have others risk their lives in our defense. We want to be involved." I repeated the familiar arguments about the fragility of the coalition. "If we don't go in and clear out the Scuds," Barak said, "Saddam may use them to deliver chemical warheads when you launch your ground offensive. They may fire nerve gas or a biological warhead at our cities. If that happens, you know what we must do."

I had a pretty good idea what he meant. Israeli missile crews were reportedly on full alert. And who knew what they would be firing?

Israel had an assault force ready to go against the Scud sites, Barak explained. Israeli planes would fly over Jordan or through Saudi airspace. Schwarzkopf had already warned me that the Saudis would never accept such an Israeli intrusion. Still, I understood the intensity of Barak's feelings. His nation had survived for the past forty years by taking no guff from its enemies. You could hear the echos of "Never again" in everything Israeli leaders said.

Finally, Barak and I rejoined the others. It was clear to our side that we had to keep Israel out of this war, and there was only one way: stop the Scuds. Norm Schwarzkopf began diverting more and more of his combat aircraft to Scud-busting, as many as a third of all missions flown. British and U.S. special operations troops slipped behind enemy lines to search out Scuds. American Patriot missile units were sent to help protect major Israeli cities. Scuds still came through, but less often.

Sometimes we fight with fury; sometimes the wisest weapon is restraint. Prime Minister Shamir showed a special brand of statesmanship in resisting heavy pressure from those around him to strike back. The forbearance of the Israelis, in the face of intense provocation, going completely against their grain, in my judgment helped keep the coalition intact.

By the third week in February, the air war had been going on uninterrupted for thirty-five days. I wanted to make sure the President understood that war was going to look a lot different once fighting began on the ground. I took advantage of one of our almost daily briefings to paint the contrast. "Once the ground war begins," I said, "we don't get these anti-septic videos of a missile with a target in the cross hairs. When a battalion runs into a firefight, you don't lose a pilot or two, you can lose fifty to a hundred men in minutes. And a battlefield is not a pretty sight. You'll see a kid's scorched torso hanging out of a tank turret while ammo cooking off inside has torn the rest of the crew apart. We have to brace ourselves for some ugly images." I also made sure that Cheney and the President understood that ground combat cannot be reported as quickly as air strikes. "There's going to be confusion. You won't know what is happening for a while. And so in the early hours, please don't press us for situation reports."

The cold bath of reality was important. Notwithstanding Panama, Cheney had never seen war on a grand scale. The President had, but only from the air during his own long-ago fighter pilot days.

As the bombing continued, one downside of air-power started to come into sharp focus, particularly what happened on February 13. That day, two of our aircraft scored direct hits on the Al Firdos bunker in Baghdad, which we regarded as a command and con-trol site and which the Iraqis claimed was an air-raid shelter. Whatever use the structure served, a large number of civilians died in the strike, which the whole world witnessed on television as victims were hauled from the smoking rubble. Schwarzkopf and I discussed this tragedy. Did we still need to pound downtown Baghdad over a month into the war? How many times could you bomb the Baath Party head-quarters, and for what purpose? No one was sitting there waiting for the next Tomahawk to hit. Schwarzkopf and I started reviewing targets more closely before each day's missions.

If nothing else, the Al Firdos bunker strike underscored the need to start the combined air/ground offensive and end the war. During a quick visit Cheney and I had made to the war zone between February 8 and 10, Schwarzkopf had told us that he would be ready to go by February 21. As soon as Cheney and I got back to Washington, we reported this date to an impatient George Bush. Three days later, however, Norm called and told me that the 21st was out.

"The President wants to get on with this," I said. "What happened?"

"Walt Boomer needs more time," Schwarzkopf answered. Boomer's 1st and 2nd Marine Divisions were deployed to drive head-on from the center of the line toward Kuwait City. But first they had to breach a savage complex of entrenchments that the Iraqis had spent months erecting. The Marines would have to penetrate belts of antipersonnel and antitank mines, tangled rolls of booby-trapped barbed wire, more minefields, and deep tank traps, and then climb twenty-foot-high berms and cross trenches filled with burning oil. All the while, they would be under fire from Iraqi troops and artillery. Boomer wanted time to shift his point of attack twenty miles to the west, where one Iraqi defensive position had been largely abandoned under air attack and another line farther back was incomplete. He also wanted more airstrikes to weaken the enemy defenses before his troops moved.

"It'll cost a few days," Norm said. He wanted to put off the ground offensive until February 24.

"Remember the strategy," I reminded him. The frontal assaults were intended only to tie down the entrenched Iraqis, and that included the Marines' mission. "If Boomer hits serious resistance, he's to stop," I said. Having engaged the enemy, his troops would have accomplished their mission by allowing VII Corps and XVIII Airborne Corps to pull off the left hook in the sparsely defended western desert. "We don't need to kill a bunch of kids singing 'The Marines' Hymn,' " I said.

One of my fundamental operating premises is that the commander in the field is always right and the rear echelon is wrong, unless proved otherwise. The field commander is on the scene, feeling the terrain, directing the troops, facing and judging the enemy. I therefore advised Cheney to accept Norm's recommendation. Cheney reluctantly went to the President and got a postponement to February 24.

I backed Norm, though I thought he was being overly cautious. Over the previous weeks, I had watched VII Corps, with its tens of thousands of troops and hundreds of tanks, pour into Saudi Arabia. We had secretly moved our armored and airborne forces to Iraq's exposed western flank, and we had been holding our breath to see if the Iraqis responded. All they did was send another under-manned division to that part of the desert. That's it, I told myself. They had been sucked in by our moves hinting at a major frontal assault and an amphibious landing on Kuwait from the Persian Gulf. They had shown us everything they had, and it was nowhere near enough to stop our left hook. Earlier we had worried that the desert soil on the western flank might not be able to support heavy armored vehicles. The engineers had tested the sands, however, and gave us a "Go." We questioned local Bedouins, and they confirmed the solidness of the terrain.

The offensive timetable was further clouded as Mikhail Gorbachev tried to play peacemaker. On February 18, the Iraqi foreign minister, Tariq Aziz, went to Moscow to hear a plan under which we would stop hostilities if the Iraqis withdrew from Kuwait. President Bush was in a bind. It was too late for this approach, he believed. After the expenditure of $60 billion and transporting half a million troops eight thousand miles, Bush wanted to deliver a knockout punch to the Iraqi invaders in Kuwait. He did not want to win by a TKO that would allow Saddam to withdraw with his army unpunished and intact and wait for another day. Nevertheless, the President could not be seen as turning his back on a chance for peace.

On February 20, Norm called saying he had talked to his commanders and needed still another delay, to the 26th. He had the latest weather report in hand, he said, and bad weather was predicted for the

24th and 25th, maybe clearing on the 26th. Bad weather equaled reduced air support, which equaled higher casualties. I was on the spot. So far, Cheney had accepted my counsel. But now I did not feel that Norm was giving me sufficiently convincing arguments to take back to Cheney and the President, first that Boomer needed to move his Marines, then that the Marines needed more air support, then that the weather was bad, and on still another occasion, that the Saudi army was not ready. What should I expect next, a postponement to the 28th?

"Look," I told Norm, "ten days ago you told me the 21st. Then you wanted the 24th. Now you're asking for the 26th. I've got a President and a Secretary of Defense on my back. They've got a bad Russian peace proposal they're trying to dodge. You've got to give me a better case for postponement. I don't think you understand the pressure I'm under."

Schwarzkopf exploded. "You're giving me political reasons why you don't want to tell the President not to do something militarily unsound!" He was yelling. "Don't you understand? My Marine commander says we need to wait. We're talking about Marines' lives." He had to worry about them, he said, even if nobody else cared.

That did it. I had backed Norm at every step, fended off his critics with one hand while soothing his anxieties with the other. "Don't you pull that on me!" I yelled back. "Don't you try to lay a patronizing guilt trip on me! Don't tell me I don't care about casualties! What are you doing, putting on some kind of show in front of your commanders?"

He was alone, Schwarzkopf said, in his private office, and he was taking as much heat as I was. "You're pressuring me to put aside my military judgment out of political expediency. I've felt this way for a long time!" he said. Suddenly, his tone shifted from anger to despair. "Colin, I feel like my head's in a vise. Maybe I'm losing it. Maybe I'm losing my objectivity."

I took a deep breath. The last thing I needed was to push the commander in the field over the edge on the eve of battle. "You're not losing it," I said. "We've just got a problem we have to work out. You have the full confidence of all of us back here. At the end of the day, you know I'm going to carry your message, and we'll do it your way." It was time to break off the conversation before one of us threw another match into the gasoline.

Within half an hour, Norm was back on the phone with the latest weather update. The 24th and the 25th did not look too bad after all. "We're ready," he said. We had a go for the 24th.

It was not my custom to show up at the White House in a turtleneck sweater and sport jacket, but I had been summoned suddenly from home for a meeting at 10:30 on Thursday evening, February 21. I found the President in his study. He had just come from Ford's Theater, where he had seen a great play, he said, Leslie Lee's *Black Eagles,* about the Tuskegee Airmen, the black fighter pilots of World War II fame. Cheney showed up next, wearing a tux, fresh from a reception for the queen of Denmark. The others arrived, rounding out the Gang of Eight. We had to make a decision about Gorbachev's pending peace proposal. The Russian leader had called Bush about it earlier in the evening. The President's problem was how to say no to Gorbachev without appearing to throw away a chance for peace.

"You've got two options," Brent Scowcroft said. "One is to tell the Russians to butt out. The other is to get better conditions and accept."

I looked at Cheney, who was sitting on the arm of a chair. I knew what he was thinking. He disliked and distrusted the Russians and hated seeing them use world opinion to pressure us and then get credit for what might turn out to be a bad solution. He preferred to throw out the Iraqis forcibly.

I could hear the President's growing distress in his voice. "I don't want to take this deal," he said. "But I don't want to stiff Gorbachev, not after he's come this far with us. We've got to find a way out."

I raised a finger. The President turned to me. "Got something, Colin?"

"We don't stiff Gorbachev," I said. I pointed out that world opinion had supported the UN's January 15 deadline for Saddam to clear out of Kuwait. "So let's put a deadline on Gorby's proposal. We say, great idea, as long as they're completely on their way out by, say, noon Saturday. If they go, you get the Nobel Peace Prize, Mr. Gorbachev. If, as I suspect, they don't move, then the flogging begins."

The room was silent as everybody seemed to chew on the idea. "What about that?" the President asked. He quickly won agreement all around, except from Cheney. "What about you, Dick?" the President asked.

Cheney looked as if he had been handed a dead rat. "I guess it's okay," he said.

At 10:40 A.M. the next morning, President Bush stood before the cameras in the Rose Garden. "The coalition will give Saddam Hussein until noon Saturday to do what he must do," a grim-visaged Bush said, "begin his immediate and unconditional withdrawal from Kuwait."

At noon on Saturday, February 23, Saddam let the Russian withdrawal proposal go by and passed the last exit. At 4:00 A.M., Riyadh time, the following day, in darkness and cold rain, U.S. Marines and an Army tank brigade, followed by Saudi, Egyptian, Kuwaiti, Syrian, and other Arab troops, crossed the border into Kuwait. Far to the west, XVIII Airborne Corps jumped off with the 82d Airborne Division and a French light armored division covering the left flank. The 101st Airborne Division (Air Assault) and the 24th Infantry Division (Mechanized) moved straight north into Iraq, heading for the Euphrates River Valley. Between these forces, VII Corps, with the British 1st Armored Division, stood poised to launch the left-hook main attack as soon as it was clear that the supporting attacks were holding the Iraqis in place. The ground war had begun.

Too keyed up to sleep, I stayed in the office and took incoming reports from Tom Kelly and Mike McConnell. I also watched CNN so that I would know the picture the rest of the world was getting.

The Marines, rather than merely pinning down the Iraqis, had broken through the enemy defenses and were already moving toward Kuwait City. The way had been prepared by Marine reconnaissance teams who, days before, had exposed themselves to terrifying risks, crawling through the barbed wire and over the oil-filled trenches to lay out cleared lanes for the assault troops to race through.

In the west, General Barry McCaffrey's 24th Infantry Division punched sixty miles into Iraqi territory on the first day. The initial penetrations were so swift and so deep that Schwarzkopf was able to move up the left-hook timetable by fifteen hours. In those twenty-four hours of land combat, ten thousand hungry, thirsty, exhausted Iraqi soldiers, stunned by thirty-eight days of air bombardment, surrendered. Gary Luck's XVIII Airborne Corps alone took 3,200 prisoners, while suffering one man wounded. Our total casualties the first day were eight dead, twenty-seven wounded.

By the morning of the second day, the 1st Marine Division was fighting in and around Kuwait City International Airport. The Marines would have fulfilled their mission even if they had only tied down Iraqi forces. Instead, by the end of the day, they had encircled Kuwait City. An amphibious feint off the Kuwaiti coast tied down more Iraqi units. XVIII Airborne Corps thrust deeper into Iraq. VII Corps, under Lieutenant General Fred Franks, had the master strategic role, the flanking attack from west to east to cut off the Iraqi army in Kuwait and kill it, particularly the vaunted Republican Guard. But VII Corps was not moving as fast as we expected.

On that second day, we suffered a heavy blow. A Soviet-made Scud missile slammed into a makeshift barracks near Dhahran, killing twenty-eight American soldiers. The casualty list presented a harsh reality of our modern army; women were among the victims.

On February 26, the third day, I called Schwarzkopf at about noon his time. I told him that I hated second-guessing field commanders, but I could not understand why VII Corps was still not fully engaged. "Can't you get Fred Franks moving faster?" I asked. Schwarzkopf himself had already been leaning hard on Franks, and was just as happy to pass along additional pressure from the chairman. He soon got back to me with word that VII Corps was finally in the thick of the fight. Franks's troops had almost completely destroyed one Republican Guard division and had driven two others into retreat.

U.S. Marines, U.S. Army Special Forces, and Saudi, Egyptian, Kuwaiti, and other Arab troops liberated Kuwait City. XVIII Airborne Corps was approaching the Euphrates River Valley. Our intelligence indicated that of forty-two Iraqi divisions in the war zone, twenty-seven had already been destroyed or overrun. We had taken 38,000 prisoners and more kept pouring in. Our casualties remained light, though we suffered disturbing losses from friendly fire. Overall, however, the casualty rate was far below even our most optimistic estimates, thanks largely to the constant pounding our air forces were inflicting on the Iraqis.

· · ·

Before the war began, someone on my staff had given me a book entitled *Every War Must End,* by Fred Iklé. I had worked with Iklé when he was undersecretary of defense for policy and I was Cap Weinberger's military assistant. The theme of his book intrigued me, because I had spent two tours in a war that seemed endless and often pointless. Warfare is such an all-absorbing enterprise, Iklé wrote, that after starting one, a government may lose sight of ending it. As he put it:

> Thus it can happen that military men, while skillfully planning their intricate operations and coordinating complicated maneuvers, remain curiously blind in failing to perceive that it is the outcome of the war, not the outcome of the campaigns within it, that determines how well their plans serve the nation's interests. At the same time, the senior statesmen may hesitate to insist that these beautifully planned campaigns be linked to some clear ideas for ending the war. . . ."

As an example, Iklé mentioned the cunningly conceived attack on Pearl Harbor, as contrasted to the scant thought the Japanese had given to how the war they started would end. I was so impressed by Iklé's ideas that I had key passages photocopied and circulated to the Joint Chiefs, Cheney, and Scowcroft. We were fighting a limited war under a limited mandate for a limited purpose, which was soon going to be achieved. I thought that the people responsible ought to start thinking about how it would end.

On the afternoon of February 27, Otis Pearson drove me to the White House for the Gang of Eight's daily military briefing. The heavy armor-plated bulletproof Cadillac held the road with a reassuring hug, around the huge Pentagon parking lot, up Route 27 over the Memorial Bridge, and into Washington. As we rode along, words from Iklé's book ran through my mind: ". . . fighting often continues long past the point where a 'rational' calculation would indicate that the war should be ended."

I had already spoken to Norm Schwarzkopf earlier in the morning and told him I sensed we were nearing endgame. The prisoner catch was approaching seventy thousand. Saddam had ordered his forces to withdraw from Kuwait. The last major escape route, a four-lane highway leading out of Kuwait City toward the Iraqi city of Basrah, had turned into a shooting gallery for our fliers. The road was choked with fleeing soldiers and littered with the charred hulks of nearly fifteen hundred military and civilian vehicles. Reporters began referring to this road as the "Highway of Death."

I would have to give the President and the Secretary a recommendation soon as to when to stop, I told Norm. The television coverage, I added, was starting to make it look as if we were engaged in slaughter for slaughter's sake.

"I've been thinking the same thing," Norm said.

I asked him what he wanted. "One more day should do it," he answered. By then he would be able to declare that Iraq was no longer militarily capable of threatening its neighbors. And he added, "Do you realize, if we stop tomorrow night, the ground campaign will have lasted five days? How does that sound, the Five-Day War?"

Since that chipped one day off the famous victory of the Israelis over the Arab states in 1967, I said, "Not bad. I'll pass it along."

At about 2:00 P.M., I rode through the gate to the West Wing entrance of the White House. Otis let me out, parked, and then discreetly brought me a big black leather map case as I waited in the lobby. I went up the stairway to the left, past the Chief of Staff's office, to avoid going through the reception room. You never knew who you might run into there, from the Soviet ambassador to a Girl Scout delegation. An Air Force officer, Major Bruce Caughman, the President's personal assistant, helped me set up an easel in the Oval Office facing the fireplace.

George Bush was upbeat and relaxed. The Gang of Eight, plus Richard Haas, Scowcroft's Middle East specialist, formed the usual U in front of the fireplace. Someone joked about the President leaving the fire to the pros. At a briefing a couple of days before, Bush had lit the fire himself, without opening the flue. The Oval Office had instantly filled with smoke. Alarms rang. Secret Service agents ran around frantically, throwing doors open, while freezing February winds blew in from the Rose Garden.

This morning, I snapped on the laser pointer and began describing the positions: the Marines and Prince Khaled's Arab force in Kuwait City, VII

Corps closing its noose around the Iraqi forces trying to flee Kuwait, with only the Republican Guard still offering any serious resistance. In the far west, XVIII Airborne Corps had driven deep into Iraq to the banks of the Euphrates. When I finished describing the military chessboard, I said, "Mr. President, it's going much better than we expected. The Iraqi army is broken. All they're trying to do now is get out."

Our forces had a specific objective, authorized by the UN, to liberate Kuwait, and we had achieved it. The President had never expressed any desire to exceed that mandate, in spite of his verbal lambasting of Saddam. We presently held the moral high ground. We could lose it by fighting past the "rational calculation" Fred Iklé had warned about. And, as a professional soldier, I honored the warrior's code. "We don't want to be seen as killing for the sake of killing, Mr. President," I said. "We're within the window of success. I've talked to General Schwarzkopf. I expect by sometime tomorrow the job will be done, and I'll probably be bringing you a recommendation to stop the fighting."

"If that's the case," the President said, "why not end it today?" He caught me by surprise. "I'd like you all to think about that," he added, looking around the room. "We're starting to pick up some undesirable public and political baggage with all those scenes of carnage. You say we've accomplished the mission. Why not end it?" He could go on the air and announce a suspension of hostilities this evening, he said.

"That's something to consider," I replied. "But I need to talk to Norm first." I excused myself and went into the President's small private study just off the Oval Office. I picked up a secure phone, and the White House military operator put me through to Riyadh.

"Norm," I said, "the President wants to know if we can end it now."

"When is now?" he asked.

"We're looking at this evening." Given the eight-hour time difference, that would mean stopping the war in the middle of the night in the Gulf region.

"I don't have any problem," Norm said. "Our objective was to drive 'em out, and we've done it. But let me talk to my commanders, and unless they've run into a snag I don't know about, I don't see why we shouldn't stop."

"Cheney and I have to go up to the Hill and brief Congress soon," I said. "We can talk again when I get back."

I did not anticipate any objection from Schwarzkopf's field commanders. Norm had just given a televised press conference from Riyadh at 1:00 P.M. Washington time, and in this now famous "mother of all briefings," he had said, "We've accomplished our mission, and when the decision-makers come to the decision that there should be a cease-fire, nobody will be happier than me." He had also said, regarding the fleeing Iraqi forces, "The gate is closed. There is no way out of here." Later, he amended this statement to: "When I say the gate is closed, I don't want to give the impression that absolutely nothing is escaping." Heavy tanks and artillery were not getting through, he said. "I'm talking about the gate that is closed on the war machine. . . ."

I went back into the Oval Office and reported to the President that the proposal looked okay to Schwarzkopf and to me, but Norm wanted to check with his commanders. No one in the room disagreed with the tentative decision to stop the war. Jim Baker was concerned about the effect on world opinion of pointless killing. Brent Scowcroft thought that fighting beyond necessity would leave a bad taste over what was so far a brilliant military operation. Cheney said that what mattered was achieving the coalition's aims, not how many more tanks we knocked out. We would meet again, however, for one last discussion after Cheney and I returned from Capitol Hill.

Before heading for the Hill, I called the vice chairman, Dave Jeremiah, and told him to brief the chiefs on the President's tentative decision to bring the war to an end. Dave called me later and said that all the chiefs concurred.

Cheney and I briefed the Senate at 3:00 P.M. and the House at 4:30 P.M. Their respective hearing rooms were packed for both presentations. We gave the members essentially the same map-and-chart show we had put on for the President. But we mentioned nothing about the war possibly ending this day.

By 5:30 P.M. we were back at the White House, where we joined the President in the small office off the Oval Office. I took note of the time the President made his final decision to suspend hostilities, 5:57. It was the commander in chief's decision to make, and he had made it. Every member of his policymaking team agreed. Schwarzkopf and I agreed. And there is no doubt in my mind that if Norm or I had had the slightest reservation about stopping now, the President would have given us all the time we needed.

We moved into the Oval Office and started discussing the timing and content of the announcement President Bush would make to the American people that night. He also began calling his coalition partners. We initially considered having the President go on the air at 9:00 P.M. to announce a "suspension of hostilities" as of 0500, February 28, in Riyadh. The word "suspension" was picked deliberately to make clear that this was not a cease-fire negotiated with the Iraqis, but a halt taken on our own initiative. I said that I would like to give Norm a few more hours of daylight so that he could check the battlefield and clean up any loose ends, which prompted an inspiration from John Sununu. "Why not make it effective midnight our time? That'll make it the Hundred-Hour War," John said. The President agreed, and shortly after 6:00 P.M., I got on the phone again with Schwarzkopf. I told him the President would speak at 9:00 our time to announce that the fighting would stop at 8:00 A.M. the following morning Riyadh time. That would give Norm almost the one more day he had asked for in our conversation earlier in the morning.

The President and then Cheney came on the line to congratulate the CINC. "Helluva job, Norm," the President said.

Schwarzkopf was soon back on the phone with a cautionary note. The gate was still slightly open, he told me. Some Republican Guard units and T-72 tanks could slip away. I told him to keep hitting them, and I would get back to him. I passed Norm's report to the President and the others. Although we were all taken slightly aback, no one felt that what we had heard changed the basic equation. The back of the Iraqi army had been broken. What was left of it was retreating north. There was no need to fight a battle of annihilation to see how many more combatants on both sides could be killed. Obviously, the President would have preferred total capitulation, the way World War II had ended. And we knew, barring a lucky bomb hit, that Saddam would likely survive the war. We further accepted that we would face criticism from some quarters for not continuing the fight. However, we had a clear mandate, and it was being achieved. The President reaffirmed his decision to end the fighting. I then called Schwarzkopf again and relayed to him that the White House understood that there would be some leakage of Iraqi forces, but that this condition was acceptable.

At 9:02 P.M., the President spoke to the nation from the Oval Office. "Kuwait is liberated. Iraq's army is defeated. Our military objectives are met," he began. "I am pleased to announce that at midnight tonight, eastern standard time, exactly one hundred hours since ground operations commenced and six weeks since the start of Operation Desert Storm, all U.S. and coalition forces will suspend offensive combat operations."

After the President's speech, he and Mrs. Bush invited the group up to the residential quarters for a quiet celebration. The ushers passed drinks around, and I sipped my usual rum and Coke. The atmosphere was one of relief more than festivity. We had not given George Bush another V-E Day. Still, he said, "I'm comfortable. No second thoughts." We had done the right thing, he believed, and we had prevailed. Within an hour I was back at Quarters 6 at Fort Myer. I wanted to tell Alma that we had just won a war. But she was already asleep.

Over 130 years after the event, historians are still debating General George Meade's decision not to pursue General Robert E. Lee's forces after the Union victory at Gettysburg. A half century after World War II, scholars are still arguing over General Eisenhower's decision not to beat the Soviet armies to Berlin. And, I expect, years from now, historians will still ask if we should not have fought longer and destroyed more of the Iraqi army. Critics argue that we should have widened our war aims to include seizing Baghdad and driving Saddam Hussein from power, as we had done with Noriega and the Panama Defense Force in Panama. The critics include Admiral Crowe, who testified in Congress for continued sanctions and against going to war; but in his memoirs he argues that we should have continued fighting and expanded the mission to go after Saddam Hussein.

Matters were not helped when, one month after the war's end, Norm Schwarzkopf appeared on a PBS program, *Talking with David Frost*. Regarding the decision to end the fighting, Norm first said, "I reported that situation to General Powell. And he and I discussed, have we accomplished our military objectives, the campaign objectives. And the answer is yes." But a moment later, Norm said, "Frankly, my recommendation had been, you know, continue the march. I mean, we had them in a rout and we could have continued, you know, to reap great destruction upon them."

The next morning the direct White House line on my console rang with that insistent shrillness that made me sit at attention. George Bush sounded more hurt than angered. What did Norm mean? He had certainly been consulted about stopping the fighting. The war would not have ended then if he had asked for more time. "I talked to Norm myself," the President said.

I shared the President's disappointment. In fact, I was mad as hell at what Schwarzkopf had told David Frost. I called Norm in Riyadh. "That story won't fly," I said. "You're saying the President made a mistake. You made it look as if you gave him a different recommendation, and he ignored it."

"That's not what I meant at all," Norm replied.

"That's what came across," I said. "And the media are beating up on him."

Norm Schwarzkopf was, deservedly, a national hero. And the criticism that the fighting had stopped too soon had chipped his pedestal. He did not like it. The President, ever loyal, learned that Norm was feeling abused and called him once again, telling him not to worry. Still, I felt it was important to keep the record straight. Schwarzkopf had been a party to the decision, and now he seemed to be distancing himself from it. I put out a public statement, after clearing it with Norm, that read: "General Schwarzkopf and I both supported terminating Desert Storm combat operations at 12:00 midnight, 27 February 1991 (EST), as did all the President's advisors. . . . There was no contrary recommendation. There was no disagreement. There was no debate."

Norm began to back off from his Frost statement, and in his book, *It Doesn't Take a Hero,* he explained his thinking:

> My gut reaction was that a quick cease-fire would save lives. If we continued to attack through Thursday, more of our troops would get killed, probably not many, but some. What was more, we'd accomplished our mission: I'd just finished telling the American people that there wasn't enough left of Iraq's army for it to be a regional military threat . . . we'd kicked this guy's butt, leaving no doubt in anybody's mind that we'd won decisively, and we'd done it with very few casualties. Why not end it? Why get somebody else killed tomorrow? That made up my mind.

Schwarzkopf was absolutely right. Yet, it is still hard to drive a stake through charges that the job was left unfinished. The truth is that Iraq began the war with an army of over a million men, approximately half of whom were committed to the Kuwait theater of operations, where they were mauled. Iraq took such a battering in the Gulf War that four years afterward, its army is half its original size. And within the Iraqi ranks, I am sure that horror stories are told about what it was like to endure the wrath from the skies and on the ground during Desert Storm. The remaining Iraqi army is hardly a force with a will to fight to the death.

In October 1994, Saddam Hussein sent twenty thousand Republican Guards toward the Kuwaiti border, a paltry attempt to look tough while trying to get relief from UN sanctions. Immediately, the cry went up from the simple-solutionists: if only Saddam had been polished off during the Gulf War, he would not be stirring up trouble now. On October 23, the *New York Times* printed on its front page a long excerpt from a book on the Gulf War coauthored by one of the paper's reporters. The book excerpt was headlined "How Iraq Escaped to Threaten Kuwait Again." In it, the authors stated that "much of Iraq's crack troops, the Republican Guard, had not been destroyed," and that was why Saddam could still wield threatening military power.

While the belief that Saddam pulled off some sort of Dunkirk at the end of Desert Storm may have a superficial attraction, I want to cut it off and kill it once and for all. It is true that more tanks and Republican Guard troops escaped from Kuwait than we expected. And yes, we could have taken another day or two to close that escape hatch. And yes, we could have killed, wounded, or captured every single soldier in the Republican Guard in that trap. But it would not have made a bit of difference in Saddam's future conduct. Iraq, a nation of twenty million people, can always pose a threat to its tiny neighbor, Kuwait, with only 750,000 people. With or without

Saddam and with or without the Republican Guard, Kuwait's security depends on arrangements with its friends in the region and the United States. That is the strategic reality. The other reality is that in 1991 we met the Iraqi army in the field and, while fulfilling the United Nation's objectives, dealt it a crushing defeat and left it less than half of what it had been.

But why didn't we push on to Baghdad once we had Saddam on the run? Why didn't we finish him off? Or, to put it another way, why didn't we move the goalposts? What tends to be forgotten is that while the United States led the way, we were heading an *international* coalition carrying out a clearly defined UN mission. That mission was accomplished. The President even hoped to bring all the troops home by July 4, which would have been dramatic but proved logistically impossible. He had promised the American people that Desert Storm would not become a Persian Gulf Vietnam, and he kept his promise.

From the geopolitical standpoint, the coalition, particularly the Arab states, never wanted Iraq invaded and dismembered. Before the fighting, I received a copy of a cable sent by Charles Freeman, the U.S. ambassador to Saudi Arabia. "For a range of reasons," Freeman said, "we cannot pursue Iraq's unconditional surrender and occupation by us. It is not in our interest to destroy Iraq or weaken it to the point that Iran and/or Syria are not constrained by it." Wise words, Mr. Ambassador. It would not contribute to the stability we want in the Middle East to have Iraq fragmented into separate Sunni, Shia, and Kurd political entities. The only way to have avoided this outcome was to have undertaken a largely U.S. conquest and occupation of a remote nation of twenty million people. I don't think that is what the American people signed up for.

Of course, we would have loved to see Saddam overthrown by his own people for the death and destruction he had brought down on them. But that did not happen. And the President's demonizing of Saddam as the devil incarnate did not help the public understand why he was allowed to stay in power. It is naive, however, to think that if Saddam had fallen, he would necessarily have been replaced by a Jeffersonian in some sort of desert democracy where people read *The Federalist Papers* along with the Koran. Quite possibly, we would have wound up with a Saddam by another name.

Often, as I travel around the country, parents will come up to me and say, "General, we want you to know our son"—or daughter—"fought in the Gulf War." I am always a little apprehensive when I ask, "I hope everything turned out all right." They usually say yes and express their thanks that their soldier came home safely. One hundred and forty-seven Americans gave their lives in combat in the Gulf; another 236 died from accidents and other causes. Small losses as military statistics go, but a tragedy for each family. I have met some of these families, and their loss is heartbreaking. Sadly, their tragedy is compounded by the high incidence of casualties caused by friendly fire. I am relieved that I don't have to say to many more parents, "I'm sorry your son or daughter died in the siege of Baghdad." I stand by my role in the President's decision to end the war when and how he did. It is an accountability I carry with pride and without apology.

Not only did Desert Storm accomplish its political objective, it started to reverse the climate of chronic hostility in the Middle East. King Hussein of Jordan and Yasser Arafat, chairman of the PLO, were the only two major Arab leaders who showed any support for the Iraqi position during the Gulf War, and both were weakened by their stance. As a result, three years later, they were trying to reach accommodations with Israel and their other neighbors. The Madrid Middle East Peace Conference, following Desert Storm, started the process that resulted in the historic agreement between Arafat and Israeli Prime Minister Rabin in September 1993 and the peace treaty between King Hussein and Israel in October 1994. The United States today enjoys access to the region denied before Desert Storm. Even the hostages in Lebanon were released in the aftermath of the conflict. And Iraq remains weak and isolated, kept in check by UN inspectors. Not a bad bottom line.

I am content with the judgment rendered on Desert Storm by probably the world's foremost contemporary military historian, John Keegan. "The Gulf War, whatever it is now fashionable to say," Keegan has written, "was a triumph of incisive planning and almost faultless execution." It fulfilled the highest purpose of military action: "the use of force in the cause of order."

Many correspondents covering the war, and their media bosses back home, complained that they were overcontrolled by the military. They were confined to press pools. They could not roam around the battle-field without military escorts. The image of World War II's legendary Ernie Pyle, filing stories from European foxholes and Pacific beachheads, was thrown in our faces by our critics. Yet, press coverage of Desert Storm was unprecedented. Of the 2,500 accredited journalists overall, 1,400 crowded the theater of operations at the peak. Compare this figure with twenty-seven reporters going ashore with the first wave at Normandy on D-Day. Desert Storm correspondents totaled nearly four times the number covering Vietnam during that war's height. And, for the record, Ernie Pyle and his fellow World War II reporters were strictly censored. In the Gulf War, stories were reviewed by the military for security purposes. Of 1,350 print stories submitted by press pool reporters, *one* was changed to protect intelligence procedures. In Desert Storm, we tried to maintain military security while handling the largest concentration of correspondents ever gathered for a combat operation.

For good or for ill, instantaneous visual communication has revolutionized news coverage in our time. Jet travel, satellites, and minicams allow live, around-the-clock coverage, like CNN, and have removed the old print media filters between the reporter and the audience.

The immediacy of television has made life more difficult for old-fashioned hard-nosed correspondents. In the old days, reporters could play the SOB, asking tough questions in a tough way to get the story. Their methods made little difference, since nobody was going to see the reporter, only the story, filtered through editors, and presented under neat column heads. But when the public got to watch journalists in action, shouting and sometimes asking unreasonable questions, even the best reporters sometimes came across as bad guys.

By the time Cheney, Norm, and I went on television, we understood the dynamics. We were talking not only to the press assembled in front of us; we were talking to four other audiences—the American people, foreign nations, the enemy, and our troops. I would never, for example, say anything for domestic consumption and ignore its impact on Iraq, or vice versa. I knew that we had won the battle for public opinion during Desert Storm when I watched a *Saturday Night Live* skit just before the ground offensive got under way. In this spoof, an Army public relations officer, "Lieutenant Colonel Pierson," appears in desert camouflage at a press conference and faces the usual forest of waving hands and shouted questions: "Colonel, where would you say our forces are most vulnerable to attack?" "Are we planning an amphibious invasion of Kuwait? And if so, where would that be?" "On what date are we going to start the ground attack?" To anyone who had watched the actual questioning at press briefings, there was a touch of truth in the hilarity. This time, the press, not some inept General Halftrack from the *Beetle Bailey* comic strip, was the butt of satire.

During the Gulf War, we auditioned military spokespersons. In the twenty-four-hour coverage of the TV world, we could no longer put just anyone, no matter how well informed, in front of the cameras. We picked the Joint Staff operations chief, Lieutenant General Tom Kelly, as our Pentagon briefer because Kelly not only was deeply knowledgeable, but came across like Norm in the sitcom *Cheers,* a regular guy whom people could relate to and trust. Kelly's partner for the press briefing, Rear Admiral Mike McConnell, was the perfect foil, playing the bookish authority to Kelly's neighborhood sage. Norm Schwarzkopf and I, eight thousand miles apart, watched Marine Brigadier General Richard "Butch" Neal brief reporters in Riyadh for the first time. He was the third candidate we had auditioned. The press roughed Butch up a bit, but an unflinching honesty came through. After Neal's debut, I called Norm and said, "I think you've got yourself a star."

Our priority, of course, was fighting. But in this new media environment we had to learn something as old as Clausewitz: how to make the people understand and support what we were doing. Polls conducted after the war suggest that we succeeded. These surveys indicated that 80 percent of Americans polled thought press coverage of the Gulf War had been good or excellent.

Even before Norm Schwarzkopf came home in triumph, he wanted to discuss his future with me. SACEUR, Supreme Allied Commander Europe, a desirable and prestigious assignment, was already taken by Jack Galvin. "You probably could be chairman at some point," I said, "but I'm not going anywhere yet. Of course, Vuono's retiring. That would

open up Army Chief of Staff." He might be interested, Norm answered. "Sure," I said, "but let me tell
you what I really think. Now is the perfect time for
you to retire. You've been away for a long time. You
don't realize what's going to happen when you come
home. You're a national idol. People are going to go
crazy over you." I knew that no slot in the Pentagon
was big enough now to contain a man of his fame and
stature. "You've got thirty-five years in," I said.
"You'll be getting all kinds of offers. Now's the time
to leave."

Shortly afterward, after talking to other friends,
Norm called me back. "I'm going to retire," he said.
"I know what you guys will have to do over the next
few years. You have to tear the services apart. I don't
have the stomach for that. And I don't want to deal
with the damn politicians and all the crap you'll have
to put up with."

I told him I hoped we would be reshaping the
forces, not tearing them apart. Still, he had made the
right decision. Norm Schwarzkopf did not suffer
fools gladly, which you can get away with in the
absolute command environment of the battlefield.
But suffering the insufferable comes with the territory in Washington.

For a moment, it looked as if the war might flare up
again. In March, the Iraqi Shiites in the south rose up
in arms to demand more recognition from Baghdad.
Saddam responded by sending in his troops to suppress the uprising. In the north, the Kurds tried to
shake off the Iraqi yoke. Neither revolt had a chance.

Nor, frankly, was their success a goal of our policy. President Bush's rhetoric urging the Iraqis to over-throw Saddam, however, may have given encouragement to the rebels. But our practical intention was to leave Baghdad enough power to survive as a threat to an Iran that remained bitterly hostile toward the United States.

Nevertheless, we could not ignore the worsening plight of the rebellious Kurds. Saddam had lashed back, driving over half a million of them from their homes to barren mountains in southern Turkey. There, lacking food, shelter, or medical care, they began dying at a rate of six hundred a day. President Bush directed us to launch a relief operation, Provide Comfort, headed by now Lieutenant General John M. Shalikashvili. The Kurds, however, could not sur-vive indefinitely in this bleak mountainscape. Their best hope was to return home. The challenge was to get them back while protecting them from Saddam's vengeance.

Jack Galvin, operating out of Mons, Belgium, as our European commander, had long-distance con-trol over our forces in this region. One Sunday after-noon, with me in Washington and Jack in Belgium, each with a map in front of us, we sketched out a "security zone," a sector around Kurdish cities in Iraq that Saddam's troops would not be allowed to enter. I felt like one of those British diplomats in the 1920s carving out nations like Jordan and Iraq on a tablecloth at a gentleman's club. I called Galvin, in his trans-European role, "Charlemagne," and I told him that now he was truly a kingdom maker. After lining out the security zone, we ordered the Iraqi military to get out. They refused. We rattled the saber, and they withdrew. In seven weeks, Provide Comfort brought nearly half a million Kurds home. I watched Shalikashvili run this political and military maze with masterful skill and concluded, once again, that here was a soldier up to any mission.

The troops came home to a wildly cheering America. I took part in victory parades in Chicago and Washington and in a ticker-tape parade up Broadway in New York. Alma and I rode in a white 1959 Buick convertible. Ahead of us were Cheney and his wife, Lynne, and behind us Norm Schwarzkopf and his wife, Brenda. Our security people wanted the men to wear armored vests. "Not me," I said. "I look chubby enough already." Norm agreed, and Cheney went along with our military judgment. It was an emotional moment to be at the center of an event I had seen only in history books and newsreels, celebrating a Lindbergh, or an Eisenhower, or a MacArthur. Norm, a New Jerseyite, and I, a New Yorker, riding through a blizzard of tape, confetti, and balloons while thousands cheered their heads off, were two hometown boys who had made good. The generals and admirals marching in the victory parades, John Yeosock, Walt Boomer, Chuck Horner, Stan Arthur, all of us, were surrogates for the real heroes, the troops of XVIII Airborne Corps, VII Corps, and the U.S. Marines, the airmen, sailors, and Coast Guardsmen, who had given back to Americans pride in their country. Our allies were also represented in the parades, and Korea and Vietnam veterans marched too, finally getting long overdue recognition.

Sitting in the stands, their contributions largely unsung, were the service chiefs who had so superbly prepared their forces and who had provided invaluable counsel to Cheney and to President Bush. The nation owes its gratitude to General Carl Vuono, Admiral Frank Kelso, General Tony McPeak, and General Al Gray, as well as to the vice chairman, Admiral Dave Jeremiah, and the Commandant of the Coast Guard, Admiral Bill Kime. Desert Storm had been a team effort involving our commands worldwide, as well as the little-known defense agencies in Washington that provided the logistics, intelligence, communications, maps, and all the other unheralded elements of victory.

All of us in uniform had been solidly backed by civilian leaders at State, the Pentagon, and the White House. Most deserving of praise was President Bush. He had kept his promise, "This will not stand," and he had led a worldwide coalition to victory.

The celebrations were no doubt out of proportion to the achievement. We had not fought another World War II. Yet, after the stalemate of Korea and the long agony in Southeast Asia, the country was hungry for victory. We had given America a clear win at low casualties in a noble cause, and the American people fell in love again with their armed forces. The way I looked at it, if we got too much adulation for this one, it made up for the neglect the troops had experienced coming home from those other wars.

That spring I was invited to throw out the first ball at Yankee Stadium in the season opener between the

Yankees and the Chicago White Sox. I am no great shakes as a jock, but I swear my pitch was a strike. Later, I rode down the East River Drive and gazed at the huge Pepsi-Cola sign across the river. Suddenly, I was a kid again, swinging a mop across the floors of the Pepsi bottling plant. The next day, I spoke at the Waldorf-Astoria Hotel to a breakfast meeting of the Association for a Better New York. "In my youth," I said, "I belonged to Local 812, International Brotherhood of Teamsters. Is there anybody here from 812?" I guess they were not expecting that, and a table of Teamster officials let out a whoop and a holler.

The most moving part of this trip was my return to Banana Kelly. The community that my parents had fled when it started to turn into a crime-infested slum was making a comeback. Our old building at 952 Kelly Street, abandoned, burned out, and finally torn down, was now the site of new garden apartments. I watched kids playing ball and skipping rope in Kelly Street Park, which had been a garbage-strewn lot just a few years before.

Afterward, I walked a couple of blocks and up the worn stone steps of Morris High School. The wooden floors still creaked, the poles for opening and closing the tall windows still hung where I remembered, and the gym, where I was to speak, had the familiar smell of sweat and disinfectant. I looked over a sea of mostly Hispanic and black faces and I recalled what it had been like to be here as a boy thirty-seven years before. "I remember this place," I told them. "I remember the feeling that you can't make it. But you can. When I was coming up, the opportunities were limited. But now they are there. You can be anything you want to be. But wanting to be isn't enough. Dreaming about it isn't enough. You've got to study for it, work for it, fight for it with all your heart and soul." I pointed out that 97 percent of GIs now were high school graduates. Their diplomas proved one thing: that they had the drive and discipline to stick it out. I appealed to them: "Don't drop out." Choose a role model, I said. "And feel free to choose a black or a white, a general or a teacher, or just the parents who brought you into the world." I do not know if I reached a single youngster that day. But I was determined to leave Morris High with a message for those kids. Reject the easy path of victimhood. Dare to take the harder path of work and commitment, a path that leads somewhere.

I had urged the kids to pick their role models from any race, because I am concerned that the admirable ideal of black pride can be carried to an extreme where it produces isolation. I am all for instilling pride and a sense of tradition in African-Americans, particularly among the young. I made the Buffalo Soldiers my cause so that blacks could look back on a proud past in another chapter of their history. I want black youngsters to learn about black writers, poets, musicians, scientists, and artists, and about the culture and history of Africa. At the same time, we have to accept that black children in America are not going to have to make their way in an African world. They are going to have to make their way in an American world. Along with their black heritage, they should know about the Greek origins of our democracy, the British origins of our judicial system, and the contributions to our national tapestry of Americans of all kinds and colors. My message to young African-Americans is to learn to live where you are and not where you might have been born three centuries ago. The cultural gap is too wide, the time past too long gone, for Africa to provide the only nourishment to the soul or mind of African-Americans. The corollary is equally true. Young whites will not be living in an all-white world. They must be taught to appreciate the struggle of minorities to achieve their birthright.

On white-majority college campuses, in our inner cities, in almost every area of social interaction, we see an unhealthy resegregation occurring, sometimes self-imposed, sometimes imposed by economics. When disillusioned blacks go off by themselves, they withdraw from the promise of America. They then allow whites to walk away too, saying, "If that's what they want, so be it." Even justified, well-intended redistricting to increase the number of blacks in Congress has allowed nonwhite members off the hook in looking after black constituent issues. The black agenda has been given over to the Congressional Black Caucus. The concerns of African-Americans stand in danger of riding again in the back of the bus. We are a nation of unlimited opportunity *and* serious unsolved social ills; and we are all in it together. Racial resegregation can only lead to social disintegration. Far better to resume the dream of Martin Luther King, Jr.: to build a nation where whites and blacks sit side by side at the table of brotherhood.

I have lived in and risen in a white-dominated society and a white-dominated profession, but not by denying my race, not by seeing it as a chain holding me back or an obstacle to be overcome. Others may use my race against me, but I will never use it against myself. My blackness has been a source of pride, strength, and inspiration, and so has my being an American. I started out believing in an America where anyone, given equal opportunity, can succeed through hard work and faith. I still believe in that America.

On the morning of May 2, I went to the kitchen, poured my coffee, and glanced at the *Washington Post* on the table. I was front-page news. Bob Woodward's book *The Commanders* was coming out in a few days, and the *Post* had a story based on it. This article proved to be the opening salvo in a publicity blitz. On May 5, the *Post*'s "Book World" made *The Commanders* its lead review. And on May 13, *Post*-owned *Newsweek* magazine had a cover story with my picture and a banner reading "The Reluctant Warrior: Doubts and Division on the Road to War." The *Post* sure takes care of its own.

I turned out to be a central figure in Woodward's story of life in the Pentagon and the White House. I had no quarrel with the total picture of me that he presented. But the emphasis in the media barrage was on the few pages of the book implying that I privately opposed the President on the Gulf War, a publicity strategy designed to propel Woodward's work into best-sellerdom through the booster rocket of controversy. The reluctant-warrior theme allowed members of Congress who had voted against the war and other opponents to say, "See, Powell really was with us."

Except for calls from a few close friends, my phone was eerily silent as I took a pounding from the media and the Beltway gossip circuit. I heard nothing from my boss, Dick Cheney. Part of me was saying, Cheney is probably happy to see me cut down to size. The better angels of my nature said, that's just Dick; you get into trouble in this league, and you get yourself out.

The same morning the story appeared, a White House operator called to say that President Bush was coming on the line. I waited uneasily. "Colin, pay no attention to that nonsense. Don't worry about it," he said. "Don't let 'em get under your skin."

"Thanks, Mr. President," I said.

"Barb says hello. See ya." Click.

Later that day, at, of all places, a gathering on agricultural policy, reporters hit the President with more questions about me, as depicted in Woodward's book. "Nobody's going to drive a wedge between [Powell] and me," he said. "I don't care what kind of book they've got, how many unnamed sources they have, how many quotes they put in the mouth of somebody when they weren't there. . . ."

I will never forget this loyalty from the President of the United States at a time when I needed a friend.

On May 22, Cheney called me up to his office. "You're going to be reappointed as chairman," he said. I was a little puzzled, since my term was not up for over four months, on September 30. I thanked Dick. "It's the President's idea," he said. "He wants to reappoint you early."

"He doesn't have to carry my baggage," I said. "He's got plenty of time to think about this one."

"You don't understand," Cheney said. "He wants to end any speculation about your standing in the administration."

"When does he want to do it?" I asked.

"Tomorrow."

The next day I found myself in the Rose Garden with George Bush pointing to me and telling the press and assembled officials, "I'm taking this step now to demonstrate my great confidence in his ability and the tremendous respect I have for him."

When the President finished, I followed with brief remarks. Brit Hume of ABC put a question to me: "General, would you care to comment on the recent account of the Gulf War suggesting that you had, at a minimum, some serious misgivings about the use-of-force option . . ."

I had started to answer when the President adroitly brushed me aside. "I just want to be on the record as saying that he spoke his mind; he did it openly," Bush said. He recalled the day I had suggested a deadline for Saddam to accept Gorbachev's peace proposal. "It was Colin Powell, more than anyone else, who I think deserves the credit . . . after all options, in my view, were exhausted, for drawing the line in the sand." The President pointed to the second floor of the White House. "Right up in that office."

That ended that line of questioning, and the controversy over *The Commanders* died down for the moment. George Bush had picked me up, dusted me off, and put his arm around me when I needed it. He is that kind of man.

For me, the war did not end on February 28, not while we still had the reverse logistical challenge of bringing thousands of troops and mountains of equipment home (which proved as hard as sending everything over), not until we had Operation Provide Comfort in place, not until the controversies quieted down. Early in June, Alma and I finally escaped to Maryland's Eastern Shore to spend a few days at the weekend home of our close friends Grant and Ginger Green. I spied a hammock that Grant had strung up between two trees near a creek. I crawled into it and felt the bone-deep exhaustion finally start to seep out of me for the first time in nearly a year. I slept the sleep of the dead. The war was finally over.

On July 22, I flew to the Soviet Union for another round of confidence-building sessions with my Soviet counterpart, Mikhail Moiseyev. Alma came with me. It was like old home week as we were reunited with Moiseyev and his wife, Galla. Once there, I was dragged through Red Army showcase exercises, paratrooper operations so choreographed that they resembled skydiving ballets; tours of mess halls where my guides would have you believe the Soviet chief quartermaster was Escoffier; inspections of fighter aircraft, T-80 tanks, and AK-47 rifles until I was ready to scream. The Soviet minister of defense, Dimitri Yazov, gave me a gift, a pistol. If I carried every weapon the Soviets had presented to me over the years, I would look like a poster boy for the National Rifle Association.

We were in the port of Vladivostok on Navy Day watching a mock sea battle among gleaming ships of the line. This exercise, like everything else we had seen, had a Potemkin-village thinness. Behind the facade, the rot was evident. I was allowed to watch elite paratroopers, but my request to see how Soviet troops who had been pulled out of Eastern Europe were living was denied. The fancy photos of seven balanced food groups displayed in the mess halls did not square with the stew ladled out to Red Army soldiers from huge communal vats. Behind the shining warships performing for us we could see dock after dock of rusting hulks. Admiral Jerry Johnson, the vice chief of naval operations, who was traveling with me, cast an expert eye around Vladivostok harbor and said, "Here's a fleet that's going bye-bye." And the Mikhail Gorbachev whom I met on this trip was not the supremely confident figure of earlier summits. He seemed beaten down by the incessant battering he was taking in this convulsed country.

During the tour, I tried to meet and talk with ordinary Russians, though Moiseyev kept steering me to armored personnel carriers. We had flown into Vladivostok on a Friday, and while we were driving into town, I noticed heavy traffic going in the opposite direction. Then, on Sunday night, as we were driving back to the airport, the pattern was reversed. I asked our driver about it. "People get private plots, maybe five hundred to six hundred square meters," he said. "So on weekends, they go out to the country and tend vegetable gardens. They can't get anything decent in the state stores. The garden gives them a little more to eat and maybe a little income. They work like ants. You should see what they produce." The fact that small individual plots were proportionately more productive than collective farms spoke volumes about the fundamental defect of communism.

As we prepared to fly home from Vladivostok on July 28, I had trouble getting one present from the Far Eastern Military District into the hold of our 707. They had given me a massive elk's head, complete with horns, mounted on a heavy wooden base. After it was crated, the elk required four burly Russian soldiers to lug it aboard.

Moiseyev and Galla were there to say goodbye, the four of us standing in a cloud of Siberian mosquitoes attracted by the floodlights. I hugged Moiseyev and said, "Misha, take care of yourself." I meant it. I had grown fond of this honest soldier, and I was worried about him. I saw a man perched on a structure that was verging on collapse. A fleeting look of sadness in his eyes told me he understood. We all embraced, and Alma and I boarded the plane for home.

As for the elk's head, it scared the devil out of my two-year-old grandson when we displayed it in Quarters 6 at Fort Myer. I finally managed to move the beast closer to home, at least symbolically. I gave it to my friend Ted Stevens, the senior senator from Alaska, to hang in his office.

I had just fallen asleep, at about twenty minutes after midnight on August 19, when I got a call from the duty officer in the National Military Command Center. A coup against the Gorbachev government was under way. President Bush was in his summer place in Kennebunkport, Maine. Vice President Quayle was in Arizona. Cheney was fishing in Canada. Jim Baker was fishing in Wyoming. I was "home alone." I called Cheney's deputy secretary, Donald Atwood, and gave him a quick fill. I hit the usual buttons and found that there had been no change in the alert status of conventional Soviet military forces. The Soviets had a system called "Chegev," using a device the size of an attaché case that allowed a handful of leaders to communicate in the event of a nuclear crisis. We were able to monitor the system and knew that there had been no change in the Soviets' nuclear posture either.

President Bush came back immediately to Washington and assumed a stance of watchful waiting. I had to go to Walter Reed Army Medical Center that day for a previously scheduled annual physical and stress test, feeling not exactly stress-free. The day after the coup, the President held a press conference and then gathered the Gang of Eight in the residence.

"What do you make of this business, Colin?" the President asked me. "Did you notice how the tanks came into Moscow?" I said, "They were rolling down the middle of the road, headed nowhere in particular. People were waving, handing the tankers flowers, chatting with them." I pointed out that no tanks had sealed off the Kremlin or the Russian parliament; no forces had taken over the central telephone exchange, standard operating procedure during coups. "What all this tells me, Mr. President," I went on, "is that the plotters don't own the army. The military is not backing this coup." I further remembered seeing the five woebegone leaders of the conspiracy on television, and they looked to me like a variation on Jimmy Breslin's book: this was *The Gang That Couldn't Plot Straight.* I doubted if these bunglers could overthrow the dog catcher and take over the pound.

Within three days, the coup collapsed, and Gorbachev was restored to power. The failed attempt marked the end of Soviet communism, the beginning of the end for Gorbachev, and the making of Boris Yeltsin. Dimitri Yazov, one of the failed conspirators, was replaced as minister of defense by my friend Misha Moiseyev. Marshal Akhromeyev, the old Leningrad veteran whom I had come to know, committed suicide in the aftermath of the coup. Moiseyev lasted one day in his new job. Evidently he had not rallied to the government's defense fast enough to suit Yeltsin. And then Moiseyev vanished.

His disappearance worried me. Maybe it was a different Russia; still, I was not sure how much the old methods of treating losers had changed. I tried to locate Moiseyev through Russians in Washington and people going to Moscow. I learned nothing. Four months later, I finally got a letter from Moiseyev telling me that he and Galla were alive and well. He subsequently became a consultant in high-tech communications, a blooming capitalist. And the last I heard, Moiseyev was rolling in rubles.

Months before, while flying back from one of our trips to the Gulf, I had sat next to Dick Cheney and remounted one of my hobbyhorses. I had ordered the Joint Staff to do a study on the usefulness of tactical nuclear weapons. The staff's recommendation was to get rid of the small, artillery-fired nukes because they were trouble-prone, expensive to modernize, and irrelevant in the present world of highly accurate conventional weapons. I circulated the report to the four service chiefs, since its conclusions affected joint military doctrine. Carl Vuono, my old buddy, mentor, and champion, had supported me on many issues, but Carl had deeper loyalties. The nukes were a matter of prestige to the artillery. I was asking his branch to give up a part of itself. Carl, the senior artilleryman in the U.S. Army, was not about to preside over the dismantling of his nukes. He managed to line up the other service chiefs against the proposal. The report went to the Pentagon policy staff, a refuge of Reagan-era hard-liners, who stomped all over it, from Paul Wolfowitz on down. This, nevertheless, was the proposal I pulled out on the plane and put in front of Cheney, a document scribbled all over with criticisms by his special assistant, David Addington, and riddled with nonconcurrences. Cheney groaned, but he began reading.

"I know you've got a four-to-one vote against me with the chiefs," I said, "so it'll be easy to over-rule me. But don't worry, I'll be back next year, because I'm right on this one."

Dick looked at me, bemused. "Not one of my civilian advisors supports you," he said.

I kidded him. "That's because they're all right-wing nuts like you." Cheney laughed and went on reading. After we got back to Washington, he rejected my proposal.

Cheney did not have a closed mind on nuclear issues. Quite to the contrary, he had demonstrated admirable vision. In November 1989, after the fall of the Berlin Wall, he ordered his civilian analysts to take a fresh look at nuclear targets in the Single Integrated Operational Plan (SIOP). In effect, Cheney posed a question that had not been answered satisfactorily for forty years: how much is enough? His staff found the cart now pulling the horse. Every time a new nuclear weapons system came on line, the SIOP targeters went looking for something else to hit, to a point that had become unjustifiable. In the event of war, we were going to aim a warhead at a Soviet bridge *and* the city hall just blocks away. Under the then current plan, nearly forty weapons were targeted for the Ukrainian capital of Kiev alone. Debates even erupted over removing targets from Eastern Europe after the Warsaw Pact had collapsed and these countries had become democracies. Cheney and his civilian analysts reversed four decades of encrusted bureaucratic thinking and put nuclear targeting on a rational basis. Today, after subsequent agreements, the United States and Russia no longer target each other at all with nuclear weapons.

Months after the Gulf War, on September 5, at a meeting of the national security team, President Bush began pushing us for more fresh thinking on arms control. The bloom was partly off the Gulf victory by now. We were back to the superpower chessboard, radically altered after the failed coup in the Soviet Union. "I want to see some new ideas on nuclear disarmament," the President said. "I don't want talk. I want solid proposals."

Within days, we had developed a proposal that far exceeded the elimination I had urged of artillery-launched nukes. The scope was sweeping. Get rid of short-range nuclear weapons, like the Army's Lance missiles. Ground the Strategic Air Command bombers that had been on alert for the previous thirty-two years, and offload their nukes. Remove nuclear weapons from all ships, except for strategic missiles on Trident submarines. Get rid of multiple-warhead intercontinental ballistic missiles and stick to single-warhead ICBMs. Shut down as many Minuteman missile silos as we dared. The chiefs, now responding to a radically changing world, signed on, as did Paul Wolfowitz and his hard-liners. Cheney was ready to move with the winds of change. Within three weeks, on September 27, President Bush announced these unilateral nuclear reductions to the world.

When I became chairman, we had 23,000 operational nuclear weapons in the armed forces. Between our own initiatives and the START treaties, we should be down to 8,000 warheads by 2003, a drop of over 65 percent.

. . .

Although President Bush had nominated me for a second two-year term, I still had to be confirmed by the Senate. Senator Sam Nunn, chairman of the Senate Armed Services Committee, a supporter of sanctions and an opponent of going to war, made sure that I did not have a routine reconfirmation. The hearings lasted two days, and during them, Nunn criticized me for my discussions with Bob Woodward as reported in Woodward's book. I did not deny talking to Woodward. Plenty of others in the administration talked to him too. The talks were no secret; Cheney and I discussed them regularly. Nunn also tried to establish that I had held the same view as he did about prolonging the sanctions policy. I reminded him that we had tried sanctions for almost six months, and they had failed to move Saddam Hussein (nor have they in the subsequent four years). Whether or not to give sanctions a longer ride was a political decision. President Bush had made that decision. My job, when it came to war, was to make sure that we would be ready. And we were. Nunn dragged the hearings out until September 30, the last day of my term. I pointed out to him that as of midnight, the nation would have an acting chairman, because, legally, I would be out of office. With that, he promptly brought my reappointment to a vote. I was unanimously confirmed by the Senate.

After the Gulf War, *Time* magazine columnist Hugh Sidey had written: "Never before has an American President stood so grandly astride this capricious world as George Bush does these days. Historians scratched their heads . . . and looked for something comparable. There was nothing." Even now, seven months later, the president's approval rating was a healthy 66 percent. With my reconfirmation, it looked as if I would be chairman well into George Bush's second term as President.

20 ☆ Change of Command

SEVERAL MONTHS AFTER Desert Storm, I was suddenly and emotionally pulled back one day to the paddies of Vietnam. In the fall of 1991, I saw again Captain Vo Cong Hieu. I had first heard from Hieu, after twenty-seven years, when he wrote me in December 1989. In that letter, Hieu congratulated me on my elevation to the chairmanship and then reported on his life in the intervening years. "While you have richly deserved such an excellent appointment," he wrote, "I find myself in a rather difficult position." Hieu had spent thirteen years in a communist reeducation camp. He and his wife had been approved by the U.S. embassy in Bangkok to emigrate to America. But, at the time, he did not have approval for his other married children and grandchildren, a total of seven family members. He asked for my help.

I went to the ever-resourceful Rich Armitage, who knew his way around the Washington bureaucratic maze and Vietnam as well as anyone. Rich was able to arrange entry into the States for the rest of Hieu's family.

About a year and a half later, in October 1991, I was in Minneapolis to speak at a program called the Minnesota Meeting. I walked into the lobby of the hotel where the event was taking place and there stood a little man swallowed up in an ill-fitting overcoat, looking lost. I recognized Hieu instantly. He waited, smiling shyly. I embraced him. We both had tears in our eyes. He thanked me for my help and told me how he had found an American sponsor for his family in Minnesota. I invited Hieu to my speech and arranged for him to sit at a table in front of the dais. I began by saying, "I ran into an old friend here, one I haven't seen for nearly thirty years. I want you to meet him, a new neighbor of yours and a new American, Vo Cong Hieu." Hieu rose to thunderous applause, looking bewildered by a fate that had brought him to a new home in the American heartland, so far from and so unlike his native land, but free at last.

On the same day that I was reconfirmed as chairman, Father Jean-Bertrand Aristide, the first democratically elected president in Haiti's history, was overthrown by a military junta after less than eight months in office. With Aristide's downfall, Haitians began boarding anything that would float in their eagerness to get to the United States. On October 29, President Bush banned all U.S. commercial trade with Haiti to punish the military dictatorship, which also made Haitians more desirous than ever to get out. The U.S. military drew the unwelcome assignment of detaining fleeing Haitians at Guantanamo Bay, the piece of Cuban territory we occupy, until the Immigration and Naturalization Service could deter-

mine if they were legitimate political refugees entitled to come to the States.

By December, the Pentagon was being asked
about military options to put Aristide back into
power. My advice to Cheney was to go slow. "We can
take over the place in an afternoon with a company or
two of Marines," I said. "But the problem is getting
out." We had intervened in Haiti in 1915 for reasons
that sounded identical to what I was hearing now—to
end terror, restore stability, promote democracy, and
protect U.S. interests—and that occupation had
lasted nineteen years. Cheney needed no arguments
from me. We both understood why Haitians were
eager to flee a country so desperately poor and politically repressive. But these conditions did not yet
justify an American invasion.

The CINC for the Atlantic Command, responsible for the Guantanamo refugee operation, Admiral
Bud Edney, wanted to name this effort "Operation
Safe Harbor," which I rejected. It was like hanging out
a welcome sign to Haitians and then locking them up
in what was beginning to resemble a concentration
camp. I wanted something neutral-sounding that
would not raise false hopes. We settled on Navy shorthand for Guantanamo; "Safe Harbor" became "Operation GTMO." Still, Haitians continued to put to sea.

Also that December, I had a call from Congressman
Ron Dellums of California. He wanted to see me at
the Pentagon. Dellums was a black representing an
essentially white middle-class district in the Oakland
area. He could talk like an ADA liberal or the Marine

he had formerly been, depending on his audience. We scrapped often in Congress, but got along beautifully outside. However, he had never asked to see me alone before.

Upon his arrival, we sat at the little round table I preferred for one-on-one encounters. "I've been speaking to the top people," Dellums began, "senior members of the Democratic Party. And you know what you are?"

I waited.

"You're our fondest dream . . . and our worst nightmare."

I kept on listening.

"You're our fondest dream," Dellums went on, "if we can get you on the ticket as Vice President. After that, there's no way we can lose. Now, here's the nightmare. You turn out to be a Republican, and you're on *their* ticket. Then, the Black Caucus can't leave the house. Dellums has to stay home. You split the black vote, and we don't have a prayer."

"Ron, keep snowing me," I said. Dellums went on for another twenty minutes. His theme was that, compared to, say, a leader like Jesse Jackson, I was a "jelly maker, not a tree shaker." "What I want to know is this," Dellums finally asked. "Are you going to be our dream, or are you going to be our nightmare? Or are you going to do nothing?"

"I'm flattered," I said, "but I'm not going to answer you because I'm a military officer on active duty. I don't want to say anything that could start rumors. My intention is to serve the country in uniform until I retire."

We shook hands, and he looked reasonably pleased. I assumed he had the message he wanted to bring back to his party. Powell will not come to us. But he won't go with them.

That Christmas Day, the unimaginable happened. The Soviet Union disappeared. Without a fight, without a war, without a revolution, it vanished as leaders of the former Soviet republics met in the remote Kazakhstan capital of Alma Ata and dissolved the world's only other superpower with the stroke of a pen. Mikhail Gorbachev was out of a job. There was nothing left for him to govern. As he had told George Shultz and me back in 1988, he would do as much as he could before someone else came along and replaced him. I don't think that Gorbachev ever imagined that the entire Soviet empire would be tossed out along with him. He was a realist who accepted that he had been handed a dying patient. He had hoped to revive the body without replacing its Marxist heart. He could not do it. Fortunately, he came along at a time when the United States had a President, in Ronald Reagan, who was willing to take risks for peace from America's position of superior strength. Together, these two men practiced a bold brand of leadership that began to end the Cold War.

It was now more important than ever, I believed, that we get the Base Force accepted by Congress. The Base Force was a realistic military posture for a future in which two superpowers would not be flexing their muscles at each other. On February 5, Cheney and I headed to Capitol Hill for yet another hearing. This time it was to testify before the House Budget Committee as we tried to maneuver the proposal through a Congress in which key members thought the Base Force did not cut deep enough, especially with our old nemesis not only down but out. As we entered the hearing room, my legislative affairs officer, Colonel Paul Kelly, tipped me off to be ready for questioning on a different subject from Congressman Barney Frank.

During most of the hearing, the questioning moved along predictable tracks—were we getting the right mix of reserve and active forces; how many troops could we bring home from Europe? Then the chair recognized Congressman Frank. The Massachusetts lawmaker turned first to Cheney. "When the Secretary was here last time," Frank began, "he said that the security argument was not part of the reason for keeping gay men and lesbians out of the military." Frank then turned to me. "Are we to some extent dealing here with a prejudice that a majority has against a group of people?" he asked. And was this prejudice "a valid reason for telling gay and lesbian people they are not wanted in the armed forces?" There it was, out in the open, the hottest social potato tossed to the Pentagon in a generation.

"I think it would be prejudicial to good order and discipline to try to integrate that in the current military structure," I said. "And I think . . ."

Frank interrupted me. "For some time, as you know, the Secretary has acknowledged there have been gay men and lesbians in the military. Is there any evidence of behavior problems?"

"No," I answered, "because as a matter of fact they have kept, so-called, in the closet. . . . If I have heterosexual young men and women who choose not to have to be in close proximity because of different sexual preferences, am I then forced to face the problem of different accommodations for homosexuals and heterosexuals, and then by sex within the homosexual community?" Congressman Frank let the subject drop for that day.

Subsequently, however, Congresswoman Pat Schroeder of Colorado sent me a letter expressing unhappiness with my testimony. Schroeder quoted a 1942 government report and claimed that the same arguments used then against racial integration in the military were being used against gays today. "Your reasoning would have kept you from the mess hall, a few decades ago," Schroeder said.

"I need no reminders concerning the history of African-Americans in the defense of their nation," I wrote back. But she had her logic wrong. "Skin color is a benign, nonbehavioral characteristic," I pointed out. "Sexual orientation is perhaps the most profound of human behavioral characteristics. Comparison of the two is a convenient but invalid argument."

The linking of gay rights and the civil rights movement got a mixed reaction in the African-American community. The Congressional Black Caucus favored removing the ban on homosexuals in the armed services. But other African-American leaders were telling me that they resented having the civil rights crusade appropriated—hijacked, some of them put it—by the gay community for its ends. I heard from black clergymen who adamantly opposed removing the ban. The battle was joined, and we had a touchy election-year issue.

America's racial legacy was raised for me in quite a different context that same year. I had first gone to Africa in 1978 as Charles Duncan's budding military assistant during the Carter years, a quick trip to the eastern half of the continent which did not have much emotional resonance for me at the time. On March 8, 1992, as chairman, I was in Africa again for official visits to Senegal, Sierra Leone, and Nigeria. Alma came with me. I was especially curious to visit Sierra Leone, our second stop, because my cousin Arthur "Sonny" Lewis, Navy enlisted man turned diplomat, had served there as the American ambassador. We arrived in Freetown, the capital, on March 9, and, it turned out, we were able to have a mini family reunion, since Sonny was in the country on business.

We went through the usual round of official receptions, banquets, toasts, and speeches. Then, early on the morning of the third day, Alma and I were picked up at the American embassy by Joe Oppala, an American Peace Corps veteran who had settled in Sierra Leone. Oppala was going to be our guide on a visit to Bunce Island. "I was one of the people who excavated and restored what you're going to see there," Oppala told us proudly.

On our arrival at the island, he led our party to an area of crumbling fortifications. "Bunce is where the slaves were brought after they were captured in the

834 · COLIN L. POWELL

hinterland," he explained. "And you see over there?" He pointed to the remains of what once must have been handsome homes. "That's where the slave traders and government officials lived." Oppala took us past tumbledown outbuildings, describing one, then another. "Here is where the slaves were inventoried. And here is where they were fed. Here is where they were examined to make sure no damaged goods took up space on the ships." He led us up the stone steps of a large building and out onto a balcony. We looked down into brick-walled pens. "The slaves were held here before they were loaded," Oppala explained. He described how the "cargo" was packed, how long the voyage took across the Atlantic, and how much "spoilage" could be expected.

I felt something stirring in me that I had not thought much about before. The previous February, Alma and I had made the trip to Jamaica. Until now, roots, to me, had always meant the West Indies, the homeland of my parents. But I now began to feel an earlier emotional pull, my link to Africa. I mentioned my reaction to Alma. "I feel the same thing," she said. Gazing down into those cattle pens for human beings, I could imagine the smells of packed bodies. I could picture the overseer, whip in hand, herding terrified men, women, and children aboard the ships. A great-great-great-great-grandfather or -grandmother of mine must have stood in a place as horrible as this.

That afternoon, I spoke at a brief departure ceremony at the Freetown airport. "As you know," I said, "I am an American. I am the son of Jamaicans who emigrated from the island to the United States.

But today, I am something more. I am an African too. I feel my roots, here in this continent."

After the visit to Nigeria, Alma and I headed home with a new awareness of our heritage. What we had witnessed of the African past was tragic. But the experience, in its way, had been uplifting too. It demonstrated, no matter how far down people are driven, how high they can rise when they are allowed to slip their chains and know freedom, in Africa or any country, including our own.

By early 1992, we were deeply into reductions to bring the armed forces down by the 25 percent the administration had announced earlier. We started paying troops to leave the service after years of paying them bonuses to stay in. We cut back on recruiting, taking in just enough new people so that we would have the required sergeants and chief petty officers come on line ten years from now. We were bringing home thousands of troops from Germany every week, along with their families, cars, pets, and other possessions. We had to have an assignment and a home waiting for them at a stateside post. I felt a part of my life vanish the day that my first post, Gelnhausen, was shut down. The keys were given to the Germans, and a U.S. rear detachment marched out to the tune of "When Johnny Comes Marching Home." The Fulda gap became a tourist attraction in the middle of a reunified Germany.

Even before the end of the Cold War, we already had too many posts. Some had been built to fight Native Americans (Indians in those days) during the westward expansion of the last century. Some bases were left over from World Wars I and II. Some were Cold War creations, such as Loring Air Force Base in Aroostook County, Maine, built to serve as a base for limited-range B-36 bombers to reach the Soviet Union. The B-36s were long gone, but we had a hard time closing Loring, which was helping to prop up that economically depressed northern Maine county. Shutting down overseas installations was a breeze compared to closing stateside bases. People in Gelnhausen did not vote in American elections and did not have congressmen fighting for the folks back home. As Congressman Les Aspin once put it to me regarding questionable defense installations, one man's pork is another man's axle grease to keep the wheels turning.

Frank Carlucci, when he was Secretary of Defense, had worked out a deal with Texas Congressman Dick Armey to create an independent commission to review, every two years, closings proposed by the Pentagon. The idea was to insulate these closings from political pressures. After presidential approval, the commission submitted a "take it or leave it" list for the Congress to vote up or down. This system worked, since the majority of members were not affected by base closures and consequently were unworried about approving the closings. Nevertheless, our having to go through this song and dance to shut down expensive but unneeded facilities is an example of Congress's shameful unwillingness to abandon the pork barrel and make the hard decisions the people elect it to make.

Cutting the National Guard and the Reserves proved even harder than base closings. President Reagan and Cap Weinberger had built up reserve strength by 250,000 troops to 1.1 million, to deal with the Soviet threat. These part-time warriors have been indispensable to our military readiness, and they showed their stuff in Desert Storm. They represent citizen soldiery at its finest. But now that the Cold War was over, we no longer needed as many guardsmen and reservists. When we tried to cut back to sensible levels, however, we had our heads handed to us by the National Guard and Reserve associations and their congressional supporters. We were threatening part-time jobs, armories, money going into communities. We managed some reductions, but could still save much more money on the Guard and Reserves without hurting national security.

Attempts to cut an unneeded program could convert a dove into a hawk overnight. Chris Dodd, the liberal Democratic senator from Connecticut, consistently lambasted us for unnecessary defense spending, as long as it was unnecessary outside of his state. When we tried to cut attack submarine production at the Electric Boat Company in Groton, Connecticut, Chris squealed to the heavens about the resulting damage to national security. Dodd was hardly alone in his deathbed conversion to preparedness. He found plenty of support among other members of Congress delighted to discover a likely ally when their pet programs might be eliminated.

On one occasion, I suggested to the admiral in charge of the Atlantic Command that we remove our

AWACS warning planes from Iceland and send them
to look for drug-running aircraft in the Caribbean. He
fought me tooth and nail. I pointed out that the only
Soviet bombers now approaching the United States
from the direction of Iceland were those on their way
to an open house at their new "sister" unit at Barksdale Air Force Base in Louisiana. He was unper-
suaded, so I just took the planes away without further
argument and reassigned them to the drug beat.

We had planned to stockpile 110 million barrels
of oil so that when World War III broke out and we
found ourselves cut off from foreign sources, we
could still operate. But with only regional wars now
likely, we could always find alternative foreign oil
supplies. Consequently, we reduced the stockpile by
50 percent and saved the taxpayers $400 million.
Another cost cutter: the Army wanted a new radio
jammer to thwart Soviet commando attacks in
NATO's rear. What attacks? What rear? What Soviets? We cut the request, and $200 million more was
saved.

Despite bureaucratic resistance, our reductions
went forward and began to bite. Bases closed, troops
and civilians left the service. Program cuts affected
the economy and would become an election issue in
1992. The reductions, however, were carefully calibrated so that we were not whacking the forces with
a meat ax as had happened before. There are still
unneeded programs in the Pentagon. There are still
pockets of waste and fraud that have given us a black
eye in the past. I hope those scandals stay in the past.
Under Cheney, the service chiefs and I tried to be

responsible stewards of the funds entrusted to us by the American taxpayer. We were determined to build a leaner, more efficient, high-quality force capable of any mission. That, I know, remains the objective of the nation's military leaders.

It was May 1. I turned on the TV set in my office, and what I saw made me sick at heart. I was watching the latest news on the riot in Los Angeles triggered the day before by the acquittal of four policemen charged with beating Rodney King. King, an ex-con and no saint, was an unlikely candidate for martyrdom. Still, no fair-minded person seeing the now famous videotape could deny that he had been the victim of excessive police force. The not-guilty verdict ignited rage in the black community.

It can't be happening, I kept thinking, as I watched the burning, rioting, and looting. It was nearly thirty-five years since President Eisenhower had sent troops into Little Rock to quell violence over school integration; twenty-nine years since Bull Connor had turned the dogs and hoses on blacks protesting Jim Crow in Alma's native Birmingham; twenty-four years since American cities had burst into flames over the assassination of Martin Luther King, Jr. And the whole ugly spectacle was being reenacted again, after we had come so far.

While I was watching, I got a phone call from the National Security Advisor, Brent Scowcroft. "Colin," Brent said, "I know this isn't your bailiwick. But we could use some help on the speech the President's going to give on the riot." The President was going on television that night, Scowcroft explained, to spell out federal action to end the turmoil. "I'm going to send you a rough draft," Brent said. "Take a look at it and come on over and give Sam Skinner your reaction." Skinner had replaced John Sununu as White House Chief of Staff the previous December.

Nancy Hughes brought me the President's speech off the fax. I read it with dismay. I thought the tone was all wrong. Yes, the rioting was criminal, and law and order had to be restored. But the violence had not incubated in isolation; it had deep social roots. The speech, as it stood, recognized only the former and ignored the latter. In this election year, I saw the fingerprints of the far right all over the draft.

I found Skinner in his West Wing office. "Sam," I said, "do the law-and-order bit. But there's language here that's only going to fan the flames." Even Rodney King, I pointed out, was preaching racial reconciliation. "You heard what he said—'Can we all get along? . . . Let's try to work it out.' " Turn down the heat, I suggested. "Get some reconciliation into the President's message."

Sam was nervous. Speech time was only hours away. He could not keep tearing the text apart and have it ready in time for the broadcast, he said. Still, he would see what he could do.

I left the White House and went home to dress for the annual Horatio Alger scholarship dinner that I was to attend that evening at the Grand Hyatt Hotel. Later that night, as soon as I could excuse myself from the dinner, I told my security agents to find me an empty room in the Hyatt where I could watch the President's speech, set for 9:00 P.M. I reached the room just in time to hear him deploring the violence. He then said, "I'm also federalizing the National Guard, and I'm instructing General Colin Powell to place all those troops under a central command." This was the first time I had ever received military orders via television, and it was a sad moment. After the upheaval of the sixties, I had hoped that we would never again have to call out American troops to restore order in an American city. To my relief, the President went on to say that the beating of King was "revolting." People were "stunned" by the acquittals, he said, "and so was I, and so was Barbara, and so were my kids." He recognized that we had to offer a better future to minority Americans, and he asked everyone "to lend their hearts, their voices, and their prayers to the healing of hatred." I felt I had earned my pay in Sam Skinner's office that afternoon.

That weekend, with Los Angeles still smoking, Alma and I traveled to Fisk University in Tennessee for her thirty-fifth class reunion. She was particularly pleased that she had managed to produce me as the commencement speaker. I took the opportunity to build on what the President had said. "The problem goes beyond Rodney King," I told the Fisk graduates. "We must remember that America is a family. There may be differences and disputes in our family. But we must not allow the family to be broken into warring factions. . . . I want you to find strength in your diversity. Let the fact that you are black or yellow or white be a source of pride and inspiration to you.

Draw strength from it. Let it be someone else's problem, but never yours. Never hide behind it or use it as an excuse for not doing your best."

George Bush was not going to win reelection on memories of Desert Storm alone. His once stratospheric job approval rating in the polls was down by May 1992 to 40 percent (with the unfavorable rating at 53 percent). He had other problems. Dan Quayle was a drag on the ticket, Bush was warned, and "Dump Dan" became a fairly loud whisper in Republican circles. The press kept mentioning my name among likely replacements. As early as November 1990, during the Gulf War buildup, *Parade* magazine raised the possibility of a Bush-Powell ticket. My long-ago mentor at OMB, Fred Malek, now managing the Bush campaign, was rumored to be supporting the move. The campaign staff did some quiet polling which showed that Jim Baker pulled better than Dan Quayle as a vice presidential candidate. But my name pulled better than Baker's. The speculation became so intense that by mid-May I felt I had to call Quayle. "Mr. Vice President," I said. "I know how uncomfortable this talk has to be for you. All I can tell you is that I'm not the source. I'm not engineering anything. I intend to stick to my job as chairman."

Quayle was gracious. "I know, Colin," he said. "It's part of the cost of doing business in this town."

All the talk about my going on the Republican ticket was strictly Beltway navel-gazing to me. George Bush stuck by people. He had stuck by me when the sharks smelled blood over the Woodward book. And I was convinced that since the Vice President made clear that he had no intention of pulling out, George Bush was going to stick by Dan Quayle.

I was, however, still getting unsolicited feelers from the other side. Vernon Jordan, a politically connected Washington lawyer and close friend, came to see me that May on behalf of the camp of Arkansas Governor Bill Clinton, who by now had the Democratic nomination sewn up. "Your polls are running off the chart," Jordan told me. "Are you interested in running as Clinton's VP?"

"Vernon," I said, "first of all, I don't intend to step out of uniform one day and into partisan politics the next. Second, I don't even know what I am politically. And third, George Bush picked me and stuck by me. I could never campaign against him."

I had had a Republican visitor many months before who made an interesting observation about my place in politics. Stu Spencer, the California sage who practically invented the modern political consultant, had stopped by my office in the Pentagon, and we talked generally about political life. Just as Stu was leaving, he said, "Colin, if you ever do go into politics, do it as a Democrat. I know you well enough, and I don't think you'd be comfortable with some of the Republican agenda. You were raised in an old-fashioned Democratic home. You're too socially conscious." He gave me an impish smile and added, "As a Republican, I shouldn't be telling you this."

On July 25, I was returning to Fort Leavenworth for a dream come true. Ten years after the idea had first struck me, the monument to the Buffalo Soldiers had become a reality. I was on my way to Kansas to take part in the unveiling ceremony. After peering into the slave pens of Africa, after the pain of the Los Angeles riots, it was deeply satisfying to be taking part in a proud achievement of African-Americans.

As my talented speechwriter, Colonel Larry Wilkerson, and I worked on my speech for the dedication, I found myself thinking about the long struggle for racial justice in the military. I thought about Ben Davis, who stuck it out for four years at West Point while his fellow cadets gave him the silent treatment. After that ordeal, Davis reported for duty to Fort Benning, where he and his wife were shunned socially by white officers. Davis, who later commanded the Tuskegee Airmen in World War II, once remarked, "Combat was not easy, but you could only get killed once. Living with the day-to-day degradation of racism was far more difficult."

I remembered the well-intentioned remarks of some of my white superiors: "Powell, you're the best black lieutenant I've ever known." Thank you, suh. But inside me, I was thinking, if you intend to measure me against only black lieutenants, you are making a mistake. I'm going to show you the best lieutenant in the Army, period. As I rose in rank, I learned to tolerate other well-intended white gambits: "Pleased to meet you, General Powell. You know, I once served with Chappie James." Or Ben Davis, or Roscoe Robinson. Why didn't they ever tell me they'd once served with George Patton or Creighton Abrams? I recognized their behavior as a gesture to establish a friendly link to me. Instead it underscored a separation. If I were to say, on meeting a white officer, "You know, I served with Gunfighter Emerson," I am sure this news would be met with a blank stare.

After Desert Storm, the American people at long last were again proud of their military, and I wanted to use this momentum to help high school youths, particularly those in troubled inner cities, by increasing the number of Junior ROTC programs. Under Junior ROTC, active duty NCOs, but mostly retired officers and noncoms teach such high school courses as citizenship, leadership, and military history. They drill the students and take them on map reading exercises and field trips.

In the spring of 1992, I called in the Joint Staff personnel officer, Brigadier General Mary Willis, and told her, "I want a plan for increasing Junior ROTC on my desk in ten days." In a week, General Willis had a proposal to take us from 1,500 to 2,900 high schools. The service chiefs bought into it. Secretary Cheney and President Bush backed the plan. And after Sam Nunn got behind the bill in the Senate, we wound up with approval for funding Junior ROTC in 3,500 high schools.

Yet, ironically, while we had a flock of programs in states with large rural areas, like Texas, we continued to meet resistance in certain urban areas. Liberal school administrators and teachers claimed that we were trying to "militarize" education. Yes, I'll admit, the armed forces might get a youngster more inclined to enlist as a result of Junior ROTC.

But society got a far greater payoff. Inner-city kids, many from broken homes, found stability and role models in Junior ROTC. They got a taste of discipline, the work ethic, and they experienced pride of membership in something healthier than a gang. Until 1993, there were still *no* Junior ROTC programs in any public school in New York City and only one private school offered the program. Finally, we broke through. Seven New York City schools presently have Junior ROTC programs, including my alma mater, Morris High School. College-level ROTC quite literally made my life. The junior program can provide a fresh start in life for thousands of endangered kids, particularly those from minorities living in crime-plagued ghettos. Junior ROTC is a social bargain.

The LA riots, Ben Davis, and kids in the inner cities were all running through my mind as I thought about what I wanted to say at the dedication of the Buffalo Soldiers monument. I arrived at Fort Leavenworth on a sweltering Kansas summer afternoon. The sky over the ceremonial site was turning dark with thunderheads. But nothing could mar the mood. A crowd of thousands engulfed the heart of the post where the monument stood. Flags snapped and bands played. A color guard from the 10th Cavalry, an original Buffalo Soldiers regiment, paraded by on horseback. The Kansas congressional delegation attended. The governor spoke. Finally, it was my turn. I looked out over the audience. Before me, bent over canes, sitting in wheelchairs, some still standing erect, were dozens of veteran Buffalo Soldiers, men in their nineties, even their hundreds. I looked up at the sky and said, "I know you're all watching that very dark cloud. Forget about it. It ain't going to rain on us, not today."

I thanked the Fort Leavenworth military historian, Colonel von Schlemmer, for nourishing my first hope to memorialize the Buffalo Soldiers, and General Dougherty, who had kept the torch of this project burning when it almost guttered out. I saved my warmest praises for Commander Carlton Philpot, U.S. Navy. "Thank you, my friend, from the very bottom of my heart, for making my modest dream into a stunning reality," I said. "There he is, the Buffalo Soldier," I went on, pointing to the magnificent eighteen-foot-tall statue, "on horseback, in his coat of blue, eagles on his buttons, crossed sabers on his canteen, rifle in hand, pistol on his hip, brave, iron-willed, every bit the soldier that his white brother was." African-Americans had answered the country's every call from its infancy, I reminded the audience. "Yet, the fame and fortune that were their just due never came. For their blood spent, lives lost, and battles won, they received *nothing*. They went back to slavery, real or economic, consigned there by hate, prejudice, bigotry, and intolerance."

Today, I pointed out, African-Americans were scaling the barriers, gaining overdue recognition. But black success stories did not drop out of the blue. "I know where I came from," I said. "All of us need to know where we came from so our young people will know where they are going. . . . I am deeply mindful of the debt I owe to those who went before me. I climbed on their backs. . . . I challenge every young person here today: don't forget their service and their sacrifice; and don't forget *our* service and sacrifice, and climb on *our* backs. Be eagles!"

What a beautiful day it was, one forever engraved in my memory.

When the political party conventions ended in August, the battle lines were drawn: Bush-Quayle versus Bill Clinton and Senator Albert Gore, enlivened by the third-party candidacy of Ross Perot. At least, with the tickets decided, political speculation about me evaporated.

August also marked a personal milestone, thirty years of marriage for Alma and me. Our kids arranged a family-and-friends anniversary celebration at home. At one point, Mike called for everybody's attention. We were about to see the saga of Alma and Colin, a videotape patched together from old home movies. I watched the grainy, jerky images of kids demolishing birthday cakes, parents grinning and waving into the camera, grandparents looking grave and dignified. I was proud of the generation we had produced. Mike was now recovered, on his feet, a family man himself, and enrolled in Georgetown Law School. Linda had made her Broadway debut in a Thornton Wilder retrospective, *Wilder, Wilder, Wilder.* Annemarie had graduated from William and Mary in May, done a stint for CNN at the political conventions, gone to work as a production coordinator for *The Larry King Show,* then joined Ted Koppel's *Nightline* staff. No wonder they had done well, I reminded them. I had been named a Father of the Year that spring by the National Father's Day Committee, which my kids thought was hilarious. Nobody is allowed to take himself too seriously around our house. When the guests were gone, Alma and I sat amid the festive debris knowing we were richly blessed. And in the lottery of love and marriage, I knew that I had been the big winner.

On Sunday morning, October 4, I was at home leafing through the *New York Times,* when an editorial headlined "At Least: Slow the Slaughter" riveted my attention. A new cloud had edged onto our radar screens, beginning in 1991 when the old Yugoslavia started to collapse in a smaller version of Soviet disintegration. Croatia and Slovenia declared themselves independent states. Then Bosnia-Herzegovina did the same. Serbs living in Bosnia, backed by a newly independent Serbia, started fighting to foreclose a Muslim-dominated state. The all-seeing eye of twenty-four-hour television kept thrusting images in our faces of rape, pillage, and murder committed by Bosnian Serbs against the region's Muslims. Photographs of skeletal Muslim prisoners held in Bosnian Serb concentration camps looked like Dachau or Auschwitz all over again.

The week before the *Times* editorial appeared, I had been interviewed by Michael R. Gordon, the *Times* defense reporter who asked me why the United States could not assume a "limited" role in Bosnia. I had been engaged in limited military involvements before, in Vietnam for starters. I told the *Times* reporter, "As soon as they tell me it's limited, it means they do not care whether you achieve a result or not. As soon as they tell me 'surgical,' I head for the bunker." I criticized the pseudo-policy of establishing a U.S. "presence" without a defined mission in trouble spots. This approach, I pointed out, had cost the lives of 241 Marines in Lebanon.

The *Times* Sunday editorial, citing this earlier interview, lumped me with American officials who continued to "dither" over Bosnia while thousands died. The editorial referred to $280 billion a year that the United States spent on defense and concluded that the American people were owed more on their investment by the armed forces than "no-can-do." "President Bush could tell General Powell what President Lincoln once told General McClellan," the editorial ended. "If you don't want to use the Army, I should like to borrow it for a while."

I reacted about as coolly as Norm Schwarzkopf had when he was accused of McClellanitis. I exploded. I headed for my study and dashed off a blistering response. As soon as I finished, I called Bill Smullen at home and read it to him.

"Sir," the always reflective Smullen said, "send that to the *Times* and you'll wind up with a letter to the editor. I suggest you tone it down, broaden the base of your argument, and maybe you'll get an op-ed piece out of it."

Which is what I did. Four days later, with Cheney's and the NSC's approval, there appeared on the *Times* op-ed page my response, headlined "Why

Generals Get Nervous" (not my title, but one concocted by a *Times* editor). But I did get my message across. Whenever the military had a clear set of objectives, I pointed out—as in Panama, the Philippine coup, and Desert Storm—the result had been success. When the nation's policy was murky or nonexistent—the Bay of Pigs, Vietnam, creating a Marine "presence" in Lebanon—the result had been disaster. In Bosnia, we were dealing with an ethnic tangle with roots reaching back a thousand years. The fundamental decision was simple, but harsh. Do we get into this war or don't we? If the political decision was to go in, I was prepared to do what I had done in Desert Storm, to lay out the military options. But the *Times* took the editorial position that we could just take a little bite. "So you bet I get nervous when so-called experts suggest that all we need is a little surgical bombing or a limited attack," I wrote. "When the desired result isn't obtained, a new set of experts then comes forward with talk of a little escalation. "History," I pointed out, "has not been kind to this approach." As for Lincoln's problem with McClellan, it arose from the fact that McClellan would not use the overwhelming force available to him *after* Lincoln had established clear political objectives. "We have learned the proper lessons of history," I concluded, "even if some journalists have not."

As I watched the presidential campaign head into its last month, I realized that George Bush was in a tailspin. The Republican Convention, with its racial overtones and troubling mix of politics and religion, had left a bad taste in the mouth of even middle-of-the-road Americans who might have favored George Bush. His Desert Storm adulation had melted like snow in the spring. The country was not recovering quickly enough from a stubborn recession, and the President was accused of playing Herbert Hoover: economy, heal thyself. Publicity gimmicks did not work, such as having Bush try to show a common touch by trotting down from Camp David to the nearest J.C. Penney's to buy socks. A troika of Fred Malek, campaign manager, Bob Teeter, campaign chairman, and Bob Mosbacher, finance chairman, had failed to get the Bush reelection effort off dead center. A reluctant Jim Baker had been drafted from the State Department to serve as campaign miracle worker, but was unable to work a miracle. Around the White House, I sensed a mood that the good ship Bush had been holed below the water line. On November 3, the President was defeated by Governor Clinton, by 43 percent to 37.4 percent of the vote, with Ross Perot taking about 19 percent.

I have often wondered if George Bush was well during the campaign. In 1991, before reappointing me as chairman, he had gone into atrial fibrillation, an irregular heart rhythm caused, in his case, by a thyroid imbalance called Graves' disease. Afterward, he was put on medication, at one point taking five drugs at once. The President himself said that the medicine had caused "a slowing down of the mental processes." After the dosage was changed, he said he felt completely alert. Still, during the campaign, I saw a passive, sometimes detached George Bush. He was not the same leader who could listen to a free-for-all debate among his advisors, cut through to the essence of the issue, and make a firm decision. The campaign foundered. The appeals of Bill Clinton and Ross Perot to a dissatisfied electorate, no longer worried about a Cold War or a desert war, proved decisive.

The day after the election, I called the President to tell him I was sorry about the outcome, but win or lose, he had well served our nation and the world.

"Thanks, Colin," he said. "Still, it hurt. It hurt like hell."

That night when I got home to Fort Myer, I mentioned this conversation to Alma. "That's interesting," she said, "because Barbara Bush just called. They want us to come up and spend the weekend at Camp David."

"I can't imagine they would want anybody but family around at this time," I said.

"And they want us to bring the kids," Alma added.

I had to give a speech in Chicago that Friday, and on my return late that afternoon, I flew into an airport near Camp David, where a Marine helicopter was standing by. Alma, in the meantime, drove up with Annemarie, Michael, Jane, and our grandson, Jeffrey, the whole Powell clan, except for an absent Linda. On my arrival, the President was waiting by the helipad in a golf cart, as was his habit. My family had just about enough time to settle into one of the cabins when the President and Mrs. Bush collected us for a power walk around the camp perimeter. He and I led the way with the Bush dogs, Millie and Ranger, yapping at our heels.

As we walked, the election loomed like the nine-hundred-pound gorilla, unmentioned but unignorable. I did not bring up the subject, since the President did not seem in the mood for postmortems. At one point, though, he said, "Y'know, I was disappointed with Bill Crowe. Thought I treated him pretty well." The President went on, "Offered to let him stay on as chairman for another term." Crowe had been my predecessor, which I suppose is why Bush brought up what was on his mind to me. Bill Clinton's draft record and personal character had been campaign issues. Admiral Crowe had led twenty-one other retired admirals and generals to support Clinton publicly, which pretty much took the curse off the draft-dodger charge and the character issue.

President Bush shook his head. "I just never thought they'd elect him." The tone of voice clearly conveyed his deep sense of rejection. "Don't understand it." He gave me a pained smile. "But life goes on."

That night, after dinner, we all gathered in the living room of the President's cabin and watched a charming movie, *Enchanted April*. The next morning, as we said our goodbyes, Barbara Bush seemed to read the question in my eyes. "We needed to be with real friends at this time," she said. "Close friends." Alma and I were deeply moved. President or not, First Lady or not, these two exceptional people would be our close friends for life.

. . .

Just two days before the election, on November 1, I had been to dinner at Vernon Jordan's home, and at one point, Jordan asked me, "Are you interested in State or Defense? Warren Christopher would like to know," he said, referring to a Carter-era State Department alumnus who was expected to be a leader of Clinton's transition team if the Arkansas governor won.

"Vernon, I don't want either job. I don't want *any* political appointment," I said. All I really wanted was to finish my term and retire from the Army in September 1993. Furthermore, the election had been so focused on the economy that I had no clear idea where the new team stood on foreign policy and defense issues.

With the Jordan conversation still fresh in mind, I was a little apprehensive when, two weeks after the election, I got word that President-elect Clinton wanted to see me. On November 19, at 3:00 P.M., ducking a heavy rain, I ran into the Hay-Adams Hotel, one block north of the White House. On entering the President-elect's suite, I was greeted by George Stephanopoulos, the Clinton deputy campaign manager, who looked like a high school valedictorian with a good tailor. "The governor's running a little behind," Stephanopoulos said. "But he's anxious to see you."

Clinton arrived shortly afterward, and Stephanopoulos left the two of us alone. The President-elect took off his jacket, asked me to sit down, and settled into an easy chair. I had never met Bill Clinton in person and found him even bigger and more vital-looking than his TV image. He seemed relaxed and unawed by what he had just accomplished.

"I've been wanting to meet you ever since I saw a tape of your Morris High School speech," he said as he poured me a cup of coffee. He went on to mention several points from my talk. I was impressed. I had given this speech over a year and a half before, when Bill Clinton was still a small state's governor. The man, as I was about to learn, had spongelike powers of absorption and retention. He put a cigar in his mouth; he constantly seemed about to light it, but never did. A plate of cookies rested on a coffee table before us. Finally, I took one. He took one. I took a second, and we began to polish off the pile.

He asked me about Bosnia. Wasn't there some way, he wanted to know, that we could influence the situation through airpower, something not too punitive? There it was again, the ever-popular solution from the skies, with a good humanist twist; let's not hurt anybody. "Not likely," I said. But not wanting to sound too negative on our first meeting, I told him that I would have my staff give the matter more thought.

We discussed Iraq, Russia, and what initiatives the new President might take to prod the peace process along in the Middle East. He was better informed on foreign policy than his campaign had suggested. When it seemed we had covered the globe, I brought up something much on my mind, especially regarding this first nonveteran American President since FDR. "Sir," I said, "to the rest of the country you'll soon be our President. But to me and millions of troops, you're also our commander in chief. You'll never find any group more faithful to your orders. So allow me to make a few suggestions. Try to meet with the Joint Chiefs and visit the troops soon. Don't keep us at arm's length."

Clinton readily agreed. Since we were on the subject of the military, he told me that he was looking over three candidates for Secretary of Defense. "What's your judgment of Sam Nunn, Dave McCurdy"— an Oklahoma congressman at the time—"and Les Aspin?" he asked.

Obviously, I had not made the short list. At least one unwanted job was out of the way. But was this an ambush? Would my endorsement, as a Reagan-Bush appointee, be the kiss of death? "Nunn's very good, but you might find him a little independent," I answered. "And I'm not sure Sam wants to give up the power he has on the Hill. But he's definitely first-class." Dave McCurdy? "Okay, but maybe a bit erratic." Les Aspin? My objectivity was being tested to the limit. Not that I had any objection to Aspin personally. This rumpled, professorial MIT Ph.D. was brilliant, and I liked him. But, except for his support of Desert Storm, Aspin had been beating my brains out almost since I had become chairman. He had tried to scuttle the Base Force. We were already cutting the services by half a million, and Aspin had primed candidate Clinton to lop off another 200,000.

"You know, Les is real smart," Clinton commented in a way that led me to believe that I knew who my next boss was going to be.

"Smart's not everything in running the Pentagon," I pointed out. I had worked with Aspin long enough to have observed the disorder in which his brilliance flourished. "Les might not bring quite the management style you're looking for," I said.

The President-elect gave me a noncommittal nod. Retirement began to look appealing. Since Clinton was thinking of putting a former adversary over me, I thought I had better make another point. "You know I've spent most of the past twelve years serving Republican Presidents," I said. "My fingerprints are all over their national security policies. But I'm a soldier first, and when you take office, you'll have my total loyalty. My term's up in September. But if you want me to go earlier, that's fine. Also, sir, anytime I find that I cannot, in good conscience, fully support your administration's policies because of my past positions, I will let you know. And I'll retire quietly, without making a fuss."

"That's all I can ask," Clinton said.

We talked for over an hour. I was amazed by Clinton's fund of knowledge. He seemed to have an interest in everything and the kind of memory that never forgets anything. Finally, an aide came in and advised the President-elect that he had a state governor waiting to see him, and he was already running half an hour behind schedule.

"Sorry we can't talk a little longer, General," Clinton said. "I was hoping Hillary would be back in time to meet you."

I rose, then hesitated. I had to say one more thing before I left. "Governor Clinton," I began, "there's something we haven't covered." During the campaign, he had promised to end the ban on gays serving in the military. "For whatever it's worth," I said, "let me give you the benefit of my thinking. Lifting the ban is going to be a tough issue for you, and it's a culture shock for the armed forces. The chiefs and the CINCs don't want it lifted. Most military people don't want it lifted. I believe a majority in Congress are against lifting the ban too. The heart of the problem is privacy. How can this change be made to work given the intimate living conditions of barracks and shipboard life?"

"I know," Clinton said, "but I want to find a way to stop discrimination against gays."

"Let me make a suggestion," I went on. "At the press conference when you announce your choice for Secretary of Defense, say right off the bat, 'And I've asked Secretary-designate so-and-so to look into this matter and have a recommendation for me in six months on whether to and how to lift the ban.' Give yourself some breathing space. Get it out of the Oval Office. Don't make the gay issue the first horse out of the gate with the armed forces."

He nodded, and I had the impression he agreed with me. I was wrong.

Within minutes, I was down the elevator and in the backseat of my car. I had been impressed. Clinton was self-assured, smart, curious, likable, and passionate about his ideas. He also seemed to be a good listener. And to my relief, he had said nothing to me about a political appointment.

The world had a dozen other running sores that fall, but television hovered over Somalia and wrenched our hearts, night after night, with images of people starving to death before our eyes. The UN had planted a humanitarian relief effort there, and the United States had committed six hundred troops and provided C-130 transports to fly in food. We rarely knew what happened to the relief supplies. Local warlords stole the food from warehouses. They hijacked relief agency trucks. The UN effort was practically at a standstill, while images of the flesh-less limbs and bloated bellies of dying children continued to haunt us. I was not eager to get us involved in a Somalian civil war, but we were apparently the only nation that could end the suffering.

The day before Thanksgiving, President Bush called a meeting that I attended with Cheney, Scowcroft, and a handful of others. The new CINC CENTCOM, General Joseph Hoar, who had replaced Norm Schwarzkopf, had readied a contingency mercy mission for Somalia, Operation Restore Hope, which I now laid out for the President. Operation Restore Hope involved putting a substantial number of U.S. troops on the ground to take charge of the place and to make sure the food got to starving Somalis.

"I like it," the President said after I finished. "We'll do it."

Brent Scowcroft looked uneasy. "Sure, we can get in," he said. "But how do we get out?"

"We'll do it, and try to be out by January 19," the President concluded. "I don't want to stick Clinton with an ongoing military operation."

Cheney and I eyed each other. "Mr. President," Dick said, "we can't have it both ways. We can't get in there fully until mid-December. And the job won't be done by January 19." I appreciated that Dick had spoken up, since after January 20 I would be the only one in the room left holding this particular bag.

By December 8, Operation Restore Hope was under way as Navy SEAL commandos, the first of an eventual 25,400 troops, went ashore at night at Somalia's capital, Mogadishu. The only resistance the SEALs encountered was from about seventy-five reporters and camera crews beaming spotlights on them, determined to broadcast a military operation live, increasing the danger to everybody. I was not all that distressed, however, since I knew that Somali warlords seeing them would be impressed by the tough-looking SEALs.

The mission succeeded from the start. We had a crack three-star Marine general in charge, Bob Johnston, Schwarzkopf's chief of staff during Desert Storm. A few days earlier we had sent in Ambassador Bob Oakley, an old NSC colleague, who had previously served as the U.S. ambassador to Somalia. Bob was called out of retirement for this mission and agreed to do it only after I swore to his wife, Phyllis, that he could come home for his daughter's wedding. In Somalia, Bob met with the warlords and persuaded them that it was not in their interest to interfere with the powerful force coming ashore. The warlords cooperated, and food began to flow to the countryside. Within weeks, we were so successful that we had upset the economics of the marketplace. So much free food came pouring into Somalia that it became tough to make a living by farming.

Brent Scowcroft's initial uneasiness, nevertheless, was justified. The famine had been provoked not by the whims of nature but by internal feuding. How were we to get out of Somalia without turning the country back to the same warlords whose rivalries had produced the famine in the first place? Clearly, we would not be gone by inauguration day.

On December 22, President-elect Clinton nominated Les Aspin as his Secretary of Defense. Les and I met the day after Christmas at the Pentagon. I had long studied Aspin in his performance as chairman of the House Armed Services Committee. The man had a fine mind and a clear command of defense issues. He was also a gadfly, capable of policy by one-liners and occasional cheap shots. And he was immune to efficient organization, counting on his congressional staff to keep him from hurtling off the rails.

"Les," I said, "I want to tell you the same thing I told the President-elect. My term's up in September. If you want your own guy, I'll leave sooner. Say the word and I'm gone."

Aspin laughed. "You're the only one around here who knows how the joint works," he said. "We know each other. We'll get along fine."

We went over the major pending defense issues, and his expression clouded only at one point. "I'm nervous about the gay business," he said. If Clinton reversed the ban on gays by executive order, he believed, Congress was not going to roll over and play dead. I repeated to him the advice I had given to the President-elect about not rushing into the swamp. We parted with this time bomb still ticking.

I had never expected to return to Phenix City, Alabama, and certainly not for the reason that brought me there in the final days of the Bush administration. Phenix City lies just across the Chattahoochee River from Fort Benning, Georgia, where I had reported in 1964 for the Infantry Officers Advanced Course. It was outside of Phenix City that Alma and I had managed to find a halfway decent house among a row of shanties. The town was typical of the Old South, a part of America where we were not allowed to live in a decent neighborhood; where after fighting in Vietnam I was refused service at a hamburger joint; where a state trooper could call an Army officer "boy" and tell him to get out of town. Twenty-eight years later, Alma and I were going back to Phenix City to dedicate the General Colin L. Powell Parkway, which intersected with Dr. Martin Luther King, Jr., Parkway.

We flew into Lawson Army Air Field at Fort Benning on January 7, 1993, a cold, drizzly afternoon. As the limousine sped us away, I gazed out at the five-mile course around the field that I used to run as a Pathfinder student. We drove across the Chattahoochee into Phenix City, where, in spite of the foul weather, a big crowd had turned out, whites and blacks. Every funeral home within fifty miles must have been hit up for the graveside canopies that people huddled under. The mayor made a gracious speech and presented me with the keys to the city (the city where, in the old days, I could not get a key to a gas station men's room).

After being feted and speechified at one event after another, Alma and I were driven back through Fort Benning. It was dusk, and through the trees we could just make out Riverside, the antebellum mansion where Fort Benning's commanding general lived. It had been Alma's dream house when I was a young officer. Now we occupied the chairman's residence at Fort Myer. I had a street named after me where, previously, I would not have been allowed to walk freely. We had persevered, and we had lived the American dream.

The waning hours of the Bush era were not particularly pleasant for me. Every day, more of my teammates over the past four years left, and I was starting to feel like the kid about to enter a new school full of strangers. And we had several loose ends still flapping. We had stemmed the Haitian refugee tide, but the clamor to put Father Aristide back in power was building pressure for U.S. intervention. We were frustrated by not knowing what we should do or could do to end the killing in Bosnia. Our troops were still enmeshed in Somalia. We even had to slap down Saddam Hussein that January after he sent aircraft into the no-fly zone and threatened UN inspection teams. I gladly passed along the order for a retaliatory missile strike on Iraqi air defense installations.

On January 14, with only six days left before the changing of the guard, I stood with Dick Cheney and other Pentagon officials in the jammed Ceremonial Hall at Fort Myer as the U.S. Army's Herald Trumpets announced the arrival of President and Mrs. Bush. We were going to do it up right for our departing commander in chief. The Army band swung into a medley of Texas tunes as the President reviewed troops representative of those who had triumphed in Desert Storm. We presented the President and the First Lady with farewell gifts from all of us in the Defense Department. And then I spoke. "Mr. President," I said, "you have sent us in harm's way when you had to, but never lightly, never hesitantly, never with our hands tied, never without giving us what we needed to do the job." I turned to Barbara Bush. "She is the First Lady and the first service wife," I said. "She is a woman who has served her nation through thick and thin, who won't take guff from anyone who tries to give it, nor deny kindness to anyone who needs it." When I finished, I introduced Dick Cheney, who gave a moving speech praising George Bush, the man, the President, the commander in chief. It was the closest I had ever seen Dick come to tears.

The George Bush I served was a patrician born to privilege in New England, yet made it on his own in Texas oil fields; a well-bred gentleman who was also full of mischief and fun to be around. He was fair-minded in his judgment and treatment of individuals, yet seemed unmindful of the racial polarization being caused by the far right wing of his party. He had given America proud victories in Panama and the Persian Gulf, presided over the end of the Cold War, and left a world safer from nuclear catastrophe.

He had sensed the public pulse on these issues just as he had missed it on America's domestic concerns. He was honored for the one and penalized for the other. As for my personal relationship with George Bush, he had entrusted me with heavy responsibility and respected my judgments. He had also shown me kindness, loyalty, and friendship. I thought the world of him and always will.

Toward the end, the chiefs and I also held a parade and farewell dinner for our departing Pentagon boss. At this time, I tried to convey what I thought lay underneath Dick Cheney's controlled exterior. "He studied weapons and strategy and techniques," I told the guests, "but . . . he learned that we are not a thing. We are not a bureaucracy. We are not a system. Instead, he learned that America's armed forces are a human organism that must be cared for, that hurts, that must be trained, that bleeds, and that must always be tended to." Dick Cheney had tended to us.

He and I had never, in nearly four years, spent a single purely social hour together. We were, however, remarkably close in our attitudes. We thought so much alike that, in the Tank or in the Oval Office, we could finish each other's sentences. I had developed not only professional respect but genuine affection for this quiet man. On the day before the inauguration, I went up to Cheney's suite to bid him goodbye. I said hello to his secretary, Kathy Villalpando, and started into his office, which was strewn with cardboard boxes holding the books and mementos accumulated over the past four years.

"Where's the Secretary?" I asked Kathy.

"Oh, Mr. Cheney left hours ago," she said. I was disappointed, even hurt, but not surprised. The lone cowboy had gone off into the sunset without even a last "So long."

The next day a young President, shaped by the sixties, took the torch from a man who had been the Navy's youngest fighter pilot in the war years of the forties. I felt like a bridge spanning the administrations and the generations.

21 ★ Mustering Out

IT WAS SUNDAY night, four days after Bill Clinton's inauguration as the forty-second President. Alma and I were having dinner at the Watergate apartment of Cap and Jane Weinberger. I was enjoying a relaxing evening with old friends, and not particularly looking forward to what I faced the next day at the White House. The phone rang, and Cap took it. "It's for you," he said. "It's the President."

I suspected why Bill Clinton was calling. The following afternoon, the Joint Chiefs were to meet with him to discuss his campaign promise to lift the ban on gays serving in the military. The already burning controversy had been heated up further that morning by the odd performance of the new Secretary of Defense, Les Aspin, on CBS's *Face the Nation.* Discussing how the administration and Congress would deal with the President's pledge,

Aspin told his interviewers, "If we can't work it out, we'll disagree, and the thing won't happen." In effect, he had publicly predicted the failure of Clinton's first presidential initiative.

I took the phone from Weinberger. "Good evening, Mr. President," I said.

"General, I've just learned that Justice Thurgood Marshall has died," Clinton told me. He went on to explain that the Marshall family was hoping the Supreme Court associate justice could be buried in Arlington National Cemetery even though he was not automatically eligible. The President's staff had advised him that a waiver was possible for distinguished Americans, but he wanted to check it out with me.

"That's right," I said. "There won't be any problem." I was pleased that the President wanted to see this civil rights giant buried at Arlington and that he was thoughtful enough to touch base with the military on a matter affecting hallowed ground.

"And I thank you and Mrs. Powell for coming to my inauguration," Clinton added, ending the conversation. He had said nothing about Aspin's interview or the gay issue.

The next afternoon, Secretary Aspin, the four service chiefs, the vice chairman, and I found ourselves arrayed on one side of the table in the Roosevelt Room of the White House, facing the President; Vice President Al Gore; the new White House Chief of Staff, Mack McLarty; Anthony Lake, the National Security Advisor; George Stephanopoulos, the White

House spokesman; and other members of the President's staff. Aspin asked me to lead off with a quick briefing on current Pentagon concerns, the status of forces, troop levels, and the defense budget. We figured the commander in chief's first meeting with his top military advisors ought at least to raise a few purely military issues. As soon as I finished, however, we spent the next 105 minutes solely on homosexuals in the armed forces.

"Mr. President," I said at one point during the discussion, "we know gays and lesbians serve ably and honorably—but not openly. If they are allowed to do so, that's going to raise tough issues of privacy." I suggested that he hear from each chief from the perspective of his service, since they were the ones who would have to make any new policy work. The chiefs spoke in turn, making clear that they were not just voicing personal opinions; they were concerned about maintaining morale and good order. They had gone back to their constituencies—the field commanders, senior NCOs, the troops, service spouses, chaplains—and they had run into a solid wall of opposition to lifting the ban. Only the last to speak, the Air Force chief, Tony McPeak, seemed somewhat conciliatory, possibly feeling sympathy for a President who had just heard an unbroken chorus of nays. I smiled to myself, since during our talks in the Tank, McPeak had been the most truculent opponent of allowing homosexuals to serve.

Throughout the meeting, the President displayed the capacity for intent listening that I had observed when we first met. When he did speak, his voice was raspy from all the inaugural ceremonies. "I made a campaign promise," he said. "And I sure want to keep it." Then, turning toward me, he added, "But I also took an oath last week as commander in chief, and I have to consider the well-being of the armed forces. I don't want to see soldiers holding hands or dancing together at military posts, but that's just a matter of regulating behavior, the same as we do for heterosexual soldiers. What I don't like is barring homosexuals who want to serve, whether they're in or out of the closet."

The talk continued, respectful but tense. I felt increasingly disappointed that this issue had been allowed to become the new administration's first priority. I also thought I understood why. Bill Clinton had already backed off from other campaign stands. For example, as a candidate, he had criticized the Bush policy of sending Haitian refugees back home, and he had already recanted on that one. With his credibility at stake, I assumed that some of his advisors must have told him, "Mr. President, you can't back down again. Just issue an executive order allowing gays to serve, and tell those generals to do it."

The chiefs continued to bring up practical problems that gay integration presented on crowded ships, in cramped barracks, and in other intimate situations. At one point I proposed a change to the current policy that Aspin, the chiefs, and I had discussed earlier. "We could stop asking about sexual orientation when people enlist," I said. Gays and lesbians could serve as long as they kept their lifestyle to themselves. This change would no doubt still be con-

demned as discriminatory by gay rights activists, and
military traditionalists would probably call it a surrender. "But," I concluded, "this way might provide a
practical compromise."

The President decided to stick to the current
policy for the time being, while the military was to
carry out a six-month study of the issue. In the meantime, he said, enlistees were not to be asked about
their sexual orientation. "I know these issues are
tough," he concluded, as the meeting broke up. "If
they were easy, somebody would have solved them
long before us."

As contentious as the issue was, the chiefs and I
left the meeting feeling optimistic. The President had
given us a fair hearing. He knew where the military
stood, and he had shown a willingness to compromise. At least he was not going to ram an immediate
end to the ban down the throats of the armed forces.

The next day, the *New York Times* hit me and the
chiefs with both barrels. A *Times* editorial charged us
with being "defiantly opposed, almost to the point of
insubordination." *Times* columnist Abe Rosenthal
said that Colin Powell would never have become
chairman but for President Truman's racial integration of the military in 1948. I came under fire from
the *Washington Post:* "Powell . . . is on the wrong
side of this issue"; the *Chicago Tribune:* "The military could use a dose of tolerance"; the *Philadelphia
Inquirer:* "Of all people, Powell should know the
arguments for dropping the ban"; the *Atlanta Constitution:* "Colin Powell, of all people, is enforcing bigotry." *Time* magazine dubbed me "the Rebellious

General." I became the target of cartoonists who portrayed me as a uniformed Neanderthal. Much of the criticism seemed to suggest that my earlier advice on this issue should be changed simply because we had changed Presidents.

Bill Clinton had asked my views and I had given them, knowing they were not what he wanted to hear. I felt honor-bound to do so. My life would have been easier if he had simply lifted the ban by executive order. The military would have said, "Yes, sir." But, as Les Aspin knew, almost immediately, Congress would have enacted a ban as a matter of law, forcing the President to veto it and confronting him with an almost certain veto override. The President and his advisors had picked the wrong issue, and they had misread the public's attitude. While I was being torn apart by the media, my office was receiving more than three thousand letters and phone calls a day, never running less than six to one in favor of keeping the ban.

My objections to removing the ban were not knee-jerk traditionalist. I did not, for example, oppose having women perform certain combat roles, such as flying fighter aircraft and serving aboard ship. And I recognized that some of those who wanted to keep the ban on gays did, in fact, spout arguments similar to those used to resist racial integration in the armed forces forty years before: "Next thing you know, they'll want to live in our housing, eat in our mess halls, go to our clubs, sit next to us in church." Nevertheless, I continued to see a fundamental distinction. Requiring people of different color to live together in intimate situations is far different from requiring people of different sexual orientation to do so.

On February 10, the *New York Times* used the gay issue as the peg for a front-page story about me that I could not let stand. The article was headlined "Joint Chiefs Head Is Said to Request Early Retirement." When I arrived at the Pentagon at 7:00 A.M., a CBS TV crew was already waiting in ambush to question me about my alleged departure. The *Times* account contained a grain of truth. I had told Aspin— and Dick Cheney even earlier—that I might ask to leave the chairmanship a month or two before my term was up, but mostly for the convenience of my successor before the next budget cycle. And Alma and I hoped to use the summer months to move into a new home we had bought in preparation for our reentry into civilian life. I flatly denied to CBS that I had any intention of quitting over the gay issue. Instead, I expected to help the President solve the problem. After talking to this network, I told Bill Smullen to get me on everything else on the air. By the end of the morning, I had appeared on all three major networks and CNN and had slam-dunked the early-retirement story.

Over the next couple of weeks, I took the most scathing public criticism of my career. As George Bush had said about losing the presidency, it hurt. Unknown to Tony McPeak, his driver asked Otis Pearson one day if he might test-drive the chairman's limo. McPeak, as Air Force Chief of Staff, was one of those mentioned in the *Times* as my possible successor.

Nine months later, Congress approved the policy we had discussed with the President that January afternoon, now shorthanded as "Don't ask. Don't tell." I expect that the courts will ultimately decide the issue once and for all. And when they do, whichever way they rule, the U.S. military will comply with the law of the land. I stand by what I have done. My position reflected my conscience and the needs of the service at the time. I say this realizing that, as time passes, public attitudes may change on this volatile subject just as they have on so many burning social controversies in recent years.

Almost my only satisfaction during the first weeks of the Clinton administration was getting rid of the uniformed guards who had been assigned to stand outside the doorways of the Secretary of Defense and the deputy secretary ever since the phony Libyan assassination hit team scare twelve years before. Weinberger, Carlucci, and Cheney had all fallen in love with these resplendent sentinels. All I saw were good troops going to waste. Since Les Aspin was oblivious to this sort of pomp, I managed to persuade his assistants to disband the guards before he noticed them.

My other victories included earning two merit badges of American pop distinction; my name was in the *New York Times* crossword puzzle, and I was the subject of a question on television's *Jeopardy*.

Soon after the inauguration, the Clinton national security team gathered in the Situation Room for the first time. The issue was Bosnia. Although I was a member of the team, I still felt a little like a skunk at the picnic. I had been up to my eyeballs in Reagan and Bush national security policies that were held in some disrepute by my new bosses. They nevertheless welcomed me, aware that my institutional memory might prove useful. This meeting was my introduction to the new administration's decision-making style. Tony Lake, the new National Security Advisor, sat in the chairman's seat, but did not drive the meeting. Warren Christopher, the Secretary of State, sat on one side of Lake, somewhat passively, quite a change from George Shultz and Jim Baker, who strode into such meetings and immediately acted as the chieftains of U.S. foreign policy. Christopher, lawyerlike, simply waited for his client group to decide what position he was to defend. Les Aspin flanked Lake on the other side. He did not try to lead either, and when Aspin did speak, he usually took the discussion onto tangents to skirt the immediate issue. The rest of the seats were filled by other members of the new national security team.

Vice President Gore arrived after we had been talking for over an hour, and we had to shuffle around the table to find a chair for him. The President showed up a little later; fortunately, by then, a place had been saved for the nation's chief executive.

This meeting set the pattern for all that were to follow. As President Reagan's National Security Advisor I had run structured meetings where the objectives were laid out, options were argued, and decisions were made. I had managed to adjust to the looser Bush-era approach, and I would somehow adapt to the Clinton style. But it was not going to be easy.

At subsequent meetings, the discussions continued to meander like graduate-student bull sessions or the think-tank seminars in which many of my new colleagues had spent the last twelve years while their party was out of power. Backbenchers sounded off with the authority of cabinet officers. I was shocked one day to hear one of Tony Lake's subordinates, who was there to take notes, argue with him in front of the rest of us.

Bosnia was the foreign policy issue over which candidate Clinton had criticized Bush most sharply. Clinton had promised more aggressive action in that tormented place. Now he had the opportunity, and the meetings we held on Bosnia were full of belligerent rhetoric. But what aggressive action were we to take, and to what end? So far, none of the European countries that had sent in troops to help the war's victims favored fighting a ground conflict or using their forces to impose a truce. They placed their faith not in might, but in diplomacy.

My own views on Bosnia had not shifted from the previous administration. In response to constant calls by the new team to "do something" to punish the Bosnian Serbs from the air for shelling Sarajevo, I laid out the same military options that I had presented to President Bush. Our choices ranged from limited air strikes around Sarajevo to heavy bombing of the Serbs throughout the theater. I emphasized that none of these actions was guaranteed to change Serb behavior. Only troops on the ground could do that.

Heavy bombing might persuade them to give in, but would not compel them to quit. And, faced with limited air strikes, the Serbs would have little difficulty hiding tanks and artillery in the woods and fog of Bosnia or keeping them close to civilian populations. Furthermore, no matter what we did, it would be easy for the Serbs to respond by seizing UN humanitarian personnel as hostages.

My constant, unwelcome message at all the meetings on Bosnia was simply that we should not commit military forces until we had a clear political objective. Aspin shared this view. The debate exploded at one session when Madeleine Albright, our ambassador to the UN, asked me in frustration, "What's the point of having this superb military that you're always talking about if we can't use it?" I thought I would have an aneurysm. American GIs were not toy soldiers to be moved around on some sort of global game board. I patiently explained that we had used our armed forces more than two dozen times in the preceding three years for war, peacekeeping, disaster relief, and humanitarian assistance. But in every one of those cases we had had a clear goal and had matched our military commitment to the goal. As a result, we had been successful in every case. I told Ambassador Albright that the U.S. military would carry out any mission it was handed, but my advice would always be that the tough political goals had to be set first. Then we would accomplish the mission.

Tony Lake, who had served on the NSC during the Vietnam War, supported my position. "You know,

Madeleine," he said, "the kinds of questions Colin is asking about goals are exactly the ones the military never asked during Vietnam." Former Secretary of Defense Robert S. McNamara, in his confessional book *In Retrospect,* admits to similar confusion over our ends in the Vietnam War, leading to the tragic results with which we are all too familiar.

I always felt more comfortable when the President was present at these discussions. Bill Clinton had the background to put history, politics, and policy into perspective. Yet, he was not well served by the wandering deliberations he permitted. He had an academic streak himself and seemed to enjoy these marathon debates. As the talk dragged on, the participants eventually persuaded themselves that they had found a solution to the problem at hand that turned a sow's ear into a silk purse. But after a few days of exposure to critical light, the solution started looking suspiciously like a sow's ear again. In one case, early in 1993, the President was persuaded to propose lifting the weapons embargo against the Bosnian Muslims and to allow air strikes against the Serbs until the Muslims were better able to defend themselves. Secretary Christopher went off to sell this strategy to our allies, even though they had made it clear it was dead on arrival. He came back a week later and we spent another Saturday thrashing out another solution.

In 1994 and 1995 the UN and NATO, at U.S. prodding, did conduct limited strikes, and the Serbs employed the expected countermeasures. The harsh reality has been that the Serbs, Muslims, and Croatians are committed to fight to the death for what they believe to be their vital interests. They have matched their military actions to their political objectives, just as the North Vietnamese did years earlier. The West has wrung its hands over Bosnia, but has not been able to find its vital interests or matching commitment. No American President could defend to the American people the heavy sacrifice of lives it would cost to resolve this baffling conflict. Nor could a President likely sustain the long-term involvement necessary to keep the protagonists from going at each other's throats all over again at the first opportunity.

At the Pentagon, Les Aspin was experiencing his own growing pains. Aspin had a management style that was the complete opposite of Cheney's. He was as disjointed as Cheney was well organized. We never knew what time Les was coming to work in the morning. Staff meetings were sporadic. When meetings were held, they turned into marathon gabfests, while attendees for subsequent meetings stacked up in the hallways. Aspin brought to the Pentagon key members of his congressional staff who acted as a palace guard. They had to be dealt with before anything got through to the Secretary of Defense. Aspin's new press secretary, Vern Guidry, made it a condition of his employment that he did not have to brief the press corps. Guidry saw his job as managing Aspin's personal public relations. These aides were slow to grasp the difference between handling Capitol Hill intrigues and running an enterprise of three million people.

One promise the new defense team had made was to exercise more civilian control over the Pentagon's military leaders, especially the guy currently in the chairman's office. Some of Aspin's assistants even considered announcing my replacement early to make me a lame duck. They quickly discovered that the civilians and the military in the Pentagon needed each other. Rather than being out of control, the generals and admirals were willing to respond to new direction and show what they could do.

Aspin's immediate problem, from the day he took over the department, was the image he projected. In a building full of neatly pressed uniforms, the top man looked out of place in his dated, rumpled tan suits and wrinkled shirts. Although Aspin had a first-class mind, he often sounded inarticulate when he addressed his new subordinates. He resisted seeing the foreign leaders streaming to Washington to meet the new Clinton team. When he did see them, Les would hunch over the table and say, "So, how's it going in your country?" The burden of conversation fell on his guests, and after forty-five minutes, they would leave, having learned little about the new administration's foreign and defense intentions. In one meeting with King Hussein of Jordan, I watched as His Majesty had to carry on a monologue while Les polished off thirteen hors d'oeuvres from a tray placed between them. Aspin's health posed a problem. He was hospitalized twice for heart irregularities. A pacemaker brought this condition under control, but not until several wobbly months had gone by. Overall, the image Aspin projected was not likely to inspire confidence in our troops or allies.

Fortunately, he was backed up by two solid deputies, Bill Perry, who subsequently succeeded him as Secretary of Defense, and John Deutch, a college chum of Aspin's whom I had met at the Department of Energy during the Carter administration. Deutch eventually became President Clinton's Director of Central Intelligence. They helped balance the flock of ambassadors and academics that Aspin brought into the department.

In the days when he was chairing the House Armed Services Committee, Aspin had labeled the Bush-Cheney-Powell Base Force concept a "dumb strategy." Now, as Secretary of Defense, his primary objective was to conduct a "Bottom Up Review" of the armed forces, fulfilling a Clinton campaign promise. Theoretically, BUR meant starting with a clean slate, as if the current armed forces did not exist, and then building a new force to match current defense missions. This approach had a test-tube reasonableness, except that instead of starting from scratch, the new administration had inherited existing strategies, forces, treaty obligations, commitments, and crises all around the world. And instead of a clean slate, Clinton had already pledged during the campaign to cut forces by 200,000 troops and tens of billions of dollars below the Base Force level. Yet, to win votes, he had also promised to restore several popular but wasteful defense projects that Bush had canceled.

The Base Force strategy called for armed forces capable of fighting two major regional conflicts "near simultaneously." The reasoning was simple: if we were fighting in one place, we still wanted to

have enough might remaining so that another potential aggressor would not be emboldened to pull a fast
one. Aspin floated the idea of a force premised on
our fighting one major conflict and a holding action
against any other enemy until we could finish the
first fight. Our South Korean allies immediately
asked if they were the ones who might be left "on
hold." Aspin's trial balloon popped. It took us nine
months to finish the BUR, and we ended up again
with a defense based on the need to fight two
regional wars, the Bush strategy, but with Clinton
campaign cuts. The Base Force disappeared as a
term, but, as Aspin acknowledged, it was the lineal
ancestor of the BUR force. What is not clear as of
this writing is whether the cuts in personnel and budget have taken us below the levels required to support
the strategy and structure the Clinton administration
have adopted. In short, do we have the strength to
accomplish the mission? That mission may well
change over the next few years. The collapse of
North Korea as a threat or a change for the better in
Iraq and Iran will certainly require an adjustment of
the two-war scenario. It will not last forty years, as
did the strategy of containment, but it is appropriate
for the present post–Cold War transition period.

Les Aspin and I got along well personally. And,
over time, his performance became more disciplined.
He became more conscious of the need to project an
image that reflected the awesome responsibility on
his shoulders as day-to-day commander of the armed
forces of the United States. Under his leadership, we
worked out the compromise on the homosexual
issue, completed the Bottom Up Review, and solved

several tough procurement problems. Still, in spite of these achievements and his considerable intellect, Les Aspin had been miscast as Secretary of Defense.

Former President George Bush's hope for a January 20 exit from Somalia became a faded memory. In April, I spent my fifty-sixth birthday in Mogadishu trying to move the operation off America's back and onto the UN's, where it had been in the first place. We had accomplished our mission by ending the civil disorder that had disrupted the production and distribution of food and led to the mass starvation. It was now up to the UN force to maintain that order. But UN Secretary General Boutros Boutros-Ghali reasoned that since the catastrophe had been provoked by feuding fourteenth-century-style warlords, the solution was a dose of twentieth-century-style democracy. The UN approved a resolution shifting the mission from feeding the hungry to "nation building," the phrase I had first heard when we went into Vietnam. From what I have observed of history, the will to build a nation originates from within its people, not from the outside. Somalia was not an African version of a Western state. Almost no institutions of law, no credible central government, and no authority existed there apart from clan leaders. Nation building might have an inspirational ring, but it struck me as a way to get bogged down in Somalia, not get out. The Somali factions were ultimately going to solve their political differences their own way.

That spring I was asked to introduce the President at the Memorial Day ceremony at the Vietnam Veterans

Memorial. Some veterans' groups charged that it dishonored the 58,191 names on that wall to have a "draft dodger" speak at the memorial. Other vets took the position that Bill Clinton was now commander in chief, and he had better show up, if only to earn absolution for his conduct during the war. I believed he should speak because he was the commander in chief. And, as a practical matter, if he did not make an appearance this first year, the issue would come up next year, and the next. I readily agreed to introduce him.

Over the past months, the President had become quite active in his role as commander in chief. He had visited the carrier U.S.S. *Theodore Roosevelt.* He had welcomed troops coming home from duty in Somalia. He was still, however, surrounded by young civilians without a shred of military experience or understanding. One day, my assistant, Lieutenant General Barry McCaffrey, went to the White House for a meeting. Walking through the West Wing, McCaffrey passed a young White House staffer and said, "Hello, there," to which she replied with upturned nose, "We don't talk to soldiers around here." McCaffrey was the winner of three Silver Stars and still bore disfiguring arm wounds suffered in Vietnam. He had commanded one of the crack divisions in Desert Storm. The young woman's comment rocketed back to the Pentagon and whipped through the place like a free electron. Bill Clinton was sufficiently sensitive to the gaffe so that McCaffrey was next seen at the Seattle economic summit jogging alongside the President.

As soon as word got out that I was going to introduce Bill Clinton at the Vietnam wall, I started taking flak—Powell, of all people, a two-tour veteran who had lost buddies in Vietnam, while Clinton was reading books at Oxford. I received a letter from a woman whom I knew well whose husband had been killed in the war. My participation at the memorial, she wrote, would be "dishonorable, inexcusable, and unforgivable." That kind of criticism bothered me, but Clinton's draft record did not. By the will of the American people, he was our commander in chief. My lack of resentment, however, went beyond merely owing him a soldier's allegiance. I had worked in the Reagan-Bush era with many hard-nosed men—guys ready to get tough with Soviets, Iranians, Iraqis, Nicaraguans, or Panamanians—all of whom were the right age, but most of whom had managed to avoid serving during the Vietnam War. Bill Clinton, in my judgment, had not behaved much differently from these men. The whole system of deferments and angles for escaping the fighting may have been technically legal. But it was class-ridden, undemocratic, and unjust.

On Memorial Day, the faithful Otis managed to speed me to the White House from the Georgetown University Law Center, where my son, Mike, had just graduated that morning (carrying little Jeffrey as he walked under his own steam across the stage to get his law degree). I joined the President in the Oval Office with about two minutes to spare for the drive to the Vietnam Veterans Memorial. Over the past months, Bill Clinton had given me several small gifts. Today, he handed me a pair of matching watches, a man's and a woman's, of some historical curiosity. The watches had been designed to commemorate the next opening of the East German Parliament, which, with the collapse of the communist bloc, never took place.

The President seemed relaxed and in good humor as we drove to the ceremony, chatting, sipping ice water from a big tumbler, and editing his speech. But as we neared the wall, where over five thousand people were waiting, I could see the muscles of his face tightening. We got out of the car to scattered applause and the boos of protesters, whom the park police had managed to keep on the fringe.

Jan Scruggs, who had led the long struggle to build the memorial, served as master of ceremonies. To me, the most poignant moment occurred when Kansas City Chiefs linebacker Derrick Thomas talked about growing up without a father, since his dad, an Air Force captain, had been killed in Vietnam. Finally, it was my turn to introduce the President.

"I never come here," I began, "without being touched to the depth of my soul as I run my hand over the name of a friend long departed but never forgotten." We were here, I noted, to honor the dead of all our wars, but particularly, on this occasion, to heal the injury Vietnam had caused us to inflict on ourselves. I quoted Abraham Lincoln's second inaugural address: "With malice toward none, with charity for all, with firmness in the right as God gives us to see the right, let us strive to finish the work we are in, to bind up the nation's wounds, to care for him who shall have borne the battle. . . ." As the senior Vietnam veteran on active duty, I concluded, "I want to introduce to you the commander in chief of the armed forces of the United States, President Bill Clinton."

The applause exceeded the jeering as the President made what I am sure was one of the most difficult speeches of his life, and it was a graceful effort. Afterward, as we drove away, I watched the tension flow out of him. "You stole my line," he said, chuckling. He took out one of his cue cards and handed it to me. On it were Lincoln's words that I had quoted. "It came better from you anyway," he said. "From me it would have been self-serving."

On June 10, 1993, I was to be the commencement speaker at Harvard. One of my aides pointed out that I would be speaking exactly fifty years after Winston Churchill had addressed the Harvard grads, a somewhat humbling thought. I decided to speak about the changes between two historic times, Churchill's World War II era and our post–Cold War present. However, I had early warnings that I would be walking into a protest from Harvard's gay and lesbian community, who had something else on their minds.

That day, on the Harvard campus, among a crowd of 25,000, a few hundred people held balloons aloft bearing the words "Lift the Ban." When I rose to give my speech, scattered catcalls erupted, but far more cheers, especially from the front rows, which were filled with alums from the Class of '43, back for their fiftieth reunion. Their presence moved me.

These were once young men who had heard Churchill speak, who had donned uniforms, and who had gone off and won a war against fascism.

I paid tribute to these proud veterans of the last "good war." I reviewed the revolutionary changes since the end of the Cold War. And then I addressed the immediate controversy. As for the American military's social record, I began, "We took on racism, we took on drugs. We took on scandals such as Tailhook, and we found answers to them . . . and we will do the same with the controversial issue of homosexuals in the military." Some people on the stage and in the audience turned their backs in protest as I spoke. But by the end, a steady chant by the gay-lesbian contingent was drowned out by waves of applause.

That summer, we started to bring American troops home from Somalia, intending to leave only about 4,200 to support the UN operation. By then, the Somalis were apparently feeling sufficiently well nourished to resume killing each other and any perceived enemies. On June 5, a shoot-out between followers of a major clan leader, Mohammed Farah Aidid, and UN forces left two dozen Pakistani soldiers dead. At U.S. urging, the UN passed a resolution authorizing a hunt for the perpetrators. This action was taken without any serious discussion among senior U.S. policymakers over expanding the Somalia commitment from nation building to hunting down Somali chieftains. The UN special envoy, retired American Admiral Jon Howe, put a $25,000 reward on Aidid's head. Howe, Turkish Lieutenant

General Cevik Bir, the UN commander, and the American commander, Major General Tom Montgomery, asked for U.S. helicopter gunships and AC-130 strike planes to attack Somali strongholds.

I supported the request, and the President approved. But when the UN command further pressed us to send in our elite counterterrorist Delta Force to capture Aidid, I resisted, as did Aspin and General Joe Hoar, CINC CENTCOM. Finding Aidid in the warrens of Mogadishu was a thousand-to-one shot. Worse, we were personalizing the conflict and getting deeper and deeper into ancient Somali clan rivalries. I tried to get our spreading commitment reviewed, but was unsuccessful. In the meantime, we started to take American casualties. In late August, I reluctantly yielded to the repeated requests from the field and recommended to Aspin that we dispatch the Rangers and the Delta Force. It was a recommendation I would later regret.

During April 14–16, former President Bush had visited Kuwait, where he was, apparently, the target of an assassination plot engineered by Iraq. Subsequent FBI and CIA investigations produced enough evidence linking the attempt to Saddam Hussein's regime to warrant retaliation. President Clinton, Vice President Gore, Tony Lake, Les Aspin, Warren Christopher, and I met in the White House residence and I walked the President through a proposed cruise missile strike against Iraqi intelligence headquarters in Baghdad. I explained what it might achieve, what could go wrong, possible Iraqi reactions, and the decisions the President would have to make at each stage. In effect, I was conducting a graduate-level tutorial for a national security freshman. I was curious to see how our young nonveteran President would handle his baptism of fire. Clinton passed the first test handily; he asked all the right questions. The real test would come as we went into countdown and lives were at stake; or, as we put it in the infantry, when he faced his first sucking chest wound.

On June 26, twenty-three missiles soared off U.S. Navy vessels in the Red Sea and Persian Gulf headed for Baghdad. The President was scheduled to make a television statement fifteen minutes after H-Hour. However, we ran into a communications glitch. Ordinarily, CNN had a crew in Baghdad that would have broadcast the results almost instantly, and we were counting on this report. The crew, however, had been pulled out, and hours would pass before our satellites could pass over and photograph the attack site. Within fifteen minutes the President was on the phone calling me. Had we hit the target? All I could answer was, "Sir, it's too soon to know." White House aides then got in touch with CNN's president, Tom Johnson, who called Amman, Jordan. The network's crew there phoned friends in Baghdad, who reported that the intelligence headquarters had indeed been hit.

This attack also presented the President with the cruelest aspect of military operations. Some of the missiles had missed the target and caused civilian casualties. I studied Bill Clinton's behavior closely throughout this operation, his decision-making and his emotions. He remained cool and resolute.

The long adventure that had filled thirty-five of my fifty-six years was approaching its end. In July, the British embassy gave a dinner honoring me and Sir Charles Powell, Prime Minister Thatcher's former private secretary. David Gergen, who had come aboard the Clinton team as chief imagemeister, stopped by to say hello. "You sure you want to leave?" Dave said. "You know, it wouldn't be hard for you to stay on." Legally, I could. The Goldwater-Nichols law allowed the chairman three two-year terms, and I had served two. But I was ready to go. I had had a good run. And though the Clinton national security team was now working reasonably well, I was sure my departure would not be mourned.

As for my successor, Aspin and Clinton spent a lot of time evaluating several highly qualified candidates. On August 11, the President announced that General John M. Shalikashvili, then Supreme Allied Commander Europe, would be the next chairman. If anyone asks me what institution in America provides the greatest opportunity, I say take a look at what the U.S. Army did for me and for Shalikashvili, who did not arrive in this country until he was in his teens and who rose to the top after entering the Army as a draftee.

The manhunt for Mohammed Farah Aidid went on. Major General Montgomery began pleading for tanks and armored vehicles to protect his supply convoys from raids by warlords. This threat understandably confused Americans. Why, since we had gone into Somalia to feed its starving people, were our troops being shot at? This was the quicksand that the UN "nation-building" mission had sucked us into. I had been urging Aspin for weeks to demand a policy review to find a way out. He, in turn, was frustrated that his policy team so far had produced nothing usable. Still, with our commander on the ground pleading for help to protect American soldiers, I had to back him, as I had with the Rangers and Delta Force. With only three days left in my term, I was in Les Aspin's office making one last pitch to him to give Tom Montgomery the armor he wanted.

"It ain't gonna happen," Aspin, the political realist, said. Many members of Congress, led by Senator Bob Byrd, were saying we had no further business in Somalia and should withdraw immediately. I had done what I had to do, a soldier backing soldiers. Aspin had done what a civilian policymaker has to do, try to meet the larger objective, in this case, to get us out of Somalia, not further into it.

I tried not to think much about my impending retirement. There were, however, repeated reminders. On September 20, the Pentagon's senior NCOs staged a colorful ceremony for me in the center courtyard. Though I had attained the highest commissioned rank in the military, that day I received symbolic rank that I considered a touching compliment. I was made an honorary sergeant major of the Army and the Marines, an honorary master chief petty officer in the

Navy and the Coast Guard, and a chief master sergeant of the Air Force.

On another day, a young major showed up from the Army personnel office to advise me of my benefits—pension, use of government stationery, wearing of the uniform, contributions toward burial costs. For retirement pay and Social Security purposes, he informed me, I had thirty-five years, three months, and twenty-one days of federal service. By the time he was finished, I expected him to hand me a gold watch. A day later, Lieutenant Colonel Gordy Coulson, the ceremonies officer for the Military District of Washington, came to review my departure ceremony. Coulson had often briefed me on other officers' farewells. As he took me through the familiar rituals, it finally sank in that we were talking about me. He saw the wistful look in my face, and we both started to tear up.

The night before my retirement, Les Aspin hosted a memorable farewell dinner for me. The next morning began routinely, as I put on my uniform with my favorite black wool pullover sweater. Otis was waiting for me outside, and we followed the well-worn grooves toward the Pentagon. On our arrival, my office had the hollow sound of moving day. The walls were bare. My aides had packed my bust of Thomas Jefferson, the shotgun from Mikhail Gorbachev, the Lincoln quote comparing horses and generals, a print of the railroaded Buffalo Soldier, Lieutenant Henry Flipper. Gone, too, were the aphorisms from under the glass top of my desk: "Fast Eddie, let's shoot some pool," "Only the mediocre are always at their best," "Never let 'em see you sweat," and the others.

Navy Captain Gregory "Grog" Johnson, my current executive assistant, came in to tell me that President Clinton wanted to see me. I was surprised. My retirement ceremony was scheduled for 4:00 P.M., and the President had graciously agreed to preside. I wondered what this meeting was about.

On my arrival at the White House, I was ushered up to the second-floor residential quarters, where I found Bill Clinton just back from his morning jog, buttoning up a fresh shirt. "Let's go sit on the porch," he said, leading me out to the Truman balcony. We did a little Kabuki dance over who was to sit where. He finally took a Kennedy rocker, and I sat in a lawn chair. The day was warm, with a hint of rain in the air. The Jefferson Memorial to the south basked in the morning sun. I wondered when I would ever have another view like this.

"I don't have any agenda," the President said. "I'm just grateful for what you've done for me and the country, and I wanted us to have some time together." He asked what my plans were.

"I'll be busy writing my autobiography," I said, "and I'll be hitting the speech circuit." I mentioned that I was also getting offers to join businesses and corporate boards "But," I said, "I'm not going to get involved until I've been out awhile and had a chance to think about how I want to spend the rest of my life." My immediate concern, I told him, was to make my family financially secure after my thirty-five years on government salary.

"There's some part-time public service you might like to think about after you retire," the President said. He mentioned my heading up the President's Foreign Intelligence Advisory Board, a prestigious body of civilians that evaluates U.S. intelligence activities. He also suggested that I might want to serve as chairman of the D-Day fiftieth anniversary observances or work with his national service program for young people.

"Mr. President," I said, "I think I'll sit it out for now. But if I were to take any of those spots it would be the youth program."

He smiled. "That's what I figured you'd say," he said.

We talked a little politics, a subject he clearly relished; and then we discussed domestic issues, with health care much on his mind. We turned to national security. Somalia was uppermost in my thoughts at the moment. I told him that we could not substitute our version of democracy for hundreds of years of tribalism. "We can't make a country out of that place. We've got to find a way to get out, and soon," I said.

The President admitted that he had not focused enough on the UN resolution back in June that had put us on a collision course with Aidid. "That complicated the whole nature of our involvement," he said.

I glanced at my watch. We had been talking for over an hour. "I feel guilty about taking up so much of your time," I said.

"This day's for you," Bill Clinton answered, as if he did not have a care in the world.

At that point, a frantic aide poked his head through the door and said, "Mr. President, it's time to go to work."

The President rose. "Colin, I'll see you this afternoon," he said.

I thanked him for his thoughtfulness, not just this day, but during the entire nine months that I had served him. In spite of early press speculation to the contrary, we had gotten along well and had become close.

Just days after this conversation, the Rangers and the Delta Force ran into a stiff firefight in Somalia and eighteen of our men were killed. Americans were horrified by the sight of a dead U.S. soldier being dragged through the streets of Mogadishu. We had been drawn into this place by television images; now we were being repelled by them.

The President immediately conducted a policy review that resulted in a plan for our withdrawal over the next six months. Les Aspin was severely criticized for not providing the reinforcements Montgomery had requested, even though faulty policy was the real problem. This setback marked the beginning of the end of Les Aspin's tenure at the Pentagon. In December, President Clinton announced that he would be replaced by Bill Perry. Aspin went on to other important assignments. He was appointed chairman of the President's Foreign Intelligence Advisory Board and a member of the congressionally mandated commission on roles and missions in the armed forces. He then was appointed chairman of another congressionally mandated commission examining the intelligence community. Les was perfect for these assignments. He was in his intellectual element. Tragically, his life was cut short by a stroke in May 1995.

.   .   .

After my visit to the White House, I held my final meetings and thanked the directors of the Joint Staff who had served me so faithfully for four years. I had my last lunch with the service chiefs and the CINCs. "I appreciate you guys standing this deathwatch with me," I said, as the hour of my retirement approached. They had a surprise for me. A smiling George Bush came striding into the dining room. The former President seemed happily adjusted to private life. After this friendly reunion with him, I went back to my office, took one last look at the blank walls, then went home to get Alma and to put on the "suit of lights" for the last time.

The parade ground at Fort Myer began to resemble the stage of the fifties television show *This Is Your Life* as Alma and I mounted the reviewing stand. My sister, Marilyn, and her family, cousins from all over, friends from the Pershing Rifles, comrades I had served with in Gelnhausen, Fort Devens, Vietnam, Fort Leavenworth, Fort Carson, and Frankfurt, White House Fellowship classmates, and church friends began showing up, along with George and Barbara Bush, Vice President and Mrs. Gore, former Vice President and Mrs. Quayle, Cap and Jane Weinberger, and Dick Cheney.

Just as the ceremony was about to begin, a White House military aide came to me and said that President Clinton would be presenting me with the Presidential Medal of Freedom, the nation's highest nonmilitary award. Too late, I said. I had already received the medal, along with Baker, Scowcroft, Cheney, and Schwarzkopf, from President Bush for our roles in Desert Storm. This award was an upgrade, the aide informed me, the Presidential Medal of Freedom with Distinction. "The President is going to hang it around your neck along with this sash," the aide said. The sash he held out was big and royal blue.

"Not the sash," I pleaded. "I'll look like the crown prince of Ruritania."

"The sash is negotiable," he said, "but the medal has to go around your neck."

With the arrival of the President and Mrs. Clinton, the ceremony began, and the sun suddenly broke through dark clouds as if on cue. Drum and bugle corps played, cannons fired a nineteen-gun salute, the President and I inspected the troops, and the Army band played, for the first and maybe the last time, "Eye of the Storm: The General Colin L. Powell March." The President hung the Medal of Freedom around my neck, without the resplendent sash. And Alma received the Army's Decoration for Distinguished Civilian Service. Bill Clinton then spoke about my career. I was most moved when he said, "He clearly has the warrior spirit and the judgment to know when it should be applied in the nation's behalf. . . . I speak for the families who entrusted you with their sons and daughters . . . you did well by them, as you did well by America."

It was now my turn to speak. As I looked out over this spectacle of color and pageantry, I would have had to be soul-dead not to marvel at the trajectory my life had followed, from an ROTC second lieutenant out of CCNY to the highest-ranking officer in the U.S. armed forces; from advising a few hundred men in the jungles of Vietnam to responsibility for over two million soldiers, sailors, airmen, and Marines; from growing up with tough kids in the South Bronx to association with leaders from all over the world; from a green officer who lost his pistol on his way to guard an atomic cannon to a National Security Advisor who helped superpower leaders move the world away from nuclear holocaust.

The troops passed in review. A flyover of jets and helicopters roared above the parade ground. And then the commander of the Old Guard came and saluted me. "Sir," he said, "this concludes the ceremony." It was over, thirty-five years, three months, and twenty-one days.

Afterward, the guests retreated to the Fort Myer Ceremonial Hall for refreshments. President Clinton quieted down the crowd and said that he had a present for me, one purchased through the generosity of my friends in the administration. An aide yanked a gray cloth away from an object in a corner. And there it stood in all its battered glory, a rusted-out '66 Volvo. I spotted a grinning Otis. The White House staff had commissioned him to find this clunker, for which I tried to express my profound gratitude.

That night, I took off the uniform for the last time. In the years I had worn it, I had benefited beyond my wildest hopes from all that is good in this country, and I had overcome its lingering faults. I had found something to do with my life that was honorable and useful, that I could do well, and that I loved doing. That is rare good fortune in anyone's life. My only regret was that I could not do it all over again.

21 ★ A Farewell to Arms

I WOKE UP the next morning without benefit of an alarm clock for the first time in memory. I got dressed in slacks, a polo shirt, and a pair of loafers, ambled down to the kitchen of the home we had bought in the Washington suburbs, and joined Alma for breakfast. I was embarking full-time on a job I had been moonlighting at for years, husband.

Alma looked up from her coffee. "The sink's stopped up," she said. "It's leaking all over the floor."

No problem, I thought. I'll call the post engineer. Then I remembered. What post engineer? I spent my first civilian morning crouched under a dripping sink. The Chairman of the Joint Chiefs had become Harry Homeowner.

When I stepped from four stars to civilian, overnight my personal staff of ninety disappeared. I left the Pentagon with my pension and a retiree ID card. Fortunately, Colonel Bill Smullen, my public affairs assistant, retired with me, and he, along with Peggy Cifrino, another Pentagon veteran, went to work, setting up a small office to manage my new life.

The change in my life was driven home on an afternoon not long after my retirement when I ran out of gas on the Beltway during the rush hour in one of my old Volvos. A Good Samaritan pulled up behind me, and we risked life and limb pushing the car onto the shoulder across three lanes of understandably impatient, honking homeward-bound commuters. I had on a baseball cap pulled low over my face, and no one, including my savior, recognized the man who could not keep a car gassed up as someone who had once moved armies. Just as I was about to call my office on a cellular phone, a traffic assistance officer arrived.

"What's the trouble?" he asked.

I pulled the cap down lower and explained. He delivered a standard never-run-out-of-gas-on-the-Beltway lecture, then went to the hood of his vehicle. He pulled out a hose about the diameter of a straw, squirted a half pint of gas into my tank, and left, also without recognizing me. I pulled off the Beltway at the nearest exit, got caught in another traffic jam, and ran out of gas again. I told myself, Mr. Powell, becoming a civilian is going to be harder than you expected.

I have retired from the Army, but not from an active life. Writing this autobiography has been a new adventure, and my speaking schedule is heavy. My personal life remains simple, by choice. Having seen much of the world and having lived on planes for years, I am no longer much interested in travel. And after a lifetime of bouncing from post to post, Alma loves building her own nest. When we do go away, it is usually for a few days to visit friends on

Long Island like the Ron Lauders or cousin Bruce Llewellyn. We will, however, walk barefoot in the snow to watch our actress daughter, Linda, perform. In 1994, while Michael and Jane were camping with us, waiting for their new home to be built, they had another son, Bryan. We are lucky enough to have our grandchildren living nearby, and we spend some of our happiest hours with them, the best of both worlds—the joy of having children, with little of the responsibility. Alma and I entertain quietly, exchanging occasional dinner invitations with a few friends. My idea of an enjoyable evening is to sink into an easy chair and watch old movies on TV, especially musicals, of which I love best the aforementioned *Music Man,* along with *Oklahoma!* and *Guys and Dolls.* I have seen *Casablanca, The Hustler, The Producers, The Lavender Hill Mob,* and *Moonstruck* so many times that I can spout the lines. If I am not watching movies, I am reading. My taste is eclectic, running to history and biographies of just about anybody, a few novels, and only an occasional military work.

I still like to have music in the background, as I did in the Pentagon, and calypso singers remain my favorites. I also enjoy Aretha Franklin, Carly Simon, Lou Rawls, Paul Simon, Anne Murray, Natalie Cole, and any music by Andrew Lloyd Webber. The appeal of hard rock and rap, however, escapes me, a generational block, I guess. I enjoy classical music, but do not ask me what I am listening to because I cannot distinguish one piece from another. I will watch football on television during the championship season, and I still find something wonderfully American about getting out to the park during the baseball season. But the days of my own modest athletic glory, a long-ball hitter in softball, a fair racquetball player, are over. Pumping the Lifecycle is the peak of my physical exertion nowadays. Getting grimy under the hood of a car remains my happiest pastime. My pride and joy these days is a 1966 Model 122 Volvo station wagon painted bile green, with about one trip to the moon on the odometer. I picked it up for $500, and only had to invest another $1,000 to get it running.

Since retirement, Alma and I have taken one trip that was like the end of a Horatio Alger dime novel. My parents kept a little safe, and one day after Mom died, I went over the contents—a few hundred dollars in cash, a couple of rings, a crude oilcloth billfold, with a dollar in it, which I had made in the second grade, and which my father could never throw away. The real treasure turned out to be the British passports that my folks carried when they came to America, containing the earliest photographs I have of them. I took out those pictures and studied them just before Alma and I left for London in December 1993. The son of those two solemn-faced black immigrants from a tiny British colony was off to be knighted by the queen of England.

On December 15, we were in our hotel getting dressed for our audience at Buckingham Palace. The usually cool Alma kept fidgeting over her outfit. I thought she looked regal. On our arrival, we were escorted to a waiting room, where the queen's equerry explained the procedure. "When you enter," he instructed us, "Her Majesty will come forward and present you with your KCB"—I was to be made a Knight Commander of the Order of the Bath. "You'll then withdraw, unless she asks you to be seated." I had heard about this distinction: dismissed meant "B" list, being asked to sit meant "A" list.

What looked like a wall suddenly opened, and we entered a room filled with ornate gilded furniture. "General and Mrs. Colin Powell," the equerry announced.

As Queen Elizabeth came toward us, she passed by a table and casually swept up something. "How nice to see you again, General and Mrs. Powell," she said, then added, "I'm pleased to give you this," and handed me a box containing my decoration.

That was it. Since I was an American, there would be no bending of the knee, no tap on the shoulder with the royal sword. And Alma did not have to master the curtsy.

"Won't you sit down," the queen said. We did and had a stimulating fifteen-minute conversation on topics ranging from the state of the world to the beastly weather. And then we left.

Had my parents remained British subjects, I would now be "Sir Colin" and Alma "Lady Powell." On the other hand, if my parents had stayed in Jamaica, I can't imagine I would ever have been knighted. If Luther and Arie had shipped out for Southampton instead of New York City, I might have made sergeant major in a modest British regiment, but not likely British chief of defense staff. I treasure my family's British roots, but I love our America, land of opportunity.

After leaving the palace, Alma and I entered a Bentley driven by a uniformed chauffeur. The driver turned, smiling, and said, "Lady Powell, where would you like to go?" Correct or not, the phrase had a pleasant ring.

"To Harrods," Alma said.

On May 10, 1994, I found myself sitting with dignitaries from all over the world in front of the Union Building on a hill over Pretoria watching the once unimaginable happen. To the cheers of tens of thousands of people filling the hillside, four white senior officers of the South African armed forces formed an honor guard to escort their country's next president, Nelson Mandela, to the stage. As an African-American, I was proud; as a member of the human race, I was inspired; and as a student of world affairs, I was amazed by this act of reconciliation.

The week before, President Clinton had invited me to join the U.S. delegation to the inauguration, which was to be led by Vice President and Mrs. Gore and would include Mrs. Clinton, several members of Congress and the cabinet, and prominent African-Americans who had long supported Mandela. It is no secret that the vast majority of American blacks are Democrats and that far more are liberal than conservative. On the flight to South Africa, my fellow passengers included the Reverend Jesse Jackson, Senator Carol Moseley-Braun, members of Congress Charles Rangel, Ron Dellums, Kweisi Mfume, Louis Stokes, and Maxine Waters, cabinet members Ron Brown and Mike Espy, and former Mayor David Dinkins of New York and Mayor Carl Schmoke of

Baltimore. I knew most of them already, and we had always gotten along well. I also knew that African-Americans were proud of the historic firsts my career represented. My fellow passengers, however, would have preferred me to have succeeded under different auspices. In the eyes of this group, I was a product of those trickle-down conservative Republicans Reagan and Bush. As Jesse Jackson put it, I should be judged as a soldier faithfully doing his duty, even if those duties required me to carry out "repressive policies."

During this long flight, though, we left rank and politics at the terminal. We had warm, funny, easy conversations. We joked about pretending to be asleep in order to avoid being trapped by Jesse Jackson's aisle monologues. C. DeLores Tucker, from the National Political Congress of Black Women, told me, "Colin, you should go into politics, and I mean as a Democrat. You're too nice to be a Republican."

On this occasion, partisan politics were secondary. We were Americans first, in Africa to watch something unfold that we had hoped for but never dared imagine. The day was brilliantly choreographed. A chorus sang the old white anthem "The Call of South Africa," and then "Nkosi Sikelel'i," "God Bless Africa," the Black Freedom national anthem. Jewish, Muslim, Hindu, and Christian clerics (including Bishop Desmond Tutu) delivered invocations. In a nine-minute inaugural address, Mandela sounded the statesman's themes of racial peace and reconciliation. Four jets flew overhead, releasing different-colored smoke representing the new South African flag, the colors mingling in the planes' wake like the hopes of this newly free nation. Apartheid was dead, and South Africa had moved from a pariah state to a role model for Africa. It was a breathtaking moment. Mandela the protester, Mandela the prisoner, was now Mandela the president.

After the inauguration, while we were waiting for the bus to the U.S. embassy, Dellums, Mfume, and I broke into our doo-wop version of "In the Still of the Night," backed by an integrated South African choir. On the flight home, I played poker with Charlie Rangel, Dave Dinkins, and Mike Espy, who was the big loser. The moral: never play cards with three brothers from New York. I enjoyed the camaraderie. C. Payne Lucas, head of the organization Africare, told me just before we left South Africa, "Know what the brothers and sisters are saying? 'Hey, Powell's all right. Forget the Reagan-Bush stuff. He's just another black kid like you and me.' " Before, we had all been friendly enough. Now they saw me as one of them.

What I witnessed in Pretoria was much on my mind a few days later when I went to deliver the commencement speech at historically black Howard University. Howard had recently become the eye of a racial hurricane after speakers on the campus connected to the Black Muslim Nation of Islam had publicly denounced Jews. The speeches had caused an uproar in the Jewish community, and Howard was being sharply criticized for providing a platform for race-baiting. One thing that had impressed me in South Africa was that Nelson Mandela had invited to his inauguration three jailers from his twenty-seven-year imprisonment. He had simply refused to let the acid of race hatred destroy his humanity. The previous week, we had witnessed Arabs and Jews put aside their ancient enmity as Israel's prime minister, Yitzhak Rabin, and the PLO's chairman, Yassir Arafat, signed a once unimaginable agreement on Palestinian self-rule. And then they shook hands. I thought about the turmoil at Howard, and I knew the message I had to deliver.

That Saturday, as I spoke on a lovely summer's day, I pulled up something from the marrow of my beliefs as a black living in a white-majority society. "African-Americans have come too far and we have too far yet to go," I said, "to take a detour into the swamp of hatred." My Howard speech received unusually wide media coverage, not because I was more eloquent than other commencement speakers that spring, but because my denouncing race hatred from any quarter was an apparently welcome message.

On Thursday, September 15, 1994, former President Jimmy Carter phoned me to ask if I would join him and Senator Sam Nunn on a mission to Haiti to stave off a potentially bloody invasion. The UN had recently authorized the use of force to topple the island's military dictatorship and to return Jean-Bertrand Aristide to power. The whole world knew that the United States was on the verge of invading. I told the former President that I would go if President Clinton wanted us to do it.

That afternoon, Bill Clinton did call. "Jimmy Carter is sometimes a wild card," he told me. "But I took a chance on him in North Korea, and that didn't turn out too badly." The President's main concern was that Carter would go to Haiti, "and the next thing you know, I'm expected to call off the invasion because he's negotiating a deal." He had no intention of halting the invasion, Clinton told me. But we could go with his blessing, provided we stuck to negotiating only how, not if, our troops would go ashore.

On Friday night, I returned home late from a speech in Ohio and had just enough time to pack and catch a few winks before joining Carter and Nunn early Saturday morning. Accompanying us were Michael Kozak, the State Department's special negotiator to Haiti; Larry Rossin, director of inter-American affairs at the NSC; Tom Ross, Secretary Harold Brown's former public affairs advisor at Defense, now with the NSC; Major General Jerry Bates, deputy operations chief of the Joint Staff; and Robert Pastor, a veteran Latin American hand. We arrived at Port-au-Prince on Saturday at 12:30 P.M. At that point, though neither we nor the Haitians knew it, H-Hour for the invasion was set for one minute after midnight, Monday, September 19, less than thirty-six hours away.

We were taken to the Haitian military headquarters and led up to a second-floor corner office to meet General Raoul Cedras, leader of the ruling junta, a lean, sallow man with a long, pointed chin and nose. He introduced us to his colleagues, including the chief of the army, Brigadier General Philippe Biamby, another junta leader, and as he did so, I noticed an M-16 assault rifle, loaded with a banana clip, leaning against the wall. The tension in the air made me decide never to be too far away from that M-16. I was also surprised to see hanging on Cedras's wall photographs of the six U.S. officers who had run Haiti during the 1915–34 occupation. I mentioned them. "We never forget our history," Cedras said with an enigmatic smile.

We sat down at a conference table, where Jimmy Carter made clear that the invasion was inevitable. Our hope, he explained, was to make it happen peacefully rather than bloodily. Carter started laying out attractive terms to persuade the junta to give up the fight, including amnesty and an offer that Cedras and the others might not be barred from returning to Haiti at some time in the future. Cedras was offended. "Our constitution does not allow exile," he said.

The first meeting broke up inconclusively at about 2:00 P.M. Thirty-four hours to H-Hour. Our party retired to the Hotel Villa Creole in the hills above the city for a courtesy meeting with Haitian parliamentarians. Later, we had dinner with prominent business leaders. What struck me was how sleek, well-fed, and well-dressed these men looked after almost three years of economic embargo had impoverished the rest of their countrymen. So much for sanctions. One useful piece of intelligence did come out of the dinner. A Haitian entrepreneur, Marc Bazin, told me, "If you want to get through to Cedras, his wife is the key."

At 11:00 P.M., we met again with Cedras and his circle. Carter had drafted an agreement, which we argued over for hours. The junta resisted having to leave Haiti as the draft required. "We will not go," Cedras said. "It is not only unconstitutional, it is a stain on our integrity."

I thought, as a fellow army officer, that I might be able to reach these men by appealing to soldierly honor. It did not matter if they had any honor, as long as they thought they did. "You have to decide what course is honorable," I said, looking around the table. "What military code calls for the senseless sacrifice of life? Let me tell you what true honor is. It means having the courage to give up power rather than cause pointless death." Cedras and the others listened intently, but conceded nothing.

Senator Nunn registered two key points from his perspective. "You should know," he said, "that the U.S. Congress will back the President." And Nunn pointed out that democracy meant more than simply replacing the junta with the elected president. "It also means allowing a functioning parliament."

I could not tell if Carter's terms, Nunn's arguments, or my psychological gambit made any dent. The meeting ended, again without resolution, but we had an invitation to come to Cedras's house early on Sunday morning, where we would meet his wife.

As we began to leave, a Colonel Dorelien, the personnel chief of the Haitian armed forces, started to shake hands with Jimmy Carter, then suddenly pulled back. "Have you shaken hands with Aristide recently?" the colonel asked.

"No," Carter said. "Why?"

"His spirit would still be on you," Dorelien said, "and I would not like to be touched by it."

It was nearly 2:00 A.M. when we parted. Twenty-two hours to H-Hour.

Early Sunday morning we were at Cedras's house, a Mediterranean-style villa set amid lush tropical gardens. Yannick Prosper Cedras, the general's wife, turned out to be a striking woman with glossy black hair and a café au lait complexion. She was the daughter of a general, she told us, and the wife of a general, and to her, honor counted above all else. She described how the night before, she and her husband had climbed into bed with their three children and told them that this could be their last night on earth. They had to be prepared to give up their lives for honor. "We would rather die with American bullets in our chests," she said, "than as traitors, with Haitian bullets in our backs."

"My wife," I responded, "would understand perfectly your loyalty as a general's wife, but I tell you, there is no honor in throwing away lives when the outcome is already determined. You and your husband should accept the inevitable and spare Haiti further suffering. Let's talk about life and not death." Carter and Nunn pressed the same argument. She remained noncommittal.

Her husband reminded us that it was time to meet with the Haitian president, Emile Jonassaint (whom the U.S. did not recognize). As we were leaving, Mrs. Cedras said, "My husband will do what is right. And whatever that is, I will support him." We had shifted her, at least, from opposition to neutrality.

At the Presidential Palace, we met Jonassaint, an eighty-one-year-old man of serene dignity who spoke elegant French and punctuated his speech with waves of his long, thin, delicately shaped hands. Then it was back to the military headquarters to try yet again to get Cedras to accept Carter's terms. It was now 9:00 A.M., fifteen hours to H-Hour. And we faced a new time bind. We were in constant touch with President Clinton, who told us we had to be out of Haiti by noon—three hours away. We asked the White House for more time.

At military headquarters, Cedras presented a completely unacceptable counterproposal. He wanted to negotiate how many American troops, tanks, and guns would be allowed ashore. That, he was told, was out of the question. It was time to lay it on the line. I leaned across the table. "Let me make sure you understand what you're facing," I said. I began ticking off on my fingers: two aircraft carriers, two and a half infantry divisions, twenty thousand troops, helicopter gunships, tanks, artillery. I kept it up, watching the Haitians' spirits sink under the weight of the power I was describing.

"We used to be the weakest nation in the hemisphere," Cedras said with a pained smile. "After this, we'll be the strongest."

At 4:00, Biamby burst into the room. "The invasion is coming!" he shouted. He had just been on the phone with a source at Fort Bragg, he told us, and American paratroopers were getting ready to board their aircraft at 5:00 P.M. Not bad intelligence, I thought, for a poor country.

With the clock running out, we hit an impasse. President Clinton had instructed us that we could not leave Carter's amnesty offer open-ended. The junta had to step down by October 15, whether the Haitian parliament granted amnesty or not. "We cannot accept," Cedras said. "This is a matter for our civilian authorities." Remembering that Jonassaint had behaved like more than a figurehead, we suggested taking up the matter with him. Cedras assented. We raced through the crowds to the cars outside to drive to the Presidential Palace. I rode with Cedras in his car. Hand grenades rolled around on the floor. And in the back was a Haitian soldier clutching an assault rifle.

We ran up the steps of the palace to Jonassaint's office, where the old leader was waiting with his ministers of foreign affairs, defense, and information. As Jimmy Carter laid out the terms for stopping the invasion, I got word to call President Clinton. I found a phone in a nearby office and managed to dial straight through to the White House. "Mr. President," I said, "I think we've got some movement here. We just need more time." Clinton was uneasy. He was not going to change the invasion timetable, he said, but we could keep talking a little longer.

When I got back to Jonassaint's office, his minister of defense was fuming, "These terms are outrageous. I'll resign first," he said.

"Then resign," Jonassaint said calmly.

The minister of information spoke up. Our proposal was "disgraceful," he charged, and he also threatened to quit. Jonassaint gave him a dismissive wave. "We have too many ministers already," he said. "I am going to sign this proposal. I will not let my people suffer further tragedy. I choose peace."

Cedras and the others yielded to Jonassaint's decision. I took that moment to tell Cedras, "We expect an ironclad assurance from you that our troops will not be attacked when they come ashore. Remember, we can turn this invasion back on as easily as we can turn it off."

"I will obey the orders of my president," he said, looking to Jonassaint.

"You have our assurance," the old man said, nodding.

English and French translations of the documents were prepared, and Carter and Jonassaint signed them. The storming of Haiti had been averted at H-Hour minus six.

The next day, American troops, led by Lieutenant General Hugh Shelton, commander of XVIII Airborne Corps, landed peacefully to the cheers of the Haitian people. Three weeks later, Cedras and his cronies were out of the country. And on October 15, President Aristide made his triumphal reentry into Port-au-Prince.

The agreement we worked out was criticized. The "thugs" supposedly got off too easily. I was attacked for playing on the honor of dishonorable men. The criticism did not bother me. Once Lieutenant General Shelton and his troops set foot in Haiti, for better or worse, we ran the place. What happened to the junta was inconsequential. Because of what we accomplished, young Americans, and probably far more Haitians, who would have died were still alive. That was success enough for me.

The real credit goes to three Presidents—Bill Clinton, for taking a politically risky eleventh-hour gamble to avoid an invasion; Jimmy Carter, for his imagination and dogged determination to find peaceful solutions to crises; and Emil Jonassaint, who was wise enough to provide his overmatched generals with the cover they needed to quit. Only time will tell, however, whether the Haitians will be successful in their quest for democracy.

I have had one other brush with foreign policy since my retirement. Near midnight on Saturday evening, December 17, 1994, I was in my study reading when the phone rang. I had a good idea who was calling. That afternoon, Vernon Jordan had stopped by the house unexpectedly and told me that President Clinton wanted to talk to me about a job in the administration. Washington at the time was swirling with rumors that Warren Christopher wanted to step down as Secretary of State. Christopher had been working tirelessly, but was taking heavy criticism for a U.S. foreign policy that seemed adrift, without coherence or consistency. Jordan confirmed to me that Christopher did in fact want to leave. State was the position the President wanted to talk about. I asked Vernon if he could derail the call. He smiled and said, "No way."

I answered the phone that evening, and a White House operator asked me to stand by for the President. When he came on the line, I said jokingly, "I hope you're not asking me to sign on for another Carter mission." The former President was about to leap into private diplomacy again, this time in Bosnia. Clinton laughed and said no, but he would like me to drop by the next morning for a chat.

I arrived at the White House diplomatic entrance at 8:00 A.M. I talked briefly with Secret Service agents, who had had a busy night. Someone had taken pot-shots at the White House the day before, and on my arrival, agents were still finding spent bullets inside.

I went up to the residential quarters, where the President greeted me and led me to his study. We sat down and chatted for a time, particularly about Bosnia and Haiti. And then he told me that Warren Christopher wanted to leave. Would I be interested in the post?

I had been giving the matter hard thought ever since Vernon Jordan's visit. I told the President that I was honored to be asked, but, respectfully, I had to decline. "I've only been out of government a little over a year," I said. I had some major commitments, particularly completing my autobiography for my publisher. Beyond that, I added, "Alma and I would really like a longer break from public life." We had finally managed to recapture a private life, and we wanted more time to enjoy our family and to think about our future. I had turned down a feeler for the same position from Jordan the year before for similar reasons.

Left unspoken were my reservations about the amorphous way the administration handled foreign policy, a style with which I was already familiar. I did not see how I could fit back into this operation without changes so radical that the President would probably have difficulty making them. Still, it was a hard call for me. If the nation had faced an immediate crisis, it would have been impossible to say no. That was not the case. The President faced a likely vacancy, not an emergency. He accepted my answer graciously, and we went on to talk of other matters. I left shortly afterward. We have continued ever since to stay in close touch, frequently discussing domestic and foreign policy issues.

As for the Secretary of State post, Warren Christopher, as deeply committed a public servant as I have ever known, agreed to stay on.

An Epilogue

From the privacy of retirement, I watch a fundamental transformation of a world I knew so well for the thirty-five years of my career. That world was defined by an historic struggle between the Soviet Union and the West with rules that structured our political, economic, and military relations. It was a dangerous period, but relatively stable, and one in which we understood the role we had to play. With the end of the Soviet Union and the death of communism as an ideology, we face a world so far without a new structure or a new set of rules. Our strategy of containment died with the Soviet Union.

Yet, however different the world, the United States remains its leader. We are still the foundation on which Western security rests, and we are increasingly looked to as the foundation upon which the newly freed nations of Eastern Europe want their security to rest. America is trusted and respected as no other nation on earth. This trust comes not only out of respect for our military, economic, and political power, but from the power of the democratic values we hold dear. The Cold War was ultimately won not by armies marching, but by triumphant democratic ideals that proved superior to every competing ideology. Democracy, the rights of men and women, and the power of free markets are proving themselves around the world. We see it happening in Latin America, Asia, parts of Africa, and wherever else these principles have the opportunity to take root.

In this new world, economic strength will be more important than military strength. The new order will be defined by trade relations, by the flow of information, capital, technology, and goods, rather than by armies glaring at each other across borders. Nations seeking power through military strength, the development of nuclear weapons, terrorism, or tyrannical governments are mining "fool's gold." They can never hope to match or challenge the military and economic power of the free world led by the United States. Despotic regimes will come to realize it in due course, when they find themselves left behind while free nations prosper and provide a better life for their people. One only has to look at China to see a nation slowly finding a place in the world, not through the strength of the People's Liberation Army or Mao's Little Red Book, but through the release of the creative entrepreneurial power of the Chinese people. In Vietnam, American businesses are being invited in to repair the economic disaster created by two decades of "victorious" communism. We should encourage and support these impulses. Only Marxist Cuba and North Korea still cling to a political and ideologic corpse, perhaps hoping for protection under the endangered species act. But even they cannot escape the tide of history, and we must begin to adjust our policies of Cold War isolation to hasten their integration into a new world.

I am heartened by the reconciliations taking place around the globe, by a fundamental shift from chronic conflict to negotiated settlements. The IRA and Britain, the Middle East peace process, South Africa, Angola, Mozambique, Cambodia, El Salvador, Nicaragua, all offer examples of once-intractable conflicts resolving themselves through the exhaustion of the protagonists and diplomatic intervention, especially on the part of the United Nations. The way ahead for these nations will not be easy or without violence, but I believe their commitment to reconciliation will prevail in the end.

Still, this is not going to be a world without war or conflict. Bosnia and Chechnya remind us of the force of factional, nationalist passions. Islamic fundamentalism, misused for political purposes, has the potential to destabilize the underbelly of Eurasia. Nuclear proliferation, although limited to a few rogue nations, still leaves a menacing cloud over the planet. And we are currently witnessing the chaos that occurs when states revert to anarchy, tribalism, and feudalism, as in Somalia, Rwanda, Burundi, Liberia, and Sierra Leone. Television delivers tragic scenes from these places into our living rooms nightly, and we naturally want to do something to relieve the suffering we witness. Often, our desire to help collides with the cold calculus of national interest. In none of these recent foreign crises have we had a vital interest such as we had after Iraq's invasion of Kuwait and the resulting threat to Saudi Arabia and the free flow of oil. These later crises do not affect any of our treaty obligations or our survival as a nation. Our humanitarian instincts have been touched, which is something quite different. Americans are willing to commit their diplomatic, political, and economic resources to help others. We proudly and readily allow our young sons and daughters in uniform to participate in humanitarian enterprises far from home. In no other way could the Somalis, for example, have been saved so quickly from starvation in 1992. But when the fighting starts, as it did in Somalia, and American lives are at risk, our people rightly demand to know what vital interest that sacrifice serves.

I believe it unlikely that a single new strategy to define our role in the world, one with the same coherence as the old strategy of containment, will emerge. Yet, this unformed, unnamed new era holds out the promise of a bright new beginning. As I write, our nation is not at war anywhere. Nor do we have the requirement imposed on us by containment to support unpalatable regimes that do not adhere to accepted democratic principles. And let us not forget the towering achievement of this past half century, our victory in the Cold War. Nuclear annihilation, the horrific possibility that hung over the world as long as East and West were locked in distrust, no longer threatens. A despotic expansionist empire, whose military might once matched our own, is gone, pulled down by its own malignancy. Free enterprise has outrun state-dominated economic systems. Individual liberty has shown its supremacy over police-state conformity. This is the victory of freedom that our generation leaves the world. I feel privileged beyond measure to have taken part in so historic an era.

During my service in both military and civilian national security posts, I studiously avoided doing or saying anything political, and it has taken me a while to shed the lifetime habits of a soldier. Gradually, however, as I speak around the country, the reticence is leaving and my philosophy is evolving. Most of all, I am impressed by our nation's present entrepreneurial vitality. Free enterprise is alive and well. Old-line firms are scraping off the barnacles and rust and becoming competitive again. New generations of Americans are bustling, taking risks, making deals, creating new businesses, determined to compete in world markets and to ride the technological wave into the future. Everything I observe affirms my belief in free enterprise. It creates new wealth, generates new jobs, enables people to live good lives, fuels demand, and triggers fresh enterprises, starting the cycle all over again. Government should not interfere with the demonstrated success of the free marketplace, beyond controls to protect public safety and to prevent distortions of competition by either labor or industry.

I am concerned, however, that the present tax burden on Americans is so high that it seriously risks dampening our entrepreneurial vitality. Every tax dollar taken away from a consumer or a business is a dollar that will be spent less efficiently than if left in private hands.

I believe so strongly in job-producing free enterprise because jobs are the best answer to most of our social ills. My parents came to this country looking not for government support, but for job opportunities. They labored all their lives at jobs provided by a thriving garment industry. They earned a modest wage, yet enough to live a good life, raise their children, and enjoy a few luxuries.

Because I express these beliefs, some people have rushed to hang a Republican label around my neck. I am not, however, knee-jerk antigovernment. I was born a New Deal, Depression-era kid. Franklin Roosevelt was a hero in my boyhood home. Government helped my parents by providing cheap public subway systems so that they could get to work, and public schools for their children, and protection under the law to make sure their labor was not exploited. My mother's International Ladies Garment Workers Union, with its right to bargain collectively secured by law, also protected her. Social Security allowed my parents to live a dignified retirement. Medicare gave them access to quality care during long, painful terminal illnesses. I received a free college education because New York taxed its citizens to make this investment in the sons and daughters of immigrants and the working class.

The great domestic political challenge of our time is to reconcile the necessity for fiscal responsibility with the explosive growth in entitlement programs, including Social Security and Medicare, which the needy and the middle class rely on so heavily. Realistically, we have only two alternatives; either we reduce the entitlement system or we raise taxes to pay for it. We cannot keep balancing the books by increasing the deficit. Yet many politicians want to exempt such programs from serious fiscal scrutiny because to do otherwise risks political suicide. However, until our leaders are willing to talk straight to the American people and the people are willing to accept hard realities, no solution will be found to relieve our children and grandchildren of the crushing debt that we are currently amassing as their inheritance. I say all this, of course, fully aware that it is easy for me to do so since, so far, I have never had to ask anyone to vote for me.

While the current call for "less government" is justified, in one role I want government to be vigorous and active, and that is in ensuring the protections of the Constitution to all Americans. Our Constitution and our national conscience demand that every American be accorded dignity and respect, receive the same treatment under the law, and enjoy equal opportunity. The hard-won civil rights legislation of the 1960s, which I benefited from, was fought for by presently derided liberals, courageous leaders who won these gains over the opposition of those hiding behind transparent arguments of "states' rights" and "property rights."

Equal rights and equal opportunity, however, mean just that. They do not mean preferential treatment. Preferences, no matter how well intended, ultimately breed resentment among the nonpreferred. And preferential treatment demeans the achievements that minority Americans win by their own efforts. The present debate over affirmative action has a lot to do with definitions. If affirmative action means programs that provide equal opportunity, then I am all for it. If it leads to preferential treatment, or helps those who no longer need help, I am opposed. I benefited from equal opportunity and affirmative action in the Army, but I was not shown preference. The Army, as a matter of fairness, made sure that performance would be the only measure of advancement. When equal performance does not result in equal advancement, then something is wrong with the system, and our leaders have an obligation to fix it. If a history of discrimination has made it difficult for certain Americans to meet standards, it is only fair to provide temporary means to help them catch up and compete on equal terms. Affirmative action in the best sense promotes equal consideration, not reverse discrimination. Discrimination "for" one group means, inevitably, discrimination "against" another; and all discrimination is offensive.

To sum up my political philosophy, I am a fiscal conservative with a social conscience.

I have found my philosophy, if not my political affiliation. Neither of the two major parties fits me comfortably in its present state. Granted, politics is the art of compromise, but for now I prefer not to compromise just so that I can say I belong to this or that party. I am troubled by the political passion of those on the extreme right who seem to claim divine wisdom on political as well as spiritual matters. God provides us with guidance and inspiration, not a legislative agenda. I am disturbed by the class and racial undertones beneath the surface of their rhetoric. On the other side of the spectrum, I am put off by patronizing liberals who claim to know what is best for society but devote little thought to who will eventually pay the bills. I question the priorities of those liberals who lavish so much attention on individual license and entitlements that little concern is left for the good of the community at large. I distrust rigid ideology from any direction, and I am discovering that many Americans feel just as I do. The time may be at hand for a third major party to emerge to represent this sensible center of the American political spectrum.

I have served three Presidents, three quite different men, each of whom I admire, however differently they filled the office. On the personal level, Ronald Reagan was a father figure to me, George Bush an older brother, and Bill Clinton, though almost ten years younger, something of a contemporary—Clinton and I were shaped by the sixties and the specter of Vietnam, though we came at the war from opposite poles. As a result of my service to these men, I have had a privileged view of the nation's highest office. I know what it demands. As I speak around the country, I am constantly questioned about my own future: specifically, am I going to run for President? I am flattered by my standing in public opinion polls. I am moved by the encouragement to run that I hear as I travel around the country. I am honored by the grass-roots draft movements that have sprung up on my behalf, though I have no personal connection to them. To be a successful politician, however, requires a calling that I do not yet hear. I believe that I can serve my country in other ways, through charities, educational work, or appointive posts.

Nevertheless, I do not unequivocally rule out a political future. If I ever do decide to enter politics, it will not be because of high popularity ratings in the polls. I am fully aware that in taking stands on issues, I would quickly alienate one interest group or another and burn off much popularity. And I would certainly not run simply because I saw myself as the "Great Black Hope," providing a role model for African-Americans or a symbol to whites of racism overcome. I would enter only because I had a vision for this country. I would enter because I believed I could do a better job than the other candidates of solving the nation's problems. I would not expect or desire to have anything handed to me; I would fight for the right to lead. And I would enter not to make a statement but to win. I understand the battlefield, and I know what winning takes.

I am fully aware of the enormous personal and family sacrifices that running for office demands. And, frankly, the present atmosphere does not make entering public service especially attractive. I find that civility is being driven from our political discourse. Attack ads and negative campaigns produce destructive, not constructive, debate. Democracy has always been noisy, but now, on television and radio talk shows, and with print chasing after broadcast audiences, demagoguery and character dismemberment displace reasoned dialogue. As you dial through the current flood of talk shows, you will hear endless whining and not much constructive advice for our country. Any public figure espousing a controversial idea can expect to have not just the idea attacked, but his or her integrity. And Lord help anyone who strays from accepted ideas of political correctness. The slightest suggestion of offense toward any group, however innocently made, and even when made merely to illustrate a historical point, will be met with cries that the offender be fired or forced to undergo sensitivity training, or threats of legal action.

Ironically, for all the present sensitivity over correctness, we seem to have lost our sense of shame as a society. Nothing seems to embarrass us; nothing shocks us anymore. Spend time switching channels on daytime television and you will find a parade of talk shows serving up dysfunctional people whose morally vacant behavior offers the worst possible models for others. None of this mass voyeurism is more offensive to me than the use of black "guests" by talk-show producers, reinforcing the most demeaning racial stereotypes. At least in the old days of *Amos 'n' Andy,* Amos was happily married and hardworking, and he and his wife together were raising sweet little Arabella, who said her prayers every night.

We say we are appalled by the rise of sexually transmitted disease, by the wave of teenage pregnancies, by violent crime. Yet we drench ourselves in depictions of explicit sex and crime on television, in movies, and in pop music. Language that I heard—and used—only on all-male Army posts is now scripted into the mouths of women, even children.

A sense of shame is not a bad moral compass. I remember how easy it was for my mother to snap me back into line with a simple rebuke: "I'm ashamed of you. You embarrassed the family." I would have preferred a beating to hearing those words. I wonder where our national sense of shame has gone.

As I travel around the country, I invite questions from my audiences, which range from trade associations to motivational seminars, from prison inmates to the youngsters at my pride and joy, the Colin L. Powell Elementary School in Woodlands, Texas. What people ask gives me a good idea of what is on America's mind. To my surprise, they seldom mention the headline issues—abortion, gun control, welfare, affirmative action, and the like. Their questions more often express a yearning. They seem to be searching for a guiding star that we have lost sight of. They see good order breaking down. They see violence so commonplace that it has lost the power to shock. They see a judicial system that threatens to become a form of public entertainment, losing its majesty and authority.

American voters channel-surfed right past a Republican President in 1992 and a Democratic Congress in 1994, looking, in my judgment, not so much for a different party but for a different spirit in the land, something better. How do we find our way again? How do we reestablish moral standards? How do we end the ethnic fragmentation that is making us an increasingly hyphenated people? How do we restore a sense of family to our national life? On the speech circuit, I tell a story that goes to the heart of America's longing. The ABC correspondent Sam Donaldson was interviewing a young African-American soldier in a tank platoon on the eve of battle in Desert Storm. Donaldson asked, "How do you think the battle will go? Are you afraid?"

"We'll do okay. We're well trained. And I'm not afraid," the GI answered, gesturing toward his buddies around him. "I'm not afraid because I'm with my family."

The other soldiers shouted, "Tell him again. He didn't hear you."

The soldier repeated: "This is my family and we'll take care of each other."

That story never fails to touch me or the audience. It is a metaphor for what we have to do as a nation. We have to start thinking of America as a family. We have to stop screeching at each other, stop hurting each other, and instead start caring for, sacrificing for, and sharing with each other. We have to stop constantly criticizing, which is the way of the malcontent, and instead get back to the can-do attitude that made America. We have to keep trying, and risk failing, in order to solve this country's problems. We cannot move forward if cynics and critics swoop down and pick apart anything that goes wrong to a point where we lose sight of what is right, decent, and uniquely good about America.

Like that soldier in Desert Storm, we have to achieve the blessings of family; and we should begin with the restoration of real families. We need to restore the social model of married parents bringing into the world a desired child, a child to be loved and nurtured, to be taught a sense of right and wrong, to be educated to his or her maximum potential in a society that provides opportunities for work and a fulfilling life. Simple to say; difficult to achieve; yet the ideal toward which we must never stop striving.

My travels since leaving the Army two years ago have deepened my love for our country and our people. It is a love full of pride for our virtues and with patience for our failings. We are a fractious nation, always searching, always dissatisfied, yet always hopeful. We have an infinite capacity to rejuvenate ourselves. We are self-correcting. And we are capable of caring about each other. In this season of our discontent, I find it heartening to look back. Remember during the sixties and seventies when people wondered how we could survive the assassinations of John, Martin, and Bobby, and a war that tore us apart, riots in front of the White House, and the resignations in disgrace of a Vice President and a President? Some counted us out, another once great empire in terminal decline. But we came roaring back, while other empires fell instead. We will prevail over our present trials. We will come through because our founders bequeathed us a political system of genius, a system flexible enough for all ages and inspiring noble aspirations for all time. We will continue to flourish because our diverse American society has the strength, hardiness, and resilience of the hybrid plant we are. We will make it because we know we are blessed, and we will not throw away God's gift to us.

Jefferson once wrote, "There is a debt of service due from every man to his country, proportioned to the bounties which nature and fortune have measured to him." As one who has received so much from his country, I feel that debt heavily, and I can never be entirely free of it. My responsibility, our responsibility as lucky Americans, is to try to give back to this country as much as it has given to us, as we continue our American journey together.

Colin Powell's Rules

1. It ain't as bad as you think. It will look better in the morning.
2. Get mad, then get over it.
3. Avoid having your ego so close to your position that when your position falls, your ego goes with it.
4. It can be done!
5. Be careful what you choose. You may get it.
6. Don't let adverse facts stand in the way of a good decision.
7. You can't make someone else's choices. You shouldn't let someone else make yours.
8. Check small things.
9. Share credit.
10. Remain calm. Be kind.
11. Have a vision. Be demanding.
12. Don't take counsel of your fears or naysayers.
13. Perpetual optimism is a force multiplier.

Acknowledgments

I thank first of all my literary agent, Marvin Josephson, for gently guiding me to decide to write this book. Without Marvin's early encouragement and patient explanations of what I was getting myself into, the memoir might have remained merely a passing idea. During the writing, Marvin continued to be a source of inspiration and constructive criticism, for which I will be forever grateful.

Once the decision to write the book was made, I had to find a collaborator. The search, in the beginning, did not go well. Then, just the day before my retirement, into my office strode Joseph E. Persico, tall, white-haired, a few years older than me, carrying an ancient briefcase, dressed like a rumpled, tweedy professor, his glasses hanging from a cord around his neck. As he crossed the room, he took it all in before turning to me for a handshake. He did not seem to be the least bit impressed by his first visit to the Pentagon and the office of the Chairman of the Joint Chiefs of Staff, or by me. I had found my collaborator. Joe is a master of the science and art of writing. He has kept me on course for the past two years. More than a collaborator, he has been my mentor, nag, minister, and above all, my partner and friend. *My American Journey* is my story, but our book. I could not have carried out this project without Joe. With him came most of the Persico family. Sylvia, Joe's wife, edited, made useful suggestions, typed, and performed countless other services, most important her loving support of Joe. Vanya Perez, Joe's eldest daughter, was our invaluable transcriber and main typist. The manuscript was finished, thank heaven, days before

Vanya's second child was born. I deeply appreciate the contribution of both these women to the work.

My editor and publisher, Harold Evans, president of the Random House Trade Group, is the best in the business. I only doubted Harry once, and that was when he said that he could edit the whole manuscript on a laptop computer while sitting on a beach in Jamaica. He did, and brilliantly, I might add. Alberto Vitale, president of Random House, and S. I. Newhouse, president of Newhouse Publications, were both unstinting in their support of this project. The manuscript benefited from a scrupulous copyediting by Edward Johnson.

Colonel (Ret.) Bill Smullen, my assistant and close friend, worked on every aspect of the book, particularly heading the research operation while also running my office, which gave me the freedom to devote myself to writing. For the past six years, Bill has been alongside me as my confidant and protector. I will never be able to thank him enough. Bill and I are both indispensably aided by the other member of my staff, Peggy Cifrino.

Several friends and members of my family read the manuscript in whole or in part, and I have profited from their suggestions. Norma Leftwich gave it a particularly sensitive reading, and others whose comments proved especially valuable include Richard Armitage, Marybel Batjer, Marilyn and Norman Berns, Kenneth Duberstein, Admiral David Jeremiah, Alton Sheek, Larry Wilkerson, my son, Michael, my daughters, Linda and Annemarie, and my wife, Alma. During the course of writing the book, Alma continued as well to provide what she had given me throughout our marriage, an anchorage of good sense, good judgment, and good advice.

Numerous people helped us with the research. Among them I particularly thank Mike Andricos, Larry Bird, Hugh Howard, Tina Lavato, Susan Lemke, and Christina Mazzola.

We benefited from the expertise of numerous people in the Department of Defense. Among them are Joan Asboth, Dr. Donald Baucom, Sheryl Blankenship, Denise Brown, Colonel Conrad Busch, Barbara Callahan, Major General Richard Chilcoat, Linda Clark, Lieutenant Colonel Gordon Coulson, Teresa Crowley, Patricia Darnell, Major Joe Davis, Commander Alan Dooley, Lieutenant Colonel Nino Fabiano, Gene Fredrickson, Lieutenant Colonel James Gleisberg, Dr. Alfred Goldberg, Major General Gregory Govan, Colonel Larry Gragg, Colonel Kevin Hanretta, Gerri Harcarik, Colonel Marvin Harris, Lieutenant Colonel Douglas Hart, Lieutenant Megan Hayes, Nancy Hughes, Colonel Larry Icenogle, Lorna Jaffe, Rear Admiral Gregory Johnson, Major General John Jumper, Ilana Kass, Dr. Susan Koch, Shari Lawrence, Dr. John Leland, Don Lenker, Colonel H. T. Linke, Captain Matt Margotta, Bruce Menning, Franklin Miller, William Ormsbee, Harvey Perritt, Carolyn Piper, Peter Probst, Michael Rodgers, Betty Skinner, Lieutenant Colonel Mary Lou Smullen, Colonel James Terry, Patricia Tugwell, Dr. Todd White, Theodore Wise, and Janet Wray.

Others who helped with the research and related tasks included Lewis Brodsky, Michael Burch, John Chapla, Dennis Daellenbach, Charles DeCicco, Donna Dillon, Frank Donatelli, Amanda Downes, Andrew Duncan, Ralph Faust, Brigadier General Lou Hennies, Tammy Kupperman, James Manley, James McGrath, Marilynn McLaren, Thomas M. Persico, Karen Pierce, Ed Rabel, Colonel Douglas Roach, Gresham Striegel, Lieutenant Colonel Robert Trotter, Colonel John Votaw, and Margrit Krewson at the Library of Congress.

Others who helped me in ways that only they know include Julius Becton, James Cannon, Sharon Krager, Camille Nowfel, Gus Pagonis, George Price, Willard Sink, Clyde Taylor, Ronald Tumelson, Harlan Ullman, and Karen Wall.

And then there are all the friends who touched my life in countless ways, to my benefit. Many are mentioned in the book, but far more could not be included without extending these pages endlessly. They know who they are, and what they did for me. And I thank them all.

About the Coauthor

JOSEPH E. PERSICO was born in Gloversville, New York, in 1930 and graduated from the State University of New York at Albany. He served as a lieutenant junior grade aboard a minesweeper during the Korean War, and later at Southern NATO headquarters in Naples. Subsequently he joined the U.S. Information Agency and was posted to Brazil, Argentina, and Washington. For eleven years he was chief speechwriter for New York Governor and later U.S. Vice President Nelson A. Rockefeller. His books are *My Enemy My Brother: Men and Days of Gettysburg; Piercing the Reich: The Penetration of Nazi Germany by American Secret Agents During World War II; The Spiderweb,* a novel; *The Imperial Rockefeller,* a biography of Nelson Rockefeller; *Edward R. Murrow: An American Original; Casey: The Life and Secrets of William J. Casey from the OSS to the CIA;* and *Nuremberg: Infamy on Trial.* Mr. Persico divides his time between homes in upstate New York and Mexico.

Index

Aaron, David, 344, 345
ABC, 816, 930
Abenina, Edgardo, 667, 672
Abernathy, William C.,
    89–91, 101, 105, 107,
    110, 307
Abrams, Creighton W.,
    205–7, 235, 480, 844
Abrams Complex, 480,
    490–91
Achalov, Vladislav A., 481,
    492, 495
    Powell's meeting with, 634
Adams, Eddie, 616
Addington, David, 514, 822
Adelman, Ken, 499, 501,
    548
Aeroflot, 257
Afanasenko, Peter, 681, 730
affirmative action, 925
Afghanistan, 378, 447, 513,
    516, 547, 572, 732
Africare, 907
Agent Orange, 130–31, 220
AGI (Annual General Inspec-
    tion), 197–98, 199,
    202–3, 404–5, 484–85
    2nd Division and, 298
Aidid, Mohammed Farah,
    888–89, 891, 895
AIPAC (American Israeli
    Political Action Com-
    mittee), 564–65

Air Defense Command,
    Soviet, 425, 426
Air Force, U.S., 309, 310,
    660, 661, 663, 717,
    892
Air Force Academy, U.S.,
    394
Akhromeyev, Sergei,
    535–37, 554, 680, 821
Albright, Madeleine,
    877–78
Alexander, Clifford, 356
all-volunteer force, 274,
    491–92
    modern management
    techniques and, 332–35
    race and, 341–42, 761–63
    see also Army, U.S.; Base
    Force
Al Shireaa, 497
American Israeli Political
    Action Committee
    (AIPAC), 564–65
American Legion, 540
Amlong, Jim, 186
Amos 'n' Andy (TV show),
    29, 928
Andrews Sisters, 20
Andropov, Yuri, 427, 558
Angola, 516, 608, 627, 920
Annenberg, Lee, 691
Annenberg, Walter, 691–92
Ann-Margret, 212

Annual General Inspection (AGI), 197–98, 199, 202–3, 404–5, 484–85
2nd Division and, 298
antiwar movement, 157, 187, 232–33, 687–88
Aquino, Corazon, 667, 668–69, 672
Arafat, Yasser, 803, 908
Ardrey, Robert, 431
Argentina, 708
Aristide, Jean-Bertrand, 827–28, 864, 908, 911, 915
Armacost, Mike, 510
Armed Forces Hostess Association, 401–2
Armey, Dick, 836
Armitage, Richard, 381, 382, 393–94, 430, 434, 475, 497, 510, 519, 565, 580, 826
Arms Control and Disarmament Agency, 499, 501–2, 548
Arms Export Control Act, 469
arms-for-hostages deal:
CIA and, 469–70, 497, 517
Iran and, 459–61, 464–66, 468–71
McFarlane and, 460–61
Reagan and, 460, 465, 469–71, 503, 519–20
Shultz and, 459, 461, 471, 508–9

Tower Report and, 508–9
Weinberger and, 459–61, 463–66, 468–71, 508–9
see also Iran-contra scandal
Army, 610
Army, U.S., 309, 439–40, 621, 660, 663, 892
Afro-Americans in, 92–95, 277, 416–21
base closings and, 835–39
black officers in, 242–43
careerism in, 221, 225–26, 235
Carlisle Report and, 234–35
casualty notification by, 181
category IV soldiers in, 274, 491
"charm school" for generals of, 368–69
command assignments in, 268–69
competition for promotion in, 314
computers and, 88
draftees vs. volunteers in, 76–77
efficiency reports and, 406–8
leadership and, 78–79
management practices in, 81–82
Navy's CENTCOM rivalry with, 579–80
officer grades in, 177

officer rank in, 146–47
officers' role in, 88–89
old vs. new, 307–8
promotion machinery of,
    411–12
Ptarmigan phone system
    deal and, 466–68
race, racism and, 92–95,
    172–73, 188–89,
    242–43, 285–94,
    341–42, 416–21, 492,
    607–8, 761–63, 844–45
RAM standards of, 166
segregation ended in, 95
staff officers in, 204
tactical nuclear weapons
    and, *see* nuclear
    weapons
tradition and ritual in,
    85–88
unit readiness report of,
    178–80, 404–5
see also all-volunteer
    force; Base Force
Army Command and Gen-
    eral Staff College,
    183–86, 192, 203
Army Department, U.S.,
    207
Army of the Republic of
    Vietnam (ARVN), 120,
    131, 132, 144, 151, 152
Army Rangers, 642, 650,
    889, 892, 896
Army Times, 203, 230
Army War College, 309
    Carlisle report of, 234–35

Arnett, Peter, 769
Arthur, Stan, 739, 809
A Shau, South Vietnam,
    120–23, 131, 135, 147,
    156
Aspen Institute Symposium,
    694–95
Aspin, Les, 836, 862, 873,
    874, 889, 891, 893
    Base Force and, 857–58,
        881–82
    Bosnia and, 875, 877
    on *Face the Nation,*
        867–68
    and gays in military, 868,
        870–71, 872
    management style of,
        879–83
    Somalia crisis and, 892,
        896
Association for a Better
    New York, 811
Association of the United
    States Army, 609
Atkins, Marie, 4
Atlanta Constitution, 871
Atlantic Command, U.S.,
    828
"At Least: Slow the Slaugh-
    ter" (*New York Times*
    editorial), 849
Atomic Energy Commis-
    sion, 371
Atwood, Donald, 725, 820
Atwood, Wesley, 136
Austria, 496
A-Vice, 233, 235

AWACS planes, 838
Aziz, Tariq, 763, 782

"Baby Letter," 141, 143, 145
Back to Bataan (film), 39
Bagnal, Chuck, 320, 334
Baker, Howard, 528, 581, 597
Baker, James A., III, 589, 641–43, 647, 665, 689, 703, 727, 728, 737, 741–44, 763, 794, 820, 842, 852, 875
Baldwin, John, 372, 391–92
Baldwin, Velma, 250, 317
Bandar Bin Sultan, Prince, 364–65, 705, 719–20, 722
Bangladesh, 745
Barak, Ehud, 777–78
Barrett, Raymond "Red Man," 79, 90, 112, 184, 307, 393, 396, 485
Bartholomees, Jim, 82
Base Force, 237, 702, 857–858
  Aspin and, 857–58, 881–882
  Cheney and, 673–74, 679, 683–86, 688–90, 694–95, 830–31
  Congress and, 830–31
  JCS and, 673, 685
Bates, Jerry, 909
Batjer, Marybel, 381–82, 393–94, 472, 492, 497, 501

Battle of the Bulge, 206, 315
Baxter, Bob, 247
Bayne, Marmaduke G., 313, 316
Bay of Pigs, 851
Bazin, Marc, 910
Beame, Abraham, 37
Beckwith, Charles, 376–77
Becton, Julius, 309, 393, 412, 416
Beirut bombing, 437–39
Bell, George, 98
Bell, Ida, 67, 360, 453
Be Luong basecamp, 135–137
Benavidez, Roy P., 379, 388
Bennett, Bob, 518
Bennett, Louise, 4
Ben-Shoshan, Abraham, 777
Bent, Joan, 7
Berle, Milton, 29
Berlin, Irving, 119
Berlin Wall, 102, 479, 664, 823
Bermúdez, Enrique, 514
Berns, Leslie, 32, 71
Berns, Lisa, 71
Berns, Marilyn Powell (sister), 9, 17, 24, 25, 31, 56, 71, 100, 105, 359, 360, 578, 626, 759, 897
  college send-off of, 22
  marriage of, 34–35
  Powell's relationship with, 15–16
Berns, Norman, 34–35, 105, 359, 578, 626

Berra, Yogi, 609
Beryl, Aunt, 13, 19, 45–46,
　100–101
Biamby, Philippe, 909, 913
"Big Bamboo, The" (song),
　20
Biggs, Corporal, 288–89
Bill (manufacturer's rep),
　166–67
Bir, Sevik, 889
Bishop, Maurice, 439
Bissell, Keith, 81
Black Eagles (Lee), 784
Blackstock, Captain, 79
Blagg, Tom, 403, 409, 410
Blitzer, Wolf, 772
Blue Ridge, U.S.S., 719
Blue Spoon, Operation, 637,
　639, 640–51; *see also*
　Just Cause, Operation
body count, 148–49,
　222–23, 226
Boese, Specialist, 522
Boomer, Walt, 739, 780–81,
　783, 809
Boren, David, 514
Boselager Cavalry competi-
　tion, 500–501
Bosnia-Herzegovina, 439,
　849, 856, 864, 875–79,
　917, 920
Bostic, James E., Jr., 246,
　247–48, 570
"Bottom Up Review"
　(BUR), 881–82
Boutros-Ghali, Boutros, 883
Boys and Sex (Pomeroy),
　329

Bradford, Zeb, 270–71
Bradley, Omar, 323, 622
Brady, Nick, 665
Brady, Peter, 4
Braim, Paul, 293
Bramlett, Bill, 317
Brash, Amy, 14
Brash, Mabel Evadne, 14,
　45
Brash, Norman, 14
Brechbuhl, Ulrich, 521–23
Brehm, William, 310
Brezhnev, Leonid, 558
Brian's Song (film), 292–93
Bridges at Toko-Ri, The
　(film), 39
Bridge Too Far, A (Ryan),
　315
Brinkerhof, John, 311
British-American Parlia-
　mentary Society, 750
Brookhart, Harold C., 40,
　49, 53, 58, 64, 624
Brooks, Elsa, 621
Brooks, Harry, 280, 416
Brooks, Jim, 451
Brooks, Ronald, 41–42,
　48–50, 53, 104, 105,
　106
　death of, 620–21
Brookshire, Grail L., 395
Brown, Arthur, 470
Brown, Cammie, 620
Brown, Colene, 357
Brown, Harold, 351–56,
　361, 367, 372, 374,
　378, 388, 422, 430,
　442, 677, 909

Brown, Harold (*cont.*):
  background and personal-
    ity of, 357–58
  Weinberger contrasted
    with, 430
Brown, H. Rap, 189, 201
Brown, Ron, 905
Brown v. *Topeka Board of
  Education,* 35
Brzezinski, Zbigniew, 347,
    351, 353, 532, 575
  Powell interviewed by,
    343–47
Buffalo Soldiers, 625
  creation of, 93–94
  history of, 416–21
  memorial dedicated to,
    419–21, 423, 690–92,
    843–48
"Bugs and Gases," 751
Bulgaria, 259, 267, 744
Bulge, Battle of the, 206, 315
BUR ("Bottom Up
  Review"), 881–82
Burke, Bobby G., 242
Burns, Ken, 747–48
Burundi, 920
Bush, Barbara, 586, 747,
    796, 841, 853–54, 865,
    897
Bush, George, 502, 511,
    590, 694–95, 810, 845,
    873, 876, 897
  assessment of, 582, 588,
    865, 926
  and decision not to pursue
    Saddam Hussein, 808

Frost-Schwarzkopf inter-
    view and, 797–99
Governor's Island meet-
    ing and, 591–96
Gulf War and, 700–702,
    705, 706–8, 711–14,
    717, 721, 726–28, 737,
    740–47, 754–61, 763–
    764, 767–69, 779–80,
    782, 784–86, 794–97
Haiti crisis and, 827
Iran-contra scandal and,
    504, 519
Kuwait visited by, 889
Los Angeles riots and,
    839–41
1992 election and, 848,
    851–54
NSR 12 and, 661
Panama crisis and,
    586–88, 628, 638, 643,
    651, 654, 657–58
Powell appointed JCS
    chairman by, 618
Powell as running mate
    of, 555, 580–82,
    829–30, 842
Powell reappointed by,
    815–17, 825
Quayle supported by,
    842–43
race, racism and, 606
Saddam Hussein demo-
    nized by, 746–47, 802
Somalia and, 860–62, 883
Soviet coup and, 820–22,
    824

Thatcher's Aspen meeting with, 694–95, 702, 707–8
Bush administration, 631, 639, 700–702
Butler, George "Lee," 662
Byrd, Bob, 892

CACDA (Combined Arms Combat Development Activity), 410, 413, 424, 609
Califano, Joseph, 369–70
Calley, William, 217
Cambodia, 920
Camp Casey, South Korea, 276, 277, 285
Canada, 721, 722
Canadian Army Cup tank competition, 500–501
Capron, Adin B., 52
Card, Andrew, 671
Carlisle, Pa., Powell's speech in, 609–11
Carlucci, Frank, 249–51, 388, 389, 392, 429, 443–44, 521, 526, 531, 534, 537, 554, 557, 584, 587, 629, 633, 677, 836, 874
background of, 384–85
CENTCOM decision and, 579–80
Iran-contra scandal and, 504–6, 508
joins Defense Department, 385
leaves Defense Department, 590–91
at NSC, 497–501, 503–6, 508
Powell's NSC appointment and, 528–29
Reagan-Gorbachev talks and, 549, 553
Carlucci, Kristin, 386
Carlucci, Marcia, 386
Carmichael, Stokely, 189
Carns, Mike, 647, 696
Carter, Jimmy, 260, 343, 357, 369–70, 379, 383, 388, 389, 526, 698, 705
Desert One fiasco and, 374–78
Haiti mission and, 908–916
Carter administration, 351, 357, 369–70, 378–79, 385, 389
Cartwright, Roscoe "Rock," 242, 416
Caruthers, Mike, 339
Casablanca (film), 902
Casey, William J., 465–66, 628
Castro, Fidel, 559
Caughman, Bruce, 791
Caulkins, Rodney L., 239, 240
Cavazos, Richard G., 411–412
CBS, 262, 657, 710, 725, 867, 873

CCNY (City College of
    New York), 36–39, 44,
    47, 48, 50–51, 53, 477
  Powell's graduation from,
    55–58
  ROTC abolished by, 245
Cedras, Raoul, 909–15
Cedras, Yannick Prosper, 912
Center for Strategic and
    International Studies,
    758
Central American Task
    Force (CIA), 513
Central Command (CENT-
    COM), U.S., 579–80,
    614, 698, 736, 860, 889
Central Intelligence Agency
    (CIA), 253, 309, 385,
    443, 465, 505, 507,
    511, 513, 542, 583,
    589–90, 611, 637, 889
  arms-for-hostages deal
    and, 469–70, 497, 517
  Gulf War and, 699–700,
    703, 710
  Noriega and, 627–28, 630
  Soviet assessments by,
    569–70
Chain, Jack, 685
Chambers, Andy, 492, 521
Chandler, John P., 236
Charlier, Joseph, 192
"charm school," 368–69
Chayefsky, Paddy, 37
Chechnya, 920
Checker, Chubby, 101
Cheney, Lynne, 809

Cheney, Richard B., 624,
    805, 809, 820, 838,
    845, 850, 873, 874,
    897, 898
  Base Force and, 673–74,
    679, 683–86, 688–90,
    694–95, 830–31
  Bush's departure from
    office and, 864–67
  character of, 556, 614–15,
    815
  Commanders controversy
    and, 815–16
  Gulf War and, 493–94,
    699–710, 735–38, 740,
    743, 746, 748–49,
    753–58, 764, 765, 767,
    772–74, 777, 779, 781,
    784–86, 789, 793
  Haiti crisis and, 828
  military budget 1991–92
    and, 683–86
  nuclear weapons and,
    822–24
  Panama crisis and, 633,
    634–41, 644–45, 648,
    650–51, 655–56
  Philippines crisis and,
    667, 669–73
  Powell recommended as
    JCS chairman by,
    616–19
  Powell's first encounter
    with, 495–96
  Powell's force reduction
    proposal and, 661,
    664–65

Somalia crisis and, 860–62
Chernenko, Konstantin, 558
Chernobyl disaster, 547
Chicago Tribune, 871
Chilcoat, Dick, 751, 769
Child Buyer, The (Hersey), 139
China, People's Republic of, 253, 256, 460, 503, 744, 919
  Powell's visit to, 263–66
Chisholm, Chris, 71
Chisholm, Donna, 71
Christopher, Warren, 855, 875, 878, 889, 916, 917
Churchill, Winston, 621, 750, 887
Churchill, Winston (grandson), 750
CID (Criminal Investigation Division), 406
Cifrino, Peggy, 900
Cilento, Barbara, 525–26
City College of New York (CCNY), 36–39, 44, 47, 48, 50–51, 53, 477
  Powell's graduation from, 55–58
  ROTC abolished by, 245
Civilian Reserve Air Fleet (CRAF), 713
Civil Rights Act (1964), 170
civil rights movement, 115–16
Civil War, U.S., 93, 737, 747

Civil War (Burns), 747–48
Clark, William, 435–36
Claude, Uncle, 7
Clausewitz, Karl von, 312–313, 457, 635, 672
Claytor, W. Graham, 372–74, 378, 383, 386
Cleaver, Eldridge, 189
Cline, Patsy, 212
Clinton, Bill, 843, 848, 853, 862, 905, 926
  Carter's Haiti mission and, 908–9, 913–14, 915–16
  and gays in military, 858–59, 862–63, 867–72
  Iraq missile strike and, 889–91
  management style of, 875–76
  Powell's meetings with, 855–59, 894–96
  Powell's retirement and, 897–900
  Vietnam Memorial speech of, 883–87
Clinton, Hillary, 858, 905
Clinton administration, 875
CNN, 539, 707, 720, 769, 772, 776, 786, 804, 848, 873, 890
Coast Guard, U.S., 892
Cobb, Howell, 417
Coffey, Vernon, 63, 95
Coker, Philip, 399, 420

Cold War, 3, 67, 71, 237, 257, 424–29, 516, 568, 608–9, 612, 830, 837, 919

Cole, Ezra, 4

Cole, Natalie, 902

"Colin Powell's Rules," 620, 933

"combat sports," 279–80, 304–5

Combined Arms Combat Development Activity (CACDA), 410, 413, 424, 609

"Come Water Me Garden" (song), 20

command, Powell on, 482–84

Commanders, The (Woodward), 729, 814

Commanders' Conference, 617

Communist Party, Soviet, 569

Conference on Security and Cooperation in Europe (CSCE), 679

Congress, U.S., 93, 232, 237, 357, 371, 374, 390, 446–48, 497, 505, 512, 531, 613, 661, 681, 684, 687, 728, 797, 813, 815
    arms exports and, 469–71
    Base Force and, 830–31
    Buffalo Soldiers and, 418
    contras and, 514, 556
    and gays in military, 858–59, 862–63, 867–68, 872, 874
    Gulf War and, 743, 749–50, 753, 759, 761–64, 768–69, 793
    JCS and, 621–22
    military manpower report to, 310–11
    military reductions and, 835–39
    Panama and, 635
    SDI and, 444–46
    SOCOM created by, 377–378
    Somalia and, 892
    Weinberger and, 445–46

Congressional Black Caucus, 813, 829, 832

Connor, Eugene T. "Bull," 114, 172, 260, 839

Constitution, U.S., 680, 924

containment strategy, 882, 918, 921

contras, 469, 497, 555, 600, 628
    Congress and, 514
    NSC and, 512–15
    Weinberger's view of, 513
    see also Iran-contra scandal

Cook, Mariana, 328

Cooke, David O. "Doc," 452–53, 472, 625

Cooper, James Fenimore, 536

Coote, Alfred, 14

Coote, Gytha, 14
Copperhead artillery
    weapon, 686
Corcione, Domenico, 722
Coulson, Gordy, 893
Couric, Katie, 339
CRAF (Civilian Reserve Air
    Fleet), 713
Craig, David, 722, 751, 766,
    767
Criminal Investigation
    Division (CID), 406
Crist, George, 579
Croatia, 849
Cropper, Dorothy, 32
Crosby, Bing, 291
Crossley, Ross W. "Bill," 481
Crowe, Bill, 530, 579, 619,
    624, 629, 674, 797, 854
Crozier, Ted "Wild Turkey,"
    319–20, 322, 334–35
C-Span, 531, 532, 541
Cuba, 3–4, 94, 439, 516,
    559, 627, 660, 744, 920
Cuban missile crisis, 113
Cummings, Ezra "Chopper,"
    96
Curtis, Adam J., 638
Curtis, Bonnie, 638
Custer, George Armstrong,
    185, 193, 414
Custer, Thomas W., 193
Czechoslovakia, 479, 610,
    687, 744

Daily, Thomas P., 647
Darman, Dick, 665

Davis, Benjamin O., 58,
    242, 844, 846
Davis, Jefferson, 417
Dawkins, Pete, 169, 422, 423
DEA (Drug Enforcement
    Agency), U.S., 628
Deaver, Michael, 388
de Chastelain, John, 722
Declaration of Indepen-
    dence, 731
Defense Department, U.S.,
    181, 370, 372, 377,
    429, 502, 507, 684, 758
arms-for-hostages deal
    and, 459–61, 463–66,
    468–71, 508, 516–18
Carlucci's arrival at,
    385–86
Carlucci's departure
    from, 590–91
charter of, 502
Cheney's arrival at, 614–
    615
Kester at, 351–57
Reagan defense budget
    and, 389–90
Reagan transition and,
    380–83
Saratoga incident and,
    373–74
Weinberger appointed
    secretary of, 380–82
see also Pentagon
Defense Intelligence
    Agency (DIA), 627
Defense Logistics Agency,
    758

Defense Reorganization Act (1986), *see* Goldwater-Nichols Act

Defense Security Assistance Agency, 468–69

de Klerk, Frederik W., 728

de la Espriella, Ricardo, 627

De Lauer, Richard, 445

Dellums, Ron, 761, 828–29, 905, 907

Delta Force, U.S., 637, 642, 889, 892, 896

Delvalle, Eric, 629

Democratic Party, U.S., 515, 556, 581, 606, 635, 829

DePace, Sandy, 96, 101

DePace, Tony, 51, 55, 96, 101, 171

Depression, Great, 18, 174

Deputies Committee, 633

DePuy, William E., 233, 235–38, 243, 248, 270, 673

Desert One, Operation, 374–78, 421, 652

Desert Shield, Operation, 716, 727, 749, 754–55, 757–59; *see also* Persian Gulf War

Desert Storm, Operation, 308, 716, 796, 801–3, 809, 837, 845, 851, 930; *see also* Persian Gulf War

Deutch, John, 881

De Villa, Renato, 672

Dewey, Arthur E., 247

DIA (Defense Intelligence Agency), 627

Diem, Ngo Dinh, 113, 151, 155–56

Dienbienphu, Battle of, 472

Dignity Battalions, 651, 653, 657

Dinkins, David, 905, 907

Distinguished Service Cross, 379

Distinguished Service Medal, 371–72, 393

Dixon, Julian, 761

Dobrynin, Anatoly, 558

Dodd, Chris, 837

Dolan, Tony, 503, 566

Dole, Robert, 381

Dollie (Zia's friend), 193

Donaldson, Sam, 539, 930

"Don't Ask. Don't Tell." policy, 874

Dorelien, Colonel, 911

Dot, Aunt, 19, 21

Dougherty, Alonzo, 423, 690, 846

Douglass, Frederick, 417–18

Douhet, Giulio, 312

Drug Enforcement Agency, U.S. (DEA), 628

Duberstein, Ken, 546, 597, 598

Dubinin, Yuri, 545–46, 591–592

Duc Pho, South Vietnam, 197–99, 201–2

Dugan, Michael, 723–26

Dukakis, Michael, 586, 606
Duncan, Bill, 178
Duncan, Charles, 352, 361–
    362, 364–67, 369–72,
    378, 833
Dunlap, Jack, 149–50
Dyke, Charles W. "Bill,"
    462

Eagleburger, Lawrence S.
    "Larry," 667, 703, 704
Early Bird, 431–32, 441
Ebbesen, Sam, 55
Economist, 689
Economy Act (1933), 469
Edney, Bud, 828
Edwards, Mickey, 514
Edwards, Robert D., 77–78,
    144, 485
Ed (Zia's friend), 193
Egypt, 361, 697, 703, 744
EIB (Expert Infantryman's
    Badge), 295–96
8th Guards Army, Soviet,
    481, 482, 489, 536,
    634, 685
8th Infantry Division (Mech-
    anized), U.S., 462, 481
XVIII Airborne Corps, U.S.,
    306, 338, 612, 637,
    739, 781, 786, 787,
    788, 792, 809, 915
Eighth Army, U.S., 269, 410
82nd Airborne Division,
    U.S., 315, 338, 642,
    650, 655, 657, 705,
    708–9, 717, 786

89th Airlift Wing, U.S., 434
Eisenhower, Dwight D., 12,
    113, 185, 315, 471–73,
    479, 480, 722, 797, 839
Eisenhower, John D., 472
Eisenhower administration,
    71
election of 1992, 838, 848,
    930
  Bush's defeat in, 851–54
  Powell as possible candi-
    date in, 555, 580–82,
    829–30, 842
  Quayle as liability in, 842
  race, racism and, 840
elections:
  of 1952, 12
  of 1960, 82
  of 1964, 170–71, 173
  of 1968, 187–88
  of 1976, 373, 378
  of 1980, 378–79
  of 1984, 457
  of 1988, 566, 580–88,
    606
  of 1990, 743
  of 1994, 930
11th Armored Cavalry Regi-
    ment, U.S., 481
11th Infantry Brigade, U.S.,
    197, 208, 216, 217, 222
Elizabeth II, Queen of
    England, 904
Ellison, Joy, 85, 101
Ellison, Richard D., 84, 85,
    101
"El Paso" (song), 137

El Salvador, 920
Emerson, Henry E. "Gunfighter," 270, 290, 292–293, 298–99, 303, 333, 338–39, 396, 458, 845
  combat sports idea of, 279–80, 304–5
  command style of, 271–273
  marriage of, 306–7
  no-medals policy of, 300–301
  Pro-Life program of, 274–75, 290
  retirement of, 339–41
  reverse cycle training and, 283
Enchanted April (film), 854
Endara, Guillermo, 631, 637, 642, 647, 648, 653, 654, 657
Energy Department, U.S., 370–72
Ermath, Fritz, 550, 551
Ervin, Sam, 266, 268–69
Espy, Mike, 905, 907
Estonia, 574, 610, 682
Ethlyn, Aunt, 92
Evers, Medgar, 172
Every War Must End (Ikle), 789–90
Expert Infantryman's Badge (EIB), 295–96
Eyadema, Gnassingbe, 695, 699
"Eye of the Storm: The General Colin L. Powell March," 898

Face the Nation (TV show), 725, 867
Fahd, King of Saudi Arabia, 364, 703, 706, 707, 708, 722, 748
Falkland Islands War, 468, 708
Fall, Bernard, 224
Federal Bureau of Investigation (FBI), 542, 889
Federal Energy Regulatory Commission, 371
Fedorova, Alla, 254, 256, 257
Fields, Jackie, 96, 97, 107
Fiers, Alan, 513
V Corps, U.S., 473–74, 477–87, 492, 495, 500, 536, 556, 614
Finland, 572
Fiorino, Sam, 27
Firebase Liz, 199, 202, 203
1st Armored Division, British, 786
1st Cavalry Division, U.S., 717
1st Division, ARVN, 120, 145
  Powell as staff officer of, 151–52
1st Infantry Division, U.S., 84–85
1st Infantry Regiment, U.S., 197
1st Marine Division, U.S., 780, 787
1st Marine Expeditionary Force, U.S., 717, 719

1st Tactical Fighter Wing, U.S., 705, 708, 719
First Flight (horse), 751–52
Fisher, Zachary, 691
Fitzgerald, F. Scott, 139
Fitzwater, Marlin, 538, 562, 598, 641
501st Airborne Infantry Regiment, U.S., 319
502nd Airborne Infantry Regiment, U.S., 319
506th Airborne Infantry Regiment, U.S., 319
Flipper, Henry O., 418–19, 692, 893
Flynn, Bill, 410–11
Flynn, Fred, 395
Follow Me, 61
Forbes, Claret, 32
Forces Command (FORSCOM), U.S., 413, 590, 605, 607–13, 614, 616, 625
Ford, Gerald, 310, 495, 530
Forrest, Colin G., 166–67
Forrestal, James, 437
Forsythe, George, 235
Fort Apache, The Bronx (film), 13
Fort Benning, Ga., 161, 162, 168, 173–74, 181
Fort Bragg, N.C., 110–11
Fort Campbell, Ky., 323, 327–28, 332, 341
Fort Carson, Colo., 392–95
Fort Leavenworth, Kans., 183–86, 192–94, 414

Buffalo soldiers monument at, 419–21, 423, 690–92, 843–48
4th Armored Division, U.S., 18
4th Infantry Company, PDF, 632
4th Infantry Division (Mechanized), U.S., 392
    mission of, 395–96
    Powell's departure from, 410–11
    see also Hudachek, John W.
4th Infantry Regiment, U.S., 84
48th Infantry Brigade, U.S., 68, 74, 76, 82
France, 113, 472, 721, 722, 744, 768
Francis, Fred, 657
Francis, H. Minton, 292–293
Francisco, Slinger (Mighty Sparrow), 20
Frank, Barney, 831–32
Frankfurter, Felix, 37
Franklin, Aretha, 188, 902
Franks, Fred, 787, 788
Franks, Gary, 763
free enterprise, 923
Freeman, Charles, 801
Friedl (bartender), 79–80
Friedman, Milton, 246–47
Frost, David, 798
Frost, Robert, 24
Fryer, John, 247

"Future Just Ain't What It Used to Be, The" (Powell), 609

Gaffney, Frank, 448, 468–469
Gaines Company, 10, 23
Galvin, Jack, 685, 806, 808
Gang of Eight, 737, 741, 763, 768, 785, 790, 791, 820
Gantt, Florence, 506, 522, 540, 550, 580
Garcia, Manny, 28
Gardner, John W., 244
Garmon, Michael, 411
Gast, Philip, 362
Gaston, A. G., 107
Gatanas, Mark, 55
Gates, Bob, 633, 641, 665, 737, 757
Gates, Darryl, 587
gays in military, 831–32, 858–59, 867–74
Gendron, Tom, 84–85
General Colin L. Powell Parkway, 863–64
General Defense Plan (GDP), 71
General Education Development (GED), 298
General Motors (GMC), 732
General Officer Management Office (GOMO), 409–10
General Services Administration, 596

George Washington University, 213, 226, 227, 229–30, 232–33
  Powell honored by, 686
Georgia, Republic of, 568, 610, 612
Gergen, David, 891
Germany, Democratic Republic of (East), 660, 664
Germany, Federal Republic of (West), 267
Germany, reunified, 835
Gettys, Charles M., 203–4, 206–8, 210–12, 219, 307, 396
Gettysburg, Battle of, 797
Ghorbanifar, Manucher, 582–84
Gianastasias, Father, 286–287, 307, 326
Giroldi Vega, Moises, 631–35, 667, 669
glasnost, 479, 558, 568, 572
Glaspie, April, 699
Glosson, "Buster," 718, 735
Goldfarb, Rich, 55
Goldwater, Barry, 170–71, 623
Goldwater-Nichols Act (1986), 623–24, 639, 664, 674, 678, 891
Gorbachev, Mikhail, 479, 510, 558, 660, 662–67, 893
  August coup and, 820–822

Governor's Island meeting and, 591–96
Gulf War and, 702, 782, 785–86, 816
INF treaty and, 516, 535, 544–45, 548
Moscow summit and, 571–72, 573–76
Powell's assessment of, 548, 818
Reagan's Springfield speech and, 567–68
Soviet internal decline and, 516, 537, 558–560, 569–70, 608–10, 830
Washington visit and, 540–55
Gorbachev, Raisa, 545–46
Gordon, Michael R., 689, 849
Gore, Albert, 848, 868, 875, 889, 897, 905
Gore, Tipper, 897, 905
Gosling, Francis G. "Goose," 236
Grant, Tony, 17, 29, 533
Grant, Ulysses S., 622
Grasser, Peter G., 290–92
Grasshopper, Operation, 123–35
Graves, Howard, 647
Gray, Alfred M., 220, 640, 664, 678, 700, 809
Great Britain, 621, 691, 920
Gulf War and, 721–22, 744

Powell's visits to, 750–51, 903–5
Ptarmigan phone system deal and, 466–68
Great Depression, 18, 174
Green, Fred, 754
Green, Ginger, 522, 817
Green, Grant, 501, 522, 817
Greenberg, Irving, 310
Green Party, German, 488
Gregg, Don, 511
Grenada, 439–40, 474, 499–500, 652
Grier, Rosie, 212
Grierson, Benjamin H., 418
Griffin, Thomas, 169, 481, 488
Griffiths, Anne Mills, 527
Griscom, Tom, 545, 552, 597–98
Gromyko, Andrei, 428
GTMO, Operation, 828
Guadalcanal Diary (film), 39
Guest, Wayne, 183
Guidry, Vern, 879
Gulf War, *see* Persian Gulf War
Gumbel, Bryant, 433
Gures, Dogan, 722
Guys and Dolls (film), 902
Gytha, Aunt, 16

Haas, Richard, 791
Haig, Alexander, 530
Haile Selassic, Emperor of Ethiopia, 34

Haiti, 827, 864, 870
  Carter's mission to,
    908–16, 917
Hallums, James D., 335–37
Hammering Hank
    (sergeant), 335–38
Hannan, James D., 208–9
Hardisty, Huntington
    "Hunt," 668, 672
Harkin, Tom, 530
Harrington, William, 692
Haruna, 18
Havel, Václav, 687
Health, Education and Wel-
    fare Department, U.S.,
    250–51, 327, 370, 380,
    385
*Heart Is a Lonely Hunter,
    The* (McCullers), 139
Helms, Jesse, 385, 386, 628,
    635
Heningburg, Alfonse, 96
Heningburg, Gustav, 96
Heningburg, Michael,
    96–98, 107
Heritage Foundation, 611
Herrera Hassan, Eduardo,
    630
Herres, Robert, 616, 640, 668
Hersey, John, 139
Hickle, Walter, 251
Hieu, Vo Cong, *see* Vo Cong
    Hieu
Hill, Charles, 591
Hine, Patrick, 760
Ho, Don, 214
Hoar, Joseph, 860, 889

Ho Chi Minh, 113, 131
Ho Chi Minh Trail, 121, 221
Holliman, John, 769
Homecoming GI (Rock-
    well), 158–59
Honeycutt, Weldon C.
    "Tiger," 319, 334, 393
Hong Kong, 154
Honor Guard Regiment,
    U.S., 95
Hoover, Herbert, 852
Hope, Bob, 211–12
Horner, Chuck, 735, 739,
    809
Horton, Willie, 606
House of Commons, British,
    750
House of Representatives,
    U.S., 516–18, 763,
    768–69, 794
  Armed Services Commit-
    tee of, 357, 373–74,
    657, 683, 862, 881
  Budget Committee of,
    831
  Permanent Select Com-
    mittee on Intelligence
    of, 495
  see also Congress, U.S.
Howard, Edie, 248
Howard, Edward, 248
Howard University, 907–8
Howe, Jon, 497, 510–11,
    888
Hudachek, Ann, 402, 404
Hudachek, John W., 392–93,
    399, 410, 411, 477

leadership style of,
398–99, 402–4
Powell's efficiency report
by, 406–9
Powell's first meeting
with, 395–96
Hue, South Vietnam,
145–46, 152–54
Hughes, Nancy, 430, 452,
765, 840
Hume, Brit, 816
Hungary, 479, 610
Hussein, King of Jordan,
703, 803, 880
Hussein, Saddam, 3, 696,
698–701, 703, 710,
715, 723, 741, 759,
766, 773, 786, 790,
796, 807, 825, 864
attempt to thwart UN
inspectors by, 3
as Bush's relative, 754
elimination of, as Gulf
War objective, 745,
747, 756, 797, 800–
801, 808
invasion of Kuwait
ordered by, 696, 697
Hustler, The (film), 902
Huyser, Robert "Dutch,"
387

Iceland, 838
"I Fall to Pieces" (song),
212
Iklé, Fred, 386, 430, 789–
790, 792

Immigration and Naturaliza-
tion Service, 827–28
Independence, U.S.S., 700
Industrial College of the
Armed Forces, 313
Infantry Board, U.S., 166,
168, 175
Infantry Officers Advanced
Course, 147, 161, 165,
168–70, 175, 185
Information Agency, U.S.,
309, 571
INF treaty, 516, 535, 538–
539, 543, 554, 567,
575, 576
Senate ratification of,
572
signing of, 546–47
In Retrospect (McNamara),
878
"Instant Thunder," 717–18
Interior Department, U.S.,
251, 436
International Brotherhood of
Teamsters, 43, 811
International Ladies Gar-
ment Workers Union,
12, 923
interservice rivalries,
310–11
"In the Still of the Night"
(song), 907
Iran, 715
arms-for-hostages deal
and, 459–61, 464–66,
468–69, 497, 512–13,
517–18

Iran (*cont.*):
  Desert One mission and,
    374–78
  fall of Shah in, 365–66,
    698
  Iraq's conflict with, 510,
    608, 696, 710, 745,
    754, 882
  Powell's visit to, 362–64
Iran-contra scandal, 461,
    469, 496–500, 504–6,
    512–13, 531, 628
  Bush and, 504, 519
  congressional hearings
    on, 516–17
  Tower Report on, 507–9
  Weinberger and,
    496–500, 517–20
Iraq, 511, 512, 696, 698–
    703, 728–29, 750, 762,
    771, 774, 782, 786,
    795–96, 799–802, 805,
    856, 889, 920
  Iran's conflict with, 510,
    608, 696, 710, 745,
    754, 882
  Kurds in, 710, 745, 807–9
  Provide Comfort Opera-
    tion and, 808, 817
  "security zone" in, 808
  UN embargo of, 713
  see also Persian Gulf
    War
Irish Republican Army
    (IRA), 920
Israel, 437, 468, 475, 630,
    697, 703, 757, 803

  Gulf War and, 724,
    741–42, 776–78
Italy, 475, 721–22
It Doesn't Take a Hero
    (Schwarzkopf), 799
Ivri, David, 777

Jackson, Andrew, 94–95
Jackson, Jesse, 563, 581,
    829, 905, 906
Jamaica, 19–20
  British culture and, 34
  Powell's visits to, 3–8,
    91–92, 834
  slavery and, 33–34
Jamaica Defense Force
    (JDF), 4
James, Daniel "Chappie,"
    242, 844
Japan, 266, 426, 621, 789
Jedi Knights, 718, 735, 739
Jefferson, Thomas, 263,
    458, 730–31, 932
Jenes, Ted, 410
Jeopardy (TV show), 874
Jeremiah, Dave, 694, 773,
    794, 809
Johns, Tiger, 81
Johnson, Alma, *see* Powell,
    Alma Johnson
Johnson, Barbara, 105, 106,
    194
Johnson, Gregory "Grog,"
    894
Johnson, H. T., 708
Johnson, Jerry, 818
Johnson, Jim, 657

Johnson, Lyndon Baines,
    170–71, 173, 176,
    187–88, 200, 203, 224,
    244, 261–62
Johnson, Mildred, 98, 104,
    105, 159, 174, 330, 450
Johnson, Robert C. "R.C.,"
    98, 104, 105–6,
    114–15, 141, 330
    death of, 450–51
Johnson, Tom, 890
Johnston, Bob, 735, 736,
    737, 738, 861
Joint Center for Political
    Studies, 534–35
Joint Chiefs of Staff (JCS),
    3, 220, 237, 339, 352,
    449, 450, 490, 510,
    616, 635, 662–63, 666,
    704, 743, 789, 857, 867
    Base Force and, 673, 685
    CENTCOM and, 579–80
    Congress and, 621–22
    Goldwater-Nichols Act
       and, 623–24, 664, 674,
       678
    history of, 621–24
    Joint Staff of, 646–48,
       659, 664, 674–75, 677,
       822–23, 897
    Powell's management
       style and, 674–79
    stationery of, 678
Jonassaint, Emile, 912,
    914–16
Jones, David, 365, 623
Jones, Don, 473

Jones, Linc, 481
Jordan, 475, 697, 703, 778,
    808
Jordan, Hal, 81
Jordan, Vernon, 843, 855,
    916–17
Jumper, John, 751–52
Juneau, U.S.S., 39
Junior ROTC, 845–46
Just Cause, Operation, 308,
    378, 646–48, 667, 673
    media and, 652–56
    opposition to, 657
    U.S. casualties in, 654
Justice Department, U.S.,
    587

KATUSA (Korean Augmen-
    tation to the U.S.
    Army), 282
Kearse, Elisha, 692
Keegan, John, 803
Kelley, P. X., 177
Kelly, Barry, 584
Kelly, Colin P., III, 400
Kelly, Colin P., Jr., 18–19, 39
Kelly, Paul, 831
Kelly, Tom, 626, 631, 640,
    641, 644, 645, 648,
    651, 667, 709–10, 738,
    765, 786, 806
Kelso, Frank, 809
Kennan, George, 687
Kennedy, Edward M. "Ted,"
    444
Kennedy, John F., 82, 102,
    113, 158, 224, 553

Kenya, 361, 365

Kerr, Dick, 511, 699

Kerwin, Walter "Dutch," 235

Kester, John, 351–57, 361, 366, 370, 378, 442, 452, 675–76

KGB, 254, 255, 257, 541–42, 627

Khalid Bin Sultan, Prince, 722, 791

Kheim, Captain, 137, 141–143

Khomeini, Ayatollah Ruhollah, 362, 460, 461, 497

Khrushchev, Nikita, 479, 553, 558

Kiltie (Weinberger's dog), 432

Kime, Bill, 809

King, Coretta, 605, 761

King, Martin Luther, Jr., 35, 141, 188, 201, 605, 761, 813, 839

King, Rodney, 839, 840, 841

King, Tom, 751

Kinzel, Arthur, 319

Kissinger, Henry, 460, 502–3, 532, 575

Klein, Melvin, 28–29

Kliest, Baron von, 386

Knott, Dick, 578–79, 584

Knott, Eleanor, 578–79, 584

Knott, Jane, *see* Powell, Jane Knott

Koch, Edward, 37

Kohl, Helmut, 560

Koppel, Ted, 848–49

Korda, Michael, 600

Korea, People's Republic of (North), 882, 920

Korea, Republic of (South), 157, 269–70, 276, 660, 696

Korean Air Lines (KAL) flight 007 shootdown, 424–29

Korean tour, 275–306
  assessment of, 307–8
  Biggs episode in, 288–89
  Bryan's Song episode in, 292–94
  combat sports and, 279–280, 304–5
  end of, 305–6
  ice rink episode in, 290–92
  see also 2nd Infantry Division, U.S.; Emerson, Henry E. "Gunfighter"

Korean War, 18, 39, 40, 220, 275, 622, 755

Kozak, Michael, 909

Kranowitz, Alan, 514

Krauthammer, Charles, 581

Kryuchkov, Vladimir A., 542

Kuhn, Jim, 599

Ku Klux Klan, 93

Kurds, 710, 745, 807–8

Kuwait, 511, 512, 564–65, 696, 707, 713, 718, 735–36, 741–45, 750,

759, 763, 764, 774, 782, 785, 790, 796, 799–800, 921
Ky, Nguyen Cao, 153, 200

Laboa, Sebastian, 656
Laird, Melvin, 244
Laitin, Joe, 261–63
Lake, Anthony, 868, 875–76, 877, 889
Langevin, Roger, 621
Lanham, C. T., 62
Laos, 121, 122, 223
Larry King Show, The (TV show), 848
Latvia, 574, 610, 682
Lauder, Aerin, 496
Lauder, Jane, 496
Lauder, Jo Carol, 496
Lauder, Ronald, 496, 902
Laurice, Aunt, 11, 14, 16, 21, 38, 45
Lavender Hill Mob, The (film), 902
Lawrence, Richard D., 204, 212, 392–93
Lawrie, Tim, 711
Laxalt, Paul, 382
leadership, 398–99
    U.S. Army and, 78–79
    Vietnam War failure of, 225–26
Leahy, William, 621
Leavenworth Historical Society, 420
Lebanon, 437–39, 457, 510, 652, 660, 803, 850, 851

Ledford, Frank, 523
Ledsky, Nelson, 550
Lee, Jim, 81, 157
Lee, Leslie, 784
Lee, Robert E., 797
Legion of Merit, 219, 221
Lehman, John, 449–50
Lenin, V. I., 558
"Letter from a Birmingham Jail" (King), 141
Lewis, Arthur S. "Sonny," 31, 626, 833
Lewis, Roger, 31
Lewis, Vernon, 109
Liberia, 530, 920
Library of Congress, 518
Libya, 443, 460, 627, 874
Liman, Arthur, 517
Lincoln, Abraham, 367, 625–26, 851, 886–87
Linhart, Bob, 550
Linton, Jalester "Old Sarge," 416–17
Lithuania, 574, 610, 682
Livsey, Tim, 693
Llewellyn, Bruce, 32, 691, 902
Llewellyn, Nessa, 32, 570
Lloyd Webber, Andrew, 902
Loeffke, Bernard, 253–54, 266
Lombardi, Arthur, 320
London, Jack, 536
Longest Day, The (Ryan), 139
Los Angeles riots, 839, 846
Los Angeles Times, 673

Louisell, William C., 74–75, 79, 82, 110
Lowder, Hank, 197, 202
Lowery, Joe, 761
loyalty, 483
Lucas, C. Payne, 907
Luck, Gary, 787
Luncheon with Alma (radio show), 98
Luxenberg, Morry, 55
LZ Dragon, 199, 200

MacArthur, Douglas, 387, 622
McAuliffe, Anthony, 315
McCaffrey, Barry, 787, 884
McCarthy, Jack, 229
McChrystal, Herbert J., 235–36, 248
McClellan, George B., 737, 850, 851
MacColl, Ray, 419
McConnell, Mike, 697, 775, 786, 806
McCullers, Carson, 139
McCurdy, Dave, 857
McFarlane, Robert C. "Bud," 436, 437, 438, 460–61, 465, 503
McGee, Frank, 190–91
McKinney, Jim, 576
McKoy, Alice, 9, 11, 13
McKoy, Edwin, 11
McKoy, Maud Ariel, *see* Powell, Maud Ariel McKoy
McLarty, Mack, 868

McLeod, David G., 526
McNamara, Robert S., 139, 156, 157, 878
McNamara's Line, 220–21
McPeak, Merrill "Tony," 726, 809, 869, 873
MACV (Military Assistance Command Vietnam), 215
Maddox, Lester, 260
MAD (Mutually Assured Destruction), 444, 543
Madrid, Middle East Peace Conference in, 803
Mahaffey, Fred, 248, 315–16
Mahan, Alfred Thayer, 312
Major, John, 751
Malamud, Bernard, 37
Malaysia, 31
Malek, Fred, 251–53, 261, 262, 266, 310, 317, 842, 852
Malta, 665, 666, 668
Management Information Directorate, 235–36
Mandela, Nelson, 687, 905–7
Manley, Michael, 3, 6
Maresca, Jack, 679, 681
Marine Corps, U.S., 219–20, 310, 439, 622, 650, 660, 661, 664, 780–81, 787, 791, 809, 892
Marine Expeditionary Forces (MEF), 220

Market Garden, Operation, 315
Marsh, John O., Jr., 390–91
Marshall, Thurgood, 868
Martin, Dave, 710
massive retaliation policy, 71
Mathis, Johnny, 291
Mavroudis, Antonio, 49, 171, 181–82, 190–91, 731
Max (Powell's cat), 478
Meade, George, 797
Medal of Honor, 379
media, 928
    Bosnia and, 849–51
    Gulf War and, 752, 771–776, 797–800, 803–6
    Just Cause Operation and, 652–56
    Powell and, 539–40, 563–564, 814–15, 849–51, 871–73
    Schwarzkopf and, 752, 805, 806
    Somalia and, 896
Mcdicare, 923
Medina, Ernest, 216, 217
Meese, Edward, 497
Meikle, Roy, 32, 36
Meikle, Vernon, 32, 36, 92
Melnyk, Ray, 651
Menetrey, Lou, 248
Merritt, Jack, 413, 609, 611
Metcalf, Joseph, 440
Meyer, Edward "Shy," 370, 372, 389, 392, 408, 421, 623

Mfume, Kweisi, 905, 907
Michel, Bob, 514
Mighty Sparrow (Slinger Francisco), 20
Military Academy, U.S., 418
Military Airlift Command (MAC), U.S., 387, 708
Military Assistance Advisory Group, U.S., 120
Military Assistance Command Vietnam (MACV), 215
Miller, Paul David, 432, 450
Miller, Tom, 68–70, 79, 112, 307, 485, 488–89
Millie (Bush's dog), 854
Minnesota Meeting, 827
Mobutu, Joseph D., 628
Moellering, John, 510
Mohica, Lou, 49–50
Mohr, Harry W. "Skip," 295
Mohr, Henry, 611
Moiseyev, Galina Iosifovna, 730, 733, 817, 822
Moiseyev, Mikhail, 680–83, 730, 817, 821, 822
Mondale, Walter, 373–74
Montagnards, 123, 131
Montgomery, Tom, 889, 891, 892, 896
Moonstruck (film), 902
Moreau, Arthur, 463–64
Morris High School, 24, 29, 846, 856
    Powell's speech at, 811–814

Morse, Wilfred C., 73
Mosbacher, Bob, 852
Moscow Summit, 556–57,
 571–77
  Reagan's Springfield
   speech and, 565–68
Moseley-Braun, Carol, 905
Mozambique, 920
Mubarak, Hosni, 703, 723
Mulroney, Brian, 561
Muriel, Cousin, 7
Murphy, Audie, 39
Murphy, James, 316, 317
Murray, Anne, 902
Muse, Kurt, 637, 642, 649
Music Man, The (film), 601,
 902
Mutually Assured Destruc-
 tion (MAD), 444, 543
My Lai Massacre, 205,
 215–18

Namibia, 608
National Academy of Sci-
 ences, 591
National Association for the
 Advancement of Col-
 ored People (NAACP),
 172
National Association of
 Black Journalists, 605
National Defense Univer-
 sity, 313, 316
National Enquirer, 754
National Father's Day Com-
 mittee, 849
National Guard, U.S., 162,
 608, 837, 841

National League of Fami-
 lies, 527
National Military Command
 Center, 424, 437, 648,
 650, 668, 765, 820
National Military Council,
 proposed, 623
National Political Congress
 of Black Women, 906
National Press Club, 457
National Security Agency
 (NSA), 463, 496,
 541–42
National Security Council
 (NSC), 343–46, 351,
 434, 464, 465, 469,
 499, 500, 505, 507–8,
 589–90, 598, 639, 647,
 728, 850, 877
 arms-for-hostages deal
  and, *see* arms-for-
  hostages deal
 assessment of, 502–3
 charter of, 502
 contras and, 512–15
 Gulf War and, 701–4
 Powell's appointment as
  head of, 528–30
 Powell's confirmation as
  head of, 531–33
 PRG and, 510–11
National Security Decision
 Directive (NSDD),
 459–60
National Security Planning
 Group, 528–29
National Security Review
 No. 12, 661

"National Strategy for the 1990's" (conference), 611
National Urban League, 607
National War College, 183, 309–11, 316
Nation of Islam, 907
NATO (North Atlantic Treaty Organization), 169, 192, 260, 321, 465, 489, 560–61, 591, 679, 685, 690, 744, 878
  expansion of, 610
  major competitions of, 500–501
Navy, U.S., 309, 310, 373–374, 439–40, 449, 621, 622, 660, 661, 663, 685, 892
  CENTCOM and, 579–80
  wound laboratory of, 432–33
Navy Department, U.S., 502
Navy Seals, 642, 650, 861
NBC, 190, 339, 657
NBC News, 562
NBC Nightly News, 562
Neal, Richard "Butch," 806
Negroponte, John D., 537
Nelson, Major, 49
New Jersey, U.S.S., 438
Newman, Paul, 13
New Orleans, Battle of, 95
Newsweek, 372, 814
Newton, Robert, 301–3
New York Daily News, 15
New York Mirror, 15
New York Post, 15

New York Times, 15, 37, 466, 530, 533, 600–601, 617, 689, 761, 800, 849–51, 871, 873, 874
Ngo Dinh Diem, 113, 151, 155–56
Ngo Dinh Nhu, 151, 156
Nguyen Cao Ky, 153, 200
Nhu, Madame, 151
Nicaragua, 469, 497, 512–15, 516, 534, 555, 559, 600, 628, 920
Nichols, Bill, 623
Nigeria, 833–35
Nightline (TV show), 849
9th Cavalry Regiment, U.S., 93–94; *see also* Buffalo Soldiers
9th Infantry Division, U.S., 612
Nixon, Richard M., 82, 95, 217, 233, 250, 266, 460, 567
  resignation of, 309–10
Nixon Administration, 268
Nofziger, Lyn, 599
no-medals policy, 300–301
No Name Club, 241
NORAD (North American Air Defense Command), 394–95, 730
Noriega, Manuel Antonio, 556, 563, 586–88, 600, 626–31, 634–35, 642, 644, 648, 652 653, 656–57, 658, 746, 797

Norman, Gene Alfred
Warren, 29, 533
Norman, Juanita, 533
North, Oliver L., 434, 436–
437, 497, 503, 505,
512, 517, 627
North American Air
Defense Command
(NORAD), 394–95,
730
North Atlantic Treaty Orga-
nization (NATO), 169,
192, 260, 321, 465,
489, 560–61, 591, 679,
685, 690, 744, 878
expansion of, 610
major competitions of,
500–501
North Vietnamese Army
(NVA), 222, 223
Nowell, William, 481
NSA (National Security
Agency), 463, 496,
541–42
NSC, see National Security
Council
NSDD (National Security
Decision Directive),
459–60
nuclear weapons, 489, 516,
547, 822–24
Gulf War and, 738
Nunn, Lee, Jr., 247
Nunn, Sam, 531–32, 749–
750, 825, 845, 857, 908

Oakley, Phyllis, 861
Oakley, Robert, 565, 861

Obey, Dave, 515
O'Brien, Tom, 412
Odom, William, 464
Office of Management and
Budget (OMB),
248–53, 266, 382, 389,
665
"oil slick" theory, 140
Oklahoma! (film), 902
101st Airborne Division,
U.S., 206, 315–26,
340, 343–44, 353, 477,
739, 786
boxing episode and, 335
history of, 315
mission of, 320
Reforger exercise and,
320–21
thermostat episode in,
324–25
193rd Infantry Brigade,
U.S., 649
On War (Clausewitz), 312
Oppala, Joe, 833
Organization of American
States, 657
Organization of Petroleum
Exporting Countries
(OPEC), 696
Osborne, Kathy, 582, 598
Osipovich, Gennady,
426–27
Otis, Glenn, 492, 524
Oxford Union, 455–56
Ozal, Turgut, 723

Page, Clarence, 581
Pagonis, Gus, 755

Pahlavi, Mohammad Reza, Shah of Iran, 362, 365–66, 698
Paige, Emmet, 416
Pakistan, 193
Palastra, Joe, 361–62
Palestine Liberation Organization (PLO), 437, 803, 908
Palmer, Bruce, 235
Panama, 308, 378, 556, 563, 586, 600, 626–27, 632, 635, 636–48, 649–54, 656–58, 669, 673, 685, 740, 771, 851
Panama Defense Force (PDF), 586, 627, 630, 632, 636–38, 642, 649–53, 657, 797
Parade, 56–57, 615, 620, 842
Pardo, John, 53–55, 485
Parvin, Landon, 508
Pastor, Robert, 909
Pat, Cousin, 7
Pathfinder course, 161, 163–165
Patriot missiles, 778
Patton, George, 185, 206, 477, 844
Pawlik, Steve, 177–78
Paz, Robert, 638
PBS, 797
PDF (Panama Defense Force), 586, 627, 630, 632, 636–38, 641–42, 649–53, 657, 797
"Peace Dividend," 684

Pearson, Otis, 487, 490, 492, 612, 662, 693–94, 699, 740–41, 791, 873, 885, 893, 899
Peers, William Ray, 217
Pentagon (building), 233, 235
    Cooke and, 452–53
    Eisenhower Corridor of, 471–73
    Powell's office in, 625
    "Tank" room of, 666
"people sniffer," 220–21
perestroika, 479, 537, 558, 568
Pérez, Carlos Andrés, 386
Perle, Richard, 448
Perot, Ross, 848, 853
Perry, J. Clyde, 106
Perry, William, 378, 881, 896
Pershing, John "Black Jack," 441
Pershing Rifles, 40–42, 47–51, 54–55, 897
Persian Gulf, 660
    Stark incident and, 512
Persian Gulf War, 177, 308, 378, 696–701
    aftermath of, 806–9
    air campaign in, 717–18, 758, 769–71, 774–76, 778–80
    airlift and buildup in, 708–13, 716–17, 754–55
    air plan for, 735–36, 742

Persian Gulf War (*cont.*):
  airpower philosophy and,
    717–18, 723–24, 735,
    756, 779
  allied coalition and, 721–
    722, 744, 757, 778, 801
  A1 Firdo bunker strike in,
    779–80
  biological weapons threat
    and, 750, 751–52,
    766–67, 771
  black soldiers in, 761–63
  and Bush's demonization
    of Saddam Hussein,
    746–47, 802
  casualties in, 771, 787,
    788, 802
  chemical weapons threat
    and, 710–11, 751, 766–
    767
  CIA and, 699–700, 703,
    710
  Commanders controversy
    and, 729, 814–15
  Congress and, 743,
    749–50, 753, 759,
    761–64, 768–69, 793
  decision to cease hostili-
    ties in, 790–97
  elimination of Saddam
    Hussein as aim of, 745,
    747, 756, 797,
    800–801, 808
  Gang of Eight and, 737,
    741–44, 763–64,
    768–69, 785–86, 791
  Great Britain and,
    721–22, 744
  ground campaign in, 758,
    786–91
  ground offensive delay in,
    779–80
  ground plan for, 735–40
  H-Hour debate in, 764
  "Highway of Death" in,
    790
  as "Hundred-Hour War,"
    795
  Instant Thunder Opera-
    tion and, 717–18
  Islamic prohibitions and,
    719–21
  Israel and, 724, 741–42,
    776–78
  Jedi Knights and, 718,
    735, 739
  Keegan's assessment of,
    803
  limited nature of, 789–90
  mail problem and,
    752–53
  Marines in, 780–81, 787,
    791
  media and, 752, 771–76,
    797–800, 803–6
  NSC and, 701–4
  nuclear option and, 738
  prelude to, 696–97
  projected casualties in,
    757–59
  public opinion and, 804–
    806
  reservists and, 716–17
  results of, 799–803
  rotation problem and,
    721

sanctions option and, 701, 727–29, 741, 744, 746, 759

Scud missile threat in, 774–76, 777, 778, 788

Soviet involvement in, 702, 730

Soviet peace proposal and, 782, 785–86

strategy decisions for, 739–42, 773–74

UN and, 702–3, 713, 741, 744–46, 763, 768–69, 792, 801

U.S.-Iraqi relations prior to, 699–700

victory celebrations for, 809–10

Vietnam stigma and, 764

Pettigrew, Albert, 288, 289, 300

Philadelphia Inquirer, 871

Philippines, 660, 851
    attempted coup in, 667–73

Phillips, Don, 95

Philpot, Carlton, 690–91, 692, 846

Piccolo, Brian, 292

Picking People, Powell's Rules for, 537–38

Piland, Sue, 599

Pisani, Joe, 472, 491

Pittsburgh Courier, 140

Planning and Programming Analysis Directorate, 235–36

Platt, Nicholas, 669

Playboy, 256

Play to Win (play), 688

PLO (Palestine Liberation Organization), 437, 803, 908

Plummer, Penelope, 212

Poelzig, Hans, 480

Poindexter, John, 465–66, 470–71, 497, 503, 508, 517, 528

Poland, 259–60, 267, 479, 610, 744

Policy Review Group (PRG), 510–11, 512, 630, 633

Popadiuk, Roman, 537

Pork Chop Hill (film), 39

Portugal, 384

Post Daily Bulletin, 328

Powell, Alma Johnson (wife), 97–115, 138, 140–41, 143, 151, 154, 159–61, 174, 175, 181–184, 190, 194–96, 207, 227, 228, 231, 238–43, 260, 269–70, 296, 308–309, 313, 317–18, 346, 366, 368, 383, 391, 395, 410–11, 414, 415, 416, 423, 424, 429, 458, 473, 493, 494, 500, 584–85, 596, 612, 618, 619, 626, 636, 648, 652, 656, 688, 723, 733, 750, 797, 809, 817, 853, 854, 863–64, 867, 873, 897, 900

Powell, Alma Johnson
    (wife), (cont.):
background of, 98–99
character of, 115
decoration awarded to,
    898
Fisk reunion and, 841–42
at Fort Carson, 401–2, 404
German lessons and,
    477–78
Great Britain trip and,
    903–5
Hawaii leave and, 214–15
Jamaica visit and, 3–8
Jane Weinberger and, 435
Michael Powell's auto
    accident and, 522–26,
    529
as mother figure, 332
Nigeria visit and, 833–35
Powell's first meeting
    with, 97–98
Powell's marriage to,
    104–7
religious conversion by,
    193
30th anniversary and,
    848–49
Powell, Annemarie (daugh-
    ter), 231, 270, 327,
    329, 401, 414, 458,
    478, 486, 500, 570,
    619, 848, 853
on Powell as father, 329
Powell, Bryan (grandson),
    902
Powell, Charles, 467, 891

Powell, Colin L.:
air assault badge earned
    by, 321–22
appointed Deputy Assis-
    tant to President for
    National Security,
    499–500
beer incident and, 26–27
Biggs episode and,
    288–89
birth of, 9
Carlisle speech of, 609–11
cars as hobby of, 331–32,
    459, 613–14, 899
childhood of, 13–18
combat notebook of,
    129–30, 132, 139, 147
on command, 482–84
court-martial assignment
    and, 72–73
"crybaby" incident and,
    16
decision-making philoso-
    phy of, 596–97
decorations and awards
    of, 219, 221, 371–72,
    393, 570, 687, 897–99
early education of, 16–17,
    24, 29, 36–39, 44,
    47–48, 51–58
"experts" rule of, 155
family of, 19–21, 31–33
first combat experience
    of, 126–28
first field command of, 68
hamburger incident and,
    162–63

in helicopter crashes, 5–6,
    207–11
on holding meetings,
    520–21
honorary degrees of, 570
illnesses of, 346–47, 493
as Infantry Board test
    officer, 165–68
infantry maxims of, 62
Intelligence Estimates
    exam and, 191–92
lost pistol incident and,
    69–70, 488–89
on loyalty, 483
marriage of, 104–7
misfired shell incident
    and, 75–76
name of, 18–19, 400
Pepsi-Cola job of, 43–44,
    371, 811
picking people rule of,
    537–38
political philosophy of,
    922–32
"prefix 5" designation
    and, 169–70
promoted to brigadier
    general, 366–68
promoted to captain, 114
promoted to colonel, 314
promoted to first lieu-
    tenant, 72
promoted to lieutenant
    colonel, 230–31
promoted to licutenant
    general, 473
promoted to major, 177

promoted to major gen-
    eral, 413, 424
racial identity of, 28–29,
    43, 51–53, 63–65
religion and, 25–26, 30,
    64, 238–41, 399–400,
    454
retirement of, 892–900
soldiering and, 40–42,
    76–78
tae kwon do experience
    of, 297
tank gunner qualification
    of, 396–97
as teacher, 176–80
vice presidency proposals
    and, 555, 580–82,
    829–30, 842
warmaking rules of, 658
wounding of, 149–51
Powell, Jane Knott (daugh-
    ter-in-law), 578,
    584–85, 612, 626, 853,
    902
Powell, Jeffrey Michael
    (grandson), 612, 853,
    885
Powell, Lewis, 313
Powell, Linda (daughter),
    175, 180, 184, 194,
    214, 231, 239, 241,
    269–70, 401, 458, 570,
    619, 853, 902
  acting career and,
    414–15, 521, 688, 848
  on Powell as father,
    328–29

Powell, Luther (father), 10,
  27, 34, 35, 51, 56–57,
  67, 72, 100, 151, 160,
  239, 903, 904
  background of, 9–10
  decline and death of,
    359–61
  family and, 22–24
  Fort Campbell visited by,
    323–24
  and move to Queens,
    46–47
  numbers betting and, 24,
    45–46
  at Powell's wedding,
    104–8
Powell, Marilyn (sister), see
  Berns, Marilyn Powell
Powell, Maud Ariel McKoy
  (mother), 8–9, 25, 26,
    27, 34, 56–57, 67, 160,
    239, 323–24, 366–68,
    903, 904
  background of, 11–12
  death of, 453–54
  described, 11
  Luther's death and, 359–
    361
  and move to Queens, 46–
    47
  at Powell's wedding, 107,
    109
Powell, Michael Kevin
  (son), 143, 160–61,
    175, 180, 184, 194,
    214, 215, 231, 239,
    241, 326–27, 458, 478,

482, 486, 493–94, 570,
  578, 612, 619, 626,
  848, 853, 885, 902
  in auto accident, 521–26,
    529
  college graduation of,
    458
  as college student, 400–
    401
  marriage of, 584
  Powell's advice to, 329–
    330
  speech on handicapped
    by, 584–85
POW/MIA issue, 527
Presidential Medal of Free-
  dom with Distinction,
  897–98
President's Daily Brief, 441
President's Foreign Intelli-
  gence Advisory Board,
  895, 896
Presley, Elvis, 83, 278
Preston, Rodney "Pee Wee,"
  336–39
Price, Bill, 639
Price, Charles, 467
Price, George B., 139–40,
  151, 171
Price, Herman, 95, 96, 101
Price, Leontyne, 140
Price, Madeline, 96, 101
Pritchard, Walter, 81,
  218–19
"Private TA-21," 83
Producers, The (film), 902
Project 14, 421, 652

Pro-Life program, 274–75, 290

Provide Comfort, Operation, 808, 817

Ptarmigan phone system, 466–68

Purviance, Stuart, 367, 625

Purvis, Joe, 735

Pyle, Bob, 209–10

Pyle, Ernie, 804

Qaddafi, Muammar, 460

Quang, Captain, 143, 144

Quayle, Dan, 582, 665, 737, 741, 820, 848, 897
  as election liability, 842
  Philippine crisis and, 667–73

Querin, Betty, 329

Quigley, Joan, 546

Rabin, Yitzhak, 803, 908

race, racism, 28–29, 58, 63–65, 98, 927, 928
  affirmative action and, 925–26
  all-volunteer force and, 341–42, 761–63
  Birmingham and, 140–41, 158
  Buffalo Soldier monument and, 844–48
  Civil Rights Act and, 171–73
  Fort Bragg experience and, 51–53

and gays in military, 832–33

Gulf War and, 761–63

hamburger incident and, 162–63

Howard speech and, 907–908

King assassination and, 188–89

1988 election and, 606

Pepsi job and, 43, 811

Powell's assessment of, 811–14

Powell's Nigeria visit and, 833–35

and Powell's NSC appointment, 529–30

Republican Party and, 606

2nd Division and, 285–294

in U.S. Army, 92–95, 172–73, 188–89, 201, 242–43, 285–94, 341–342, 416–21, 492, 607–608, 761–63, 844–45

Vietnam War and, 201

West Indian culture and, 33–34

after World War II, 95

Ramirez, Victor, 28

Ramos, Fidel, 670, 672

Randolph, A. Philip, 37

Rangel, Charles, 905, 907

Ranger (Bush's dog), 854

Rangers, Army, 642, 650, 889, 892, 896

Rapid Deployment Joint
    Task Force, 698
Raspberry, William, 581
Rastafarian movement, 34
Rather, Dan, 267
Rawls, Lou, 902
Raymond "the Bagel Man,"
    37
Reagan, Nancy, 527–28, 538,
    577
  astrologer consulted by,
    546
  Raisa Gorbachev and,
    545–46
Reagan, Ronald, 193, 379–
    380, 388–89, 466, 501,
    503, 529, 538, 557,
    582, 583, 587, 590,
    606, 629, 691, 830,
    837, 926
  arms-for-hostages deal
    and, 460, 465, 469–71,
    503, 519–20
  assessment of, 600–601
  Finding of Necessity
    signed by, 469–71, 519
  Geneva Summit and, 480
  Governor's Island meet-
    ing and, 591–96
  Grenada visited by, 474
  INF treaty and, 516, 535,
    543–45, 547–55
  Iran-contra scandal and,
    496–510, 519–20
  KAL 007 shootdown and,
    428
  Moscow Summit and,
    571–76

Nancy Reagan's devotion
    to, 577
  at NATO conference, 561
  Powell's introduction to,
    449
  POW/MIA issue and, 527
  SDI and, 444–45
  Springfield speech of,
    565–68
  Weinberger and, 440
Reagan administration, 387,
    460, 463–66, 470–71,
    591, 592, 614
  assessment of, 476–77
Reaume, Judi, 490, 497
Redman, Charles, 557
Reforger (Return of Forces
    to Europe) exercise,
    320–21
Regan, Donald, 504
Republican Guard, Iraqi,
    697, 701, 788, 792,
    795, 800, 801
Republican National
    Convention (1992),
    851–52
Republican Party, U.S., 388,
    555, 581, 635
  racism of, 606
Reserve Officers Training
    Corps (ROTC), 39–42,
    47–53, 458, 478
  abolished by CCNY,
    245
  Junior, 845–46
  Vietnam War and, 55
Restore Hope, Operation,
    860–62

Return of Forces to Europe (Reforger) exercise, 320–21
reverse cycle training, 283
Reykjavik Summit (1986), 544
Rice, Don, 726
Rickover, Hyman G., 260–261
Ridgway, Rozanne, 571–72, 574, 591
Rita phone system, 467
Ritchie, Ivie, 7
Robbins, Marty, 137
Robinson, Edward G., 37
Robinson, Jackie, 688
Robinson, John "Dave," 662
Robinson, Roscoe, 416, 844
Rockefeller, Nelson, 511
Rockwell, Norman, 158
Roger, Cousin, 21
Rogers, Bernard, 235, 353, 356–57, 408
Romero, Gabby, 621
Roosevelt, Franklin D., 12, 99, 249–50, 621, 923
Roosevelt, Teddy, 94
Roque, Victor, 31
Rosenthal, Abe, 37, 871
Ross, M. Collier, 407–8, 411, 412
Ross, Tom, 357, 358, 909
Rossin, Larry, 909
Rostow, Nick, 537
ROTC (Reserve Officers Training Corps), 39–42, 49–53, 458, 478

abolished by CCNY, 245
Junior, 845–46
Vietnam War and, 55
Rowan, Carl, 530
Rowen, Harry, 668, 670
Rucker, John Anthony, 193–94
Rudman, Warren, 514, 515
"Rum and Coca–Cola" (song), 20
Rumsfeld, Donald, 318
Rupee, Uncle, 92
Rutherford, Jerry, 489
Rwanda, 920
Ryan, Cornelius, 139

Saba, Joseph, 517
Sabah, Saad Al abdullah Al-Salim Al-, 565
SAC (Strategic Air Command), U.S., 824
Safe Harbor, Operation, 828
Saint, Butch, 617
St. Margaret's Church (South Bronx), 25–26, 454
St. Margaret's Episcopal Church (Woodbridge), 238–41
Sakharov, Andrei, 591
Salk, Jonas, 37
Same Mud, Same Blood (TV documentary), 190–91
Sandinistas, 512–13, 555, 559, 628
Saratoga, U.S.S., 373–74
Saturday Evening Post, 158

Saturday Night Live (TV show), 805
Saudi Arabia, 361, 364, 701–9, 711, 713, 714–15, 734, 735, 801, 921
  missile sale to, 564–65
Sayers, Gale, 292
Scabbard and Blade, 40
Schlesinger, James, 318, 370
Schmitt, Maurice, 722
Schmoke, Carl, 905
Schroeder, Pat, 832
Schwar, Joe, 81, 111–14, 143
Schwar, Joey, 112
Schwar, Kevin Michael, 112, 143
Schwar, Pat, 81, 111–12, 114, 143
Schwar, Steve, 112
Schwartz, Walter, 28
Schwarzenegger, Arnold, 658–59, 688, 752
Schwarzkopf, Brenda, 809
Schwarzkopf, H. Norman, 225, 611, 617, 685, 706, 711, 716–19, 734–35, 736, 768, 770–71, 787, 788, 809, 860, 898
  casualty projections and, 757–58
  command ability of, 722
  ending of hostilities and, 790–94

  Frost's interview of, 797–800
  Grenada invasion and, 440
  ground attack delay and, 779–80
  McClellan gibe and, 737, 850
  media and, 752, 805, 806
  named CENTCOM commander, 580
  onset of Gulf War and, 697–701
  retirement of, 806–7
  Scud threat and, 774–76
  subordinates and, 748–49
  temper of, 748, 765
Scott, Bill, 55
Scott, Bruce, 485, 490
Scowcroft, Brent, 530, 590, 593, 598, 615, 633, 641, 643, 650, 655–56, 665, 703, 704, 705, 712, 725, 727, 737, 741–43, 746, 757, 785, 789, 791, 794, 839–40, 860, 862, 898
Scruggs, Jan, 886
Scud missiles, 775–77, 778, 788
SDI (Strategic Defense Initiative), 444–46, 480, 543–44, 547, 551–53
Congressional hearings on, 445
2nd Armored Cavalry Regiment, U.S., 478

2nd Armored Rifle Battalion, U.S., 68
2nd Aviation Battalion, U.S., 301–3
2nd Infantry Brigade, U.S., 84, 86
2nd Infantry Division, U.S., 269, 270–73, 306
 AGI and, 298
 educational development and, 297–98
 EIB earned by, 295–96
 Korean troops in, 282
 racial friction in, 285–94
 reverse cycle training in, 283, 294
 short-term AWOLs and, 306
 Soldier of the Month in, 299–300
 see also Emerson, Henry E. "Gunfighter"; Korean tour
2nd Infantry Regiment, U.S., 88, 90, 110
2nd Marine Division, U.S., 780
Secret Service, U.S., 542, 592
Sedgwick, Clyde, 281
Semple, Robert, 732
Senate, U.S., 170, 176, 385, 517–18, 530, 763, 768, 794
 Armed Services Committee of, 531–32, 749–50
 INF treaty ratified by, 572

 Powell confirmed as JCS chairman by, 624
 Powell confirmed as National Security Advisor by, 531–32
 Powell reconfirmed by, 825
Senegal, 745, 833
7th Infantry Division, U.S., 642, 650, 653
VII Corps, U.S., 478, 492, 521, 781, 786, 787, 791–92, 809
Sevareid, Eric, 267
Shaft (film), 277
Shalikashvili, John M., 612, 808, 891
Shamir, Yitzhak, 697, 778
Shaw, Bernard, 769
Sheafer, Ted, 640
Sheek, Alton J., 136, 142
Shelton, Hugh, 915
Sheridan, Philip, 185, 414
Sherman, William Tecumseh, 414
Shevardnadze, Eduard, 535, 558, 568, 744
Shirley, Uncle, 21
Shomron, Dan, 697
Shooting Star (Stegner), 139
Shriver, Maria, 688
Shultz, George, 629, 875
 arms-for-hostages deal and, 459, 461, 471, 508–9
 Beirut bombing and, 438, 456–57

Shultz, George (*cont.*):
  contras as seen by,
    512–13
  Governor's Island meet-
    ing and, 591–92
  INF treaty and, 535, 548,
    549, 553, 554
  KAL shootdown and, 426
  Noriega deal and, 587–88
  Powell and, 556
  Reagan-Gorbachev talks
    and, 566–68, 574, 575,
    830
  Weinberger's rivalry with,
    427–28, 438, 440,
    456–57
Sickser, Jay, 27–28
Sickser's, 27–28, 42
Sidey, Hugh, 267, 825–26
Siemer, Deanne, 370
Sierra Leone, 31, 626, 833,
  920
Sihelnik, Stephen A., 526
Silver Star, 221
Simon, Carly, 902
Simon, Paul, 902
Sinclair, Upton, 37
Single Integrated Opera-
  tional Plan (SIOP), 823
Sink, Willard, 121–23, 129,
  136
Skinner, Sam, 840, 841
Slide for Life exercise, 59,
  63
Slovenia, 849
Smith, A. A. "Tony," 236,
  237

Smith, Carl, 352, 367, 387,
  422, 423, 430
Smith, Charles, 240
Smith, Ike, 81
Smith, R. Jeffrey, 689
Smullen, F. William, 674,
  710, 760, 773, 850,
  873, 900
Social Security, 923
SOCOM (Special Opera-
  tions Command),
  377–78, 614, 639
Soldier's Medal, 219
Solis Palma, Manuel, 629
Somalia, 745, 859–62, 864,
  883, 884, 888–89, 892,
  895, 920, 921
Somoza, Anastasio, 514
Sonny, Cousin, 21
Sorzano, José, 513–14
South Africa, 660, 728, 746,
  905–7, 920
South Bronx, N.Y., 13–15
Southern Christian Leader-
  ship Conference, 761
Southern Command
  (SOUTHCOM), 627,
  647, 657
Soviet Union, 266–67, 362,
  439, 447, 461, 479,
  503, 513, 515–16, 528,
  566–67, 573, 610, 660,
  682, 684, 698, 732
  Afghanistan invaded by,
    378
  August coup in, 820–22,
    824

CIA assessments of, 569–70

demise of, 608–9, 687, 830, 918

Dobrynin on foreign policy of, 558–60

Gulf War and, 702, 730, 782, 785–86

INF treaty and, *see* INF treaty

KAL 007 shootdown and, 425–29

Powell's visits to, 253–59, 817

Spadafora, Hugo, 628

Spanish-American War, 94

Spears, Lieutenant Colonel, 146–47

Special Operations Command (SOCOM), 377–78, 614, 639

Spencer, Stu, 843

Sputnik, 71

Standing Firm (Quayle), 667

Stark, U.S.S., 512

Starks, Tiffani, 647

START treaty, 554, 824

Star Wars, *see* Strategic Defense Initiative

State Department, U.S., 309, 438, 502–3, 511, 548, 557, 571, 591, 643, 647, 668, 669, 696, 701, 852, 916–17

Stegner, Wallace, 139

Stempler, Jack, 357–58

Stephanopoulos, George, 855, 868

Stevens, John, 16

Stevens, Paul, 505, 537

Stevens, Steve, 81

Stevens, Ted, 514, 515, 555, 581, 820

Stewart, Imagene, 541

Stilwell, Joseph, Jr., 84, 85, 307

Stilwell, Joseph "Vinegar Joe," 84

Stiner, Carl, 612, 637, 642, 648, 651, 655, 658

Stivers, Don, 625

Stofft, Bill, 81, 625

Stokes, Louis, 905

Strategic Air Command (SAC), U.S., 824

Strategic Airlift Command, U.S., 685

Strategic Army Corps (STRAC), U.S., 86, 153

Strategic Defense Initiative (SDI), 444–46, 480, 543–44, 547, 551–53

Congressional hearings on, 445

"Strategic Overview— 1994," 660, 662–64, 666, 696

Street Without Joy (Fall), 224

Stuart, Reginald, 534–35

Stukel, Don, 247

Sudderth, James, 166, 168

Sullivan brothers, 39
Sununu, John, 633, 641,
    665, 671, 712, 728,
    737, 795, 840
Superfly (film), 277
Supreme Court, U.S., 868
Surratt, Mary, 311
Swain, Carrol, 203
Syria, 438, 721, 744, 801

Taft, William Howard, IV,
    249, 250–51, 385, 429,
    450, 473, 528, 591, 615
Talking with David Frost
    (TV program), 797–98
"Tank," 666
Teeter, Bob, 852
Teitelbaum sisters, 16
Tender Is the Night (Fitzger-
    ald), 139
10th Cavalry Regiment,
    U.S., 93–94, 418–20,
    625, 846; *see also* Buf-
    falo Soldiers
Territorial Imperative
    (Ardrey), 431
terrorism, terrorists, 437–38,
    439, 465, 486, 497, 527
Tet Offensive, 186–87, 616
Thatcher, Margaret, 455,
    479, 553, 569, 751, 891
  Bush's Aspen meeting
    with, 695, 702, 707–8
  Ptarmigan phone deal
    and, 466–68
  Weinberger and, 466–68
Thayer, Paul, 429

Theodore Roosevelt, U.S.S.,
    884
Theologos, John, 55
*Theoretical Framework for
    Monetary Analysis, A*
    (Friedman), 247
3rd Armored Division, U.S.,
    67, 481, 488
3rd Infantry Regiment,
    ARVN, 120
Third Army, U.S., 611, 708
32nd Infantry Regiment,
    U.S., 269, 281
  and Aviation Battalion's
    brawl with, 301–4
Thirty Seconds Over Tokyo
    (film), 39
Thomas, Derrick, 886
Thompson, E. P., 455
Thurman, Max, 248, 470,
    626, 631–36, 638–39,
    642, 644–46, 648, 651,
    655, 657–58
Tillman, Jacqueline, 580,
    582
Time, 518, 825, 871
Timmes, Charles M., 120
"Tiny Bubbles" (song), 214
Today (TV show), 433
Togo, 695, 699
Tong Du Chon, South
    Korea, 277–79, 285–87
Tonkin Gulf Resolution,
    176, 200
Tower, 29
Tower, John, 504, 591, 614
Tower Commission, 507–9

Trachtenberg, Stephen, 687
"Tracking Victorio"
    (Stivers), 625
Training and Doctrine Command (TRADOC),
    U.S., 413, 424
Transportation Command,
    U.S. (TRANSCOM),
    639, 708
Treadwell, Jack, 208, 210
Trost, Carl, 640, 663
Truman, Harry, 95, 871
Tucker, C. Delores, 906
Tucker, Henry B. "Sonny,"
    341–42, 346
Tumelson, Ron, 204, 208,
    210
Tunisia, 475, 697
Turkey, 722, 723, 745, 808
Turner, Stansfield, 385
Tuskegee Airmen, 94, 844
Tutu, Desmond, 906
TV Guide, 691
Twain, Mark, 536
12th Cavalry Regiment,
    U.S., 75
21st Air Force, U.S., 708,
    710
22nd Air Force, U.S., 708,
    710
23rd Infantry (Americal)
    Division, U.S.,
    197–207, 224–25
history of, 204–5
24th Infantry Division
    (Mechanized), U.S.,
    440, 717, 719, 787

24th Infantry Regiment,
    U.S., 93–94
25th Infantry Regiment,
    U.S., 93–94

Ukraine, 610
Ullman, Harlan, 312,
    313–14
Ullman, Julian, 313–14
United Arab Emirates
    (UAE), 696, 700
United Nations (UN), 3,
    559, 592–93, 657, 864,
    920
  Bosnia and, 877–79
  Gulf War and, 702–3,
    713, 741, 744–45, 763,
    768–69, 792, 801
  Haiti and, 908–9
  Iraqi Embargo and,
    713–14
  Resolution 678 of, 744
  Somalia and, 860, 883,
    888–89, 892, 895
Unit Readiness Report,
    178–80, 404–5
Urcioli, George, 51
USA-Canada Institute, 258
"U.S. Policy Toward Iran"
    (NSDD), 458–59
Utgoff, Victor, 351
Utley, Robert, 84–85

Van Cleave, William, 380,
    381, 385
Van Dam, Bruce, 524, 526
Venezuela, 386

Vernon, Cousin, 21
Vessey, John, 448
Veterans Affairs Department, U.S., 732
Vic, Uncle, 14, 18
Viet Cong, 121, 122, 125–127, 131–34, 147–48, 156, 186–87, 198, 199, 222, 616
Vietnam, Democratic Republic of (North), 113, 176
Vietnam, Republic of (South), 102, 113, 158, 200–201
  Diem assassination and, 156
Vietnam, Socialist Republic of, 919–20
Vietnam Veterans Against the War, 232
Vietnam Veterans Memorial, 731
  Clinton's speech at, 883–87
Vietnam War, 82, 85, 275, 379, 614, 623, 704, 851, 878, 926
  antiwar movement and, 157, 187, 232, 687–88
  assessment of, 156–58, 200–201, 218–26
  body count statistic and, 148–49, 222–23, 226
  bombing halt in, 203
  career noncoms and, 218
  casualties in, 157, 181

Clausewitz's principles and, 312–13
  decorations awarded in, 221
  Diem assassination and, 156
  Grasshopper Operation in, 123–35
  leadership failure in, 225–26
  McNamara era and, 156–158
  McNamara Line in, 220–221
  My Lai Massacre in, 215–18
  "oil slick" theory and, 140
  onset of U.S. involvement in, 113
  Powell's introduction to, 119–23
  racial friction and, 201
  ROTC and, 55
  Tet Offensive in, 186–87, 616
  Tonkin Gulf Resolution and, 176
  Vietnamese military command and, 153
  "Vietnamization" of, 233
Villalpando, Kathy, 866–867
Vincennes, U.S.S., 429
Vincent, Richard, 760
Vo Cong Hieu, 121–22, 123, 124, 127, 129, 133,

134, 136–37, 141, 143, 224, 826, 827
von Kliest, Baron, 386
von Schlemmer, Robert, 419–20, 847
Vuono, Carl, 248, 353, 424, 589, 609, 616, 617, 618, 640, 663, 666, 806, 810, 822

Wagner, Raymond H., 302–3
Wagner, Robert, Jr., 37
Waldheim, Kurt, 496
Walker, Costelle "Coz," 96
Wallace, Chris, 562–63
Wallace, George C., 114, 260
Wallechinsky, David, 615, 620
Waller, Cal, 739
Walrop, Chumley W., 303
Walsh, Lawrence, 518–19
Warden, John, 717–18, 735
War Department, U.S., 502
Warner, John, 533
Warsaw Pact, 260, 610, 660, 679, 687, 823
Washington, George, 93, 680
Washington Post, 262, 358, 365, 432, 433, 466, 492, 505, 636, 689, 723–25, 814, 871
Watergate scandal, 266, 267–68, 309–10, 343
Waters, Maxine, 905

Watson, Barbara, 31
Watson, Captain, 79
Watson, Grace, 31
Watson, James, 31
Webb Patrol, 40
Webster, Bill, 668, 703
Weeden, Father, 25, 26, 51
Wehrkunde conference, 386
Weinberger, Caspar, 249, 250–51, 385, 387–88, 422–23, 429, 463, 471, 472, 475–77, 627, 645, 672, 677, 837, 869–70, 874, 897
appointed Secretary of Defense, 380–82
arms-for-hostages deal and, 459–61, 463–66, 468–71, 508–9
Beirut bombing and, 437–38, 456–57
Brown contrasted with, 430
Congress and, 445–46
contras as seen by, 513
defense budget and, 389–90
"diary" of, 461, 517–19
Iran-contra scandal and, 496–500, 517–19
KAL 007 shootdown and, 425, 427–28
Lehman and, 450
management style of, 380–81
Navy's dog experiment and, 432–33

Weinberger, Caspar (*cont.*):
  Oxford Union debate and,
    454–56
  personality of, 440–42
  Poindexter appointment
    and, 465–66
  Reagan and, 440
  resignation of, 527–28,
    529
  Schultz's rivalry with,
    427–28, 438, 440,
    456–57
  SDI and, 444–46
  staff meetings of, 430–31
  Thatcher and, 466–68
  Tower report and, 508–9
  warfare guidelines of,
    456–58
Weinberger, Jane, 387,
    434–35, 527, 869, 897
Welch, Larry, 615, 640, 663,
    723
"Welcome Baby" letters,
    89–90
Wellington, Arthur Welles-
    ley, Duke of, 198
West Indies, 33–34
Westmoreland, William,
    235
Wetzel, Eileen, 478
Wetzel, Robert L. "Sam,"
    477, 478–79, 487, 500
Whelan, Donald, 192
Whiddon, Orren R. "Cot-
    ton," 481
White, Thomas, 481
White, Tom, 656, 681

"White Christmas" (song),
    119, 291
White House Fellowship
    program, 243–70
  China visit and, 263–66
  Laitin's criticism of,
    262–63
  Soviet tour and, 253–59
White House Military
    Office, 576
"Why Generals Get
    Nervous" (Powell),
    850–51
Wick, Charles C., 571
Wickham, John, 316–20,
    323, 324, 334, 343,
    345–47, 353, 413,
    421–23, 462, 473,
    498–99, 507, 609, 686
Wiehl, Bill, 281
Wiener Family, 46
Wilder, Thornton, 848
Wilder, Wilder, Wilder
    (Wilder), 848
Wilkerson, Larry, 844
Will, George, 581
Williams, Pete, 639, 653,
    772
Willis, Mary, 845
Willson, Meredith, 601
Wilson, Charles, 446–48
Wisconsin, U.S.S., 719
Wishart, Leonard, 692
Witte, Uncle, 92
Wofsey, Marvin, 230, 233
Wolfowitz, Paul, 639, 661,
    694, 702, 777, 822, 824

Woodmansee, Jack, 491, 501
Woodward, Bob, 636, 729,
    814, 825, 842–43
World Affairs Council of
    Western Mas-
    sachusetts, 565–66
World War II, 18, 39, 205,
    220, 275, 621, 682,
    722, 732, 744, 797,
    844, 887
Wruble, Bernard, 370–71

XM 571 Articulated Carrier,
    166–68

Yazov, Dimitri, 634, 818,
    821
Year 2000 Institute, 259
Yeltsin, Boris, 821
Yemen, 703, 744
Yeosock, John, 611, 717,
    739, 809
Young, John, 225
Young, Whitney, 607
Yugoslavia, 439, 610, 849

Zaire, 628, 745
Zia ul-Haq, Mohammad,
    193